SOUTH-WESTERN

Keeping FINANCIAL Records

FOR

BUSINESS

Robert A. Schultheis
Professor, Department of Management Information Systems
Southern Illinois University
Edwardsville, Illinois

Burton S. Kaliski
Dean, Undergraduate School
New Hampshire College
Manchester, New Hampshire

Daniel H. Passalacqua
Instructor/Regional Occupational Program Coordinator
Oak Grove High School
San Jose, California

South-Western Publishing Co.

Vice-President/Editor-in-Chief: Dennis M. Kokoruda
Senior Developmental Editor: Carol Volz
Developmental Editor: Bob Sandman
Art Director: John Robb
Design Coordinator: Darren Wright
Marketing Manger: Larry Qualls
Coordinating Editor: Mark Beck
Production Manager: Carol Sturzenberger
Production Editor: Laurie Wendell
Associate Director/Photo Editing: Devore Nixon
Photo Editor: Fred M. Middendorf

Cover Design: Graphica

Internal Design: Circa 86

Photo Research: Meyers Photo-Art

ISBN: 0-538-63313-1

Library of Congress Catalog Card Number: 94-066105

7 8 9 10 11 12 RRDW 05 04 03 02 01 00

Printed in the United States of America

◼▶ TO THE STUDENT

♦♦♦

This text will give you a thorough background in the basic record keeping skills used in business. The skills presented will also serve as a sound background for employment in office jobs.

HOW TO USE THIS TEXT

This textbook is carefully designed to function as a learning tool. It is organized into 16 chapters, with three to nine jobs per chapter. Each chapter begins with a brief introduction that describes the skills you will study in the chapter and why those skills are important to learn. Each skill is discussed in detail in its own job.

Each job begins with an **Applied Math Preview**, a set of problems that provides practice in the kinds of math you will need to use in the job. Printed at the start of most jobs is a **Business Terms Preview**, a list of new terms that are defined and used within the job. Next, there is a set of **Goals**, or learning objectives, that describe what you will learn in studying the job. Your work on each job should begin with solving the Applied Math Preview problems and reading the Business Terms Preview and Goals. Applied Math Preview answers are provided in Appendix E.

Each job is divided into three sections as follows:

- **Understanding the Job** provides definitions of terms and background information on the skill being presented.
- The **Sample Problem** (found in all except Job 1) gives step-by-step instructions for performing the skill.
- **Application Problems** provide the opportunity to practice using the skill demonstrated in the job.

In addition, many illustrations highlight concepts in the job. Note that each illustration is referred to within the job and has a caption that describes what is being illustrated. All new record keeping vocabulary terms are printed in bold type. The term and its definition also appear in the margin as a **Key Term** so that these definitions can easily be found for later reference.

The following features within the job enhance the learning experience:

- In the margins, **Tips** contain hints, reminders, or math information.
- At the ends of jobs, **Building Your Business Vocabulary** sections require you to match definitions to Key Terms and provide you practice with important vocabulary words.
- **Problem Solving Models** list all the steps demonstrated in the Sample Problem. For easy reference, the Problem Solving Models appear just before the Application Problems.
- **Checkpoints** can be found in the margins of the Application Problems. They provide partial answers so that you can tell if you are working the problems correctly.

REINFORCEMENT ACTIVITIES

These special activities appear at the end of each chapter:

- **Discussion** contains questions that help you review concepts presented in the chapter.
- **Professional Business Ethics** and **Critical Thinking** are real-life business situations that require you to stretch your knowledge and apply reasoning skills. Each chapter contains one or the other of these features.
- **Applied Communications** provides opportunities to write memos, directions, and letters related to record keeping.
- **Record Keeping Careers** covers job hunting and workplace skills.
- A **Global Business** feature is provided in five chapters. This activity provides information you will need to work with coworkers, customers, and vendors in foreign countries.
- **Reviewing What You Have Learned** is a matching exercise to help you test your understanding of Key Terms used in the chapter.
- **The Mastery Problem** ties together two or more related concepts from the chapter.

SPECIAL FEATURES

Additional special features appear throughout the textbook:

- **Multicultural Insights** describe the contributions of a variety of cultures to record keeping and business. Some of these features focus on historical contributions while others describe a situation in the United States today. This feature will help strengthen your awareness of the value of diversity in the work force and in society.

- **Interviews** describe individuals in a variety of occupations in the business world today. The careers of these individuals show how a record keeping background can be useful when starting your own business or advancing in your career.
- **Calculator Tips** show how to use calculator shortcuts and special keys.

- This icon identifies a problem that can be solved using the *Automated Accounting 6.0* (or higher) software. Data for 40 Application and Mastery Problems are available on the *Keeping Financial Records for Business* template disk.

REFERENCE MATERIAL

Reference material at the end of the book includes five appendices, a glossary of terms, and an index:

- **Appendix A: Paying Your Income Taxes** provides instruction on filing a personal income tax return.
- **Appendix B: Applied Math Skills** provides a review of basic math skills.
- **Appendix C: Using Electronic Spreadsheets** introduces electronic spreadsheets and shows how to create them for record keeping activities, such as budgeting.
- **Appendix D: Using a Calculator and Computer Keypad** discusses desktop calculators, hand-held calculators, and different kinds of computer keypad layouts. There is also a section on the ten-key touch system.
- **Appendix E: Applied Math Preview Answers** lists the solutions to the Applied Math Previews that appear at the beginning of each job.
- The **Glossary** lists all the Key Terms, their definitions, and the page numbers on which the terms first appear.
- The **Index** shows the page location for each topic in the text. This can be useful if you need to look up a topic but do not know where to find it.

ACKNOWLEDGMENTS

We thank the following individuals who contributed to the review process for this edition:

Mr. Robert Brown
Crosby High School
Waterbury, Connecticut

Ms. Carmela Chartowick
E. Syracuse Minoa High School
East Syracuse, New York

Mrs. Joanna Dunlap
Nitro High School
Nitro, West Virginia

Mrs. Doretha H. Eason
Apopka High School
Apopka, Florida

Mr. Mike Fladlien
Muscatine High School
Muscatine, Iowa

Mr. Robert A. Franklin
Los Banos High School
Los Banos, California

Ms. Carol Hernandez
Whitesboro High School
Marcy, New York

Mrs. Diana Hicks
Weslaco High School
Weslaco, Texas

Mr. Jim Leone
Ellison High School
Killeen, Texas

We also appreciate the ongoing feedback provided by the classroom professionals who use *Keeping Financial Records for Business* every day.

Robert A. Schultheis

Burton S. Kaliski

Daniel H. Passalacqua

CONTENTS

C H A P T E R

Basic Record Keeping Skills

*N*early every person keeps records—store clerks, farmers, factory workers, and business owners. Schools, clubs, and organizations keep records, also. Keeping records plays an important role in both your personal life and in your business career. That is why it is important to learn the necessary skills.

In Chapter 1, you will learn how to enter record keeping information both manually and by using a computer. You will also learn how to file information numerically, chronologically, and alphabetically. Each job in the chapter begins with an Applied Math Preview. This preview will help improve your math skills, which you will need to be successful in record keeping.

JOB 1 ▶ RECORD KEEPING AND THE COMPUTER

APPLIED MATH PREVIEW

Copy and answer each problem. Do your work neatly.

1.	2.	3.	4.	5.
17	5,174	2.04	$970.21	$2,008.46
33	56	16.7	7.34	5,107.09
82	279	0.92	25.86	0.29
45	1,036	208.004	200.45	356.98
+ 38	+ 209	+ 3.05	+ 0.78	+ 119.05

▲▲▲▲▲
TIP
▼▼▼▼▼

Make sure that you align the decimal points when you copy the numbers in each problem.

BUSINESS TERMS PREVIEW

- Computer printout • Electronically • Enter • Manually •
- Merchandise • Position • Record • Record keeping jobs •

GOALS

1. To learn about record keeping positions.
2. To learn why records are important.
3. To introduce you to careers in record keeping and computers.

No matter what kind of **position** or job you take when you graduate, you will probably have to keep some records as part of your work.

A **record** is a form on which information has been **entered**, or recorded. Many records are still completed and kept by hand, or **manually**. When records are kept manually, the information is usually recorded on paper.

Many records are also completed and kept by computers, or **electronically**. When records are kept electronically, the information is usually entered into a computer and stored on a disk.

A *sales clerk* in one store may fill out a sales slip for a customer manually. A sales clerk in another store may fill out a sales slip for a customer using a computer.

The sales slip prepared with the computer has the same types of information as the sales slip prepared manually. Knowing what a sales slip is and how to fill it out correctly is important to learn, whether you will use a computer or a pencil or pen to do it. You can also see that knowing about computers is very important in most jobs.

You might ask, "Why do we need to keep so many records?" The answer is that we need all kinds of information to run our stores, farms, factories, businesses, schools, and other organizations. For example, we need information to know:

a. How much we have sold
b. What our expenses are
c. If we are making a profit
d. How much our customers owe us
e. How much we owe others
f. How much cash we have
g. How much tax we owe
h. If we have enough goods on hand to sell to our customers

Because of the large number of records we must keep, computers are often used to help complete and keep records. Computers have become common in homes, factories, farms, and offices because they help us keep records faster and more accurately. However, you should remember that we must keep the same information whether it is kept manually or on a computer.

K E Y   Terms

Position. Job.

Record. A form on which information is recorded.

Enter. To record information on a form or into a computer.

Manually. By hand.

Electronically. By computer.

K E Y *Terms*

Merchandise. Goods that a business sells.

Computer printout. A document prepared by a computer.

Record keeping jobs. Jobs where handling records is most of the work.

Because computers are so common, nearly every job involves computers in some way. Some workers may use computers directly in their work. For example, an *order entry clerk* is a worker who prepares sales order forms for customers ordering **merchandise**, or goods that the business sells. Some order entry clerks may take an order over the phone from a customer and enter that order directly into the computer.

Other workers may use the computer indirectly. For example, a *stock clerk* may use a list of merchandise stored in the computer to find an item that a customer wants.

The list prepared by the computer is called a **computer printout.** Whatever the computer prints on a printer is called a printout. Knowing how to read and use computer printouts is very useful since they are used in many jobs today.

Nearly every job requires the use and handling of records. Those jobs in businesses, farms, factories, and offices in which workers spend most of their time handling records are called **record keeping jobs**. Look at the list of record keeping jobs shown in Illustration 1A, below.

Illustration 1A
A computer printout listing some record keeping jobs

```
Employees who keep records about customers and the goods they buy:
        Billing Clerk
        Accounts Receivable Clerk
        Invoice Clerk
        Order Entry Clerk

Employees who keep records about employees:
        Time Clerk
        Benefits Clerk
        Commission Clerk
        Payroll Clerk
        Personnel Clerk

Employees who keep records about the goods the firm buys:
        Purchase Order Clerk
        Receiving Clerk
        Stock Clerk

Employees who keep records about cash:
        Cashier
        Teller
        Cashier Checker
        Ticket Clerk

Employees who keep other kinds of records:
        Data Entry Clerk
        Posting Clerk
        Records Clerk
        Administrative Clerk
        Office Assistant
        Voucher Clerk
        Accounts Payable Clerk
```

To get and keep a record keeping job, you usually will need:

a. A high school diploma
b. Some training in record keeping principles and practices
c. Some knowledge of computer terms and equipment
d. The ability to operate office machines such as the typewriter, telephone, and calculator
e. The ability to meet people, talk to them, and cooperate with others
f. The ability to read and follow directions
g. These work habits and attitudes:
   —accuracy in your math
   —accuracy in copying numbers and names
   —neatness in your writing, math, and record keeping
   —checking all your work all the time
   —promptness in getting to work
   —completing all your work all the time

The knowledge, skills, and work habits you will learn in this course will help you get and keep that first record keeping job. The same knowledge, skills, and work habits will also help you advance in your work to jobs with more responsibility and higher pay.

BUILDING YOUR BUSINESS VOCABULARY

On a sheet of paper, write the headings **Statement Number** and **Words**. Next, choose the words that match the statements. Write each word you choose next to the statement number it matches. The first one is done for you to show you how. Be careful; not all the words listed should be used.

	Statement Number	Words
Sample Answer:	1	enter

Statements	Words
1. To record information on a form or into a computer	computer printout
	electronically
2. Forms on which information is recorded	enter
3. Goods that a business is selling	manually
4. A job	merchandise
5. By hand	position
6. Anything the computer has printed	record keeping jobs
7. By computer	records
8. Jobs in which workers spend most of their time handling records	sales clerk
	stock clerk

APPLICATION PROBLEMS

PROBLEM | **I-I** ▶ Working papers are available for completing the problems in each job of this textbook. If the working papers are used, you do not have to copy headings or prepare forms on sheets of paper.

Directions

CHECKPOINT ✓

I-I
Four answers are true.

Write the numbers 1 through 10 on a sheet of paper. Next to each number place a *T* if the statement is true or an *F* if the statement is false.

1. Only a few jobs require you to use records.
2. A form prepared with a computer usually contains the same information as that same form would if it were prepared manually.
3. Any job in which records are kept is a record keeping job.
4. Knowing how to do math accurately is not important anymore, since computers do all the math in record keeping jobs.
5. One reason records are kept is to find out how much tax you owe.
6. Persons who do record keeping work alone. They do not need to be able to work with others.
7. A high school diploma is usually needed to get a record keeping job.
8. A promotion usually means more responsibility but not more pay.
9. Knowledge of computers is not important in record keeping jobs.
10. Knowing how to operate office machines is important in record keeping work.

PROBLEM | **I-2** ▶ Juanita works in the stock room of a large business. One of her duties is to record the amount of each item that the business has in stock on a stock record. This is a form which lists the item number, the item description, and the amount of the item on the shelves.

When Juanita is finished recording the amount of each item that the business has on the stock records, she gives the forms to another employee who records when the business buys or sells the item.

Directions

CHECKPOINT ✓

I-2 (4)
Promptness is an example of a work habit.

Write the numbers 1 through 4 on a sheet of paper. Write your answer to each of the following questions next to the correct number.

1. Look at the list of job titles in Illustration 1A, page 3. What might the title of Juanita's job be?
2. What is the name of one record that Juanita must keep?

3. What might happen if Juanita makes a mistake in counting and recording the amount of any stock item?
4. What are three work habits a person working in Juanita's position should have?

PROBLEM | 1-3 ▶ Sheila works in the marketing department of a small business. One of her duties is to take customer orders over the phone. Sheila completes a sales order form for every customer who orders merchandise.

When Sheila receives a telephone call from a customer, she records the information on the sales order form.

Directions

1-3 (2)
A computer is an office machine.

Write the numbers 1 through 5 on a sheet of paper. Write your answer to each of the following questions next to the correct number.

1. Look at the job titles listed in Illustration 1A, page 3. What might the title of Sheila's job be?
2. What are three types of office machines that Sheila might use?
3. What are three work habits which would be important for anyone in Sheila's position?
4. What is the name of one record that Sheila must use?
5. What might happen if Sheila makes a mistake entering the information?

APPLIED MATH PREVIEW

Copy and complete each problem. Write the numbers legibly.

1.	2.	3.	4.
423	56.91	3,007.198	$ 87,106.54
− 85	− 27.34	− 502.64	− 23,900.48

▲▲▲▲▲
TIP
▼▼▼▼▼

Check your subtraction in each problem by adding the answer you got to the number you subtracted. For example, 76 - 46 = 30. To check the subtraction, 46 + 30 = 76.

BUSINESS TERMS PREVIEW

- Data • Data entry clerks • Double ruling • Footing • MICR •
- Money column • OCR • Optical mark recognition • UPC •

GOALS

1. To learn how to enter and correct data on business forms.
2. To learn to read special data processing symbols.

𝒰NDERSTANDING THE JOB

KEY Terms

Data. Information.

Data entry clerks. Workers who enter data using a computer.

A frequent task of record keepers is to enter information, or **data**, into forms or records. Sometimes data are entered manually. For example, a store clerk may enter data about a sale onto a sales slip with a pen. Sometimes data are entered using a computer. For example, school office workers may enter data from student enrollment forms using a computer so that printouts of class schedules and class lists can be made. Workers who enter data using a computer terminal are called **data entry clerks**.

The important thing about entering data is that it must be done accurately and neatly. Entering accurate data in a computer is especially important. If you enter incorrect data into a computer, all printouts using that data will be incorrect.

In this job you will first learn how to enter data onto forms manually. Then you will learn about special symbols used to enter data with computers.

Peggy Knowles is a record keeper for the El Paso Jays, a minor league baseball team. Knowles was asked to make a list of the bills that the team owes at the end of the month for the team treasurer. On December 31, Knowles prepared the list shown in Illustration 2A.

Illustration 2A   List of bills due

El Paso Jays Baseball Team					
List of Bills Due					
December 31, 19--					
NAME	AMOUNT DUE				
Arlington Hotel	1	5	3	4	19
Cassens Transportation Service, Inc.		8	0	2	89
Fairmont Uniform Company		4	8	2	80
Jepel Sporting Goods, Inc.			9	4	39
Total Bills Due	2	9	1	4	27

Now let's see how Knowles did this job:

STEP 1 ▶ *Enter the heading.*

On most business forms there is a heading which tells WHO, WHAT, and WHEN about the form. The first line answers WHO. The second line answers WHAT. The third line answers WHEN. The heading that Knowles entered was:

> WHO the form is for: El Paso Jays Baseball Team
> WHAT the form contains: List of Bills Due
> WHEN the form was completed: December 31, 19--

STEP 2 ▶ *Enter the names and amounts.*

Knowles took each bill and entered the name of the company to whom the bill was owed in the Name column. Then she entered the amount owed to each company in the column headed Amount Due.

A column on a form used for recording amounts of money is called a **money column**. A money column has vertical lines which help you keep the amounts of money you enter aligned. Look at Illustration 2B.

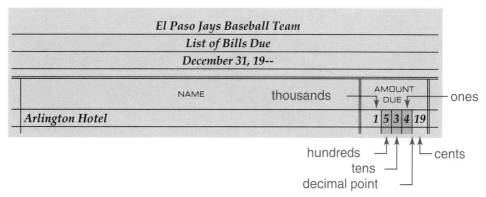

K E Y *Terms*

Money column. A column on a form used for recording amounts of money.

Footing. Total of money column written in small, neat figures.

To enter the amount of the first bill, $1,534.19, Knowles went to the thousands space and wrote "1," for $1,000. She then entered the rest of the amount. Knowles found the place to enter the 1 quickly because she knew that the thousands place is the first space to the left of the four vertical lines. Notice that these lines separate the hundreds, tens, and ones. There are no special lines to separate thousands, ten thousands, or more. There is also no line separating ten cents from one cent.

STEP 3 ▶ *Check the names and number of items listed.*

Knowles checked to see that she had spelled the name of each company correctly. She also counted the bills she had and compared that count with the number of bills she listed on the form. She counted four bills and found that she had listed four names on the form. She did this to make sure that she did not skip a bill or list a bill twice.

STEP 4 ▶ *Rule the money column.*

When Knowles had entered all the bills due, she drew a line under the last amount. The line shows that the amounts are to be added. Knowles used a ruler to make the ruling neat and straight.

STEP 5 ▶ *Foot the column.*

Knowles added the amounts in the column and put the total in small figures just below the line. These figures are called **footings**. Record keepers use a sharp pencil to make their footings in small, neat figures.

STEP 6 ▶ Check the total.

To check the total, Knowles added the amounts again. This time she added *from the bottom up* and got the same total.

STEP 7 ▶ Write in the final total.

Since Knowles got the same answer as before, she wrote the words "Total Bills Due" in the Name column and then wrote the final total below the footings.

Sometimes a total or an amount is negative. This can happen when you return goods to the seller. For example, the El Paso Jays may have returned $100.00 in goods bought from Jepel Sporting Goods, Inc. at an earlier date. This means that they really owe Jepel Sporting Goods nothing. In fact, Jepel Sporting Goods owes them $5.61, or the difference between the $100.00 of goods returned and the $94.39 bill owed.

When amounts are negative, record keepers often show them in parentheses. (See Illustration 2C.)

Illustration 2C   Entering negative amounts

| Jepel Sporting Goods, Inc. | | (5 61) |

STEP 8 ▶ Double rule the money column.

Knowles used a ruler to draw a double line under the final total. The double line shows that the record keeper is finished. Record keepers call this double line a **double ruling**.

You should notice some other things about the way the form was completed. Notice that

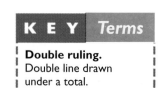

KEY *Terms*

Double ruling. Double line drawn under a total.

1. No dollar signs were entered. When using a lined money column, it is understood that the amounts shown are money.
2. No commas or decimal points were entered. When using lined money columns, the vertical lines replace the commas and decimal points.

Making Corrections

When record keepers make corrections in amounts on forms, they usually do not erase the old amount. Instead, they cross out the old amount and write the correct amount above or beside it. For example, after completing the List of Bills Due, Knowles found that the amount owed to Fairmont Uniform Company should have been $482.08 instead of $482.80. To correct the error, she did not erase the amount. Instead, the old amount was crossed out and the correct amount was written above it. Then the columns were re-added, the old total was crossed out, and the correct total was written beside it. Look at Illustration 2D.

El Paso Jays Baseball Team					
List of Bills Due					
December 31, 19--					

NAME	AMOUNT DUE				
Arlington Hotel	1	5	3	4	19
Cassens Transportation Service, Inc.		8	0	2	89
Fairmont Uniform Company		4 8	8 2	2	08 80
Jepel Sporting Goods, Inc.			9	4	39
Total Bills Due 2913.55	2	9	1	4	27

By making corrections this way, anyone can see exactly what happened. Another record keeper can quickly see that the old amount was changed, and so was the total. Anyone examining Knowles's work could check the old bill for the El Paso Jays and see why the change was made.

Entering Data with Computers

Record keepers working with computer forms often have to read and write using a different set of numbers than those we normally use.

For example, the letter *O* looks much like the number 0. To avoid having a zero entered into a computer incorrectly as a letter *O*, record keepers may put a slash through the zero. In this way, a person entering data into a computer will know that a Ø is a zero, not an *O*. Other numbers may also be confused with letters of the alphabet, and so they may be written differently. For example, look at these numbers:

Ø   1   7

zero   one   seven

Notice that the number one has been drawn with a base and a top to it. This may be done to make sure that the letter l is not entered instead of the number one. Also notice that a slash has been drawn through the seven. This is done so that it is not mistaken for a poorly written nine or a poorly written one.

Numbers may also be printed in a special way so that they can be read directly by the computer. Thus, they will not have to be entered by a person at a computer. One way to print numbers so they can be read directly by the computer is to use Magnetic Ink Character Recognition (**MICR**) numbers. Here is how the numbers 0 through 9 look in MICR:

Banks print checking account numbers and their bank number on the bottom of checks in MICR. (See Illustration 2E.) This speeds their processing of all the checks that are brought into the banks.

K E Y *Terms*

MICR. Magnetic Ink
Character Recognition.

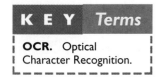
Another way to print numbers so that they can be read directly by a computer is to use Optical Character Recognition (**OCR**) numbers. There are many styles of OCR numbers. Here is how one style of OCR numbers from 0 through 9 looks:

0 1 2 3 4 5 6 7 8 9

Illustration 2E   A check printed with MICR numbers

I-CHEN K. WU
6093 Hunt Street, N.
Portland, OR 97203-1893

Date _October 15,_____ 19 __

No. **3889**

12-332
1260

Pay to the order of _Tanner Apparel Company_____ $ _81.67_

_Eighty-one 67/100_____ **Dollars**

For Classroom Use Only

MOUNTAIN NATIONAL BANK
MD   Portland, OR 97223-8912

I-Chen K. Wu

⑈012600635⑈ 208⑈145

Bank Number   Checking Account Number

Credit card account numbers are often embossed, or pressed into the card, in OCR form. The style of OCR numbers used on credit cards is shown in Illustration 2F. •

Illustration 2F   A credit card embossed with the account number in OCR

Seasons Department Store

0046062-1

L. J. RAMEY

When a customer pays by using a credit card, salespersons in stores usually check the credit card account number by using a computer or a book. The book lists those credit cards that have been lost or stolen. Many office and sales workers must know how to read OCR numbers as part of their jobs.

KEY Terms

Optical mark recognition Allows pencil marks to be read by special machines.

UPC Bar code read by special cash registers.

There are a number of other ways in which numbers and letters may be printed so that they can be read directly by a computer. These include optical mark recognition and the Universal Product Code as shown in Illustration 2G.

Optical mark recognition is often used by water and gas meter readers and by persons who take tests. Pencils are used to mark numbers or letters on forms which can be read by special machines. The Universal Product Code, or **UPC**, is a bar code marked on store products which can be read by special cash registers. It is also used to mark railroad cars so that they can be tracked by computer.

Illustration 2G   Optical mark recognition and the Universal Product Code

Optical marks

Bar codes

ⒷUILDING YOUR BUSINESS VOCABULARY

On a sheet of paper, write the headings **Statement Number** and **Words**. Next, choose the words that match the statements. Write each word you choose next to the statement number it matches. Be careful; not all the words listed should be used.

Statements	Words
1. Columns on a form used for recording amounts of money	data
2. The total of a money column written in small figures	data entry clerk
3. A set of lines used to show that the math on a form has been completed	double ruling
4. Information	electronically
5. To record something on a form	enter
6. By computer	footing
7. Magnetic Ink Character Recognition	MICR
8. Optical Character Recognition	money columns
9. A worker who enters data into a computer system	OCR
10. A bar code placed on products which can be read by special cash registers	optical mark recognition
11. Allows pencil marks to be read by special machines	output
	printer
	UPC

PROBLEM SOLVING MODEL FOR: *Entering Record Keeping Data*

Use the Problem Solving Model as a reminder when you are working on the Application Problems or studying for a test.

▲▲▲▲▲
TIP
▼▼▼▼▼

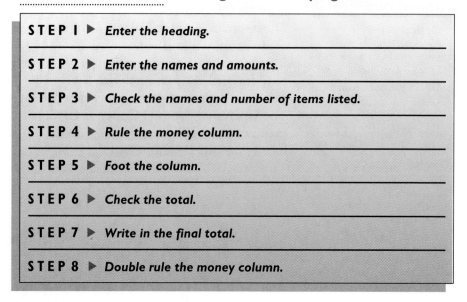

STEP 1 ▶ *Enter the heading.*

STEP 2 ▶ *Enter the names and amounts.*

STEP 3 ▶ *Check the names and number of items listed.*

STEP 4 ▶ *Rule the money column.*

STEP 5 ▶ *Foot the column.*

STEP 6 ▶ *Check the total.*

STEP 7 ▶ *Write in the final total.*

STEP 8 ▶ *Double rule the money column.*

APPLICATION PROBLEMS

PROBLEM **2-1** ▶ You are a clerk in the receiving department of Dolphin Supplies, Inc. At the end of the month, the department must prepare a list of how much money was spent and what the money was spent for.

Directions

a. On a sheet of paper, make a form with the headings and columns shown below. The form should have 3 lines at the top for the heading and 10 lines for the other entries.

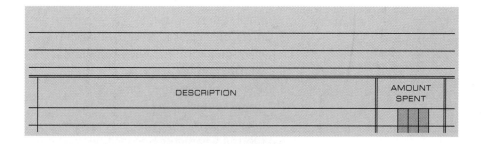

DESCRIPTION	AMOUNT SPENT

b. Enter this heading on the top three lines of the form:

Receiving Department
List of Expenses
March 31, 19--

c. Copy the following names and amounts in the correct columns of the form.

Names of Expenses	Amounts
Employee Wages	$54,208.42
Postage	1,977.29
Travel Expenses	808.65
Service Contracts	4,008.13
Telephone	2,569.01
Supplies	3,419.96
Delivery Service	1,003.08
Other Expenses	430.48

d. Check your work by comparing the names and amounts above to the names and amounts you listed on the form. Then count the number of expenses above and the number of expenses on the form.

e. Draw a line under the last amount in the Amount Spent column. Add the amounts and write the total as a footing just under the line.

CHECKPOINT ✔

2-1
Total expenses = $68,425.02

f. Check the total by re-adding the amounts in the Amount Spent column starting from the bottom of the column and adding up. If you get the same answer as you did the first time, write "Total" in the Description column and write the final total below the footing, but on the same line.

g. Draw a double ruling below the final total.

PROBLEM | 2-2 ▶ You are an accounting clerk for Sitka Pottery, Inc. One of your duties is to make a List of Amounts Owed at the end of the week, September 15, 19--. On the following page is a list of companies and the amounts Sitka Pottery owes to them.

Directions

a. On a sheet of paper, make a form with the headings and columns shown below. The form should have 3 lines at the top for the heading and 10 lines for the other entries.

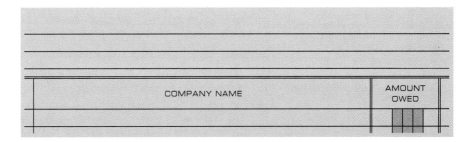

COMPANY NAME

AMOUNT OWED

b. Enter the heading on the top three lines of the form. The heading should include the name of the company, the name of the form, and the date.

c. Copy the names of and amounts owed to the following companies in the correct columns of the form.

Companies	Amounts Owed
Arnesta Craft Shops, Inc.	$ 2,730.78
Juneau Clay Mining Company	14,027.19
Seattle Shipping Corporation	2,245.61
Sheldon Brothers, Inc.	34.88
Tucson Designs, Limited	207.85
Desert Colors, Inc.	9.89
Western Outlet Store Corporation	4,304.57

d. Check your work by comparing the names and amounts above to the names and amounts on the form. Then count the number of companies above and the number of companies on the form.

e. Draw a line under the last amount in the Amount Owed column. Add the amounts and write the total as a footing just under the line.

CHECKPOINT

2-2
Total = $23,560.77

f. Check the total by re-adding the amounts in the Amount Owed column starting from the bottom of the column and adding up. If you get the same answer as you did the first time, write "Total" in the Company Name column and write the final total below the footing, but on the same line.

g. Draw a double ruling below the final total.

PROBLEM   **2-3** ▶ You are a sales clerk for a discount store. When customers pay with credit cards instead of cash, you must check to see if the credit card numbers are on a special list. This is a list of lost or stolen credit cards.

Directions

CHECKPOINT

2-3
One card is lost or stolen.

a. On a sheet of paper, write the headings "Credit Cards," "Lost or Stolen," and "OK." Then write the numbers 1 through 10 under the Credit Cards heading.

b. On the left on page 17 are ten credit card account numbers written in OCR. On the right is a list of lost or stolen credit cards. Compare each credit card number on the left to the list on the right. If you find the card number on the list, place a check mark under the Lost or Stolen heading. If you don't find the credit card number on the list, place a check mark under the OK heading.

Credit Cards

1. 467 388 309 82
2. 478 388 398 28
3. 447 287 375 28
4. 498 403 128 01
5. 445 103 323 54
6. 508 791 898 31
7. 447 101 224 64
8. 476 343 311 90
9. 439 971 989 13
10. 433 101 422 46

List of Lost or Stolen Cards

431	374	183	49	467	382	021	98
432	375	287	31	467	388	309	82
432	377	301	28	471	343	410	88
433	101	603	82	476	343	311	99
434	402	101	11	477	101	224	12
444	403	128	01	477	997	351	63
445	488	323	19	478	103	322	54
446	791	898	31	478	383	398	54
447	101	224	46	498	101	422	64
449	103	323	33	508	971	898	13

Problems 2-4 and 2-5 may be found in the Working Papers.

APPLIED MATH PREVIEW

Copy and complete each problem.

1. 35 × 94 =
2. 103 × 420 =
3. 50 × 200 =
4. 45 × $1.20 =
5. 10 × $45.89 =

6. 100 × $3.67 =
7. 1,000 × $4.80 =
8. $350 × 0.01 =
9. $14.20 × 0.05 =
10. $308.50 × 0.20 =

▲▲▲▲▲
T I P
▼▼▼▼▼

When you multiply, your answer should have the same number of decimal places as the total number of decimal places in both numbers you multiplied. If you multiply 5.26 × 0.10, your answer should have four decimal places in it: 0.5260

BUSINESS TERMS PREVIEW

- Data processing • Input • Output • Processing •
- Source documents • Transposition error • Verify •

GOALS

1. To learn about the data processing cycle.
2. To improve your verifying skills.

 **U**NDERSTANDING THE JOB

K E Y *Terms*

Data processing.
Doing things to data to make them more useful.

In business, information is usually called data. When a business does something to data to make them more useful, that is called **data processing**. For example, all these tasks are data processing activities:

1. Recording data on a business form.
2. Comparing data on one business form to data on another.
3. Copying data from one business form to another.

All data processing activities, whether they are done manually or electronically, are done in a series of steps. These steps are called the *data processing cycle*. The steps in the cycle are shown in Illustration 3A.

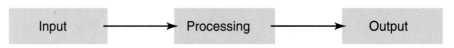

Illustration 3A   Steps in the data processing cycle

Input. First step of the data processing cycle.

Source documents. Forms from which you get data.

MULTICULTURAL INSIGHT

Scribes, persons who could read and write, were very important people in the ancient civilizations of Asia Minor and northern Africa. Most scribes recorded transactions on a small lump of moist clay, which was then dried to create a somewhat permanent record. These scribes are an example of the earliest record keepers.

For example, suppose that you go to your counselor to plan your class schedule for next year. After deciding what courses you should take, your counselor writes your name and the courses you are to take on an enrollment form like the one in Illustration 3B, below.

The counselor takes all the enrollment forms for the students to the school office. There, an office assistant enters the information from the enrollment forms into the computer. This is the **input** step, and it is the first step of the data processing cycle. The office assistant calls the enrollment forms **source documents** since these forms are the source of the information entered into the computer.

**ARLINGTON HIGH SCHOOL
STUDENT ENROLLMENT FORM**

Student Name _Melissa Brown_   Student No. _1076_

Street Address _350 Cay Boulevard_

City _Miami_   State _FL_ Zip Code _33134-5893_

Date of Enrollment _9_/_1_/_--_/

Course Choices:

1. _English II_   4. _Record Keeping_
2. _Social Studies II_   5. _Physical Education_
3. _Business Math_   6. _General Science_

Illustration 3B   Enrollment form (source document)

KEY Terms

Processing. Second step of the data processing cycle.

Output. Third step of the data processing cycle.

Verify. To check for accuracy.

Once all the student enrollment data have been entered into the computer, the computer assigns every student to a class. This is the **processing** step and the second step of the data processing cycle.

Finally, the computer prints out a class schedule for every student and class lists for the teachers. This is the **output** step and the third step of the cycle.

Notice that the computer started with the enrollment forms, or *source documents*, and finished with the class lists and student schedules, or *computer printouts*.

Workers who enter data into computers must check, or **verify**, their work very carefully. Errors made in entering data can cause many problems when the computer does its processing. You can see that just a few errors in entering student enrollment forms would throw the whole high school schedule off. In business, errors usually cost money. Look at Illustration 3C (page 20).

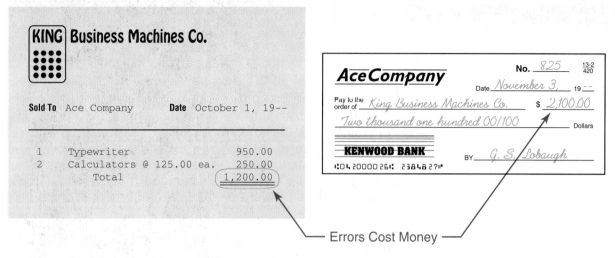

Illustration 3C   Errors in entering data cost money

Verifying your work and the work of others is an important record keeping skill, whether you do your work manually or with a computer. There are several steps which record keepers take to verify their own and others' work. Some of these steps follow:

1. *Verify the accuracy of the math.* For example, add a column of figures the second time from the bottom up.

2. *Check to see if there are omissions.* For example, check each item on a form to make sure that it is filled in. You can also count the number of source documents to make sure that one was not skipped.

3. *Check to see if there are duplications.* Count the number of source documents to make sure that one was not entered twice.

4. *Compare the information recorded* against the source document, number for number, letter for letter. Look out for a common data entry error in which the order of two numbers or letters is switched. For example, when the source document shows "1023 Clark St." and you enter "1032 Calrk St." These are known as **transposition errors**.

Illustration 3D shows a computer printout of a class list and an attendance list made by a teacher on the first day of class at Bremen High School. Sally Saunders, the school's office assistant, was asked to verify the information on the two lists. She did this by comparing the names on the class list with the names on the attendance list.

Let's look at the two steps Sally Saunders used to complete this task.

STEP 1 ▶ Prepare checklist.

Sally prepared the checklist shown in Illustration 3D. She used the following column headings: Student No., Correct, Error, Not in Class.

STEP 2 ▶ Compare data.

Sally completed the checklist by comparing the names of the students on the class list to the attendance list.

Illustration 3D   A class list and an attendance list

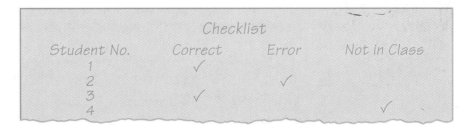

```
        Class List
Student No.  Student Name
     1       Sharon Arnold
     2       Edith Barn
     3       Garry Conners
     4       Lisa Donnel
```

Attendance List
9/5/--

Sharon Arnold
Edith Bran
Garry Conners

Checklist			
Student No.	Correct	Error	Not in Class
1	✓		
2		✓	
3	✓		
4			✓

When Sally compared the first name, Sharon Arnold, she found that the name was on both lists and compared exactly. So, she put a check mark in the Correct column on the line for Student No. 1 of the checklist.

When Sally compared the second name, she found Edith Barn's name on both lists. However, the name was not spelled correctly on the attendance list. Therefore, she put a check mark in the Error column on the line for Student No. 2 of the checklist.

When Sally compared the third name, she found Garry Conner's name on both lists compared exactly. So, she put a check mark in the Correct column on the line for Student No. 3 of the checklist.

When Sally tried to compare Lisa Donnel's name, she found that it was on the class list but not on the attendance list. Sally put a check mark on the line for Student No. 4 under the Not in Class column.

BUILDING YOUR BUSINESS VOCABULARY

On a sheet of paper, write the headings **Statement Number** and **Words**. Next, choose the words that match the statements. Write each word you choose next to the statement number it matches. Be careful; not all the words listed should be used.

Statements	Words
1. The first step in the data processing cycle	data
2. A job	data processing
3. A form on which information is kept	electronically
4. To check for accuracy	input
5. Doing something to data to make them more useful	manually
	merchandise
6. The forms from which you get the data you enter into the computer	output
	position
7. The third step in the data processing cycle	processing
8. By computer	record
9. Information	source documents
10. When numbers, letters, or other characters are switched in order	transposition error
	verify
11. The second step in the data processing cycle	

PROBLEM SOLVING MODEL FOR: *Verifying Data*

STEP 1 ▶ *Prepare checklist.*

STEP 2 ▶ *Compare data.*

PROBLEM **3-1** ▶ You are a records clerk at Belon High School. One of your duties is to verify the accuracy of the class lists on the first day of classes.

Directions

a. Make a checklist like the one in the Sample Problem using the same headings. Then write the numbers for 15 students under the Student No. heading.

```
              Class List
    Student No.  Student Name
         1        Trudy Andrews
         2        Christie Bell
         3        Renee Calvin
         4        Jeffrey Huang
         5        Fred Kennedy
         6        Susan Larmont
         7        Victor Lyman
         8        Madelin Frobel
         9        Ira Norstein
        10        Roberta Oliver
        11        Janet Petroff
        12        Robert Quigley
        13        Terry Romano
        14        Stuart Simons
        15        Vera Talent
```

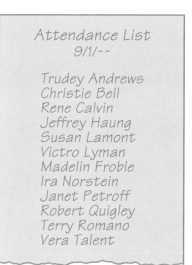

Attendance List
9/1/--

Trudey Andrews
Christie Bell
Rene Calvin
Jeffrey Haung
Susan Lamont
Victro Lyman
Madelin Froble
Ira Norstein
Janet Petroff
Robert Quigley
Terry Romano
Vera Talent

CHECKPOINT ✓

3-1
If your work is correct, you should have 6 checks in the **Correct** column, 6 checks in the **Error** column, and 3 checks in the **Not in Class** column.

b. A class list prepared by a computer and a class attendance list made by the teacher on the first day of class appear above. Complete the checklist by comparing the names of the students on the class list to the attendance list. If the names are on both lists and are exactly the same, put a check mark in the Correct column. If the names are on both lists but are not exactly the same, put a check mark in the Error column. If a name on the class list is not on the attendance list, put a check mark in the Not in Class column.

PROBLEM **3-2** ▶ You are an accounts payable clerk at Shasta Products Company. One of your duties is to maintain a list of vendors, or businesses which sell merchandise to your company.

CHECKPOINT ✔

3-2
There are 4 errors.

```
               New Vendor List
  Vendor          Vendor Name
  No.              and Address
   105        Avon Estates, Inc.
              15 Briar Lane
   106        Award Design Co.
              205 Seattle Drive
   107        Axle Products Co.
              3152 First St.
   108        Axon Machinery, Inc.
              2 South Waters St.
   109        Aztec Vendors, Inc.
              3402 Drury Avenue
   110        Azure Plumbing Supplies
              203 Freeman Boulevard
   111        Bacloff Computer Center
              One Technology Drive
   112        Baffin Color Displays
              10678 Machine St.
   113        Bagley Brothers, Inc.
              2287 River Road
   114        Bagnelle Window Co.
              1001 Vellow St.
```

New Vendor List

Avon Estates, Inc.
15 Briar Lane

Award Desing Co.
250 Seattle Drive

Axle Products Co.
3152 First Street

Avon Machinery, Inc.
2 South Waters Street

Aztec Vendors, Inc.
4302 Drury Avenue

Azure Plumbing Supplies
203 Freeman Boulevard

Backloff Computer Ctr.
One Technology Drive

Bagley Brothers, Inc.
2287 River Road

Directions

a. Make a checklist like the one in the Sample Problem but with these headings: Vendor No., Correct, Error, and Not on List. Write the numbers for 10 vendors under the Vendor No. heading, starting with 105.

b. A new vendor list prepared by the computer and another prepared by the accounts payable department are shown above. Complete the checklist by comparing the names and addresses of the vendors on the computer list to the department list. If the names and addresses are on both lists and are exactly the same, put a check mark in the Correct column. If the names and addresses are on both lists but are not exactly the same, put a check mark in the Error column. If a name on the computer list is not on the department list, put a check mark in the Not on List column.

Problems 3-3, 3-4, and 3-5 may be found in the Working Papers.

J O B **4** ▶ FILING NUMERIC DATA

APPLIED MATH PREVIEW

Copy and complete each problem.

1. 28 ÷ 4 =
2. 620 ÷ 5 =
3. $36.00 ÷ 6 =
4. $49.00 ÷ 10 =
5. $3,400 ÷ 100 =

6. $5,230.00 ÷ 1,000 =
7. $480 ÷ 40 =
8. $72.60 ÷ 12 =
9. $640 ÷ 160 =
10. $3,795 ÷ 23 =

When dividing by 10, 100, or 1,000, move the decimal point in the number to be divided one, two, or three places to the *left*. The number of places to the left is determined by the number of zeros in the number you are dividing by. For example,
$120.00 ÷ 10 = $12.00;
$120.00 ÷ 100 = $1.20;
$120.00 ÷ 1,000 = $0.12.

TIP

BUSINESS TERMS PREVIEW

- **Alphabetically** • **Central processing unit** • **Chronologically** •
- **Computer program** • **Computer system** • **Guides** •
- **Input device** • **Numerically** • **Output device** •
- **Printer** • **Sort** • **Tickler file** •

GOALS

1. To learn the names and uses of common computer equipment.
2. To learn how to file by numbers and by dates.

𝒰NDERSTANDING THE JOB

You learned in the last job that all data processing follows a set of definite steps:

Input ⟶ Processing ⟶ Output

KEY Terms

Input device. Used to enter data into a computer.

To do these data processing steps, you need tools. If you are doing manual data processing, you may use a pencil to record input data, a calculator to process the data, and a sheet of paper for the results or output.

In the same way, electronic data processing uses tools to complete the steps in the data processing cycle. For example, in the last job, the office assistant in the school office used a computer to enter the enrollment data. The keyboard or mouse is called an **input device**.

KEY Terms

Central processing unit. Part of a computer that processes data.

Computer program. Set of instructions.

Printer. An output device.

Output device. Used to get data out of a computer.

Computer system. Input devices, central processing unit, and output devices.

Sort. File data in some order.

Chronologically. By date.

Numerically. By number.

Alphabetically. By the alphabet.

Guides. Tabs to help find records.

The processing that is done, such as assigning students to the right classes, is performed by the **central processing unit** of the computer.

The central processing unit processes the data it is given according to a set of instructions. This set of instructions is called a **computer program**. For example, in order for the computer to process the enrollment data and print out the class lists and schedules, it has to be given a computer program which tells it how to do those tasks.

Another type of data processing tool is a **printer**. The printer is an **output device**. An output device is used to get information out of the computer.

The input devices, central processing unit, and output devices put together are called a **computer system**. The whole computer system is needed to complete the data processing cycle of input, processing, and output.

Large firms often use large computer systems. Smaller firms may use smaller computer systems known as minicomputers. Very small firms and many individuals use even smaller computer systems known as microcomputers.

One kind of processing which people and computers do is to **sort**, or file data in some kind of order. When the data are dates, they may be sorted in order of time, or **chronologically**. When the data are numbers, they may be sorted from the lowest number to the highest, or **numerically**. When the data are names, they may be sorted using the alphabet, or **alphabetically**.

You will learn about numerical and chronological sorting in this job. You will learn about alphabetic sorting in Job 5.

Numeric Filing

When people file records, they sort them in some way. Numeric filing means sorting records in numerical order. In this system, each record to be sorted must have a number. The records are first sorted in numerical order and then may be placed in a file with the *lowest number* at the *beginning* of the file.

Look at the numeric file in Illustration 4A (page 27). Notice that there are special tabs with numbers in the file. These are called **guides** and are used to help the record keeper find records faster.

Notice that the first guide reads 1-10; the second guide, 11-20; the third guide, 21-30; and so on. If you wanted to find a record numbered 9, you would find it behind the guide labeled 1-10. The record numbered 9 would be placed just after the record numbered 8.

If you were looking for a record numbered 27, you would look behind the guide labeled 21-30. There you would find the record numbered 27 right after the record numbered 26.

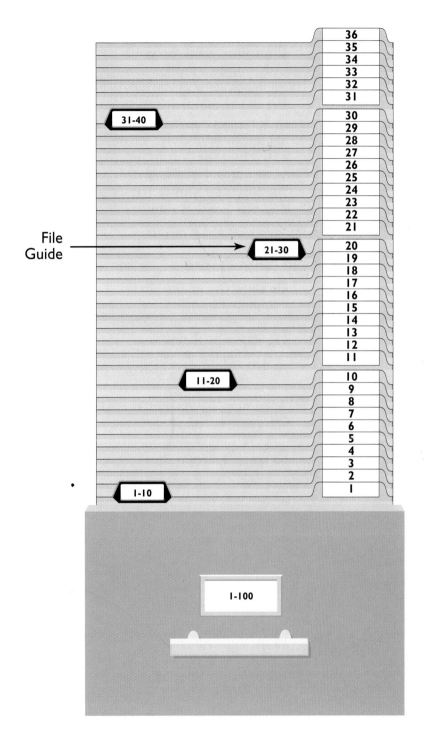

File
Guide

You are a stock clerk for the Archer Products Company. One of your duties is to prepare and file records for new products at the end of each month. The records should be sorted numerically by stock number, with the stock item with the lowest number first and the highest number last.

STEP 1 ▶ *Prepare the records.*

On the left is an unsorted list of new stock items. On the right are the completed records for the new stock items.

Archer Products Company
List of New Products
August 31, 19--

Stock No.	Description
2193	Bracket
1734	Angle iron
1683	Cutter
1922	Fastener

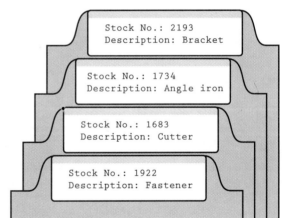

Stock No.: 2193
Description: Bracket

Stock No.: 1734
Description: Angle iron

Stock No.: 1683
Description: Cutter

Stock No.: 1922
Description: Fastener

STEP 2 ▶ *Verify your work.*

After completing the stock records, verify that you have copied the data correctly by

1. Comparing the numbers and descriptions on the records to the data on the list to see if you copied them correctly.
2. Counting the stock items on the list and comparing that count to the count of records you completed. This will let you know if you skipped an item or copied one twice.

STEP 3 ▶ *File the stock records by stock number.*

To file these stock items numerically, search through the records for the lowest stock number (1683). Put this record at the beginning of the other records. Then find the record with the next lowest stock number (1734), and place this record after the first one. File each of the remaining records in the same way.

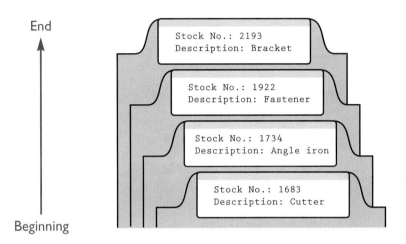

End

↑

Beginning

Stock No.: 2193
Description: Bracket

Stock No.: 1922
Description: Fastener

Stock No.: 1734
Description: Angle iron

Stock No.: 1683
Description: Cutter

Chronological Filing

Filing records chronologically means sorting them according to the date that is on them. If you borrow books from a library, you are allowed to keep the books for a limited time, such as two weeks. Do you know how the librarian knows which books must be returned on any one day? Have you wondered how a record keeper remembers which bills must be paid by a certain date?

Look at the chronological file in Illustration 4B (page 30). This file is used by librarians to help them remember what books are due on any date. It is called a chronological file, **tickler file**, or follow-up file.

Notice that there is a guide for each month. Behind the guide labeled January, there are guides for each day of the month. If you receive a bill on January 10 that has to be paid on January 20, you would place the bill behind the guide numbered 20. When January 20 comes, you will look behind the guide for that day and pay the bills you find there.

After paying the bills due on January 20, you would take the guide for that day and put it behind the guide for February. As each day goes by, the numbered guide for that day would be shifted to the next month. By the end of January, all the numbered guides would have been shifted behind the guide for February. That is why there is only one set of guides numbered 1 through 31 in the file.

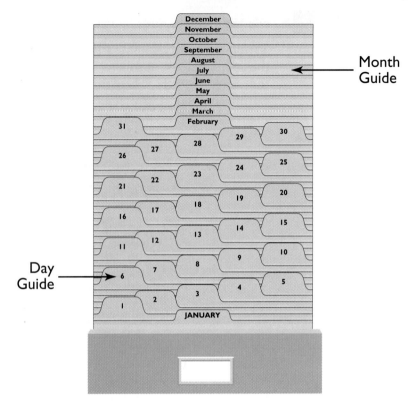

Illustration 4B   Chronological file with guides

SAMPLE PROBLEM 2

You are an office assistant for the Mountain Travel Tour Company. One of your duties is to make a schedule which shows which tours are being held on what dates. The tours should be listed *chronologically* by date.

 ► **Enter the heading.**

On a sheet of paper, write the heading:

Mountain Travel Tour Company
Summer Tour Schedule
April 1, 19--

STEP 2 ▶ *File the tours by date.*

List the tours, recording the tour with the earliest date first and the tour with the latest date last. The unsorted list of tours on the left has been sorted in chronological order on the right.

Unsorted List of Tours	Sorted List of Tours
June 4, Hidden Valley Tour	May 15, River Raft Tour
May 21, River Cave Tour	May 21, River Cave Tour
May 15, River Raft Tour	June 4, Hidden Valley Tour
July 8, Mountain Ridge Tour	July 8, Mountain Ridge Tour

STEP 3 ▶ *Verify your work.*

After the tours have been sorted by date, verify your work by:

1. Comparing the tour dates and names on both lists to make sure you have copied each date and tour name correctly.
2. Counting the tours on both lists to make sure that you have not copied one twice or failed to copy one at all.

𝓑UILDING YOUR BUSINESS VOCABULARY

On a sheet of paper, write the headings **Statement Number** and **Words**. Next, choose the words that match the statements. Write each word you choose next to the statement number it matches. Be careful; not all the words listed should be used.

Statements	Words
1. By number	alphabetically
2. By date	central processing unit
3. To file in some order	chronologically
4. A group of input devices, output devices, and a central processing unit	computer program
	computer system
5. By the alphabet	data
6. The part of the computer system that does the processing of data	guides
	input device
7. Used to get data out of a computer	manually
8. A set of instructions that the computer follows to process the data	numerically
	output device
9. Used to help find records in a file	printer
10. A chronological file which reminds workers of important dates	sort
	tickler file
11. Used to enter data into a computer	
12. An output device	

PROBLEM SOLVING MODEL FOR: *Filing Numeric Data*

STEP 1 ▶ *Prepare the records.*

STEP 2 ▶ *Verify your work.*

STEP 3 ▶ *File the records by number.*

APPLICATION PROBLEMS

PROBLEM **4-1** ▶ You are a records clerk in the payroll department of the Northern Tour Company. One of your duties is to keep lists of employees sorted alphabetically and numerically. You are given the list of employees below which is sorted alphabetically by the employee name. Your job is to make another list sorted numerically by employee number.

CHECKPOINT ✔

4-1

If your work is correct, the first employee on your *numerically* arranged list should be Olga Herman (234). The last employee should be Maria Aponte (498).

Directions

a. On a sheet of paper, write the heading:

> Northern Tour Company
> Employees by Number
> January 31, 19--

b. Under the heading, write the column headings "Employee Number" and "Employee Name."

Employee Number	Employee Name
498	Aponte, Maria
243	Barton, Don
308	Charles, Tina
380	Dressler, Lamont
497	Eller, Chris
489	Franklin, Tyrone
334	Ginsberg, Irving
234	Herman, Olga
409	Isaacs, Joel
388	Kinsey, Martha

c. Sort the employees numerically by employee number. Place the employee with the lowest number first.

d. Verify your work by comparing the numbers and names in the original list to your list and counting the names in both lists.

PROBLEM **4-2** ▶ You are a clerk in the sales department of Raker Communications Company. You are given the lists of salespeople in each sales territory below. Rewrite each list so that it is sorted numerically by employee number.

Employees by Sales Territories			
North	South	East	West
1078 Johnson	1108 Billings	2710 Canter	2061 Yankle
2716 Wu-ling	1008 Edison	1072 Rodriguez	1066 Quible
2218 Capolo	1072 O'Hara	1027 Bernstein	1606 Powers
1087 Faraday	1801 Elmwood	1109 Davis	2606 Vasson
2128 Washington	1782 Granger	1081 Walen	2616 Munson

Directions

a. On a sheet of paper, write the heading:

Raker Communications Company
Salespeople by Territory
February 28, 19--

CHECKPOINT ✔

4-2
The last employee in the West territory should be Munson (2616).

b. Write the headings for each territory (North, South, East, West).
c. Sort the employees in each territory numerically by employee number. Record the employee with the lowest number in each territory first.
d. Verify your work by (1) comparing the original list of names to your list, and (2) counting the number of employees on both lists to be sure you did not copy a name twice or forget a name.

Problems 4-3, 4-4, and 4-5 may be found in the Working Papers.

APPLIED MATH PREVIEW

Change each percent to a decimal.

1. 20%	6. 63%	11. 70%	16. 7%
2. 25%	7. 4%	12. 30%	17. 3%
3. 50%	8. 12%	13. 10%	18. 1%
4. 75%	9. 82%	14. 52%	19. 4.5%
5. 29%	10. 91%	15. 19%	20. 7.51%

▲▲▲▲▲
TIP
▼▼▼▼▼

To change a percent to a decimal, move the decimal point two places to the left and drop the percent sign.

BUSINESS TERMS PREVIEW

- **Documents** • **Indexing** • **Record clerks** •
- **Retrieve** • **Store** • **Surname** •

GOAL

To learn basic rules for filing documents alphabetically in a manual filing system.

UNDERSTANDING THE JOB

KEY *Terms*

Record clerks. Workers specially trained to store and retrieve documents.

Documents. Business papers.

Store. File.

Retrieve. Find.

Almost everyone does some filing. Secretaries, managers, supervisors, stock clerks, salespersons, homeowners—all must file papers that are important to their job or personal life.

The job of filing is often done by special workers called **record clerks**. Record clerks are trained to keep data in an orderly way. They must be able to find information quickly and easily when it is needed.

Record clerks often use special terms in their work. They may call letters, bills, invoices, and other business papers **documents**. (See Illustration 5A on page 35.) When they file a document, they may say that they have **stored** it. When they get a document from the files, they may say that they have **retrieved** it.

Record clerks may store documents in many ways. They may store paper documents in file folders. They may store documents in *microfilm* form. They may also store documents using a computer system.

In this job you will learn how to file documents alphabetically. You will learn how filing is done with computer systems in the next job.

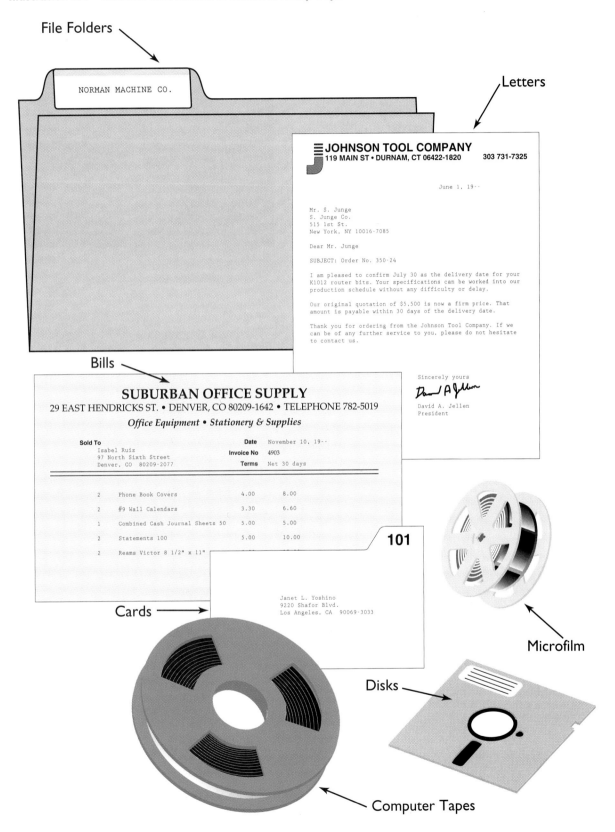

File Folders

NORMAN MACHINE CO.

Letters

≡JOHNSON TOOL COMPANY
119 MAIN ST • DURNAM, CT 06422-1820   303 731-7325

June 1, 19--

Mr. S. Junge
S. Junge Co.
515 1st St.
New York, NY 10016-7085

Dear Mr. Junge

SUBJECT: Order No. 350-24

I am pleased to confirm July 30 as the delivery date for your
K1012 router bits. Your specifications can be worked into our
production schedule without any difficulty or delay.

Our original quotation of $5,500 is now a firm price. That
amount is payable within 30 days of the delivery date.

Thank you for ordering from the Johnson Tool Company. If we
can be of any further service to you, please do not hesitate
to contact us.

Sincerely yours

David A. Jellen
President

Bills

SUBURBAN OFFICE SUPPLY
29 EAST HENDRICKS ST. • DENVER, CO 80209-1642 • TELEPHONE 782-5019
Office Equipment • Stationery & Supplies

Sold To	Date	November 10, 19--
Isabel Ruiz	Invoice No	4903
97 North Sixth Street		
Denver, CO 80209-2077	Terms	Net 30 days

2	Phone Book Covers	4.00	8.00
2	#9 Wall Calendars	3.30	6.60
1	Combined Cash Journal Sheets 50	5.00	5.00
2	Statements 100	5.00	10.00
2	Reams Victor 8 1/2" x 11"		

101

Janet L. Yoshino
9220 Shafor Blvd.
Los Angeles, CA 90069-3033

Cards

Microfilm

Disks

Computer Tapes

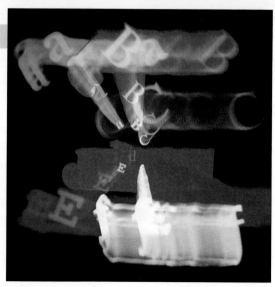

Filing documents alphabetically means sorting them according to the letters of the alphabet. Look at the alphabetic file in Illustration 5B. Notice that there is a guide for each letter of the alphabet and that each guide is arranged in alphabetical order: "B" is after "A"; "C" is after "B"; and so forth.

Illustration 5B
Alphabetic file with guides

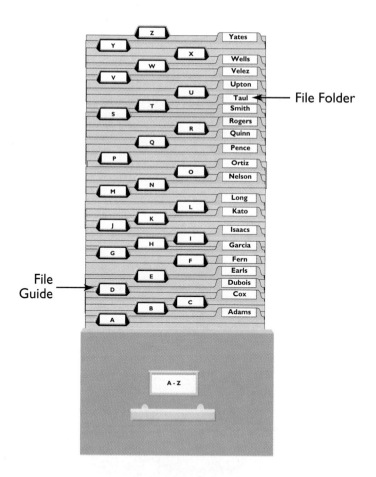

File Folder

File Guide

Now let's learn the rules to use this system.

RULE 1 ▶ *File papers by the last name (surname).*

If you need a document that was sent to your company by Alice Baker, where in the files would you look for it? Behind guide "A" for Alice, or behind guide "B" for Baker?

Rule 1 tells you that you file documents according to the last name, or **surname**. So you would look behind the "B" guide for Alice Baker's document.

Notice that on the tab of the file folder below, Alice Baker's last name was put first. Arranging the parts of a name so that they are in filing order is called **indexing**. Alice Baker's name has been put in indexing order on the file folder tab below.

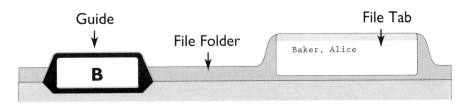

RULE 2 ▶ *When the surnames of people begin with the same first letter, use the second letter in the name to decide which name is to be filed in front of the other. If both the first and second letters are the same, use the third letter, and so forth.*

Suppose that you had to retrieve documents sent to your company from Vicki Cole and Judy Carmen. Using Rule 1, you would look at the surnames. Since both begin with "C," you would use Rule 2 and look at the second letter in each last name. Since the second letter of Carmen is an "a" and the second letter of Cole is an "o," you would find the document from Cole behind the document from Carmen.

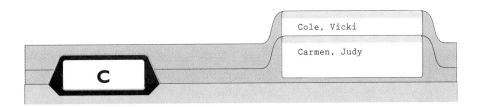

In the same way, you would find a document from Yolanda Roland behind a document from Amanda Robley. In this case, you had to go to the third letter in each name to find a difference.

RULE 3 ▶ *File "nothing" before "something."*

Suppose that you wanted to store documents from Lucia Ramos and from Lucia Ramosa. Using Rule 3, you would file Lucia Ramos before Lucia Ramosa since *nothing* follows the "s" in Ramos, but an "a" follows the "s" in Ramosa.

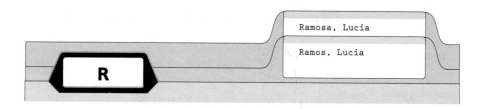

In the same way, a document from Roger Marti*n* would be stored before one from Roger Marti*nez*.

RULE 4 ▶ *If the surnames of people are the same, compare the first letters of the first names to decide how to file them. If the first letter of the first names is the same, use the second letter, and so forth.*

If you had to retrieve documents from Leroy Travis and Michael Travis, you would find the one from Leroy Travis before the one from Michael Travis. The last names are the same. So the first three rules do not apply. You must look at the first names of the persons. Since "L" in Leroy comes before "M" in Michael, the document from Leroy Travis would be found before the one from Michael Travis.

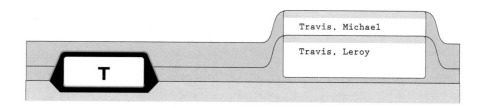

In the same way, a document from *Michi* Nozaki would be found before one from *Oki* Nozaki.

Do you know why a document from I. Rubenstein would be found before a document from Ira Rubenstein? Using Rule 3 (nothing comes before something), *I.* Rubenstein would be stored before *Ira* Rubenstein. This is because no letter follows the "I" in I. Rubenstein while the letter "r" follows the "I" in Ira Rubenstein.

RULE 5 ▶ *A middle name or middle initial is used to decide alphabetic order only if the surnames and first names are both the same.*

Suppose you had to retrieve documents from Andrea Vera Schmidt and Andrea Julia Schmidt. Since both surnames and first names are alike, you would have to use the middle names to decide the order. You would find the document from Andrea *Julia* Schmidt before the one from Andrea *Vera* Schmidt.

If a document from Andrea J. Schmidt was to be stored in the file, you would place it before the document from Andrea Julia Schmidt. Rule 3 tells you that nothing is filed before something. Since the surnames and first names are alike, you would use the middle names or initials to decide the order. The "J" in Andrea J. Schmidt had no letters after it, while the "J" in Andrea Julia Schmidt had a "u" after it.

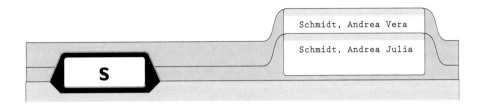

RULE 6 ▶ *When a person's whole name appears in a business name, treat the name as if it were by itself.*

Suppose you had to store documents from Denise Breimer Company and Denise Breimer in a file. Which one would you file first? Using Rule 6, you would first index the documents this way:

> Breimer, Denise
> Breimer, Denise, Company

Then, using Rule 3, you would file the document from Denise Breimer before the document from Denise Breimer Company, because you file nothing before something.

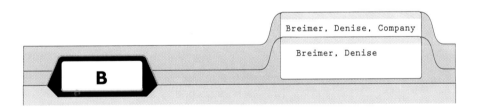

RULE 7 ▶ *Business names that do not contain the whole names of persons are filed according to their first words. If the first words are the same, the second words are compared, and so forth.*

You store a document from the Apex Solvent Company behind the "A" guide because the first word of the company name begins with "A." A document from the A One Solvent Company would be filed behind the "A" guide also, since the first word of this company name begins with "A." The document from the A One Solvent Company would be filed before the document from the Apex Solvent Company. The first word in the A One Solvent Company is "A." The first word in the Apex Solvent Company is "Apex." Since Rule 3 shows that nothing comes before something, the document beginning with the word "A" comes before the document beginning with the word "Apex."

You would place a document from the Apex Solvent Company before a document from the Apex Transportation Company. Since both company names have the same first word, you must compare the next word in both company names. Since "S" comes before "T," the solvent company document would be placed before the transportation company document.

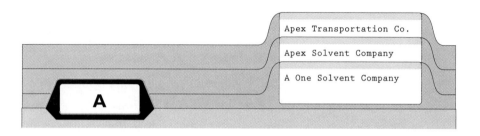

Apex Transportation Co.

Apex Solvent Company

A One Solvent Company

A

BUILDING YOUR BUSINESS VOCABULARY

On a sheet of paper, write the headings **Statement Number** and **Words**. Next, choose the words that match the statements. Write each word you choose next to the statement number it matches. Be careful; not all the words listed should be used.

Statements	Words
1. Workers trained to store and retrieve data	data entry clerks
2. Letters, bills, and business papers	documents
3. To file a document	double rulings
4. To find a document	footing
5. Metal tabs used to help record clerks find documents	guides
	indexing
6. A chronological file used to remind workers of important dates	money columns
	OCR
7. Workers who enter data in a computer system	record clerks
	retrieve
8. Used for recording amounts of money on a form	store
	surname
9. The total of a column written in small figures	tickler file
10. Arranging the parts of a name so that it can be filed	
11. Last name	

RULE 1 ▶ *File papers by the last name (surname).*

RULE 2 ▶ *When the surnames of people begin with the same first letter, use the second letter in the name to decide which name is to be filed in front of the other. If both the first and second letters are the same, use the third letter, and so forth.*

RULE 3 ▶ *File "nothing" before "something."*

RULE 4 ▶ *If the surnames of people are the same, compare the first letters of the first names to decide how to file them. If the first letter of the first names is the same, use the second letter, and so forth.*

RULE 5 ▶ *A middle name or middle initial is used to decide alphabetic order only if the surnames and first names are both the same.*

RULE 6 ▶ *When a person's whole name appears in a business name, treat the name as if it were by itself.*

RULE 7 ▶ *Business names that do not contain the whole names of persons are filed according to their first words. If the first words are the same, the second words are compared, and so forth.*

APPLICATION PROBLEMS

| PROBLEM | 5-1 ▶ You are a records clerk for Marshall College. You store and retrieve documents about students. You have been asked by your supervisor to make a card file for the new students below.

Directions

CHECKPOINT ✓

5-1
The first name on the list should be Adams, Stanley. The last name should be West, Thomas.

a. Copy on 3" x 5" cards, or separate pieces of paper, each name below. Write the names in indexing order (surname first, followed by a comma and the first name or initial); for example, Evans, Betty.

Arlene Smith	Thomas West
Wilma Brandt	Laverne Washington
Stanley Adams	Clay Monroe
Anna Marino	Wilma Brant
Raul Morales	Timothy O'Reilly
Olga Svenson	Francis Kowalski

b. Arrange the cards or slips of paper in alphabetical order using Rules 1 and 2.

c. List each name in alphabetical order on another sheet of paper.

PROBLEM 5-2 ▶ You work as an office assistant for a job placement office. Your supervisor gives you the following list of job applicants and asks you to make a card file for them.

Directions

a. Copy on 3" x 5" cards, or separate pieces of paper, the name of each job applicant below. Write the names in indexing order (surname first, followed by a comma and the first name or initial).

Clyde Trane	Henry Thompson
Laura Truman	Gregg Trumon
Henry Thomson	Susan Trolan
Carole Thomas	Thomas Travis
Sandra Tollman	Adele Tromain
Frank Tolan	Sophia Trevis

b. Using Rules 1 and 2, arrange the cards or slips of paper in alphabetical order.

c. After sorting the names in alphabetical order, list each name in alphabetical order on another sheet of paper.

PROBLEM 5-3 ▶ You are employed by the Effingham Raiders, a professional football team. At the start of summer training, you are given the names of the new team members below and asked to make a card file for them.

Directions

a. Copy on 3" x 5" cards, or separate pieces of paper, the name of each player below. Write the names in indexing order (surname first, followed by a comma and the first name or initial).

Edmund Pagan	Vincent Pagano
Randolph Comisky	Oren Stein
Anton Comiski	Allen Palen
Daniel Campbell	Robert Steinberg
Gary Paganos	Tyrone Patterson
Aaron Domski	Albert Steinman

b. Using Rules 1, 2, and 3, arrange the cards or slips of paper in alphabetical order.

c. After sorting the names in alphabetical order, list each name in alphabetical order on another sheet of paper.

Problems 5-4, 5-5, and 5-6 may be found in the Working Papers.

JOB 6 ▶ ENTERING AND FILING DATA ELECTRONICALLY

APPLIED MATH PREVIEW

Change each decimal to a percent.

1. 0.80	6. 0.29	11. 0.07	16. 0.03
2. 0.25	7. 0.02	12. 0.40	17. 0.035
3. 0.50	8. 0.10	13. 0.15	18. 0.09
4. 0.75	9. 0.08	14. 0.19	19. 0.095
5. 0.47	10. 0.05	15. 0.99	20. 0.0751

BUSINESS TERMS PREVIEW

- Characters • Cursor • Data base • Field • File • Key •
- Magnetic media • Menu • Record • Update • Vendor •

GOAL

To learn how data are entered and stored in a data processing system.

UNDERSTANDING THE JOB

In a manual filing system, you file documents in file folders. Then you file the folders in file cabinets.

A computer filing system is like a manual filing system in many ways. A document in a computer filing system looks a lot like a paper document. The difference is that the document in a computer filing system may be shown on the monitor of a computer instead of on a piece of paper, and is called a record instead of a form.

Look at the Student Enrollment Record on the screen in Illustration 6A on page 44. You can see that the data are arranged in about the same way as they were on the paper enrollment form in Illustration 3B in Job 3, page 19.

```
        STUDENT ENROLLMENT RECORD
    STUDENT NUMBER    1 2 6 5
    STUDENT NAME      J U L I E    R A Y
    STREET ADDRESS    1 5 7 5    C O R D O V A    A V E N U E
    CITY              G L E N D A L E
    STATE             C A
    ZIP CODE          9 1 2 0 7 - 3 8 0 7
    ENROLLMENT DATE   0 8 / 2 3 / - -
    FIRST COURSE      R E C O R D    K E E P I N G
    SECOND COURSE     T Y P I N G    I
    THIRD COURSE      E N G L I S H    I I
    FOURTH COURSE     S O C I A L    S T U D I E S
    FIFTH COURSE      B U S I N E S S    M A T H
    SIXTH COURSE      P H Y S I C A L    E D U C A T I O N
    SEVENTH COURSE    A R T
```

K E Y   Terms

Magnetic media.
What a computer stores
data on.

However, the computer does not store data in a filing cabinet. Instead, the computer stores data on **magnetic media** which are usually disks.

Data processing workers use special terms when they talk about documents in computer filing systems:

1. The blanks that have to be filled in on the enrollment form are called **fields**.
2. The enrollment form for any one student in the file is called a **record**.
3. A group of related records may be called a **file**.
4. If the disk contains many files, it may be called a **data base**.

Special Terms for Electronic Filing

Field = A group of numbers and letters
Examples: student number, student name

Record = A group of fields
Examples: student enrollment record, student grade sheet

File = A group of records
Examples: student enrollment records, student grade records

Data Base = A group of files
Example: A set of disks containing student files for enrollment, grades, absences, medical history, and test scores

Illustration 6B Field, record, file, and data base in a computer system

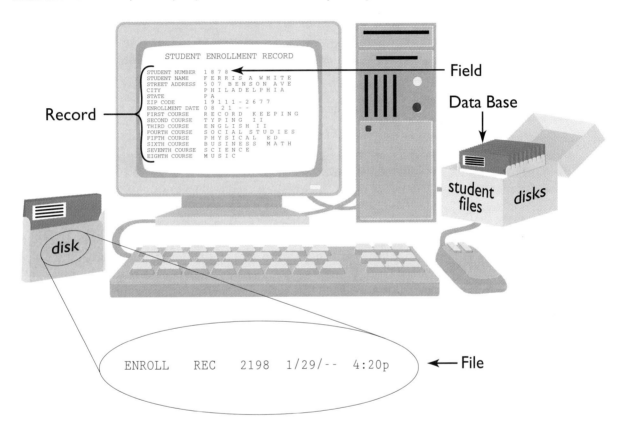

STUDENT ENROLLMENT RECORD

STUDENT NUMBER 1 8 7 8
STUDENT NAME F E R R I S A W H I T E
STREET ADDRESS 5 0 7 B E N S O N A V E
CITY P H I L A D E L P H I A
STATE P A
ZIP CODE 1 9 1 1 1 - 2 6 7 7
ENROLLMENT DATE 0 8 2 1 - -
FIRST COURSE R E C O R D K E E P I N G
SECOND COURSE T Y P I N G I I
THIRD COURSE E N G L I S H I I
FOURTH COURSE S O C I A L S T U D I E S
FIFTH COURSE P H Y S I C A L E D
SIXTH COURSE B U S I N E S S M A T H
SEVENTH COURSE S C I E N C E
EIGHTH COURSE M U S I C

Field

Data Base

Record

student files disks

disk

ENROLL REC 2198 1/29/-- 4:20p ← File

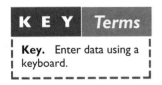

K E Y *Terms*

Key. Enter data using a keyboard.

The most important difference between a computer file and a manual file is that you do not have to sort the records in a computer file. The computer program will do that for you. If you enter many records into the file, the computer program will take care of placing them in proper order. After having to sort records in the last job, you can see that a computer filing system can save a lot of time.

You may enter data into a record in a computer file in a number of ways. One way is to type, or **key**, the data from the source document into the electronic form that is on the screen.

SAMPLE PROBLEM

Dan Worrell is a general office assistant for the El Paso Jays, the minor league baseball team you learned about in Job 2. One of his jobs is to key in data about new equipment that was purchased into the team equipment file. Here is how he does that job:

STEP 1 ▶ *Choose the correct menu item.*

Worrell starts by turning on the computer. When he does, the screen looks like the one in Illustration 6C.

    The information on Worrell's screen is a list of tasks that can be done with the Equipment File. This list of choices is called a **menu**. The menu shown is the first menu in the program and is called the *main menu*.

    The main menu shows that the program will let you add, update, and display equipment records, or print reports about equipment records. **Update** means to replace old data in a record with new data.

    At the bottom of the screen is a flashing marker called a **cursor**. The cursor shows Worrell where he is on the screen. The cursor in Illustration 6C tells Worrell that a choice must be made from the list. Since Worrell is entering data about new equipment, he will have to add new equipment records. So he strikes the 1 key. When he does, the screen displays a blank equipment record like the one shown in Illustration 6D on the next page.

KEY *Terms*

Menu. A list of choices on a computer screen.

Update. Replace old data with new data.

Cursor. Flashing marker on the display screen.

Illustration 6C
Equipment menu

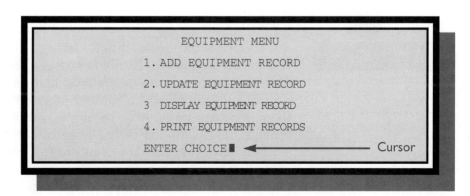

```
                EQUIPMENT MENU

        1. ADD EQUIPMENT RECORD

        2. UPDATE EQUIPMENT RECORD

        3  DISPLAY EQUIPMENT RECORD

        4. PRINT EQUIPMENT RECORDS

    ENTER CHOICE ■  ◄──────────────  Cursor
```

```
                    EQUIPMENT RECORD
      EQUIPMENT NUMBER  ■ □ □
                                                   Cursor
      EQUIPMENT TYPE  □ □ □ □ □ □ □ □ □ □ □ □ □ □
      DESCRIPTION     □ □ □ □ □ □ □ □ □ □ □ □ □ □
      AMOUNT          □ □ □ □
      DATE PURCHASED  □ □/□ □/□ □
      VENDOR          □ □ □ □ □ □ □ □ □ □ □ □ □ □
```

STEP 2 ▶ *Key data into the first field.*

Worrell starts keying data into the blank record for the new equipment the team has just bought. His source documents are the bills that the team received from the sellers. The first bill shows that the team just purchased 3,000 white baseballs, equipment number 23, from Amdex Sports, Inc. on July 17 of the current year.

Worrell looks at the data on the first line of the bill from Amdex Sports, Inc., which is the equipment number. He keys that number into the first field on the screen. As he does so, the numbers that are entered appear on the screen.

EQUIPMENT NUMBER   *0 2 3*

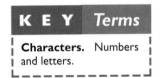

K E Y   Terms

Characters. Numbers and letters.

Each box on the screen is a space for a number or letter. Numbers and letters are called **characters**. Worrell cannot key more characters than the spaces provided for each field.

Notice that the first field contains space for only three numbers. When the computer program for the equipment file was written, the first field was given three spaces because the team had only 250 types of equipment. Only three spaces were needed to let Worrell key any equipment number. In the same way, the Amount field was given only four spaces, since the team would never have more than 9,999 of any item of equipment on hand.

Worrell keys the Equipment Number, 023, into the first field and presses the ENTER key on the keyboard. This tells the computer that the operator is finished entering data in that field.

Notice that he entered *023* instead of just *23*. Had Worrell entered 23, these characters would have been placed in the first two spaces in the field. The computer would have read these characters as 230.

As soon as Worrell presses ENTER, the screen looks like Illustration 6E on page 48.

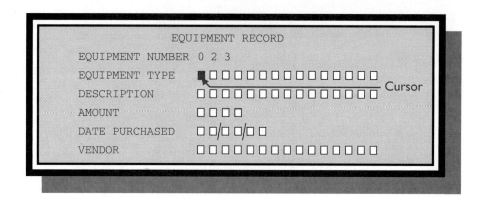

Notice that the cursor has moved to the next field, Equipment Type. As each field is filled in, the cursor moves down the form.

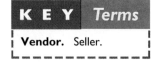 ▶ **Key data into the remaining fields.**

Worrell now keys data into the Equipment Type, Description, Amount, Date Purchased, and Vendor fields using the bills as the source documents. The **Vendor** field is used for the name of the company that sold the equipment to the team. The word vendor means seller.

Notice that the Equipment Type, Description, and Vendor fields have all been given different amounts of space. Notice also that the Date field has only six spaces. The six spaces are divided into groups of two spaces each. The first two spaces are for the month, the next two are for the day, and the last two are for the year.

The baseballs were purchased on July 17 of the current year. To make it easier and faster, numbers are used for each month instead of keying the whole name of the month. Here are the numbers that are used:

01	January	07	July
02	February	08	August
03	March	09	September
04	April	10	October
05	May	11	November
06	June	12	December

Since July is the seventh month of the year, Worrell keys 07 in the first two spaces for the date. The operator must key *07* instead of *7*. If just 7 was keyed in the first space, the computer would think that the number entered was 70.

Worrell then keys 17 in the middle two spaces for the day. If the day had been July 7, he would enter 07. He then enters the last two numbers of the current year in the last two spaces. To save time, the year is not entered in full. When the date is entered completely, Worrell strikes the ENTER key.

K E Y *Terms*

Vendor. Seller.

When the data are entered into the last field and Worrell strikes the ENTER key, a blank equipment data screen will appear. Worrell will then enter the data from the next bill. When all data from all the bills have been entered, the computer program will place each record in the file. Then the computer program will display the main menu like the one in Illustration 6C.

If Worrell had made a mistake, Worrell would key 2 from the main menu. If Worrell needed to know how many bats the team had just bought, he would key 3. If Worrell needed to print the record for a piece of equipment, he would key 4.

BUILDING YOUR BUSINESS VOCABULARY

On a sheet of paper, write the headings **Statement Number** and **Words**. Next, choose the words that match the statements. Write each word you choose next to the statement number it matches. Be careful; not all the words listed should be used.

Statements	Words
1. A list of choices on a display screen	characters
2. Enter data using a keyboard	cursor
3. A group of files	data base
4. A flashing marker on a display screen	field
5. A group of fields	file
6. A group of numbers and letters	guides
7. Kinds of magnetic storage, such as disks	indexing
8. To replace old data with new data	key
9. Metal tabs used to help record clerks find something	magnetic media
	menu
10. Arranging the parts of a name so that it can be filed	record
	retrieve
11. A computer word for numbers and letters	tickler file
12. A seller	update
13. A group of records	vendor

PROBLEM SOLVING MODEL FOR: *Entering Data Electronically*

> **STEP 1** ▶ *Choose the correct menu item.*
>
> **STEP 2** ▶ *Key data into the first field.*
>
> **STEP 3** ▶ *Key data into the remaining fields.*

𝓐PPLICATION PROBLEMS

PROBLEM **6-1** ▶ You are a stock clerk for Redenbacker Service Company. It is your job to key in data about new equipment items the company has bought, using a computer terminal.

Directions

6-1
Use 4 characters for amounts.

a. Make two blank equipment-record screens like the one shown in Illustration 6D.
b. Enter the data for the two new equipment items listed below into the screens. Use the current year. Print all the characters you enter. To avoid confusion, use these special symbols:

For the letter O	O
For the number 0	Ø
For the number 1	1
For the number 7	7

New Equipment Items

Field	a.	b.
Equipment Number:	108	74
Equipment Type:	Catcher's mask	Bat weights
Description:	Large	1 lb.
Amount:	4	12
Date Purchased:	May 5, 19--	May 7, 19--
Vendor:	Carlton, Inc.	Spellman Bros.

PROBLEM **6-2** ▶ You are a clerk in the enrollment office of Emerson College. Part of your job is to enter student enrollment data into a student enrollment file.

Directions

6-2
Use 6 characters for dates.

a. Make two blank student enrollment record screens like the one shown on page 51.
b. Enter the data for two new students listed on page 51 into the screens. Use the current year. Print all the characters you enter. To avoid confusion, use these special symbols:

For the letter O	O
For the number 0	Ø
For the number 1	1
For the number 7	7

New Students

Field	a.	b.
Student number:	245-45-1907	247-34-2076
Last name:	Sanders	Feldman
First name:	Randy	Sidney
Middle initial:	T.	R.
Home street address:	16 Barker St.	405 Iona Ave.
Home city:	Newark	Wilmington
Home state:	DE	DE
Home zip code:	19711-4547	19808-3627
Date admitted:	June 6, 19--	June 8, 19--
Dormitory assignment:	Marshall Hall	Beadle Hall

```
                    STUDENT  ENROLLMENT  RECORD
    STUDENT NUMBER         □□□ - □□ - □□□□
    LAST NAME             □□□□□□□□□□□□□□□□
    FIRST NAME           □□□□□□□□□□□□□□□□
    MIDDLE INITIAL        □
    HOME STREET ADDRESS   □□□□□□□□□□□□□□□□
    HOME CITY            □□□□□□□□□□□□□□□□
    HOME STATE           □□
    HOME ZIP CODE         □□□□□  □□□□
    DATE ADMITTED        □□/□□/□□
    DORMITORY ASSIGNMENT □□□□□□□□□□□□□□□□
```

PROBLEM **6-3** ▸ You are a data entry clerk for the Weller Police Department. Part of your job is to enter data about arrests into an arrest incidence file. You use the arrest forms completed by police officers as your source documents.

Directions

Look at the partial screen on page 52, and answer the questions that follow.

1. The screen shows that you have entered part of the arrest number. What key should you press when you finish entering the number?
2. In what field is the cursor shown?
3. How many fields are shown on the partial screen?
4. How many spaces have been given for the Arresting Officer field?
5. How many spaces have been given for the Time Of Arrest field?

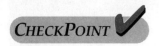

6-3 (6)
Be sure to use zeros when you enter the date.

6. To enter May 9 of the current year, in the Date Of Arrest field, what would you key into these spaces: □ □/□ □/□ □?
7. When you finish keying in data in all the fields on the Arrest Incidence Record, what will appear on the screen?

```
                    ARREST INCIDENCE RECORD
        ARREST NUMBER           2 0 8 ■
        DATE OF ARREST          □ □/□ □/□ □
        TIME OF ARREST          □ □:□ □ □ □
        ARRESTING OFFICER       □ □ □ □ □ □ □ □ □ □ □ □ □ □
        OFFICER BADGE NUMBER    □ □ □ □ □
```

Problems 6-4, 6-5, and 6-6 may be found in the Working Papers.

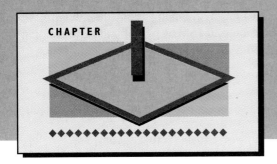

Reinforcement Activities

DISCUSSION

1. Entering data accurately into a manual or electronic data processing system is very important. What might happen if a clerk entered:
   a. A larger amount on a customer's bill than the customer owed?
   b. A smaller amount on a customer's bill than was owed and the salesperson was paid a commission on the amount of the sale?

2. Now that you have learned some of the jobs that record keepers do, think about what knowledge, skills, and attitudes you would look for in a record keeper if you were the one doing the hiring. List at least five of these. Then arrange them in their order of importance, with the most important being listed first.

3. You have begun to see how computers can save time in keeping records. Can you list other advantages of the computer to:
   a. The business owner?
   b. The record keeper?
   c. The customer?

4. What disadvantages might use of the computer have for:
   a. The business owner?
   b. The record keeper?
   c. The customer?

PROFESSIONAL BUSINESS ETHICS

Bill Workman has been a record keeper for Ellison Sales, Inc. for the last six months. Bill's job is to take customer orders over the phone and type them on a customer order form. He likes his work and his supervisor feels that he is very good at it.

The company is planning to install a computer system soon and wants Bill to use a computer to enter the customer orders. Bill has never used a computer before, and he is afraid to learn. In talking about his job with you, he is thinking of pretending to be sick so that he will miss the training sessions. Bill asks you what he should do. What might you tell him?

APPLIED COMMUNICATIONS

You were a beginning office assistant for a manufacturing company for the last year. Your job was to enter data about customers into a computer. You have now been promoted to the job of supervising other beginning office assistants who do the same work.

One of your duties as supervisor is to teach new clerks how to enter data into the computer. This includes how to enter a date into a field like this: □ □/□ □/□ □. Write what you might say to a new worker to explain how to enter the date into this type of field. You should not use more than one page for your explanation.

RECORD KEEPING CAREERS

Record keepers who spend most of their time entering data into computers are called data entry clerks. There are many different types of data entry clerks. Most of these workers do not have the job title "Data Entry Clerk." Instead, the job titles they hold are usually related to the kind of data they enter.

For example, data entry clerks who enter sales orders are usually called *order entry clerks*. Some other examples are:

Job Title	Type of Data Entered
Time clerk	The hours employees work
Inventory clerk	The merchandise bought for resale to customers
Premium clerk	The amounts people pay for insurance
Cashier	The goods bought by people and how much they paid for them

> **KEY** *Terms*
>
> **Entry-level jobs.** Jobs in which first-time workers are placed.

Young people who get their first jobs are often placed in data entry clerk positions. Jobs in which first-time workers are placed are called **entry-level jobs**.

Below is an advertisement for an order entry clerk position found in the Help Wanted section of a newspaper.

> **ORDER ENTRY CLERK**
> Take customer orders over the phone. Computer keyboard skills. Ability to deal with people. Good math skills. High school diploma required. Call 555-3208, 8-12 and 1-5.

Answer these questions about the order entry position:

1. What is the job title of the position?
2. What are three skills the position requires?
3. What education does the position require?
4. How do you apply for the position?

REVIEWING WHAT YOU HAVE LEARNED

On a sheet of paper, write the headings **Statement Number** and **Words**. Next, choose the words that best complete the statements. Write each word you choose next to the statement number it completes. Be careful; not all the words listed should be used.

Statements	Words
1. Nearly everyone must keep some _____ .	alphabetically
2. A worker who spends most of the time filing documents is called (a,an) _____ .	central processing unit
3. In an electronic filing system, a group of files is called (a,an) _____ .	chronologically
4. A group of records is called (a,an) _____ .	data base
5. When you sort documents by the names of the persons on the documents, you are sorting the documents _____ .	file
6. A computer system is made up of input devices, (a,an) _____ , and output devices.	menu
7. A list of program choices on a display screen is called (a,an) _____ .	numerically
8. A document prepared by a computer printer is called (a,an) _____ .	printout
9. A computer needs (a,an) _____ to process data.	program
10. When you sort documents by the dates on the documents, you are sorting _____ .	records
	records clerk
	terminal

MASTERY PROBLEM

Valdez Publications publishes and sells a magazine for do-it-yourself homeowners. You are a records clerk for the firm. Part of your job is keying data to print cards for customers who subscribe to the magazine. The computer data cards that are printed out contain the customer's account number, name, and the date on which the magazine subscription runs out.

Directions

(b)

There are 3 errors.

a. Make a checklist with these headings: No., Correct, Error. Write the numbers 1-10 under the No. heading.

b. Compare the handwritten customer data with the printout on the right. If both the handwritten data and printout are the same, put a check mark in the Correct column of your checklist. If they are not exactly the same, put a check mark in the Error column.

Handwritten Customer Data	Computer Printout
No. Data	
1. 35978 Bernard Malone October 16, 19X1	35987 Bernard Malone October 16, 19X1
2. 39122 Rhonda Macone April 15, 19X2	39122 Rhonda Malone April 15, 19X2
3. 34078 B. Malone Hardware, Inc. September 30, 19X1	34078 B. Malone Hardware, Inc. September 30, 19X1
4. 39578 Brenda M. Malone September 30, 19X2	39578 Brenda M. Malone September 30, 19X2
5. 39212 Brenda P. Malone October 6, 19X1	39212 Brenda P. Malone October 6, 19X1
6. 39222 Brenda P. Maloney April 1, 19X1	39222 Brenda P. Maloney April 16, 19X1
7. 37048 Rhonda Malone April 5, 19X2	37048 Rhonda Malone April 5, 19X2
8. 37804 R. Malone Lumber, Inc. October 16, 19X2	37804 R. Malone Lumber, Inc. October 16, 19X2
9. 32919 Malone Kitchen Company October 1, 19X2	32919 Malone Kitchen Company October 1, 19X2
10. 32199 Maloney Lumber Company April 1, 19X2	32199 Maloney Lumber Company April 1, 19X2

The company keeps three copies of every customer card. One copy is filed in numerical order using the customer account number. A second copy is filed in chronological order using the date the subscription ends. A third copy is filed in alphabetical order by customer name.

(c)
Account number 39578 is
last.

(d)
October 16, 19X2, is the
last date.

(f)
Maloney Lumber Company
is the last customer.

c. Using the handwritten customer data, print the data on blank cards so that the cards are filed in numerical order. The top card should be the customer with the lowest account number. The first line of each card should contain the account number; the second line, the customer name; the third line, the date.

d. Using the handwritten customer data, print the data on blank cards so that the cards are filed in chronological order. The top card should be the customer with the earliest cancellation date. The first line of each card should contain the date; the second line, the account number; and the third line, the customer name. Sometimes 19X1, 19X2, and so on, are used instead of using a current year such as 1995. 19X1 represents year 1 and 19X2 represents year 2.

e. Using the handwritten customer data, print the customer names in indexing order.

f. Print the data about the customers on blank cards so that they are filed in alphabetical order. The first line should contain the customer name in *indexing* order; the second line, the account number; and the third line, the date.

REVIEWING YOUR BUSINESS VOCABULARY

This activity may be found in the Working Papers.

CHAPTER

Budget Records

*Y*ou may get an allowance each week to buy your lunches, school supplies, and other items. If you are careful and plan your spending, you will have enough money for the things you *need*. If you are not careful, you may spend too much money early in the week on things you *want*. That is why you need to learn how to complete a budget. A budget is a plan for spending your money. Many families use budgets to make sure that there is enough money on hand to pay the bills. Businesses also keep budgets for the same reason.

In Chapter 2, you will learn how to make budgets and to record receipts and payments. Budgets for an individual, for a family, and for a business will be covered. You will also learn how to use a calculator to save time and improve accuracy when you add up budget totals.

JOB 7 ▶ KEEPING A PERSONAL BUDGET

APPLIED MATH PREVIEW

Copy and complete the problem below. Check your work by crossfooting.

1. $2.60 + $20.25 + $140.04 + $386.31 =
2. 2.30 + 58.71 + 308.19 + 74.10 =
3. 0.56 + 5.09 + 8.98 + 370.20 =
4. 8.34 + 27.18 + 377.78 + 801.33 =
5.

▲▲▲▲▲
TIP
▼▼▼▼▼

The total you get when you add down the numbers in the column at the far right should be the same as the total you get when you add across the totals of the first four columns.

BUSINESS TERMS PREVIEW

• Budget • Crossfooting • Estimating • Extend an amount •
• Payments • Receipts •

GOALS

1. To learn why you should keep a budget.
2. To learn how to keep a record of receipts and payments.

KEY Terms

Estimating. Making a careful guess.

Budget. A plan for receiving and spending money.

Receipts. Amounts received.

Payments. Amounts spent.

When you budget, you plan how to make your weekly allowance cover your weekly expenses. This means **estimating** how much money you will receive and how much you will spend. It also means deciding what you really need and making sure that your plan provides money for those needs. Money that is left over can be saved or spent on things that you want.

When people plan in advance how much money they will receive and how they will spend their money, they are making a **budget**. When people budget their income, they must keep careful records of their **receipts** (the amounts they receive) and **payments** (the amounts they spend). This way they can compare the amounts they spent with the amounts they planned to spend. They do this to see if they are really *living within their budget* and to see if their estimates were practical.

*S*AMPLE PROBLEM

Ron Velez, a high school student, gets an allowance each week. Velez also earns money by mowing lawns. The money he receives must cover all his expenses except clothing. Velez decides to budget his total receipts so that he does not overspend his money on his wants and then not have enough money left for his needs. Here is how he does it:

STEP 1 ▶ *Estimate receipts.*

Velez knows that he will get an allowance of $15.00 a week from his parents. He also estimates that he can earn about $15.00 a week by mowing lawns. So, Velez feels that he can count on receipts of $30.00 a week.

Weekly allowance	$ 15.00
Estimated income from mowing lawns	+ 15.00
Total estimated receipts for week	$ 30.00

Estimate payments.

Velez lists the payments that he expects to make during the week. His list looks like this:

Lunches	$ 8.50
School supplies	7.50
Entertainment	9.00
Savings	5.00
Total estimated payments	$30.00

STEP 3 ▶ *Record the headings.*

Velez decides to keep a detailed record of his actual receipts and payments in a form like the one shown in Illustration 7A, below. Velez used the top of the form for a heading containing:

WHO: Ron Velez
WHAT: Record of Receipts and Payments
WHEN: Week of September 4, 19--

Notice that Velez used separate columns for each type of estimated payment. At the end of the week, Velez will be able to look at the total of each payment column to find out how much money he spent on each type of payment.

Illustration 7A   Record of receipts and payments

Ron Velez
Record of Receipts and Payments
Week of September 4, 19--

DATE		EXPLANATION (ESTIMATED)	TOTAL RECEIPTS ($30.00)	TOTAL PAYMENTS ($30.00)	TYPE OF PAYMENT LUNCHES ($8.50)	SCHOOL SUPPLIES ($7.50)	ENTER-TAINMENT ($9.00)	SAVINGS ($5.00)
19-- Sept.	4	Weekly allowance	15 00					
	5			1 75	1 75			
	6			3 75	1 75		2 00	
	7			7 25	1 75	5 50		
	7	Mowing job	6 00					
	8			6 25	1 75	4 50		
	9			1 75	1 75			
	10	Mowing job	10 00					
	10			3 00				3 00
	10			6 00	2 00		4 00	
	10	Totals for week	31 00 31 00	29 75 29 75	10 75 10 75	10 00 10 00	6 00 6 00	3 00 3 00
	11	Balance	1 25					

▶ *Record the estimated budget amounts.*

To help him remember the amounts that he had estimated for receipts and payments, Velez wrote them in parentheses under the column headings. For example, the $30.00 under the heading Total Receipts means that Velez hopes to have $30.00 to spend for the week. If he receives less than $30.00, he will have to reduce his spending to *live within his budget.*

Velez wrote $30.00 under the Total Payments heading because he plans to spend $30.00 during the week. If you add all the amounts under each of the headings in the Type of Payment columns, the total will be $30.00. This amount equals the $30.00 in the Total Payments column.

STEP 5 ▶ *Record each receipt.*

Velez had these actual receipts and payments during the week beginning Monday, September 4, 19--:

Sept. 4 Received an allowance of $15.00 for the week.
      5 Paid $1.75 for lunch.
      6 Paid $1.75 for lunch and $2.00 for a ticket to a high school football game.
      7 Paid $1.75 for lunch and $5.50 for school supplies.
      7 Earned $6.00 for mowing a lawn after school.
      8 Paid $1.75 for lunch and $4.50 for school supplies.
      9 Paid $1.75 for lunch.
    10 Earned $10.00 for mowing lawns.
    10 Put $3.00 in savings account.
    10 Paid $2.00 for lunch and $4.00 for a movie.

Velez entered these receipts and payments in the record shown in Illustration 7A.

The first money that Velez received during the week was a $15.00 allowance from his parents. To record that amount, Velez entered the date in the Date column. He recorded the year and the month at the beginning of the record. He will not enter the year and month again unless they change.

Velez then wrote the words "Weekly allowance" in the Explanation column and entered the amount of money he received in the Total Receipts column. He followed the same steps on September 7 and 10 when he received money for mowing lawns.

STEP 6 ▶ *Record each payment.*

Velez recorded the payment he made on September 5 on the second line of the record. He entered the date, 5, in the Date column. He did not enter the year or month since they had not changed.

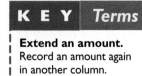
Since he only spent $1.75 on that day, he wrote $1.75 in the Total Payments column. Velez also entered $1.75 again, or **extended** the payment for lunch into the Lunches column. Notice that every payment is recorded twice: once in the Total Payments column and once more in a Type of Payment column. Velez wrote nothing in the Explanation column since the heading of the Type of Payment column showed how the money was spent.

Often, Velez makes several payments in one day. For example, on September 6, he spent $1.75 for a school lunch and $2.00 for a ticket to a football game. He recorded both payments on one line. He recorded the total amount he spent, $3.75, in the Total Payments column. He extended $1.75 into the Lunches column and $2.00 into the Entertainment column. Velez wrote nothing in the Explanation column for September 6 since the column headings showed how the money was spent.

Velez followed the same procedures for the other payments he made during the week. *Notice that the amount Velez enters in the Total Payments column must equal the sum of all the payments he extends into the Type of Payment columns.*

STEP 7 ▶ Total and foot each money column.

At the end of the week, Velez ruled a single line across the money columns to show that he was ready to total them. Then Velez totaled each money column and wrote each total in small figures directly below the line.

STEP 8 ▶ Verify the totals.

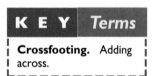
Velez verified the column totals by **crossfooting**. The total of all amounts extended into the Type of Payment columns should have been recorded in the Total Payments column. Thus, the total of all the Type of Payment columns should be the same as the total of the Total Payments column:

Lunches	$10.75
School supplies	10.00
Entertainment	6.00
Savings	3.00
Total of Type of Payment columns	$29.75
Total of Total Payments column	$29.75

Sometimes people make errors when they record numbers or add them. You need to know how to find errors when they are made. Let's suppose that Velez did not get $29.75 when he added the Type of Payment columns totals. What would he do to find the error or errors?

Velez would first verify the addition in every column by re-adding them. If he had added down the first time, he would add the columns up to verify them.

If Velez still did not find the error, he would verify that he had copied the amounts correctly to the Type of Payment columns. For example, he might have transposed numbers when he copied the amount spent on lunch on September 5. He might have entered $1.57 instead of $1.75 in the Lunches column.

Next, he would verify that he had added the amounts extended into the Type of Payment columns correctly and had written the correct total in the Total Payments column. For example, he might have added the amounts spent for a lunch ($1.75) and a football ticket ($2.00) incorrectly and entered that wrong total into the Total Payments column.

STEP 9 ▶ *Complete the record.*

After verifying the totals, Velez entered them below the footings. To show that the math was done, Velez ruled a double line across all the money columns.

STEP 10 ▶ *Record the balance of cash on hand.*

Velez recorded the balance of money that he had left at the end of the week. To find out how much he had left, he subtracted the total payments ($29.75) from the total receipts ($31.00):

Total receipts	$31.00
Total payments	- 29.75
Balance of cash	$ 1.25

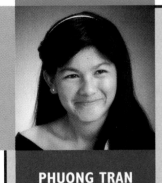

He then entered the next date, 11, in the Date column, wrote "Balance" in the Explanation column, and put $1.25 in the Total Receipts column. Now Velez is ready to record the receipts and payments for the next week.

Velez compared his actual and estimated receipts and payments by using the totals of the Type of Payment columns. This is how they compared:

	Estimated	Actual
Total receipts	$30.00	$31.00
Payments:		
Lunches	$ 8.50	$10.75
School supplies	7.50	10.00
Entertainment	9.00	6.00
Savings	5.00	3.00
Totals	$30.00	$29.75

Velez can now decide whether he is living within his budget. He can also decide whether he has to change any of the estimated budget amounts.

Each week Velez puts money into a *savings account* at his bank. The bank pays him interest on the money he has in the savings account. He uses the savings account to help pay for unexpected expenses and for those things he wants instead of needs.

BUILDING YOUR BUSINESS VOCABULARY

On a sheet of paper, write the headings **Statement Number** and **Words**. Next, choose the words that match the statements. Write each word you choose next to the statement number it matches. Be careful; not all the words listed should be used.

Statements	Words
1. To check for accuracy	budget
2. The total of a money column written in small figures	crossfooting
	cursor
3. Making a careful guess	double ruling
4. A plan for receiving and spending money	estimating
5. A column on a form used for recording amounts of money	extend an amount
	footing
6. A flashing marker on a display screen	money column
7. Amounts spent	payments
8. Adding across	receipts
9. To record an amount again in a second column	retrieve
	verify
10. A double line drawn under a total to show that the math on a form is done	

PROBLEM SOLVING MODEL FOR: *Keeping a Personal Budget*

STEP 1 ▶	*Estimate receipts.*
STEP 2 ▶	*Estimate payments.*
STEP 3 ▶	*Record the headings.*
STEP 4 ▶	*Record the estimated budget amounts.*
STEP 5 ▶	*Record each receipt.*
STEP 6 ▶	*Record each payment.*
STEP 7 ▶	*Total and foot each money column.*
STEP 8 ▶	*Verify the totals.*
STEP 9 ▶	*Complete the record.*
STEP 10 ▶	*Record the balance of cash on hand.*

*A*PPLICATION PROBLEMS

PROBLEM **7-1 ▶** Mimi Regna is a high school student. She also works part-time at a service station and is saving money for college expenses. Her estimated receipts and payments for the week of April 14, 19-- are

Estimated Receipts		Estimated Payments	
From allowance	$10.00	Lunches	$ 9.00
From part-time job	28.00	School supplies	2.50
		Entertainment	7.50
		Savings	19.00
Total estimated receipts	$38.00	Total estimated payments	$38.00

Directions

a. Prepare a record of receipts and payments for Regna like the one shown in Illustration 7A (page 60).
b. Enter the heading on the top three lines.
c. Record the estimated budget amounts under the column headings.
d. Record the actual receipts and payments shown on page 66:

April 14 Received an allowance of $10.00 for the week.
15 Paid $1.80 for lunch.
16 Paid $1.80 for lunch and $3.00 for notebook paper.
16 Received $30.00 in pay from part-time job.
17 Paid $1.80 for lunch and $4.50 for an audio tape.
18 Paid $1.80 for lunch and $.75 for a pen.
19 Paid $1.80 for lunch and put $18.00 in a savings account.
20 Paid $2.50 for a matinee movie.

CHECKPOINT

7-1
Total Payments = $37.75

e. Rule and foot the money columns.
f. Verify the totals by crossfooting.
g. Write the totals below the footings and double rule the money columns.
h. Find the balance of cash on hand by subtracting the total of the Total Payments column from the total of the Total Receipts column.
i. Record the balance of cash on hand on the line below the double ruling. Use April 21 as the date and write "Balance" in the Explanation column.
j. Answer these questions:

   1. What amount was spent for entertainment?
   2. How much was spent for lunches?
   3. On which item(s) did Regna spend more than she had planned?
   4. Did Regna put more or less savings in the bank than planned?
   5. Did Regna receive more or less income than she had planned?

PROBLEM **7-2** ▶ Sarah Ichiro lives at home with her parents and commutes to Barnett Business College. To help pay for her education, Ichiro works part-time at a restaurant. Her estimated receipts and payments for the week of September 20, 19-- are

Estimated Receipts		Estimated Payments	
From allowance	$ 40.00	Auto expenses	$ 30.00
From part-time job	90.00	Lunches	12.50
		Books and supplies	31.25
		Entertainment	25.00
		Piano lessons	8.75
		Savings	22.50
Total estimated receipts	$130.00	Total estimated payments	$130.00

Directions

a. Prepare a record of receipts and payments with the following column headings:

DATE	EXPLANATION (ESTIMATED)	TOTAL RECEIPTS [ ]	TOTAL PAYMENTS [ ]	TYPE OF PAYMENT					
				AUTO EXPENSES [ ]	LUNCHES [ ]	BOOKS AND SUPPLIES [ ]	ENTER-TAINMENT [ ]	PIANO LESSONS [ ]	SAVINGS [ ]

b. Enter the heading on the top three lines.

c. Record the estimated budget amounts in parentheses under the column headings.

d. Record the actual receipts and payments:

Sept. 20 Received an allowance of $40.00 for the week.
21 Paid $3.75 for lunch and $20.00 for a book.
22 Paid $4.75 for lunch and $6.50 for a notebook and paper.
22 Received $95.00 in pay from part-time job.
23 Paid $2.25 for lunch and $15.00 for gasoline.
24 Paid $3.80 for lunch.
25 Paid $2.50 for lunch, $8.75 for piano lessons, and put $40.00 in savings account.
26 Paid $15.00 for a football ticket and $5.00 for a parking sticker.

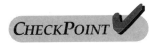

CHECKPOINT

7-2 (h)
Balance = $7.70

e. Rule and foot the money columns.

f. Verify the totals by crossfooting.

g. Write the totals below the footings and double rule the money columns.

h. Find the balance of cash on hand by subtracting the total of the Total Payments column from the total of the Total Receipts column.

i. Record the balance of cash on hand on the line below the double ruling. Use September 27 as the date and write "Balance" in the Explanation column.

j. Answer these questions:

1. What amount was spent for auto expenses?
2. How much was spent for books and supplies?
3. On which items did Ichiro spend less than planned?
4. Did Ichiro put more or less savings in the bank than planned?
5. Did Ichiro receive more or less income than planned?

Problems 7-3 and 7-4 may be found in the Working Papers.

APPLIED MATH PREVIEW

Copy and complete the problem below.

1. $ 42.00 + $ 16.02 + $ 20.58 + $ 38.05 =
2.   10.88 +   30.70 +   91.47 +   90.64 =
3.   107.56 +   410.10 +   375.20 +   714.87 =
4.   259.10 +   60.81 +   582.08 +   27.34 =
5.

Check your work by crossfooting. The answer you get when you add the last column on the right should be the same as the answer you get when you add the bottom row of totals.

BUSINESS TERMS PREVIEW

• **Classified** • **Personal computer** • **Scrolling** •
• **Spreadsheet** •

GOAL

To learn how to keep budget records for a family.

UNDERSTANDING THE JOB

Keeping a record of receipts and payments for a family is a lot like keeping one for a person. However, the headings used in the Type of Payment columns may be different. A family record of receipts and payments will usually have Type of Payment headings such as household expenses, clothing, savings, health and personal expenses, education, entertainment, transportation, and gifts.

The types of payments usually **classified**, or grouped together, under these headings are shown on page 69.

Many families keep records to help them live within their budget. Some families keep these records manually. Others use a microcomputer, or **personal computer**. In this job, you will learn about keeping family budgets in both ways.

KEY Terms

Classified. Grouped together.

Personal computer. Microcomputer.

Household Expenses:

Energy (electricity, gas)
Furniture and appliances
Groceries
Home repair and maintenance
Homeowner's insurance
Kitchen utensils (dishes, pots, pans)
Property taxes
Rent or mortgage payments
Telephone service
Utilities (water, sewer)

Gifts:

Contributions
Personal gifts

Health and Personal:

Beauty salon and barber shop expenses
Doctor and dentist bills
Glasses, contact lenses
Health and accident insurance
Hospital expenses
Medicines

Education:

School lunches
School supplies
Textbooks
Tuition and fees for college

Clothing:

Clothes for all family members
Clothing repairs and dry cleaning

Transportation:

Car and bus fare
Car insurance
Car payments
Car repairs, cleaning
Oil and gasoline

Entertainment:

Audio and video tapes, disks
Computer games
Dining out
Hobbies
Magazines, newspapers
Movies
Vacation trips

Savings:

Stocks and bonds
Savings accounts

𝒮AMPLE PROBLEM

Jules and Eve Frieden are married and have one child. Jules manages a hardware store and receives $2,100.00 in pay each month. Eve Frieden is a supervisor at a manufacturing plant and receives $600.00 in pay a week. They have decided to keep a budget to see if they can spend their money more wisely.

Here are the steps they follow to keep their budget:

STEP 1 ▶ *Prepare an estimate of receipts and payments.*

Based on past experience, the Friedens estimated how their income would be spent. A budget that they felt they could live within for the month of June is shown in Illustration 8A.

The Friedens know that some payments, like household expenses, will be almost the same each month. Other payments, like entertainment, will change from month to month. If they want to take a vacation trip, they must spend less than the usual amount on entertainment for several months. That way the money for the trip will be available when they need it. Successful budgeting means looking ahead and planning for these large payments.

Illustration 8A   The Frieden's budget for June

Budget for June

Estimated Receipts		Estimated Payments	
Eve Frieden, wages ($600 x 4)	$2,400.00	Household expenses	$2,500.00
Jules Frieden, wages	2,100.00	Clothing	190.00
		Transportation	540.00
		Health and personal	110.00
		Entertainment	325.00
		Education	275.00
		Gifts	135.00
		Savings	425.00
Total estimated receipts	$4,500.00	Total estimated payments	$4,500.00

STEP 2 ▶ *Record receipts and payments.*

After the budget was prepared, the Friedens recorded their receipts and payments so they could compare their estimated and actual figures. To record the amounts, they used a Record of Receipts and Payments form.

The Friedens had to decide how they would record their receipts and payments. They could have recorded them each day, once each week, or once a month. They decided to:

1. Record all receipts on the day they are received.
2. Record all payments once each week on Saturday.
3. If the last day of a month isn't a Saturday, record payments made after Saturday at the end of the month.
4. Total and balance the record on the last day of the month.

Here are the receipts and payments made by the Friedens during the month of June, beginning with June 1, 19--:

June	1	There was a balance of $230.70 left from last month.	
	2	Jules received his monthly paycheck for $2,100.00.	
	3	Eve received her weekly paycheck for $600.00.	
	6	The payments made since May 31 were:	
		Groceries	$ 136.00
		Mortgage payment	1,524.41
		Gas, electric	272.26
		Sweaters, skirts	108.77
		Gasoline for cars	26.00
		Cough drops, cold medicine	8.67
		Two video tapes	8.00
		School lunches	10.00
		Deposit in savings account	70.00
	10	Eve received her weekly paycheck for $600.00.	
	13	The payments made since last week were:	
		Groceries	$165.54
		Blue jeans, shirts	94.58
		Gasoline for cars	27.00
		Beauty salon	25.00
		Visit to doctor	25.00
		Newspapers, magazines	31.00
		Computer games	45.66
		School lunches	10.00
		School supplies	10.17
		Contribution	40.00
		Gift for Grandma	20.00
		Deposit in savings account	80.00
	17	Eve received her weekly paycheck for $600.00.	
	20	The payments made since last week were:	
		Groceries	$106.48
		Telephone, insurance bills	178.29
		Work shoes, dress shoes	134.98
		Gasoline for cars, car repair	87.92
		Medicine, visit to doctor	29.00
		Dinner out for family	45.00
		School lunches, paper supplies	13.88
		Gifts for mother's birthday	45.19
		Deposit in savings account	60.00
	24	Eve received her weekly paycheck for $600.00.	
	27	The payments made since last week were:	
		Groceries	$152.08
		New living room table	152.44
		Jogging outfit, shoes	182.89
		Gasoline for cars	23.90
		Barber shop, beauty salon	48.00
		Baseball game for family	24.00
		School lunches	10.00
		Contribution	15.00

	Deposit in savings account	75.00
30	The payments made since the 27th were:	
	Groceries	$ 24.90
	Gutter repairs on house	289.54
	Gasoline for cars	14.50
	Newspapers	4.80
	School lunches	6.00

The completed record is shown in Illustration 8B:

Jules and Eve Frieden
Record of Receipts and Payments
For June, 19--

DATE		EXPLANATION (ESTIMATED)	TOTAL RECEIPTS ($4,500.00)	TOTAL PAYMENTS ($4,500.00)	HOUSE-HOLD EXPENSES ($2,500.00)	CLOTHING ($190.00)	TRANS-PORTATION ($540.00)	HEALTH & PERSONAL ($110.00)	ENTER-TAINMENT ($325.00)	EDUCA-TION ($275.00)	GIFTS ($135.00)	SAVINGS ($425.00)
19-- June	1	Balance	230 70									
	2	Jules' pay	2100 00									
	3	Eve's pay	600 00									
	6	Since 5/31		2164 11	1932 67	108 77	26 00	8 67	8 00	10 00		70 00
	10	Eve's pay	600 00									
	13	Since 6/6		573 95	165 54	94 58	27 00	50 00	76 66	20 17	60 00	80 00
	17	Eve's pay	600 00									
	20	Since 6/13		700 74	284 77	134 98	87 92	29 00	45 00	13 88	45 19	60 00
	24	Eve's pay	600 00									
	27	Since 6/20		683 31	304 52	182 89	23 90	48 00	24 00	10 00	15 00	75 00
	30	Since 6/27		339 74	314 44		14 50			4 80	6 00	
	30	Totals	4730 70	4461 85	3001 94	521 22	179 32	135 67	158 46	60 05	120 19	285 00
July	1	Balance	268 85									

Illustration 8B Completed record of receipts and payments

Let's look at the Record of Receipts and Payments shown in Illustration 8B so that you can keep one like it. Take a close look at:

1. **The heading.** Notice that the heading on the top three lines answers the questions: Who? What? When?
2. **The beginning balance.** Notice that the Friedens entered a balance of $230.70 in the Total Receipts column on June 1. This amount is the difference between the total receipts and total payments for the month of May. Since the Friedens did not spend the money in May, it is available to spend in June.

Enter receipts on separate lines.

3. **How receipts are entered.** Notice that the Friedens entered a receipt every time they received money. For example, Jules received his monthly paycheck for $2,100.00 on June 2. Eve received four weekly paychecks of $600.00 each. Each was recorded on the day it was received.

4. **The Total Payments column.** Notice that each amount in the Total Payments column is equal to all of the amounts in the Type of Payment columns on the same line. For example, the amount, $2,164.11, shown in the Total Payments column for June 6 was found by adding these amounts:

Groceries	$ 136.00
Mortgage payment	1,524.41
Gas, electric	272.26
Sweaters, skirts	108.77
Gasoline for cars	26.00
Cough drops, cold medicine	8.67
Two video tapes	8.00
School lunches	10.00
Deposit in savings account	70.00
Total payments for week	$2,164.11

5. **How the amounts were classified and entered.** Each payment for a week was classified and entered in the proper column. When two or more amounts were classified as the same type, only the total was entered. For example, the amounts spent for groceries, mortgage payment, and gas and electric were grouped together as household expenses. These amounts were then added and entered into the Household Expenses column.

Groceries	$ 136.00
Mortgage payment	1,524.41
Gas, electric	272.26
Household expenses	$1,932.67

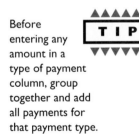

Before entering any amount in a type of payment column, group together and add all payments for that payment type.

TIP

6. **The rulings and totals.** On the last day of the month, the Friedens:

   a. Totaled each money column.
   b. Footed each money column.
   c. Verified the totals by crossfooting.
   d. Wrote the totals below the footings.
   e. Double ruled the money columns.
   f. Entered the balance for the next month.

7. **The ending balance.** The balance on July 1 ($268.85) was found by subtracting the total monthly payments from the total monthly receipts.

STEP 3 ▶ *Compare the budget estimates with the actual figures.*

At the end of each month, the Friedens compare their actual receipts and payments with their budget estimates. This helps them to decide if they need to adjust their spending or their budget estimates.

Calculator TIPS

Adding and crossfooting the totals in a record of receipts and payments takes time. Many record keepers use calculators to make this task easier.

You probably have used calculators before and can add a column of numbers using a calculator. If you can, you know that a calculator helps you add faster and more accurately. But did you know that you could use a calculator to find the totals of the Type of Payment columns and crossfoot those totals at the same time? If your calculator has *memory keys*, you can do this.

Many calculators have memory keys. Some have three memory keys and others have four:

MR/C   M–   M+   or   MC   MR   M–   M+

Here is how you can use the memory keys to crossfoot the Type of Payment totals.

STEP 1 ▶ *Add the first Type of Payment column.*

Add the first Type of Payment column in Illustration 8B (page 72), Household Expenses, by pressing these keys in order:

a. 1 9 3 2 • 6 7 +

b. 1 6 5 • 5 4 +

c. 2 8 4 • 7 7 +

d. 3 0 4 • 5 2 +

e. 3 1 4 • 4 4 +

The total, 3001.94, will appear in the calculator's window or display.

STEP 2 ▶ *Add the total to the calculator's memory.*

Press the M+ key. This adds the column total, 3001.94, to the calculator's memory.

STEP 3 ▶ *Add the other column totals to memory.*

Now add each of the other Type of Payment columns. When you get each column total, press the M+ key. This adds each column total to memory.

STEP 4 ▶ *Display the total of memory.*

When you have added every column total to memory, press the MR (memory recall) key or the MR/C (memory recall/clear) key once.

When you do, your calculator display will show 4461.85. This is the total of all the Type of Payment columns. This amount should be the same as the total of the Total Payments column.

STEP 5 ▶ *Clear memory.*

To clear the calculator's memory, press the MC (memory clear) key. If your calculator has an MR/C key, press that key twice. When you press the MR/C key once, the display shows the contents of memory. When you press the MR/C key twice, you clear, or erase, the amount in memory.

Using a Computer for Budgeting

Many people, families, and businesses keep budgets on computers using a computer program called a **spreadsheet**. A spreadsheet program lets you create forms like budgets and enter information into the rows and columns of the forms. If the Friedens used a spreadsheet to keep their budget, their Record of Receipts and Payments might look like the computer screen in Illustration 8C below.

The entire record does not show up on the screen since the record is too big. The Friedens would move the record shown on the screen from left to right and up and down to display the part of the record they want. Moving a record on the computer this way is called **scrolling.**

The nice part of using the spreadsheet program is that the Friedens only have to enter the amounts they receive or spend. All the math is done for them by the program. The totals for each column are added by the computer program and shown on the screen automatically.

In the Using Electronic Spreadsheets appendix, you will learn how to use computer spreadsheet programs to keep budgets for persons, families, and businesses.

> **KEY Terms**
>
> **Spreadsheet.** A computer program which lets you create and enter data into forms.
>
> **Scrolling.** Moving a record around on a computer screen.

	A	B	C	D	E	F
1:	Jules and Eve Frieden					
2:	Record of Receipts and Payments					
3:	For June, 19--					
4:						
5:			Total	Total	Household	
6:	Date	Explanation	Receipts	Payments	Expenses	Clothing
7:		(Estimated)	(4500.00)	(4500.00)	(2500.00)	(190.00)
8:	June 1	Balance	230.70			
9:	2	Jules's pay	2100.00			
10:	3	Eve's pay	600.00			
11:	6	Since 5/31		2164.11	1932.67	108.77
12:	10	Eve's pay	600.00			
13:	13	Since 6/6		573.95	165.54	94.58
14:	17	Eve's pay	600.00			
15:	20	Since 6/13		700.74	284.77	134.98
16:	24	Eve's pay	600.00			
17:	27	Since 6/20		683.31	304.52	182.89
18:	30	Since 6/27		339.74	314.44	
19:		Totals	4730.70	4461.85	3001.94	521.22
20:	July 1	Balance	268.85			

Illustration 8C   A record of receipts and payments on a personal computer

On a sheet of paper, write the headings **Statement Number** and **Words.** Next, choose the words that match the statements. Write each word you choose next to the statement number it matches. Be careful; not all the words listed should be used.

Statements	Words
1. Making a careful guess	budget
2. When items which are alike are grouped together	classified
	crossfooting
3. Amounts of money received	estimating
4. The total of a column of numbers written in small figures	extend an amount
	field
5. To record an amount again in a second column	footing
	money columns
6. Adding a row of figures across a business form	personal computer
	printout
7. A careful plan, made in advance, of cash receipts and cash payments	receipts
	scrolling
8. To check	spreadsheet
9. Columns on a form used to record amounts of money	verify
10. A microcomputer	
11. A computer program which lets you create and enter data into forms	
12. Moving a record around on a computer screen	

PROBLEM SOLVING MODEL FOR: *Keeping a Family Budget*

STEP 1 ▶ *Prepare an estimate of receipts and payments.*

STEP 2 ▶ *Record receipts and payments.*

STEP 3 ▶ *Compare the budget estimates with the actual figures.*

APPLICATION PROBLEMS

PROBLEM | 8-1 ▶ Dick and Marie Rice have agreed to keep a record of receipts and payments like the one in Illustration 8B (page 72). Dick Rice is attending college and Marie Rice manages a local discount department store.

Directions

a. Prepare a record of receipts and payments. Use a ruled sheet of paper with ten money columns.

b. Use as the heading for your record:

Dick and Marie Rice
Record of Receipts and Payments
For March, 19--

c. Enter the column headings and estimated totals below using Illustration 8B (page 72) as a guide.

1.	Date	7.	Transportation ($450.00)
2.	Explanation	8.	Health/personal ($150.00)
3.	Total Receipts ($2,400.00)	9.	Entertainment ($120.00)
4.	Total Payments ($2,400.00)	10.	Education ($50.00)
5.	Household expenses ($1,300.00)	11.	Gifts ($30.00)
6.	Clothing ($200.00)	12.	Savings ($100.00)

d. Record the following receipts and payments for March, 19--:

Mar. 1 Balance of cash, $378.56.

4 Marie Rice received her paycheck for $553.85.

8 The payments made since February 28 were:

Groceries	$105.88
Mortgage payment	500.00
Toaster	39.95
Gasoline, oil for car	15.10
Barber shop	15.00
Newspapers	5.23
Textbook	21.00
City museum donation	20.00

11 Marie Rice received her paycheck for $553.85.

15 The payments made since last week were:

Groceries	$ 93.72
Gas, electric	137.17
Dry cleaning	45.00
Gasoline for car	18.00
Automobile insurance	160.00
Car repairs	65.48
Cosmetics	12.00
Magazine subscription	14.00
Movie	9.00
Notebook paper	5.25
Charitable contribution	8.00

18 Marie Rice received her paycheck for $553.85.

22 The payments made since last week were:

Groceries	$108.13
Water bill	24.68

Gasoline for car, car wash	15.91
Dentist visit	35.00
Toothpaste, toothbrushes	7.36
Newspaper subscription	10.46
Video tape rental	12.00
Charitable contribution	4.00
Savings account deposit	200.00

25 Marie Rice received her paycheck for $553.85.

29 The payments made since last week were:

Groceries	$101.08
Telephone bill	52.13
Shoe repair	9.25
Gasoline for car	13.88
Car insurance	65.00
Visit to doctor, medicine	53.67
Beauty salon	25.00
Newspapers, magazines	14.18
Charitable contribution	4.00

31 The payments made since the 29th were:

Food	$16.31
Gasoline, oil for car	18.29
Newspapers	5.23
Movie	9.00
Dinner out	35.00

CHECKPOINT

8-1
New balance = $464.62

e. Rule and foot the columns. Verify the totals by crossfooting.
f. Write in the totals below the footings and double rule the columns.
g. Record the new balance for April 1.

PROBLEM 8-2 ▶ Linda and Tony Nero decide to keep a record of receipts and payments like the one in Illustration 8B (page 72). Linda Nero is a customer service representative and Tony is a computer operator for the same manufacturing company. Linda is studying for a degree in business at a nearby college.

Directions

a. Prepare a record of receipts and payments. Use a ruled sheet of paper with ten money columns.
b. Use as the heading for your record:

Linda and Tony Nero
Record of Receipts and Payments
For July, 19--

c. Enter the following column headings and estimated totals using Illustration 8B (page 72) as a guide.

1.	Date	7.	Transportation ($350.00)
2.	Explanation	8.	Health/personal ($150.00)
3.	Total Receipts ($2,000.00)	9.	Entertainment ($75.00)
4.	Total Payments ($2,000.00)	10.	Education ($150.00)
5.	Household expenses ($1,000.00)	11.	Gifts ($40.00)
6.	Clothing ($135.00)	12.	Savings ($100.00)

d. Record the following receipts and payments for July, 19--:

July   1   Balance of cash, $288.74.

         4   The Neros received their paychecks (Linda, $192.31; Tony, $269.23). Use one line for each paycheck.

         7   The payments made since June 30 were:

Groceries	$ 93.18
Rent	575.00
Electric knife	23.36
Gasoline, oil for car	14.67
Barber shop	9.00
Newspapers	5.50
Movie	7.00
Textbooks	46.00
Laboratory fees	15.00
Charitable contribution	5.00

    11   The Neros received their paychecks (Linda, $192.31; Tony, $269.23). Use one line for each paycheck.

    14   The payments made since last week were:

Groceries	$101.74
Utility bill	128.91
Skirt	36.95
Gasoline for car	12.21
Automobile insurance	145.00
Aerobics session at fitness center – health	10.00
Dinner out	24.65
Notebooks, paper	12.72
Charitable contribution	5.00

    18   The Neros received their paychecks (Linda, $192.31; Tony, $269.23). Use one line for each paycheck.

    21   The payments made since last week were:

Groceries H	$87.99
TV repair H	55.40
Gasoline for car, car wash T	14.51
Doctor visit P	21.00
Medicine P	15.75
Magazines E	14.00
Newspapers E	5.50
Rock concert E	44.00
Charitable contribution G	5.00

25 The Neros received their paychecks (Linda, $192.31; Tony, $269.23). Use one line for each paycheck.

28 The payments made since last week were:

Groceries H	$ 87.37
Telephone bill H	36.88
Dry cleaning C	43.00
Gasoline for car T	13.01
Car payment T	148.33
Cosmetics P	16.77
Newspapers E	5.50
Charitable contribution	5.00
Savings account deposit	100.00

31 The payments made since the 28th were:

Groceries	$51.82
Gasoline, oil for car	14.71
Video tape rental	10.00
Anniversary gift for Linda's parents	40.28

e. Rule and foot the columns. Verify the totals by crossfooting.

f. Write the totals below the footings and double rule the columns.

g. Record the new balance for August 1.

Problems 8-3 and 8-4 may be found in the Working Papers.

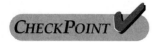

CHECKPOINT

8-2

New balance = $28.19

JOB 9 ▶ KEEPING A BUSINESS BUDGET

TIP

▲▲▲▲▲

Combine numbers that equal ten when possible to make your adding easier. For example, when crossfooting the first row of numbers ($1,078.44 + $2,451.15 + $15,063.46), combine the 4 cents with the 6 cents to make 10 cents. Then add the 5 cents to make 15 cents.

APPLIED MATH PREVIEW

Copy and complete the problem below.

1. $1,078.44 + $2,451.15 + $15,063.46 =
2. 2,008.07 + 1,980.91 + 32,182.42 =
3. 4,321.82 + 3,848.25 + 12,340.84 =
4. 1,549.31 + 1,101.48 + 14,214.32 =
5.

BUSINESS TERMS PREVIEW

- Cash budget • Cash flow • Crossfooting •
- Fixed payments • Negative cash flow • Positive cash flow •
- Quarter • Variable payments •

GOALS

1. To learn how businesses use budgets.
2. To learn how to complete a business budget.

𝒰NDERSTANDING THE JOB

Persons and families usually keep budgets for two major reasons:

1. They wish to make sure that there is enough money on hand to pay the bills.
2. They want help in spending their money wisely.

Businesses keep budgets for these same reasons. To help prepare a budget, businesses may estimate their cash receipts and cash payments for a period of time, such as three months, six months, or one year.

Carmen Lamas owns the Lamas Painting Company. Lamas Painting Company paints home and business interiors and exteriors. The company usually has these types of cash receipts:

Interior Sales: Sales of painting services for the insides of homes and businesses

Exterior Sales: Sales of painting services for the outsides of homes and businesses

The company usually has these types of cash payments:

Wages: Payments to regular and part-time workers
Rent: Payments for the office and the supply room
Utilities: Payments for heat and electricity
Supplies: Payments for paints, brushes, paint clothes, and other painting supplies
Office Expenses: Payments for telephone service, typing paper, ribbons, paper clips, file folders, and other supplies
Repairs: Payments for repairing painting equipment
Insurance: Payments for insurance on equipment
Taxes: Payments for local, state, and federal taxes
Equipment: Payments for the purchase of equipment, such as trucks, ladders, and sprayers

K E Y *Terms*

Quarter. Three months.

In December, Lamas wanted to plan how the company would operate for the first three months, or first **quarter**, of next year. Lamas needed to know if the company would have enough money *at the right time* to pay the bills that would come due. To find out, Lamas began a budget for the three-month period from January through March. The partially prepared budget is shown in Illustration 9A on page 83.

Lamas estimated what the cash receipts and cash payments for the company would be, month by month, for the quarter. Lamas entered the estimated amounts for each type of cash receipt and cash payment in the correct monthly column.

You might wonder how Lamas came up with these figures. Lamas first looked at what the business had received and spent in previous first quarters. Lamas then estimated how much more or

DESCRIPTION	JANUARY	FEBRUARY	MARCH	TOTAL
Receipts:				
Interior Sales	7 2 0 0 00	7 5 0 0 00	4 4 0 0 00	
Exterior Sales	2 4 0 0 00	2 7 0 0 00	6 8 0 0 00	
Total Receipts				
Payments:				
Wages	5 8 0 0 00	5 8 0 0 00	6 5 0 0 00	
Rent	1 2 0 0 00	1 2 0 0 00	1 2 0 0 00	
Utilities	2 1 0 00	2 1 0 00	1 5 0 00	
Supplies	3 0 0 00	3 0 0 00	5 0 0 00	
Office Expenses	9 0 00	9 0 00	1 0 0 00	
Repairs	2 0 0 00	2 0 0 00	5 5 0 00	
Insurance	3 7 5 00	3 7 5 00	3 7 5 00	
Taxes	1 1 6 0 00	1 1 6 0 00	1 3 0 0 00	
Equipment			7 5 0 00	
Total Payments				
Balance				

less the cash receipts and cash payments would be during the upcoming quarter.

Notice that Lamas estimated that the cash receipts from exterior painting would be lower in some months than in others. For example, the cash receipts for exterior painting in January and February are estimated to be lower than in March. From past experience, Lamas knows that more customers have the exteriors of their homes and businesses painted in the warmer months.

Lamas also estimated that the business would spend $5,800.00 during January and February for wages. Lamas estimated that the cash payments for wages would increase in March to $6,500.00. From past experience, Lamas knows that her business will increase during the warmer months. She also knows that she will have to hire more people in the warmer months to handle that business. Payments, like wages, which change from month to month are called **variable payments**.

Some cash payments are the same each month. For example, the amounts spent on rent and insurance are estimated to be the same for each month. These types of payments are known as **fixed payments** because they do not change.

When business persons estimate cash receipts and cash payments as Lamas did, they are estimating the **cash flow** of their businesses. (See Illustration 9B on page 84.) The report they prepare that shows the cash flow is called a **cash budget**. Lamas will use the cash

KEY Terms

Variable payments. Payments which change from month to month.

Fixed payments. Payments which do not change.

Cash flow. How money is received and spent over time.

Cash budget. A report of the cash flow.

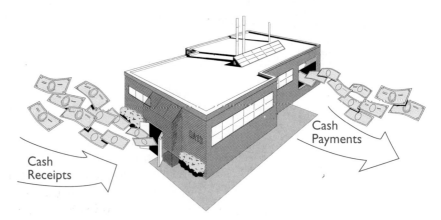

Cash
Receipts

Cash
Payments

budget to find out whether there will be enough cash flowing into the business each month (cash receipts) to cover the cash flowing out of the business each month (cash payments). This will let Lamas know in which months there may be more cash receipts than are needed to pay the bills. It will also let Lamas know in which months there may not be enough cash receipts to pay the bills.

After Lamas estimated the cash receipts and payments for each month, she gave the cash budget to Leroy Brady, her record keeper. Lamas asked Brady to complete the cash budget by filling in the heading and finding the totals and balances. The completed cash budget is shown in Illustration 9C.

Illustration 9C
Completed cash budget
for Lamas Painting
Company

Lamas Painting Company				
Cash Budget				
For First Quarter, 19--				
DESCRIPTION	JANUARY	FEBRUARY	MARCH	TOTAL
Receipts:				
Interior Sales	7 2 0 0 00	7 5 0 0 00	4 4 0 0 00	19 1 0 0 00
Exterior Sales	2 4 0 0 00	2 7 0 0 00	6 8 0 0 00	11 9 0 0 00
Total Receipts	9 6 0 0 00	10 2 0 0 00	11 2 0 0 00	31 0 0 0 00
Payments:				
Wages	5 8 0 0 00	5 8 0 0 00	6 5 0 0 00	18 1 0 0 00
Rent	1 2 0 0 00	1 2 0 0 00	1 2 0 0 00	3 6 0 0 00
Utilities	2 1 0 00	2 1 0 00	1 5 0 00	5 7 0 00
Supplies	3 0 0 00	3 0 0 00	5 0 0 00	1 1 0 0 00
Office Expenses	9 0 00	9 0 00	1 0 0 00	2 8 0 00
Repairs	2 0 0 00	2 0 0 00	5 5 0 00	9 5 0 00
Insurance	3 7 5 00	3 7 5 00	3 7 5 00	1 1 2 5 00
Taxes	1 1 6 0 00	1 1 6 0 00	1 3 0 0 00	3 6 2 0 00
Equipment			7 5 0 00	7 5 0 00
Total Payments	9 3 3 5 00	9 3 3 5 00	11 4 2 5 00	30 0 9 5 00
Balance	2 6 5 00	8 6 5 00	(2 2 5 00)	9 0 5 00

Let's see what steps Brady took to complete the cash budget.

STEP 1 ▶ ***Complete the heading.***

Brady entered the name of the business, Lamas Painting Company, on the first line at the top of the form. He entered the name of the form, Cash Budget, on the next line.

Notice that the form is not called a record of receipts and payments. The reason is that the form is not used to record *actual* receipts and payments. It is used to record *estimated* receipts and payments.

Brady entered "For First Quarter, 19--" on the bottom line of the heading since the form includes the estimated cash receipts and cash payments for the first three months of the year.

STEP 2 ▶ ***Total the estimated cash receipts for each month.***

Brady ruled and totaled the cash receipts columns. For example, Brady added the two cash receipts amounts for January, $7,200.00 + $2,400.00, and entered the total, $9,600.00, on the Total Receipts line in the column for January. In the same way, he entered the totals for the other months in the proper columns.

STEP 3 ▶ ***Total each type of estimated cash receipt.***

Brady **crossfooted** the amounts of cash receipts for interior sales and entered the total, $19,100.00, in the Total column at the right. He then crossfooted the amounts for exterior sales and entered the total, $11,900.00, in the Total column.

STEP 4 ▶ ***Total the estimated cash receipts for the period.***

Brady ruled the Total column and added the two amounts he had just entered, $19,100.00 + $11,900.00. The total, $31,000.00, is the total cash receipts Lamas expects for the first quarter.

STEP 5 ▶ ***Verify the estimated cash receipts.***

Brady verified the total receipts for the first quarter, $31,000.00, by crossfooting the total cash receipts amounts for each month:

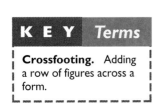

KEY Terms

Crossfooting. Adding a row of figures across a form.

Total estimated cash receipts, January	$ 9,600.00
Total estimated cash receipts, February	10,200.00
Total estimated cash receipts, March	11,200.00
Total	$31,000.00

Since the two totals agreed, Brady was reasonably confident that he had made no mistakes. Brady then double ruled the receipts columns to show that he was done with those amounts.

STEP 6 ▶ *Total the estimated cash payments for each month.*

Brady ruled the payments columns and added the payments for each month. He entered these totals on the Total Payments line of the form. For example, the total estimated payments for January were $9,335.00. Brady entered this amount on the Total Payments line in the column for January.

STEP 7 ▶ *Total each type of estimated cash payment.*

Brady crossfooted the amounts for each type of cash payment and entered the totals on the proper line of the Total column at the right. For example, he crossfooted the cash payments amounts for wages and entered the total, $18,100.00, in the Total column on the Wages line.

STEP 8 ▶ *Total the estimated cash payments for the period.*

Brady ruled the Total column and added the cash payment amounts. He entered the total, $30,095.00, on the Total Payments line in the Total column at the right.

STEP 9 ▶ *Verify the estimated cash payments.*

Brady crossfooted the total payments for each month. The total, $30,095.00, was compared to the total cash payments he found in Step 8. Since the two amounts agreed, he was reasonably confident that he had made no errors. He then double ruled the payments columns.

STEP 10 ▶ *Find the estimated balance for each month.*

Brady saw that the estimated receipts were greater than the estimated payments for every month except March. When there are more receipts than payments in a period, it is called a **positive cash flow**. For months with a positive cash flow, Brady subtracted the total payments from the total receipts. He then entered the balance on the Balance line of the form. For example, in January, the receipts were $9,600.00, and the payments were $9,335.00. Brady subtracted the payments from the receipts and entered the difference on the Balance line in the January column.

Total estimated cash receipts in January	=	$9,600.00
Total estimated cash payments in January	=	- 9,335.00
Estimated balance for January	=	$ 265.00

In March, the payments were greater than the receipts. When there are more payments than receipts in a period, it is called a **negative cash flow**. Brady subtracted the total receipts from the total payments.

Total estimated cash payments in March	=	$11,425.00
Total estimated cash receipts in March	=	- 11,200.00
Estimated balance for March	=	$ (225.00)

Brady entered $225.00 on the Balance line in the March column. Because the balance was negative, Brady put parentheses around the balance.

STEP 11 ▶ *Find the estimated balance for the period.*

Brady subtracted the total cash payments for the three months, $30,095.00, from the total cash receipts for the three months, $31,000.00. He entered the difference, $905.00, on the Balance line in the Total column. This balance is the estimated amount of cash that Lamas should have left at the end of the three months.

STEP 12 ▶ *Verify the balances.*

Brady added the positive monthly balances together. Then Brady subtracted the negative monthly balance from the total of the positive monthly balances. The difference should equal the balance for the three months which Brady found in Step 11.

Positive balances		
January	$ 265.00	
February	+ 865.00	
Total of positive balances		$1,130.00
Negative balance		- 225.00
Balance for three months		$ 905.00

Since the balances agreed, Brady was confident that he had made no mistakes on the form.

Lamas can now look at the cash budget for the three-month period which Brady has completed. She can quickly see in which months she will probably have a positive cash flow and in which months she will probably have a negative cash flow. Lamas must plan to save enough money from the positive months to cover the difference in the negative months.

𝓑UILDING YOUR BUSINESS VOCABULARY

On a sheet of paper, write the headings **Statement Number** and **Words**. Next, choose the words that match the statements. Write each word you choose next to the statement number it matches. Be careful; not all the words listed should be used.

Statements	Words
1. Amounts of money received	cash budget
2. Cash payments that change from period to period	cash flow
	crossfooting
3. When cash receipts are greater than cash payments	estimating
	extend an amount
4. A report showing the estimated cash flow of a business	fixed payments
	money columns
5. When cash payments are greater than cash receipts	negative cash flow
	positive cash flow
6. To record an amount again in a second column	quarter
	receipts
7. Adding a row of figures across a business form	variable payments
8. Cash payments that are the same from period to period	
9. A three-month period	
10. How money is received and spent over time	

PROBLEM SOLVING MODEL FOR: *Keeping a Business Budget*

....

STEP 1 ▶ *Complete the heading.*

STEP 2 ▶ *Total the estimated cash receipts for each month.*

STEP 3 ▶ *Total each type of estimated cash receipt.*

STEP 4 ▶ *Total the estimated cash receipts for the period.*

STEP 5 ▶ *Verify the estimated cash receipts.*

STEP 6 ▶ *Total the estimated cash payments for each month.*

STEP 7 ▶ *Total each type of estimated cash payment.*

STEP 8 ▶ *Total the estimated cash payments for the period.*

STEP 9 ▶ *Verify the estimated cash payments.*

STEP 10 ▶ *Find the estimated balance for each month.*

STEP 11 ▶ *Find the estimated balance for the period.*

STEP 12 ▶ *Verify the balances.*

APPLICATION PROBLEMS

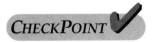

PROBLEM | **9-1** ▶ It is March, and you are the record keeper for Lamas Painting Company. Carmen Lamas wants to plan for the second quarter of the year. She has estimated the cash receipts and payments for the Lamas Painting Company for April through June. She has asked you to complete the cash budget.

Directions

a. Copy and complete the cash budget below. Follow Steps 1-12 in the Sample Problem. Use Illustration 9C (on page 84) as a guide.

CHECKPOINT ✔

9-1
Total estimated balance = $2,755.00

b. Answer these questions about the completed cash budget:

1. Which cash payments are fixed cash payments?
2. Which cash payments are variable cash payments?
3. What are the total estimated cash receipts from interior sales for the quarter?
4. What are the total estimated cash payments for repairs for the quarter?
5. In what month(s) is there a positive cash flow?
6. In what month(s) is there a negative cash flow?
7. Is the cash flow for the entire quarter positive or negative?

DESCRIPTION	APRIL	MAY	JUNE	TOTAL
Receipts:				
Interior Sales	3 6 0 0 00	3 5 0 0 00	4 5 0 0 00	
Exterior Sales	7 0 0 0 00	7 4 0 0 00	9 3 0 0 00	
Total Receipts				
Payments:				
Wages	6 5 0 0 00	6 5 0 0 00	7 0 0 0 00	
Rent	1 2 0 0 00	1 2 0 0 00	1 2 0 0 00	
Utilities	1 0 0 00	1 0 0 00	1 0 0 00	
Supplies	5 0 0 00	5 0 0 00	5 5 0 00	
Office Expenses	9 0 00	9 0 00	9 0 00	
Repairs	2 0 0 00	1 5 0 00	1 5 0 00	
Insurance	3 7 5 00	3 7 5 00	3 7 5 00	
Taxes	1 3 0 0 00	1 3 0 0 00	1 5 0 0 00	
Equipment		1 1 0 0 00		
Total Payments				
Balance				

PROBLEM **9-2** ▶ You are the record keeper for Astra Computer Services, a business that installs and services computer systems for businesses and government agencies. The owner, Wally Turner, has estimated the cash receipts and cash payments for the company for the first quarter of next year. He has asked you to complete the cash budget.

Directions

a. Copy and complete the cash budget below. Follow Steps 1-12 in the Sample Problem. Use Illustration 9C (page 84) as a guide.

b. Answer these questions about the completed cash budget:

1. Which cash payments are fixed cash payments?
2. Which cash payments are variable cash payments?
3. What are the total estimated cash receipts from business sales for the quarter?
4. What are the total estimated cash payments for taxes for the quarter?
5. In what month(s) is there a positive cash flow?
6. In what month(s) is there a negative cash flow?
7. Is the cash flow for the entire quarter positive or negative?

CHECKPOINT ✓

9-2 (b. 3)
Total estimated receipts =
$31,600.00

DESCRIPTION	JANUARY	FEBRUARY	MARCH	TOTAL
Receipts:				
Business Sales	6 5 0 0 00	6 5 0 0 00	6 7 0 0 00	
Government Sales	3 9 0 0 00	4 2 0 0 00	3 8 0 0 00	
Total Receipts				
Payments:				
Wages	6 2 0 0 00	6 2 0 0 00	6 2 0 0 00	
Rent	1 0 0 0 00	1 0 0 0 00	1 0 0 0 00	
Insurance	4 0 0 00	4 0 0 00	4 0 0 00	
Telephone	2 5 0 00	2 5 0 00	2 5 0 00	
Utilities	1 7 0 00	1 7 0 00	1 3 0 00	
Taxes	1 1 0 0 00	1 1 0 0 00	1 3 5 0 00	
Equipment	1 0 0 00	3 0 0 00	3 0 0 00	
Supplies	6 0 0 00	6 0 0 00	6 0 0 00	
Other		1 1 0 0 00		
Total Payments				
Balance				

PROBLEM 9-3 ▶ You continue to work as the record keeper for Astra Computer Services. (See Problem 9-2.) It is now March, and Wally Turner has estimated the cash receipts and cash payments for the company for the next three months. He has asked you to complete the cash budget.

Directions

a. Copy and complete the cash budget below. Follow Steps 1-12 in the Sample Problem. Use Illustration 9C (page 84) as a guide.

b. Answer these questions about the completed cash budget:

9-3 (b. 7)
Cash flow for the quarter is positive.

1. Which cash payments are fixed cash payments?
2. Which cash payments are variable cash payments?
3. What are the total estimated cash receipts from government sales for the quarter?
4. What are the total estimated cash payments for taxes for the quarter?
5. In what month(s) is there a positive cash flow?
6. In what month(s) is there a negative cash flow?
7. Is the cash flow for the entire quarter positive or negative?

DESCRIPTION	APRIL	MAY	JUNE	TOTAL
Receipts:				
Business Sales	7 0 0 0 00	7 2 0 0 00	7 5 0 0 00	
Government Sales	3 8 0 0 00	3 8 0 0 00	3 8 0 0 00	
Total Receipts				
Payments:				
Wages	6 2 0 0 00	6 2 0 0 00	6 2 0 0 00	
Rent	1 0 0 0 00	1 0 0 0 00	1 0 0 0 00	
Insurance	4 0 0 00	4 0 0 00	4 0 0 00	
Telephone	2 5 0 00	2 5 0 00	2 5 0 00	
Utilities	1 0 0 00	7 0 00	5 0 00	
Taxes	1 1 0 0 00	1 1 0 0 00	1 3 5 0 00	
Equipment	1 0 0 00	1 0 0 00	5 0 0 00	
Supplies	6 0 0 00	6 0 0 00	6 0 0 00	
Other	2 1 0 0 00			
Total Payments				
Balance				

Problem 9-4 may be found in the Working Papers.

APPLIED MATH PREVIEW

Find the totals of each column. The amounts in parentheses are negative amounts. If an answer is negative, put it in parentheses.

1.	2.	3.	4.
$350.00	$189.40	$ 9.25	$ 23.30
4.00	(56.70)	(36.70)	(45.10)
(20.00)	1.75	(65.80)	(305.90)
150.00	835.98	(268.35)	(55.20)
(6.00)	(45.25)	52.35	(4.60)

TIP

Add all positive numbers. Then add all negative numbers. Then subtract the smaller total from the larger total. If the larger total is positive, the answer will be positive. If the larger total is negative, the answer will be negative.

BUSINESS TERMS PREVIEW

• **Budget variance report** • **Variance** •

GOAL

To learn how to compare budgeted amounts with actual amounts.

UNDERSTANDING THE JOB

Many companies compare their actual cash receipts and payments with amounts on their cash budget to see if they have received or spent more than they had planned. In this way, they can make their budgets more realistic. They may also find that they must adjust their spending to bring future payments into line with their budget.

A form that compares budgeted amounts with actual amounts is called a **budget variance report**. This report shows how actual receipts and payments *vary*, or are different, from budgeted receipts and payments. A budget variance report for the Lamas Painting Company is shown in Illustration 10A.

KEY Terms

Budget variance report. Compares budgeted amounts to actual amounts.

Lamas Painting Company
Budget Variance Report
For January, 19--

	BUDGETED	ACTUAL	VARIANCE
Receipts:			
Interior Sales	7 2 0 0 00	7 3 2 0 00	1 2 0 00
Exterior Sales	2 4 0 0 00	2 3 7 0 00	(3 0 00)
Total Receipts	9 6 0 0 00	9 6 9 0 00	9 0 00
Payments:			
Wages	5 8 0 0 00	5 8 0 0 00	0 00
Rent	1 2 0 0 00	1 2 0 0 00	0 00
Utilities	2 1 0 00	1 9 0 00	(2 0 00)
Supplies	3 0 0 00	1 4 0 00	(1 6 0 00)
Office Expenses	9 0 00	1 2 0 00	3 0 00
Repairs	2 0 0 00	1 2 0 00	(8 0 00)
Insurance	3 7 5 00	3 7 5 00	0 00
Taxes	1 1 6 0 00	1 1 8 0 00	2 0 00
Equipment	0 00	0 00	0 00
Total Payments	9 3 3 5 00	9 1 2 5 00	(2 1 0 00)
Balance	2 6 5 00	5 6 5 00	3 0 0 00

SAMPLE PROBLEM

Carmen Lamas asks her record keeper, Leroy Brady, to prepare a budget variance report for January. Here is how Brady completed the job:

STEP 1 ▶ Complete the heading.

Brady entered the name of the business, Lamas Painting Company, on the first line of the report. He entered the name of the report, Budget Variance Report, on the next line. Brady entered "For January, 19--" on the last line of the heading. The budget variance report compares the differences between budgeted and actual amounts for the whole month of January.

STEP 2 ▶ Enter the budgeted amounts.

Brady entered the budgeted amounts for January receipts in the Budgeted column. He got these amounts from the cash budget form. (See Illustration 9C on page 84.) For example, he entered $7,200.00 on the Interior Sales line of the Receipts section in the Budgeted column.

Brady then entered the budgeted amounts for January payments. For example, he entered $5,800.00 on the Wages line of the Payments section in the Budgeted column.

Finally, Brady entered the planned balance for January, $265.00, on the Balance line in the Budgeted column.

STEP 3 ▶ Enter and total the actual cash receipts and payments.

Brady copied the actual cash receipts and payments for January from the company records. He entered each amount in the Actual column on the correct budget line. Then he ruled and totaled the cash receipts and cash payments amounts.

STEP 4 ▶ Find the actual cash balance.

Brady subtracted the actual cash payments from the actual cash receipts to find the actual cash balance. He entered this amount, $565.00, on the Balance line in the Actual column.

Actual Cash Receipts	$9,690.00
Actual Cash Payments	- 9,125.00
Actual Cash Balance	$ 565.00

STEP 5 ▶ Find the variance for each cash receipt.

For each cash receipt, Brady found the **variance**, or difference, between the budgeted amount and the actual amount. Brady follows these rules to find variances:

KEY Terms

Variance. Difference.

1. Always subtract the smaller amount from the larger amount.

    For example, Brady subtracted the smaller amount for interior sales, $7,200.00, from the larger amount, $7,320.00. The difference, or variance, was $120.00. Brady entered $120.00 in the Variance column on the Interior Sales line.

2. If the actual amount is larger than the budgeted amount, the variance is positive.

    Brady knew that the variance was positive because the actual amount, $7,320.00, was more than the budgeted amount, $7,200.00.

3. If the actual amount is smaller than the budgeted amount, the variance is negative. Negative variances are placed in parentheses.

    Brady found the variance for exterior sales by subtracting the smaller amount, $2,370.00, from the larger amount, $2,400.00. The variance was $30.00. Since the actual amount was less than the budgeted amount, the variance was negative. Brady put parentheses around it.

STEP 6 ▶ Find and verify the total variance for cash receipts.

Brady found the total variance for cash receipts by subtracting the negative amount, $30.00, from the positive amount, $120.00. The difference was $90.00. This means that the company received $90.00 more in cash receipts than it had planned.

To verify his work, Brady subtracted the total budgeted cash receipts from the total actual cash receipts.

When actual receipts exceed budgeted receipts, the variance is positive.

TIP

Total actual cash receipts	$9,690.00
Total budgeted cash receipts	- 9,600.00
Total variance for cash receipts	$ 90.00

Since this amount was also $90.00, Brady was confident that he had done his work correctly. So, he entered the $90.00 in the Variance column on the Total Receipts line.

STEP 7 ▶ Find the variance for each cash payment.

Next, Brady found the variance for each cash payment. When there is *no difference* between the budgeted and actual amounts, there is no variance. Brady put 0.00 in the Variance columns for wages, rent, insurance, and equipment, since there were no differences between the budgeted amounts and the actual amounts spent on these items.

When actual payments exceed budgeted payments, the variance is positive.

TIP

Brady found the variances for the other cash payments using the rules explained earlier. For example, Brady found the variance for office expenses by subtracting the smaller amount, $90.00, from the larger amount, $120.00. The difference was $30.00. He entered the difference in the Variance column on the Office Expenses line. Brady knew that this variance was positive because the actual cash payment, $120.00, was larger than the budgeted cash payment, $90.00.

Brady found the variance for utilities by subtracting the smaller amount, $190.00, from the larger amount, $210.00. He entered the variance, $20.00, on the Utilities line in the Variance column. Brady knew this variance was negative because the actual cash payment, $190.00, was less than the budgeted cash payment, $210.00. Brady put the variance in parentheses.

STEP 8 ▶ Find and verify the total variance for cash payments.

Brady added every positive amount in the Variance column for cash payments: $30.00 + $20.00. These are the items on which the company spent more than it had planned. The total was $50.00.

Brady then added the negative amounts (the amounts in parentheses): $20.00 + $160.00 + $80.00. These are the items on which the company spent less than it had planned. The total was $260.00.

Brady subtracted the smaller total, $50.00, from the larger total, $260.00. The difference, $210.00, is the total variance for cash payments. Because the larger amount was negative, Brady knew that the difference must be negative. This means that the company spent $210.00 less cash than it had planned in January.

To verify his work, Brady subtracted the total actual cash payments from the total budgeted cash payments.

Total budgeted cash payments	$9,335.00
Total actual cash payments	- 9,125.00
Total variance for cash payments	$ 210.00

Since this amount was also $210.00, Brady was reasonably confident that he had done his work correctly. So, he entered the $210.00 in the Variance column on the Total Payments line. Because the actual total cash payments were less than the budgeted total cash payments, the variance was negative. Brady put parentheses around it.

STEP 9 ▶ *Find the variance in the cash balance.*

The budgeted cash balance was $265.00. The actual cash balance was $565.00. Brady subtracted the smaller amount from the larger amount.

When the actual cash balance exceeds the budgeted cash balance, the variance is positive.

TIP

Actual cash balance	$565.00
Budgeted cash balance	- 265.00
Cash balance variance	$300.00

Since the actual cash balance was larger than the budgeted cash balance, Brady knew that the variance was positive. The variance means that there was more cash on hand than had been budgeted. The company had $300.00 more cash on hand in January than they had expected. Brady entered the cash balance variance, $300.00, on the Balance line in the Variance column.

If the actual cash balance had been less than the budgeted cash balance, the variance would have been negative. For example, if the actual cash balance had been $120.00, Brady would have subtracted the actual cash balance from the budgeted cash balance:

When the actual cash balance is less than the budgeted cash balance, the variance is negative.

TIP

Budgeted cash balance	$265.00
Actual cash balance	- 120.00
Cash balance variance	$145.00

In this case, the company has less cash than it had expected. The amount of the shortage is $145.00. Brady would have entered the cash balance in the Variance column and placed parentheses around it.

On a sheet of paper, write the headings **Statement Number** and **Words**. Next, choose the words that match the statements. Write each word you choose next to the statement number it matches. Be careful; not all the words listed should be used.

Statements	Words
1. A form that compares budgeted amounts with actual amounts	budget
	budget variance report
2. Cash payments that change from period to period	crossfooting
	extend an amount
3. To record an amount again in a second column	fixed payments
	negative cash flow
4. Adding a row of figures across a business form	positive cash flow
	quarter
5. A plan for receiving and spending money	receipts
6. When cash payments are greater than cash receipts for a period	variable payments
	variance
7. Amounts of money received	
8. A three-month period	
9. Difference	

PROBLEM SOLVING MODEL FOR: *Analyzing Budgets*

STEP 1 ▶ *Complete the heading.*

STEP 2 ▶ *Enter the budgeted amounts.*

STEP 3 ▶ *Enter and total the actual cash receipts and payments.*

STEP 4 ▶ *Find the actual cash balance.*

STEP 5 ▶ *Find the variance for each cash receipt.*

STEP 6 ▶ *Find and verify the total variance for cash receipts.*

STEP 7 ▶ *Find the variance for each cash payment.*

STEP 8 ▶ *Find and verify the total variance for cash payments.*

STEP 9 ▶ *Find the variance in the cash balance.*

APPLICATION PROBLEMS

PROBLEM | **10-1** ▶ You are the record keeper for Johnson Roofing Company. You have been asked to complete the company budget variance report for March.

Directions

a. Complete the budget variance report below. Follow the steps in the Sample Problem, and use Illustration 10A (page 93) as a guide.

b. Answer these questions about your completed budget variance report:

1. Which cash receipts had a positive variance?
2. Which cash payments had no variance?
3. Which cash payments had a negative variance?
4. Which cash payment had the largest positive variance?
5. Was the actual cash balance greater or less than the budgeted cash balance?

CHECKPOINT ✔

10-1

Total cash balance
variance = $2,100.00

	BUDGETED	ACTUAL	VARIANCE
Receipts:			
Business Sales	66 8 0 0 00	66 2 8 0 00	
Home Sales	22 0 0 0 00	23 5 4 0 00	
Total Receipts	88 8 0 0 00		
Payments:			
Wages	54 5 0 0 00	54 5 0 0 00	
Mortgage Payment	2 3 9 0 00	2 3 9 0 00	
Gas and Electric	7 5 0 00	6 8 0 00	
Roofing Supplies	12 5 0 0 00	11 9 0 0 00	
Office Expenses	7 9 0 00	8 6 0 00	
Equipment	1 5 0 0 00	1 0 2 0 00	
Insurance	2 3 0 0 00	2 3 0 0 00	
Taxes	12 7 5 0 00	12 7 5 0 00	
Telephone	3 5 0 00	3 5 0 00	
Total Payments	87 8 3 0 00		
Balance	9 7 0 00		

PROBLEM 10-2 ▶ You work in the finance department of the Ralston Paper Company. Your supervisor has asked you to complete the company budget variance report for November.

Directions

a. Complete the budget variance report below. Follow the steps in the Sample Problem, and use Illustration 10A (page 93) as a guide.

b. Answer these questions about your completed budget variance report:

1. Which cash receipts had no variance?
2. Which cash payments had no variance?
3. Which cash payments had a negative variance?
4. Which cash payment had the largest negative variance?
5. Was the actual cash balance greater or less than the budgeted cash balance?

CHECKPOINT ✔

10-2 (b. 5)
The actual cash balance was less than the budgeted cash balance.

	BUDGETED	ACTUAL	VARIANCE
Receipts:			
Sales of Pulp	148 350 00	148 350 00	
Sales of Boxes	69 200 00	72 250 00	
Total Receipts	217 550 00		
Payments:			
Wages	110 000 00	115 000 00	
Rent	15 800 00	15 800 00	
Gas and Electric	3 250 00	3 380 00	
Paper Supplies	45 700 00	46 400 00	
Office Expenses	4 850 00	4 550 00	
Equipment Repair	2 500 00	2 145 00	
Insurance	5 760 00	5 760 00	
Taxes	23 750 00	22 480 00	
Telephone	1 490 00	1 560 00	
Total Payments	213 100 00		
Balance	4 450 00		

Problems 10-3 and 10-4 may be found in the Working Papers.

Reinforcement
Activities

DISCUSSION

KEY *Terms*

Division of labor.
Dividing a job among
several workers.

In each problem in Job 9, the owner or manager worked with the record keeper to prepare the cash budget for the business. The owner provided the estimated amounts for cash receipts and cash payments. The record keeper completed the cash budget by filling in the heading and totaling and verifying the amounts. Dividing a job up like this is called **division of labor**. Can you think of any advantages of having division of labor in preparing a cash budget?

CRITICAL THINKING

John McKay has just been hired as a record keeper for Bering Machine Corporation. You have been asked to train John to complete cash budget reports. While you are teaching John how to verify the totals in the cash budget by crossfooting, John suggests that this step is not needed. He says that since you are using a calculator to find the totals, you cannot make any mistakes. He feels that it is a waste of time to verify the work by crossfooting the totals.

1. Is John right?
2. If John is not right, what errors could you make in finding the totals of the cash budget even if you are using a calculator?

APPLIED COMMUNICATIONS

Herbert Jackson and you are record keepers for the Trendair Company. Jackson was given the job of completing the cash budget form by the manager, Lynn Voss. When Voss looked at Jackson's work, she found a number of math errors. Voss was upset about these errors and let Jackson know that there was no excuse for making them.

Later, Jackson complained to you that Voss was not very fair to have scolded him for the errors. Jackson felt that he had worked very hard to do a good job and had not made the errors on purpose. "After all," he said, "everybody makes errors once in a while."

What would you say to Jackson about

1. How he could have avoided making math errors on the cash budget report?
2. How important accuracy is on the cash budget report?

RECORD KEEPING CAREERS

Imagine that you work as a record keeper for Banner Bank. You are paid $700 per month. You are also given a number of *fringe benefits*. For example, you are given free parking, free hospital insurance, free life insurance, and a free pension plan. The fringe benefits amount to 25% of your monthly salary.

You are offered a job at Loren Bank at $750 per month. The fringe benefits of this job include free hospital insurance and a free pension plan. These fringe benefits amount to 15% of the salary offered.

1. What is your real monthly pay in each job?
2. Which job offers the greatest total yearly income, and how much more is it per year?
3. Which job do you think is best, and why?

REVIEWING WHAT YOU HAVE LEARNED

On a sheet of paper, write the headings **Statement Number** and **Words**. Next, choose the words that best complete the statements. Write each word you choose next to the statement number it completes. Be careful; not all the words listed should be used.

Statements	Words
1. A form used to keep track of actual cash receipts and cash payments is called a _____ .	budget variance report cash budget cash flow
2. A report which compares actual cash receipts and payments to budgeted cash receipts and payments is called a _____ .	division of labor fixed payments
3. Cash payments which change from month to month are called _____ .	negative cash flow positive cash flow
4. Cash payments which stay the same from month to month are called _____ .	receipts record of receipts and payments
5. A form which shows the cash flows for a period of time is called a _____ .	variable payments
6. Dividing a job up so that each part is done by a different person is called _____ .	
7. When estimated cash receipts are greater than estimated cash payments, a business is said to have a _____ .	
8. When estimated cash payments are greater than estimated cash receipts, a business is said to have a _____ .	

MASTERY PROBLEM

Phase 1: Budgeting for a Family

Ria and Ben Stein decide to keep a record of receipts and payments to help them spend their money more wisely. Ria is a word processing supervisor, and Ben owns and operates an accounting service. Ria is also studying for a business degree at a community college.

Directions

a. Prepare a record of receipts and payments. Use a ruled sheet of paper with ten money columns.

b. Complete the headings for their record. Enter these estimated totals:

1. Date
2. Explanation
3. Total Receipts ($4,100.00)
4. Total Payments ($4,100.00)
5. Household Expenses ($2,100.00)
6. Clothing ($250.00)
7. Transportation ($800.00)
8. Health and Personal ($200.00)
9. Entertainment ($200.00)
10. Education ($200.00)
11. Gifts ($50.00)
12. Savings ($300.00)

c. Record the following receipts and payments for July of the current year.
   July 1 The balance of cash was $303.18
        6 The Steins received their weekly paychecks which together totaled $975.00.

7 The payments made since June 30 were

Contributions	$ 25.00
Haircut	12.00
Groceries	185.64
College textbooks	75.33
Rent	650.00
Gasoline, oil for cars	48.16
Newspapers, magazines	14.57
Notebooks, paper	22.55
Savings account deposit	75.00

13 The Steins received their weekly paychecks which together totaled $975.00.

14 The payments made since last week were

Savings account deposit	$ 75.00
Electric bill	163.59
Groceries	107.16
Jacket	110.89
Gasoline for cars	47.61
Automobile insurance	157.23
Dentist visit	42.00
Beauty salon	40.00
Baseball game	12.75
College laboratory fees	65.00

20 The Steins received their weekly paychecks which totaled $975.00.

21 The payments made since last week were

Groceries	$118.77
Car repair	212.15
Doctor visit, medicine	37.91
Telephone bill	63.15
Magazines, newspapers	6.78
Gasoline for cars	49.71
Dinner out	35.95
Savings account deposit	75.00

27 The Steins received their weekly paychecks which together totaled $975.00.

28 The payments made since last week were

Groceries	$149.81
Gasoline for cars	42.09
Movie	12.00
Hat, shoes	86.77
VCR	326.18
Magazine subscription	36.00
Savings account deposit	75.00

31 The payments made since the 28th were

Groceries	$ 41.48
Gasoline for cars	22.18
College textbooks	75.99

d. Rule and foot the columns. Verify the totals by crossfooting.
e. Write the totals below the footings and double rule the columns.
f. Record the new balance for August 1.

Phase 2: Budgeting for a Business

Ben Stein also wants to plan the budget for his business, Stein's Accounting Service, Inc., for the third quarter of the current year. The firm provides income tax and accounting services to individuals and small businesses. He has estimated the firm's receipts and payments for July, August, and September. Copy and complete the cash budget.

Total estimated balance =
$3,450.00

DESCRIPTION	JULY	AUGUST	SEPTEMBER	TOTAL
Receipts:				
Income Taxes	4 5 0 0 00	5 0 0 0 00	5 0 0 0 00	
Accounting	5 5 0 0 00	6 0 0 0 00	6 5 0 0 00	
Total Receipts				
Payments:				
Wages	5 7 0 0 00	5 7 0 0 00	5 7 0 0 00	
Rent	1 2 0 0 00	1 2 0 0 00	1 2 0 0 00	
Loans	4 0 0 00	4 0 0 00	4 0 0 00	
Insurance	3 0 0 00	3 0 0 00	3 0 0 00	
Utilities	2 1 0 00	2 2 5 00	1 7 5 00	
Telephone	4 1 5 00	4 2 5 00	4 5 0 00	
Repairs	5 0 00	5 0 00	5 0 00	
Supplies	1 5 0 00	1 5 0 00	1 5 0 00	
Taxes	1 2 5 0 00	1 2 5 0 00	1 2 5 0 00	
Total Payments				
Balance				

CHECKPOINT ✔

Total cash balance
variance = $40.00

Phase 3: Analyzing a Budget

Ben Stein has entered the budgeted and actual receipts and payments for July. Copy and complete the report.

	BUDGETED	ACTUAL	VARIANCE
Receipts:			
Income Taxes	4 5 0 0 00	4 2 3 0 00	
Accounting	5 5 0 0 00	5 8 4 0 00	
Total Receipts			
Payments:			
Wages	5 7 0 0 00	5 7 0 0 00	
Rent	1 2 0 0 00	1 2 0 0 00	
Loans	4 0 0 00	4 0 0 00	
Insurance	3 0 0 00	3 0 0 00	
Utilities	2 1 0 00	2 5 5 00	
Telephone	4 1 5 00	4 3 5 00	
Repairs	5 0 00	7 5 00	
Supplies	1 5 0 00	9 0 00	
Taxes	1 2 5 0 00	1 2 5 0 00	
Total Payments			
Balance			

REVIEWING YOUR BUSINESS VOCABULARY

This activity may be found in the Working Papers.

C H A P T E R 3

Credit Records

If you buy a camera on credit, you get the camera now but pay for it at some later date. Credit is common in today's world and is used by individuals, families, businesses, and governments. One way for individuals to buy on credit is to use a credit card. Another way is to buy on the installment plan. A third way is to borrow money from a bank.

In Chapter 3, you will learn about the advantages and disadvantages of using a credit card, how to apply for credit, and the way that stores and banks decide who gets credit. You will learn how to read and check credit card statements. Calculator Tips will also be given for figuring your payments when you borrow money.

JOB 11 ▶ APPLYING FOR BANK CREDIT CARDS

TIP

To round a number to the nearest cent, use the *Rule of 5*. When the number to the right of the cents place is 5 or more, drop that number and add a penny to the answer. For example, to round $1.465 to the nearest cent, drop the 5 and add one cent to the answer. The answer becomes $1.47. When the number to the right of the cents place is 4 or less, drop that number and leave the answer as it is. For example, $1.784 is rounded to $1.78.

APPLIED MATH PREVIEW

Copy and complete the problems below. When necessary, round your answers to the nearest cent.

1. $500.00 × 52 =
2. $450.00 × 52 =
3. $375.00 × 52 =
4. $428.65 × 52 =
5. $471.17 × 52 =

6. $24,000.00 ÷ 12 =
7. $15,756.00 ÷ 12 =
8. $18,540.00 ÷ 12 =
9. $22,524.12 ÷ 12 =
10. $14,258.86 ÷ 12 =

BUSINESS TERMS PREVIEW

- **Annual** • **Authorize** • **Charge account** • **Credit** •
- **Credit application** • **Credit card** • **Creditor** •
- **Good credit risk** • **Joint account** •

GOALS

1. To learn what factors are used in granting credit.
2. To learn how to apply for credit.
3. To learn the advantages and disadvantages of using a credit card.

When you buy something now and pay for it later, you are using **credit**. You use credit when you borrow money and pay it back later. For example, you may borrow money to buy a car. You use the money to get the car right away, but you pay back the money to the lender later.

Buying on credit must be done carefully. If you are not careful, you can buy too much and get very deeply in debt. You must be sure that you can pay for the item later.

Another disadvantage of buying on credit is that it may be more expensive. The stores that accept your credit cards have to pay the credit card companies a service fee of 3% to 5% of the purchase amount. Some stores will offer you a discount if you pay for your purchases with cash. Most credit card companies usually charge each user an **annual**, or yearly, fee. The fee charged is often between $25.00 and $45.00. Finally, credit card companies charge interest on any balance that is not paid when it is due. The interest rates that credit card companies charge may range from 8% to 20% a year.

On the other hand, buying on credit has many advantages. You do not need to carry cash for a credit purchase. If you plan to buy something that is very expensive, you do not have to shop with a large amount of cash. Buying on credit also allows you to spread out your payments. A person may not have saved enough money to buy a $1,000 kitchen appliance with cash. The person may, however, be able to afford to pay $100 a month for the appliance. Buying the appliance on credit allows the person to get the appliance right away but pay for it over time. Also, buying on credit provides you with detailed records of your purchases.

There are many sources of credit available. You may borrow money from banks, insurance companies, credit unions, or personal finance companies. You can also borrow money from stores and credit card companies. When you buy an article on credit, you are really borrowing the money from the store. You get the article right away, but the store does not get its money until later. Sources of credit are called lenders or **creditors**.

KEY Terms

Credit. Buy now, pay later.

Annual. Yearly.

Creditor. Lender.

Charge account. A form of credit offered by stores.

Credit card. Identifies the person buying on credit.

Charge or Credit Cards

A common form of credit offered by department and chain stores is a charge account. A **charge account** allows you to purchase items now and pay for them later. When people buy using a charge account from stores, they may say they have bought an item "on account." This means that they have used the store charge account to make the purchase. Sometimes the store issues a charge card or **credit card** to the customer, like the one shown in Illustration 11A on page 108. This card contains the customer's name and account number, which are often printed in special raised characters on the card. Credit

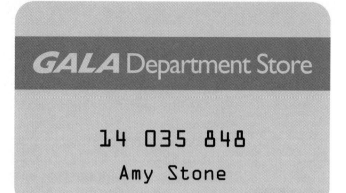

GALA Department Store

14 035 848
Amy Stone

cards are used to identify the person who is making the credit purchase. Store credit cards can typically be used only in the store that
issues them. For example, a chain department store may issue credit
cards to customers for use in any of their stores.

Two other types of credit cards commonly used are gasoline
credit cards and bank credit cards. Gasoline credit cards can usually
be used only to purchase gas, oil, or other items from service stations. Bank credit cards are credit cards issued by banks. These cards
are designed to be accepted at many stores and businesses for many
different types of services and products. However, not all stores
accept every bank credit card.

Applying for Credit

When you open an account with a creditor, such as a store, you usually complete a **credit application** form. The credit application form
provides the lender or creditor with information about your ability
to pay the money you owe. A completed credit application form is
shown in Illustration 11B on page 110.

An employee in the credit department of the store will use the
information from the credit application to decide whether or not you
are a **good credit risk**. A good credit risk is a person who is very
likely to pay the money owed. A bad credit risk is not likely to pay
the money owed.

Lenders usually look at many factors before they grant you credit, including your income, the value of the things you own, the
amount you already owe, and your past credit history. Successful
businesses and people who own a lot, owe others little, and have
steady incomes are likely to pay off their debts. They are good credit
risks. Those who have paid off their debts in the past promptly and
fully are likely to do the same in the future. They are also good credit
risks.

K E Y *Terms*

Credit application.
Provides information
about your ability to
pay debts.

Good credit risk.
Person likely to pay
debts.

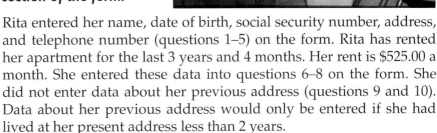

Rita Valesquez is applying for a ValuCard from the Carlsbad National Bank. To get the Valu-Card, Rita completed the credit card application form shown in Illustration 11B on page 110. Here is how she did it:

STEP **1** ▶ *Complete the Applicant section of the form.*

Rita entered her name, date of birth, social security number, address, and telephone number (questions 1–5) on the form. Rita has rented her apartment for the last 3 years and 4 months. Her rent is $525.00 a month. She entered these data into questions 6–8 on the form. She did not enter data about her previous address (questions 9 and 10). Data about her previous address would only be entered if she had lived at her present address less than 2 years.

Rita then entered the data about her current full-time job: the name, address, and telephone number of her employer, how long she had been employed, her job title, and her income (questions 11–16). The amount of pay that Rita receives each week after deductions is $345.00. This is her weekly net pay. The form asks for her monthly net pay. So, Rita had to calculate her monthly net pay.

To calculate monthly net pay, some people multiply the weekly net pay by 4 because there are 4 whole weeks in each month. For example, $345.00 x 4 = $1,380.00. However, this amount is really less than their true monthly net pay. The reason is that most months have more than four weeks in them. To be accurate, you must

1. Multiply your weekly net pay by 52 (the number of weeks in a year) to find your yearly net pay.

    $345.00 x 52 = $17,940.00 yearly net pay

2. Divide your yearly net pay by 12 (the number of months in a year) to get your monthly net pay.

    $17,940.00 ÷ 12 = $1,495.00 monthly net pay

Rita previously worked for 3 years for Red Rock Distributors, Inc. as a record keeper. She entered the company name, address, and telephone number, her job title, length of time employed, and monthly pay into questions 17–22 of the form.

Carlsbad National Bank VALUCARD

APPLICANT:

1. Name (Last)	(First)	(Initial)	2. Birthdate	3. Social Security No.
Valesquez	Rita	N.	3/5/68	264-87-1533

4. Address (Street)	(City)	(State)	(Zip)
234 Kinder Street	San Antonio	TX	78247-3121

5. Area Code/Tel. Number	6. Lived At Present Address	7. __Own _✓_Rent __Other	8. Monthly Payment
512-555-8934	3 Years 4 Months		$525.00

9. Previous Street Address (if less than 2 years at present address)	10. Lived At Previous Address
	Years Months

11. Present Employer	12. How Long Employed	13. Job Title	14. Monthly Net Income
Superior Furnishings, Inc.	2 Years 1 Months	Supervisor	$1,495.00

15. Employer's Address (Street)	(City)	(State)	(Zip)	16. Area Code/Tel. Number
45 New Ridge Road	San Antonio	TX	78238-6511	512-555-3074

17. Previous Employer	18. How Long Employed	19. Job Title	20. Monthly Net Income
Red Rock Distributors, Inc.	3 Years 0 Months	Record Keeper	$1,207.00

21. Employer's Address (Street)	(City)	(State)	(Zip)	22. Area Code/Tel. Number
80778 Arroyo Boulevard	San Antonio	TX	78232-3341	512-555-5078

23. Other Sources Of Income	24. Net Income Per Month
Brevet's Department Store	$208.00

CO-APPLICANT: Complete this section only if a joint account is requested. (Spouse can be a co-applicant.)

25. Name (Last)	(First)	(Initial)	26. Birthdate	27. Social Security No.

28. Address (Street)	(City)	(State)	(Zip)

CREDIT REFERENCES:

48. Savings Account (Institution Name)	(Account No.)	(Balance)
Butte Savings and Loan Co.	20781	$957.88

49. Checking Account (Institution Name)	(Account No.)	(Balance)
Verona National Bank	342-787	$307.12

LOANS AND OUTSTANDING DEBTS: List all debts owing. Attach additional sheet if necessary.

50. Auto Make, Model, & Year	51. Financed By	52. Account No.	53. Balance	54. Monthly Payment
Ford Taurus, 19--	Halperin City Bank	3461-89	$6,859.00	$350.00

55. Name of Creditor/Lender	56. Account No.	57. Balance	58. Monthly Payment
Farmington's Department Store	23078	$128.50	$50.00

The above information is given to obtain credit privileges. I (we) hereby authorize the obtaining of information about any statements made herein, and I (we) agree to be bound by the terms of the National Credit Card agreement. Signers shall be jointly and severally liable.

Rita N. Valesquez	8/19/--	1
Applicant's Signature	Date	Authorized User(s)

Co-Applicant's Signature	Date	Relationship to Applicant	No. of Cards Requested

Illustration 11B   A completed credit card application form

Rita also earns $48.00 a week in net pay working part-time at Brevet's Department Store. Rita found the monthly net pay for her part-time job and entered these data into questions 23 and 24 of the form. Here are her calculations:

$48.00 x 52 = $2,496.00 yearly net part-time pay

$2,496.00 ÷ 12 = $208.00 monthly net part-time pay

STEP 2 ▶ *Complete the Co-Applicant section of the form.*

If two people are applying for the same credit card, information about the other person, or co-applicant, is entered into this section. If Rita were married, she might have applied for a **joint account** with her husband. Information about her husband would then be entered into the Co-Applicant section. This section has almost the same questions as the Applicant section. Since Rita is applying for a credit card for herself only, she left the Co-Applicant section blank. Because the

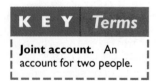

KEY *Terms*

Joint account. An account for two people.

Co-Applicant section was not used, it is not fully shown in Illustration 11B (page 110).

STEP 3 ▶ *Complete the Credit References section of the form.*

Rita listed the bank names, account numbers, and balances of her savings and checking accounts in questions 48 and 49.

STEP 4 ▶ *Complete the Loans and Outstanding Debts section of the form.*

Rita pays $350.00 a month on her Ford Taurus. She has $6,859.00 left to pay on her car loan which is financed by the Halperin City Bank. Rita entered the data about her car and her car loan in questions 50–54 of the form.

Rita also has a $128.50 balance in her charge account with Farmington's Department Store. She makes payments of $50.00 a month on the balance. She entered the data about the charge account in questions 55–58.

STEP 5 ▶ *Sign the form and return it to the credit firm.*

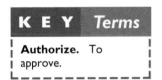

K E Y *Terms*

Authorize. To approve.

When Rita had finished entering the data, she checked the form over to make sure that she had completed it correctly. Then, she signed and dated the form. She also showed that she was the only person approved, or **authorized**, to use the credit card and asked that only one card be sent to her. She then mailed the application form to the Carlsbad National Bank.

*B*UILDING YOUR BUSINESS VOCABULARY

On a sheet of paper, write the headings **Statement Number** and **Words**. Next, choose the words that match the statements. Write each word you choose next to the statement number it matches. Be careful; not all the words listed should be used.

Statements	Words
1. Buy now and pay later	annual
2. A source of credit; lender	authorize
3. A form of credit offered by stores	bank credit cards
4. Credit cards issued by banks	budget
5. Used to identify the person buying on credit	cash flow
	charge account
6. People likely to pay off their debts	credit
7. Provides information about your ability to pay your debts	credit application
	credit card
8. An account for two people	creditor
9. To approve	good credit risks
10. Yearly	joint account

PROBLEM SOLVING MODEL FOR: *Applying for Bank Credit Cards*

STEP 1 ▶ *Complete the Applicant section of the form.*

STEP 2 ▶ *Complete the Co-Applicant section of the form.*

STEP 3 ▶ *Complete the Credit References section of the form.*

STEP 4 ▶ *Complete the Loans and Outstanding Debts section of the form.*

STEP 5 ▶ *Sign the form and return it to the credit firm.*

APPLICATION PROBLEMS

PROBLEM **11-1** ▶ The weekly pay for 5 people is listed below.

Directions

Find the yearly and monthly pay for each person. Round to the nearest cent when necessary.

11-1
(A. Berle) Yearly pay =
$14,300.00; monthly
pay = $1,191.67

Name	Weekly Pay	Yearly Pay	Monthly Pay
A. Berle	$275.00		
B. Coster	$226.00		
C. Dazai	$286.90		
D. Espino	$340.60		
E. Frisch	$490.80		

PROBLEM **11-2** ▶ Frank Reiner is applying for a ValuCard from the Carlsbad National Bank.

Directions

Complete a credit application form for Frank Reiner using the data provided. Be sure to compute his monthly net pay accurately and to sign and date the form 7/18/--. Frank wants only one card and is the only authorized user.

Applicant Section Data:

Name: Frank G. Reiner
Birthdate: 3/22/66
Social Security Number: 304-45-9846
Address: 3070 Ivany Street

City: Charleston
State: West Virginia
Zip Code: 25312-9087
Telephone Number: 304-555-1225
Other Data: Has rented his present apartment for 4 years and 6 months at
$426.00 a month
Present Employer: R. B. Crouse, Inc., 2207 Citadel Street, Charleston, WV
25313-7839, telephone 304-555-2601
Present Job: Credit Clerk II for 1 year and 2 months with a weekly net pay
of $254.88
Previous Employer: Tallworks, Inc., 1600 Montana Boulevard, Charleston,
WV 25302-9922, telephone 304-555-6133
Previous Job: General Office Clerk for 3 years and 1 month with a weekly
net pay of $212.43
Other Sources of Income: Part-time delivery person for Danville Delivery
Service with a weekly net pay of $64.00

Credit References Section Data:

Savings Account: Account No. 32108 with a balance of $429.08 at
Torrence Savings and Loan
Checking Account: Account No. 12-8907 with a balance of $139.03 at
Edgemont Bank and Trust Co.

Loans and Outstanding Debts Section Data:

Auto Loan: A balance of $3,508.91, with monthly payments of $276.25, in
loan account No. 12078 for a 19-- Buick Riviera with Edgemont Bank and
Trust Co.
Other Lender: A $227.00 balance, with monthly payments of $35.00, in
account No. 44729 with Valley Electronics

PROBLEM | 11-3 ▶ Amy Weinstein is applying for a TotalCard from Fredonia City Bank.

Directions

Complete a credit application form for Amy Weinstein using the
data provided. Be sure to compute her monthly net pay accurately
and to sign and date the form 1/31/--. Amy wants only one card and
is the only authorized user.

Applicant Section Data:

Name: Amy V. Weinstein
Birthdate: 9/16/68
Social Security Number: 342-12-5611
Address: 15 Azalea Lane
City: Madison
State: Wisconsin
Zip Code: 53711-3414
Telephone Number: 608-555-3978
Other Data: Has rented her present apartment for 2 years and 1 month at

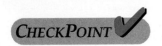
$495.00 a month
Present Employer: Telos Company, 1503 Oro Drive, Madison, WI 53714-2531, telephone 608-555-8898
Present Job: Solderer for 1 year and 2 months with a weekly net pay of $284.88
Previous Employer: Borkin Bros., Inc., 437 Merton Avenue, Madison, WI 53716-4077, telephone 608-555-8787
Previous Job: Line worker for 3 years and 1 month with a weekly net pay of $231.87
Other Sources of Income: Part-time airport limousine driver for Reo Limousine Service with a weekly net pay of $102.64

Credit References Section Data:

Savings Account: Account No. 12-899 with a balance of $271.73 at Churchill State Bank
Checking Account: Account No. 22-3075 with a balance of $301.33 at Churchill State Bank

Loans and Outstanding Debts Section Data:

Auto Loan: A balance of $4,078.24, with monthly payments of $285.95, in loan account No. 6051 for a 19-- Olds Calais with Churchill State Bank
Other Lender: A $147.35 balance, with monthly payments of $25.00, in account No. 2158 with Ferrel Furniture Co.

Problem 11-4 may be found in the Working Papers.

APPLIED MATH PREVIEW

Copy and complete these problems.

1.	2.	3.	4.	5.
$40.65	$331.98	$104.75	$277.28	$1.43
- 40.56	- 313.98	- 104.57	- 272.78	- 1.34

BUSINESS TERMS PREVIEW

- Chronological • Credit card statement • Embossed •
- Imprinter • Overcharged • Sales slip • Transaction •
- Unauthorized charges • Undercharged •

GOALS

1. To learn how to find the common errors on credit card statements.
2. To learn how to find the correct credit card balance.

UNDERSTANDING THE JOB

KEY Terms

Sales slip. Written record of a sale.

Each time you use your credit card, a sales clerk completes a written record of the sale called a **sales slip**. For example, Victor Perini has a bank credit card from the Crestwood Bank. On April 2, 19--, he used the card to buy a book from Belden's Book Store. The store clerk at Belden's completed the bank credit card sales slip shown in Illustration 12A. Notice that the total amount of the sale, $15.73, is shown at the bottom and the top of the sales slip.

ACCOUNT NUMBER	SALE AMOUNT	INVOICE NUMBER
5489 784 022	00015.73	507907

4/X1   4/X3

VICTOR PERINI

0037971
BELDEN'S BOOK STORE
14 CASSEN STREET
MOBILE, AL 36617-2239

DATE	AUTHORIZATION NO.	SALES CLERK	DEPT.
4/2/--	--	72	6

QUAN.	DESCRIPTION	PRICE	AMOUNT
1	Book	14.98	14 98

SIGN HERE X *Victor Perini*

	SUBTOTAL	14 98
	SALES TAX	75
SALES SLIP	TOTAL	15 73

VISA OR MasterCard

MERCHANT COPY · BANK COPY · CUSTOMER COPY

MERCHANT: RETAIN THIS COPY FOR YOUR RECORDS

Illustration 12A   A bank credit card sales slip

<table>
<tr><td>

K E Y *Terms*

Embossed. Printed in raised characters.

Imprinter. A device which prints data from a charge card onto a sales slip.

Credit card statement. Shows the transactions and balances of a credit card account.

</td></tr>
</table>

The customer's account number, name, and other data may be **embossed**, or printed in raised characters, on a charge card. This allows the clerk to print some of the data on the sales slip automatically, using an **imprinter**. This device prints customer data from the charge card onto the sales slip. The imprinter also prints the store's name, address, and account number, and the sale amount on the sales slip. You will learn in Chapter 7 that many businesses now use special electronic devices to read credit card information.

The store clerk gave Victor a copy of the sales slip, kept one copy for store records, and sent a third copy to the credit card company. After the month was over, the credit card company sent Victor a **credit card statement** listing each sales slip, the sales slip amount, any payments Victor made, and the total amount that Victor owes. The statement Victor received for the month of April is shown in Illustration 12B.

VISA — Crestwood Bank — MasterCard

Transaction Date	Reference	Transaction Description		New Loans, Fees, & Purchases	Payments & Credits
04/02/--	03078912	Belden's Book Store	Mobile, AL	15.73	
04/06/--	07989721	Ventnor Car Repairs	Mobile, AL	157.45	
04/07/--	207078T2	Payment -- Thank You			103.44
04/18/--	10798372	T & R Electronics	Mobile, AL	88.98	
04/21/--	00391782	Shipley's Sporting Goods	Houston, TX	24.56	
04/27/--	91074392	Reppenour Restaurant	Mobile, AL	35.56	
04/27/--		Annual Fee		25.00	

How We Arrived At Your Finance Charge	Monthly Rate	Annual Percentage Rate	Balance to Which Monthly Rate Applied	Finance Charge

Previous Balance	Payments & Credits	New Loans, Fees, & Purchases	Finance Charge	New Balance	Minimum Payment Due
103.44	103.44	347.28	0.00	347.28	25.00

Billing Date	Date Payment Due	Credit Line	Account Number	In case of billing error, write to this address: P.O. Box 10787, Mobile, AL 36616-2978
04/30/--	05/25/--	2000	5489 784 022	Direct telephone inquiries to 1-800-555-1987

Illustration 12B   Credit card statement

116   Chapter 3 Credit Records

Each purchase that Victor made was called a **transaction**. A transaction is something that happens in a business that a record keeper records, like sales, purchases, and payments of bills. The first transaction for Victor in April was the purchase of the book from Belden's Book Store. The total amount of the purchase, $15.73, was recorded in the New Loans, Fees, & Purchases column.

On April 7, Victor paid the credit card company $103.44. This amount was the previous balance due from the March statement. The payment was recorded in the Payments & Credits column.

On April 27, Victor was charged his annual credit card fee. This amount, $25.00, was recorded in the New Loans, Fees, & Purchases column.

*S*AMPLE PROBLEM

Before Victor paid the new balance due for the month of April, he examined the statement to make certain that the balance owed was correct. He used a credit card statement work sheet, like the one shown in Illustration 12C on page 118, to help him. Here is how he did this job:

STEP 1 ▶ *Complete the heading.*

Victor entered the heading at the top of the work sheet. He wrote "For April, 19--" because the work sheet included transactions for the whole month of April.

STEP 2 ▶ *Verify the sales slips.*

Victor saves the copies of the sales slips for every purchase he makes. When he receives his statement, he sorts the sales slips in **chronological** order. He then verifies that each sales slip is listed on the statement.

Victor's first sales slip was for the book he bought. He checked the statement to see that the sales slip was recorded. Since it was, he placed a check mark next to the date in the Transaction Date column.

Victor put aside those sales slips which are dated after the billing date shown on the statement, April 30, 19--. These sales slips will be shown on the next credit card statement that Victor receives.

KEY Terms

Unauthorized charges. Transactions not approved.

Overcharged. When you are charged more than you should be.

From time to time, Victor has found that sales slips for other people have been recorded on his statement. Because Victor did not approve these transactions, they are called **unauthorized charges**. For April, he found that the transaction dated April 21, 19--, should not have been listed on his statement. He found no sales slip for this transaction and did not make the purchase. Victor listed the date, store, and amount of the sales slip on the line "Unauthorized charges listed on statement." He also listed the amount, $24.56, on the line "Less: Unauthorized charges" in the section "Calculating the correct new balance."

STEP 3 ▶ *Verify the amount of each transaction on the statement.*

Victor has also found that occasionally the amount on the statement does not agree with the amount on the sales slip. For example, Victor found that the transaction dated April 27 was incorrectly listed as $35.56. The actual sales slip shown in Illustration 12D shows a correct total of only $35.16. Victor was charged more than he should have been, or **overcharged**. Victor entered $35.56 on the "Charge on statement" line under the heading "For an overcharge." He then entered the correct amount, $35.16, under the incorrect amount and

---

Victor Perini
Credit Card Statement Work Sheet
For April, 19--

a. Unauthorized charges listed on statement:

Date	Store		Amount
4/21/--	Shipley's Sporting Goods	$	24.56
		$	

b. Corrections to amounts on statement:

For an overcharge:			For an undercharge:		
Charge on statement	$	35.56	Charge on sales slip	$	
Charge on sales slip	$	35.16	Charge on statement	$	
Amount overcharged	$	.40	Amount undercharged	$	

c. Calculating the correct new balance:

New balance from statement		$	347.28
Less: Unauthorized charges	$ 24.56		
Overcharge on statement	$ .40		
		$	24.96
		$	322.32
Add: Undercharge on statement		$	
Correct new balance		$	322.32

Illustration 12C   Victor Perini's credit card statement work sheet

K E Y *Terms*

Undercharged.
When you are charged
less than you should be.

subtracted to find the amount overcharged, $.40. He entered the overcharge on the line "Overcharge on statement" in the section "Calculating the correct new balance."

If the amount on the statement had been less than the amount on the sales slip, there would have been an **undercharge**. Victor would then have subtracted the amount on the statement from the amount on the sales slip, entering the data under the heading "For an undercharge."

STEP 4 ▶ *Verify other charges.*

Victor examined the statement for other charges. He found that he was charged $25.00 for his annual fee. He knew that this was the correct amount, and he also knew that he should be charged the fee in April. His card membership is renewed every April.

STEP 5 ▶ *Verify the payments.*

Victor looked at his checkbook to make certain that the payment listed for April 7 was correct. He also checked to make certain that $103.44 was the only payment he made during that month.

STEP 6 ▶ *Calculate the correct new balance.*

Victor then calculated the amount he owed, or the correct new balance, in the section "Calculating the correct new balance." He entered the new balance from the statement, $347.28. He added the unauthorized charge and the overcharge and put the sum, $24.96, below the $347.28 and subtracted. Since there was no undercharge on the statement, the result, $322.32, is the correct new balance. He entered the correct new balance on the bottom line of the work sheet.

If there had been an undercharge, Victor would have entered it on the line "Add: Undercharge on sales slip" and added it to get the correct new balance.

Victor wrote a letter to the credit card company explaining why the new balance was incorrect. He included a copy of the sales slip for the restaurant meal as proof that he was charged too much.

Illustration 12D   Sales slip for April 27

Victor could have called the credit card company using the telephone number provided on the statement. A representative of the company would have then advised him on how to handle the errors he found on his statement. However, by telephoning he may not have been able to protect all of his legal rights.

You have learned how to check credit card statements in this job. In a later job you will learn how to complete credit card sales slips as a store clerk.

BUILDING YOUR BUSINESS VOCABULARY

On a sheet of paper, write the headings **Statement Number** and **Words**. Next, choose the words that match the statements. Write each word you choose next to the statement number it matches. Be careful; not all the words listed should be used.

Statements	Words
1. A written record of a sale	annual
2. A form showing the transactions and balances for a credit card account	authorize
	bank credit card
3. To check for accuracy	chronological
4. Something that happens in a business that is recorded	credit
	credit card statement
5. When you are charged more than you should be	creditor
6. When you are charged less than you should be	embossed
	imprinter
7. A credit card issued by a bank	joint account
8. When you buy now and pay later	overcharged
9. Yearly	sales slip
10. A lender	transaction
11. A device for recording a credit card sale	unauthorized charges
12. By date	undercharged
13. Printed in raised characters	verify
14. Transactions not approved	

PROBLEM SOLVING MODEL FOR: *Checking Your Credit Card Statement*

STEP I ▶ *Complete the heading.*

STEP 2 ▶ *Verify the sales slips.*

STEP 3 ▶ *Verify the amount of each transaction on the statement.*

STEP 4 ▶ *Verify other charges.*

STEP 5 ▶ *Verify the payments.*

STEP 6 ▶ *Calculate the correct new balance.*

ＡPPLICATION PROBLEMS

PROBLEM | 12-1 ▶ **Directions**

Complete the following table by putting the amount overcharged or undercharged in the correct column.

 CHECKPOINT ✔

12-1 (1)
Undercharge = $0.09

	Total of Sales Slip	Amount Charged on Statement	Overcharge	Undercharge
1	$123.87	$123.78		
2	$309.18	$309.81		
3	$16.59	$116.59		
4	$72.06	$72.00		
5	$8.93	$8.98		

PROBLEM | 12-2 ▶ Jill Wilson has saved each of her credit card sales slips for the month of June. Jill renews her card membership every June for a fee of $35.00. Her checkbook shows that she made a payment of $237.20 on June 15. She wants to verify her credit card statement for June.

Directions

CHECKPOINT ✔

12-2
Correct new balance = $234.13

a. On pages 122 and 123, you are given Jill's credit card statement and the top sections of her sales slips for June. Use a work sheet like the one in Illustration 12C (page 118) to verify the statement.
b. List the date, store, and amount of every transaction which should not appear on the statement.
c. Compare the "sale amounts" on the sales slips to the amounts on the statement. If an amount is incorrect, find the overcharge or

undercharge. Do not compare the "Amount" on the slips with the statement. The "Amount" and "sales amount" may differ because the bottom sections of the slips, showing sales taxes and totals, are not provided.

d. Find the correct new balance for the statement.

ACCOUNT NUMBER 4810 078 172	SALE AMOUNT 00015.20		INVOICE NUMBER 186271			
6/X1 6/X3	DATE 6/3/--	AUTHORIZATION NO. --	SALES CLERK 12		DEPT. 55	
JILL WILSON	QUAN.	DESCRIPTION	PRICE		AMOUNT	
0079182	1	Book	12.48	12	48	
TOLL'S BOOKSTORE	1	Calendar	2.00	2	00	

ACCOUNT NUMBER 4810 078 172	SALE AMOUNT 00012.52		INVOICE NUMBER 279183			
6/X1 6/X3	DATE 6/4/--	AUTHORIZATION NO. --	SALES CLERK 3		DEPT. 2	
JILL WILSON	QUAN.	DESCRIPTION	PRICE		AMOUNT	
0019728	--	Gasoline	12.52	12	52	
RON'S 77 GAS						

ACCOUNT NUMBER 4810 078 172	SALE AMOUNT 00021.20		INVOICE NUMBER 280188			
6/X1 6/X3	DATE 6/8/--	AUTHORIZATION NO. --	SALES CLERK --		DEPT. --	
JILL WILSON	QUAN.	DESCRIPTION	PRICE		AMOUNT	
0020189	--	Dinner	20.19	20	19	
TRES BON RESTAURANT						

ACCOUNT NUMBER 4810 078 172	SALE AMOUNT 00112.16		INVOICE NUMBER 700893			
6/X1 6/X3	DATE 6/18/--	AUTHORIZATION NO. 2017983	SALES CLERK 4		DEPT. 6	
JILL WILSON	QUAN.	DESCRIPTION	PRICE		AMOUNT	
0088493	1	Portable TV	106.82	106	82	
TOWN TV AND RADIO						

ACCOUNT NUMBER 4810 078 172	SALE AMOUNT 00010.16		INVOICE NUMBER 280343			
6/X1 6/X3	DATE 6/22/--	AUTHORIZATION NO. --	SALES CLERK 3		DEPT. 2	
JILL WILSON	QUAN.	DESCRIPTION	PRICE		AMOUNT	
0019728	--	Gasoline	10.16	10	16	
RON'S 77 GAS						

ACCOUNT NUMBER 4810 078 172	SALE AMOUNT 00027.89		INVOICE NUMBER 330911			
6/X1 6/X3	DATE 6/29/--	AUTHORIZATION NO. --	SALES CLERK 10		DEPT. 1	
JILL WILSON	QUAN.	DESCRIPTION	PRICE		AMOUNT	
0044909	1	FRAME	26.56	26	56	
HILL ART STUDIO						

BANK of the MOUNTAIN

Transaction Date	Reference	Transaction Description		New Loans, Fees, & Purchases	Payments & Credits
06/03/--	20719834	Toll's Bookstore	Atlanta, GA	15.20	
06/04/--	91702930	Ron's 77 Gas	Atlanta, GA	12.52	
06/08/--	33307922	Tres Bon Restaurant	Atlanta, GA	22.10	
06/15/--	51072983	Payment -- Thank You			237.20
06/16/--		Annual Membership Fee		35.00	
06/18/--	20179833	Town TV and Radio	Atlanta, GA	112.16	
06/20/--	00982719	Range Riding Stables	Yuma, AR	45.00	
06/22/--	31057434	Ron's 77 Gas	Atlanta, GA	10.16	
06/29/--	15324150	Hill Art Studio	Atlanta, GA	27.89	

How We Arrived At Your Finance Charge	Monthly Rate	Annual Percentage Rate	Balance to Which Monthly Rate Applied	Finance Charge

Previous Balance	Payments & Credits	New Loans, Fees, & Purchases	Finance Charge	New Balance	Minimum Payment Due
237.20	237.20	280.03	0.00	280.03	25.00

Billing Date	Date Payment Due	Credit Line	Account Number	In case of billing error, write to this address: P.O. Box 3011A, Atlanta, GA 30307-1421
06/30/--	07/25/--	1500	4810 078 172	Direct telephone inquiries to 1-800-555-9811

PROBLEM **12-3** ▶ Marvin Freeman has saved each of his credit card sales slips for the month of May. Marvin renews his card membership every May for a fee of $30.00. His checkbook shows that he made a payment of $312.77 on May 12. He wants to verify his credit card statement for May.

Directions

a. On pages 124 and 125, you are given Marvin's credit card statement and the top sections of his sales slips for May. Use a work sheet like the one in Illustration 12C (page 118) to verify the statement.

b. List the date, store, and amount of every transaction which should not appear on the statement.

c. Compare the "sale amounts" on the sales slips to the amounts on the statement. If an amount is incorrect, find the overcharge or undercharge. Do not compare the "Amount" on the slips with the statement. The "Amount" and "sales amount" may differ because the bottom sections of the slips, showing sales taxes and totals, are not provided.

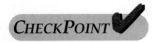

CHECKPOINT

12-3
Correct new balance =
$541.19

d. Find the correct new balance for the statement.

ACCOUNT NUMBER 3308 102 448	SALE AMOUNT 00167.98			INVOICE NUMBER 220325	
5/X1 5/X3	DATE 5/5/--	AUTHORIZATION NO. 339134	SALES CLERK 23	DEPT. 12	
MARVIN FREEMAN	QUAN.	DESCRIPTION	PRICE	AMOUNT	
0408855 EMORY CLOTHING	1	Jacket	159.98	159 98	

ACCOUNT NUMBER 3308 102 448	SALE AMOUNT 00017.33			INVOICE NUMBER 797985	
5/X1 5/X3	DATE 5/7/--	AUTHORIZATION NO. --	SALES CLERK 2	DEPT. 2	
MARVIN FREEMAN	QUAN.	DESCRIPTION	PRICE	AMOUNT	
8839001 7TH ST. STATION	--	Gasoline	17.33	17 33	

ACCOUNT NUMBER 3308 102 448	SALE AMOUNT 00247.23			INVOICE NUMBER 079313	
5/X1 5/X3	DATE 5/9/--	AUTHORIZATION NO. 107988	SALES CLERK 3	DEPT. 5	
MARVIN FREEMAN	QUAN.	DESCRIPTION	PRICE	AMOUNT	
3930119 V & R REPAIRS	--	Car Repairs	235.46	235 46	

ACCOUNT NUMBER 3308 102 448	SALE AMOUNT 00019.98			INVOICE NUMBER 635726	
5/X1 5/X3	DATE 5/15/--	AUTHORIZATION NO. --	SALES CLERK 8	DEPT. 10	
MARVIN FREEMAN	QUAN.	DESCRIPTION	PRICE	AMOUNT	
8839979 SUNDAY COMPUTERS	1	Box Computer Disks	19.03	19 03	

ACCOUNT NUMBER 3308 102 448	SALE AMOUNT 00033.60			INVOICE NUMBER 879116	
5/X1 5/X3	DATE 5/25/--	AUTHORIZATION NO. --	SALES CLERK 7	DEPT. --	
MARVIN FREEMAN	QUAN.	DESCRIPTION	PRICE	AMOUNT	
4351569 TICKET-O-RAMA	4	Baseball Tickets	8.40	33 60	

ACCOUNT NUMBER 3308 102 448	SALE AMOUNT 00025.07			INVOICE NUMBER 761001	
5/X1 5/X3	DATE 5/29/--	AUTHORIZATION NO. 841928	SALES CLERK 14	DEPT. 9	
MARVIN FREEMAN	QUAN.	DESCRIPTION	PRICE	AMOUNT	
6179763 MORE-MART STORES	6	Video Tapes	3.98	23 88	

CRESTVIEW BANK & TRUST COMPANY

Transaction Date	Reference	Transaction Description		New Loans, Fees, & Purchases	Payments & Credits
05/05/--	78121991	Emory Clothing	Detroit, MI	167.98	
05/07/--	44158742	7th St. Station	Detroit, MI	13.77	
05/09/--	99785127	V & R Repairs	Detroit, MI	247.23	
05/12/--	84571128	Payment -- Thank You			312.77
05/14/--	81672661	Staten's Body Shop	Boston, MA	113.98	
05/15/--	51641554	Sunday Computers	Detroit, MI	19.98	
05/20/--		Annual Fee		30.00	
05/25/--	61265993	Ticket-O-Rama	Detroit, MI	33.60	
05/29/--	37114987	More-Mart Stores	Lansing, MI	25.07	

How We Arrived At Your Finance Charge	Monthly Rate	Annual Percentage Rate	Balance to Which Monthly Rate Applied	Finance Charge

Previous Balance	Payments & Credits	New Loans, Fees, & Purchases	Finance Charge	New Balance	Minimum Payment Due
312.77	312.77	651.61	0.00	651.61	65.00

Billing Date	Date Payment Due	Credit Line	Account Number	In case of billing error, write to this address: P.O. Box 3872A, Detroit, MI 48223-6152
05/30/--	06/25/--	3000	3308 102 448	Direct telephone inquiries to 1-800-555-1987

Problem 12-4 may be found in the Working Papers.

GOALS

1. To learn how to find finance charges on installment purchases.
2. To learn how to find the total cost of buying on the installment plan.
3. To learn how to verify the amounts on installment contracts.

UNDERSTANDING THE JOB

KEY Terms

Installment plan. When you pay for an item by the month.

Cash price. The amount an item would cost if you paid cash for it.

Finance charge. The difference between cash and installment prices.

Installment contract. A form describing the time, place, and amounts of an installment purchase.

One way to buy on credit is to buy on the **installment plan**. When you buy on the installment plan, you pay for an item in monthly payments or installments. For example, a person or business may want to buy a car that costs $8,500.00. The person or business may not have $8,500.00 in the bank to pay cash for the car, but can afford monthly payments of $350.00. Buying the car on credit in this way allows the person or business to have the car right away but pay for it over many months.

When you buy on the installment plan, you are really borrowing the seller's money and paying it back over time. For that reason, the installment price is usually more than the **cash price**, or the amount the item would cost if you paid cash for it. The difference between the cash price and installment price of an item is called the **finance charge**.

An installment buyer is usually asked to sign an **installment contract** like the one shown in Illustration 13A. You need to know how the amounts on an installment contract are found so that you can check them before you sign it.

Illustration 13A   Part of
an installment contract

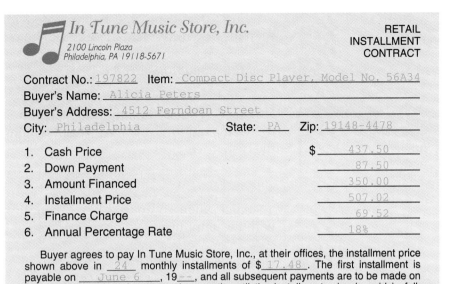

In Tune Music Store, Inc.
2100 Lincoln Plaza
Philadelphia, PA 19118-5671

RETAIL
INSTALLMENT
CONTRACT

Contract No.: 197822   Item: Compact Disc Player, Model No. 56A34
Buyer's Name: Alicia Peters
Buyer's Address: 4512 Ferndoan Street
City: Philadelphia   State: PA   Zip: 19148-4478

1.	Cash Price	$ 437.50
2.	Down Payment	87.50
3.	Amount Financed	350.00
4.	Installment Price	507.02
5.	Finance Charge	69.52
6.	Annual Percentage Rate	18%

Buyer agrees to pay In Tune Music Store, Inc., at their offices, the installment price shown above in ___24___ monthly installments of $ 17.48 . The first installment is payable on ___June 6___, 19__, and all subsequent payments are to be made on the same day of each consecutive month until the installment price is paid in full, subject to the conditions on the reverse side of this contract.

Signed _Alicia Peters_

SAMPLE PROBLEM

Alicia Peters bought a compact disc player priced at $437.50 from the In Tune Music Store. The store asked her to pay 20% down and the rest in monthly payments of $17.48 for two years. The store also asked her to sign the installment contract shown in Illustration 13A.

Here is how Alicia checked the amounts on the contract before she signed it:

STEP **1** ▶ **Find the amount of the down payment.**

The **down payment** is part of the purchase price that you must pay right away. The down payment for the compact disc player is 20% of the cash price, which is $437.50. To find the down payment, Alicia multiplied the cash price by the down payment percent.

$437.50 x 0.20 = $87.50   down payment

KEY *Terms*

Down payment. Part of purchase price paid at sale.

Alicia then compared the down payment amount she calculated with the down payment amount shown on the contract.

STEP 2 ▶ *Find the amount financed.*

The amount that you borrow from the seller is called the **amount financed**. This is the amount Alicia must repay over time. Alicia found the amount financed by subtracting the down payment from the cash price.

K E Y *Terms*

Amount financed.
Amount borrowed.

$$\$437.50 - \$87.50 = \$350.00 \quad \text{amount financed}$$

Alicia then compared her calculation of the amount financed with the amount shown on the contract.

STEP 3 ▶ *Find the installment price.*

The **installment price** is the down payment plus the total of all the monthly payments. Alicia found the installment price by multiplying the monthly payment, $17.48, by 24 months (2 years). She then added that amount and the down payment.

K E Y *Terms*

Installment price.
Down payment plus
total monthly payments.

$$
\begin{array}{rl}
\$17.48 \times 24 = \$419.52 & \text{total of the monthly payments} \\
+\ 87.50 & \text{down payment} \\
\hline
\$507.02 & \text{installment price}
\end{array}
$$

Alicia then compared her calculation of the installment price with the amount shown on the contract.

STEP 4 ▶ *Find the finance charge.*

The finance charge is the difference between the installment price, $507.02, and the cash price, $437.50. Alicia subtracted the cash price from the installment price to find the finance charge.

Finance
charge =
installment
price – cash price

▲▲▲▲▲
T I P
▼▼▼▼▼

$$\$507.02 - \$437.50 = \$69.52 \quad \text{finance charge}$$

Alicia then compared her calculation of the finance charge with the amount shown on the contract. Since all of the amounts that Alicia calculated agreed with the amounts on the contract, Alicia signed the contract.

If Alicia had found an error in one of the amounts, she would have crossed out that amount and written the correct amount to the right of the incorrect amount. She would then have corrected any amounts after, or **subsequent** to, the incorrect amount on lines 1–5 of the contract. For example, if the installment price had been incorrectly shown on the contract as $502.70 and the finance charge as $65.20, Alicia would have made these corrections:

K E Y *Terms*

Subsequent. After or
following.

3. Amount Financed	350.00
4. Installment Price	~~502.70~~ 507.02
5. Finance Charge	~~65.20~~ 69.52
6. Annual Percentage Rate	18%

Calculator
TIPS

Verifying the calculations of down payment, amount financed, installment price, and finance charge is easier when you use a calculator. The calculations in the Sample Problem could have been completed this way:

STEP 1 ▶ *Find the amount of the down payment.*

Press these keys in order:

4	3	7	•	5	x	•	2	=

The answer that appears in the display is $87.50, the down payment amount. Notice that it was not necessary to enter the ending zeros after .5 and .2.

STEP 2 ▶ *Find the amount financed.*

Press these keys in order:

4	3	7	•	5	–	8	7	•	5	=

The display now shows $350.00, the amount financed.

STEP 3 ▶ *Find the installment price.*

Press these keys in order:

1	7	•	4	8	x	2	4	=

The display now shows $419.52, the total of the monthly payments. Leave the display as it is and press these keys in order:

+	8	7	•	5	=

The display now shows $507.02, the installment price.

STEP 4 ▶ *Find the finance charge.*

Leave the installment price in the display and press these keys:

–	4	3	7	•	5	=

The display now shows $69.52, the finance charge.

The store would then have had to prepare a new, corrected contract for Alicia to sign.

Alicia will pay $69.52 more for the compact disc player on the installment plan than she would if she paid cash. If Alicia saved her money and waited until she could buy the player for cash, she would save $69.52. However, she would not get the use of the compact disk player until the needed cash was saved.

The finance charge is the cost you pay to borrow money from the seller. The finance charge is also shown as a percent on the contract and is called the **annual percentage rate** or APR. The annual percentage rate listed on the contract shown in Illustration 13A (page 127) is 18%. To find the APR on an installment contract, you must use a formula and a table. You will not be expected to find the APR for installment contracts in this job.

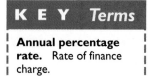

BUILDING YOUR BUSINESS VOCABULARY

On a sheet of paper, write the headings **Statement Number** and **Words**. Next, choose the words that match the statements. Write each word you choose next to the statement number it matches. Be careful; not all the words listed should be used.

Statements	Words
1. A form of credit in which you pay for an item in monthly payments	amount financed
2. The amount an item costs if bought for cash	annual percentage rate
	bank credit card
3. The difference between the cash and installment prices of an item	cash price
4. A form which describes the time, place, and amounts for an installment purchase	credit
	creditor
5. The part of the installment price paid at the time an item is bought	down payment
6. After or following	finance charge
7. The amount borrowed from the seller in an installment purchase	installment contract
	installment plan
8. The down payment plus the total of all monthly payments	installment price
9. When you buy now and pay later	subsequent
10. The annual finance charge shown as a rate or percent	

PROBLEM SOLVING MODEL FOR: *Buying on the Installment Plan*

STEP 1 ▶ *Find the amount of the down payment.*

STEP 2 ▶ *Find the amount financed.*

STEP 3 ▶ *Find the installment price.*

STEP 4 ▶ *Find the finance charge.*

*A*PPLICATION PROBLEMS

PROBLEM | **13-1** ▶ Linda Gorman bought an electronic keyboard priced at $312.50 from Searles Equipment Company. The store asked her to pay 20% down and the rest in monthly payments of $22.58 for one year. The store also asked her to sign the installment contract shown in this problem.

13-1
Finance charge = $20.96

Directions

a. Verify the down payment, the amount financed, the installment price, and the finance charge on the contract. If you find an error, cross out the incorrect amount and write the correct amount to the right of it. Correct any subsequent amounts on lines 1–5 of the contract in the same way.

b. If you find no errors in the amounts, sign Gorman's name to the contract.

SEARLES ▮▮▮▮▮▮
241 Gardenia Street • Warwick, RI 02888-2978

RETAIL INSTALLMENT CONTRACT

Contract No.: 34078 Item: Electronic Keyboard, Model TR-3411
Buyer's Name: Linda Gorman
Buyer's Address: 23 Cordell Avenue
City: Warwick   State: RI   Zip: 02886-6598

1. Cash Price	$	312.50
2. Down Payment		62.50
3. Amount Financed		250.00
4. Installment Price		333.46
5. Finance Charge		29.60
6. Annual Percentage Rate		15%

Buyer agrees to pay Searles Equipment Company, at their offices, the installment price shown above in __12__ monthly installments of $__22.58__. The first installment is payable on __August 12__, 19__, and all subsequent payments are to be made on the same day of each consecutive month until the installment price is paid in full, subject to the conditions on the reverse side of this contract.

Signed _____

Barry Young bought a copy machine for his business priced at $3,000.00 from Ortiz Office Equipment Company. The store asked him to pay 10% down and the rest in monthly payments of $133.50 for two years. The store also asked him to sign the installment contract shown in this problem.

CHECKPOINT ✔

13-2
There are 2 errors.

Directions

a. Verify the down payment, the amount financed, the installment price, and the finance charge on the contract. If you find an error, cross out the incorrect amount and write the correct amount to the right of it. Correct any subsequent amounts on lines 1–5 of the contract in the same way.

b. If you find no errors in the amounts, sign Young's name to the contract.

OOE ORTIZ OFFICE EQUIPMENT COMPANY
1212 Richards Boulevard • Cincinnati, OH 45244-0288

RETAIL INSTALLMENT CONTRACT

Contract No.: 918022 Item: Desktop Copier, Model No. 44508-1
Buyer's Name: Barry Young
Buyer's Address: 14-78 Locale Road
City: Cincinnati   State: OH   Zip: 45247-3361

1.	Cash Price	$ 3000.00
2.	Down Payment	300.00
3.	Amount Financed	2700.00
4.	Installment Price	3554.00
5.	Finance Charge	554.00
6.	Annual Percentage Rate	17%

   Buyer agrees to pay Ortiz Office Equipment Company, at their offices, the installment price shown above in __24__ monthly installments of $_133.50_. The first installment is payable on _February 2_, 19__, and all subsequent payments are to be made on the same day of each consecutive month until the installment price is paid in full, subject to the conditions on the reverse side of this contract.

Signed _____

Problems 13-3, and 13-4 may be found in the Working Papers.

APPLIED MATH PREVIEW

Copy and complete each problem. Round your answers to the nearest cent when necessary.

1. $3,000.00 \times 0.15 =$
2. $4,500.00 \times 0.18 =$
3. $2,189.78 \times 0.12 =$
4. $1,000.00 \times 0.10 \times 1.5 =$
5. $1,500.00 \times 0.15 \times 2 =$
6. $3,108.33 \times 0.12 \times 0.5 =$
7. $1,893.25 \times 0.18 \times 2.5 =$
8. $2,219.58 \times 0.08 \times 0.25 =$
9. $10,207.71 \times 0.05 \times 1.5 =$
10. $25,387.10 \times 0.09 \times 0.5 =$

BUSINESS TERMS PREVIEW

- **Amount due** • **Date of note** • **Due date** • **Interest** •
- **Principal** • **Promissory note** • **Time of note** •

GOALS

1. To learn about promissory notes.
2. To learn how to find the interest on a promissory note.
3. To learn how to find the amount due on a promissory note.

𝒰NDERSTANDING THE JOB

KEY Terms

Promissory note. A written promise to pay.
Interest. Money paid for the use of money.

Businesses and people sometimes need to borrow money. A chain of clothing stores may need the money to buy merchandise in order to open a new store. A restaurant may need to buy equipment for a new kitchen so that it can serve more customers. In their personal lives, people may need money to improve their homes or cover large medical expenses.

When you borrow money from a bank for personal or business reasons, you usually sign a **promissory note** like the one shown in Illustration 14A on page 134. A promissory note is your written promise to pay back the loan.

You usually have to pay for the use of the money you borrow. The amount you pay is called **interest**. The rate of interest that banks charge varies with changes in the economy. When interest rates go up, businesses and individuals may borrow less. When interest rates go down, businesses and individuals may borrow more.

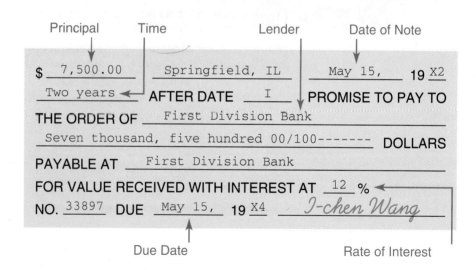

Principal Time   Lender   Date of Note

$ __7,500.00__   Springfield, IL   May 15, __ 19 X2

__Two years__ ◄ **AFTER DATE** __I__ **PROMISE TO PAY TO**

THE ORDER OF __First Division Bank__

__Seven thousand, five hundred 00/100-------__ **DOLLARS**

PAYABLE AT __First Division Bank__

FOR VALUE RECEIVED WITH INTEREST AT __12__ **%** ◄

NO. __33897__ **DUE** __May 15,__ **19** __X4__   *I-chen Wang*

Due Date   Rate of Interest

SAMPLE PROBLEM

KEY Terms

Principal. Amount borrowed.

Date of note. Day the note was signed.

Time of note. Time for which money was borrowed.

Due date. Date note must be paid.

I-chen Wang wants to borrow $7,500.00 to expand her business. Her bank, the First Division Bank of Springfield, Illinois, will lend her the money using the promissory note shown in Illustration 14A.

Let's look at the promissory note. The amount that I-chen borrowed, $7,500.00, is called the **principal**. The day the note was signed, May 15, 19X2, is called the **date of the note**. The time for which the money is borrowed, two years, is called the **time of the note** or just the *time*. The date the note must be paid, May 15, 19X4, is called the **due date**.

How much will I-chen have to pay in interest? How much will she have to pay the bank when the note comes due? To find the answers to these questions, I-chen followed these steps:

STEP 1 ▶ *Calculate the interest.*

I-chen found the amount of interest by using the formula

$$I = P \times R \times T$$
$$\text{Interest} = \text{Principal} \times \text{Rate} \times \text{Time}$$

The rate of interest shown on a note is always an annual rate, unless it is clearly stated that it is not. So, if you borrow $1,000.00 for one year at 10% interest, the interest is found this way:

$$I = P \times R \times T$$
$$I = \$1{,}000.00 \times 0.10 \times 1$$
$$I = \$100.00$$

The amount of interest you pay depends on how long you borrow the money. If you borrow the $1,000.00 for $1\frac{1}{2}$ years at 10% interest, you must pay $1\frac{1}{2}$ (1.5) times the interest for one year:

$$I = P \times R \times T$$
$$I = \$1{,}000.00 \times 0.10 \times 1.5$$
$$I = \$150.00$$

If you borrow the money for six months, you must pay $^6/_{12}$, or $\frac{1}{2}$ (0.5), of the interest for one year:

$$I = P \times R \times T$$
$$I = \$1{,}000.00 \times 0.10 \times 0.5$$
$$I = \$50.00$$

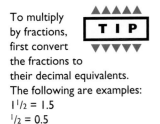

To multiply by fractions, first convert the fractions to their decimal equivalents. The following are examples:
$1\frac{1}{2} = 1.5$
$^1/_2 = 0.5$
$^1/_4 = 0.25$

If you borrow the money for three months, you must pay $^3/_{12}$, or $^1/_4$ (0.25), of the interest for one year:

$$I = P \times R \times T$$
$$I = \$1{,}000.00 \times 0.10 \times 0.25$$
$$I = \$25.00$$

Since I-chen borrowed $7,500.00 at 12% interest for two years, she found the interest this way:

$$I = P \times R \times T$$
$$I = \$7{,}500.00 \times 0.12 \times 2$$
$$I = \$1{,}800.00$$

STEP 2 ▶ *Find the amount due on the due date.*

I-chen must pay the First Division Bank the principal plus the interest owed on the due date, May 15, 19X4. The amount she pays on the due date is called the **amount due**. To find the amount due on the due date, I-chen added the interest for the two years to the principal.

$$\$7{,}500.00 + \$1{,}800.00 = \$9{,}300.00$$

KEY Terms

Amount due. Principal + interest owed on due date.

So, I-chen will have to pay the First Division Bank $9,300.00 on May 15, 19X4 to pay off the promissory note.

Using a calculator to find the amount of interest and the amount due on the due date makes the job easier. Here's how you would find I-chen's interest and amount due with a calculator:

STEP 1 ▶ *Calculate the interest for one year.*

Press these keys in order:

| 7 | 5 | 0 | 0 | x | • | 1 | 2 | = |

The answer that appears in the display is $900.00. This is the amount of interest on $7,500.00 for one year.

STEP 2 ▶ *Calculate the interest for two years.*

Leave the amount in the display, and press these keys in order:

| x | 2 | = |

The amount that appears in the display is $1,800.00. This is the amount of interest on $7,500.00 for two years.

STEP 3 ▶ *Find the amount due on the due date.*

Leave the amount in the display, and press these keys in order:

| + | 7 | 5 | 0 | 0 | = |

The amount that appears in the display is $9,300.00, which is the amount that I-chen must pay the bank when the note comes due.

If the time of the note was six months, you would multiply the annual interest by $1/2$ year, or 0.5, instead of two years.

If your calculator has a *percent key*, you can find interest even faster by using it. Here is how to use the percent key on most calculators to find the interest for one year as you did in Step 1.

Press these keys in order:

| 7 | 5 | 0 | 0 | x | 1 | 2 | % |

The answer that appears in the display is $900.00. Notice that you did not need to convert 12% into the decimal 0.12. You only had to enter the interest rate and press the percent key.

Notice also that you did not have to press the equals key. Pressing the percent key displayed the answer automatically.

On a sheet of paper, write the headings **Statement Number** and **Words**. Next, choose the words that match the statements. Write each word you choose next to the statement number it matches. Be careful; not all the words listed should be used.

Statements	Words
1. A written promise to pay	amount due
2. Money paid for the use of money	annual
3. The amount borrowed on a note	annual percentage rate
4. The day a note is signed	date of note
5. The amount of time for which money is borrowed on a note	down payment
	due date
6. The date a note must be paid	interest
7. Principal plus interest owed on the due date	principal
	promissory note
8. Yearly	time of note

PROBLEM SOLVING MODEL FOR: *Paying Back a Loan*

STEP 1 ▶ *Calculate the interest.*

STEP 2 ▶ *Find the amount due on the due date.*

APPLICATION PROBLEMS

PROBLEM | **14-1** ▶ Roland Keith wants to borrow money to improve his home using the promissory note shown below.

$ __8,250.00__   Boise, Idaho   October 15, __19 X2__

__1 1/2 years__ AFTER DATE __I__ PROMISE TO PAY TO

THE ORDER OF __Norris Trust Company__

__Eight thousand, two hundred fifty 00/100-------__ DOLLARS

PAYABLE AT __Norris Trust Company__

FOR VALUE RECEIVED WITH INTEREST AT __11__ %

NO. __238-298__ DUE __April 15,__ __19 X4__ _Roland Keith_

Directions

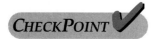

CheckPoint ✔

14-1 (5)
Amount due = $9,611.25

Answer these questions:

1. What is the principal of the note?
2. What is the time of the note?
3. What is the due date of the note?
4. How much interest must be paid when the note is due?
5. What is the amount due on the due date?

PROBLEM | **14-2** ▶ Eunice Hamilos wants to borrow money to start a gift shop using the promissory note shown below.

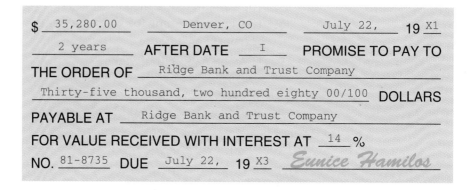

$ __35,280.00__ ___Denver, CO___ ___July 22,___ 19 _X1_

__2 years__ **AFTER DATE** __I__ **PROMISE TO PAY TO**

THE ORDER OF __Ridge Bank and Trust Company__

__Thirty-five thousand, two hundred eighty 00/100__ **DOLLARS**

PAYABLE AT __Ridge Bank and Trust Company__

FOR VALUE RECEIVED WITH INTEREST AT __14__ %

NO. __81-8735__ **DUE** __July 22,__ 19 _X3_ _Eunice Hamilos_

Directions

CheckPoint ✔

14-2 (4)
Interest = $9,878.40

Answer these questions:

1. What is the principal of the note?
2. What is the annual rate of interest?
3. What is the date of the note?
4. How much interest must be paid when the note is due?
5. What is the amount due on the due date?

PROBLEM | **14-3** ▶ Tyrone Wilson wants to borrow money to modernize his office using the promissory note shown below.

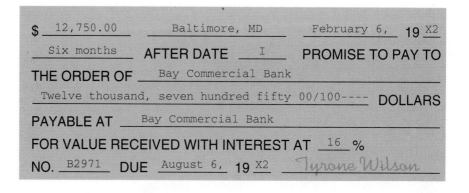

$ __12,750.00__ ___Baltimore, MD___ ___February 6,___ 19 _X2_

__Six months__ **AFTER DATE** __I__ **PROMISE TO PAY TO**

THE ORDER OF __Bay Commercial Bank__

__Twelve thousand, seven hundred fifty 00/100----__ **DOLLARS**

PAYABLE AT __Bay Commercial Bank__

FOR VALUE RECEIVED WITH INTEREST AT __16__ %

NO. __B2971__ **DUE** __August 6,__ 19 _X2_ _Tyrone Wilson_

14-3 (5)
Amount due
= $13,770.00

Directions

Answer these questions:

1. What is the annual rate of interest?
2. What is the due date of the note?
3. What is the time of the note?
4. How much interest must be paid when the note is due?
5. What is the amount due on the due date?

Problems 14-4 and 14-5 may be found in the Working Papers.

CHAPTER 3

Reinforcement
Activities

DISCUSSION

When you do not pay the balance on your credit card statement, the company will charge you interest. After all, you are borrowing their money.

Suppose that on your March statement, you had a balance of $100.00. Suppose also that you did not pay this balance during March. This is what part of your April statement would look like when you receive it:

How We Arrived At Your Finance Charge	Monthly Rate	Annual Percentage Rate	Balance to Which Monthly Rate Applied	Finance Charge
Previous Balance	1.5%	18%	$100.00	$1.50

Notice that the credit card company charged you 1.5% *per month* on the previous, unpaid balance you have in your account ($100.00 × 0.015 = $1.50). The monthly rate of 1.5% is equal to 18% *per year* (1.5% × 12 = 18%).

Answer these questions:

1. If your previous balance had been $300.00, how much interest would your April statement show that you owe?
2. If your previous balance had been $500.00 and the credit card interest rate was 2% *per month*, how much interest would your April statement show that you owe?
3. If the credit card interest rate was 2% per month, what would be the *annual* percentage rate shown on the statement?

PROFESSIONAL BUSINESS ETHICS

You work for a business that has a very large credit department. The manager of the department, Alicia Rodriguez, supervises a large number of employees from many different cultural backgrounds. Alicia enjoys the many cultures represented in her department and wants the other members of the department to appreciate them as well. She thinks that it would be fun to have a cultural potluck luncheon next Friday. She wants to ask each employee in the department to bring a food dish from her or his culture to share. Alicia discusses her idea with you and asks you to do the following:

1. Take a sheet of paper and draw a line down the middle from the top to the bottom.
2. On the left side of the paper, write the word *Advantages* at the top.
3. On the right side of the paper, write the word *Disadvantages* at the top.
4. On the left side of the paper, list all the advantages and positive outcomes of the luncheon.
5. On the right side of the paper, list all the disadvantages and any problems that you can think of.
6. Look at the advantages and disadvantages and write a brief recommendation either for or against the luncheon.

APPLIED COMMUNICATIONS

Suppose you were Victor Perini and received the incorrect credit card statement shown in Illustration 12B on page 116 of Job 12. Write a letter to your credit card company, Crestwood Bank, describing the two errors that were found on the statement. In your letter, show what the correct amount of the new balance should be.

RECORD KEEPING CAREERS

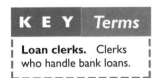

KEY *Terms*

Loan clerks. Clerks who handle bank loans.

Banks and other lending institutions hire clerks who handle bank loans. Often these clerks are called **loan clerks**. Loan clerks calculate interest on loans, handle loan payments from customers, and answer questions about loan balances. The two want ads that follow, taken from a city newspaper, describe two such positions:

Commercial Loan Clerk

Local bank is seeking a qualified person to work in our Commercial Loan Department. This position is clerical in nature but is above the beginning level. 1-2 years experience in loan operations required. Good math skills, ability to deal with loan customers, experience in using a computer. Excellent salary and benefits.

Write: Personnel Department,
        P.O. Box 3407, Topeka, KS 66605
        Equal Opportunity Employer

Loan Service Clerk

Lending institution is seeking personable individual with experience who is good with figures. Must have experience with personal computers. We offer complete benefits package. Call Personnel for appointment at 555-3389 between 1 and 4 pm.
Equal Opportunity Employer

Answer these questions about these two want ads:

1. Are either of the jobs entry-level jobs?
2. What does the commercial loan clerk job require that the loan service clerk job does not?
3. What do both jobs require?
4. How do you apply for the commercial loan clerk job?
5. How do you apply for the loan service clerk job?

GLOBAL BUSINESS: INTERNATIONAL TELEPHONE CALLS

You work for a large corporation that has many sales offices in Canada and Mexico. These offices send their budget information and credit card slips to your department. From time to time, you must call or send a fax to one of the sales offices to verify information. You can call offices in these countries by dialing directly, without the assistance of an operator.

For the offices in Canada, dial 1 + a three-digit area code + a seven-digit telephone number. To call Toronto, for example, dial 1-416-555-1234. This procedure is the same as placing a long-distance call within the United States.

When calling Mexico, or other foreign countries, the procedure is a bit more complicated. To make an international call, you must dial

1. 011, the International Access Code
2. the country code
3. the city code
4. the local telephone number.

To call Mexico City, for example, dial 011-52-5-555-1234.

Not all countries allow direct dialing. Before making international phone calls, check with your local telephone company for information. The following chart shows selected country codes and city codes:

City	Country Code	City Code
Addis Ababa, Ethiopia	251	1
Caracas, Venezuela	58	2
Guatemala City, Guatemala	502	2
Rome, Italy	39	6
Tokyo, Japan	81	3
Sydney, Australia	61	2

An International Telephone Calling Activity can be found in the Working Papers.

On a sheet of paper, write the headings **Statement Number** and
Words. Next, choose the words that best complete the statements.
Write each word you choose next to the statement number it completes.
Be careful; not all the words listed should be used.

Statements	Words
1. When you borrow money, the lender will usually charge you _____ for using the money.	annual percentage rate
	date of note
	down payment
2. A written promise to pay back the money you borrowed is called (a, an) _____ .	due date
	finance charge
	good credit risks
3. People who pay off their debts promptly and fully are considered _____ .	interest
	promissory note
4. The interest rate for a year is often called the _____ .	sales slip
	undercharged
5. The date on which a promissory note must be paid is called the _____ .	
6. The cost of borrowing money on an installment plan is called _____ .	
7. A written record of a sale is called (a, an) _____ .	

MASTERY PROBLEM

Rose Stroud has a ShoppersCard from Heron Farmer's Bank that she
uses to make personal purchases. She also owns Stroud's Trucking Company,
which is a moving company specializing in household furniture and business
equipment.

Phase 1: Checking a Credit Card Statement

Rose Stroud has saved each of her credit card sales slips for the month of
June. Rose renews her card membership every June for a fee of $30.00.
Her checkbook shows that she made a payment of $308.33 on June 6. She
wants to verify her credit card statement for June.

Directions

a. On pages 144 and 145, you are given Rose's credit card statement and
the top sections of her sales slips for June. Use a credit card statement
work sheet to verify the statement.

b. List the date, store, and amount of every transaction which should not
appear on the statement.

c. Compare the "sale amounts" on the sales slips to the amounts on the
statement. If an amount is incorrect, find the overcharge or

undercharge. Do not compare the "Amount" on the slips with the statement. The "Amount" and "sales amount" may differ because the bottoms of the slips, showing sales taxes and totals, are not provided.

d. Find the correct new balance for the statement.

(d)
Correct new balance =
$544.79

ACCOUNT NUMBER		SALE AMOUNT		INVOICE NUMBER	
3375 885 322		00200.81		641877	
6/X1 6/X4	**DATE** 6/2/--	**AUTHORIZATION NO.** 337802	**SALES CLERK** 32	**DEPT.** 13	
ROSE STROUD	**QUAN.**	**DESCRIPTION**	**PRICE**	**AMOUNT**	
1780928	1	Mantle Clock	139.89	139 89	
NORTHSIDE FURNITURE	2	Candle Holders	25.68	51 36	

MERCHANT COPY

ACCOUNT NUMBER		SALE AMOUNT		INVOICE NUMBER	
3375 885 322		00014.88		999812	
6/X1 6/X4	**DATE** 6/5/--	**AUTHORIZATION NO.** --	**SALES CLERK** --	**DEPT.** --	
ROSE STROUD	**QUAN.**	**DESCRIPTION**	**PRICE**	**AMOUNT**	
0871116	--	Gasoline	14.88	14 88	
RT. 45 SERVICE					

MERCHANT COPY

ACCOUNT NUMBER		SALE AMOUNT		INVOICE NUMBER	
3375 885 322		00185.73		641093	
6/X1 6/X4	**DATE** 6/9/--	**AUTHORIZATION NO.** 718372	**SALES CLERK** 12	**DEPT.** 21	
ROSE STROUD	**QUAN.**	**DESCRIPTION**	**PRICE**	**AMOUNT**	
0798902	1	Coat	176.89	176 89	
BARNEFF'S					

MERCHANT COPY

ACCOUNT NUMBER		SALE AMOUNT		INVOICE NUMBER	
3375 885 322		00018.78		226179	
6/X1 6/X4	**DATE** 6/20/--	**AUTHORIZATION NO.** --	**SALES CLERK** 8	**DEPT.** 1	
ROSE STROUD	**QUAN.**	**DESCRIPTION**	**PRICE**	**AMOUNT**	
0756641	--	Dinner	17.89	17 89	
CASTLE INN					

MERCHANT COPY

ACCOUNT NUMBER		SALE AMOUNT		INVOICE NUMBER	
3375 885 322		00011.98		336419	
6/X1 6/X4	**DATE** 6/24/--	**AUTHORIZATION NO.** --	**SALES CLERK** 8	**DEPT.** 1	
ROSE STROUD	**QUAN.**	**DESCRIPTION**	**PRICE**	**AMOUNT**	
0046007	--	Gasoline	11.98	11 98	
BLUFF ROAD SERVICE					

MERCHANT COPY

ACCOUNT NUMBER		SALE AMOUNT		INVOICE NUMBER	
3375 885 322		00082.61		711209	
6/X1 6/X4	**DATE** 6/28/--	**AUTHORIZATION NO.** --	**SALES CLERK** 14	**DEPT.** 21	
ROSE STROUD	**QUAN.**	**DESCRIPTION**	**PRICE**	**AMOUNT**	
0023617	1	Mirror	78.68	78 68	
AARON'S FINE THINGS					

MERCHANT COPY

HERON FARMER'S BANK

VISA | MasterCard

Transaction Date	Reference	Transaction Description		New Loans, Fees, & Purchases	Payments & Credits
06/02/--	37816228	Northside Furniture	Tulsa, OK	200.81	
06/05/--	39712564	Rt. 45 Service	Enid, OK	14.88	
06/06/--	33307922	Payment -- Thank you			308.33
06/09/--	71282255	Barneff's	Tulsa, OK	185.73	
06/16/--		Annual Membership Fee		30.00	
06/19/--	89989112	Brown Theaters, Inc.	Chicago, IL	77.23	
06/20/--	70029812	Castle Inn	Tulsa, OK	18.78	
06/24/--	00879806	Bluff Road Service	Tulsa, OK	19.18	
06/28/--	85769123	Aaron's Fine Things	Tulsa, OK	82.61	

How We Arrived At Your Finance Charge	Monthly Rate	Annual Percentage Rate	Balance to Which Monthly Rate Applied	Finance Charge

Previous Balance	Payments & Credits	New Loans, Fees, & Purchases	Finance Charge	New Balance	Minimum Payment Due
308.33	308.33	629.22	0.00	629.22	25.00

Billing Date	Date Payment Due	Credit Line	Account Number	In case of billing error, write to this address: P.O. Box 1422, Tulsa, OK 74101-7341
06/30/--	07/25/--	2800	3375 885 322	Direct telephone inquiries to 1-800-555-6500

Phase 2: Checking an Installment Contract

Rose bought a big screen TV priced at $4,250.00 from Lockhart Electronics. The store asked her to pay 20% down and the rest in monthly payments of $212.92 for one and one-half years. The store also asked her to sign the installment contract shown in this problem.

Directions

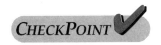

CHECKPOINT

(a)
Finance charge = $432.56

a. Verify the down payment, the amount financed, the installment price, and the finance charge on the contract. If you find an error, cross out the incorrect amount and write the correct amount to the right side of it. Correct any subsequent amounts on lines 1–5 of the contract in the same way.

b. If you find no errors in the amounts, sign Stroud's name to the contract.

Phase 3: Borrowing on a Promissory Note

Rose wants to borrow money to improve her business office using the promissory note shown below.

$ 17,200.00   Tulsa, OK   June 22, 19 X1

6 months   AFTER DATE ___I___ PROMISE TO PAY TO

THE ORDER OF _____ Western Mining Bank and Trust Co. _____

Seventeen thousand, two hundred and no/100----- DOLLARS

PAYABLE AT   Western Mining Bank and Trust Co.

FOR VALUE RECEIVED WITH INTEREST AT 12 %

NO. 44718 DUE December 22, 19 X1   *Rose Stroud*

CHECKPOINT ✔

(5)
Amount due =
$18,232.00

Answer these questions:

1. What is the principal of the note?
2. What is the time of the note?
3. What is the due date of the note?
4. How much interest must be paid when the note is due?
5. What is the amount due on the due date?

REVIEWING YOUR BUSINESS VOCABULARY

This activity may be found in the Working Papers.

COMPREHENSIVE PROJECT 1

Comprehensive Project 1 has been designed to reinforce major concepts of this and previous chapters. The Comprehensive Project is found in the Working Papers.

C H A P T E R

4

Cash Receipts Records

*M*any record keeping students are qualified to become cashiers. The main tasks of a cashier are to receive and pay out money. In a large business, one person may receive money while another person may pay out money. If the cashier works in a small business, both tasks may be done by the same person.

In Chapter 4, you will learn about the forms, machines, and procedures that cashiers use on the job. Various cashier positions in businesses will also be described. Calculator Tips will be given so that you may complete a record of cashier's collections, prove cash, and complete a tally sheet.

JOB 15 ▶ PREPARING AND RECORDING RECEIPTS

APPLIED MATH PREVIEW

Copy and complete the following problems.

▲▲▲▲▲
TIP
▼▼▼▼▼

The sum of all the columns added across must equal the sum of all the rows added down. For example:

3 + 4 = 7
2 + 5 = 7
5 + 9 = 14

1. Add:
$ 40.10
307.88
2,170.83
645.29
+ 3,602.10

2. Add across and then down:
a. 4 + 3 + 10 + 30 =
b. 20 + 40 + 50 + 60 =
c. 76 + 16 + 36 + 86 =
d. 97 + 27 + 57 + 67 =
e. 19 + 99 + 29 + 89 = ____
f.

BUSINESS TERMS PREVIEW

- Cash box • Cashier • Duplicate •
- Grand total • Receipt • Stub •

GOALS

1. To learn how to prepare receipts when you receive money.
2. To learn how to record receipts.

UNDERSTANDING THE JOB

KEY Terms

Cashier. Employee who receives and pays out money.

The main tasks of a **cashier** are to receive and to pay out money. Some employees do both tasks because of their job responsibilities. For example, salespeople in retail stores usually collect money from customers and give back change when merchandise is sold.

There are many jobs in business in which cashiers receive money from other employees who also collect money. For example, cashiers may receive cash from news carriers who collect it from customers on their routes. Other cashiers may receive cash from employees who collect it from food vending machines, newspaper vending machines, subway turnstiles, and parking meters.

Most cashiers must meet and talk with customers and other employees as part of their jobs. The job of the cashier is important because cash must be handled accurately and carefully. It is also important because the cashier represents the business to customers.

Successful cashiers must know how to

a. Make change rapidly and accurately
b. Write numbers and words legibly
c. Recognize counterfeit money
d. Verify checks
e. Check their work
f. Listen to others
g. Greet people
h. Dress for the job

SAMPLE PROBLEM

You are the cashier for the Rafael Vending Company, which maintains food vending machines in a large city. The company hires employees to refill vending machines and collect the money deposited in them. Your job is to receive money from these employees when they return to the office after servicing the  machines on their routes. The work is divided among a number of cashiers. You handle all the money received from routes on the east side of town.

On Monday, June 7, 19--, cash is brought to you by these route employees:

Route	Amount	Carrier
105	$1,056.25	Louise Bentley
106	972.40	Ralph Smith
108	1,065.60	Lance Chen
110	236.40	Ira Schwartz
111	1,272.65	Danice Johnson
114	776.65	Allen Morgan

Here is how you would do your job:

STEP 1 ▶ Count the money.

When you are handed the money by the employee for Route 105, count the money to make certain that it adds up to $1,056.25, as the employee claims.

STEP 2 ▶ Make out a receipt.

KEY Terms

Receipt. A form issued for cash received.

After you make sure that you have received the correct amount, make out a **receipt**, using a *receipt book*. Office supply stores sell many kinds of receipt books. Illustration 15A shows the form used by the Rafael Vending Company.

No. **1078**

Date: *June 7,* 19 --

Received from: *Louise Bentley*

Route: 105

Amount: $ *1,056.25*

Rafael Vending Company

No. **1078**

Date: *June 7,* 19 --

Received from: *Louise Bentley* $ *1,056.25*

One thousand, fifty-six 25/100 ————— Dollars

Route: 105   For: *Route collections*

————— *(Your Name)* —————
Cashier

Illustration 15A   A receipt and stub

Notice how you complete the receipt:

1. The amount is written both in figures and in words. This spelling list might help you to complete receipts in this job:

one	eleven	ten
two	twelve	twenty
three	thirteen	thirty
four	fourteen	forty
five	fifteen	fifty
six	sixteen	sixty
seven	seventeen	seventy
eight	eighteen	eighty
nine	nineteen	ninety

2. In the written amount, only the first word, "One," is capitalized.
3. A comma is used after the word "thousand" in the written amount. Commas are used in written amounts in the same places as they are used in figures.
4. A hyphen is used in "fifty-six." Hyphens are used when you write out the numbers twenty-one through ninety-nine.
5. The cents are written as a fraction, $^{25}/_{100}$.
6. A line is drawn from the cents to the word "Dollars."

Hand the receipt to Louise Bentley, the employee for Route 105, leaving the **stub** in the receipt book.

Another commonly used form of receipt does not use a stub. Instead, a duplicate receipt is made using carbon or carbonless paper. The original receipt is torn out while the **duplicate** remains in the book. The duplicate receipt takes the place of the stub. The important thing to remember is that the cashier must have a record of every receipt issued.

STEP 3 ▶ *Put the money in a cash box.*

After you issue the receipt to Louise Bentley, put the $1,056.25 in a **cash box**. Cash boxes have compartments so that you can keep the different types of coins and bills arranged neatly. This reduces the chance of giving out the wrong change. Always make certain the money you receive is put in the cash box before you take care of the next route employee.

STEP 4 ▶ *Record the amounts shown on the stubs in a record of cashier's collections.*

At the end of each day, record the information found on the stubs in a record of cashier's collections. For example, you would record the route numbers, employee names, and amounts received on Monday, June 7, in the first three columns of the form. The completed record of cashier's collections for the week of June 7 is shown in Illustration 15B on page 151.

STEP 5 ▶ *Total and verify each column total.*

Total the amounts in the column for Monday by adding them from the top down. Record the total, $5,379.95, as a footing on the Totals line of the form. Then, verify the total by adding the amounts again from the bottom up. When you are sure that the total is correct, write it again below the footing. This means that you, the cashier, must have $5,379.95 in your cash box at the end of Monday, June 7.

You will repeat this procedure at the end of each day.

Rafael Vending Company
RECORD OF CASHIER'S COLLECTIONS

Cashier _(Your Name)_   Week of _June 7,_   19 _ _ _

Route	Employee	Monday	Tuesday	Wednesday	Thursday	Friday	TOTALS
105	Louise Bentley	1056 25		788 25			1844 50
106	Ralph Smith	972 40			1077 45		2049 85
107	Arlene Jones		1151 85			1734 55	2886 40
108	Lance Chen	1065 60		809 45		652 80	2527 85
109	Sonia Velez		686 35		1290 90		1977 25
110	Ira Schwartz	236 40		1007 85		378 15	1622 40
111	Danice Johnson	1272 65		978 40		897 60	3148 65
112	Sam Vance			448 20		1450 80	1899 00
113	Martha O'Reilly		942 60		890 25		1832 85
114	Allen Morgan	776 65		480 90		820 80	2078 35
	TOTALS	5379 95	2780 80	4513 05	3258 60	5934 70	21867 10
		5379 95	2780 80	4513 05	3258 60	5934 70	21867 10

← Grand Total

Illustration 15B   Completed record of cashier's collections

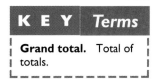 **STEP 6** ▶ *Find the weekly total for each route.*

At the end of the week, find the total received from each route employee for the week. For example, you would crossfoot the amounts received during Monday through Friday for Route 105 and place the total, $1,844.50, in the Totals column at the right side of the form.

STEP 7 ▶ *Find and verify the grand total and double rule the form.*

Add the route totals that are in the Totals column and enter that amount as a footing at the bottom of the column. To prove your work, crossfoot the daily totals and compare that amount to the total of the Totals column. This amount is called a **grand total** because it is the total of other totals. In this case, the total of the route totals and the total of the daily totals must be equal.

> Total of Route Totals $21,867.10
> Total of Daily Totals $21,867.10

Since they are equal, write the grand total below the footing and double rule the money columns.

Calculator TIPS

You can use the memory keys on your calculator, as you have before, to find the total receipts from each route and the grand total.

This is how you can do it:

S T E P 1 ▶ *Add the receipts for the first route.*

Add the amounts in the row for Route 105 by pressing these keys in order:

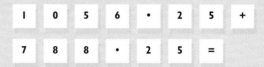

The total, 1,844.50, will appear in the calculator's display. Record this amount in the Totals column for Route 105.

S T E P 2 ▶ *Add the total to the calculator's memory.*

Press the M+ key. This adds the column total, $1,844.50, to the calculator's memory.

S T E P 3 ▶ *Record and add the other row totals to memory.*

Now add each row for the other routes. When you get each row total, record it in the Totals column and press the M+ key. This adds each route total to memory.

S T E P 4 ▶ *Display the total of memory.*

When you have added every route total to memory, press the MR (memory recall) or the MR/C (memory recall/clear) key once. When you do, your calculator display will show 21,867.10. This is the grand total. This amount should equal all the column totals for the days of the week.

S T E P 5 ▶ *Clear memory.*

To clear the calculator's memory, press the MC (memory clear) key. If your calculator has a MR/C key, press that key twice. When you press the MR/C key once, the display shows the contents of memory. When you press the MR/C key twice, you clear or erase the amount in memory.

On a sheet of paper, write the headings **Statement Number** and **Words**. Next, choose the words that match the statements. Write each word you choose next to the statement number it matches. Be careful; not all the words listed should be used.

Statements	Words
1. The part of the receipt which stays in the book	amount due
2. A form issued for cash received	budget
3. The total of a column of numbers written in small figures	cash box
4. To add a row of figures across a business form	cashier
5. A box in which cash is kept	crossfoot
6. A person who receives and pays out money	duplicate
7. An exact copy	footing
8. To check for accuracy	grand total
9. A total of other totals	receipt
	stub
	verify

PROBLEM SOLVING MODEL FOR: *Preparing and Recording Receipts*

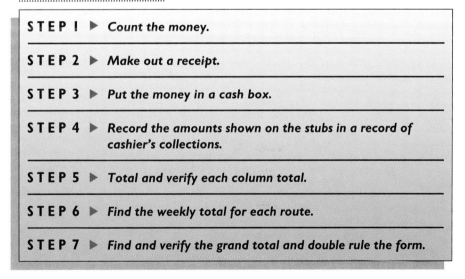

STEP 1 ▶ *Count the money.*

STEP 2 ▶ *Make out a receipt.*

STEP 3 ▶ *Put the money in a cash box.*

STEP 4 ▶ *Record the amounts shown on the stubs in a record of cashier's collections.*

STEP 5 ▶ *Total and verify each column total.*

STEP 6 ▶ *Find the weekly total for each route.*

STEP 7 ▶ *Find and verify the grand total and double rule the form.*

APPLICATION PROBLEMS

PROBLEM **15-1** ▶ You are a cashier collecting cash from route employees for the Rafael Vending Company.

Directions

a. Use a record of cashier's collections form like the one in Illustration 15B (page 151). Complete the heading by using your name as cashier and November 2, as the week. Record the route numbers 105–114 in the Route column. Be sure to record the numbers in numerical order (105, 106, etc.).

b. You received money on Monday, November 2, as shown below.

Route No.	Employee	Amount
107	Arlene Jones	$1,027.80
110	Ira Schwartz	977.15
111	Danice Johnson	1,278.35
114	Allen Morgan	808.30

Make a receipt for each employee. Be sure to fill out the stub first. The starting number for your receipts will be 101. Sign your own name as cashier.

c. Enter the information found on the stubs in the record of cashier's collections.

d. Foot, verify, and enter the total for the column headed Monday.

e. Fill in the record of cashier's collections for the rest of the week in the same way using the information given below. You are not required to make any more receipts.

Tuesday, November 3

Route No.	Employee	Amount
105	Louise Bentley	$ 823.85
106	Ralph Smith	1,100.40
111	Danice Johnson	201.45
112	Sam Vance	1,307.25
113	Martha O'Reilly	650.65

Wednesday, November 4

Route No.	Employee	Amount
107	Arlene Jones	$ 440.95
108	Lance Chen	1,370.75
110	Ira Schwartz	704.75

Thursday, November 5

Route No.	Employee	Amount
105	Louise Bentley	$1,222.50
109	Sonia Velez	387.65
114	Allen Morgan	1,002.75

Friday, November 6

Route No.	Employee	Amount
106	Ralph Smith	$ 790.80
111	Danice Johnson	1,372.25
112	Sam Vance	600.35

f. Find the total collected from each route for the week by crossfooting.

g. Foot the grand total for the week by adding the amounts in the Totals column.

CHECKPOINT ✓

15-1

Grand total = $16.067.95

h. Check your addition by crossfooting the totals for each day. The answer should agree with the grand total found in *g*. If the answer agrees, write the grand total below the footing. If the totals do not agree, find the error by re-adding all the columns.

i. Answer these questions about the completed record:

1. On which route was the most money collected for the week?
2. On which route was the least money collected for the week?
3. On which day was the most money collected?
4. On which day was the least money collected?

PROBLEM 15-2 ▶ You have been hired as a cashier for the City of St. Joseph. Parking meters throughout the city are maintained by St. Joseph. Your job is to count the money collected daily from the route collectors and keep a weekly record of the collections.

Directions

a. Use a record of cashier's collections form like the one in Illustration 15B (page 151). Complete the heading by using your name as cashier and April 22, as the week. Head the second column Collector instead of Employee. Record the route numbers 312–321 in the Route column in numerical order.

b. You received money on Monday, April 22, as shown below.

Route No.	Collector	Amount
312	R. Dahl	$118.25
314	M. Edwards	45.80
320	C. Ting	110.10
321	J. Valdez	85.25

Make a receipt for each collector. Be sure to fill out the stub first. The starting number for your receipts will be 1201. Sign your own name as cashier.

c. Enter the information found on the stubs in the record of cashier's collections.

d. Foot, verify, and enter the total for the column headed Monday.

e. Fill in the record of cashier's collections for the rest of the week in the same way using the information given below and on the next page. You are not required to make any more receipts.

Tuesday, April 23				Wednesday, April 24		
Route No.	Collector	Amount		Route No.	Collector	Amount
313	G. Hiel	$28.50		312	R. Dahl	$86.45
315	I. Baum	75.25		314	M. Edwards	92.15
316	R. O'Hare	29.95		317	A. Paulo	53.55
318	U. Tiros	74.30		320	C. Ting	37.10
319	N. Nye	28.65		321	J. Valdez	62.35

Thursday, April 25				Friday, April 26		
Route No.	Collector	Amount		Route No.	Collector	Amount
315	I. Baum	$35.00		312	R. Dahl	$44.75
316	R. O'Hare	90.70		313	G. Hiel	82.25
319	N. Nye	66.25		318	U. Tiros	38.05
				320	C. Ting	30.85
				321	J. Valdez	67.15

f. Find the total collected from each route for the week by crossfooting.

g. Foot the grand total for the week by adding the amounts in the Totals column.

h. Check your addition by crossfooting the totals for each day. The answer should agree with the grand total found in *g*. If the answer agrees, write the grand total below the footing. If the totals do not agree, find the error by re-adding all the columns.

i. Answer these questions about the completed record:
1. On which route was the most money collected for the week?
2. On which route was the least money collected for the week?
3. On which day was the most money collected?
4. On which day was the least money collected?

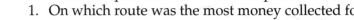

CHECKPOINT ✔

15-2 (i. 1)
Route 312 collected the most money.

Problems 15-3 and 15-4 may be found in the Working Papers.

JOB 16 ▶ USING A CASH REGISTER

APPLIED MATH PREVIEW

Copy and complete the following problems.

1. $1.88	2. $ .45	3. $3.78	4. $2.09	5. $4.81
.59	.98	1.68	2.18	.54
3.79	1.09	5.16	1.76	1.98
4.19	2.28	.19	2.31	.79
.77	.16	.48	4.12	2.47
2.39	3.28	.27	5.85	.93

BUSINESS TERMS PREVIEW

- Amount tendered • Cash register • Cash register receipt •
- Subtotal • Universal Product Code •

GOALS

1. To learn how a cash register is used to record sales.
2. To learn how to make change.

UNDERSTANDING THE JOB

KEY Terms

Cash register. A machine used to handle money.

Cash register receipt. A printed record of transactions.

When cashiers must handle large amounts of money rapidly, they usually use a **cash register** instead of a cash box. A cash register helps to reduce errors and safeguard cash.

An electronic cash register used in a small business is really a microcomputer with a cash drawer, special keyboard, printer, and special displays. Cash registers used in large businesses are often terminals which are connected to minicomputers.

Cash registers provide printed receipts recording every transaction, called **cash register receipts** or cash register tapes. The cashier usually gives you the receipt, like the ones shown in Illustrations 16A and 16B on page 158. The receipt lists the amount charged for each item and shows the final total.

Many electronic cash registers print a very detailed receipt, like the one shown in Illustration 16B on page 158, listing the name of each item bought and its price. This allows customers to check their purchases easily.

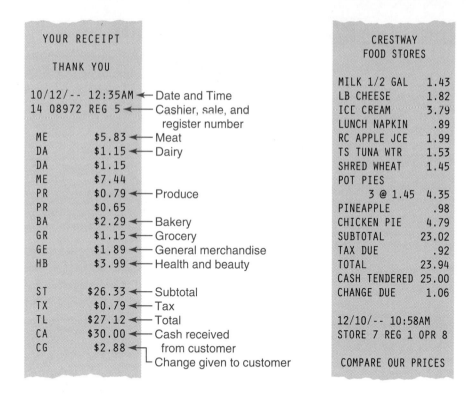

```
YOUR RECEIPT

  THANK YOU

10/12/--  12:35AM  ← Date and Time
14 08972 REG 5  ← Cashier, sale, and
                      register number
   ME      $5.83  ← Meat
   DA      $1.15  ← Dairy
   DA      $1.15
   ME      $7.44
   PR      $0.79  ← Produce
   PR      $0.65
   BA      $2.29  ← Bakery
   GR      $1.15  ← Grocery
   GE      $1.89  ← General merchandise
   HB      $3.99  ← Health and beauty

   ST     $26.33  ← Subtotal
   TX      $0.79  ← Tax
   TL     $27.12  ← Total
   CA     $30.00  ← Cash received
   CG      $2.88  ┐   from customer
                  └ Change given to customer
```

```
        CRESTWAY
       FOOD STORES

MILK 1/2 GAL    1.43
LB CHEESE       1.82
ICE CREAM       3.79
LUNCH NAPKIN     .89
RC APPLE JCE    1.99
TS TUNA WTR     1.53
SHRED WHEAT     1.45
POT PIES
     3 @ 1.45   4.35
PINEAPPLE        .98
CHICKEN PIE     4.79
SUBTOTAL       23.02
TAX DUE          .92
TOTAL          23.94
CASH TENDERED  25.00
CHANGE DUE      1.06

12/10/--  10:58AM
STORE 7 REG 1 OPR 8

COMPARE OUR PRICES
```

Many cash registers have special keys for each department in a store, like the one shown in Illustration 16C on page 159. For example, supermarkets may have cash registers with special keys for sales of:

1. *Meat* (various fish and meat products)
2. *Dairy products* (butter, cheese, cream, eggs, milk, etc.)
3. *Produce* (fresh vegetables and fruits)
4. *Bakery products* (cakes, pies, donuts, etc.)
5. *Groceries* (canned foods, cereals, etc.)
6. *Health and beauty* (toothpaste, shampoo, bath soap, etc.)
7. *General merchandise* (items which are not included in the other departments, such as dishwashing soaps, laundry detergents, paper napkins, brushes, and soda)

The cashier must depress not only the keys for the selling price of each item, but also a key for the name of the department in which the item is found. For example, to record the sale of a half-gallon of milk for $1.43, the cashier would depress

If you watch the register display, you will see the selling price of the milk appear with the word "DAIRY."

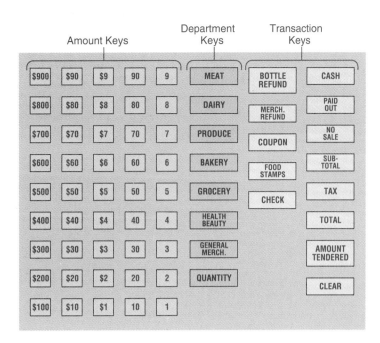

Amount Keys   Department Keys   Transaction Keys

SAMPLE PROBLEM

You are a checkout cashier at Frank's Market. A customer just bought cottage cheese for $1.79, a package of meat for $5.89, and a loaf of bread for $1.12.

Here is how you handled the customer's sale:

STEP 1 ▶ *Enter each sale item.*

You entered each sale item in the register by pressing the correct amount and department keys. For example, you entered the first item, cottage cheese, by pressing these keys:

As you entered each item, the amount and type for each item were shown in the cash register display. They were also printed out on the cash register receipt.

STEP 2 ▶ *Find the total of the sale.*

After entering all the items, you pressed the Subtotal, Tax, and Total keys in that order. The register calculated the subtotal ($8.80), the sales tax ($0.35), and the total ($9.15), and showed these amounts in the register display. These amounts were also printed out on the cash register receipt, as shown below.

DA	$1.79
ME	$5.89
BA	$1.12
ST	$8.80
TX	$0.35
TL	$9.15

A **subtotal** is a total on which other calculations will be made. You will learn more about sales tax in Chapter 7.

STEP 3 ▶ *Accept the amount tendered by the customer and give the correct change.*

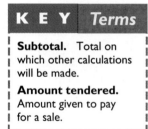

KEY Terms

Subtotal. Total on which other calculations will be made.

Amount tendered. Amount given to pay for a sale.

The customer gave you a ten-dollar bill. This amount is called the **amount tendered**, or the amount that is given in payment of a sale. You placed the bill on the cash register but did not put it in the cash drawer of the register. You then pressed these keys:

$10   **AMOUNT TENDERED**

As you entered the amount tendered, $10, it was shown on the register display. It was also printed out on the cash register receipt.

BA	$1.12
ST	$8.80
TX	$0.35
TL	$9.15
CA	$10.00

The register calculated the amount of change the customer should receive ($0.85) and displayed this amount. It also printed the amount out on the receipt.

TL	$9.15
CA	$10.00
CG	$0.85

You handed the customer the receipt and the $0.85, using a half-dollar, a quarter, and a dime. As you handed the customer the change, you said, "Fifty, seventy-five, and eighty-five."

Older cash registers, which are not electronic, do not figure the correct change. If you use an older cash register, you must figure the change yourself. Cashiers usually figure the change mentally by adding coins and dollars to the total sale until they have reached the amount tendered. In the Sample Problem, you would have given the customer a dime, a quarter, and a half-dollar, saying, "$9.15 (the amount of sale), $9.25 ($9.15 plus the dime), $9.50 ($9.25 plus the quarter), $10.00 ($9.50 plus the half-dollar)."

Cashiers should never put paper money in the cash register until after they have given the change to the customer. In the Sample Problem, if the customer claims to have given you more than $10, you can show the customer the actual $10 bill.

Cashiers also should try to give the customer change with the least number of coins and bills possible. The customer does not usually want to receive a lot of small coins and bills as change.

Many items sold in supermarkets today have a special code printed on them. This code, called the **Universal Product Code** *(UPC)*, can be read and recorded by a special cash register system.

In this system, an electronic cash register and a scanner are connected to a minicomputer. As each item is scanned, the code tells the computer the department, the brand, and the size of the product being bought. The computer finds the price of each item and figures the total amount owed. These amounts are shown in lighted numbers on the cash register display so that the cashier and the customer can see them.

Cashiers who use electronic cash registers must still know how to operate the register keyboard and to classify sales into departments. After all, some items sold may not have a UPC label on them (for example, fresh vegetables and fruit). Also, the bar code on some items may be damaged and cannot be read by the scanner.

In chain store systems, such as fast food chain stores, the data from each electronic cash register is sent to a central computer located in a central office. (See Illustration 16D on page 162.) There the data are used by managers to keep track of each store's sales, items which are selling quickly, and items which are selling slowly. This information allows managers to improve the sales of the chain.

K E Y *Terms*

Universal Product Code. A bar code.

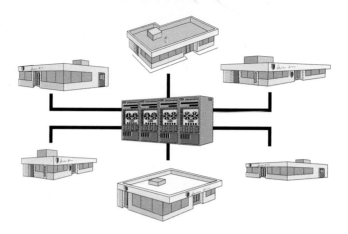

BUILDING YOUR BUSINESS VOCABULARY

On a sheet of paper, write the headings **Statement Number** and **Words**. Next, choose the words that match the statements. Write each word you choose next to the statement number it matches. Be careful; not all the words listed should be used.

Statements	Words
1. The amount given to pay a bill	amount tendered
2. A machine used to handle money	cash register
3. An exact copy	cash register receipt
4. A special bar code read by electronic cash registers	cashier
5. A written record of transactions printed by a cash register	crossfoot
6. A total of other totals	duplicate
7. A form issued for cash received	grand total
8. The part of the receipt which stays in the book	receipt
9. A total on which other calculations will be made	stub
10. Something that happens in a business that should be recorded	subtotal
	transaction
	Universal Product Code

PROBLEM SOLVING MODEL FOR: *Using a Cash Register*

STEP 1 ▶ *Enter each sale item.*

STEP 2 ▶ *Find the total of the sale.*

STEP 3 ▶ *Accept the amount tendered by the customer and give the correct change.*

APPLICATION PROBLEMS

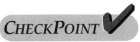

PROBLEM | 16-1 ▶ You are the cashier at the Fredway Superfood Store. You use a cash register with the keys shown in Illustration 16C on page 159.

Directions

CHECKPOINT ✔

16-1 (a)
Use the **General Merch.** key for paper cups.

a. A customer buys the items shown below. Copy the items and prices, and next to each item, write the name of the department key you would use to enter the item into your cash register.

Items Bought		Department Keys Used
$ .78	Paper cups	
$2.59	Meat	
$1.56	Cheese	
$ .88	Carrots	
$2.88	Detergent	

b. After entering each item, your register shows a total sale of $8.69. The amount tendered by the customer is $10.00. List the types and numbers of the bills or coins you should give the customer for change.

PROBLEM | 16-2 ▶ You are the cashier at the Nationway Store. You use a cash register with the keys shown in Illustration 16C on page 159.

Directions

a. A customer buys the items shown below. Copy the items and prices, and next to each item, write the name of the department key you would use to enter the item into your cash register.

Items Bought		Department Keys Used
$ .87	Cucumbers	
$1.49	Cereal	
$ .79	Soup	
$1.77	Toothpaste	
$7.99	Roast beef	

CHECKPOINT ✔

16-2 (b)
The change should include I five-dollar bill.

b. After entering each item, your register shows a total sale of $12.91. The amount tendered by the customer is $20.00. List the types and numbers of the bills or coins you should give the customer for change.

Problems 16-3, 16-4, and 16-5 may be found in the Working Papers.

HANDLING REFUNDS, COUPONS, AND CHECKS

APPLIED MATH PREVIEW

Copy and complete the following problems.

1. $ 1.89	2. $ 0.56	3. $ 5.66	4. $75.00	6. $50.00
0.45	2.78	2.18	− 62.14	− 31.84
7.48	9.19	0.39		
8.99	0.59	1.49		
+ 1.22	+ 1.38	+ 0.29	5. $100.00	7. $ 25.00
			+ 77.79	+ 12.56

BUSINESS TERMS PREVIEW

- **Check-cashing privilege card** • **Debit cards** •
- **Policies** • **Refund** • **Third-party checks** •

GOALS

1. To practice making change.
2. To learn how to verify checks.
3. To learn how cashiers handle coupons and refunds.

UNDERSTANDING THE JOB

KEY *Terms*

Debit cards. Allow immediate payment from checking account.

Stores may allow customers to pay for their purchases in many ways. For example, food stores may allow customers to pay for part of their purchases with coupons, food stamps, bottle refunds, refunds of merchandise, checks, and even credit cards.

Some stores also accept **debit cards**. Debit cards are issued by banks and allow you to make payments from your checking account without checks or cash. Debit cards are similar to credit cards except that the amount of your purchase is subtracted from your checking account immediately instead of being added to a bill sent to you at the end of the month.

In some stores, you can pay for your purchase simply by inserting your debit card into a special terminal connected to your bank's computer system. The bank's computer system subtracts the amount of your purchase immediately from your checking account and adds the same amount to the store's bank account.

In this job you will learn how to handle refunds, coupons, and checks. You will learn more about credit card sales in Chapter 7.

SAMPLE PROBLEM

Suppose that you are still working as a checkout cashier at Frank's Market as you did in Job 16. You are using a register with the keyboard shown in Illustration 17A.

Frank's Market allows customers to return bottles and get a **refund**, or money back. You may give the customer cash for the bottles, or if the customer is buying other items, you can deduct the refund from the total amount due.

Frank's Market also accepts vendor coupons for items bought in the store. For example, a customer might buy a box of cereal for $1.25 and give you $1.00 plus a coupon. The coupon gives the customer 25¢ off the purchase price of the cereal.

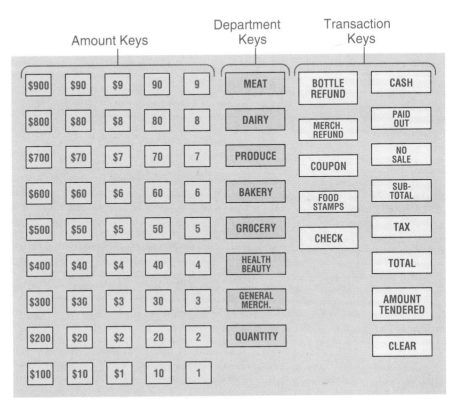

Illustration 17A Cash register keyboard

Customers can cash checks at Frank's Market only if they have a special **check-cashing privilege card**, like the one shown in Illustration 17B. Customers must apply for the card in advance of their purchases. Frank's Market checks the credit histories of the customers. If they are found to be good credit risks, they are issued the card.

Illustration 17B   A check-cashing privilege card

Frank's Market

No. 1836
**Check-Cashing
Privilege Card**

This card allows: Andrew Luann
1289 Hardy Street
Allentown, PA 18104-0423

To cash checks for purchases according to the restrictions printed on the back of this card.

Customer
Signature *Andrew Luann* Date *March 16,* 19 _ _

Other businesses may have other check-cashing **policies**, or sets of rules for accepting checks. For example, some may accept personal checks from customers if they provide some identification and the checks are from local banks. The identification required may be a driver's license or employee identification card from a local employer.

Frank's Market accepts personal checks from customers as long as the checks are completed properly, are made out to Frank's Market, are from local banks, are not dated for some future date, and are for no more than $25.00 over the sale amount. Local banks are banks in the same town as Frank's Market: Allentown, Pennsylvania. In addition, only customers who have been given a check-cashing privilege card are allowed to cash checks in the store.

Frank's Market does not accept checks which are made out to other people. They only accept the checks of their customers which are made out to Frank's Market. For example, they do not accept employment checks or government checks. Checks from people other than their customers are called **third-party checks**.

Checks which do not meet the store's check-cashing policies must be given to your supervisor. The supervisor then decides whether the check can be authorized, or approved for cashing.

On July 19, Andrew Luann bought these items: a loaf of bread for $1.49, a bunch of celery for $0.79, and a half-gallon of milk for $0.85. He gave you a coupon, a bottle refund, and a $10.00 check. Here is how you handled the sale:

STEP 1 ▶ *Enter each sale item.*

You entered each sale item by pressing these keys:

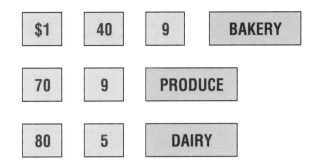

| $1 | 40 | 9 | BAKERY |

| 70 | 9 | PRODUCE |

| 80 | 5 | DAIRY |

STEP 2 ▶ *Enter each coupon and refund slip.*

Andrew Luann gave you a coupon for 15¢ off the loaf of bread. He also gave you a bottle refund slip for 28¢. You pressed these keys in order:

| 10 | 5 | COUPON |

| 20 | 8 | BOTTLE REFUND |

INTERVIEW

BEN ALBRECHT

Ben Albrecht was born and raised in San Francisco, California. At the age of twelve, Ben helped support his family by buying and selling newspapers. It was through his newspaper business that Ben realized the importance of accurate inventory, correct billing, customer satisfaction, and good business management. Ben used these skills to build his route from 57 customers to over 100.

During high school and college, Ben began selling peanuts for a concessions company at baseball games and gradually worked his way up to selling souvenirs and programs. Ben worked at football games, boxing matches, hockey games, ice follies, and even county fairs. Because of his record keeping experience with inventory, sales, commissions, and profitable concession placement, Ben was promoted to concession manager.

At the age of 23, Ben started a long career in the baking industry. He began with the entry-level position of route salesman. His hard work and knowledge of sales resulted in many promotions over the years. Eventually, he became president of the Parisian French Bread Company, headquartered in San Francisco. After eight years as president, Ben decided to go into business for himself. He found a partner, invested $35,000, and started his own baking ingredient company. During his first year of business, sales reached $400,000. Now six years later, annual sales are $12 million. Hard work and a good understanding of basic record keeping have helped Ben Albrecht become the financial success he is today.

You then placed the coupon and bottle refund slip in the back of the cash drawer of the cash register.

STEP 3 ▸ **Find the total for the customer.**

You pressed the subtotal, tax, and total keys in that order. The results, printed out on the cash register receipt, looked like this:

BA	$1.49
PR	$0.79
DA	$0.85
CO	-$0.15 ←—— Coupon
BR	-$0.28 ←—— Bottle Refund
ST	$2.70
TX	$0.14
TL	$2.84

STEP 4 ▸ **Verify the check tendered by the customer.**

Andrew Luann showed you his check-cashing privilege card (Illustration 17B, page 166) and gave you the following check.

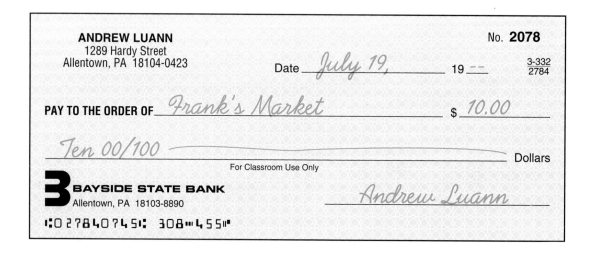

You wrote the check-cashing privilege card number on the back of the check. You then verified the check using the checklist which was posted on your cash register:

CHECK VERIFICATION CHECKLIST

If any of the items below are true, call your supervisor:

1. The customer's name or address is not printed on the check.
2. The name, address, or customer signature on the card does not match the name, address, or signature on the check.
3. The amount of the check in writing is not the same as the amount in figures.
4. The date on the check is a future date.
5. The check is not from a local bank.
6. The check is for more than $25 over the total sale.
7. The check is not made out to Frank's Market.

Since none of the items on the checklist were true, you accepted it for payment. Had one or more of these items been true, you would have called your supervisor. The supervisor may have authorized the check after talking with the customer. The supervisor may also have asked the customer to make out a new check or refused to accept the check at all.

STEP 5 ▶ *Enter the amount of the check and give the correct change.*

You then entered the amount of the check in the register and pressed the Check key. The correct change to give the customer was shown on the display. The cash register receipt looked like this:

ST	$2.70
TX	$0.14
TL	$2.84
CK	$10.00	◀—— The amount of the check tendered
CG	$7.16	◀—— The correct amount of change to give the customer

You gave the customer the cash register receipt and the correct change in these amounts: a $5 bill, two $1 bills, a dime, a nickel, and a penny. You then placed the check in the cash drawer.

On a sheet of paper, write the headings **Statement Number** and **Words.** Next, choose the words that match the statements. Write each word you choose next to the statement number it matches. Be careful; not all the words listed should be used.

Statements	Words
1. Allow payments to be made from checking accounts immediately	amount tendered
	authorize
2. Money given back to a customer for returned bottles or merchandise	check-cashing privilege card
3. A total on which other calculations will be made	debit cards
	grand total
4. Rules or procedures	policies
5. Approve	refund
6. Amount given to pay a bill	stub
7. Allows you to cash checks at a store	subtotal
8. Checks from people other than customers	third-party checks

PROBLEM SOLVING MODEL FOR: *Handling Refunds, Coupons, and Checks*

STEP 1 ▶ *Enter each sale item.*

STEP 2 ▶ *Enter each coupon and refund slip.*

STEP 3 ▶ *Find the total for the customer.*

STEP 4 ▶ *Verify the check tendered by the customer.*

STEP 5 ▶ *Enter the amount of the check and give the correct change.*

*A*PPLICATION PROBLEM

PROBLEM | **17-1** ▶ On May 17, you were a cashier at Frank's Market and handled the five customers in this problem.

Customer 1:

After entering each item bought by Karla Hansen, your register displayed a total sale of $66.04. Karla gave you the check-cashing privilege card and check that appear on the next page.

Directions

a. On a separate sheet of paper, write the heading "Check-Cashing Policies." Under the heading, write the numbers 1–7 for the seven check-cashing policies of Frank's Market shown in the checklist in Step 4 (page 169) of the Sample Problem. Verify the check against these seven policies by placing a check mark next to any policy found to be true.

b. On the same sheet of paper, write the headings "Bills and Coins" and "Number Used." Then list the type and number of each bill or coin you should give the customer for change if you accept the check or if it is authorized by your supervisor.

Frank's Market

No. 1892
Check-Cashing Privilege Card

This card allows: Karla Hansen
415 Audrey Land
Allentown, PA 18103-1048

To cash checks for purchases according to the restrictions printed on the back of this card.

Customer
Signature *Karla Hansen*   Date *June 8,*   19 ⎯⎯

KARLA HANSEN   No. **3398**
507 Cole Street
Allentown, PA 18102-6612
                                    Date *May 17,*   19 ⎯⎯   3-332
                                                                        1977

PAY TO THE ORDER OF *Frank's Market* $ *75.00*

Seventy-five 00/100 ――――――――――――――――――――― Dollars
For Classroom Use Only

fcb
FARMERS CITY BANK
Bethlehem, PA 18015-6623   *Karla Hansen*

⑈019770745⑈ ⑈133⑈657⑈

Customer 2:

After entering each item bought by Sonny Boneli, your register displayed a total sale of $37.88. Sonny gave you the check-cashing privilege card and check that appear on the next page.

Directions

a. On a separate sheet of paper, write the heading "Check-Cashing Policies." Under the heading, write the numbers 1–7 for the seven check-cashing policies of Frank's Market shown in the checklist in Step 4 (page 169) of the Sample Problem. Verify the check against these seven policies by placing a check mark next to any policy found to be true.

b. On the same sheet of paper, write the headings "Bills and Coins" and "Number Used." Then list the type and number of each bill or coin you should give the customer for change if you accept the check or if it is authorized by your supervisor.

Frank's Market

No. 0786

Check-Cashing Privilege Card

This card allows: Sonny Boneli
238 Taylor Boulevard
Allentown, PA 18103-2298

To cash checks for purchases according to the restrictions printed on the back of this card.

Customer
Signature *Sonny Boneli* Date *April 1*, 19 --

SONNY BONELI   No. **124**

Date _*May 17,*_____ 19 __   3-332 / 2075

Pay to the
Order of _*Frank's Market*_____ $ *50.00*_____

_*Fifty 00/100*_____ Dollars

For Classroom Use Only

Sandhill State Bank
Allentown, PA 18105-3108

Sonny Boneli

⑆020750745⑆ 912⑈008⑈

The problem material for Customers 3, 4, and 5 may be found in the Working Papers.

BUSINESS TERMS PREVIEW

- Cash count report • Cash overage • Cash shortage •
- Change fund • Denomination • Detailed audit tape •
- Proof of cash •

GOAL

To learn how a cashier proves that the amount of money in a cash register at the end of the day is correct.

NDERSTANDING THE JOB

KEY *Terms*

Detailed audit tape. Record of all cash register transactions.

In addition to being recorded on the cash register receipts that are given to customers, each transaction is also recorded on a **detailed audit tape** inside the cash register. What is recorded on this tape varies with each store. However, usually every item sold, its department, its price, the total amount of each sale, and the cashier's number are recorded.

The detailed audit tape is used to help the cashier prove that the amount of money in the cash register at the end of the day is correct. The detailed audit tape can also be used as a source document for keeping records of the business' total cash received and total sales of each kind of item. Being able to verify the money in the cash register and record total items sold are two more advantages of using a cash register. Businesses such as gas stations and convenience stores handle many cash transactions every day. Keeping cash records by hand would take a great deal of time. There would also be a greater chance of errors. Keeping records with a machine, such as a cash register, makes it much easier to keep track of totals and prepare proofs of cash.

SAMPLE PROBLEM

Sandy Wilmer is cashier number 26 and operates register no. 14 for Albany Casuals. Each morning Sandy is given $100.00 in different coins and bills by the manager of the store. She will use this $100.00 as a **change fund**, or a source of money, from which she can give customers change. Here are the steps Sandy will follow each day to check her work:

K E Y Terms

Change fund.
Amount cashier starts with.

STEP 1 ▶ *Verify the change fund at the beginning of the day.*

Sandy verifies that she has been given $100.00 in her change fund before she puts the money into the register. After counting the change fund, she puts the money in the cash drawer in the correct compartments.

STEP 2 ▶ *Find the total sales for the day.*

At the end of the day, Sandy finds the total sales from the detailed audit tape in her register. The tape shows that she sold $1,922.90 during the day.

STEP 3 ▶ *Find the cash paid out for the day.*

Customers who return merchandise may have the amounts returned subtracted from their purchases. However, customers who are not buying anything may be paid cash for their returns.

At the end of the day, Sandy finds the total amount of money that she has paid out to customers for returns from the detailed audit tape. The tape shows that she paid $23.50 in refunds to customers.

STEP 4 ▶ *Find the total cash to be accounted for.*

Although Sandy's total sales were $1,922.90, she must account for $1,999.40 because

Sales for the day	$1,922.90
Plus: Change fund in register, start of day	+ 100.00
	$2,022.90
Less: Cash paid out during day	- 23.50
Equals: Total cash to be accounted for	$1,999.40

STEP 5 ▶ *Count the actual cash in the register at the end of the day.*

Since Sandy knows how much cash she is supposed to have, she empties all the compartments in the cash register and sorts the bills and coins into their **denominations**, or values. She also sorts and counts the checks. This is what she finds:

Bills and Coins:

Quantity	Denomination
28	$20.00 bills
21	$10.00 bills
17	$ 5.00 bills
31	$ 1.00 bills
7	$ 0.50 coins
20	$ 0.25 coins
25	$ 0.10 coins
32	$ 0.05 coins
80	$ 0.01 coins

Total Checks: $1,100.00

She enters the quantity of each denomination of the bills and coins on the **cash count report** shown in Illustration 18A and multiplies the denomination by the quantity to get the amount. Then she enters the total amount of the checks.

Illustration 18A   Cash count report showing actual cash count

ALBANY CASUALS, INC.
Cash Count Report

Date: _August 21,_____ 19 _--_
Cashier No.: _26_____   Register No.: _14_____

Quantity	Denomination	Amount	
28	$20.00 Bills	560	00
21	$10.00 Bills	210	00
17	$5.00 Bills	85	00
31	$1.00 Bills	31	00
7	$0.50 Coins	3	50
20	$0.25 Coins	5	00
25	$0.10 Coins	2	50
32	$0.05 Coins	1	60
80	$0.01 Coins		80
	Checks	1,100	00
Total Cash in Cash Drawer		1,999	40

Signature: _Sandy Wilmer_____

Prepare the proof of cash.

Sandy now compares the amount of cash she should have (Step 4) with the amount of cash she actually has (Step 5). She does this by preparing the **proof of cash** shown in Illustration 18B. She will turn in the cash proof form with her actual cash.

Since the cash in Sandy's register agrees with the amount she is supposed to have, the cash is neither short nor over.

<table>
<tr><td>**K E Y** | **Terms**</td></tr>
</table>

Proof of cash. Compares amount of cash you should have with actual cash.

ALBANY CASUALS, INC.
Cash Proof Form

Date: _August 21,_ 19 _--_

Change fund	100	00
Add total cash sales from audit tape	1,922	90
Total	2,022	90
Less cash paid out from audit tape	23	50
Cash that should be in register	1,999	40
Cash actually in register	1,999	40
Cash short	0	00
Cash over	0	00

Cash Register No.: _14_   Cashier No.: _26_

Signature: _Sandy Wilmer_

Illustration 18B   Proof of cash form

Sometimes the cashier will find that the actual cash in the register does not agree with the cash that should be in the register. Suppose the cash in the register at the end of the day had been $1,998.90. The cashier would have completed the last part of the proof of cash form this way:

Cash that should be in register	1,999	40
Cash actually in register	1,998	90
Cash short	0	50

<table>
<tr><td>**K E Y** | **Terms**</td></tr>
</table>

Cash shortage. Less cash on hand than there should be.

Since Sandy would not have enough money, she would enter the $0.50 on the Cash Short line of the form. This amount is called a **cash shortage**.

If the actual cash in the register had been $1,999.45, Sandy would have completed the proof of cash form this way:

Cash that should be in register	1,999	40
Cash actually in register	1,999	45
Cash short	0	00
Cash over	0	05

Since Sandy would have too much money, she would enter the $0.05 on the Cash Over line of the report. This amount is called a **cash overage**.

You can use a calculator to make the job of preparing the proof of cash form easier. The calculator will let you add and subtract amounts the way you need to on a proof of cash form. For example, use the data from the Sample Problem, except let the actual amount found in the cash drawer at the end of the day be $1,999.45. Here is how you can use a calculator to find the amounts on the proof of cash form.

STEP 1 ▶ *Add the amounts for the change fund and total cash received.*

Press these keys in order:

| 1 | 0 | 0 | + | 1 | 9 | 2 | 2 | • | 9 | = |

The answer that appears in the display is 2022.90. Enter this amount on the Total line of the cash proof form.

STEP 2 ▶ *Subtract the cash paid out.*

Without clearing the calculator, press these keys in order:

| – | 2 | 3 | • | 5 | = |

The answer that appears in the display is 1999.40. Enter this amount on the Cash That Should Be In Register line of the form.

STEP 3 ▶ *Subtract the cash actually in the drawer.*

Without clearing the calculator, press these keys in order:

| – | 1 | 9 | 9 | 9 | • | 4 | 5 | = |

The answer that appears in the display is -0.05. This is really a minus five cents. This means that you have five cents more than you should in the drawer. Whenever the number is negative, you will know that there is a cash overage. Enter 0.05 in the Cash Over line of the form.

If the answer had no minus sign, you would have a cash shortage. You would then enter the amount on the Cash Short line of the form.

On a sheet of paper, write the headings **Statement Number** and **Words**. Next, choose the words that match the statements. Write each word you choose next to the statement number it matches. Be careful; not all the words listed should be used.

Statements	Words
1. The value of a coin or bill	cash count report
2. A record of all cash register transactions	cash overage
3. A form on which you compare how much cash you are supposed to have with what you actually have in the register	cash register
	cash shortage
	cashier
4. A machine used to reduce errors and safeguard money	change fund
	denomination
5. A form issued for cash received	detailed audit tape
6. An amount given to a cashier at the beginning of the day for making change	proof of cash
	receipt
7. Something that happens in a business that should be recorded	transaction
8. When there is less cash in the register at the end of the day than there should be	
9. Used to find the amount of cash in the drawer	

PROBLEM SOLVING MODEL FOR: *Preparing Proofs of Cash*

STEP 1 ▶ *Verify the change fund at the beginning of the day.*

STEP 2 ▶ *Find the total sales for the day.*

STEP 3 ▶ *Find the cash paid out for the day.*

STEP 4 ▶ *Find the total cash to be accounted for.*

STEP 5 ▶ *Count the actual cash in the register at the end of the day.*

STEP 6 ▶ *Prepare the proof of cash.*

APPLICATION PROBLEMS

PROBLEM | 18-1 ▶ You are cashier no. 21 at register no. 6 at Bradford Foodmart. At the end of the day on March 16, your cash drawer contained these items:

Quantity	Denomination
28	$20.00 bills
18	$10.00 bills
12	$ 5.00 bills
48	$ 1.00 bills
12	$ 0.50 coins
43	$ 0.25 coins
24	$ 0.10 coins
78	$ 0.05 coins
122	$ 0.01 coins

Total checks: $245.00

Directions

Prepare a cash count report like the one shown in Illustration 18A on page 175.

PROBLEM | **18-2** ▶ You are the cashier in Problem 1. On March 16, you started the day with a change fund of $150.00. At the end of the day, your register's detailed audit tape showed total cash sales of $980.20 and total cash paid out of $12.80. At the end of the day, your cash drawer contained the amount shown in the cash count report you completed in Problem 1.

Directions

Prepare a proof of cash like the one shown in Illustration 18B on page 176.

PROBLEM | **18-3** ▶ You are cashier no. 18 at cash register no. 4 for Burgos Discount Store. On June 6, you started the day with a change fund of $100.00. At the end of the day, your register's detailed audit tape showed total cash sales of $2,598.50 and total cash paid out of $45.90. Your cash drawer contained these items: 38 $20.00 bills; 24 $10.00 bills; 15 $5.00 bills; 75 $1.00 bills; 56 $0.50 coins; 22 $0.25 coins; 57 $0.10 coins; 81 $0.05 coins; 233 $0.01 coins; and checks totalling $1,459.00.

Directions

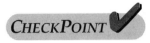

a. Prepare a cash count report like the one shown in Illustration 18A on page 175.
b. Prepare a proof of cash like the one shown in Illustration 18B on page 176.

Problems 18-4, 18-5, and 18-6 may be found in the Working Papers.

JOB 19 ▶ Preparing Cashier Reports

APPLIED MATH PREVIEW

Copy and complete the following problems.

1. 134.50 + 356.78 + 82.18 + 1,089.88 =
2. 1,779.20 + 4.56 + 314.72 + 29.19 =
3. 8.35 + 1,200.88 + 41.62 + 3.77 =
4. 2,030.87 + 1,802.98 + 322.76 + 654.41 =
5. 839.29 + 674.22 + 78.21 + 723.56 =

GOAL To learn how to prepare daily cashier reports for a store with many departments.

UNDERSTANDING THE JOB

Cashiers complete a number of reports about their work each day. These include the *cash count report* and the *proof of cash*, which you have already studied. These reports help cashiers verify the amounts in their cash registers.

Businesses use reports such as the cash count report and the proof of cash to provide control of their cash. It is very important for businesses not to waste or lose any of their cash. Cash registers, checking accounts (discussed in Chapter 5), petty cash funds (discussed in Chapter 6), and sales slips (discussed in Chapter 7) are other examples of ways to control cash.

There are four basic requirements in a good cash control system. First, there should be more than one person responsible for cash. The person who handles cash should not also be the person responsible for all the cash record keeping. Second, all cash received should be deposited in a bank that day. Third, no cash should be paid out unless approved by a supervisor or other authorized person. Fourth, cash records should be checked from time to time. Ways of checking cash include surprise counts of cash on hand, verification of cash-related source documents, and comparison of bank records with business records.

Cashiers also complete reports that are helpful to managers. For example, cashiers may complete *departmental sales reports* for their registers. These reports may, in turn, be used to complete a *summary of departmental sales* for the entire store. These two reports show the total sales made during the day for each department. They help managers spot departments that are selling more or less than expected.

Randall Gorman is the manager of Randy's Sporting Goods. At the end of each day, each cashier completes a departmental sales report for each cash register. The cashiers complete their reports by copying the total sales for each department from their detailed audit tapes. A departmental sales report for register no. 1 is shown in Illustration 19A on page 182.

On October 5, the cashiers gave Randall their departmental sales reports, their detailed audit tapes, and the cash from their cash registers. Randall completed the summary of departmental sales report shown in Illustration 19B on page 182.

To complete the report, Randall followed these steps:

STEP 1 ▶ *Verify the amounts and totals on each departmental sales report.*

Randall compared the amounts shown on each departmental sales report to the amounts on the detailed audit tape for the same register. For example, he compared the detailed audit tape shown in Illustration 19C (page 182) from register no. 1 with the departmental sales report completed by the cashier for register no. 1 (Illustration 19A on page 182).

Randall found that the cashier had copied the total sales for tennis incorrectly from the tape to the report. The cashier had copied the total sales amount correctly, however. Randall corrected the departmental sales report for register no. 1 by crossing out the amount for tennis and writing the correct amount next to it.

STEP 2 ▶ *Copy the amounts to the summary of departmental sales report.*

Randall copied the amounts from the departmental sales reports to the summary of departmental sales report. For example, Randall copied the total sales for bicycling, $780.00, from the departmental sales report for register no. 1 to the line for bicycling in the column for register no. 1 in the summary report.

STEP 3 ▶ *Find and verify the daily total for each register.*

Randall added the columns for each register in the summary report and compared them to the totals shown on the departmental sales reports. He did this to insure that he had copied the amounts correctly.

RANDY'S SPORTING GOODS
Departmental Sales Report

Cashier No.: _4_   Register No.: _1_

Department	Total
Bicycling	$ 780.00
Running	1,280.00
Tennis	980.00
Swimming	420.00
General	380.00
Total	$3,750.00

Signature: _Lamont White_

Date: _October 5,_   19 _--_

Illustration 19B
Summary of
departmental
sales report

RANDY'S SPORTING GOODS
Summary of Departmental Sales
October 5, 19--

Department	Registers								Department Total	
	1		2		3		4			
Bicycling	780	00	245	89	451	98	101	90	1 579	77
Running	1 280	00	448	99	812	43	209	34	2 750	76
Tennis	890	00	1 009	58	212	45	1 298	33	3 410	36
Swimming	420	00	128	12	498	53	509	63	1 556	28
General	380	00	598	39	308	66	876	42	2 163	47
Total	3 750	00	2 430	97	2 284	05	2 995	62	11 460	64
	3 750	00	2 430	97	2 284	05	2 995	62	11 460	64

For example, Randall added the column for register no. 1 and entered the total, $3,750.00, as a footing. He then compared that total to the total on the departmental sales report for register no. 1. Since they were equal, he wrote the total below the footing on the summary of departmental sales report.

STEP 4 ▶ Find the daily total for each department.

Randall found the total sales for each department by adding across. For example, he added the bicycling department sales from each register. The total sales for bicycling for the day were $1,579.77. He entered this amount in the Department Totals column on the line for bicycling.

Illustration 19C
Detailed audit tape
showing departmental
sales totals

BI	780.00	◀—— Total bicycling sales
RU	1280.00	◀—— Total running sales
TE	890.00	◀—— Total tennis sales
SW	420.00	◀—— Total swimming sales
GE	380.00	◀—— Total general sales
TL	3750.00	◀—— Total sales, register 1
10/05/--	RG1	◀—— Date and register number

Department	Total
Bicycling	$ 780.00
Running	1,280.00
Tennis	~~980.00~~ 890.00
Swimming	420.00
General	380.00
Total	$3,750.00

STEP 5 ▶ **Find and verify the grand total and double rule the form.**

Randall added the amounts in the Department Totals column and entered that total, $11,460.64, as a footing at the bottom of the column. This amount is a grand total since it is the total of the Department Totals column and the total of the register column totals. To prove his work, Randall crossfooted the totals of the register columns and compared that amount to the total of the Department Totals column. Since these amounts were equal, Randall entered the grand total below the footing and double ruled the form.

BUILDING YOUR BUSINESS VOCABULARY

On a sheet of paper, write the headings **Statement Number** and **Words.** Next, choose the words that match the statements. Write each word you choose next to the statement number it matches. Be careful; not all the words listed should be used.

Statements	Words
1. Money given back to a customer for returned bottles or merchandise	amount tendered
	cashier
2. A total of other totals	change fund
3. A special bar code read by electronic cash registers	crossfooting
	detailed audit tape
4. The amount of cash given to the cashier by the customer	footing
	grand total
5. A form on which you compare how much cash you are supposed to have with what you actually have in the register	proof of cash
	refund
	subtotal
6. A person who receives and pays out money	transaction
	Universal Product Code
7. Adding a row of figures across a business form	
8. An amount given to a cashier at the beginning of the day for making change	
9. A record of all cash register transactions	

PROBLEM SOLVING MODEL FOR: *Preparing Cashier Reports*

STEP 1 ▶	**Verify the amounts and totals on each departmental sales report.**
STEP 2 ▶	**Copy the amounts to the summary of departmental sales report.**
STEP 3 ▶	**Find and verify the daily total for each register.**
STEP 4 ▶	**Find the daily total for each department.**
STEP 5 ▶	**Find and verify the grand total and double rule the form.**

APPLICATION PROBLEMS

PROBLEM | **19-1** ▶ You are an office assistant for City Market. The manager has asked you to prepare a summary of departmental sales report, like the one shown in Illustration 19B (page 182), for May 24.

Directions

a. Verify each of the following departmental sales reports by comparing it to the detailed audit tape shown below it. Correct any departmental sales reports that contain errors.

Cashier No.: _4_   Register No.: _1_

Department	Total
Meat	$ 679.23
Produce	407.21
Dairy	303.67
Grocery	449.21
General	117.82
Total	$1,956.96

Signature: _Raymond Dugan_

Date: _May 24,_   19 _--_

Cashier No.: _2_   Register No.: _2_

Department	Total
Meat	$ 599.29
Produce	210.06
Dairy	507.88
Grocery	221.87
General	439.76
Total	$1,978.86

Signature: _Rita Delgado_

Date: _May 24,_   19 _--_

```
      ME      679.23
      PR      407.12
      DA      303.67
      GR      449.12
      GE      117.82
      TL     1956.96

   05/24/--        RG1
```

```
      ME      599.29
      PR      210.06
      DA      507.88
      GR      221.87
      GE      439.76
      TL     1978.86

   05/24/--        RG2
```

| Cashier No.: 1 | Register No.: 3 |
Department	Total
Meat	$ 1,209.98
Produce	731.54
Dairy	488.12
Grocery	508.34
General	333.80
Total	$3,271.78

Signature: *Victor Moran*

Date: May 24, 19 --

| Cashier No.: 3 | Register No.: 4 |
Department	Total
Meat	$1,003.39
Produce	598.23
Dairy	823.19
Grocery	399.31
General	629.11
Total	$3,453.23

Signature: *Shirley Brown*

Date: May 24, 19 --

```
ME        1209.98
PR         731.54
DA         488.12
GR         508.34
GE         333.80
TL        3271.78

05/24/--        RG3
```

```
ME        1003.39
PR         598.23
DA         823.19
GR         399.31
GE         629.11
TL        3453.23

05/24/--        RG4
```

CHECKPOINT

19-1
Grand total = $10,660.83

b. Copy the amounts from the departmental sales report for each register to the summary of departmental sales report for the whole store.

c. Find the column, line, and grand totals. Verify them by crossfooting, and double rule the report.

 PROBLEM 19-2 ▶ You are a clerk in the manager's office at Russo's Discount Electronics. The manager has asked you to prepare a summary of departmental sales report, like the one shown in Illustration 19B (page 182), for June 6.

Directions

a. Verify each departmental sales report that appears on the following page by comparing it to the detailed audit tape shown below it. Correct any departmental sales reports that contain errors.

CHECKPOINT

19-2
TV and VCR Department total = $22,702.88

b. Copy the amounts from the departmental sales report for each register to the summary of departmental sales report for the whole store.

c. Find the column, line, and grand totals. Verify them by crossfooting, and double rule the report.

Cashier No.: 2	Register No.: 1
Department	**Total**
TV and VCR	$ 3,801.34
Sound Systems	4,228.91
Computer Systems	12,010.99
Appliances	2,078.43
General	851.76
Total	$22,071.43

Signature: _Philip Tanner_

Date: _June 6,_ 19 _ _

```
TV      3801.34
SO      4228.91
CO     12010.99
AP      2078.43
GE       851.76
TL     22971.43

06/06/--        RG1
```

Cashier No.: 4	Register No.: 2
Department	**Total**
TV and VCR	$ 4,211.31
Sound Systems	8,145.98
Computer Systems	9,208.23
Appliances	1,897.45
General	2,301.87
Total	$25,773.84

Signature: _Lorraine Varner_

Date: _June 6,_ 19 _ _

```
TV      4211.31
SO      8154.98
CO      9208.23
AP      1897.45
GE      2301.87
TL     25773.84

06/06/--        RG2
```

Cashier No.: 3	Register No.: 3
Department	**Total**
TV and VCR	$ 5,389.01
Sound Systems	4,207.98
Computer Systems	9,114.41
Appliances	2,781.31
General	1,506.82
Total	$22,999.53

Signature: _Manny Duran_

Date: _June 6,_ 19 _ _

```
TV      5389.01
SO      4207.98
CO      9114.41
AP      2781.31
GE      1506.82
TL     22999.53

06/06/--        RG3
```

Cashier No.: 1	Register No.: 4
Department	**Total**
TV and VCR	$ 9,301.22
Sound Systems	3,109.00
Computer Systems	6,981.98
Appliances	3,113.01
General	1,556.65
Total	$24,062.85

Signature: _Betsy O'Mara_

Date: _June 6,_ 19 _ _

```
TV      9301.22
SO      3109.99
CO      6981.98
AP      3113.01
GE      1556.65
TL     24062.85

06/06/--        RG4
```

Problem 19-3 may be found in the Working Papers.

APPLIED MATH PREVIEW

Copy and complete the following problems.

1. 81 × $100.00 =	5. 214 × $10.00 =
2. 23 × $50.00 =	6. 131 × $5.00 =
3. 101 × $0.50 =	7. 322 × $0.10 =
4. 114 × $0.25 =	8. 812 × $0.01 =

▲▲▲▲▲
TIP
▼▼▼▼▼

When you multiply by 10 or 100, move the decimal point in the number multiplied to the right as many places as there are zeros in the number you multiply by. For example, 54 × 10 = 540. When you multiply by 0.01, move the decimal point in the number being multiplied to the left as many decimal places as there are in the number you multiply by. For example, 123 × 0.01 = 1.23.

BUSINESS TERMS PREVIEW

• Bank deposit • Deposit slip • Loose bills and coins •
• Tally sheet •

GOALS

1. To learn how to prepare a tally sheet.
2. To learn how to prepare a bank deposit slip.

UNDERSTANDING THE JOB

KEY Terms

Bank deposit. Money placed in a bank account.

The cash you collect using a cash drawer, cash register, or other means should be deposited, or placed, in the bank at the end of each day. It is not good business practice to keep large amounts of cash on hand after business hours. After proving cash and preparing the daily cash reports, you must prepare a **bank deposit** so that the cash collected can be deposited in the bank.

Many banks offer the use of a night deposit safe. A night depository (also called a *deposit slot* or *deposit box*) is usually located outside the bank. The bank supplies the customer with a safety deposit bag that can be locked. After the safety deposit bag has been placed in the night deposit slot, the bag moves to a vault within the bank. A bank employee will remove the bag from the vault during the next day's banking hours. A night deposit slot is especially useful for businesses that do not have their own safes and that collect large sums of cash that cannot be deposited during banking hours. Examples of such businesses are restaurants, gas stations, and movie theaters.

Susan Sims is the cashier for Elbery's Cash and Carry Barn. One of her jobs is to prepare a bank deposit of the money she receives daily. Here are the steps she follows on March 22:

STEP **1** ▶ *Separate and wrap the bills.*

Susan removes from the cash register all the bills that are to be deposited. She arranges them according to denominations so that $20 bills, $10 bills, $5 bills, and $1 bills are all in separate stacks. The bills are placed face up and counted in stacks of a hundred bills to a package. (Some banks prefer fifty bills to a package.) Susan uses wrappers supplied by the bank to wrap the money.

Susan usually finds that there are not enough bills of one denomination to make one complete package. For example, she may have 156 $1 bills. Only 100 of these bills are needed to make a full package. That means that 56 $1 bills are left over. Susan wraps the first 100 $1 bills in a wrapper. She places the 56 $1 bills left in a $1 wrapper also, but marks the wrapper "$56.00 only", as shown in Illustration 20A.

Illustration 20A
Wrapped bills

Mark packages that do not have the full number of bills

STEP **2** ▶ *Separate and wrap the coins.*

Susan removes from the cash register all the coins that are to be deposited. She uses the table below to help her sort out the coins and put them in the wrappers correctly.

Coin	Color of Wrapper	Number of Coins in Full Wrapper	Value of Coins in Full Wrapper
Half-Dollars	Tan	20	$10.00
Quarters	Orange	40	10.00
Dimes	Green	50	5.00
Nickels	Blue	40	2.00
Pennies	Red	50	0.50

Usually there will not be enough coins of one denomination to make a full roll. For example, if there are 28 quarters, Susan cannot prepare a full roll of quarters because 40 quarters are needed to make one roll. Susan puts the 28 quarters in a quarter wrapper and writes "$7.00 only" on the wrapper to show how much money is inside, as shown in Illustration 20B.

 **STEP 3** ▶ *Tally the money to be deposited.*

Susan sorts and wraps the money this way:

Bills	Coins
3 packages of $10 bills	7 rolls of half-dollars
5 loose $10 bills	5 loose half-dollars
1 package of $5 bills	8 rolls of quarters
6 loose $5 bills	13 loose quarters
1 package of $1 bills	15 rolls of dimes
34 loose $1 bills	11 loose dimes
	12 rolls of nickels
	21 loose nickels
	21 rolls of pennies
	24 loose pennies

Susan lists the sorted bills and coins on a **tally sheet**, or checklist of money (Illustration 20C on page 190). She enters the bills first. For example, she enters 3 in the Number column on the line for full packages of $10 bills. She multiplies the number of full packages (3) by the amount of a full package ($1,000.00) and enters the total ($3,000.00) in the first money column.

Then Susan enters the data for the loose $10 bills. She enters 5 in the Number column on the line for loose $10 bills. She multiplies the number of loose $10 bills (5) by their value ($10.00) and enters the total ($50.00) in the first money column.

Susan enters the data for the rest of the bills and coins in the same way. Notice that Susan finds the totals for both the bills and coins separately and enters these totals in the second money column.

Notice also that Susan lists the wrappers that were not full as **"loose" bills and coins** on her tally sheet. Of course, the bills and coins are not really loose. They are wrapped and specially marked. However, this is what bills and coins that do not fill their wrappers are called.

Illustration 20B   Wrapped coins

Mark rolls that do not have
the full amount of coins

Illustration 20C   Tally sheet

TALLY SHEET		Date: March 22,	19 --		
NO.	**BILLS**				
	Packages of $100 bills x $10,000.00				
	Loose $100 bills				
	Packages of $50 bills x $5,000.00				
	Loose $50 bills				
	Packages of $20 bills x $2,000.00				
	Loose $20 bills				
3	Packages of $10 bills x $1,000.00	3 000	00		
5	Loose $10 bills	50	00		
1	Packages of $5 bills x $500.00	500	00		
6	Loose $5 bills	30	00		
1	Packages of $1 bills x $100.00	100	00		
34	Loose $1 bills	34	00		
	Total bills to be deposited			3 714	00
NO.	**COINS**				
7	Rolls of half-dollars x $10.00	70	00		
5	Loose half-dollars	2	50		
8	Rolls of quarters x $10.00	80	00		
13	Loose quarters	3	25		
15	Rolls of dimes x $5.00	75	00		
11	Loose dimes	1	10		
12	Rolls of nickels x $2.00	24	00		
21	Loose nickels	1	05		
21	Rolls of pennies x $0.50	10	50		
24	Loose pennies		24		
	Total coins to be deposited			267	64
	Total cash to be deposited			3 981	64

STEP 4 ▶ *Prepare the deposit slip.*

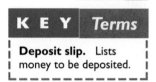

K E Y   Terms

Deposit slip. Lists
money to be deposited.

Once Susan completes the tally sheet, she prepares a **deposit slip** (Illustration 20D). A deposit slip is a form used to list all money placed in a bank account. The bank used by Elbery's Cash and Carry Barn supplies Susan with the deposit slips.

To complete the deposit slip, Susan enters the date, the totals for the bills and coins, and the total deposit. Everything else is preprinted on the slip.

Notice that the totals for bills and coins are shown separately on the deposit slip. Susan gets these totals from the tally sheet. There is also a special place to list checks to be deposited. You will learn how to deposit checks in the next chapter.

For DEPOSIT to the Account of					1-5 / 210
				Dollars	Cents
	ELBERY'S CASH AND CARRY BARN		BILLS	3,714	00
			COINS	267	64
	DATE March 22, 19 --		Checks as Follows Properly Endorsed		
	FIRST COMMERCE STATE BANK New York, New York				
	Subject to the Terms and Conditions of this Bank's Collection Agreement				
	⑆0210 0625⑆ 2418⑈639⑈		**TOTAL DEPOSIT**	3,981	64

Notice also that the deposit slip Susan completes has the bank account number of the business printed in Magnetic Ink Character Recognition (MICR) on the bottom left side. The bank provides the business with deposit slips preprinted with its account number in MICR. When Susan takes the money and deposit slip to the bank teller, the bank will enter the total deposit in MICR on the slip. The bank's computer system can then read the account number and total deposit directly from the deposit slip.

Calculator TIPS

The calculator can be used to make the job of completing a tally sheet much easier. Here is how you can use a calculator to complete the tally sheet used in the Sample Problem.

STEP 1 ▶ *For each line of bills, multiply the number of bills by the value and store the total in memory.*

For each denomination of bills, there is a line for a full package and a line for loose bills. For the full package, multiply the number of packages by the total value of the package. For example, multiply 3 by $1,000 to find the total for 3 packages of $10 bills. Do this by pressing these keys in order:

$$3 \quad \times \quad 1 \quad 0 \quad 0 \quad 0 \quad =$$

The answer that appears in the display is 3000, or $3,000.00. Enter this on the line for full packages of $10 bills. Then add the total to memory by pressing the M+ key:

$$M+$$

For loose bills, multiply the number of bills by the denomination. For example, multiply 5 x $10 to find the total for 5 $10 bills. Do this by pressing these keys in order:

$$5 \quad \times \quad 1 \quad 0 \quad =$$

The answer that appears in the display is 50, or $50.00. Enter this on the line for loose $10 bills. Then add the total to memory by pressing the M+ key.

Follow these steps for each full package and loose dollar denomination.

STEP 2 ▶ *Find the total bills.*

Find the total bills by finding the total of the amounts you have been adding to memory. Do this by pressing the MR/C or MR key:

MR/C   or   MR

The answer that appears in the display is 3714, or $3,714.00. Enter this amount on the Total bills to be deposited line of the form.

STEP 3 ▶ *Clear memory.*

Now clear the memory by pressing the MC key once or by pressing the MR/C key twice.

STEP 4 ▶ *For each line of coins, multiply the number of coins by the value and store the total in memory.*

Calculate the totals for each full wrapper of coins and for the loose coins in the same way that you found the totals for bills. Enter each total in the form. After you find each total, press the M+ key to store the amount in memory.

STEP 5 ▶ *Find the total coins.*

Find the total coins by pressing the MR or MR/C key. The answer that appears in the display is 267.64. Enter this amount on the Total coins to be deposited line of the report.

STEP 6 ▶ *Clear memory.*

Clear memory by pressing the MC key once or the MR/C key twice.

STEP 7 ▶ *Add the total bills to total coins.*

Find the total amount of the deposit by pressing these keys in order:

3   7   1   4   +   2   6   7   •   6   4   =

The answer that appears in the display, 3981.64, is the total amount to be deposited. Enter this on the Total Cash To Be Deposited line of the form.

On a sheet of paper, write the headings **Statement Number** and **Words**. Next, choose the words that match the statements. Write each word you choose next to the statement number it matches. Be careful; not all the words listed should be used.

Statements	Words
1. Bills and coins that do not fill their wrappers	amount tendered
2. A form issued for cash received	bank deposit
3. A checklist of money to be deposited	cash overage
4. Money placed in a bank account	cash shortage
5. A form which lists all money deposited in a bank account	change fund
6. When there is more cash in the register at the end of the day than there should be	crossfooting
7. The amount of cash given to the cashier by the customer	deposit slip
8. Magnetic Ink Character Recognition	detailed audit tape
9. Adding a row of figures across a business form	loose bills and coins
10. A record of all cash register transactions	MICR
	receipt
	tally sheet

PROBLEM SOLVING MODEL FOR: *Preparing Bank Deposits*

STEP 1 ▶ *Separate and wrap the bills.*

STEP 2 ▶ *Separate and wrap the coins.*

STEP 3 ▶ *Tally the money to be deposited.*

STEP 4 ▶ *Prepare the deposit slip.*

APPLICATION PROBLEMS

PROBLEM | **20-1** ▶ You are a cashier for Velma's Speedy Shop. The store has an account at Denison City Bank. At the close of each day, you must sort the cash in your cash register and prepare the money for deposit.

Directions

20-1

Total cash for Oct. 5 = $2,638.75

The cash to be tallied and deposited for three days of the week is listed in this problem. For each day:

a. Prepare a tally sheet like the one in Illustration 20C (page 190).
b. Prepare a deposit slip like the one in Illustration 20D (page 191).

October 5:		October 6:		October 7:	
Quantity	Denomination	Quantity	Denomination	Quantity	Denomination
8	$50.00 bills	3	$100.00 bills	12	$100.00 bills
57	$20.00 bills	4	$ 50.00 bills	25	$ 50.00 bills
48	$10.00 bills	28	$ 20.00 bills	41	$ 20.00 bills
87	$ 5.00 bills	39	$ 10.00 bills	22	$ 10.00 bills
121	$ 1.00 bills	101	$ 5.00 bills	62	$ 5.00 bills
82	$ 0.50 coins	145	$ 1.00 bills	74	$ 1.00 bills
45	$ 0.25 coins	67	$ 0.50 coins	59	$ 0.50 coins
67	$ 0.10 coins	29	$ 0.25 coins	21	$ 0.25 coins
33	$ 0.05 coins	55	$ 0.10 coins	88	$ 0.10 coins
215	$ 0.01 coins	102	$ 0.05 coins	78	$ 0.05 coins
		325	$ 0.01 coins	189	$ 0.01 coins

Problem 20-2 may be found in the Working Papers.

CHAPTER 4

Reinforcement Activities

DISCUSSION

1. For five days last week, a new cashier had cash shortages of $4.25 and $3.12 and cash overages of $5.67, $3.14, and $4.45.
   a. What is one possible consequence of the cash overages?
   b. What is one possible consequence of the cash shortages?
   c. If you were the cashier's supervisor, what possible actions might you take if the shortages and overages continue?

2. Cashiers must know how to handle money accurately. One step that a cashier can take to insure accuracy is to count all money that is received from others before a receipt is given.

   Suppose that you are a cashier, and another employee gives you some cash and tells you that it amounts to $113.56. What might happen if you write a receipt for $113.56 and give it to the employee without counting the money first?

CRITICAL THINKING

In order to make a good choice or decision, it is very important to carefully study all the factors involved. By not doing so, a wrong choice might be made. For example, before buying an item of clothing, you probably think about the price, size, style, store location, return policy, color, opinions of friends, and other factors before purchasing. By considering these factors, you are more likely to make a decision you are happy with. Imagine that you never considered the size of a clothing item before purchasing. You probably wouldn't be too happy with the fit.

This critical thinking strategy of *studying all the factors involved* before making a decision can be applied to many different types of situations. For example, what are the factors you would study before purchasing a new automobile? In this case you might consider price, gas mileage, or color. Make a list of all the other items that you would consider before buying a car. At this time, do not worry about their importance.

Suppose that you are a cashier at a store. A customer whose purchases total $7.14 gives you a $10 bill.

1. Write what you would say to the customer as you hand back the change if you were using a cash register that automatically figured the correct change.
2. Write what you would say to the customer as you hand back the change if you were using a cash register that did not figure change.

RECORD KEEPING CAREERS

Using the newspapers that are in your school library or at home, find the want ad section. Then:

1. Identify three titles of jobs that require the handling of cash.
2. List the requirements for each job on a sheet of paper. Then cross out those that are the same or very similar.
3. Be prepared to discuss the job titles and the job requirements in class.

REVIEWING WHAT YOU HAVE LEARNED

On a sheet of paper, write the headings **Statement Number** and **Words**. Next, choose the words that best complete the statements. Write each word you choose next to the statement number it completes. Be careful; not all the words listed should be used.

Statements	Words
1. When a cashier receives bills from a customer, the cashier should put the bills _____ .	amount tendered
2. When the cashier receives money, it should be _____ before a receipt is given.	authorized
3. When a receipt is given for cash, the _____ is made out first and left in the receipt book.	cash register
4. The money that a cashier is given at the start of the day is called the _____ .	change fund
5. When a store uses a cash register with a scanner and products with the _____ , the cashier does not have to enter the data about each item sold.	counted
6. The cashier can find out the total sales by reading the _____ .	detailed audit tape
7. The bank account number is usually printed on the deposit slip in _____ .	loose bills and coins
8. Some stores will not cash _____ .	MICR
	on the register
	stub
	third-party checks
	Universal Product Code

Statements	Words

9. The bills and coins left over after all others have been placed in full wrappers or rolls are called _____ .
10. The amount of money the customer gives the cashier in payment of a bill is called the _____ .

MASTERY PROBLEM

Vera Dunlap is cashier no. 6 at Palmer's SuperMart. Vera uses cash register no. 1 with the keys shown in Illustration 16C on page 159. On April 9, Vera serves customers, makes change, and proves cash.

Phase 1: Making Change

Directions

a. A customer buys the items shown below. Copy the items and prices; next to each item, write the name of the department key Vera should use to enter the item into her cash register.

Items Bought		Department Keys Used
$8.19	Roast beef	
$0.98	Pineapple	
$0.88	Eggs	
$2.89	Battery	5.58
$1.48	Milk	

(a)
Use the GENERAL
MERCH. key for the
battery.

b. After entering each item, Vera's register shows a total sale of $14.42. The amount tendered by the customer is $20.00. List the types and numbers of bills or coins Vera should give the customer for change.

Phase 2: Proving Cash

Vera started the day with a change fund of $150.00. At the end of the day, her register's detailed audit tape showed total cash sales of $1,978.34 and total cash paid out for bottle refunds of $51.67. She found the cash listed as follows in the drawer. There were no checks.

(b)
Cash short = $1.00

Quantity	Denomination	Quantity	Denomination
5	$50.00 bills	72	$ 0.50 coins
27	$20.00 bills	88	$ 0.25 coins
81	$10.00 bills	96	$ 0.10 coins
33	$ 5.00 bills	13	$ 0.05 coins
239	$ 1.00 bills	342	$ 0.01 coins

CHECKPOINT

Directions

a. Prepare a cash count report.
b. Prepare a proof of cash.

Phase 3: Preparing a Summary of Departmental Sales Report

Sam Loeb is the manager of Palmer's SuperMart. Sam must prepare a summary of departmental sales report for the four cash registers of the store on April 9.

Directions

a. Verify each departmental sales report by comparing it to the detailed audit tape shown following it. Correct any reports that contain errors.

Cashier No.: 6	Register No.: 1
Department	**Total**
Meat	$ 512.89
Dairy	307.14
Produce	222.76
Bakery	202.18
Grocery	217.89
Health and beauty	310.20
General merchandise	205.28
Total	$1,978.34

Signature: *Vera Dunlap*

Date: *April 9,* 19 --

Cashier No.: 4	Register No.: 2
Department	**Total**
Meat	$ 821.25
Dairy	407.12
Produce	388.98
Bakery	310.22
Grocery	289.99
Health and beauty	448.12
General merchandise	376.98
Total	$3,042.66

Signature: *Andy Armstrong*

Date: *April 9,* 19 --

ME	512.89
DA	307.14
PR	222.76
BA	202.18
GR	217.89
HE	310.20
GE	205.28
TL	1978.34
04/09/--	RG1

ME	821.25
DA	407.12
PR	388.98
BA	310.22
GR	289.99
HE	448.12
GE	376.98
TL	3042.66
04/09/--	RG2

Cashier No.: 7	Register No.: 3
Department	**Total**
Meat	$ 641.41
Dairy	325.11
Produce	387.01
Bakery	135.66
Grocery	333.51
Health and beauty	278.87
General merchandise	448.91
Total	$2,550.48

Signature: *Edna O'Brien*

Date: *April 9,* 19 --

Cashier No.: 2	Register No.: 4
Department	**Total**
Meat	$ 701.68
Dairy	390.09
Produce	412.81
Bakery	200.18
Grocery	339.98
Health and beauty	100.98
General merchandise	414.54
Total	$2,568.27

Signature: *Deane Formen*

Date: *April 9,* 19 --

```
ME        641.41              ME        701.68
DA        325.11              DA        390.09
PR        387.01              PR        412.81
BA        135.66              BA        200.18
GR        333.51              GR        339.98
HE        278.87              HE        108.99
GE        448.91              GE        414.54
TL       2550.48              TL       2568.27

04/09/--        RG3           04/09/--        RG4
```

b. Copy the amounts from the departmental sales report for each register to the summary of departmental sales report for the whole store.

c. Find the column, line, and grand totals. Verify them by crossfooting, and double rule the report.

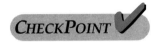

CHECKPOINT ✔

(c)
Grand total = $10,139.75

Phase 4: Tallying and Depositing the Cash

Palmer's SuperMart has an account at Federal Bank and Trust Co. At the close of April 9, Sam must sort the cash in the registers and prepare the money for deposit. The sorted cash is listed below.

Directions

CHECKPOINT ✔

(a)
Total cash = $11,139.75

a. Prepare a tally sheet.
b. Prepare a deposit slip.

Quantity	Denomination
63	$50.00 bills
165	$20.00 bills
325	$10.00 bills
184	$ 5.00 bills
367	$ 1.00 bills
178	$ 0.50 coins
199	$ 0.25 coins
71	$ 0.10 coins
56	$ 0.05 coins
410	$ 0.01 coins

REVIEWING YOUR BUSINESS VOCABULARY

This activity may be found in the Working Papers.

CHAPTER 5

Checking Account Records

*I*n today's world, it is not always convenient or safe to use cash when paying for items. Imagine for a moment that you just purchased a new automobile and that your payments will be $451.78 a month. Would you feel comfortable putting that much cash in an envelope and mailing it? Would you want to drive across your state every month to pay your bill in person? Fortunately, there is an easier way.

The safest and most convenient way for you to pay your bills is to write checks and mail them directly to the companies. By using checks, you can avoid the expense and trouble of visiting each company's office to pay cash. Checks also provide you with a record of your expenses. And since your money is in the bank, it is well protected.

In Chapter 5, you will learn how to open a checking account, prepare deposit slips, write checks, and make sure your checking account is accurate. Learning how to properly handle a checking account is a skill that you will use the rest of your life. A Calculator Tip will be given for doing the math on check stubs.

JOB 21 ▶ OPENING A BANK CHECKING ACCOUNT

APPLIED MATH PREVIEW

Copy and complete these problems.

1. $3,500.00	2. $251.50	3. $ 0.95	4. $324.58	5. $1,235.87
+ 250.00	+ 0.90	+ 0.87	10.90	923.33
			+ 0.89	+ 200.08

BUSINESS TERMS PREVIEW

- **ABA number** • **Forged signature** • **Individual checking account** •
- **Joint checking account** • **Personalized deposit slip** • **Signature card** •

GOALS

1. To learn how to open a bank checking account.
2. To learn how to complete a signature card.
3. To learn how to complete a deposit slip for a personal checking account.

Dave Rodman is a full-time office worker. On June 1, Dave decides to open his own typing and word processing service. He plans to do typing and word processing out of his home. To start his business, Dave must pay these bills:

> $1,975.00 for a word processing system and printer
> $350.00 to Allied Office Supply Company for an office desk
> $82.45 for office supplies

The safest and most convenient way for Dave to pay these bills is to write checks and mail them directly to the companies. In this way, Dave will not have the expense and trouble of visiting each company's office. Also, Dave's money will be protected since it is in a bank.

To be able to pay bills by check, Dave must open a bank checking account. Dave can open either an individual checking account or a joint checking account. An **individual checking account** lets only Dave write checks on the account. A **joint checking account** lets Dave share the account with another person or persons.

The first step in opening a checking account is to select a bank that will meet your needs. In choosing a bank, ask such questions as

—Is the bank convenient to your home or business?
—Does the bank provide the services you need?
—Does the bank charge for a checking account?

KEY Terms

Individual checking account. Used by only one person.

Joint checking account. Used by two or more persons.

SAMPLE PROBLEM

Dave considered the questions above and decided to open his checking account at the Fifth National Bank. After work on Wednesday, Dave went to the Fifth National Bank to open his account under the name of Dave's Word Processing Service. Dave asked the bank's receptionist about opening an account, and she took him to see Ms. Carla Miller. Ms. Miller is a bank employee who handles all new accounts. Ms. Miller told Dave he needed to do two things to open a checking account:

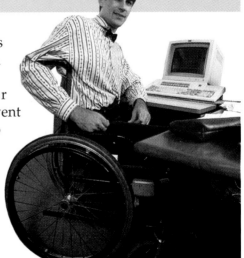

1. Fill out a **signature card**.
2. Make an opening deposit of money.

Filling Out a Signature Card

Ms. Miller asked Dave to fill out and sign a signature card like the one shown in Illustration 21A. Dave learned that a signature card is a very important document because it allows the bank to make sure that signatures on Dave's checks are actually his. The bank would be held responsible if payment was made on a check with a **forged signature**.

▓▓▓▓▓ F I F T H	ACCOUNT NUMBER ___156-8284___
▓▓▓▓ NATIONAL BANK	
411 Peachtree Road NE, Atlanta, GA 30303-0411	

AUTHORIZED SIGNATURE FOR:

NAME ___Dave's Word Processing Service___

ADDRESS ___212 Dobbs Court, Atlanta, GA 30304-0212___

TELEPHONE ___(404) 555-1711___

SIGNATURE ___Dave Rodman___

DATE ___June 1, 19--___

Illustration 21A   A signature card

Ms. Miller typed in all information except for the signature itself. She entered the business name, address, phone number, and the date. She also gave Dave an account number. The signature card was signed only by Dave. This means that no one other than Dave can write checks on the account. So, Dave has opened an individual checking account with his bank.

Making Deposits

Dave is now ready to make his first deposit. He decided to take $2,500.00 in cash from his savings. He also has a $150.00 check written out to him for typing business letters last month. Dave decided to deposit the $2,500.00 from his savings and also his $150.00 check. Thus, Dave's opening deposit will be for $2,650.00 ($2,500.00 + $150.00).

When money is deposited in a checking account, a deposit slip must be completed. Most banks today use personalized deposit slips. A **personalized deposit slip** is one on which the depositor's name, address, and account number are printed. This makes it easier for banks to process deposits and helps ensure that deposits will be processed correctly.

Dave completed a personalized deposit slip like the one shown in Illustration 21B on page 203. Since different types of money can be deposited (bills, coins, and checks), each type is listed separately on the deposit slip.

For DEPOSIT to the Account of

37-502
0810

Dave's Word Processing Service
212 Dobbs Ct.
Atlanta, GA 30304-0212

DATE _June 1_____ 19 _ _

FIFTH
NATIONAL
BANK
Atlanta, GA

**Subject to the Terms and Conditions of this Bank's
Collection Agreement**

⑆081001351⑆ 1568⑈284⑈

	Dollars	Cents
BILLS	2,500	00
COINS		
Checks as Follows Properly Endorsed		
Roy Golden	150	00
TOTAL DEPOSIT	2,650	00

Dave followed these steps in completing the deposit slip:

STEP 1 ▶ **Enter the date.**

Dave recorded June 1, 19--, in the Date space.

STEP 2 ▶ **Enter bills deposited.**

Dave recorded $2,500.00 on the Bills line.

STEP 3 ▶ **Enter coins deposited.**

You learned how to record coins deposited in Job 20. Dave had no coins to deposit, so he left the Coins line blank.

STEP 4 ▶ **Enter checks deposited.**

Dave is depositing a check for $150.00, so he entered this amount on the first line for checks. For future reference, Dave wrote the name of the person who gave him the check, Roy Golden, in the space provided. Some banks require that you enter instead a number assigned to the bank of the person who wrote the check. The number is called the **ABA number**. Fifth National Bank's ABA number, listed at the top of the deposit slip, is 37-502/0810. If Roy Golden's bank had an ABA number of 2-146/3624, Dave would enter 2-146 (leaving out 3624 to save space) on the line with the $150.00. (See Illustration 21C.)

K E Y Terms

ABA number A number assigned to banks.

	Dollars	Cents
BILLS		
COINS		
Checks as Follows Properly Endorsed		
2-146	150	00
TOTAL DEPOSIT		

Many deposits include more than just a few checks. If this occurs, the back of the deposit slip is used. The back is usually filled with 15 to 20 additional lines for checks. The total of the back is then recorded on the front side.

STEP 5 ▶ **Calculate and enter the total.**

Dave then added the bills, coins, and checks, and entered the total, $2,650.00, on the Total Deposit line.

After making his deposit, Dave received a receipt for the deposit from the bank. Most banks today use a machine that prints out a receipt like the one shown in Illustration 21D below.

The number 156-8284 is Dave's account number which appears on both his signature card (Illustration 21A on page 202) and on his personalized deposit slip (Illustration 21B on page page 203).

Illustration 21D Dave's deposit receipt

FIFTH NATIONAL BANK

The receipt of deposit should be held until verified with your next statement of account. Checks and other items are received for deposit subject to the terms and conditions of this bank's collection agreement.

JUNE 01, 19-- #156-8284 $2,650.00

This is a Receipt for Your Deposit

BUILDING YOUR BUSINESS VOCABULARY

On a sheet of paper, write the headings **Statement Number** and **Words**. Next, choose the words that match the statements. Write each word you choose next to the statement number it matches. Be careful; not all the words listed should be used.

Statements	Words
1. A name falsely signed by someone else	ABA number
2. A number assigned to banks	coins
3. An account used by two or more people	deposit
4. An account used by only one person	deposit slip
5. A form completed when a deposit is made	forged signature
6. A form used to indicate to the bank which signatures to accept on signed checks	individual checking account
7. A deposit slip on which the depositor's name and address are preprinted	joint checking account
	personalized deposit slip
	signature card

PROBLEM SOLVING MODEL FOR: *Completing a Deposit Slip*

STEP 1 ▶ *Enter the date.*

STEP 2 ▶ *Enter bills deposited.*

STEP 3 ▶ *Enter coins deposited.*

STEP 4 ▶ *Enter checks deposited.*

STEP 5 ▶ *Calculate and enter the total.*

APPLICATION PROBLEMS

PROBLEM | **21-1** ▶ You are opening your own checking account.

Directions

21-1
Make sure to fill in every line and use the current year for the date

Prepare a signature card like the one shown in Illustration 21A on page 202.

a. Enter your account number, 495-8486, on the Account Number line.
b. Print your name on the Name line.
c. Print your complete address on the Address line.
d. Enter your complete telephone number on the Telephone line.
e. Sign your name on the Signature line.
f. Enter the date, March 1, 19--, on the Date line.

PROBLEM | **21-2** ▶ On March 1, your employer, Sam Rosenberg, asks you to prepare the opening deposit for Sam's Sailboats.

Directions

21-2
If your work is correct, the total deposit should equal $255.69

Prepare a deposit slip for the following items:

| Bills: | $175.00 | Checks: | $50.00 from Sue Linzer |
| Coins: | $ 5.00 | | $25.69 from Donald Ingrum |

On July 15, Griffin Taylor started his own bicycle shop. In order to pay bills by check, Griffin opened a checking account under the name Griffin Cyclery. You have been hired as his record keeper.

CHECKPOINT ✔

21-3
If your work is correct, the total deposit should equal $537.68

Directions

Prepare a deposit slip for Griffin. He is depositing the following items on July 15:

Bills:	1	$50 bills	Coins:	$ 25.00 in dimes
	3	$20 bills		
	5	$10 bills	Checks:	$245.68 from Lisa Todd
	3	$ 5 bills		$ 80.00 from Lane Kirkland
	12	$ 1 bills		

Problems 21-4 and 21-5 may be found in the Working Papers.

APPLIED MATH PREVIEW

Copy and complete these problems.

1.	2.	3.	4.
$3,458.89	$4,638.70	$6,394.58	$2,911.52
485.49	- 729.58	- 938.48	- 318.00
4,234.87			
254.68	+ 346.92	+ 714.60	+ 945.39
596.34			
+ 867.50			

BUSINESS TERMS PREVIEW

- Check • Check protector • Check stub • Checkbook •
- Drawee • Drawer • Issue • Legible • Payee •
- Postdated • Void •

GOALS

1. To learn how to complete check stubs.
2. To learn how to write checks.

UNDERSTANDING THE JOB

KEY Terms

Checkbook. A book of checks.

In Job 21, you learned that a bank checking account is a safe and convenient way to pay bills. You also learned that to open a checking account you must fill out a signature card and make a deposit of money. In Job 22, you will learn how to write checks and keep a record of checks in a checkbook.

On June 1, Dave Rodman opened a checking account at the Fifth National Bank. He was asked to fill out the signature card shown in Illustration 21A on page 202 in Job 21. Dave was asked to fill out a deposit slip and make an opening deposit. (See Illustration 21B on page 203, Job 21.) The bank then gave Dave a supply of deposit slips and a **checkbook** with pages of checks like the one shown in Illustration 22A on page 208.

The example in this job is a checking account for a business. However, checking accounts can be useful in your personal life, too. Paying your bills with checks is safer and more convenient than sending cash in the mail.

The steps for opening an account that were presented in Job 21 and the steps for writing checks that are presented in this job apply to personal checking accounts as well as business checking accounts.

Illustration 22A   Check and stub

Notice that there are two parts to each check in Dave's checkbook:

1. The **check stub** which remains in the checkbook as a permanent record of checks written.
2. The **check** which will be detached from the stub and sent to the company or person to whom Dave owes the money.

The stub gives Dave a record of the important facts about any check that he writes. Careful people always fill out the stub before writing the check. If they did not do this, they might mail the check and then find they have no record of the details about it.

Dave is now ready to use his checking account to pay his bills. Study the completed check shown in Illustration 22B.

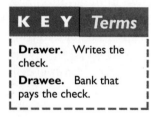

> **KEY Terms**
>
> **Check stub.** Part of check kept by depositor.
> **Check.** A written order by the depositor to his or her bank to pay a company or person.

Illustration 22B   Three parties to a check

> **KEY Terms**
>
> **Drawer.** Writes the check.
> **Drawee.** Bank that pays the check.

Notice there are three parties involved in the check:

1. The **drawer**. The drawer is the person who writes the check. Dave has ordered the Fifth National Bank to *draw* $350.00 out of his account and pay it to Allied Office Supply Company.
2. The **drawee**. The drawee is the bank that is ordered to pay a check from an account. The Fifth National Bank has been ordered by Dave to pay $350.00 out of his account.

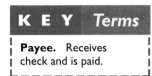

K E Y Terms

Payee. Receives check and is paid.

3. The **payee**. The payee is the one who will be paid. Allied Office Supply Company will receive $350.00 when this check is presented for payment.

*S*AMPLE PROBLEM

K E Y Terms

Issue. To send out.

On June 6, Dave **issued** Check No. 1 for $350.00 to Allied Office Supply Company for an office desk. The completed check and check stub are shown in Illustration 22C below. Here are the steps Dave used to complete the stub and check.

| NO. 1 | $ *350.00* | | Dave's Word Processing Service | | No. **1** |

Dave's Word Processing Service
212 Dobbs Ct.
Atlanta, GA 30304-0212

NO. 1 $ *350.00*
DATE *June 6, 19--*
TO *Allied Office Supply Company*
FOR *office desk*

	DOLLARS	CENTS
BAL. BRO'T. FOR'D.		
AMT. DEPOSITED	*2650*	*00*
TOTAL	*2650*	*00*
AMT. THIS CHECK	*350*	*00*
BAL. CAR'D. FOR'D.	*2300*	*00*

No. **1**
Date *June 6* 19 -- 37-502 / 0810

PAY TO THE ORDER OF *Allied Office Supply Company* $ *350.00*

Three hundred fifty 00/100 ——— Dollars
For Classroom Use Only

FIFTH NATIONAL BANK
Atlanta, GA

Dave Rodman

⑆08100135⑆ 1568284⑈

NO. 2 $ _____
DATE _____
TO _____
FOR _____

	DOLLARS	CENTS
BAL. BRO'T. FOR'D.	*2300*	*00*
AMT. DEPOSITED		
TOTAL		
AMT. THIS CHECK		
BAL. CAR'D. FOR'D.		

Dave's Word Processing Service
212 Dobbs Ct.
Atlanta, GA 30304-0212

No. **2**
Date _____ 19 ___ 37-502 / 0810

PAY TO THE ORDER OF _____ $ _____

_____ Dollars
For Classroom Use Only

FIFTH NATIONAL BANK
Atlanta, GA

⑆08100135⑆ 1568284⑈

Illustration 22C   A portion of Dave's checkbook

STEP 1 ▶ *Complete the top half of the stub.*

Notice that the top half of the stub contains the following facts:

1. *Check number:* No. 1
2. *Amount:* $350.00
3. *Date:* June 6, 19--
4. *Payee's name:* Allied Office Supply Company
5. *The reason the check is issued:* office desk

Fill in the required information on the top half of the stub.

STEP 2 ▶ *Complete the bottom half of the stub.*

After filling in the top half of the stub, complete the bottom half of the stub. Notice that the bottom half of the stub contains

1. *Balance Brought Forward (Bal. Bro't. For'd.).* Usually this space shows the amount of money left in the checking account after the last check was written. Since this was a new account, there was no previous balance to be brought forward. So, no amount was written in this space.
2. *Amount Deposited (Amt. Deposited).* The $2,650.00 recorded in this space is the amount Dave deposited on June 1. Although no space is provided for the date of the deposit, some record keepers like to show the date on the stub. The number 6 in "6/1" stands for June because June is the sixth month of the year. It is a good idea to memorize the number for each month. You can use this shortcut for writing dates when the lack of space makes it necessary.
3. *Total.* Dave found the total by adding the balance brought forward to the deposit of $2,650.00. Since there was no amount to be brought forward, the total is $2,650.00.
4. *Amount of This Check (Amt. This Check).* Dave wrote the amount of the check, $350.00, in this space.
5. *Balance Carried Forward (Bal. Car'd. For'd.).* Dave found this amount by subtracting the amount of the check from the total:

Total	$2,650.00
Amt. This Check	- 350.00
Bal. Car'd. For'd.	$2,300.00

Since checks are always subtracted from the total, a minus sign is not used on the check stub. Notice that this amount, $2,300.00, is shown as the balance brought forward on the stub of Check No. 2. After each check stub is completed, the new balance is always carried forward to the next check stub. Before Dave issues Check No. 2, he will be able to look at this amount and see if there is enough money left in the account to pay the check.

Once Dave completed the stub, he then filled in the check using the following steps. His completed check is shown in Illustration 22C on page 209.

STEP 3 ▶ *Always use ink.*

Checks should always be written in permanent ink. Names, dates, or amounts written in pencil or erasable ink can be easily changed. Avoid using broad felt-tipped pens as their broad tip makes it easier to forge a signature.

STEP 4 ▶ *Write legibly.*

Write **legibly**. Checks that cannot be read will not be accepted or paid by the bank.

STEP 5 ▶ *Use the current date.*

Write the current date on all checks. Checks with old dates may not be accepted by businesses. Checks that are **postdated**, that is, marked with a future date, often cause problems when they are cashed early. For example, if the checkholder cashes the check before the written date, there may not be enough money in the account to pay it. This can result in serious legal problems for the owner of the checking account.

STEP 6 ▶ *Write the name of the payee.*

After the words "Pay to the Order of," write the name of the payee. Remember, the payee is the person or business to whom a check is issued.

STEP 7 ▶ *Write the amount of the check in figures.*

Write the amount of dollars in figures close to the printed dollar sign, so that no other number can be added. Write the amount of cents after the decimal point.

STEP 8 ▶ *Write the amount of the check in words.*

Start writing the amount of the check in words at the left margin of the check. Write the number of cents as a fraction. Fill the unused space with a line all the way to the printed word "Dollars":

Three hundred fifty 00/100————————Dollars

Only the first letter of the entire amount is capitalized. When you write the amount in words, remember to write the numbers twenty-one through ninety-nine with a hyphen.

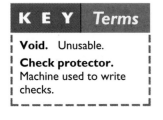

STEP 9 ▶ *Sign your name.*

Sign your name to the check in exactly the way that it appears on the signature card.

If you make an error in writing a check, make the check unusable by writing **VOID** in large letters on both the stub and check. A check with an erasure or correction will be questioned by the bank. Most people destroy voided personal checks, but businesses usually keep all voided checks for their records.

Look at the number, 37-502/0810, shown in the upper right corner of the check in Illustration 22D below. This is called the ABA number. ABA numbers are assigned to banks by the American Bankers Association. They are used to help sort checks so that they can be sent to the right bank for collection. As you learned in Job 21, the top two parts of the ABA number may be used to list checks for deposit.

K E Y | *Terms*

Void. Unusable.
Check protector. Machine used to write checks.

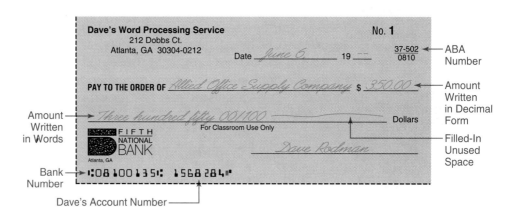

Illustration 22D   Rules of check writing

The numbers in the lower left corner of the check, 0810 0135 and 1568 284, are the bank number and Dave's account number, respectively. These numbers are printed in MICR so that they can be read by the bank's computer. The ABA number, bank number, and Dave's account number are also printed on all his deposit slips.

On June 12, Dave issued Check No. 2 for $82.50 to the Superior Book Company for word processing books. The check and stub for Check No. 2 are shown in Illustration 22E on page 213. (Notice that the check stub for Check No. 1 is still in the checkbook even though Dave has already mailed the check.) Dave carried forward the balance of $2,217.50 to the stub of Check No. 3.

Businesses that issue many checks may use a machine known as a check writer or **check protector**. This machine prints the amount on the check in a way that makes changes impossible.

Other businesses may prepare their checks using a computer. Printers are used in a computerized system to print paychecks and checks to those companies to whom the business owes money.

Check Stub No. 1

NO. 1	$ 350.00
DATE	June 6, 19--
TO	Allied Office Supply Company
FOR	office desk

	DOLLARS	CENTS
BAL. BRO'T. FOR'D.	6/1	
AMT. DEPOSITED	2650	00
TOTAL	2650	00
AMT. THIS CHECK	350	00
BAL. CAR'D. FOR'D.	2300	00

Check Stub No. 2

NO. 2	$ 82.50
DATE	June 12, 19--
TO	Superior Book Company
FOR	word processing book

	DOLLARS	CENTS
BAL. BRO'T. FOR'D.	2300	00
AMT. DEPOSITED		
TOTAL	2300	00
AMT. THIS CHECK	82	50
BAL. CAR'D. FOR'D.	2217	50

Check No. 2

Dave's Word Processing Service
212 Dobbs Ct.
Atlanta, GA 30304-0212

No. 2

37-502
0810

Date June 12 19 --

PAY TO THE ORDER OF Superior Book Company $ 82.50

Eighty-two 50/100 _____ Dollars

For Classroom Use Only

FIFTH NATIONAL BANK
Atlanta, GA

Dave Rodman

⑆081001351⑆ 1568284⑈

Check Stub No. 3

NO. 3	$
DATE	
TO	
FOR	

	DOLLARS	CENTS
BAL. BRO'T. FOR'D.	2217	50
AMT. DEPOSITED		
TOTAL		
AMT. THIS CHECK		
BAL. CAR'D. FOR'D.		

Check No. 3

Dave's Word Processing Service
212 Dobbs Ct.
Atlanta, GA 30304-0212

No. 3

37-502
0810

Date _____ 19 ____

PAY TO THE ORDER OF _____ $ _____

_____ Dollars

For Classroom Use Only

FIFTH NATIONAL BANK
Atlanta, GA

⑆081001351⑆ 1568284⑈

Illustration 22E   Dave's checkbook on June 12

BUILDING YOUR BUSINESS VOCABULARY

On a sheet of paper, write the headings **Statement Number** and **Words**. Next, choose the words that match the statements. Write each word you choose next to the statement number it matches. Be careful; not all the words listed should be used.

Statements	Words
1. The person who writes the check	ABA number
2. The part which remains in the checkbook when a check is issued	check
	check protector
3. The person to whom a check is made out and who will receive the money	check stub
	checkbook
4. The word you print across the check and the check stub when you make an error	deposit
	drawee
5. The party who is ordered to pay the amount on the check	drawer
	issue
6. A special number assigned to a bank by the American Bankers Association	legible
	MICR
7. Clear and easy to read	payee
8. To send out	postdate
9. A machine used to write checks	void
10. A written order by the drawer to the drawee to pay the payee	
11. To record a future date on a document	

PROBLEM SOLVING MODEL FOR: *Completing Check Stubs and Checks*

STEP 1 ▶ *Complete the top half of the stub.*
STEP 2 ▶ *Complete the bottom half of the stub.*
STEP 3 ▶ *Always use ink.*
STEP 4 ▶ *Write legibly.*
STEP 5 ▶ *Use the current date.*
STEP 6 ▶ *Write the name of the payee.*
STEP 7 ▶ *Write the amount of the check in figures.*
STEP 8 ▶ *Write the amount of the check in words.*
STEP 9 ▶ *Sign your name.*

*A*PPLICATION PROBLEMS

PROBLEM | **22-1** ▶ A list of amounts, in figures, is written in Column 1 of the following table. Copy each amount on a sheet of paper. Then, in Column 2, write each amount in words as it would appear on a check.

Column 1	Column 2	
1. $ 5.00	_____	Dollars
2. $ 40.00	_____	Dollars
3. $190.00	_____	Dollars
4. $ 19.50	_____	Dollars
5. $160.90	_____	Dollars
6. $ 85.47	_____	Dollars
7. $ 63.84	_____	Dollars
8. $ 47.50	_____	Dollars
9. $ 91.10	_____	Dollars
10. $240.80	_____	Dollars

PROBLEM 22-2 ▶ You are a record keeper for Pattie Fisher, who owns a sailboat rental business. On June 1, Pattie opens a checking account at the First Union State Bank with a deposit of $950.00. She puts you in charge of keeping the checkbook. You are authorized to sign the checks with your own name.

CHECKPOINT

22-2
If your work is correct, the **Bal. Car'd. For'd.** on Check Stub No. 3 should equal $506.00

Directions

a. On June 1, enter the opening deposit of $950.00 in the space for "Amt. Deposited" on the stub of Check No. 1. Fill in the total.
b. On June 5, write Check No. 1 for $75.00 to Central Power Company for utilities. Bring the new balance forward to the stub of Check No. 2.
c. On June 9, write Check No. 2 for $322.00 to Dobbs Motor Company for truck supplies. Bring the new balance forward to Check No. 3.
d. On June 12, write Check No. 3 for $47.00 to the *Star Journal* for a newspaper advertisement.

PROBLEM 22-3 ▶ You are a record keeper for Ed Ockerman, who owns and operates a sandwich shop. On October 1, Ed opens a checking account at the Cold Springs National Bank with a deposit of $860.00. He puts you in charge of keeping the checkbook. You are authorized to sign the checks with your own name.

CHECKPOINT

22-3
If your work is correct, the **Bal. Car'd. For'd.** on Check Stub No. 3 should equal $482.25

Directions

a. On October 1, enter the opening deposit of $860.00 in the space for "Amt. Deposited" on the stub of Check No. 1. Fill in the total.
b. On October 2, write Check No. 1 for $118.25 to Baker Restaurant Suppliers for linen supplies.
c. On October 5, write Check No. 2 for $97.50 to the Magic Oven Bakery for baked goods.
d. On October 6, write Check No. 3 for $162.00 to the Sterling Tableware Company for silverware.

Problems 22-4 and 22-5 may be found in the Working Papers.

APPLIED MATH PREVIEW

Copy and complete these problems.

1. $ 3,485.94	2. $ 2,495.28	3. $ 6,295.30	4. $ 8,211.45
+ 1,599.35	+ 4,695.49	- 4,566.75	- 3,254.19
- 1,579.20	- 3,678.59	+ 3,588.75	+ 4,445.60

BUSINESS TERMS PREVIEW

• **Insufficient funds** • **Voucher** • **Voucher check** •

GOALS

1. To practice making additional deposits in a checkbook.
2. To practice writing checks.
3. To learn the meaning of a voucher check.

𝒰NDERSTANDING THE JOB

KEY *Terms*

Insufficient funds.
When there is not
enough money in the
checking account to
pay a check.

You need to know the exact amount of money in a checking account before issuing a check. A business owner needs to make decisions about buying supplies or paying for personal expenses. If the balance recorded in the checkbook is lower than the correct balance, the owner may unnecessarily put off buying items necessary for business success. If the balance recorded in the checkbook is higher than the correct balance, the owner may purchase items with money that is not really available.

The bank will not pay a check that you issue unless there is enough money in your account to cover the amount of the check. If you issue a check without enough money in your account, the bank will return the check to the payee marked **"insufficient funds."** The bank will then charge you an extra fee for every check marked "insufficient funds."

If you regularly write checks that are returned for having insufficient funds, vendors may become angry if they cannot cash your checks. You may hurt your chances of obtaining loans and buying on credit in the future. Also, it is illegal to intentionally write a check that cannot be covered.

For this reason, you must keep an up-to-date record of the balance of your checking account. In this job, you will practice keeping the checkbook balance up-to-date as you record additional deposits and write checks.

SAMPLE PROBLEM

Tricia Close, who owns and operates an aerobics studio, has a checking account at the Idaho State Bank. On June 1, there was a balance of $840.00 in her checking account. On June 5, Tricia deposited the following cash:

Quantity	Denomination
18	$10.00 bills
25	$ 5.00 bills
30	$ 0.50 coins
40	$ 0.25 coins

Here are the steps Tricia Close took to make the deposit and record it in her checkbook:

STEP 1 ▶ **Prepare the deposit slip.**

Tricia counted the bills and coins to be deposited and filled out the deposit slip shown in Illustration 23A.

Illustration 23A
Deposit slip

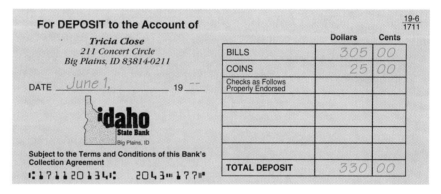

STEP 2 ▶ **Record the total deposit on the check stub.**

The total amount of the deposit, $330.00, was recorded as one amount on the stub of Check No. 71 as shown in Illustration 23B.

Illustration 23B Additional deposit on a check stub

	DOLLARS	CENTS
NO. 71		
DATE		
TO		
FOR		
BAL. BRO'T. FOR'D.	840	00
AMT. DEPOSITED 6/5	330	00
TOTAL	1,170	00
AMT. THIS CHECK		
BAL. CAR'D. FOR'D.		

STEP 3 ▶ **Add the balance brought forward to the deposit.**

Look at the Total line of the check stub in Illustration 23B on page 217. You can see that the total of $1,170.00 was found by adding the balance brought forward of $840.00 and the deposit of $330.00.

Bal. Bro't. For'd.	$ 840.00
Amt. Deposited	+ 330.00
Total	$1,170.00

Illustration 23C   A page of check stubs

NO. **71** $ _229.00_
DATE _June 6, 19--_
TO _Maximum Sound_

FOR _audio cassettes_

	DOLLARS	CENTS
BAL. BRO'T. FOR'D.	840	00
AMT. DEPOSITED ⁶/⁵	330	00
TOTAL	1,170	00
AMT. THIS CHECK	229	00
BAL. CAR'D. FOR'D.	941	00

NO. **72** $ _699.00_
DATE _June 10, 19--_
TO _Gym World_

FOR _mats and weights_

	DOLLARS	CENTS
BAL. BRO'T. FOR'D.	941	00
AMT. DEPOSITED		
TOTAL	941	00
AMT. THIS CHECK	699	00
BAL. CAR'D. FOR'D.	242	00

NO. **73** $ _275.00_
DATE _June 17, 19--_
TO _Cash_

FOR _personal use_

	DOLLARS	CENTS
BAL. BRO'T. FOR'D.	242	00
AMT. DEPOSITED ⁶/¹⁵	600	00
TOTAL	842	00
AMT. THIS CHECK	275	00
BAL. CAR'D. FOR'D.	567	00

Study the check stubs in Illustration 23C. The check stubs show how Tricia Close recorded the following checks and an additional deposit:

June 6 Issued Check No. 71 for $229.00 to Maximum Sound for audio cassettes.
    10 Issued Check No. 72 for $699.00 to GymWorld for exercise mats and hand weights.
    15 Deposited $600.00.
    17 Issued Check No. 73 for $275.00 for personal use.

Look at the stub for Check No. 73 shown in Illustration 23C. The stub shows that the check was made payable to the order of "Cash" for $275.00. This is a common procedure when cashing a check for personal use.

All of Tricia Close's business receipts are deposited in her checking account. One way she can withdraw funds from her checking account for her personal use is to cash a check at the bank. She does this by making the check payable to herself or by simply writing the word "Cash" after the words "Pay to the order of." Checks made payable to "Cash" must be handled with great care. If the check is lost, anyone finding the check may try to cash it.

Voucher Checks

Some businesses use a special kind of check called a **voucher check**. A voucher check has a special stub, or **voucher**, attached to it. The voucher shows the purpose of the check and gives a description of the payment. A voucher check is shown in Illustration 23D.

Illustration 23D
Voucher check

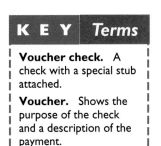

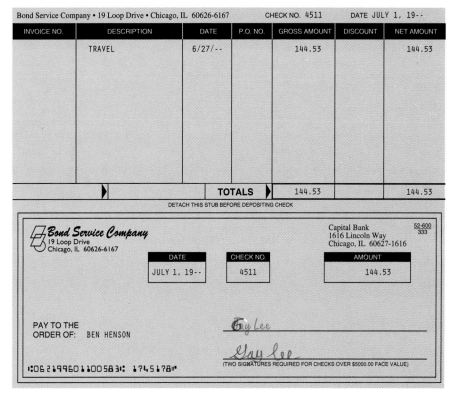

Bond Service Company • 19 Loop Drive • Chicago, IL 60626-6167   CHECK NO. 4511   DATE JULY 1, 19--

INVOICE NO.	DESCRIPTION	DATE	P.O. NO.	GROSS AMOUNT	DISCOUNT	NET AMOUNT
	TRAVEL	6/27/--		144.53		144.53
			TOTALS	144.53		144.53

DETACH THIS STUB BEFORE DEPOSITING CHECK

Bond Service Company
19 Loop Drive
Chicago, IL 60626-6167

Capital Bank
1616 Lincoln Way
Chicago, IL 60627-1616   52-600 / 333

DATE	CHECK NO.	AMOUNT
JULY 1, 19--	4511	144.53

PAY TO THE
ORDER OF: BEN HENSON

Gay Lee

Gay Lee

(TWO SIGNATURES REQUIRED FOR CHECKS OVER $5000.00 FACE VALUE)

⑆062199601⑆100583⑈ 1745178⑈

TIPS

You can use your calculator to help you do the math on check stubs. Here is how you would fill out Stubs 71, 72, and 73 in Illustration 23C with the help of your calculator.

STEP 1 ▶ *Key in the Balance Brought Forward.*

Key in the Bal. Bro't. For'd. by pressing these keys in order:

8 4 0 +

STEP 2 ▶ *Add the June 5 deposit.*

Add the June 5 deposit by pressing these keys in order:

3 3 0 =

The total, 1,170.00, will appear in the calculator's display. Record this amount in the Total space on Check Stub No. 71. *Do not clear your display.*

STEP 3 ▶ *Subtract the June 6 check.*

Subtract the June 6 check by pressing these keys in order:

-	2	2	9	=

The difference, 941.00, will appear in the calculator's display. Record this amount in the Bal. Car'd. For'd. space on Stub No. 71. Record it also in the Bal. Bro't. For'd. space on Stub No. 72. *Do not clear your display.*

STEP 4 ▶ *Subtract the June 10 check.*

Subtract the June 10 check by pressing these keys in order:

-	6	9	9	=

Record the difference, 242.00, in the proper spaces on Stubs 72 and 73. *Do not clear your display.*

STEP 5 ▶ *Add the June 15 deposit.*

Add the June 15 deposit by pressing these keys in order:

+	6	0	0	=

Record the total, 842.00, on the Total line of Stub No. 73. *Do not clear your display.*

STEP 6 ▶ *Subtract the June 17 check.*

Subtract the June 17 check by pressing these keys in order:

-	2	7	5	=

Record the difference, 567.00, on Stub No. 73 in the proper space. Now that you are finished, clear your display by pressing the C key once or the CE/C key twice.

ℬUILDING YOUR BUSINESS VOCABULARY

On a sheet of paper, write the headings **Statement Number** and **Words**. Next, choose the words that match the statements. Write each word you choose next to the statement number it matches. Be careful; not all the words listed should be used.

Statements	Words
1. The person to whom the check is made out and who will receive the money	balance brought forward
2. The word you print across a check when you have made an error	drawee
	drawer
3. The person who writes the check	insufficient funds
4. To send out	issue
5. A check that has a special stub attached	payee
6. The new checkbook balance which is recorded on the next check stub	verify
	voucher
7. The part of a voucher check that shows a description of the payment	voucher check
	void
8. When there is not enough money in the checking account to pay a check	

PROBLEM SOLVING MODEL FOR: *Keeping a Checkbook*

> **STEP 1** ▶ *Prepare the deposit slip.*
>
> **STEP 2** ▶ *Record the total deposit on the check stub.*
>
> **STEP 3** ▶ *Add the balance brought forward to the deposit.*

APPLICATION PROBLEMS

PROBLEM **23-1** ▶ On May 1, Leigh Ann King, who owns a catering business, had a balance of $3,890.57 in a checking account. She issued checks and made a deposit as follows:

CHECKPOINT

23-1
If your work is correct, the **Bal. Car'd. For'd.** on Check Stub No. 93 should equal $1,717.23

May	5	Issued Check No. 91 for $234.69 to the Huddle Shop for new uniforms.
	8	Deposited $511.35.
	14	Issued Check No. 92 for $450.00 to Carter Realty Co. for shop rent.
	21	Issued Check No. 93 for $2,000.00 to Russell Motor Company for down payment on a car.

Directions

Complete the check stubs for Check Nos. 91–93 as they would appear in Leigh Ann's checkbook.

PROBLEM **23-2** ▶ On June 1, Alfred West, a lawyer, had a balance of $1,865.40 in his checking account. He issued checks and made a deposit as follows:

23-2
If your work is correct, the
Bal. Car'd. For'd. on
Check Stub No. 173 should
equal $1,162.90

June   4   Issued Check No. 171 for $877.20 to Heckman's Travel Service
           for travel to a convention.
      10   Deposited $635.50.
      13   Issued Check No. 172 for $335.80 to Soundniques for an
           intercom system.
      25   Issued Check No. 173 for $125.00 to cash for personal use.

Directions

Complete the check stubs for Check Nos. 171–173 as they would
appear in Alfred's checkbook.

PROBLEM   **23-3** ▶   You are a record keeper for the Carlson Company. On September 1,
the Carlson Company opened a checking account at the Knoxville
National Bank with a deposit of $4,500.00. You are placed in charge
of keeping the checkbook. You are authorized to sign the checks with
your own name.

Directions

23-3
If your work is correct, the
Bal. Car'd. For'd. on
Check Stub No. 103 should
equal $3,565.12

a.   On September 1, enter the opening deposit on the stub of Check
     No. 101.
b.   On September 4, write Check No. 101 for $700.00 to King Realty
     for office rent.
c.   On September 8, write Check No. 102 for $495.78 to Consolidated
     Products Company for office supplies.
d.   On September 15, you deposit the following cash:

Quantity	Denomination
5	$20.00 bills
15	$10.00 bills
18	$ 5.00 bills
42	$ 1.00 bills
18	$ 0.50 coins
16	$ 0.25 coins
30	$ 0.10 coins
21	$ 0.05 coins

Prepare the deposit slip. Enter the total amount of the deposit on
the stub of Check No. 103, and enter the new balance on the Total
line.
e.   On September 25, write Check No. 103 for $138.15 to Lakewood
     Service Company for repairs to the air conditioning system.

Problem 23-4 may be found in the Working Papers.

USING A CHECK REGISTER

BUSINESS TERM PREVIEW

• **Check register** •

GOALS

1. To learn how to use a check register.
2. To learn how to write checks for less than one dollar.

𝒰NDERSTANDING THE JOB

KEY Terms

Check register. Book for recording checks and deposits when stubs are not used.

In Jobs 22 and 23, you learned that you can keep an up-to-date record of your checking account by completing a check stub each time you write a check. Another way to keep an up-to-date record is to keep a **check register**. Most people who open a personal checking account will use a check register instead of check stubs.

A check with a check stub is somewhat different from a check used with a check register. The check stub is attached to the check. The check is removed to make a payment. The check stub stays in the checkbook. A checkbook with stubs is usually more expensive than a checkbook with a check register. Also, a checkbook with stubs is often too big to fit in a purse or pocket.

A check used with a check register has no stub attached. The check register is a book that is separate from the pad of checks. The same information that is recorded on a stub is recorded in the check register. The check register, therefore, contains a record of each check that is written and each deposit that is made. A checkbook with a check register is usually less expensive than a checkbook with stubs. Also, a checkbook with a check register is small enough to fit in a purse or pocket.

In this job, you will practice keeping the check register up-to-date as you record additional deposits and write checks.

On March 1, Juan Chevere has a balance of $584.19 in his personal checking account. Juan uses a check register to keep an up-to-date balance of his checking account. The check register in Illustration 24A shows how Juan recorded the following checks and additional deposit.

**Illustration 24A
Completed check register**

RECORD ALL CHARGES OR CREDITS THAT AFFECT YOUR ACCOUNT

NUMBER	DATE	DESCRIPTION OF TRANSACTION	PAYMENT/DEBIT (−)	√ T	FEE (IF ANY) (−)	DEPOSIT/CREDIT (+)	BALANCE $ 584 19
121	19-- 3/1	TO Computer World	$ 150 00		$	$	− 150 00
		FOR w. p. program					434 19
122	3/5	TO Windsor Men's Shop	55 00				− 55 00
		FOR clothes					379 19
123	3/9	TO Lakeside Grocery	85 00				− 85 00
		FOR food					294 19
—	3/15	TO Salary				680 00	+680 00
		FOR					974 19
		TO					
		FOR					

March 1 Issued Check No. 121 for $150.00 to Computer World for the purchase of a personal word processing program.

5 Issued Check No. 122 for $55.00 to the Windsor Men's Shop for clothes.

9 Issued Check No. 123 for $85.00 to Lakeside Grocery for food.

15 Deposited salary check in the amount of $680.00.

Here are the steps Juan followed in completing the check register:

STEP **1** ▶ *Record the balance.*

The first thing Juan did was to record the balance of $584.19 on the first line of the check register in the space headed "Balance." Juan copied the amount (brought forward) from the previous page of the check register.

STEP 2 ▸ Subtract the checks issued.

Before Juan wrote each check, he recorded all the facts about the check in the check register. Juan recorded the amount of the check in the Payment/Debit column and again on the top of the same line in the Balance column.

When the word "debit" is used by a bank, it means that your account balance is reduced. In the Balance column, Juan found the new balance by subtracting the amount of the check from the previous balance. This is why, on March 1, you see the following arithmetic for Check No. 121:

Balance	584.19
Check No. 121	- 150.00
Balance	434.19

On March 5, Juan again found the new balance of $379.19 by subtracting $55.00, the amount of Check No. 122, from the old balance of $434.19.

Balance	434.19
Check No. 122	- 55.00
Balance	379.19

On March 9, Juan found the balance of $294.19 by subtracting $85.00, the amount of Check No. 123, from the old balance of $379.19.

You should remember to record each check in the check register *before* you write the check, just as you completed check stubs before writing checks.

STEP 3 ▸ Add the deposits.

When Juan deposited his salary of $680.00, he recorded the amount in the Deposit/Credit column. Since Juan was recording a deposit and not a check issued, he put a dash in the Number column. He labeled the deposit "Salary" to show where the money came from. He also recorded the amount of the deposit on the top of the same line in the Balance column. He found the new balance by adding the amount of the deposit to the old balance.

When the word "credit" is used by a bank, it means that your account balance is increased. This is why, on March 15, you see the following arithmetic in the Balance column:

Balance	294.19
Deposit	+ 680.00
Balance	974.19

Some people use a home computer to keep their check register. Using a computer this way allows them to keep a record of their income and expenses. The computer records may then be used to help complete their income tax forms at the end of the year.

Writing a Check for Less than One Dollar

Most payments by check are for more than one dollar. Sometimes, however, you must write a check for less than one dollar. For example, on March 16, Juan wanted a reprint of a newspaper article in *The Daily News* to be mailed to him. The cost of the reprint was 90 cents. He wrote the check shown in Illustration 24B for this amount since coins might be lost in the mail.

Notice that the number for 90 cents is shown as a fraction. It is written in words on the next line with the word "Only" before it, the word "cents" after it, and the printed word "Dollars" crossed out.

Illustration 24B A check for less than one dollar

Juan Chevere	No. **124**
911 Mead Ct.	
Chicago, IL 60626-6167	

Date *March 16,* 19 -- $\frac{64\text{-}60}{0710}$

PAY TO THE ORDER OF *The Daily News* $ *90/100*

Only ninety cents ──────────────── Dollars

For Classroom Use Only

GREAT LAKES
N A T I O N A L   B A N K
2101 Lakeview Drive, Chicago, IL 60627-6166

Juan Chevere

⑆071041376⑆ 5172261

BUILDING YOUR BUSINESS VOCABULARY

On a sheet of paper, write the headings **Statement Number** and **Words**. Next, choose the words that match the statements. Write each word you choose next to the statement number it matches. Be careful; not all the words listed should be used.

Statements	Words
1. To send out	balance brought forward
2. When there is not enough money in the checking account to pay a check	check
3. The new checkbook balance which is recorded on the Balance line	check register
4. A book for recording checks when stubs are not used	deposit slip
5. The part of a voucher check that shows a description of the payment	drawee
6. The person who writes a check	drawer
7. The word you print across a check when you have made an error	insufficient funds
8. A written order by the drawer to the drawee to pay the payee	issue
	payee
	void
	voucher

PROBLEM SOLVING MODEL FOR: *Using A Check Register*

STEP 1 ▶ **Record the balance.**

STEP 2 ▶ **Subtract the checks issued.**

STEP 3 ▶ **Add the deposits.**

*A*PPLICATION PROBLEMS

PROBLEM **24-1** ▶ Write out the following amounts in words as you would when writing a check. Use Illustration 24B as an example. Remember to use a hyphen in numbers from twenty-one through ninety-nine.

CHECKPOINT ✔

24-1 (1)
Only thirty-five cents

1. _____ $\$^{35}/_{100}$ Dollars

2. _____ $\$^{75}/_{100}$ Dollars

3. _____ $\$^{98}/_{100}$ Dollars

4. _____ $\$^{72}/_{100}$ Dollars

5. _____ $\$^{30}/_{100}$ Dollars

6. _____ $\$^{83}/_{100}$ Dollars

7. _____ $\$^{44}/_{100}$ Dollars

8. _____ $\$^{67}/_{100}$ Dollars

9. _____ $\$^{56}/_{100}$ Dollars

10. _____ $\$^{08}/_{100}$ Dollars

PROBLEM **24-2** ▶ You have a personal checking account at the Grand Canyon State Bank. You use a check register to keep an up-to-date balance of your account. On July 1, you have a balance of $784.96 in your account.

CHECKPOINT ✔

24-2
If your work is correct, the balance in your check register on July 25 should equal **$873.46**

Directions

a. Enter the July 1 balance on the first line of the check register in the column headed "Balance."

b. On July 5, issue Check No. 201 for $72.25 to Dr. S. Graves for a medical checkup. Enter the check in the check register and find the new balance.

c.   On July 10, issue Check No. 202 for $127.80 to the Auto Doctor for auto repairs. Enter the check in the check register and find the new balance.

d.   On July 15, issue Check No. 203 for $12.75 to Rosenberg Book Store for school supplies. Enter the check in the check register and find the new balance.

e.   On July 25, enter the deposit of your salary of $301.30 in the check register. Label the deposit "Salary." Find the new balance. Remember to put a dash in the Number column.

PROBLEM 24-3 ▶ You have a personal checking account at the Parker National Bank. You use a check register to keep an up-to-date record of your account. On November 1, you have a balance of $554.17 in your account.

Directions

24-3
If your work is correct, the balance in your check register on November 28 should equal $796.37

a.   Enter the November 1 balance on the first line of the check register in the column headed "Balance."

b.   On November 8, issue Check No. 309 for $86.55 to Dr. Matt Goldberg for an office visit. Enter the check in the check register and find the new balance.

c.   On November 12, issue Check No. 310 for $40.00 to The Edwardsville Cougars for baseball tickets. Enter the check in the check register and find the new balance.

d.   On November 15, enter the deposit of your salary of $475.10 in the check register. Label the deposit "Salary." Find the new balance. Remember to put a dash in the Number column.

e.   On November 28, issue Check No. 311 for $106.35 to Jenn's Clothing Store for new clothes. Enter the check in the check register and find the new balance.

Problem 24-4 may be found in the Working Papers.

JOB **25** ► ENDORSING CHECKS

APPLIED MATH PREVIEW

Copy and complete these problems.

1. $ 560.00	2. $ 195.00	3. $ 745.00	4. $1,475.00
175.00	47.62	111.86	201.19
415.00	110.91	57.75	43.87
17.50	31.75	96.21	106.55
19.97	68.24	411.18	71.92
+ 104.10	+ 415.92	+ 604.12	+ 806.48

BUSINESS TERMS PREVIEW

- Blank endorsement • Canceled checks • Clearinghouse •
- Endorsement • Full endorsement • Leading edge • Negotiable •
- Restrictive endorsement • Split deposit • Trailing edge •

GOALS

1. To learn how to transfer checks from one party to another.
2. To learn how to cash or deposit a paycheck.

UNDERSTANDING THE JOB

KEY Terms

Endorsement.
Signature on the back of a check.

Negotiable.
Transferable to another party.

What do you do with a check that you receive? For example, you receive your paycheck. You can cash the check for its full amount at the bank, deposit the full amount of the check, or deposit part of the amount and receive cash for the remainder. In order to do any of these three, you must transfer your ownership of the check to the bank. This transfer can be made by signing the back of the check. The signature on the back of a check that transfers ownership is called an **endorsement**.

A check can be endorsed (transferred) because of the words "Pay to the order of" that appear in front of the payee's name. Look at Maria Delgado's paycheck in Illustration 25A (on page 230). The check reads "Pay to the order of Maria Delgado." These words allow Maria to "order" the transfer of her check ownership to another party (such as the bank). Because the ownership of a check is transferable to another party, it is said to be **negotiable**. The three ways Maria can transfer the ownership of her check are shown in this job.

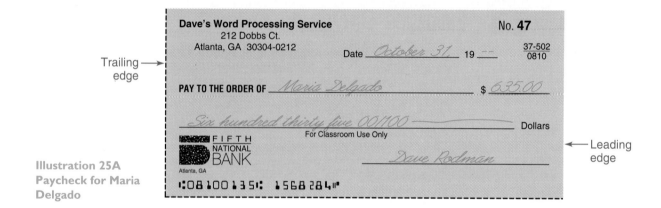

Dave's Word Processing Service
212 Dobbs Ct.
Atlanta, GA 30304-0212

No. **47**

Date _October 31_ 19 __

37-502
0810

Trailing → edge

PAY TO THE ORDER OF _Maria Delgado_ $ _635.00_

_Six hundred thirty five 00/100_____ Dollars

For Classroom Use Only

FIFTH
NATIONAL
BANK
Atlanta, GA

Dave Rodman

← Leading edge

⑆081001351⑆ 1568284⑈

Illustration 25A Paycheck for Maria Delgado

SAMPLE PROBLEM 1

Cashing a Paycheck

Maria decides to get cash for the full amount of the paycheck. She goes to her bank, Second National Bank, turns the check over, and signs her name at the top of the **trailing edge** of the check. (See Illustration 25A above.) She can use only the top $1\frac{1}{2}''$ of the check for her signature.

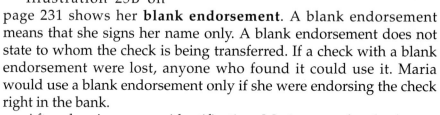

Illustration 25B on page 231 shows her **blank endorsement**. A blank endorsement means that she signs her name only. A blank endorsement does not state to whom the check is being transferred. If a check with a blank endorsement were lost, anyone who found it could use it. Maria would use a blank endorsement only if she were endorsing the check right in the bank.

After showing proper identification, Maria turns the check over to the bank and leaves with $635.00 in cash. The Second National Bank must now collect the $635.00 from the drawer's bank. Dave Rodman has ordered the Fifth National Bank to pay the money. Therefore, the Second National Bank needs a way to get the money from the Fifth National Bank. The Second National Bank will start by encoding the amount of the check in MICR so that a computer can be used in the collection process. (See Illustration 25D on page 232.)

Next, the Second National Bank will endorse the back of the check in the section for Bank of First Deposit. The endorsement will be made by either computer or endorsement stamp. Illustration 25C on page 231 shows the endorsement stamp for the bank.

▲▲▲▲▲
TIP
▼▼▼▼▼

MICR stands for Magnetic Ink Character Recognition.

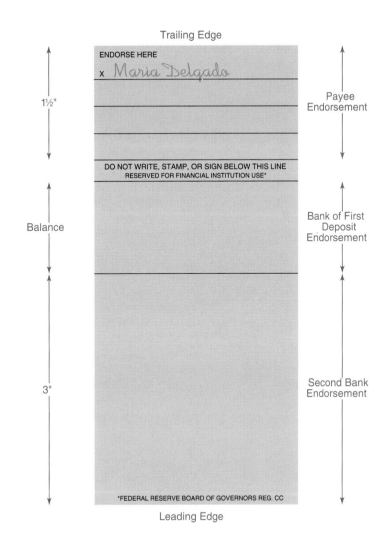

Trailing Edge

1½"

Balance

3"

ENDORSE HERE

x Maria Delgado

DO NOT WRITE, STAMP, OR SIGN BELOW THIS LINE
RESERVED FOR FINANCIAL INSTITUTION USE*

*FEDERAL RESERVE BOARD OF GOVERNORS REG. CC

Leading Edge

Payee
Endorsement

Bank of First
Deposit
Endorsement

Second Bank
Endorsement

Second National Bank
Atlanta, Georgia
0715 13612

K E Y *Terms*

Clearinghouse.
Central place where
banks exchange checks.

In a simpler world, a worker from the Second National Bank would walk across town to the Fifth National Bank and collect the amount of the check. But, with billions of checks written daily, this personal touch is impossible. Instead, banks arrange a central place, called a **clearinghouse**, where they distribute and exchange checks every day. Computers read the bank numbers printed in MICR and sort the checks rapidly according to the banks on which they were drawn. Funds are transferred from one bank to another on the central

KEY Terms

Leading edge. Right side of check.

Canceled check. Checks that have been paid by the bank.

computer of the clearinghouse. Thus, money is transferred from the Fifth National Bank to the Second National Bank. The clearinghouse endorsement is then made in the Second Bank Endorsement section of the back of the check, near the **leading edge** of the check.

The check is sent from the clearinghouse to the Fifth National Bank, where it is deducted from Dave Rodman's business checking account. The check is stamped "PAID" by Dave's bank, which makes the check a **canceled check**. Illustration 25D shows the canceled check. At the end of each month, all canceled checks are returned to Dave Rodman. Illustration 25E shows the route of this check.

Illustration 25D   Face of canceled check

Amount of check in MICR

Illustration 25E
Diagram of check's route

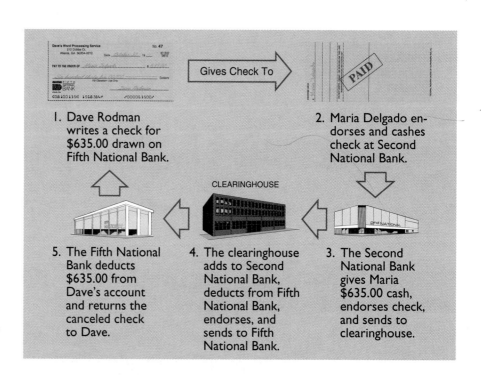

Gives Check To

1. Dave Rodman writes a check for $635.00 drawn on Fifth National Bank.

2. Maria Delgado endorses and cashes check at Second National Bank.

CLEARINGHOUSE

5. The Fifth National Bank deducts $635.00 from Dave's account and returns the canceled check to Dave.

4. The clearinghouse adds to Second National Bank, deducts from Fifth National Bank, endorses, and sends to Fifth National Bank.

3. The Second National Bank gives Maria $635.00 cash, endorses check, and sends to clearinghouse.

MULTICULTURAL
INSIGHT

Over 7,000 years ago, the Babylonian civilization in Asia Minor had banks and a method for drafts to be drawn in one place and paid in another. The Babylonians required that most business transactions be put in writing and signed by the parties involved. This was the first verified use of source documents.

SAMPLE PROBLEM 2

Depositing a Paycheck

Instead of cashing her paycheck, Maria may decide to deposit the paycheck. If she does, she will follow three steps:

STEP **1** ▶ *Endorse the check.*

To deposit her check, Maria must endorse it. As you see in Illustration 25F, Maria writes "For Deposit Only" and then signs her name. She is using a **restrictive endorsement**. A restrictive endorsement limits the use of the check. In this case, it can only be used for deposit to her account. No one finding the check could cash it and keep the money.

ENDORSE HERE
x *For Deposit Only*
Maria Delgado
DO NOT WRITE, STAMP, OR SIGN BELOW THIS LINE RESERVED FOR FINANCIAL INSTITUTION USE*

Illustration 25F   Restrictive endorsement

STEP **2** ▶ *Prepare a deposit slip.*

Maria prepares a deposit slip, as shown in Illustration 25G. Notice that she has listed the check by the ABA number, using the top part of that number.

Illustration 25G
Completed deposit slip

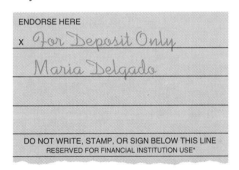

For DEPOSIT to the Account of

$\frac{64\text{-}61}{0715}$

Maria Delgado
519 Axel Road
Atlanta, GA 30301-0519

DATE ___October 31,___ 19___

2nd
NATIONAL BANK
ATLANTA, GA

Subject to the Terms and Conditions of this Bank's Collection Agreement

⑇071513612⑇ 411⑈20731⑈

	Dollars	Cents
BILLS		
COINS		
Checks as Follows Properly Endorsed		
37-502	635	00
TOTAL DEPOSIT	635	00

Record the deposit in the check register.

Maria records the deposit in her check register. She adds the deposit to her previous balance, as shown in Illustration 25H.

		RECORD ALL CHARGES OR CREDITS THAT AFFECT YOUR ACCOUNT						
NUMBER	DATE	DESCRIPTION OF TRANSACTION	PAYMENT/DEBIT (−)	√ T	FEE (IF ANY) (−)	DEPOSIT/CREDIT (+)	BALANCE $195 00	
—	19-- 10/31	TO *Paycheck*	$		$	$635 00	+635	00
		FOR					830	00
		TO						
		FOR						

Illustration 25H   Check register showing deposit

𝒮AMPLE PROBLEM 3

Depositing Part of a Paycheck

Assume that this time, Maria wants to deposit all of the paycheck except for $100.00, which she wants in cash. Maria is making a **split deposit**. She will follow three steps again.

STEP 1 ▶ **Endorse the check.**

Maria will use a blank endorsement since she wants some cash back and since she is at the bank.

STEP 2 ▶ **Prepare a deposit slip.**

Illustration 25I shows the way a deposit slip is prepared for a split deposit. Notice that the full amount of the check is listed. Then the amount of cash to be received is deducted. The bottom line shows the amount to be deposited.

BILLS		
COINS		
Checks as Follows Properly Endorsed		
37-502	635	00
Cash	(100	00)
TOTAL DEPOSIT	535	00

Illustration 25I   Deposit slip for a split deposit

Record the deposit in the check register.

Maria will add $535.00 to the balance of the check register.

There are times when a bank will not allow you to receive any cash on the day of the deposit. In such cases, you must deposit your check and wait one or more days to receive cash. The purpose of this rule is to prevent your receiving cash for someone's check that may not be backed by sufficient funds. However, if you have an account in the bank with a balance equal to or greater than the cash you want, the check can be cashed.

There is another type of endorsement used when you want to transfer a check to a specific person. For example, suppose that you are Elliott Reed. You receive a check for your birthday, but you have no bank account. So, you decide to endorse the check to your mother, Elaine Reed, and she will give you cash for it. You cannot use a restrictive endorsement ("For Deposit Only"), and you do not want to use a blank endorsement ("Elliott Reed") in case the check is lost. So you use a **full endorsement**, writing "Pay to the order of" in front of your mother's name. Illustration 25J shows a full endorsement.

ENDORSE HERE

x *Pay to the order of*

Elaine Reed

Elliott Reed

DO NOT WRITE, STAMP, OR SIGN BELOW THIS LINE
RESERVED FOR FINANCIAL INSTITUTION USE*

Illustration 25J   Full endorsement

BUILDING YOUR BUSINESS VOCABULARY

On a sheet of paper, write the headings **Statement Number** and **Words**. Next, choose the words that match the statements. Write each word you choose next to the statement number it matches. Be careful; not all the words listed should be used.

Statements	Words
1. The right side of a check	blank endorsement
2. A central place where banks exchange checks	canceled checks
	clearinghouse
3. Checks that have been paid by the bank	endorsement
4. A deposit that is part cash received, part deposit	full endorsement
	leading edge
5. An endorsement which limits use of a check	legible
6. An endorsement by signature only	negotiable
7. An endorsement which names the person to whom the check is transferred	restrictive endorsement
	split deposit
8. The left side of a check	trailing edge
9. Signature on the back of a check	voucher check
10. Transferable to another party	

PROBLEM SOLVING MODEL FOR: *Endorsing Checks*

STEP 1 ▶ *Endorse the check.*

STEP 2 ▶ *Prepare a deposit slip.*

STEP 3 ▶ *Record the deposit in the check register.*

APPLICATION PROBLEMS

PROBLEM | **25-1** ▶ Adam Sandler has received three checks today. The first is his pay-check, which he will cash at the bank, so he will use a blank endorsement. The second is a check from a part-time job, which he will deposit; therefore, he will use a restrictive endorsement. The third is a check that he is giving to his sister, Louise Sandler, for money he owes her, so he will use a full endorsement.

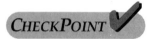

CHECKPOINT ✔

25-1
If your work is correct, the full endorsement for Check 3 should read:
Pay to the order of
Louise Sandler
Adam Sandler

Directions

Prepare the endorsements that Adam will write on the back of each check.

PROBLEM | **25-2** ▶ Joan Hadgis has received four checks today. The first is a check from a friend; she is going to deposit this check. The second is a check that she wants to transfer to her mother, Ellen Hadgis. The third is one of her paychecks that she wants to cash right at the bank. The fourth is another paycheck that she wants to transfer to Midtown Community College for a tuition payment.

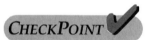

CHECKPOINT ✔

25-2
Hint: One is blank, one is restrictive, and two are full

Directions

Prepare the endorsements that Joan will write on the back of each check. Use the proper endorsement each time.

PROBLEM | **25-3** ▶ Tony Buckley is preparing a bank deposit on May 12, 19--. He is depositing cash and two checks.

Cash:	Quantity	Denomination	
	4	$10.00 bills	40.
	6	$ 5.00 bills	30
	19	$ 1.00 bills	19
	14	$ 0.25 coins	3.50
	8	$ 0.10 coins	.80
	7	$ 0.05 coins	.35
	21	$ 0.01 coins	21

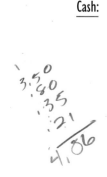

CHECKPOINT ✔

25-3
If your work is correct, the total deposit should equal $296.36

Checks:	ABA Number	Denomination
1	4-11	$ 75.00
2	15-91	$127.50

Directions

a. Prepare the endorsements that Tony will write on the back of each check to deposit them.
b. Complete the deposit slip.

Problems 25-4 and 25-5 may be found in the Working Papers.

SAVINGS ACCOUNTS AND OTHER BANK SERVICES

APPLIED MATH PREVIEW

Copy and complete these problems.

	1.	2.	3.	4.
	$ 42.00	$1,872.80	$ 122.00	$1,305.00
	2.98	33.21	5.39	63.78
	312.85	312.55	65.23	124.55
	4.64	42.38	+ 230.00	+ 25.43
	166.14	145.78	- 50.00	- 70.00
	+ 7.30	+ .40		

BUSINESS TERMS PREVIEW

- ATM access card • Automated teller machine (ATM) •
- Cashier's check • Electronic funds transfer •
- Personal identification number (PIN) • Savings account •
- Service charge • Stop-payment order • Traveler's checks •
- Withdrawal • Withdrawal slip •

GOALS

1. To learn how to select the proper type of savings account.
2. To learn how to open a savings account.
3. To learn how to prepare deposit and withdrawal slips.
4. To learn about other services that banks provide to their customers.

𝒰NDERSTANDING THE JOB

Brian Corey is a sophomore at American High School. Last week he started a part-time job at the House of Pizza. Brian decided to find a job because he has two goals he wants to achieve by the time he graduates. His first goal is to earn money to purchase a used automobile. His second goal is to earn money to pay the expenses for his first year at the local community college.

Brian's parents suggested that he open a **savings account** at Heritage National Savings, a bank near their home. A savings account at the bank would provide Brian with the following benefits:

> A safe place to keep his earnings.
> An opportunity to earn interest.
> A place where Brian can deposit his work checks and withdraw cash.

K E Y   Terms

Savings account. A bank account that earns interest.

SAMPLE PROBLEM

After school on Wednesday, Brian went to Heritage National Savings. He went to the desk in the bank that was identified with the sign NEW ACCOUNTS AND INFORMATION. There he introduced himself to Keri Monahan, the customer service representative. Brian completed the following steps to open his savings account:

STEP 1 ▶ *Select a savings plan.*

Brian described his new job to Keri. He also discussed with her his savings goals. To help Brian make a good decision, Keri explained the following four types of savings plans offered by Heritage National Savings:

> **K E Y** *Terms*
>
> **Service charge.** A fee for bank services.
>
> **Withdrawal.** To take money out of an account.

1. **Regular Savings Account:** This interest-earning account at Heritage National Savings is opened with a minimum deposit of $300. Money may be added or taken out from a regular savings account at any time. However, the bank charges a fee, or **service charge**, of $1.00 per month unless a minimum of $300.00 is kept in the account.

2. **Money Market Account:** This account pays a higher interest rate than does a regular savings account. Heritage National Savings requires a minimum deposit of $750.00. An important advantage of the money market account is that the money in the account can be taken out by writing a check. **Withdrawals** by check, however, are limited. Money can be added to the money market account at any time. Heritage National Savings charges a service charge of $2.00 per month unless a minimum of $1,000.00 is kept in the account.

3. **Certificate of Deposit:** Currently, this account pays the highest interest rate at Heritage National Savings. A minimum deposit of $1,000.00 is required to open a certificate of deposit. Money cannot be added or withdrawn at anytime. The money in the certificate earns a fixed rate of interest. However, the money must be kept in the certificate for a fixed period of time. There is no monthly service charge for having a certificate of deposit.

4. **Special Savings Account:** Because Brian is 16 years old and has only $74.53 to deposit, Keri recommended that he open a special student savings account. This special savings account, offered only to students, requires a minimum opening deposit of $50.00. There is no service charge until Brian is 21 years of age. Money may be added or withdrawn from the account at any time.

Notice that interest rates, service charges, minimum deposits and minimum balances are different for each type of savings account. Furthermore, each bank has different rules for its savings plans. It is wise to compare these items before selecting a bank and an account. Select an account that best meets your savings goals. Bank employees can be very helpful to you in making a good decision.

STEP 2 ▶ *Provide a form of identification.*

Keri told Brian that before he opened a student savings account, he must show some form of identification. Keri explained that Brian could use a driver's license or student identification card.

STEP 3 ▶ *Complete a signature card.*

After showing Keri his driver's license, Brian provided the information for the signature card like the one shown in Illustration 26A. Notice that it is very similar to a signature card for a checking account. Keri typed all the information except for the signature. She also gave Brian an account number. The signature card was signed only by Brian. The single signature means that Brian opened an individual savings account and that only he can make withdrawals from the account.

Illustration 26A
Signature card

HERITAGE
National Savings
457 Liberty Drive
Erie, PA 16502-1712

Account No.: _____32-4065_____

AUTHORIZED SIGNATURE FOR:

Name _Brian E. Corey_

Address _568 Hale Avenue, Erie, PA 16502-1710_

Telephone _(814) 555-2246_

Account Type _Student Savings_   Mother's Maiden Name _Gregory_

Soc. Sec. No. _766-22-4444_   I.D. _P754094_

Birthdate and Place _08/28/78; Holyoke, MA_

Signature _Brian E. Corey_

Date _October 17, 19--_

STEP 4 ▶ **Make an opening deposit.**

After the signature card was completed, Brian made his opening deposit of $74.53. He deposited $20.00 in bills, $3.57 in coin, and his first paycheck (ABA #12-210/4588) for $50.96. Just like checking deposits, savings deposits are recorded on a deposit slip. Brian's completed deposit slip is shown in Illustration 26B. Whenever Brian wants to receive money back from his paycheck, he will fill in the amount he wants next to "Less cash received" and sign the deposit slip in front of the teller.

SAVINGS DEPOSIT		ACCOUNT NO.: 3 2 - 4 0 6 5		
		List checks by bank no.	Dollars	Cents
October 17, 19-- DATE		BILLS	20	00
Brian E. Corey NAME (please print)		COINS	3	57
568 Hale Avenue ADDRESS		CHECKS *12-210*	50	96
Erie, *PA* *16502-1710* CITY STATE ZIP CODE				
X _____ Please sign in teller's presence for cash received		**Subtotal**	74	53
		Less cash received		
HERITAGE *National Savings*		**TOTAL DEPOSIT**	74	53

Illustration 26B   Completed savings deposit slip

Withdrawals

K E Y *Terms*

Withdrawal slip. A bank form used to withdraw money from an account.

On January 12, Brian made his first withdrawal of $25.00. To take money out of his savings account, Brian first completed a **withdrawal slip**. A withdrawal slip is a bank form showing the date, your account number, the amount to be withdrawn, and your name and address. Brian's completed withdrawal slip is shown in Illustration 26C. Brian signed the withdrawal slip to show that he received $25.00 in cash. If necessary, his signature could be compared to the one on his signature card.

SAVINGS WITHDRAWAL	ACCOUNT NO.: 3 2 - 4 0 6 5
	January 12, 19-- DATE
Twenty-five 00/100 _____ DOLLARS	$ 25 ⁰⁰/₁₀₀
For Classroom Use Only	
X *Brian E. Corey* Please sign in teller's presence for cash received	*Brian E. Corey* NAME (please print) *568 Hale Avenue* ADDRESS
HERITAGE *National Savings*	*Erie,* *PA* *16502-1710* CITY STATE ZIP CODE

Illustration 26C   Completed savings withdrawal slip

Job 26 Savings Accounts and Other Bank Services   241

Bank Services

As you have learned, banks offer checking accounts and savings accounts for businesses and for individuals. However, there are some other common banking services with which you should be familiar.

Automated Teller Machines

As a convenience to customers, banks use **automated teller machines** or **ATMs**. These machines, found outside banks and in supermarkets, shopping malls, and restaurants, give you 24-hour banking. The depositor, using a special **ATM access card** and **personal identification number** or **PIN**, can make deposits, withdraw cash, or transfer money from one account to another.

Debit Cards

Some ATM access cards can also be used as a debit card. A debit card (as explained in Chapter 4, Job 17), when passed through a computer terminal, automatically subtracts the amount from your bank account. It is like writing a check without having actually written one.

A debit card is one example of **electronic funds transfer**, which means that a computer is used to transfer money from one party to another. In this case, money is going from your bank account to the bank account of the party whom you want to pay.

Remember, if you use electronic funds transfer, you must subtract these payments in your checkbook. An example of how to record an ATM withdrawal on a check stub is shown in Illustration 26D. Notice that the words "Amt. Deposited" were crossed out. The date of the withdrawal and the initials ATM were written in. The amount of the withdrawal, $40.00, was recorded in parentheses and subtracted from the Bal. Bro't. For'd.

Safe Deposit Boxes

For a fee, you may rent a safe deposit box. It is kept in the vault of the bank. You may put jewelry and valuable papers in the box. To get in the box two keys are required. You have one and the bank has one. When you want to access the box, you identify yourself by signature. Then, you and a bank employee go together to open it.

Illustration 26D
Check stub with ATM withdrawal

NO. 231 $ _____		
DATE _____		
TO _____		
FOR _____		
	DOLLARS	CENTS
BAL. BRO'T. FOR'D.	463	72
~~AMT. DEPOSITED~~ *9/21 ATM*	(40	00)
TOTAL	423	72
AMT. THIS CHECK		
BAL. CAR'D. FOR'D.		

Stop-Payment Orders

What should you do if the person to whom you sent a check tells you that the check is lost? You should notify your bank at once, before someone finding the check can try to forge a signature and cash it. At the bank, you can fill out a **stop-payment order**. The bank will then refuse payment on the check. Banks usually charge a fee for stop-payment orders.

Cashier's Checks

What should you do if someone will not accept your personal check because she or he is not certain that you have enough money in your account to pay for it? You ask your bank for a **cashier's check**. A cashier's check is guaranteed by your bank for payment. The amount of the cashier's check is immediately deducted from your account and transferred to a special account at the bank. This guarantees that the money will be available when the cashier's check is presented for payment. You will pay a fee for this guarantee.

Traveler's Check

Finally, what should you do if you are planning a trip, do not want to deal with cashier's checks, and do not want to take a lot of cash? You can purchase **traveler's checks** from your bank. Traveler's checks are much like dollars. These checks are accepted most places as if they were cash. You will pay a small fee for the purchase of traveler's checks. Each traveler's check must be signed twice by you. When you buy one you sign it in front of the teller. Then, when you use one, you sign it again. Thus only you can use this safe form of cash. However, the best advantage of using traveler's checks is that if you lose them, they can be replaced.

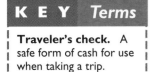

K E Y *Terms*

Traveler's check. A safe form of cash for use when taking a trip.

$\mathcal{B}$UILDING YOUR BUSINESS VOCABULARY

On a sheet of paper, write the headings **Statement Number** and **Words**. Next, choose the words that match the statements. Write each word you choose next to the statement number it matches. Be careful; not all the words listed will be used.

Statements	Words
1. A card that allows you to use an automated teller machine to make deposits, withdraw cash, or transfer money	ATM access card
2. Use of a computer to transfer money from one party to another	automated teller machine (ATM)
3. A bank account that earns interest	cashier's check
4. A form instructing the bank not to pay a check	debit card
5. Taking money out of an account	electronic funds transfer
6. A fee for bank services	interest
7. A secret code that allows you to use an automated teller machine	personal identification number (PIN)
8. A machine that allows 24-hour banking	savings account
9. A check guaranteed by the bank	service charge
10. A safe form of cash for use when taking a trip	stop-payment order
11. A bank form used to withdraw money from an account	traveler's check
	withdrawal
	withdrawal slip

PROBLEM SOLVING MODEL FOR: *Opening a Savings Account*

STEP 1 ▶ *Select a savings plan.*

STEP 2 ▶ *Provide a form of identification.*

STEP 3 ▶ *Complete a signature card.*

STEP 4 ▶ *Make an opening deposit.*

*A*PPLICATION PROBLEMS

PROBLEM **26-1** ▶ Pablo Flores has a savings account at Coastal Savings and Loan. His account number is 17-2891. His address is 2140 Bridgeport Avenue, Newark, DE 19710-1402.

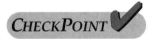

26-1
July 6 deposit = $327.99

Directions

Prepare savings deposit slips for the following deposits made by Pablo:

July	6	Bills	$ 42.00
		Coins	6.58
		Checks (ABA# <u>71-45</u>) 3400	245.21
		(ABA# <u>68-99</u>) 3307	34.20
July	13	Bills	$ 29.00
		Coins	1.04
		Checks (ABA# <u>77-40</u>) 1705	36.72
		(ABA# <u>71-45</u>) 3400	251.33
July	20	Checks (ABA# <u>71-45</u>) 3400	$229.89
		(ABA# <u>2-421</u>) 1789	107.33
		Less cash received	75.00

(Sign Pablo's name on the proper line for cash received.)

PROBLEM | 26-2 ▶ Denise Zrolka has a savings account at Rocky Mountain Bank. Her account number is 46-0671. Her address is 715 Williams Street, Denver, CO 80221-6173.

Directions

Prepare savings withdrawal slips for the following withdrawals made by Denise. Sign her name on the proper line for cash received.

March 11 $200.00
March 28 $137.82

PROBLEM | 26-3 ▶ You have a checking account and an ATM access card. You use your check stubs to record your checking account entries.

Directions

a.   Enter a balance brought forward of $842.18 on Check Stub No. 235.
b.   Record each of the following events on your check stubs:

CHECKPOINT ✔

26-3
Bal. Car'd. For'd. from Stub
237 = $660.01

December 9 Issued Check No. 235 for $35.28 to Cary's Department Store for a gift.
            11 Deposited $175.43 (Record deposit on Stub No. 236)
            12 issued Check No. 236 for $86.09 to A & Z Supermarket for groceries.
            14 Withdrew $60.00 using your ATM access card. (Record ATM withdrawal on Stub No. 237. Use Illustration 26D, page 242, as a guide).
            16 Issued Check No. 237 for $176.23 to Harvard Automotive for auto repairs.

Problem 26-4 may be found in the Working Papers.

► RECONCILING BANK STATEMENTS

APPLIED MATH PREVIEW

Copy and complete these problems.

1. Balance	$ 568.14	2. Balance	$ 971.36	3. Balance	$ 410.12
Deposit	+ 279.89	Check #1	- 451.47	Check #1	- 199.97
Balance		Balance		Balance	
Check #1	- 141.17	Check #2	- 310.19	Deposit	+ 755.86
Balance		Balance		Balance	
Check #2	- 97.18	Deposit	+ 575.50	Check #2	- 381.09
Balance		Balance		Balance	

BUSINESS TERMS PREVIEW

- Bank reconciliation statement • Bank statement •
- Bank statement balance • Checkbook balance •
- Outstanding checks • Reconciled •

GOALS

1. To learn how to read a bank statement.
2. To learn how to find which checks are outstanding.
3. To learn how to prepare a bank reconciliation statement.

UNDERSTANDING THE JOB

KEY Terms

Bank statement. Detailed record of the checking account from the bank.

Bank statement balance. Money left in account per bank's records.

In Job 25, you learned that after a bank pays a check written by one of its depositors, it marks the check "Paid." The canceled check is then returned to the depositor. However, instead of returning canceled checks one at a time, most banks hold all of them for a period of about thirty days. At the end of that period, all of the canceled checks are returned at one time, along with a **bank statement**. A bank statement is shown in Illustration 27A.

All banks use computers to prepare bank statements. Data about all checks paid and all deposits received are entered into the computer in order to keep the depositor's account up-to-date. All of the data that are stored in the computer are printed out on the bank statement.

The bank statement shows the depositor's beginning balance, individual and total deposits, individual and total checks, and the ending balance. The ending balance, called the **bank statement balance**, is the amount of money left in the checking account according to the bank's records.

2nd NATIONAL BANK
2136 Pine Street • St. Paul, MN 55110-4236

ACCOUNT OF:	STATEMENT DATE:	03/31/--

EVAN VARGAS INTERIOR DECORATING
76 SHELDON STREET
ST. PAUL, MN 55108-4062

ACCOUNT NO.: 317-4271

BEGINNING BALANCE:	3,715.00
TOTAL DEPOSITS/CREDITS:	1,465.00
TOTAL CHECKS/DEBITS:	777.00
ENDING BALANCE:	4,403.00

Date	Checks/Debits	Deposits/Credits	Balance
03/01/--			3,715.00
03/05/--	350.00		3,365.00
03/09/--	175.00		3,190.00
03/16/--		1,465.00	4,655.00
03/20/--	55.00		4,600.00
03/27/--	197.00		4,403.00

As you know, the depositor also has a record of deposits, checks, and balances. This record is kept either on check stubs or in a check register. The ending balance, called the **checkbook balance**, is the amount of money left in the checking account according to the depositor's records.

There will usually be differences between the checkbook balance and the bank statement balance. In this job, you will begin to learn how to explain these differences by preparing a **bank reconciliation statement**. This statement is used to bring the checkbook and bank statement balances into agreement.

$AMPLE PROBLEM

You are the record keeper for Evan Vargas Interior Decorating. Part of your job is to keep the checkbook and prepare the bank reconciliation statement. The stubs in the checkbook for checks written in March are shown in Illustration 27B on page 248.

NO. 307 $ 350.00
DATE March 2, 19--
TO James Company
FOR wallpaper

	DOLLARS	CENTS
BAL. BRO'T. FOR'D.	3,715	00
AMT. DEPOSITED		
TOTAL	3,715	00
AMT. THIS CHECK	350	00
BAL. CAR'D. FOR'D.	3,365	00

NO. 308 $ 175.00
DATE March 6, 19--
TO Midwest Electric
FOR electric bill

	DOLLARS	CENTS
BAL. BRO'T. FOR'D.	3,365	00
AMT. DEPOSITED		
TOTAL	3,365	00
AMT. THIS CHECK	175	00
BAL. CAR'D. FOR'D.	3,190	00

NO. 309 $ 55.00
DATE March 17, 19--
TO King Company
FOR picture frames

	DOLLARS	CENTS
BAL. BRO'T. FOR'D.	3,190	00
AMT. DEPOSITED 3/15	1,465	00
TOTAL	4,655	00
AMT. THIS CHECK	55	00
BAL. CAR'D. FOR'D.	4,600	00

NO. 310 $ 310.00
DATE March 18, 19--
TO Barres and Willis
FOR insurance

	DOLLARS	CENTS
BAL. BRO'T. FOR'D.	4,600	00
AMT. DEPOSITED		
TOTAL	4,600	00
AMT. THIS CHECK	310	00
BAL. CAR'D. FOR'D.	4,290	00

NO. 311 $ 197.00
DATE March 21, 19--
TO Jim's Garage
FOR truck repair

	DOLLARS	CENTS
BAL. BRO'T. FOR'D.	4,290	00
AMT. DEPOSITED		
TOTAL	4,290	00
AMT. THIS CHECK	197	00
BAL. CAR'D. FOR'D.	4,093	00

NO. 312 $ 210.00
DATE March 30, 19--
TO James Company
FOR draperies

	DOLLARS	CENTS
BAL. BRO'T. FOR'D.	4,093	00
AMT. DEPOSITED		
TOTAL	4,093	00
AMT. THIS CHECK	210	00
BAL. CAR'D. FOR'D.	3,883	00

The following canceled checks were returned to Evan in the same envelope with the bank statement:

Check No.	Payee	Amount
307	James Company	$350.00
308	Midwest Electric	175.00
309	King Company	55.00
311	Jim's Garage	197.00

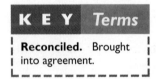

KEY Terms

Reconciled. Brought into agreement.

You can see that the March 30 checkbook balance of $3,883.00 (from stub #312) does not agree with the March 31 bank statement balance of $4,403.00 (from Illustration 27A on page 247). You must find out why the balances do not agree. They must be brought into agreement, or **reconciled**. Here is how you proceed:

STEP 1 ▶ **Compare the deposits.**

Compare the deposits recorded on the check stubs with the deposits recorded on the bank statement. In this case, there is just one deposit of $1,465.00, and it is recorded in both places. On Check Stub No. 309, place a small check mark to the right of $1,465.00 to show that it is recorded by the bank. In Job 28, you will learn how to handle a deposit not recorded by the bank.

STEP 2 ▶ **Arrange the canceled checks in order.**

Look at the check numbers and arrange the canceled checks in numerical order. Notice that all of the canceled checks returned are listed on the bank statement. You may wonder why the dates of the checks on the bank statement do not agree with the dates listed on your check stubs. This is because the dates on the bank statement show when the bank paid the checks, rather than when you wrote the checks.

STEP 3 ▶ **Compare the canceled checks with the stubs.**

Compare the canceled checks with the check stubs. Make a small check mark in the lower right corner of the stub if the canceled check has been returned and the amounts agree. In Job 29, you will learn how to handle a situation where the amounts do not agree.

STEP 4 ▶ **Find the outstanding checks.**

The check stubs without check marks indicate which checks have not been returned by the bank. These checks are called **outstanding checks**. They have been issued by the drawer and subtracted from the balance on the check stubs. However, the bank has not yet paid them nor subtracted them from your balance by the date of the bank statement. Check Nos. 310 and 312 are outstanding checks.

STEP 5 ▶ **Prepare a bank reconciliation statement.**

Check Nos. 310 and 312 have been subtracted from the checkbook balance, but not from the bank statement balance. Now, you must subtract them from the bank statement balance so that the two balances will be reconciled. The subtraction is done on the bank reconciliation statement. Illustration 27C on page 250 shows a completed bank reconciliation statement.

The heading of the bank reconciliation statement answers these questions:

WHO?   Evan Vargas Interior Decorating
WHAT?   Bank Reconciliation Statement
WHEN?   March 31, 19--

Evan Vargas Interior Decorating								
Bank Reconciliation Statement								
March 31, 19--								
Checkbook balance	3 8 8 3 00	Bank statement balance		4 4 0 3 00
		Less outstanding checks:		
		#310	$310.00	
		#312	210.00	
		Total outstanding checks		5 2 0 00
Adjusted checkbook balance	3 8 8 3 00	Adjusted bank statement balance		3 8 8 3 00

Illustration 27C   Bank reconciliation statement

The left side of the statement is used to show adjustments to the checkbook balance. None were needed on this statement. In Job 29, you will learn to make some adjustments to the checkbook balance.

The right side of the statement is used to show adjustments to the bank statement balance. Notice that the outstanding checks are listed separately and totaled. The total of the outstanding checks ($520.00) is subtracted from the bank statement balance ($4,403.00) to give an adjusted bank statement balance of $3,883.00. This amount is equal to the checkbook balance, so the balances are reconciled. Notice that the two equal adjusted balances are recorded, single ruled, and double ruled on the same line.

If the two balances could not be reconciled, you would have to find an error in either balance. If there is a bank error, notify the bank immediately. If there is a checkbook error, it should be corrected on the next check stub. Errors will be discussed in Job 29.

Although the bank statement shows that you have $4,403.00 in the bank, the outstanding checks will be deducted shortly. Therefore, you cannot write checks for more than the adjusted balance of $3,883.00, or you will be notified by the bank that you have insufficient funds.

BUILDING YOUR BUSINESS VOCABULARY

On a sheet of paper, write the headings **Statement Number** and **Words**. Next, choose the words that match the statements. Write each word you choose next to the statement number it matches. Be careful; not all the words listed should be used.

Statements	Words
1. Money left in an account per bank's records	bank reconciliation statement
2. Checks that have been paid by the bank	bank statement
3. A book for recording checks when stubs are not used	bank statement balance
	canceled checks
4. A statement that brings the checkbook and bank statement balances into agreement	check register
	check stub
	checkbook balance
5. Brought into agreement	negotiable
6. Detailed record of a checking account from the bank	outstanding checks
	reconciled
7. Checks issued by the drawer but not yet paid by the bank	
8. Money left in an account per depositor's records	

PROBLEM SOLVING MODEL FOR: *Reconciling Bank Statements*

STEP 1 ▶ *Compare the deposits.*

STEP 2 ▶ *Arrange the canceled checks in order.*

STEP 3 ▶ *Compare the canceled checks with the stubs.*

STEP 4 ▶ *Find the outstanding checks.*

STEP 5 ▶ *Prepare a bank reconciliation statement.*

*A*PPLICATION PROBLEMS

PROBLEM 27-1 ▶

CHECKPOINT ✔

27-1
If your work is correct, the adjusted balances should both equal $1,700.00

You are the record keeper for Bilodeau Company. Part of your job is to keep the checkbook and prepare the bank reconciliation statement. On March 31, the checkbook balance is $1,700.00. The bank statement shows a balance of $2,310.00. After comparing the canceled checks with the check stubs, you find that the following checks are outstanding:

#195 $75.00   #199 $365.00   #201 $170.00

bank balance

Directions

Prepare a bank reconciliation statement as of March 31. Use Illustration 27C (page 250) as a model.

PROBLEM | **27-2** ▶ You are the record keeper for Lou's Camera Shop. Part of your job is to keep the checkbook and prepare the bank reconciliation statement. On April 30, the checkbook balance is $1,950.63. The bank statement shows a balance of $2,216.89. After comparing the canceled checks with the check stubs, you find that the following checks are outstanding:

CHECKPOINT ✔

27-2
If your work is correct, the adjusted balances should both equal $1,950.63

| #506 | $7.95 | #509 | $108.11 | #512 | $150.20 |

Directions

Prepare a bank reconciliation statement as of April 30.

PROBLEM | **27-3** ▶ You are the record keeper for Exotic Travel Agency. Part of your job is to keep the checkbook and prepare the bank reconciliation statement. The check stubs show that the following checks were issued during August:

AUTOMATED

#504	$ 18.75	#507	$311.16	#510	$210.45
#505	102.40	#508	275.10	#511	75.85
#506	75.00	#509	87.10	#512	96.70

On August 31, the checkbook balance is $2,164.10. The bank statement shows a balance of $2,610.90. The following canceled checks were returned with the bank statement:

| #504 | $ 18.75 | #507 | $311.16 | #510 | $210.45 |
| #505 | 102.40 | #509 | 87.10 | #511 | 75.85 |

CHECKPOINT ✔

27-3
If your work is correct, the adjusted balances should both equal $2,164.10

Directions

Prepare a bank reconciliation statement as of August 31. (To find outstanding checks, compare the list of checks issued with the list of canceled checks.)

Problem 27-4 may be found in the Working Papers.

APPLIED MATH PREVIEW

Copy and complete the following problems.

1.	Balance	$2,105.90		2.	Balance	$5,110.90		3.	Balance	$4,316.78
	Deposit	+ 965.18			Check #1	- 98.12			Check #1	- 1,100.00
	Balance				Balance				Balance	
	Check #1	- 711.27			Check #2	- 1,473.16			Deposit	+ 955.90
	Balance				Balance				Balance	
	Check #2	- 406.98			Deposit	+ 750.00			Check #2	- 837.10
	Balance				Balance				Balance	

BUSINESS TERM PREVIEW

• **Outstanding deposit** •

GOALS

1. To learn how to prepare a bank reconciliation statement when a deposit is outstanding.
2. To learn how to use a bank-supplied reconciliation form.

$\mathcal{U}$NDERSTANDING THE JOB

KEY Terms

Outstanding deposit.
Deposit not shown on
bank statement.

In Job 27, you learned how to prepare a bank reconciliation statement when there are outstanding checks. There will also be times when a deposit that you have recorded in your checkbook is not yet recorded by the bank on your bank statement. This will happen when you make a deposit on the last day of a month or when you make a deposit after banking hours at the end of the month. Such a deposit is called an **outstanding deposit**. Outstanding deposits are another reason why the bank statement balance and the checkbook balance must be brought into agreement.

Outstanding deposits are included in the checkbook balance but not in the bank statement balance. An outstanding deposit must be added to the bank statement balance in order to reconcile it with the checkbook balance. The Sample Problem shows how a bank reconciliation statement with both outstanding checks and an outstanding deposit is handled.

SAMPLE PROBLEM

You are the record keeper for the Greg Woodward Book Store. Part of your job is to keep the checkbook and prepare the bank reconciliation statement.

On July 31, the checkbook balance is $3,755.00. The bank statement shows a balance of $3,765.00.

STEP 1 ▶ *Compare the deposits.*

Add outstanding deposits.

After comparing deposits shown on the bank statement with deposits shown on the check stubs, you find that a deposit of $270.00 has not been recorded by the bank. This is an outstanding deposit of $270.00 that must be added to the bank statement balance.

STEP 2 ▶ *Compare the canceled checks.*

After recording the outstanding deposit, you compare your canceled checks with the check stubs and find these checks to be outstanding:

| #409 | $75.00 | #412 | $110.00 | #416 | $95.00 |

STEP 3 ▶ *Complete the reconciliation.*

Subtract outstanding checks.

The checks are listed, totaled, and subtracted. The completed bank reconciliation statement is shown in Illustration 28A.

Many banks supply their own reconciliation forms. Illustration 28B shows one such form and how the bank reconciliation statement for the Greg Woodward Book Store would appear in that form. Notice how all of the places are labeled for balances and outstanding items. Like most bank-supplied reconciliation forms, there is no place for a heading; however, this form is usually used by individuals, not businesses.

In this form, you do not begin with two balances, but only with the bank statement balance. After adding outstanding deposits and subtracting outstanding checks, you arrive at an adjusted balance that should agree with your checkbook balance if no errors have been made.

Greg Woodward Book Store
Bank Reconciliation Statement
July 31, 19--

Checkbook balance	3 7 5 5 00	Bank statement balance		3 7 6 5 00
		Add outstanding deposit		2 7 0 00
		Total		4 0 3 5 00
		Less outstanding checks:		
		#409	$ 75.00	
		#412	110.00	
		#416	95.00	
		Total outstanding checks		2 8 0 00
Adjusted checkbook balance	3 7 5 5 00	Adjusted bank statement balance		3 7 5 5 00

Illustration 28A   Bank reconciliation statement

Illustration 28B   A bank-supplied reconciliation form

CHECKING ACCOUNT RECONCILIATION

CHECKS OUTSTANDING	
NUMBER	AMOUNT
409	75 00
412	110 00
416	95 00
TOTAL	280 00

ENTER BALANCE THIS STATEMENT $ 3,765.00

ADD DEPOSITS NOT CREDITED ON THIS STATEMENT   1 270.00

2 _____

3 _____

TOTAL   4,035.00

→ SUBTRACT CHECKS OUTSTANDING   280.00

BALANCE $ 3,755.00

SHOULD AGREE WITH YOUR CHECKBOOK BALANCE

IF YOUR ACCOUNT DOES NOT BALANCE

• HAVE YOU CORRECTLY ENTERED THE AMOUNT OF EACH CHECK IN YOUR CHECK REGISTER?

• DO THE AMOUNTS OF YOUR DEPOSITS ENTERED IN YOUR CHECK REGISTER AGREE WITH YOUR STATEMENT?

• HAVE ALL CHECKS BEEN DEDUCTED FROM YOUR CHECK REGISTER BALANCE?

• HAVE YOU CARRIED THE CORRECT BALANCE FORWARD FROM ONE CHECK REGISTER STUB TO THE NEXT?

• HAVE YOU CHECKED ALL ADDITIONS AND SUBTRACTIONS IN YOUR CHECK REGISTER?

• HAVE YOU REVIEWED LAST MONTH'S RECONCILEMENT TO MAKE SURE ANY DIFFERENCES WERE CORRECTED?

ANY ERRORS OR EXCEPTIONS SHOULD BE REPORTED IMMEDIATELY TO THE BANK

On a sheet of paper, write the headings **Statement Number** and **Words**. Next, choose the words that match the statements. Write each word you choose next to the statement number it matches. Be careful; not all the words listed should be used.

Statements	Words
1. Money left in an account per bank's records	bank reconciliation statement
2. Brought into agreement	bank statement
3. The party who is ordered to pay the amount on the check	bank statement balance
4. Detailed record of a checking account from the bank	checkbook balance
5. Checks issued by the drawer but not yet paid by the bank	drawee
6. A statement that brings the checkbook and bank statement balances into agreement	drawer
7. A deposit not shown on the bank statement	outstanding checks
8. Money left in an account per depositor's records	outstanding deposit
	payee
	reconciled

PROBLEM SOLVING MODEL FOR: *Handling Outstanding Deposits*

STEP 1 ▶ *Compare the deposits.*

STEP 2 ▶ *Compare the canceled checks.*

STEP 3 ▶ *Complete the reconciliation.*

APPLICATION PROBLEMS

PROBLEM 28-1 ▶ You are a record keeper for Skateboards, Ltd. Part of your job is to keep the checkbook and prepare the bank reconciliation statement.

Directions

Prepare the bank reconciliation statement as of May 31 from the following information. Use Illustration 28A (page 255) as a model.

Checkbook balance	$2,177.92
Bank statement balance	2,604.18
Outstanding deposit	342.71
Outstanding checks:	
#62	147.94
#64	621.03

PROBLEM **28-2** ▶ You are a record keeper for Conway Company. Part of your job is to keep the checkbook and prepare the bank reconciliation statement.

AUTOMATED

Directions

Prepare the bank reconciliation statement as of July 31 from the following information. Use Illustration 28A (page 255) as a model.

Checkbook balance	$3,772.19
Bank statement balance	3,616.91
Outstanding deposit	510.82
Outstanding checks:	
#77	316.11
#81	39.43

PROBLEM **28-3** ▶ You are preparing your own bank reconciliation statement.

Directions

Use the following information to prepare a February 28 statement. Use a bank-supplied form as shown in Illustration 28B (page 255).

Checkbook balance	$410.55
Bank statement balance	478.41
Outstanding deposit	75.00
Outstanding checks:	
#111	41.75
#116	92.16
#120	8.95

Problems 28-4 and 28-5 may be found in the Working Papers.

► HANDLING BANK SERVICE CHARGES, INTEREST, AND ERRORS

APPLIED MATH PREVIEW

Copy and complete these problems.

	1.			2.			3.	
	Balance	$417.11		Balance	$611.85		Balance	$3,175.10
	Service charge	- 10.50		Interest	+ 3.10		Check #62	- 281.60
	Balance	$		Balance	$		Balance	$
	Interest	+ 2.55		Deposit	+ 175.63		Service charge	- 5.25
	Balance	$		Balance	$		Balance	$
	Check #17	- 110.19		Service charge	- 4.50		Deposit	+ 511.10
	Balance	$		Balance	$		Balance	$
	Deposit	+ 410.37		Check #41	- 208.19		Interest	+ 14.11
	Balance			Balance			Balance	

BUSINESS TERM PREVIEW

• **Interest** •

GOALS

1. To learn how to prepare a bank reconciliation statement with bank service charges and interest earned.
2. To learn how to correct errors made in recording checks.

UNDERSTANDING THE JOB

In the previous two jobs, you have learned how to prepare a bank reconciliation statement when checks and deposits were outstanding. Both outstanding items are recorded on the bank statement balance side of the bank reconciliation statement.

There are two items that are recorded by the bank and appear on the bank statement before the depositor has recorded them. One is the bank service charge, or the bank's fee for handling the account. The amount of the service charge is already deducted from the bank statement balance. You must deduct it from your checkbook balance on a bank reconciliation statement.

The second item is interest earned on your bank account. **Interest** is money paid for the use of money. Many checking accounts earn interest. The amount of interest is added to the bank statement balance. You must add it to your checkbook balance on a bank reconciliation statement.

KEY Terms

Interest Money paid for the use of money.

In summary, four items will usually appear on a bank reconciliation statement. Here is how they are handled:

Item	Treatment
Outstanding checks	Subtract from bank statement balance
Outstanding deposits	Add to bank statement balance
Bank service charge	Subtract from checkbook balance
Interest	Add to checkbook balance

In this job, you will see how all four items are recorded. You will also learn how to handle errors you make in your check stubs.

SAMPLE PROBLEM

You are the record keeper for Lynn Meserve Florist. Part of your job is to keep the checkbook and prepare the bank reconciliation statement.

On May 31, the checkbook balance is $4,179.60. The bank statement shown in illustration 29A (page 260) shows a balance of $3,830.00. After comparing deposits shown on the bank statement with deposits shown on the check stubs, you discover an outstanding deposit of $550.00.

A comparison of canceled checks returned by the bank with checks written by the company shows two outstanding checks:

#57 $130.00   #59 $75.00

You also discover that Check No. 58, a canceled check, was for $76.00. You had incorrectly recorded it in your checkbook as $67.00. You also notice on the bank statement a deduction for a service charge of $11.50 and an addition of $15.90 for interest earned.

Illustration 29B (page 260) shows the bank reconciliation statement you would prepare.

Here are the steps you would follow to prepare the statement:

STEP 1 ▶ Enter the heading and the balances; handle outstanding deposits and checks.

You are familiar with this step from Jobs 27 and 28.

FIRST MASHPEE BANK
1100 Cape Drive • Mashpee, MA 02649-110

ACCOUNT OF:

STATEMENT DATE: 05/31/--

LYNN MESERVE FLORIST
54 TYLER DRIVE
MASHPEE, MA 02649-3254

ACCOUNT NO.: 312-6027

BEGINNING BALANCE:	3,562.20
TOTAL DEPOSITS/CREDITS:	1,750.90
TOTAL CHECKS/DEBITS:	1,483.10
ENDING BALANCE:	3,830.00

Date	Checks/Debits	Deposits/Credits	Balance
05/01/--			3,562.20
05/05/--	600.00		2,962.20
05/10/--	362.60		2,599.60
05/13/--		1,735.00	4,334.60
05/19/--	433.00		3,901.60
05/24/--	76.00		3,825.60
05/31/--	11.50 SERVICE CHARGE		3,814.10
05/31/--		15.90 INTEREST	3,830.00

Illustration 29B   Bank reconciliation statement

Lynn Meserve Florist
Bank Reconciliation Statement
May 31, 19--

Checkbook balance	4179 60	Bank statement balance		3830 00
Less service charge	11 50	Add outstanding deposit		550 00
	4168 10	Total		4380 00
Add interest earned	15 90	Less outstanding checks:		
Total	4184 00	#57	$130.00	
Add incorrect check #58	67 00	#59	75.00	
Total	4251 00	Total outstanding checks		205 00
Less correct check #58	76 00			
Adjusted checkbook balance	4175 00	Adjusted bank statement balance		4175 00

STEP 2 ▶ Subtract the service charge from the checkbook balance.

Since the bank has already subtracted the service charge from its balance, you must now subtract $11.50 from your balance. Record the difference, $4,168.10. If there were no more adjustments, $4,168.10 would be your adjusted checkbook balance.

STEP 3 ▶ Add the interest earned to the checkbook balance.

Since the bank has already added the interest earned to its balance, you must add $15.90 to your balance. Record the total, $4,184.00. If there were no more adjustments, $4,184.00 would be your adjusted checkbook balance.

STEP 4 ▶ Handle any errors.

Add wrong amount. Subtract right amount.

▲▲▲▲▲
TIP
▼▼▼▼▼

You wrote a check for $76.00, but recorded it on your check stub as $67.00. Since it is your error, the correction must be made on the checkbook side of the bank reconciliation statement. There are different ways to correct the error. One way, shown here, is to *add back* the wrong amount and then *subtract* the right amount. Notice how the $67.00 amount is added and the $76.00 amount is subtracted.

STEP 5 ▶ Finish the bank reconciliation statement.

Write your adjusted balances, single rule, and double rule on the same line on both sides of the statement.

STEP 6 ▶ Correct your check stubs or check register.

All items that have been listed on the checkbook side of the bank reconciliation statement must now be entered in your check stubs or check register. Illustration 29C shows how your check stub would appear with all items entered.

Illustration 29C
Corrected check stub

NO. 60	$	
DATE		
TO		
FOR		

	DOLLARS	CENTS
BAL. BRO'T. FOR'D.	4,179	60
SERVICE AMT. DEPOSITED	(11	50)
INTEREST TOTAL	15	90
	4,184	00
Check 88 AMT. THIS CHECK	67	00
5/31/--	(76	00)
BAL. CAR'D. FOR'D.	4,175	00

The Bal. Bro't. For'd. is the checkbook balance listed on the bank reconciliation statement, $4,179.60. Each item listed on the left side of the bank reconciliation statement is entered on the check stub, one at a time. Additions are shown without parentheses; subtractions are shown with parentheses. The date is entered by the adjusted checkbook balance, $4,175.00. There is little room for all of these changes. If you had more changes, such as another error correction, you would use the next stub.

Illustration 29D shows how you would record these items in a check register. Notice that additions are entered in the Deposit/Credit column. Subtractions are entered in the Payment/Debit column. Once again, the final balance, $4,175.00, agrees with the adjusted checkbook balance on the bank reconciliation statement.

Illustration 29D
Corrected check register

RECORD ALL CHARGES OR CREDITS THAT AFFECT YOUR ACCOUNT

NUMBER	DATE	DESCRIPTION OF TRANSACTION	PAYMENT/DEBIT (–)	√ T	FEE (IF ANY) (–)	DEPOSIT/CREDIT (+)	BALANCE $ 4,179 60
—	19-- 5/31	TO Service charge FOR	$ 11 50		$	$	– 11 50 4,168 10
—	5/31	TO Interest earned FOR				15 90	+ 15 90 4,184 00
—	5/31	TO Check 58 error FOR				67 00	+67 00 4,251 00
—	5/31	TO Check 58 error FOR	76 00				– 76 00 4,175 00
		TO FOR					

BUILDING YOUR BUSINESS VOCABULARY

On a sheet of paper, write the headings **Statement Number** and **Words**. Next, choose the words that match the statements. Write each word you choose next to the statement number it matches. Be careful; not all words listed should be used.

Statements	Words
1. A check with a special stub attached	ABA number
2. A number assigned to banks	canceled checks
3. A form instructing a bank not to pay a check	certified check
	insufficient funds
4. A safe form of cash for use when taking a trip	interest
5. Checks issued by the drawer but not yet paid by the bank	outstanding checks
	PIN
6. A check that is guaranteed by a bank	service charge
7. Money paid for the use of money	stop-payment order
8. Checks that have been paid by the bank	traveler's checks
9. Fee for bank services	voucher check

PROBLEM SOLVING MODEL FOR: *Handling Bank Service Charges, Interest, and Errors*

> **STEP 1** ▶ Enter the heading and the balances; handle outstanding deposits and checks.
>
> **STEP 2** ▶ Subtract the service charge from the checkbook balance.
>
> **STEP 3** ▶ Add the interest earned to the checkbook balance.
>
> **STEP 4** ▶ Handle any errors.
>
> **STEP 5** ▶ Finish the bank reconciliation statement.
>
> **STEP 6** ▶ Correct your check stubs or check register.

APPLICATION PROBLEMS

PROBLEM 29-1 ▶ You are a record keeper for McDermott Veterinary Clinic. Part of your job is to keep the checkbook and prepare a bank reconciliation statement.

Directions

Prepare the bank reconciliation statement as of October 31 from the following information. Use Illustration 29B (page 260) as a guide.

Checkbook balance	$1,475.80
Bank statement balance	1,116.70
Service charge	5.00
Interest earned	7.05
Outstanding deposit	511.10
Outstanding checks:	
#611	41.65
#613	108.30

CHECKPOINT ✓

29-1
If your work is correct, the adjusted balances should both equal $1,477.85

PROBLEM 29-2 ▶ You are a record keeper for the Newman Company. Part of your job is to keep the checkbook and prepare a bank reconciliation statement.

Directions

Prepare the bank reconciliation statement as of July 31 from the following information:

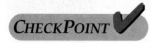
Checkbook balance	$2,771.16
Bank statement balance	3,430.06
Service charge	4.50
Interest earned	13.95
Outstanding deposit	107.90
Outstanding checks:	
#708	102.17
#709	610.10
#714	45.08

PROBLEM **29-3** ▶ You are a record keeper for the Melrose Company. Part of your job is to keep the checkbook and prepare a bank reconciliation statement.

Directions

a. Prepare a bank reconciliation statement as of January 31 from the following information:

Checkbook balance	$1,610.45
Bank statement balance	1,823.31
Service charge	6.50
Interest earned	6.05
Outstanding deposit	127.10
Outstanding checks:	
#146	14.95
#147	206.11
#150	119.35

b. Enter a balance brought forward of $1,610.45 in the check register.
c. Record the service charge and the interest earned in the check register. After subtracting the service charge and adding the interest earned, you should record a total that matches the adjusted checkbook balance. (Use Illustration 29D on page 262 as a model.)

Problems 29-4 and 29-5 may be found in the Working Papers.

Reinforcement Activities

DISCUSSION

Willie Abrams is your assistant record keeper at work. His job is to keep the check stubs and write the checks. You discover that twice during the past month, Willie has sent out checks but has not filled out the check stubs. What would you say to Willie to explain why it is necessary to fill out the check stubs? Also, tell him how to avoid this error in the future.

PROFESSIONAL BUSINESS ETHICS

You are a record keeper in charge of checks. As you are getting ready to go home today, you find a check on the floor that you had made out to Ellen Sigler, another employee. Ellen had signed a blank endorsement on the check. Write what you would do about this check and what you would tell Ellen.

APPLIED COMMUNICATIONS

You are a record keeper in charge of your company's checking account. You have just read that Lionel Company has gone out of business. The problem that this gives you is that you just wrote a large check along with a completed order for goods to Lionel Company today. You want to stop payment on this check. Write a letter to your bank asking that payment be stopped.

RECORD KEEPING CAREERS

Most of the jobs written about in this text are record keeping jobs in business. However, record keepers are employed in many public positions as well. For example, schools have record keepers (such as your school clerk). So does the federal government. Many clerks in the federal government are called "civil service clerks." In short, any organization that has an office may have a clerk.

Try to name four other organizations, other than businesses, that would need record keepers.

REVIEWING WHAT YOU HAVE LEARNED

On a sheet of paper, write in the headings **Statement Number** and **Words**. Next, choose the words that best complete the statements. Write each word you choose next to the statement number it completes. Be careful; not all words listed should be used.

Statements	Words
1. A check is written by the ____ .	bank reconciliation
2. When you endorse by signature only, you make (a, an) ____ .	statement
	bank statement
3. When you do not have enough money in your account to pay a check, you have ____ .	bank statement balance
	blank endorsement
	canceled checks
4. An endorsement which limits the use of a check is the ____ .	check register
	check stub
5. When you write on the back of a check, you are making (a, an) ____ .	checkbook balance
	drawee
6. The part of a check kept by the depositor is the ____ .	drawer
	endorsement
7. A deposit not shown on the bank statement is (a, an) ____ .	full endorsement
	insufficient funds
8. The words "Pay to the order of" make a check ____ .	negotiable
	outstanding checks
9. A check that is unusable is marked ____ .	outstanding deposit
10. To instruct your bank not to pay a check, use (a, an) ____ .	payee
	restrictive endorsement
11. The detailed record of your checking account sent by the bank is the ____ .	split deposit
	stop-payment order
12. Checks that have been paid by the bank are ____ .	void
	voucher
13. Instead of using check stubs to record checks, you can use (a, an) ____ .	voucher check
14. When you cash part of a check and deposit the rest, you have made (a, an) ____ .	
15. To bring the bank and checkbook balances into agreement, prepare (a, an) ____ .	
16. The bank that pays a check is known as the ____ .	
17. The money in your account per the bank's records is the ____ .	

18. Checks that you have written, but that are not returned with your bank statement are _____ .
19. The money in your account per your records is the _____ .
20. A check with a special stub attached is (a, an) _____ .

MASTERY PROBLEM

AUTOMATED

You are a record keeper for Lazenby Company. Part of your job is to keep the checkbook and prepare the bank reconciliation statement. Your bank account is at the Summit National Bank.

Directions

a. Enter a balance on March 1, 19--, on Check Stub No. 477 of $4,177.26.
b. Prepare a deposit slip for a March 3 deposit of the following:

Cash:	12	$20.00 bills
	17	$10.00 bills
	24	$ 5.00 bills
	11	$ 1.00 bills
	6	$ 0.50 coins
	37	$ 0.25 coins
	71	$ 0.10 coins
	56	$ 0.05 coins
	34	$ 0.01 coins
Checks:	3-16	$ 575.12
	5-71	1,146.19
	12-83	204.77

c. Record the deposit on Check Stub No. 477.
d. Record and write Checks 477–481 as follows:

Check No.	Date	Payee	For	Amount
477	March 6	Jones Realty	rent	$ 114.10
478	12	Willis Company	merchandise	611.18
479	15	Manson Company	merchandise	1,477.19
480	19	Vielleux Company	display case	971.16
481	26	Key Hardware	lock repair	57.25

e. Record (without preparing a deposit slip) a March 30 deposit of
$1,911.08 on Check Stub No. 482.

f. Write Check No. 482 dated March 31 for $111.25 to Kane Office
Supplies for stationery.

g. You receive the following bank statement on March 31, 19--. Prepare a
bank reconciliation statement as of March 31. (Find the outstanding
checks and deposits.)

summit NATIONAL BANK

2279 Nottingham Road, Newark, DE 19711-2585

ACCOUNT OF:		STATEMENT DATE:	03/31/--

LAZENBY COMPANY
1402 EIGHTEENTH AVENUE
NEWARK, DE 19710-1402

ACCOUNT NO.: 204-1714

BEGINNING BALANCE:	4,177.26
TOTAL DEPOSITS/CREDITS:	2,499.57
TOTAL CHECKS/DEBITS:	3,178.63
ENDING BALANCE:	3,498.20

Date	Checks/Debits	Deposits/Credits	Balance
03/01/--			4,177.26
03/04/--		2,489.57	6,666.83
03/10/--	114.10		6,552.73
03/15/--	611.18		5,941.55
03/20/--	1,477.19		4,464.36
03/30/--	971.16		3,493.20
03/31/--	5.00 SERVICE CHARGE		3,488.20
03/31/--		10.00 INTEREST	3,498.20

h. On Check Stub No. 483, record the service charge and interest earned
that appear on the bank statement.

REVIEWING YOUR BUSINESS VOCABULARY

This activity may be found in the Working Papers.

CHAPTER 6

Petty Cash Records

In Chapter 5, you learned that a check provides a written record for a cash payment. Businesses use these written records, or checks, to help make decisions about how to spend their money. Sometimes, however, it is not convenient or practical to write a check. For example, would you use a check to buy a piece of bubble gum? In this instance, it is easier to use cash for such a small payment.

In Chapter 6, you will learn how businesses handle small cash payments—through petty cash funds. You will learn how to group these business expenses and prepare special reports for making small cash payments. Finally, you will learn that records of *all* cash payments, whether large or small, are very important to a business. A Calculator Tip will be given for summarizing a petty cash book, which is used to record and classify petty cash payments and receipts.

JOB 30 ▶ WRITING PETTY CASH VOUCHERS

APPLIED MATH PREVIEW

Copy and complete these problems.

1. $ 7.95	2. $ 12.86	3. $ 150.00	5. $ 75.00
15.80	7.24	- 97.75	- 39.97
33.17	51.10		
4.95	39.05		
18.27	6.19	4. $125.00	6. $200.00
+ 15.91	+ 18.64	- 83.16	- 71.94

BUSINESS TERMS PREVIEW

• Currency • Petty • Petty cash box • Petty cash clerk •
• Petty cash fund • Petty cash voucher •

GOALS

1. To learn the use of a petty cash fund.
2. To learn how to record payments made from a petty cash fund.

Currency. Bills and coins.

Petty. Small.

Petty cash fund. Currency set aside for making small payments.

Petty cash box. A storage box for petty cash.

Petty cash clerk. Keeps records of petty cash.

You learned in Chapter 5 that businesses make most payments by check. Sometimes it is not convenient to write a check to make a small payment. At these and other times, it is necessary to pay in **currency**. Currency means bills and coins. Such payments in currency are made in small, or **petty**, amounts. They are called "petty cash payments."

Petty cash payments are made from a **petty cash fund**. The fund is the actual currency set aside for these payments. To start the fund, the business will estimate how much currency is needed for a certain time period, such as a week or a month. A check will then be written for the amount of the estimate. The check will be cashed and the actual currency placed in a **petty cash box**.

Recording Payments

Petty cash voucher. Record of payment from petty cash fund.

Careful records must be kept for petty cash payments. The **petty cash clerk** will keep these records. Every time someone is given money from the petty cash fund, that person must sign a printed record. This record is called a **petty cash voucher**.

SAMPLE PROBLEM

You are Alice Meehan, and you work for Marie Towle, a lawyer. On July 1, Marie starts a petty cash fund by cashing a check for $100.00. She places the currency in a petty cash box and puts you in charge of the fund. On July 1, Steve O'Leary bought office stationery from Jones Supplies with his own money. On July 2, Steve comes to you and asks for $9.65 in cash to reimburse him. Here are the steps that you will follow to handle Steve's request:

STEP 1 ▶ Ask for a receipt to prove the request.

Try to collect a receipt for all money paid out of the petty cash fund. For example, when you ask Steve for a receipt, he presents you with the receipt shown in Illustration 30A. (STA stands for stationery.)

```
JONES SUPPLIES

07/01/--

STA           5.15
STA           3.87
TAX            .63
TOTAL         9.65
CASH         10.00
CHANGE         .35

147 2186  9:15 AM
```

STEP 2 ▶ *Fill out the petty cash voucher.*

Complete the petty cash voucher by filling in the following spaces (see Illustration 30B):

Illustration 30B
Completed petty cash
voucher

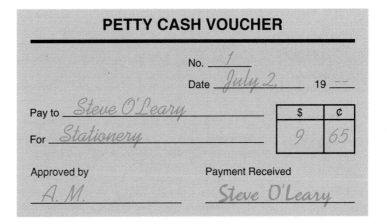

1. **No.**—Write in the number of the voucher, 1. In some cases, the vouchers are printed with numbers, so this step will not be necessary.
2. **Date**—Write "July 2, 19--," the date on which money is being paid out.
3. **Pay to**—Enter Steve O'Leary's name, the person who is being paid.
4. **For**—Write "Stationery," the expense for which you are paying.
5. **$, ¢**—Enter the amount paid out, $9.65. Notice that no dollar sign, cents sign, or decimal point is used.
6. **Approved by**—Enter your initials, A.M.
7. **Payment Received**—Have Steve O'Leary sign his name when he is handed the money.

STEP 3 ▶ *Attach the receipt to the petty cash voucher.*

Attach Steve's receipt to the voucher and file them both in the petty cash box. The receipt is additional proof of payment. There will be times when a receipt is not available, such as for tips or bus fares. But, when there is a receipt, attach it.

Proving the Petty Cash Fund

Another responsibility of the petty cash clerk is to check the balance of the fund daily. At the end of the day, count the currency in the box. Then, add the amounts of the petty cash vouchers in the box and find a total. *The sum of the currency and the vouchers should equal the original balance of the fund.*

You began the day with $100.00 in currency. When you count the currency at the end of the day, you find $79.90. When you add your vouchers, you get a total of $20.10. You then add these two figures.

Currency in box	$ 79.90
Plus: Total of vouchers	20.10
Equals: Original balance	$100.00

Because your total is $100.00, you have done your work accurately. If your total did not add up to $100.00, an error has been made. Handling errors is discussed in Job 33.

BUILDING YOUR BUSINESS VOCABULARY

On a sheet of paper, write the headings **Statement Number** and **Words**. Next, choose the words that match the statements. Write each word you choose next to the statement number it matches. Be careful; not all the words listed should be used.

Statements	Words
1. Currency set aside for making small cash payments	currency
	deposit
2. Quantity times unit price	extension
3. Bills and coins	outstanding check
4. Record of payment from the petty cash fund	petty
	petty cash box
5. Small	petty cash clerk
6. A storage box for petty cash	petty cash fund
7. Keeps records of petty cash	petty cash voucher

PROBLEM SOLVING MODEL FOR: *Writing Petty Cash Vouchers*

STEP 1 ▶ *Ask for a receipt to prove the request.*

STEP 2 ▶ *Fill out the petty cash voucher.*

STEP 3 ▶ *Attach the receipt to the petty cash voucher.*

*A*PPLICATION PROBLEMS

PROBLEM | **30-1** ▶ You work for Ellen Simons, an engineer. She puts you in charge of the petty cash fund, which was started on May 1 with a balance of $100.00.

Directions

30-1
The money spent plus the money left in the fund should equal $100.00.

a. Fill out a petty cash voucher for each of the following payments made from the petty cash fund. Approve each voucher with your own initials, but do not fill in the signature. Start with Voucher No. 1.

May   4   Paid $11.50 to Marc Joyce, an office clerk, for pencils and pens.
      9   Paid $9.50 to Jiffy Mail Services for overnight mail.
     16   Paid $12.65 to Ann Cormier, a salesperson, for cab fare.
     25   Paid $14.95 to Luis Santos, an office clerk, for typewriter ribbons.

b.   Answer the following questions:

   1.   How much money have you spent in May? (Find this amount by adding the vouchers.)
   2.   How much money is left in the fund?

PROBLEM | **30-2** ▶ You work for Annette O'Neal, a real estate agent. She puts you in charge of the petty cash fund, which was started on June 1 with a balance of $200.00.

Directions

30-2
The money spent plus the money left in the fund should equal $200.00.

a. Fill out a petty cash voucher for each of the following payments made from the petty cash fund. Approve each voucher with your own initials, but do not fill in the signature. Start with Voucher No. 1.

June   5   Paid $27.40 to Basil Thorpe, an office clerk, for mailing packages.
      12   Paid $6.95 to Charlene Ferrer, an agent, for cab fare.
      17   Paid $36.18 to Midtown Caterers for a catered lunch.
      26   Paid $17.12 to Ike Ofoje, an office clerk, for office supplies.

b.   Answer the following questions:

   1.   How much money have you spent in June?
   2.   How much money is left in the fund?

Problem 30-3 may be found in the Working Papers.

JOB 31 ▶ CLASSIFYING BUSINESS EXPENSES

APPLIED MATH PREVIEW

Copy and complete these problems.

1. $ 8.05	2. $ 9.18	3. $ 19.50	5. $ 11.16
12.70	12.21	37.19	27.91
1.95	6.56	+ 28.55	+ 18.04
16.80	21.37		
37.10	19.04		
16.05	4.82	4. $ 41.10	6. $ 57.16
21.19	6.95	19.11	39.22
+ 4.95	+ 0.75	+ 18.47	+ 24.83

BUSINESS TERMS PREVIEW

• Classifications • Petty cash record •

GOAL

To learn how to classify business expenses using a petty cash record.

MULTICULTURAL INSIGHT

The Egyptians, from northern Africa, invented papyrus, a form of paper made from the pith of the papyrus plant. The Egyptians were able to keep more detailed records than the Babylonians because papyrus was easier to handle than clay tablets. Egyptian scribes also kept very careful records because the records of different scribes were compared and had to match. Scribes could be punished for their errors.

UNDERSTANDING THE JOB

A petty cash clerk pays out money for business expenses and fills out a petty cash voucher to record each payment. At any time, the petty cash clerk can add up the vouchers to find the total amount spent from the petty cash fund. However, an employer needs to know more than just the total spent. An employer needs to know the amounts spent for each type of expense. For this reason, it is necessary to group or classify the information on the petty cash voucher to find the totals for different kinds of expenses.

For example, money spent for pencils, stamps, computer paper, and other office supplies would be classified as an *office expense*. Money spent for wrapping paper, twine, labels, cartons, and other shipping supplies would be classified as a *shipping expense*. Some typical **classifications** of expenses are:

Office Expense—money spent on supplies used in the office, such as pens, pencils, stationery, typing supplies, computer supplies, and stamps.

KEY Terms

Classification. The name for a group of similar items.

Shipping Expense—money spent on supplies used for shipping, such as cartons, tape, wrapping paper, cord, and shipping labels.

Delivery Expense—money spent on delivering packages, such as gas, oil, bridge tolls, repairs for the delivery truck, and bus or taxi fares for employees making deliveries. •

General Expense—money spent on items that do not fit under any of the other classifications. Such expenses might include first-aid supplies, window repairs, paper towels, light bulbs for the office or warehouse, cleaning supplies, lock repairs, soap for the washroom, paint, and flowers.

*S*AMPLE PROBLEM

You are the petty cash clerk for Aaron Tolliver, an architect. At the end of the week, you find the following petty cash vouchers in the petty cash box:

Voucher Number	Paid For	Amount
1	Stamps for office	$ 5.00
2	Gas for truck	15.00
3	Cab fare for delivery	11.25
4	Office light bulbs	7.50
5	Office stationery	5.95
6	Floor cleaning in office	25.00
7	Truck repair	17.50
8	Pencils for office	2.95

Mr. Tolliver asks you to report how much was spent this week for each of these classifications:

> Office Expense
> Delivery Expense
> General Expense

K E Y *Terms*

Petty cash record.
Form used to record and classify petty cash payments.

One way to give this report is to use a form called a **petty cash record**. This form is used to record each petty cash payment and classify it. The data for the petty cash record are taken from the petty cash vouchers. Illustration 31A shows how a petty cash record would look after it was completed. Notice that there is a special column in the petty cash record for each classification. By entering the amount of each payment under one of the classifications and then totaling the columns, you can see how much was spent for each type of expense.

Here are the steps you would follow to complete a petty cash record:

STEP 1 ▶ Record vouchers in numerical order.

In the petty cash record shown in Illustration 31A, each voucher is listed in numerical order. The number of each petty cash voucher is entered in the Vo. No. column. The items that the vouchers were issued for are entered in the Paid For column.

PETTY CASH RECORD

PAID FOR	VO. NO.	TOTAL PAYMENTS	DISTRIBUTION OF PAYMENTS		
			OFFICE EXPENSE	DELIVERY EXPENSE	GENERAL EXPENSE
Stamps for office	1	5 00	5 00		
Gas for truck	2	15 00		15 00	
Cab fare for delivery	3	11 25		11 25	
Office light bulbs	4	7 50			7 50
Office stationery	5	5 95	5 95		
Floor cleaning in office	6	25 00			25 00
Truck repair	7	17 50		17 50	
Pencils for office	8	2 95	2 95		
Totals	–	90 15	13 90	43 75	32 50

Illustration 31A Petty cash record

STEP 2 ▶ Enter the amount of each payment twice.

The amount of each voucher is entered twice on the same line. The Total Payments column is used each time for one entry of the amount. The second entry is in the column that describes the type of expense.

Look at how Voucher No. 1 is recorded. First, $5.00 is entered in the Total Payments column. Then, since stamps are used in the office, it is entered in the Office Expense column.

In the same way, for Voucher No. 2, the $15.00 spent for gas for the truck is entered twice. It is first entered in the Total Payments column and then in the Delivery Expense column.

Amounts are entered twice on the same line.

TIP

For Voucher No. 4, the $7.50 is first entered in the Total Payments column. It is then entered in the General Expense column because the payment is neither an office expense nor a delivery expense. You might wonder why the expense is not an office expense, since the light bulbs are for the office. The answer is that Office Expense includes supplies used for the normal, everyday paperwork in the office. Light bulbs are not an everyday expense.

STEP 3 ▶ Rule and foot the amount columns.

Single ruling shows addition.

TIP

Each of the four amount columns is single ruled and totaled. A single ruling indicates that all amounts above the ruling are to be added. The totals are first written as footings just below the single ruling. The footings should be written in clear, small figures.

STEP 4 ▶ Check totals by crossfooting.

Add the totals of the three Distribution of Payments columns. If your math is accurate, the sum of these three totals should be $90.15, the total of the Total Payments column.

Total of Office Expense column	$13.90
Total of Delivery Expense column	43.75
Total of General Expense column	32.50
Total of Total Payments column	$90.15

If the three totals do not equal $90.15, find your error by working in reverse:

1. Re-add the three totals.
2. Check that you copied your footed totals correctly.
3. Foot all four amount columns again.
4. Check to see that the amount of each voucher was entered twice.

STEP 5 ▶ Record final totals and double rule the amount columns.

Double ruling shows record is complete.

TIP

After the totals have been checked, they are written again just below the footings. The word "Totals" is written in the Paid For column, and a dash (-) is entered in the Vo. No. column. A double ruling is then drawn across all four amount columns just below the totals. The double ruling shows that the totals have been checked and all work is complete.

On a sheet of paper, write the headings **Statement Number** and **Words**. Next, choose the words that match the statements. Write each word you choose next to the statement number it matches. Be careful; not all the words listed should be used.

Statements	Words
1. Record of payment from the petty cash fund	classifications
2. Drawn under a total to show that a record is complete	crossfooting
3. The total of an amount column written in small figures	currency
4. The names for groups of similar items	double ruling
5. Drawn under an amount column to show addition	footing
6. Currency set aside for making small cash payments	petty cash box
7. Adding a row of figures across a form	petty cash fund
8. Form used to record and classify petty cash payments	petty cash record
	petty cash voucher
	single ruling

PROBLEM SOLVING MODEL FOR: *Using a Petty Cash Record*

STEP 1 ▶ *Record vouchers in numerical order.*

STEP 2 ▶ *Enter the amount of each payment twice.*

STEP 3 ▶ *Rule and foot the amount columns.*

STEP 4 ▶ *Check totals by crossfooting.*

STEP 5 ▶ *Record final totals and double rule the amount columns.*

APPLICATION PROBLEMS

PROBLEM **31-1** ▶ You are in charge of the petty cash fund for Betty Pierce, who owns a catering business.

Directions

a. Enter the petty cash vouchers listed on page 279 in a petty cash record with the same headings shown in Illustration 31A (page 276).

Voucher Number	Paid For	Amount
I	Postage stamps for office	$ 7.95
2	Office stationery	16.20
3	Gas for truck	14.75
4	Truck repairs	21.90
5	Light bulbs for office	5.05
6	Soap for washroom	7.95
7	Envelopes for office	11.00
8	Typewriter ribbons for office	13.10

b. Rule and foot the amount columns.
c. Check your totals by crossfooting.
d. If the totals agree, record the final totals and double rule the amount columns.

PROBLEM **31-2** ▶ You are in charge of the petty cash fund for the Elgin Manufacturing Company.

Directions

a. Enter the petty cash vouchers listed below in a petty cash record with the same headings shown in Illustration 31A (page 276).

Voucher Number	Paid For	Amount
I	Truck tire repair	$15.00
2	File folders for office	12.50
3	Office light bulbs	14.95
4	Gas for truck	18.00
5	Paint for office	25.00
6	Cleaning supplies	12.50
7	Office stationery	11.75
8	Pencils for office	4.75

b. Rule and foot the amount columns.
c. Check your totals by crossfooting.
d. If the totals agree, record the final totals and double rule the amount columns.

PROBLEM **31-3** ▶ You are in charge of the petty cash fund for the Brereton Packing Company.

Directions

a. Prepare a petty cash record with Distribution of Payments columns for Office Expense, Delivery Expense, Shipping Expense, and General Expense. Enter the petty cash vouchers listed on page 280 in this record.

Voucher Number	Paid For	Amount
1	Wrapping paper	$14.75
2	Cab fare for deliveries	5.95
3	Office stationery	27.50
4	Computer paper	18.95
5	Paper towels	14.75
6	Gas for truck	16.50
7	Shipping labels	21.05
8	Flowers	25.00
9	Cartons for shipping	23.75
10	Typewriter ribbons	19.40

b. Rule and foot the amount columns.

c. Check your totals by crossfooting.

d. If the totals agree, record the final totals and double rule the amount columns.

Problem 31-4 may be found in the Working Papers.

GOAL

To learn how to use a petty cash book.

UNDERSTANDING THE JOB

KEY *Terms*

Petty cash book.
Form used to record and classify petty cash payments and receipts.

In Job 31, you learned how to use a petty cash record to record and classify petty cash payments. In this job, you will learn how to use a **petty cash book**. As you see in Illustration 32A on page 282, a petty cash book is used to record and classify petty cash payments and receipts.

A petty cash book may be used by any kind of business. An advertising office may use a petty cash book to record payments for small services, such as printing photographs from slides. A printing plant may use a petty cash book to record the purchase of gas for a delivery truck. A school office may use a petty cash book to record postage for mailing a videotape back to a library. Because any business may make small payments for miscellaneous items, any business may need to use a petty cash book.

The petty cash book is similar to the petty cash record. However, the petty cash book has some additional columns: a Date column, a Receipts column, and the Other Items columns. The Date column is used to record the date of each receipt or payment. The Receipts column is used to record the amount to start the fund, any money added to the fund, and the balance of the fund. You will see how the Other Items columns are used as you study the Sample Problem.

PETTY CASH BOOK

DATE		EXPLANATION	VO. NO.	RECEIPTS	PAYMENTS	DISTRIBUTION OF PAYMENTS			
						OFFICE EXPENSE	DELIVERY EXPENSE	OTHER ITEMS	
								ITEM	AMOUNT
19-- May	1	Check #306	—	100 00					
	3	Stamps for office	1		5 00	5 00			
	7	Gas for truck	2		15 00		15 00		
	10	Cab fare for delivery	3		11 25		11 25		
	12	Office light bulbs	4		7 50			General Expense	7 50
	16	Office stationery	5		5 95	5 95			
	19	Floor cleaning in office	6		25 00			General Expense	25 00
	20	Truck repair	7		17 50		17 50		
	31	Pencils for office	8		2 95	2 95			
	31	Totals	—	100 00 100 00	90 15 90 15	13 90 13 90	43 75 43 75		32 50 32 50
June	1	Balance	—	9 85					

Illustration 32A Petty cash book

SAMPLE PROBLEM

You are in charge of the petty cash fund for Aaron Tolliver, an architect. In Job 31, you recorded Mr. Tolliver's petty cash payments in a petty cash record. Mr. Tolliver has now told you that he prefers a petty cash book.

On May 1, he cashed a $100.00 check to start a petty cash fund. The check number was 306. You then made the following payments during May. They are classified as office expense, delivery expense, or general expense.

Illustration 32A above shows how the petty cash book would appear after all the vouchers and other amounts are recorded. You would follow these six steps to complete the petty cash book:

Voucher Number	Date	Paid For	Amount
1	May 3	Stamps for office	$ 5.00
2	7	Gas for truck	15.00
3	10	Cab fare for delivery	11.25
4	12	Office light bulbs	7.50
5	16	Office stationery	5.95
6	19	Floor cleaning in office	25.00
7	20	Truck repair	17.50
8	31	Pencils for office	2.95

STEP 1 ▶ Record the opening balance.

Before you record the vouchers, you must record the $100.00 check that was cashed to start the fund. Since this is the first entry in the petty cash book, you must write the complete date in the Date column. The year is written above the month. The year and the month will not be written again until a new page is started or the year or month changes. After recording the date, "Check #306" is written in the Explanation column. The amount, $100.00, is entered in the Receipts column. A dash (-) is recorded in the Vo. No. column.

STEP 2 ▶ Record the payments.

For each voucher, enter the date in the Date column. Record what the voucher was paid for in the Explanation column, and enter the voucher number in the Vo. No. column. (Vouchers are always recorded in numerical order.) Next, enter the amount of the voucher twice, once in the Payments column and once in the correct Distribution of Payments column. For example, the payment of $5.00 on May 3 for stamps for the office is extended to the Office Expense column.

Recording the payments on May 12 and May 19 presents a special problem. Each item is a general expense, but there is no column with the heading "General Expense." This is a situation where you use the Other Items columns. The Other Items columns are used whenever there is no **special column** for a payment.

Notice that there are two columns under the heading "Other Items." The Item column is used to enter the classification of the expense. The Amount column is used to enter the amount of the expense.

KEY Terms

Special column. A column for a specific expense.

STEP 3 ▶ Rule and foot the amount columns.

Draw a single ruling under all five money columns and foot each column using small figures.

STEP 4 ▶ Check the totals by crossfooting.

Check the totals by adding the totals of the columns in the Distribution of Payments section. The sum of these totals should add up to the total of the Payments column, $90.15.

Office Expense column total	$13.90
Delivery Expense column total	43.75
Other Items Amount column total	32.50
Sum of Distribution of Payments totals	$90.15

If the sum did not equal $90.15, you could find the error by following these steps:

1. Re-add the Distribution of Payments totals.
2. Re-add each column in the petty cash book.
3. Check to see that each expense was extended correctly from the Payments column to one of the Distribution of Payments columns.

STEP **5** ▶ *Record the final totals and double rule the amount columns.*

After the footings have been checked, write the final totals. Draw a double ruling under the final totals. Enter the same date as the last payment date in the Date column. Write the word "Totals" in the Explanation column, and enter a dash in the Vo. No. column.

STEP **6** ▶ *Find and enter the new balance.*

Calculate the new balance by subtracting total payments from total receipts.

Receipts column total	$100.00
Payments column total	- 90.15
New balance	$ 9.85

Enter the new balance in the petty cash book on the line below the double ruling. Enter the date in the Date column. Use the day *after* the last payment, June 1. Write the word *Balance* in the Explanation column, and enter a dash in the Vo. No. column. Record the balance, $9.85, in the Receipts column. This balance should be compared with what is actually in the petty cash box on the morning of June 1.

ℬUILDING YOUR BUSINESS VOCABULARY

On a sheet of paper, write the headings **Statement Number** and **Words**. Next, choose the words that match the statements. Write each word you choose next to the statement number it matches. Be careful; not all the words listed should be used.

Statements	Words
1. Form used to record and classify petty cash payments and receipts	classifications
2. Entered again in a special column	crossfooting
3. Types of business expenses	extended
4. A column for a specific expense	petty cash book
5. Record of payment from the petty cash fund	petty cash box
6. Currency set aside for making small cash payments	petty cash fund
7. Form used to record and classify petty cash payments	petty cash record
	petty cash voucher
	special column

PROBLEM SOLVING MODEL FOR: *Using a Petty Cash Book*

STEP 1 ▶ *Record the opening balance.*

STEP 2 ▶ *Record the payments.*

STEP 3 ▶ *Rule and foot the amount columns.*

STEP 4 ▶ *Check the totals by crossfooting.*

STEP 5 ▶ *Record the final totals and double rule the amount columns.*

STEP 6 ▶ *Find and enter the new balance.*

APPLICATION PROBLEMS

PROBLEM | **32-1** ▶ You are in charge of the petty cash fund for the Zermatt Food Store. On June 1, your employer cashed Check No. 207 for $100.00 to start the petty cash fund. Each payment from the fund must be classified as an office expense, delivery expense, or general expense.

Directions

a. Prepare a petty cash book with the same headings as shown in Illustration 32A on page 282. (General expenses must be entered in the Other Items columns.)

b. Record the opening balance.

c. Record the following vouchers issued in June:

Voucher Number	Date	Paid For	Amount
1	June 3	Stamps for office	$ 7.50
2	7	Gas for truck	10.35
3	9	Stationery for office	9.15
4	12	Office cleaning	16.95
5	14	Light bulbs	5.10
6	18	File folders for office	16.10
7	22	Truck repairs	18.95
8	30	Gas for truck	12.00

d. Rule and foot the amount columns.
e. Check the totals by crossfooting.
f. Record the final totals and double rule the amount columns.
g. Find the new balance and enter it in the petty cash book as of July 1.

PROBLEM **32-2** ▶ You are in charge of the petty cash fund for Ryan TV Store. On October 1, your employer cashed Check No. 472 for $175.00 to start the petty cash fund. Each payment from the fund must be classified as a shipping expense, delivery expense, office expense, or general expense.

Directions

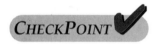
a. Prepare a petty cash book with special column headings for Shipping Expense and Delivery Expense. (Office expenses and general expenses must be entered in the Other Items columns.)
b. Record the opening balance.
c. Record the following vouchers issued in October:

Voucher Number	Date	Paid For	Amount
1	Oct. 4	Office cleaning	$17.50
2	6	Shipping labels	5.95
3	7	Light bulbs	4.10
4	10	Truck repairs	21.60
5	14	Gas for truck	18.95
6	17	Shipping supplies	14.10
7	24	Office stationery	21.00
8	31	Cartons for shipping	16.25

d. Rule and foot the amount columns.
e. Check the totals by crossfooting.
f. Record the final totals and double rule the amount columns.
g. Find the new balance and enter it in the petty cash book as of November 1.

PROBLEM | **32-3** ▶

You are in charge of the petty cash fund for Melrose Moving Company. On August 1, your employer cashed Check No. 1047 for $250.00 to start the petty cash fund. Each payment from the fund must be classified into one of these four categories:

Travel Expense—expenses of drivers for meals and tolls while on the road

Van Expense—gas and repairs for delivery vans

Telephone Expense—phone calls made by drivers while on the road

Office Expense—stationery and stamps

Directions

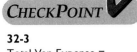

CHECKPOINT ✔

32-3
Total Van Expense =
$106.50

a. Prepare a petty cash book with special column headings for Travel Expense, Van Expense, and Telephone Expense. (Office expenses must be entered in the Other Items columns.)
b. Record the opening balance.
c. Record the following vouchers issued in August:

Voucher Number	Date	Paid For	Amount
1	Aug. 4	Gas for van	$25.90
2	7	Meals and tolls	41.75
3	12	Driver phone calls	11.65
4	17	Repairs to van	35.10
5	20	Stamps for office	15.00
6	24	Driver phone calls	10.90
7	26	Meals and tolls	63.95
8	31	Tire for van	45.50

d. Rule and foot the amount columns.
e. Check the totals by crossfooting.
f. Record the final totals and double rule the amount columns.
g. Find the new balance and enter it in the petty cash book as of September 1.

Problem 32-4 may be found in the Working Papers.

J O B **33** ▶ REPLENISHING AND MAINTAINING THE PETTY CASH FUND

APPLIED MATH PREVIEW

Copy and complete these problems.

1. $47.16 + $15.25 + $19.91 + $36.12 =
2. $18.12 + $19.11 + $31.04 + $97.16 =
3. $ 9.97 + $11.16 + $71.10 + $ 4.12 =
4. $12.11 + $17.09 + $30.97 + $24.16 =

BUSINESS TERM PREVIEW

• **Replenish the fund** •

GOALS

1. To learn how to calculate and record petty cash shortages and overages.
2. To learn how to record the entry for replenishing a petty cash fund.
3. To practice keeping a petty cash book for more than one month.

𝒰NDERSTANDING THE JOB

In this job, you will learn how to keep a petty cash book for more than one month for the same business. In order to do so, you will learn how to compare the money that is supposed to be in the fund at the end of the month with the money that is actually in the petty cash box. If there is less money in the box than the balance shown in the petty cash book, you must record a cash shortage. If there is more money in the box than the balance shown in the petty cash book, you must record a cash overage.

Even when a petty cash clerk makes an effort to be careful, errors may be made. An error may be made in counting the money to reimburse someone who presents a petty cash voucher. Money may be paid out without being recorded in the petty cash book. The money may be recorded, but the wrong amount may be entered. Currency may be lost or mislaid. A person may withdraw petty cash in advance of a purchase, receive too much change from the purchase, and put the extra money in the petty cash fund. There is always the possibility of a cash shortage because of theft, but most petty cash shortages are caused by honest mistakes.

After recording any cash shortage or cash overage, you will receive from your employer a check to **replenish the fund**. This term means to add an amount of money to bring the fund back to its original balance. The Sample Problems will show these procedures.

K E Y *Terms*

Replenish the fund.
Add an amount to bring the fund back to its original balance.

SAMPLE PROBLEM 1

Replenishing the Fund—No Cash Shortage or Overage

You are in charge of the petty cash fund for Natt Hot Air Balloons, Inc. The petty cash book for March has just been completed. It is time to start the petty cash book for April. The original balance in the fund was $150.00. On March 31, the balance shown in the petty cash book is $6.50. A count of the currency in the petty cash box shows $6.50. Your employer cashes Check No. 375 for $143.50 to replenish the fund. Here is how you would record these items:

STEP 1 ▶ *Carry the balance to a new page.*

As you see in Illustration 33A, the $6.50 balance from the March petty cash book is entered on the first line of the April petty cash book. The year and month are both recorded, since you are on a new page. The day, 1, is also entered. The word *Balance* is written in the Explanation column and a dash is entered in the Vo. No. column. The amount, $6.50, is then entered in the Receipts column.

PETTY CASH BOOK

DATE		EXPLANATION	VO. NO.	RECEIPTS	PAYMENTS	OFFICE EXPENSE	SHIPPING EXPENSE	DELIVERY EXPENSE	OTHER ITEMS ITEM	AMOUNT
19-- Mar.	1	Check #279	–	150 00						
	31	Totals	–	150 00 150 00	143 50 143 50	37 25 37 25	46 19 46 19	32 41 32 41		27 65 27 65
Apr.	1	Balance	–	6 50						

PETTY CASH BOOK

DATE		EXPLANATION	VO. NO.	RECEIPTS	PAYMENTS	OFFICE EXPENSE	SHIPPING EXPENSE	DELIVERY EXPENSE	OTHER ITEMS ITEM	AMOUNT
19-- Apr.	1	Balance	–	6 50						
	1	Check #375	–	143 50						

Illustration 33A   Starting a new page and replenishing the fund

STEP 2 ▶ *Calculate and record cash shortage or cash overage.*

Compare the balance recorded in the petty cash book with the amount of currency in the petty cash box. Since both amounts are $6.50, there is no cash shortage or cash overage.

STEP 3 ▶ *Calculate and record replenishing the fund.*

Subtract the new balance from the original balance to find how much is needed to replenish the fund.

Original balance	$150.00
New balance	- 6.50
Amount needed to replenish fund	$143.50

Enter the check cashed for $143.50 in the April petty cash book. Record the day, 1, in the Date column. Write "Check #375" in the Explanation column. Enter a dash in the Vo. No. column and record the amount, $143.50, in the Receipts column. When totaled, the two amounts in the Receipts column will add up to the original balance of $150.00.

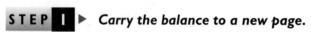

SAMPLE PROBLEM 2A

Replenishing the Fund—Cash Shortage

You are still working for Natt Hot Air Balloons, Inc. The original balance in the petty cash fund was $150.00, and on March 31, the balance shown in the petty cash book is $6.50. But, there is only $5.50 in the petty cash box on April 1. So, Check # 375 is written for $144.50 to replenish the fund. Here is how you would record the cash shortage:

STEP 1 ▶ *Carry the balance to a new page.*

Follow the same procedures as in Step 1 of Sample Problem 1.

STEP 2 ▶ *Calculate and record cash shortage or cash overage.*

Compare the balance recorded in the petty cash book with the amount of currency in the petty cash box. They are not the same. Subtract to find the difference.

						Balance recorded in petty cash book	$ 6.50
						Currency in petty cash box	- 5.50
						Cash shortage	$ 1.00

Cash
shortage
occurs when
balance in book is
greater.

TIP

The difference is a shortage because the currency in the box was *less* than the balance in the petty cash book. Record the shortage in the petty cash book as shown in Illustration 33B. Enter the day, 1, in the Date column. Write "Cash shortage" in the Explanation column. Enter a dash in the Vo. No. column, and enter the amount, $1.00, in parentheses in the Receipts column. Parentheses show a subtraction. Draw a single rule under ($1.00). On the line below the cash shortage entry, record the day once again. Write "Corrected balance" in the Explanation column, and enter a dash in the Vo. No. column. Subtract and record $5.50 in the Receipts column.

PETTY CASH BOOK

DATE		EXPLANATION	VO. NO.	RECEIPTS	PAYMENTS	DISTRIBUTION OF PAYMENTS				
						OFFICE EXPENSE	SHIPPING EXPENSE	DELIVERY EXPENSE	OTHER ITEMS	
									ITEM	AMOUNT
19-- Apr.	1	Balance	–	6 50						
	1	Cash shortage	–	(1 00)						
	1	Corrected balance	–	5 50						
	1	Check #375	–	144 50						

Illustration 33B   Recording a cash shortage

STEP 3 ▶ *Calculate and record replenishing the fund.*

Subtract the *corrected balance* from the original balance to find how much is needed to replenish the fund.

Original
balance -
corrected
balance = amount
needed to
replenish fund

TIP

Original balance	$150.00
Corrected balance	- 5.50
Amount needed to replenish fund	$144.50

Record the replenishment as you did in Sample Problem 1. The amount of the check ($144.50) plus the corrected balance ($5.50) equals the original balance ($150.00).

Replenishing the Fund—Cash Overage

You are still working for Natt Hot Air Balloons, Inc. All facts remain the same, except there is $8.75 in the petty cash box on April 1 and Check No. 375 is written for $141.25 to replenish the fund. Here is how you would record this cash overage:

STEP 1 ▶ *Carry the balance to a new page.*

Follow the same procedures as in Step 1 of Sample Problem 1.

STEP 2 ▶ *Calculate and record cash shortage or cash overage.*

Compare the balance recorded in the petty cash book with the amount of currency in the petty cash box. They are not the same. Subtract to find the difference.

▲▲▲▲▲
T I P
▼▼▼▼▼

Cash overage occurs when currency in box is greater.

Balance recorded in petty cash book	$ 6.50
Currency in petty cash box	- 8.75
Cash overage	$ 2.25

The difference is an overage because the currency in the box was *more* than the balance in the petty cash book. Record the overage in the petty cash book as shown in Illustration 33C on page 293. It is recorded in the same way as a shortage, except the words "Cash overage" are written in the Explanation column, no parentheses are used, and the overage is added to the April 1 balance to find the corrected balance of $8.75.

STEP 3 ▶ *Calculate and record replenishing the fund.*

Subtract the corrected balance from the original balance to find how much is needed to replenish the fund.

Original balance	$150.00
Corrected balance	- 8.75
Amount needed to replenish fund	$141.25

Record the replenishment as you did in the previous problems. The amount of the check ($141.25) plus the corrected balance ($8.75) equals the original balance ($150.00).

PETTY CASH BOOK

DATE		EXPLANATION	VO. NO.	RECEIPTS	PAYMENTS	DISTRIBUTION OF PAYMENTS				
						OFFICE EXPENSE	SHIPPING EXPENSE	DELIVERY EXPENSE	OTHER ITEMS	
									ITEM	AMOUNT
19-- Apr.	1	Balance	–	6 50						
	1	Cash overage	–	2 25						
	1	Corrected balance	–	8 75						
	1	Check #375	–	141 25						

Illustration 33C   Recording a cash overage

TIPS

A calculator can help you save time when summarizing a petty cash book. Here is how you can use a calculator to add expense totals and find the ending balance in the petty cash book. Assume that you begin with $100.00 and have expense column totals of $17.95, $12.75, and $31.10.

STEP 1 ▶ *Enter the original balance into memory.*

Enter the original balance into memory by pressing these keys:

$$\boxed{1}\ \boxed{0}\ \boxed{0}\ \boxed{\cdot}\ \boxed{0}\ \boxed{0}\ \boxed{M+}$$

Press the C key to clear the display.

STEP 2 ▶ *Enter the expense column totals.*

Enter each total as follows:

$$\boxed{1}\ \boxed{7}\ \boxed{\cdot}\ \boxed{9}\ \boxed{5}\ \boxed{+}$$

$$\boxed{1}\ \boxed{2}\ \boxed{\cdot}\ \boxed{7}\ \boxed{5}\ \boxed{+}$$

$$\boxed{3}\ \boxed{1}\ \boxed{\cdot}\ \boxed{1}\ \boxed{0}\ \boxed{+}$$

Your display will show 61.8, the sum of the vouchers. Check this total against the total of the Payments column.

STEP 3 ▶ *Place the total of the expense columns into memory.*

Press the M- key. You have placed your total in the memory as a subtraction.

STEP 4 ▶ *Find the ending balance.*

Press the MR or MR/C key. The number 38.2, or 38.20, appears in the display. Enter this amount in the petty cash book as the ending balance.
Remember to press the MC or MR/C key to clear the memory and the C key to clear the display before going on to any other problems.

BUILDING YOUR BUSINESS VOCABULARY

On a sheet of paper, write the headings **Statement Number** and **Words**. Next, choose the words that match the statements. Write each word you choose next to the statement number it matches. Be careful; not all the words listed should be used.

Statements	Words
1. Actual currency is less than balance in petty cash book	cash overage
2. Currency set aside for making small cash payments	cash shortage
3. Bills and coins	currency
4. Add an amount to bring the fund back to its original balance	extended
5. Actual currency is more than balance in petty cash book	petty cash book
6. Form to record and classify petty cash payments and receipts	petty cash box
	petty cash fund
	replenish the fund

PROBLEM SOLVING MODEL FOR: *Replenishing the Petty Cash Fund*

STEP 1 ▶ *Carry the balance to a new page.*

STEP 2 ▶ *Calculate and record cash shortage or cash overage.*

STEP 3 ▶ *Calculate and record replenishing the fund.*

APPLICATION PROBLEMS

PROBLEM **33-1** ▶ **Directions**

On each line, calculate the amount of cash overage or cash shortage, the corrected balance, and the amount needed to replenish the fund. The first two lines are done for you as an example.

	Original balance	Balance, petty cash book	Currency in box	(Shortage) Overage	Corrected balance	Amount to replenish
a.	$100.00	$ 5.00	$ 5.00	-0-	$5.00	$ 95.00
b.	$150.00	$ 7.00	$ 6.00	($1.00)	$6.00	$144.00
c.	$200.00	$ 9.00	$ 9.00	_____	_____	_____
d.	$150.00	$ 7.50	$ 5.50	_____	_____	_____
e.	$ 50.00	$ 9.50	$12.50	_____	_____	_____
f.	$ 75.00	$15.75	$17.95	_____	_____	_____
g.	$125.00	$12.60	$12.60	_____	_____	_____
h.	$250.00	$37.25	$36.95	_____	_____	_____
i.	$175.00	$41.18	$40.97	_____	_____	_____
j.	$100.00	$56.19	$57.21	_____	_____	_____

PROBLEM **33-2** ▶ You are the petty cash clerk for Carmen's Lumber Yard. On March 1, your employer starts the petty cash fund by cashing Check No. 517 for $150.00. Each payment from the fund is classified as an office expense, delivery expense, shipping expense, or general expense.

Directions

33-2
May 1 Balance = $15.70.

a. Prepare a petty cash book with special column headings for Office Expense, Delivery Expense, and Shipping Expense.
b. Record the opening balance.
c. Record the following vouchers issued in March:

Voucher Number	Date	Paid For	Amount
1	March 3	Postage stamps	$ 5.00
2	7	Floppy disks for office	15.00
3	12	Gas for truck	12.50
4	16	Filing labels for office	8.75
5	18	Shipping supplies	17.90
6	19	Truck repairs	35.00
7	27	Floor cleaning	25.00
8	31	Cartons for shipping	17.75

d. Rule and foot the amount columns.
e. Check your totals by crossfooting.
f. Record the final totals and double rule the amount columns.
g. Find the new balance and enter it as of April 1.

h. Begin a new page of the petty cash book for April and enter the new balance.
i. A count of currency in the box adds to $13.10. Calculate and record any cash shortage or overage and find, if necessary, the corrected balance.
j. Your employer cashes Check No. 619 to replenish the fund. Calculate the amount of this check and record it in the petty cash book.
k. Record the following vouchers issued in April:

Voucher Number	Date	Paid For	Amount
9	April 6	Gas for truck	$14.50
10	10	Typewriter ribbons	10.25
11	16	Office stationery	15.00
12	17	Shipping supplies	17.40
13	18	Cab fare for deliveries	7.50
14	24	Shipping labels	9.65
15	27	Office door repair	15.00
16	30	Truck tune-up	45.00

l. Rule and foot the amount columns.
m. Check your totals by crossfooting.
n. Record the final totals and double rule the amount columns.
o. Find the new balance and enter it as of May 1.

Problems 33-3 and 33-4 may be found in the Working Papers.

Reinforcement Activities

DISCUSSION

You are the petty cash clerk for Anderson Company. Irene Duganos, a new employee, asks you why you always prepare a petty cash voucher before you issue any money from the petty cash fund. She wonders why you just don't give out the cash. "After all," she tells you, "it's only small change." What would you say to Irene to explain why you handle petty cash the way that you do?

CRITICAL THINKING

You have learned that in order to make a good decision, it is important to *study all the factors involved*. In the Critical Thinking problem at the end of Chapter 4, you prepared a list of all the factors you would study before buying a new car. This list might have included such items as price, gas mileage, and color. However, some of the items on your list are more important than others when making the decision to buy. For example, you might feel that the price of an automobile is more important than its color. Identifying the most important items on your list can help you make a better decision about which car to buy.

Make a list of all the items that you should consider before buying a car, such as price, gas mileage, and color. List as many as you can. (You may use the same list you created for the Critical Thinking problem at the end of Chapter 4.) Pick the five most important items on your list. Explain why each item is important to you. If you wish, write them in order of importance. These five items are the ones that you must deal with first when deciding which car to buy. Because people are different, not everyone's list will be the same.

You are checking the work of your assistant petty cash clerk, Thomas Axton. Tom's job is to arrange vouchers in numerical order and then classify them. The classifications used are office expense, delivery expense, shipping expense, telephone expense, and general expense. Tom has made several errors in classification. Write a letter to Tom, explaining why it is important to classify expenses accurately. Also, explain to him what is classified under office, delivery, shipping, telephone, and general expenses.

RECORD KEEPING CAREERS

Every worker wants to "move up the ladder." The ladder referred to is a career ladder. A career ladder is a planned series of steps to better and better jobs. Each job higher up the ladder will usually pay more money. It will also require more responsibility on the part of the worker.

An example of a move up the ladder is from assistant petty cash clerk to petty cash clerk and then to head cashier. Moving up usually requires education and experience.

1. Why would a job higher up the ladder require more responsibility by the worker?
2. Why would education usually be required to climb the ladder?
3. Why would experience usually be required to climb the ladder?

GLOBAL BUSINESS: INTERNATIONAL BANKING

Gloria Sierra is a clerk for a plastic-box manufacturing company that has many customers around the world. These customers send checks that pay in foreign currencies. To deposit the checks, Gloria uses international services from her company's bank, First International. Many U.S. banks, mostly those located in large cities, have international banking departments to help customers such as Gloria. At First International, there is an international banking expert who guides Gloria and her company through the procedures of conducting business in other countries, receiving checks from foreign customers, and writing checks to foreign vendors.

If Gloria had to deal directly with foreign banks, she would have to cope with differences of language and culture and with money exchange rates. Because she is not an expert in international banking, Gloria would spend extra time dealing with these differences and working especially slowly and carefully to avoid mistakes. Having an international banking expert's help is very worthwhile for Gloria's company.

An International Banking Activity can be found in the Working Papers.

On a sheet of paper, write the headings **Statement Number** and **Words**. Next, choose the words that best complete the statements. Write each word you choose next to the statement number it completes. Be careful; not all the words listed should be used.

Statements	Words
1. To record and classify petty cash payments and receipts, use (a, an) _____ .	cash overage
2. When currency in the petty cash box is more than the balance in the petty cash book, you have (a, an) _____ .	cash shortage
	classifications
	currency
	extended
3. Expenses are sorted in groups or _____ .	petty
4. Bills and coins are also called _____ .	petty cash book
5. When you _____ , you are bringing a petty cash fund back to its original balance.	petty cash box
	petty cash clerk
6. An amount that is entered again in a second column is said to be _____ .	petty cash fund
	petty cash record
7. A record of payment from the petty cash fund is the _____ .	petty cash voucher
	replenish the fund
8. Payments that are not recorded in the Other Items columns of a petty cash book are recorded in (a, an) _____ .	special column
9. The person who is in charge of small cash payments is the _____ .	

MASTERY PROBLEM

You are the petty cash clerk for Zippola Trading Company. On June 1, your employer cashes Check No. 311 for $150.00 to start a petty cash fund. Each payment from the fund must be classified as an office expense, general expense, shipping expense, or delivery expense.

Directions

CHECKPOINT

(k)
Check No. 412 = $132.05

a. Prepare a petty cash voucher for each of the following payments made from the petty cash fund. Approve each voucher with your own initials, but do not fill in the signature. Begin with Voucher No. 1.

June 4 Paid $11.95 to Rowena Russell, office clerk, for a window screen
7 Paid $31.60 to Swann Company for shipping supplies.
9 Paid $14.75 to Bill's Lock Shop for a lock repair.
12 Paid $25.00 to A-One Cleaning Service for office cleaning
16 Paid $17.50 to Main Street Supply Shop for office supplies.
22 Paid $8.95 to Jose Martinez for cab fare on a delivery.
27 Paid $10.35 to Jean Pagliano, office clerk, for postage.
30 Paid $12.05 to Carl Carson, secretary, for typing ribbons.

b. Prepare a petty cash book with special column headings for Office Expense, General Expense, and Shipping Expense. (Delivery expenses must be entered in the Other Items columns.)
c. Record the opening balance in the petty cash book.
d. Record the petty cash vouchers in the petty cash book.
e. Rule and foot the amount columns.
f. Check your totals by crossfooting.
g. Record the final totals and double rule the amount columns.
h. Find the new balance as of July 1 and enter it in the petty cash book.
i. Begin a new page in the petty cash book and enter the new balance as of July 1.
j. A count of currency in the petty cash box shows $17.95. Calculate and record any cash shortage or overage and find, if necessary, the corrected balance.
k. Your employer cashes Check No. 412 to replenish the fund. Calculate the amount of this check and record it in the petty cash book.

REVIEWING YOUR BUSINESS VOCABULARY

This activity may be found in the Working Papers.

COMPREHENSIVE PROJECT 2

Comprehensive Project 2 has been designed to reinforce major concepts of this and previous chapters. The Comprehensive Project is found in the Working Papers.

CHAPTER 7

Record Keeping for Salesclerks

*C*ompleting a sales slip is an important task of a salesclerk. Salesclerks need to know how to complete a sales slip manually and by using a computer. They must also learn how to complete a sales slip for a cash sale and for a charge sale.

In Chapter 7, you will learn how to complete a cash sales slip and a charge sales slip. You will also learn how to compute sales taxes and make refunds on charge card sales. Calculator Tips will be given for finding extensions, totaling a sales slip, and calculating sales taxes.

JOB 34 ▶ COMPLETING SALES SLIPS

APPLIED MATH PREVIEW

Copy and complete these problems. Round your answers to the nearest cent.

1. $4.88 × 3 =	5. $3.78 × 2½ =	9. $2.76 × 6.5 =	
2. $1.59 × 2 =	6. $5.70 × 4½ =	10. $4.80 × 5.5 =	
3. $3.28 × 4 =	7. $1.89 × 4¾ =	11. $3.60 × 3.75 =	
4. $2.98 × 2 =	8. $2.27 × 3¼ =	12. $7.54 × 1.25 =	

BUSINESS TERMS PREVIEW

• C • Extension • Gross • M • POS terminal • Prompts •
• Ream • Sales slip • Sales slip register • Unit price • Wand •

GOAL

To learn how to complete sales slips for retail stores.

K E Y **Terms**

Sales slip. Written record of a sale.

Sales slip register. A mechanical device used to record sales.

POS terminal. Point of sale computer.

Prompts. Questions or orders on a display screen.

Most retail store owners keep a written record of each sale. This record is called a **sales slip**. Some stores use blank sales slips that are bound in pads with an original and a copy for each sale. When a sale is made, the salesclerk gives the original to the customer. This is the customer's record of the sale. Many stores require customers to present the sales slip when they exchange or return merchandise. The copy of the sales slip is kept by the store as a record of the sale.

Each sales slip has a printed number. The original and the copy will both have the same number. The numbers on the sales slips are printed in numerical order so that the salesclerk will know if any slips are missing.

Some stores use a mechanical device called a **sales slip register**. Numbered, blank sales slips are locked inside the register. After a sales slip is filled out, the salesclerk gives the original sales slip to the customer, while the copy rolls to where it is safely stored inside the machine.

Many stores use computers to complete sales slips. These computers are usually called point-of-sale terminals or **POS terminals**. POS terminals are special types of electronic cash registers. They include a keyboard, a display screen, a cash drawer, and a printer to print the sales slips.

The POS terminal may lead the salesclerk, step by step, through each sales transaction by displaying questions or orders (called **prompts**) on the display screen, like the one shown in Illustration 34A. This ensures that the salesclerk does not forget anything.

Bob's Bikes No. 6891
3821 Madison Road
Schenectady, NY 12307-1221

SOLD TO:	Sam Hess		Oct. 1,	19 --
STREET:	1319 Ridge			
CITY, STATE, ZIP:	Schenectady, NY 12307-2436			

CLERK	RK	CASH	✓	CHARGE	
QUANTITY	DESCRIPTION	UNIT PRICE		AMOUNT	
1	Shorts	17	99	17	99
2	Inner tubes	4	49	8	98
	TOTAL			26	97

This slip must accompany all returns

Customer Signature

Illustration 34A   POS display screen showing prompts

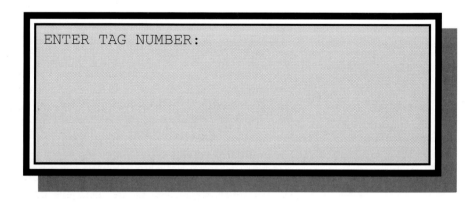

ENTER TAG NUMBER:

K E Y **Terms**

Wand. A scanner that reads bar codes on tags.

POS terminals, like electronic cash registers, may use scanners to read data from bar codes. One type of scanner used by POS terminals is a **wand**. The wand reads bar codes printed on tags attached to merchandise. The wand is attached by wire to the terminal. When a wand is used, the salesclerk does not input the name or price of merchandise being sold. This is done automatically by the computer.

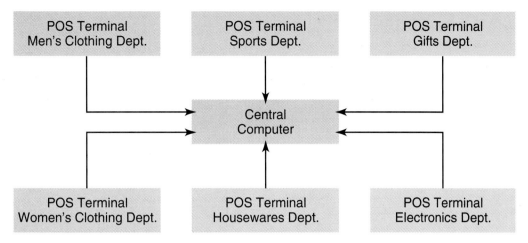

Illustration 34B   POS terminals in large store

In large stores, the POS terminals may be connected to a central computer in the same way that electronic cash registers in chain stores are connected to central computers. (See Illustration 34B.)

The central computer collects data from each of the POS terminals at the end of the day. The central computer uses the data collected to

1. Prepare a bill to be sent to the customer later if the customer is not paying cash.
2. Keep a record of total sales made.
3. Keep track of the amount of merchandise that the store has on hand. The computer will let the store know when the amount of stock gets low so that more merchandise can be ordered.
4. Keep track of sales taxes and let the store know how much tax must be sent to state and local governments.
5. Compute commissions. If the salesclerk is paid a commission on the sales that are made, the computer will keep track of the total commissions owed to the salesclerk.

Whether you complete sales slips using pads, sales slip registers, or POS terminals, the same data are used. Because these data are used in many ways, it is very important that you enter these data accurately.

In many stores, the selling price is shown on each item. However, some stores do not place the selling price on each article. These stores scan each article, and the computer inputs the price. Other stores provide their salesclerks with a price list so that they can find the price of each item.

Vince Khan is a salesclerk for Bricker's Office Supplies. He uses a pad of sales slips and the following price list:

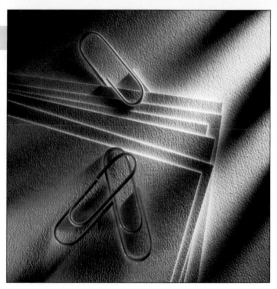

Price List

Item	Unit	Unit Price
Pencils	dozen (dz.)	$ 2.10
Copy paper	ream (rm.)	4.89
File folders	hundred (C)	7.50
Labels	thousand (M)	1.78
Pencil sharpener	each (ea.)	19.89
Paper clips	box	1.09
Ball-point pens	dozen (dz.)	3.98
Bond paper	ream (rm.)	8.60
Paper cutter	each (ea.)	22.79
Index cards	package (pkg.)	.75
Memo pads	dozen (dz.)	2.48
Memo pads	gross (12 dozen)	25.99
3-ring binder	each (ea.)	4.88
Sales slip pads	each (ea.)	3.15
Stapler	each (ea.)	9.85

On May 15, Vince sold the following items to Donna Lewis, 1478 Fortune Street, Waterloo, IA 50701-6278:

4	reams of copy paper
1	paper cutter
200	file folders
3000	labels
2$\frac{1}{2}$	dozen pencils
2	gross memo pads

Donna Lewis paid for the items with cash. Vince recorded the sale on the sales slip as shown in Illustration 34C.

Illustration 34C
Completed sales slip

BRICKER'S OFFICE SUPPLIES
800 Hoffman Avenue
Waterloo, IA 50701-7781
555-2245

No. 33089

SOLD TO: _Donna Lewis_ _May 15,_ 19 --
STREET: _1478 Fortune Street_
CITY, STATE, ZIP: _Waterloo, IA 50701-6278_

SOLD BY VK	CASH ✓	CHARGE	COD	DELIVER BY	
QUANTITY	DESCRIPTION		UNIT PRICE	AMOUNT	
4 rms.	Copy paper		4 89	19 56	
1 ea.	Paper cutter		22 79	22 79	
2 C	File folders		7 50	15 00	
3 M	Labels		1 78	5 34	
2-1/2 dz.	Pencils		2 10	5 25	
2 gross	Memo pads		25 99	51 98	
	TOTAL			119 92	

This slip must accompany all returns

_____
Customer signature for charge sales

Vince followed these steps to complete the sales slip:

STEP 1 ▶ *Record the date of the sale and the customer's name and address.*

In the spaces provided, Vince wrote the date of the sale (May 15, 19--), the customer's name (Donna Lewis), and her address.

STEP 2 ▶ *Record the salesclerk's initials and mark the sale as cash or charge.*

Vince wrote his initials in the Sold By box to show that he was the salesclerk who made the sale. Some stores give each salesclerk a number to use instead of their initials. Since the customer paid with cash, Vince placed a check mark in the box labeled "Cash." If Donna Lewis had paid by check, Vince would have written the word "check" in this space.

STEP 3 ▶ *Record the quantity, description, and unit price for each item.*

In the column headed "Quantity," Vince entered the total number of each item sold. You can see that items on the price list are sold in different units. For example, paper cutters are sold individually, copy paper is sold by the **ream**, file folders are sold by the hundred (**C**), labels are sold by the thousand (**M**), and memo pads are sold by the **gross** (12 dozen or 144).

Vince then recorded the description and the unit price for each item. The **unit price** is the selling price which Vince found on the price list.

STEP 4 ▶ *Extend the amount for each item.*

The total amount for each type of item sold is called the **extension**. It is found by multiplying the quantity by the unit price. Since the unit price of a ream of copy paper is $4.89, Vince found the extension of 4 reams of copy paper by multiplying 4 x $4.89 = $19.56. Extensions are entered in the Amount column.

Vince could have found the extension for $2\frac{1}{2}$ dozen pencils by multiplying the unit price, $2.10, first by $\frac{1}{2}$, then by 2, and adding these totals:

$$
\begin{aligned}
&1. \quad \$2.10 \times \tfrac{1}{2} = \$1.05 \\
&2. \quad \$2.10 \times 2 \ = \ \underline{4.20} \\
& \underline{\$5.25}
\end{aligned}
$$

He also could have found the extension by first changing $2\frac{1}{2}$ to a decimal (2.5) and then multiplying $2.10 x 2.5 = $5.25.

Often a solution will not come out evenly in dollars and cents. For example, $2\frac{1}{2}$ x $2.13 = 5.32\frac{1}{2}$. Since you cannot charge someone for a fraction of a cent, you must round the answer to the nearest cent. When the amount is $\frac{1}{2}$ cent or more, drop the fraction and add one cent to the total amount. When the fraction is less than $\frac{1}{2}$ cent, simply drop it. For example:

Rounding With Fractions	Rounding With Decimals
8.28\frac{1}{2}$ = $8.29	$8.285 = $8.29
5.16\frac{1}{4}$ = $5.16	$5.1625 = $5.16
7.88\frac{3}{4}$ = $7.89	$7.8875 = $7.89

STEP 5 ▶ *Total the sales slip.*

Vince added the extensions on the sales slip. The total was $119.92.

When he said this amount to the customer, Donna Lewis, she gave him $120.00 in cash. Vince gave the customer $.08 in change. Since this was a cash sale, Vince did not have to get the customer's signature on the sales slip. Vince gave Donna Lewis the original copy of the sales slip along with her change.

You can use the calculator to find extensions and the total of a sales slip. You multiply each quantity by the unit price and record the extension. You also store each extension in memory. To find the total of the bill, you recall the amount in memory. Here are the steps to follow:

STEP 1 ▶ *Find the first extension.*

Multiply the quantity (4) by the unit price ($4.89) by pressing these keys in order:

| 4 | x | 4 | • | 8 | 9 | = |

The extension, 19.56, will appear in the display. Record this extension in the Amount column of the sales slip.

STEP 2 ▶ *Add the extension to the calculator's memory.*

Press the M+ key to add the extension, 19.56, to memory.

STEP 3 ▶ *Find and record the extensions for the other items bought and add the extensions to memory.*

Now find the extension for each of the other items bought. Record the extensions in the Amount column of the sales slip. When you find each extension, press the M+ key to add it to memory.

STEP 4 ▶ *Find the total bill.*

When you have added each extension to memory, press the MR (memory recall) or MR/C (memory recall/clear) key once. When you do, the display will show 119.92. This is the total of all the extensions. Draw a line under the extensions on the sales slip. Write the word "Total" in the Description column and record the total, $119.92, in the Amount column.

STEP 5 ▶ *Clear memory.*

To clear the calculator's memory for the next sales slip, press the MC (memory clear) key. If your calculator has a MR/C key, press that key twice. When you press the MR/C key once, the display shows the contents of memory. When you press it twice, you clear or erase memory.

On a sheet of paper, write the headings **Statement Number** and **Words**. Next, choose the words that match the statements. Write each word you choose next to the statement number it matches. Be careful; not all the words listed should be used.

Statements	Words
1. The price for each unit	C
2. A computer for completing sales slips	crossfoot
3. Thousand	estimate
4. A written record of a sale	extension
5. Quantity times unit price	gross
6. A mechanical device used to record a sale	M
7. About 500 sheets of paper	POS terminal
8. An input device attached by wire to a POS terminal and used to read bar codes	prompts
	ream
9. Questions or orders on a display screen of a computer	sales slip
	sales slip register
10. Hundred	unit price
11. Twelve dozen or 144	wand

PROBLEM SOLVING MODEL FOR: *Completing Sales Slips*

STEP 1 ▶ *Record the date of the sale and the customer's name and address.*

STEP 2 ▶ *Record the salesclerk's initials and mark the sale as cash or charge.*

STEP 3 ▶ *Record the quantity, description, and unit price for each item.*

STEP 4 ▶ *Extend the amount for each item.*

STEP 5 ▶ *Total the sales slip.*

Vince Khan is still a salesclerk for Bricker's Office Supplies. He completes a sales slip for each sale he makes. He uses a sales slip form like the one in the Sample Problem.

Directions

CHECKPOINT ✔

34-1 Sale #1
Total = $68.07

On May 16, Vince made the following eight sales. Complete a sales slip for each sale using the price list found in the Sample Problem. If needed, use two lines for an item. Every customer paid cash. Begin numbering the sales slips with 33122.

Sale #1	**Sale #2**
Customer's name V-Tech, Inc.	Customer's name Tom Ingram
Address 414 Doran Street	Address 5401 Bowler Avenue
Waterloo, IA 50703-6611	Waterloo, IA 50707-5613
Items sold 15 boxes paper clips	Items sold 3 C file folders
2 pencil sharpeners	4 rms. bond paper
3 dz. ball-point pens	2 staplers
Sale #3	**Sale #4**
Customer's name Karen Hamm	Customer's name Paramount Company
Address 4322 Grand Boulevard	Address 450 Pinetree Street
Waterloo, IA 50701-3136	Waterloo, IA 50703-8891
Items sold 6$\frac{1}{2}$ dz. pencils	Items sold 5 ea. 3-ring binders
1 gross memo pads	6 pkgs. index cards
3 rms. copy paper	2 M labels
Sale #5	**Sale #6**
Customer's name Best & Co.	Customer's name Seawood Markets
Address 5123 Osage Avenue	Address 12006 Hammond Avenue
Waterloo, IA 50703-2287	Waterloo, IA 50701-1542
Items sold 25 sales slip pads	Items sold 8 rms. bond paper
2 paper cutters	6 rms. copy paper
5$\frac{1}{4}$ dz. ball-point pens	1 gross memo pads
Sale #7	**Sale #8**
Customer's name R & R Sports	Customer's name Ultimate Shops, Inc.
Address 4812 Franklin Street	Address 1323 Lake Avenue
Waterloo, IA 50707-8882	Waterloo, IA 50707-1089
Items sold 10 dz. pencils	Items sold 3 pencil sharpeners
9 dz. ball-point pens	6 pkgs. index cards
25 boxes paper clips	4 staplers

APPLIED MATH PREVIEW

Copy and complete these problems. Round your answers to the nearest cent.

1. $7.48 × 8 =
2. $1.89 × 5 =
3. $9.18 × 2 =
4. $4.79 × 4 =

5. $4.50 × $4\frac{1}{2}$ =
6. $8.12 × $6\frac{1}{4}$ =
7. $2.77 × $2\frac{1}{2}$ =
8. $5.83 × $4\frac{1}{4}$ =

BUSINESS TERMS PREVIEW

• Retailers • Sales tax •

GOALS

1. To learn how to find the amount of sales tax on a retail sale.
2. To learn how to complete sales slips when sales taxes are charged.

UNDERSTANDING THE JOB

KEY Terms

Retailers. Store owners who sell directly to consumers.

Sales tax. Percent of selling price collected by retailer for governments.

There are many places where **retailers** must collect a **sales tax** from each customer on all or certain types of sales. The tax is based on the selling price of the merchandise sold.

The sales tax collected is usually a state sales tax. All retailers in the state must collect the tax from each customer and send it to the state government. Tax rates vary from state to state because the tax laws are not the same in each state.

In many places, there is also a local (city or county) sales tax. The money collected for local taxes is turned over to the local government. Where both state and local sales taxes are charged, the taxes are usually combined so that the retailer may collect them as one amount.

Each sales slip must show the amount of the sale and the amount of the sales tax. Sales tax charts like the one shown in Illustration 35B (page 312) help salesclerks determine the amount of sales tax to charge for each sale.

You are a salesclerk for the Art Loft in a state which charges a 5% sales tax. You sold two small frames for $2.43 each and two small prints for $4.99 each. The sales slip you completed is shown in Illustration 35A.

STEP 1 ▶ *Compute the sales tax.*

The sales tax of $.74 on the sale of $14.84 was found by using the sales tax chart (Illustration 35B) in this way:

Tax on $14.00 (14 x $.05)	$ 0.70
Tax on $.84 (Tax chart, $.70-$.89)	+ 0.04
Total tax	$ 0.74

Illustration 35A
Completed sales slip
showing sales tax

No. **4078** **ART LOFT**
13089 Franklin Road
Boise, ID 83709-5162
555-3939

SOLD TO: _Trudy Boren_ _June 17,_ 19 _--_
STREET: _Apt. 6, 210 Camas Street_
CITY, STATE, ZIP: _Boise, ID 83705-1928_

SOLD BY 12	CASH ✓	CHECK		CHARGE	DELIVER BY	
QUANTITY	DESCRIPTION		UNIT PRICE		AMOUNT	
2 ea.	Frames		2	43	4	86
2 ea.	Prints		4	99	9	98
	Amount of sale				14	84
	5% sales tax					74
	Total				15	58

_____
Customer signature for charge sales

THIS SLIP MUST ACCOMPANY ALL RETURNS

5% Sales Tax Chart	
Amount of Sale	Tax
$.00 - $.09	No Tax
.10 - .29	$.01
.30 - .49	.02
.50 - .69	.03
.70 - .89	.04
.90 - 1.00	.05

On a sale over $1.00, take $.05 for each full dollar plus the tax given in the chart above for the amount over an even dollar.

T I P

You must round to the nearest cent.

If you do not have a tax chart, you must find the tax by multiplying the amount of the sale, $14.84, by the tax rate of 5%:

Amount of sale	$14.84
Tax rate, 5%	x 0.05
Sales tax	$ 0.742 = $0.74

STEP 2 ▶ *Add the sales tax to the amount of the sale.*

Amount of sale	$14.84
Sales tax	+ .74
Total	$15.58

Calculator **TIPS**

You can use the calculator to complete sales slips that include sales taxes. Here is how you would use the calculator to complete the sales slip in the Sample Problem.

STEP I ▶ *Find the extensions.*

Multiply the unit price ($2.43) times the quantity (2) to find the extension for the frames by pressing these keys in order:

| 2 | • | 4 | 3 | x | 2 | = |

The extension, 4.86, will appear in the display. Enter this amount on the sales slip. Then, add the extension to memory by pressing the M+ key.

Now find the second extension in the same way. When you do, add the extension to memory by pressing the M+ key.

STEP 2 ▶ *Find the amount of the sale.*

Press the MR or MR/C key once. The total of the extensions, 14.84, now appears in the display. Enter this amount on the sales slip.

STEP 3 ▶ *Find the amount of the sales tax.*

The total, 14.84, is still in the display. Multiply the total by the sales tax rate, 5%, by pressing these keys in order:

x	•	0	5	=

The amount of the sales tax, 0.742, will appear in the display. Round the amount to the nearest whole cent, .74, and enter the rounded amount on the sales slip. Now add the unrounded amount of the sales tax to memory by pressing the M+ key.

STEP 4 ▶ *Find the total of the sales slip.*

Press the MR or MR/C key once. The total amount of the sales slip, 15.582, will appear in the display. Round the amount off to the nearest cent, 15.58, and enter it on the Total line of the sales slip.

STEP 5 ▶ *Clear memory.*

Press the MC key once or the MR/C key twice. This will clear memory and prepare you for the next sales slip.

BUILDING YOUR BUSINESS VOCABULARY

On a sheet of paper, write the headings **Statement Number** and **Words**. Next, choose the words that match the statements. Write each word you choose next to the statement number it matches. Be careful; not all the words listed should be used.

Statements	Words
1. A store owner who sells directly to the consumer	crossfoot
2. Quantity times unit price	extension
3. The price of each unit	merchandise
4. A written record of a sale	ream
5. A percentage of the selling price collected by the retailer for the state and/or local government	retailer
	sales slip
	sales slip register
	sales tax
6. An input device attached to a POS terminal and used to read bar codes	unit price
	wand
7. A mechanical device used to record a sale	

PROBLEM SOLVING MODEL FOR: *Computing Sales Tax on Merchandise*

STEP 1 ▶ *Compute the sales tax.*

STEP 2 ▶ *Add the sales tax to the amount of the sale.*

*A*PPLICATION PROBLEMS

 **PROBLEM** | **35-1** ▶ | **Directions**

Complete the following form by finding the sales tax and the total amount for each sale. Use the 5% sales tax chart in Illustration 35B (page 312) to find the sales tax.

CHECKPOINT ✔

35-1 (1)
Sales Tax = $0.02

No.	Amount of Sale		Amount of Sales Tax		TOTAL	
1		30				
2		08				
3		45				
4		89				
5	2	78				
6	8	98				
7	1	19				
8	12	67				
9	25	36				
10	147	57				

 **PROBLEM** | **35-2** ▶ | **Directions**

Complete the following form by finding the sales tax and the total amount for each sale. Use the 5% sales tax chart in Illustration 35B (page 312) to find the sales tax.

CHECKPOINT ✔

35-2 (1)
Total = $0.84

No.	Amount of Sale		Amount of Sales Tax		TOTAL	
1		80				
2		73				
3		06				
4	2	29				
5	6	38				
6	36	76				
7	56	88				
8	215	59				
9	486	72				
10	593	41				

Directions

35-3
Sales Slip No. 99082
Total = $46.81

Complete the following four sales slips. Find the sales tax by multiplying the amount of the sale by the sales tax rate of 8%.

Billy's Better Bookstore   Cash and Carry Only
1208 Framingham Road

DATE _April 4,_____ 19 _--_

SOLD TO: _Sandra Bellows_____
STREET: _4503 Frontage Road_____
CITY, STATE, ZIP: _El Paso, TX 79922-2093_____

SOLD BY 4	CASH ✓	CHECK	DELIVER BY
QUANTITY	DESCRIPTION		AMOUNT
4	Book covers @ .89		
2	Dictionaries @ $19.89		
	Amount of sale		
	8% sales tax		
	Total		

99082

Billy's Better Bookstore   Cash and Carry Only
1208 Framingham Road

DATE _April 4,_____ 19 _--_

SOLD TO: _Frank Delouise_____
STREET: _Apt. 4B, Wrentzle Street_____
CITY, STATE, ZIP: _El Paso, TX 79924-8492_____

SOLD BY 4	CASH	CHECK ✓	DELIVER BY
QUANTITY	DESCRIPTION		AMOUNT
1	Mystery @ $15.78		
2	Science fiction		
	paperbacks @ $3.98		
	Amount of sale		
	8% sales tax		
	Total		

99083

Billy's Better Bookstore   Cash and Carry Only
1208 Framingham Road

DATE _April 4,_____ 19 _--_

SOLD TO: _Amelia Rivera_____
STREET: _2190 Katrin Street_____
CITY, STATE, ZIP: _El Paso, TX 79927-1027_____

SOLD BY 4	CASH ✓	CHECK	DELIVER BY
QUANTITY	DESCRIPTION		AMOUNT
2	Book holders @ $1.98		
3	Leather bookmarks		
	@ $2.19		
	Amount of sale		
	8% sales tax		
	Total		

99084

Billy's Better Bookstore   Cash and Carry Only
1208 Framingham Road

DATE _April 4,_____ 19 _--_

SOLD TO: _Gerald Taylor_____
STREET: _22189 Frankfort Avenue_____
CITY, STATE, ZIP: _El Paso, TX 79903-4461_____

SOLD BY 4	CASH ✓	CHECK	DELIVER BY
QUANTITY	DESCRIPTION		AMOUNT
3	Western paperbacks		
	@ $2.98		
2	Video cassettes		
	@ $4.99		
	Amount of sale		
	8% sales tax		
	Total		

99085

Problem 35-4 may be found in the Working Papers.

JOB **36** ► COMPUTING SALES TAXES ON GOODS AND SERVICES

APPLIED MATH PREVIEW

Copy and complete these problems. Round your answers to the nearest cent.

1. $449.00 × 0.01 =
2. $116.50 × 0.07 =
3. $109.19 × 5% =
4. $268.74 × 4% =
5. $115.00 × .055 =
6. $307.50 × .0315 =
7. $156.30 × 5.7% =
8. $143.50 × 6.25% =

BUSINESS TERM PREVIEW

• Bill •

GOALS

1. To learn how to find the amount of sales tax on sales of goods and services.
2. To learn how to complete sales slips that include goods, services, and sales taxes.

𝒰NDERSTANDING THE JOB

Some states charge a sales tax on both retail goods and services. For example, if you had your car repaired in New York, you would have to pay a sales tax on the total amount charged for the repair. This would include the amount charged for goods (materials and parts), as well as the amount charged for services (labor).

INTERVIEW

KAREN J. SANDER

Karen J. Sander is a native of Colombia, South America. Karen is of German descent, but speaks Spanish, German, French, Hebrew, Portuguese, and English.

After high school, Karen came to the United States and took her first job as a receptionist at the cardiology department of Boston's Children's Hospital. She then became a customer service representative to Latin America for a pub-lishing company. In this job, Karen kept sales records, account balances, and worked with the credit department. Her third major job was with Modicon, Inc., an automation systems firm. There, she served as international sales coordinator and sales project manager.

Karen has taken courses at Harvard University and Berklee College of Music. Currently, she is a senior at New Hampshire College with a major in International Business.

One key to Karen J. Sander's success has been her ability to speak several languages. Another important key to her job success has been her excellent ability to keep records.

Many states do not charge sales taxes on everything sold to consumers. For example, some states do not charge sales taxes on food or prescription drugs. Other states do not tax services. In these states, you must separate the charges that are to be taxed from those that are not taxed. For example, in states that do not tax services, you must separate the charges for labor from the charges for parts when you prepare a car repair bill. Then you compute the sales tax only on the charge for parts.

SAMPLE PROBLEM 1

Tax on Goods and Services

You are a cashier for Central Motors in Schenectady, New York. You complete a sales slip, or **bill**, for Annice Mays. Annice had her car repaired and must be charged for parts and labor. Schenectady has a 7% sales tax on *both goods and services*. The completed bill is shown in Illustration 36A.

Illustration 36A
Completed bill showing sales tax on parts and labor

CENTRAL MOTORS
1501 Lark Street
Schenectady, NY 12306-8856

NO. **71928**

NAME _Annice Mays_
ADDRESS _1590 Fifth Street_
Schenectady, NY 12303-1561

YEAR	MAKE	LICENSE NO.	MILEAGE	DATE
1994	Chevrolet	287-198	22,780	3/28/--

DESCRIPTION	PARTS		LABOR	
Change oil and filter	14	85	17	50
Replace coolant reservoir	8	95	19	50
TOTALS	23	80	37	00
PARTS FORWARD ————————————————→			23	80
SUBTOTAL			60	80
SALES TAX — 7%			4	26
TOTAL BILL			65	06

STEP 1 ▶ *Compute the sales tax.*

The sales tax of $4.26 was based on the total charge for parts and labor. The tax on $60.80 is $4.256, or $4.26 ($60.80 x 0.07).

STEP 2 ▶ *Add the sales tax to the amount of the sale.*

The amount of the sale was $60.80 for parts and labor. The sales tax is $4.26 on parts and labor. The total bill is $65.06 ($60.80 + $4.26).

𝒮AMPLE PROBLEM 2

Tax Only on Goods

You work for Hudson's Auto Repairs in St. Louis, Missouri. You must complete a bill for John Martin, who had his car repaired. In St. Louis, a 5.725% sales tax is charged *only on goods.* Services are not taxed. The completed bill is shown in Illustration 36B.

Illustration 36B
Completed bill showing
sales tax only on parts

Hudson's 8545 Lindberg Boulevard
St. Louis, MO 63125-6588

NO. **36459**

NAME *John Martin*

ADDRESS *8782 Lindell Boulevard*
St. Louis, MO 63121-1315

YEAR	MAKE	LICENSE NO.	MILEAGE	DATE
1995	*Ford*	*337-871*	*15,120*	*5/17/--*

DESCRIPTION	PARTS		LABOR	
Repair front door locks	*24*	*89*	*24*	*80*
Align front end			*47*	*90*
TOTALS	*24*	*89*	*72*	*70*
PARTS FORWARD ——————————————→			*24*	*89*
SUBTOTAL			*97*	*59*
SALES TAX — 5.725% (ON PARTS ONLY)			*1*	*42*
TOTAL BILL			*99*	*01*

STEP 1 ▶ Compute the sales tax.

The sales tax, $1.42, was based only on the charge for parts. The tax on $24.89 is $1.42 ($24.89 X 0.05725).

STEP 2 ▶ Add the sales tax to the amount of the sale.

The amount of the sale is $97.59 for parts and labor. The sales tax is $1.42 on parts only. The total bill is $99.01 ($97.59 + $1.42).

BUILDING YOUR BUSINESS VOCABULARY

On a sheet of paper, write the headings **Statement Number** and **Words**. Next, choose the words that match the statements. Write each word you choose next to the statement number it matches. Be careful; not all the words listed should be used.

Statements	Words
1. A store owner who sells directly to the consumer	bill
	extension
2. A sales slip	merchandise
3. A total on which other calculations will be made	retailer
	sales slip register
4. A percentage of the selling price collected by retailers for state or local governments	sales tax
	subtotal
5. Quantity times unit price	unit price
6. A mechanical device used to record a sale	

PROBLEM SOLVING MODEL FOR: *Computing Sales Taxes on Goods and Services*

> **STEP 1** ▶ *Compute the sales tax.*
>
> **STEP 2** ▶ *Add the sales tax to the amount of the sale.*

APPLICATION PROBLEMS

PROBLEM | **36-1** ▶ You work for a store in a state with a 4% sales tax. The tax is charged on both goods and services. On the following page is a chart to help you find the tax.

Directions

Complete the table shown below by finding the subtotal, sales tax, and final total for each sale. Use the 4% sales tax chart to find the sales tax.

4% SALES TAX CHART	
Amount of Sale	**Tax**
$ .01 – $ .12	No tax
.13 – .37	$ .01
.38 – .62	.02
.63 – .87	.03
.88 – 1.00	.04

On a sale over $1.00, take $ .04 for each full dollar plus the tax given in the chart above for the amount over an even dollar.

Bill No.	Labor		Parts		Total Labor and Parts (Subtotal)		Sales Tax		FINAL TOTAL	
Example	15	00	8	20	23	20		93	24	13
1	4	80	26	90						
2	85	89	37	48						
3	118	67	55	85						
4	179	21	29	18						
5	282	62	77	59						

PROBLEM 36-2 ▶ You work in the cashier's office of Dart Auto Repair, Inc., in Schenectady, New York. As part of your job, you complete bills for auto repairs. The sales tax is 7%. The sales tax is charged for both goods and services.

CHECKPOINT ✓

36-2 Bill #1
Total = $86.03

Directions

Copy and complete the four bills below and on the next page. Find the sales tax by multiplying the total sale by 7%.

Bill #1

DART AUTO REPAIR, INC. NO. **22605**
1598 Washington Avenue
Schenectady, NY 12305-1208
NAME _Paul Schultz_
ADDRESS _12209 Staten Street_
Schenectady, NY 12307-8912

YEAR	MAKE	LICENSE NO.	MILEAGE	DATE
1994	Plymouth	981-221	44,980	11/8/--

DESCRIPTION	PARTS		LABOR	
Rotate tires			14	70
Replace front brake pads	38	95	26	75
TOTALS				
PARTS FORWARD ——————▶				
SUBTOTAL				
SALES TAX — 7%				
TOTAL BILL				

Bill #2

DART AUTO REPAIR, INC. NO. **22606**
1598 Washington Avenue
Schenectady, NY 12305-1208
NAME _Victor Kelley_
ADDRESS _1308 Rosemarie Avenue_
Albany, NY 12211-3381

YEAR	MAKE	LICENSE NO.	MILEAGE	DATE
1994	Buick	101-454	13,750	11/8/--

DESCRIPTION	PARTS		LABOR	
Replace wiper blades	25	89	5	50
Repair tail lights	28	78	8	50
TOTALS				
PARTS FORWARD ——————▶				
SUBTOTAL				
SALES TAX — 7%				
TOTAL BILL				

Bill #3

DART AUTO REPAIR, INC.			NAME	Tony Barola		NO. **22607**
1598 Washington Avenue			ADDRESS	120 Osborg Boulevard		
Schenectady, NY 12305-1208				Schenectady, NY 12306-3141		

YEAR	MAKE	LICENSE NO.	MILEAGE	DATE
1993	Eagle	445-090	23,120	11/8/--

DESCRIPTION	PARTS		LABOR	
Change oil and oil filter	15	90	18	85
Replace rear window	175	88	75	65
TOTALS				
PARTS FORWARD ————————→				
SUBTOTAL				
SALES TAX — 7%				
TOTAL BILL				

Bill #4

DART AUTO REPAIR, INC.			NAME	Sally Walgren		NO. **22608**
1598 Washington Avenue			ADDRESS	344 Sugar Street		
Schenectady, NY 12305-1208				Albany, NY 12209-7463		

YEAR	MAKE	LICENSE NO.	MILEAGE	DATE
1992	Pontiac	345-109	35,270	11/8/--

DESCRIPTION	PARTS		LABOR	
Replace belts	33	89	24	60
Repair door handle	18	95	12	25
TOTALS				
PARTS FORWARD ————————→				
SUBTOTAL				
SALES TAX — 7%				
TOTAL BILL				

PROBLEM **36-3** ▶

CHECKPOINT ✔

36-3 Bill #1
Total = $37.77

You work in the cashier's office of Jackson's Appliance Repair Company in Fairview Heights, Illinois. It is part of your job to complete the bills for appliance repairs. The sales tax that you must charge is 6.5% on parts only. No sales tax is charged on services.

Directions

Copy and complete the following four bills. Find the sales tax by multiplying the total sale of parts by 6.5%.

Bill #1

Jackson's Appliance Repair Co.		NO. **11096**
2020 Wabash Street		
Fairview Heights, IL 62208-1425		
	NAME Joyce Fidler	
APPLIANCE Floor waxer/polisher	ADDRESS 901 Wilkins Street	
DATE January 25, 19 --	Fairview Heights, IL 62208-4918	

DESCRIPTION	PARTS		LABOR	
Repair floor waxer/polisher			24	70
Replace wax container	8	75	3	75
TOTALS				
PARTS FORWARD ————————→				
SUBTOTAL				
SALES TAX — 6.5% (ON PARTS ONLY)				
TOTAL BILL				

Bill #2

Jackson's Appliance Repair Co.		NO. **11097**
2020 Wabash Street		
Fairview Heights, IL 62208-1425		
	NAME Wilma Schneider	
APPLIANCE Snow blower	ADDRESS 1303 Federenko Avenue	
DATE January 25, 19 --	Fairview Heights, IL 62208-9891	

DESCRIPTION	PARTS		LABOR	
Replace rotor	15	98	21	19
Replace chain	20	89	6	50
TOTALS				
PARTS FORWARD ————————→				
SUBTOTAL				
SALES TAX — 6.5% (ON PARTS ONLY)				
TOTAL BILL				

Bill #3

Jackson's Appliance Repair Co.		NO. **11098**
2020 Wabash Street		
Fairview Heights, IL 62208-1425		
	NAME Samuel Blome	
APPLIANCE Log splitter	ADDRESS 288 Cabre Boulevard	
DATE January 25, 19 --	Fairview Heights, IL 62208-2917	

DESCRIPTION	PARTS		LABOR	
Tune up	15	79	35	12
Replace wheel	16	99	3	85
TOTALS				
PARTS FORWARD ————————→				
SUBTOTAL				
SALES TAX — 6.5% (ON PARTS ONLY)				
TOTAL BILL				

Bill #4

Jackson's Appliance Repair Co.		NO. **11099**
2020 Wabash Street		
Fairview Heights, IL 62208-1425		
	NAME Mark Newman	
APPLIANCE Chain saw	ADDRESS 15 Rubylan Court	
DATE January 25, 19 --	Fairview Heights, IL 62208-4918	

DESCRIPTION	PARTS		LABOR	
Replace blade	8	99	4	00
Clean fuel system	1	99	6	75
TOTALS				
PARTS FORWARD ————————→				
SUBTOTAL				
SALES TAX — 6.5% (ON PARTS ONLY)				
TOTAL BILL				

APPLIED MATH PREVIEW

Copy and complete these problems. Round your answers to the nearest cent.

1. $\$138.70 \times 0.10 \quad =$
2. $\$672.00 \times 0.01 \quad =$
3. $\$250.00 \times 0.065 \quad =$
4. $\$125.00 \times 0.0625 =$
5. $\$973.26 \times 10\% \quad =$
6. $\$733.41 \times 1\% \quad =$
7. $\$260.00 \times 6\frac{1}{2}\% =$
8. $\$\ 74.00 \times 6\frac{1}{4}\% =$

BUSINESS TERMS PREVIEW

- Authorization number • Bank credit cards • Charge sales •
- Credit card sales slip • Credit card verification terminal •
- Expiration date • Triplicate • Warning bulletin •

GOAL

To learn how to handle charge sales in a retail business.

UNDERSTANDING THE JOB

KEY Terms

Charge sales. Sales on credit. Buy now, pay later.

Credit cards authorize customers to buy on credit.

TIP

You have already learned, as a customer, how to apply for credit and to verify your credit card statements. In this job, you will learn how to handle credit sales as a retail store clerk.

Many retail stores, such as department stores, encourage their customers to buy on credit; that is, to buy now and pay later. Retailers call these sales **charge sales**.

You have already learned that large department stores may issue their own credit cards. The customer's name and charge account number are usually embossed in OCR on the card. There is also a space, usually on the back of the card, for the customer's signature.

The salesclerk must always compare the signature on the card with the customer's signature on the sales slip. This is to make sure that someone is not unlawfully using someone else's credit card and forging the signature.

Stores that issue their own credit cards must keep careful records of how much each customer owes and bill them accordingly. Customers who use a store credit card send their payments directly to the store.

Many stores also accept **bank credit cards**, such as VISA or MasterCard. When a customer charges sales using a bank credit card, copies of the sales slips are sent to the bank that issued the card. The bank pays the store the amount owed by the customer less a fee for the bank's service. The bank then sends a monthly statement to the charge customer. The customer sends payments for the amount due directly to the bank that issued the card.

SAMPLE PROBLEM 1

Store Credit Cards

You are a salesclerk in the computer department of Valuerite Department Store. A customer, Chris Everard, is purchasing a box of computer disks. When you ask, "Cash or charge?" Chris says, "Charge," and gives you a Valuerite credit card shown in Illustration 37A.

Illustration 37A   Store credit card

ValueRite

23-802-023
CHRIS EVERARD

Here are the steps you take to complete the sale:

STEP 1 ▶ *Imprint the sales slip.*

You place the credit card and a blank sales slip into an imprinter. All the letters and numbers on the card are transferred or *imprinted* onto the sales slip.

STEP 2 ▶ Complete the sales slip.

You complete the sales slip as you learned to do in Jobs 34 and 35. However, for charge sales, you place a check mark in the box for charge sales and ask the customer to sign the sales slip.

Illustration 37B shows how the completed sales slip looks after Chris Everard signs it. Chris Everard's name and account number (23-802-023) are imprinted from her charge card.

If a computer were used, a POS terminal would print out a sales slip for the charge sale like the one shown in Illustration 37C.

ValueRite
2201 Highler Boulevard

367186

Date: May 21,
19 --

23-802-023

SOLD TO: CHRIS EVERARD
STREET: 231 Riverton Drive
CITY, STATE, ZIP: Providence, RI 02910-4458

SOLD BY 28	CASH		CHECK		CHARGE ✓	
QUANTITY	DESCRIPTION				AMOUNT	
1 box	5-1/4 inch diskettes				14	89
1 ea.	Printer ribbon				5	89
	Subtotal				20	78
	6% sales tax				1	25
	Total				22	03

THIS SLIP MUST ACCOMPANY ALL RETURNS
Chris Everard

Illustration 37B   Sales slip for charge sale

ValueRite
2201 Highler Boulevard

C H A R G E	23 802 023			
	CHRIS EVERARD			
T O	PURCHASER'S SIGNATURE X Chris Everard			

TYPE OF SALE	SALES PERSON	STORE LOC.	TERM	TRANS
CHARGE	000028	07 019	00347	10892

DATE 05/21/--   TIME 03:45 PM

DEPT.		DESCRIPTION	QTY.	AMOUNT
9/3	30799	COMPUTER MDSE.	1	14.89
9/3	30720	COMPUTER MDSE.	1	5.89
		SUBTOTAL		20.78
		6.00 TAX		1.25
		TOTAL CHARGE		22.03

C U S T O M E R   C O P Y

AUTH. SIG AND NO.	CR. AUTH.	
3392		$22.03

Illustration 37C   Sales slip printed by POS terminal

STEP 3 ▶ Verify the customer's signature.

You must verify the customer's signature by comparing the signature on the sales slip to the signature on the credit card. If the signatures are different, give the card to your supervisor who will handle the problem.

You find that the signatures for Chris Everard match, so you give her a copy of the sales slip and return her credit card. The store's copy of the sales slip will be used by the bookkeeping department to keep a record of the amount due.

AMPLE PROBLEM 2

Bank Credit Cards

You are a salesclerk at Levy Motorcycle Shop. Ben Pevo, a customer, is purchasing a motorcycle, Stock Number 5607, for $1,500.00. When you ask how he wants to pay for the motorcycle, he says, "By credit card," and gives you the bank credit card shown in Illustration 37D.

Illustration 37D   A bank credit card

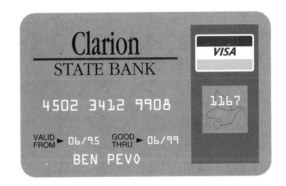

Here are the steps you take to complete the sale:

STEP 1 ▶ *Check the expiration date.*

Check the last day on which the card can be used. This is called the **expiration date**. Ben's card shows "GOOD THRU 06/99," which means that the card may be used up to the last day in June of 1999.

STEP 2 ▶ *Check for lost or stolen cards.*

A list of lost or stolen card numbers is printed in a booklet called a **warning bulletin**. You compare the numbers on Ben's card, 4502-3412- 9908-1167, with the list of numbers in the warning bulletin and find that Ben's card number is not on the list. If you had found that the card was listed as lost or stolen, you would have given the card to your supervisor who would have handled the problem.

K E Y *Terms*

Expiration date. Last day card can be used.

Warning bulletin. List of lost or stolen bank credit cards.

STEP 3 ► **Obtain the authorization number.**

If the amount of the sale is over a certain amount, usually $50.00, you must get authorization from the bank to charge the sale. You do this by telephoning a special number. If the customer's credit is good, you will be given an **authorization number** to record in the proper space on the sales slip. Ben's credit is good, so you are given authorization number 028918.

STEP 4 ► **Imprint the bank credit card sales slip.**

You use the imprinter to transfer Ben's name and bank credit card number and also the store's name and identification number to a special sales slip form used with bank credit cards. This special form is called a **credit card sales slip** and is prepared in **triplicate** (three copies):

> Copy 1 is kept by the store owner.
> Copy 2 is sent to the bank that issued the card.
> Copy 3 is given to the customer.

STEP 5 ► **Complete the credit card sales slip and verify the customer's signature.**

After you fill in all the information on the sales slip, you ask the customer, Ben Pevo, to sign the slip. Illustration 37E shows how the completed sales slip looks after Ben Pevo signs it. Notice that the VISA symbol was circled to show that a VISA card was used.

Illustration 37E
Completed bank credit card slip

ACCOUNT NUMBER 4502 3412 9908 1167	SALE AMOUNT 01575.00		INVOICE NUMBER 507907	
6/95 6/99	DATE 9/7/--	AUTHORIZATION NO. 028918	SALES CLERK 14	DEPT. 9
BEN PEVO	QUAN.	DESCRIPTION	PRICE	AMOUNT
	1	Motorcycle-5607	1,500.00	1,500 00
0897125 LEVY'S MOTORCYCLE SHOP 398 WILCO STREET INDIANAPOLIS, IN 46222-9838				
	SIGN HERE **X** *Ben Pevo*		SUBTOTAL	1,500 00
			SALES TAX	75 00
	SALES SLIP		**TOTAL**	1,575 00

MERCHANT: RETAIN THIS COPY FOR YOUR RECORDS

VISA OR MasterCard

MERCHANT COPY

You then compare Ben's signature with the signature on the back of his bank credit card. If the signatures match, you give Ben the copy of the sales slip marked "customer copy" and return his card to him. If the signatures do not match, you would turn the problem over to your supervisor.

So, the sales clerk must check the customer's bank credit card for

1. The expiration date.
2. Whether or not the card is lost or stolen.
3. Whether or not the customer's credit is good.

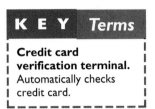
This checking takes time and keeps the customer waiting. To speed up the checking of the credit card, many businesses use a special **credit card verification terminal** that does this automatically. This special terminal is hooked up by telephone to a computer at the bank.

Some credit card verification terminals allow the salesclerk to insert the credit card into the terminal. Others require the salesclerk to key in the customer's card number. The terminal then automatically checks the customer's card number. If everything is alright, the terminal displays an authorization number for the salesclerk to use. If there is a problem with the card, the computer will display the reason for the problem on the screen.

BUILDING YOUR BUSINESS VOCABULARY

On a sheet of paper, write the headings **Statement Number** and **Words**. Next, choose the words that match the statements. Write each word you choose next to the statement number it matches. Be careful; not all the words listed should be used.

Statements	Words
1. A machine that transfers data from a credit card to a sales slip	authorization number
	bank credit cards
2. Means customer's credit is good	bill
3. Credit cards issued by banks	charge sales
4. Credit sales	credit card sales slip
5. The last day on which a credit card can be used	credit card verification terminal
6. A total on which other calculations will be made	expiration date
7. A special form used with credit card sales	imprinter
8. A list of lost and stolen bank credit cards	subtotal
9. Automatically checks credit cards	triplicate
10. Three copies	warning bulletin

PROBLEM SOLVING MODEL FOR: *Handling Charge Sales on Bank Credit Cards*

STEP 1 ▶	Check the expiration date.
STEP 2 ▶	Check for lost or stolen cards.
STEP 3 ▶	Obtain the authorization number.
STEP 4 ▶	Imprint the bank credit card sales slip.
STEP 5 ▶	Complete the credit card sales slip and verify the customer's signature.

*A*PPLICATION PROBLEMS

PROBLEM | 37-1 ▶ You are a salesclerk for Langley's Department Store, 141 Statler St., Tacoma, WA 98409-2298. Your salesclerk number is 167.

Directions

CHECKPOINT ✔

37-1 Sale #1
Total = $6.04

a. Complete sales slips for the following four charge sales made on September 8. Each customer used a Langley store credit card. The customer's name and credit card number are imprinted on the sales slip from the credit card. All other information must be filled in manually. Fill in all data except the customer's signature. Find the sales tax by multiplying the amount of the sale by 6.5%.

Sale #1	**Sale #2**

Address 218 Breckenridge St.
          Tacoma, WA 98466-4847
	Address 912 Hosmer Street
	          Tacoma, WA 98405-6712

Items sold 3 dz. Ribbons @ $.89
          4 ea. Cards @ $.75
	Items sold 2 ea. Jeans @ $17.99
	          3 ea. Shirts @ $19.99

Sale #3	**Sale #4**

Address 15 Morgan Lane
          Tacoma, WA 98404-5621
	Address 707 York Avenue
	          Tacoma, WA 98466-0891

Items sold 1 ea. Car seat @ $19.99
          1 ea. Crib @ $159.99
          3 ea. Sheets @ $7.59
	Items sold 3 rms. Copy paper @
	          $4.80
	          4 dz. Pencils @ $1.99
	          2 dz. Memo pads @
	          $4.89

b. Answer this question: After completing the sales slip and obtaining the customer's signature, what should you do?

You are a salesclerk for the CompuTech Systems of Portland, Maine. CompuTech accepts MasterCard or VISA for charge sales. However, you must get an authorization number for all charge sales over $50.00. Your sales clerk number is 108, and you work in department number 7.

Directions

CHECKPOINT

37-2 Sale #1
Total = $282.10

Complete credit card sales slips for the following four charge sales made on January 15. Each customer used a MasterCard or VISA card. The customer's name and credit card number, the invoice number, and the store name and identification number are imprinted on the sales slip from the credit card and the imprinter. All other information must be filled in manually. Fill in all data except the customer's signature. Find the sales tax by multiplying the amount of the sale by 5%.

Sale #1	**Sale #2**
Items sold 2 ea. Floppy drives @ $99.89 (stock no. 46602) 1 ea. Modem @ $68.89 (stock no. 38804)	Items sold 2 ea. Hard disk cards @ $339.87 (stock no. 18976) 1 ea. Tape backup @ $849.29 (stock no. 41978)
Authorization No. 071982 Card used VISA	Authorization No. 073978 Card used MasterCard
Sale #3	**Sale #4**
Items sold 4 sets Memory chips @ $108.48 (stock no. 67069) 2 ea. Memory boards @ $289.99 (stock no. 08199)	Items sold 4 ea. EGA boards @ $375.89 (stock no. 77891)
Authorization No. 388726 Card used MasterCard	Authorization No. 074868 Card used MasterCard

JOB 38 ▶ MAKING REFUNDS ON CHARGE CARD SALES

APPLIED MATH PREVIEW

Copy and complete these problems. Round your answers to the nearest cent.

1. $250.00 × 0.01 =	5. $834.91 × 1% =
2. $458.00 × 0.10 =	6. $631.88 × 10% =
3. $310.78 × 0.045 =	7. $582.42 × 4½% =
4. $425.15 × 0.0525 =	8. $ 38.56 × 5¼% =

BUSINESS TERM PREVIEW

• Credit slip •

GOAL

To learn how to complete a credit slip.

UNDERSTANDING THE JOB

If a customer pays cash for merchandise and later decides to return it, the store will usually give the customer the money back. If the customer used a bank charge card to buy the goods, returning merchandise is not quite so simple.

When a customer buys goods using a bank credit card, the customer does not pay the store cash. Instead, the customer is billed for the purchase by the credit card company. When the customer returns goods, the store usually will not give the customer cash back. Instead, it will give the customer a **credit slip** like the one shown in Illustration 38A.

KEY Terms

Credit slip. Gives customer credit for return.

Illustration 38A A bank credit card credit slip

```
ACCOUNT NUMBER                    CREDIT SLIP          CREDIT SLIP NUMBER
2210 901 203                                                 649179

11/94      11/97        DATE          CLERK          REG/DEPT
                        10/5/--         3                 2
OLGA STEIN
                    QUAN.   DESCRIPTION    UNIT PRICE   AMOUNT
0798876             2 ea.  Swim goggles      2.89        5  78
AMY'S AQUATICS
2507 YAKLE BLVD.
RUTLAND, VT 05701-1985
                    CUSTOMER'S X            SUBTOTAL     5  78
                    SIGNATURE               SALES TAX       23
MERCHANT'S X           SALES SLIP        TOTAL          6  01
SIGNATURE

        MERCHANT: RETAIN THIS COPY FOR YOUR RECORDS    VISA  OR  MasterCard
```

The form is called a credit slip because the customer will receive credit for the return on the customer's next credit card statement. That means that it will be recorded in the Payments and Credits column of the statement and reduce the balance owed. (See Illustration 38B.)

VISA	HILLSIDE BANK				MasterCard
Transaction Date	Reference	Transaction Description		New Loans, Fees, & Purchases	Payments & Credits
10/02/--	07139827	Happy's Ski Lodge	Rutland, VT	35.89	
10/03/--	82647362	Boulevard Motors	Rutland, VT	138.95	
10/04/--	15243416	Payment -- Thank You			103.44
10/05/--	60798986	Amy's Aquatics	Rutland, VT		6.01
10/11/--	10183928	Fifth Street Station	Rutland, VT	18.86	
10/17/--	38563847	Cleremont TV	Rutland, VT	19.76	

Illustration 38B   Section of credit card statement showing credit

Completing a credit slip for returned merchandise is very much like completing a credit card sales slip for a sale of merchandise. The Sample Problem will show you how.

SAMPLE PROBLEM

Ben Feldman is a sales-clerk at Amy's Aquatics. Olga Stein purchased merchandise from the shop two days ago and wants to return two of the items today. Here are the steps Ben followed to handle the return:

STEP 1 ▶ **Check the sales slip.**

Ben asked for Olga's copy of the credit card sales slip, which was prepared when Olga purchased the merchandise. Ben also asked for Olga's MasterCard credit card. Ben verified that the customer name and account number shown on the sales slip were the same as those shown on the card. Ben also verified that the goods that Olga wanted to return were listed on the sales slip.

STEP 2 ▶ *Imprint the credit slip.*

Ben used the imprinter to transfer Olga's name, account number, and the store's name and identification number to the credit slip. Like the credit card sales slip, the credit slip is prepared in triplicate. Copy 1 is given to the customer. Copy 2 is sent to the bank that issued the card. Copy 3 is kept by the store.

STEP 3 ▶ *Complete the credit slip.*

Ben filled in the information on the credit slip and asked Olga to sign it. The completed credit slip is shown in Illustration 38A on page 330. Notice that Ben figured the extension for the items returned and also calculated the sales tax. Since the customer had been charged for the item plus the sales tax, the total amount deducted from the customer's account must include both the amount of the return and the sales tax. Notice also that the MasterCard symbol at the bottom right of the form was circled.

Ben compared the signature on the credit slip to the signature on Olga's card. Since the signatures matched, he gave Olga the copy of the credit slip marked "customer copy" and returned her card. If the signatures had not matched, Ben would have turned the problem over to his supervisor.

Some stores require that salesclerks fill out one or more additional forms for each return of merchandise. These forms usually require that the salesclerk find out why the goods were returned. This information helps the store owner decide what merchandise to buy and where to buy it in the future.

*B*UILDING YOUR BUSINESS VOCABULARY

On a sheet of paper, write the headings **Statement Number** and **Words**. Next, choose the words that match the statements. Write each word you choose next to the statement number it matches. Be careful; not all the words listed should be used.

Statements	Words
1. Credit cards issued by banks	bank credit cards
2. A form used to return merchandise bought with a bank credit card	bill
	charge sales
3. A machine that transfers data from a credit card to a sales slip	credit card sales slip
	credit card verification
4. A total on which other calculations will be made	terminal
	credit slip

Statements	Words
5. A special form used with credit card sales	expiration date
6. Automatically checks credit cards	imprinter
7. The last day on which a credit card can be used	subtotal
8. Three copies	triplicate
9. Credit sales	warning bulletin
10. A list of lost and stolen bank credit cards	

PROBLEM SOLVING MODEL FOR: *Making Refunds on Charge Card Sales*

STEP 1 ▶ *Check the sales slip.*

STEP 2 ▶ *Imprint the credit slip.*

STEP 3 ▶ *Complete the credit slip.*

APPLICATION PROBLEMS

PROBLEM **38-1** ▶ Janice Chandler is a salesclerk for Dart Stores, Inc., of Camden, New Jersey. Her salesclerk number is 8, and she works at register no. 7.

Directions

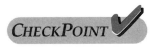

38-1 Return #1
Total = $12.49

Complete credit slips for the following four VISA charge sale returns made on May 21 for Janice. The customer's name and credit card number are already imprinted on the credit slip from the credit card. All other information must be filled in manually. Fill in all data except the customer's signature. Sign Janice's name in the blank for merchant's signature. Find the sales tax by multiplying the amount of the sale by 6%.

Return #1		**Return #2**	
Items returned	2 rms. Paper @ $5.89	Items returned	5 ea. Bulbs @ $.89

Return #3		**Return #4**	
Items returned	4 ea. Glasses @ $1.35	Items returned	3 ea. Scarves @ $3.89

PROBLEM	38-2 ▶

Brooke Tolen is a salesclerk for Vernon's Department Store. Vernon's is located in Spokane, Washington. Her salesclerk number is 2, and she works at register no. 5.

38-2 Return #1
Total = $5.45

Directions

Complete credit slips for the following four MasterCard charge sale returns made on August 8 for Brooke. The customer's name and credit card number are already imprinted on the credit slip from the credit card. All other information must be filled in manually. Fill in all data except the customer's signature. Sign Brooke's name in the blank for merchant's signature. Find the sales tax by multiplying the amount of the sale by 6.5%.

Return #1		**Return #2**	
Items returned	4 ea. Felt pens @1.28	Items returned	1 ea. Clock @ $19.89

Return #3		**Return #4**	
Items returned	2 ea. Books @15.89	Items returned	2 ea. Umbrellas @ $8.58

CHAPTER 7

Reinforcement
Activities

DISCUSSION

Retailers do not usually receive the full amount of each sale made using a bank credit card. The bank credit card company keeps a small percentage of the total sale as a fee for its services. This fee may be as much as 5% of the total amount of the sale.

Suppose that a customer purchased a $100.00 lamp using a bank credit card and the credit card company charged a 5% fee. Suppose also that the salesclerk must verify the customer's available credit for all sales over $50.00.

1. How much would the store owner receive from the sale?
2. How much would the customer have to pay the credit card company for the lamp?
3. Since the credit card company charges a fee, why do you think a store would let customers use a bank credit card?
4. Why do you think salesclerks are required to check the customer's credit only on sales over $50.00? Why are they not required to check the customer's credit on all sales?

CRITICAL THINKING

You are a manager of a store that accepts bank credit cards. The store is in a city that has an 8% sales tax. The store requires that salesclerks get an authorization number for all sales over $50.00.

An angry customer shows you the credit card sales slip shown on page 336. The slip shows that the customer had just bought two items from the store using his VISA card. After leaving the store, the customer noticed that the slip had not been completed correctly.

The salesclerk who completed the slip is on lunch break.

There are three errors on the sales slip. What are they?

What would you say to the customer?

ACCOUNT NUMBER	SALE AMOUNT				INVOICE NUMBER
8193 181 656	00068.52				179322

DATE	AUTHORIZATION NO.	SALES CLERK	DEPT.
5/9/--		D1	2

3/94   3/97

EDMUND VOLLINI

0191228
VALLEY PET STORE
324 JANWAY DRIVE
EL PASO, TX 79925-1922

QUAN.	DESCRIPTION	PRICE	AMOUNT
2 ea.	Leashes	4.98	9 96
2 ea.	Cat shelters	24.89	49 78

SIGN HERE X *Edmund Vollini*

	SUBTOTAL	59 74
	SALES TAX	4 78
SALES SLIP	**TOTAL**	68 52

MERCHANT COPY

MERCHANT: RETAIN THIS COPY FOR YOUR RECORDS

VISA OR MasterCard

APPLIED COMMUNICATIONS

If you were the manager of the store in the Critical Thinking Activity, what would you say to the salesclerk when the salesclerk returns from lunch?

RECORD KEEPING CAREERS

People who complete sales slips may work in many different types of stores. They may also work in many different types of departments within a business and have many different job titles.
For example:

1. A person who sells goods over the counter at a department store completes sales slips and may be called a *salesclerk*.
2. A person who sells goods to customers by visiting the customer's home or business may complete sales slips and be called a *field representative*.
3. A person who sells goods to customers who order the goods by telephone may complete sales slips and be called an *order entry clerk*.
4. A person at a cash register in a restaurant may complete bank credit card sales slips for customers who pay for their meals by bank credit cards. This person may be called a *cashier*.
5. A person who sells computer equipment for a dealer may complete sales slips and be called a *customer service representative*.

On a separate sheet of paper, write these two headings: (1) Business or Place and (2) Job Description. Then choose five jobs that you know about in which workers complete sales slips. For each job, list the name of the business where the job is found, and describe each job by listing some of the duties of the worker in the job.

On a sheet of paper, write the headings **Statement Number** and **Words**. Next, choose the words that best complete the statements. Write each word you choose next to the statement number it completes. Be careful; not all the words listed should be used.

Statements	Words
1. Most stores require the customer to present (a, an) _____ in order to return or exchange merchandise.	authorization number
2. The original of the sales slip should be given to the _____ .	customer
	extension
	retailer
3. For credit card sales over a certain amount, salesclerks must get (a, an) _____ .	sales slip
4. In some states, sales taxes are charged on both goods and _____ .	sales tax
	services
5. Salesclerks usually check a customer's credit card by looking up the card number in (a, an) _____ .	wand
6. A device which is attached to a POS terminal by a cable and reads bar codes is called (a, an) _____ .	warning bulletin
7. Salesclerks multiply the unit price by the quantity to find the _____ .	

MASTERY PROBLEM

You are a salesclerk for C & C Hardware Store in Charleston, West Virginia. Your salesclerk number is 9 and your register number is 4. On May 14, 19--, you handle the following sales and returns. Use a sales tax rate of 5% on all goods.

Sales Slip #1
Type of sale: Cash
Customer name: Garry Apple
Address: 56-24 Visitor Street
            Charleston, WV 25302-7892
Items sold: 2 dz. Stakes @ $12.89
                1 ea. Rake @ $8.99

Return #1
Type of return: VISA
Items returned: 1 ea. Hammer @ $7.88
                      1 ea. Pliers @$4.78

Sales Slip #2
Type of sale: VISA
Items sold: 3 ea. Bird feeders @ $7.59
                2 Bags of bird seed @ $3.99

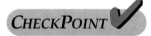

CHECKPOINT ✔

(a)
(#1) Total = $36.51

Directions

a. Complete a sales slip for each sale. If a customer uses a bank credit card, the following information is imprinted on the sales slip from the credit card and the imprinter: the customer's name and credit card number, the invoice number, and the store name and identification number. All other information must be filled in manually. Fill in all data except the customer's signature.

b. Complete a credit slip for the VISA charge sale return. The customer's name and credit card number, the credit slip number, and the store name and identification number are imprinted on the credit slip from the credit card and the imprinter. All other information must be filled in manually. Fill in all data except the customer's signature. Sign your name in the blank for merchant's signature.

REVIEWING YOUR BUSINESS VOCABULARY

This activity may be found in the Working Papers.

CHAPTER

8

Record Keeping for Retail Charge Sales

*S*tores that sell on credit must keep careful records to know how much each charge customer owes. Stores do this by keeping a separate record for each customer showing the customer's purchases, payments, and returns. In addition, retailers usually send each charge customer a monthly statement showing all the transactions recorded in the customer's account during the month and requesting a payment.

In Chapter 8, you will learn how to keep records for charge customers. You will learn how to record purchases, payments, and returns. You will also learn how to prepare customer statements. A Calculator Tip will be given for finding running balances in customer accounts.

JOB **39** ▶ ## KEEPING RECORDS FOR CHARGE CUSTOMERS

APPLIED MATH PREVIEW

Copy and complete these problems.

1. $ 387.54	2. $ 512.09	3. $2,567.19 + $2,651.87 =
13.78	208.54	
10.82	85.62	4. $1,100.56 + $2,719.60 =
562.59	48.29	
72.62	301.08	5. $3,228.60 - $408.01 =
+ 281.67	+ 20.40	6. $9,002.76 + $7,990.59 =

BUSINESS TERMS PREVIEW

- Account balance • Accounts receivable account •
- Accounts receivable clerk • Credit • Debit •
- Payment on account • Running balance • Three-column account •

GOAL

To learn how to keep records for charge customers.

The record that stores keep of a customer's purchases and payments is called an account. For charge customers, these records are called **accounts receivable accounts**. The word *receivable* is used to show that the amounts due from customers are to be *received*.

If you are employed to help keep records for charge customers, you may be called an **accounts receivable clerk**. You may keep accounts receivable records manually or with a computer. Regardless of the way you keep the records, the same concepts of recording are used. You will learn these concepts in this job.

One form of account used by many businesses to keep track of charge customers is the **three-column account**. This type of account has three amount or money columns: a Debit column, a Credit column, and a Balance column. A three-column account is shown in Illustration 39A. Notice that special columns are provided for the date, item, and amounts.

Charge sales, or increases in a customer account, are recorded in the **Debit** column. Payments from customers, or decreases in a customer account, are recorded in the **Credit** column.

The advantage of the three-column account is that it has a special column for the **account balance**, or the amount owed by the customer. Each time a debit is recorded, it is added to the balance. Each time a credit is recorded, it is subtracted from the balance. As a result, the account always shows an up-to-date balance. This is called a **running balance**.

Illustration 39A   Three-column account

NAME	Randolph Vordell		ACCOUNT NO.	1078
ADDRESS	458 Vineyard Ave., Los Angeles, CA 90019-3847			

DATE		ITEM		DEBIT	CREDIT	BALANCE
19-- May	1	Inv. #1924		2 1 3 45		2 1 3 45
	12	Inv. #2108		1 5 0 89		3 6 4 34
	25	Cash			1 7 5 00	1 8 9 34
	28	Inv. #2281	548.50	1 8 4 16		3 7 3 50
	31	Cash	350.00		1 7 5 00	1 9 8 50
			198.50	5 4 8 50	3 5 0 00	

Charge Sale ⌐   Balance ⌐
Payment Received ⌐

- Add debits.
- Subtract credits.
- Inv. = Invoice

Computers are often used to process customer accounts. If a computer were used to keep accounts, Randolph Vordell's account might look like the display screen shown in Illustration 39B.

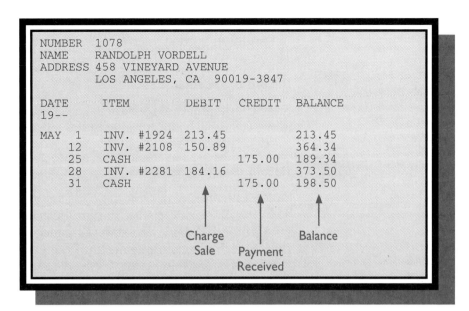

```
NUMBER   1078
NAME     RANDOLPH VORDELL
ADDRESS  458 VINEYARD AVENUE
         LOS ANGELES, CA  90019-3847

DATE     ITEM         DEBIT   CREDIT   BALANCE
19--

MAY  1   INV. #1924   213.45           213.45
    12   INV. #2108   150.89           364.34
    25   CASH                 175.00   189.34
    28   INV. #2281   184.16           373.50
    31   CASH                 175.00   198.50
```

Charge Sale   Payment Received   Balance

SAMPLE PROBLEM

Sandy Temple is an accounts receivable clerk for Fenton's Department Store. On May 1, the store opened a charge account for Randolph Vordell. The following charge sales and payments were made by Randolph during May:

K E Y *Terms*

Payment on account.
Part payment.

May 1 Sold merchandise on credit to Randolph Vordell for $213.45; invoice no. 1924.

12 Sold merchandise on credit to Randolph Vordell for $150.89; invoice no. 2108.

25 Received a check from Randolph Vordell for $175.00 in **payment on account**.

28 Sold merchandise on credit to Randolph Vordell for $184.16; invoice no. 2281.

31 Received a check from Randolph Vordell for $175.00 in payment on account.

Illustration 39A (page 340) shows how Sandy recorded these facts in Randolph Vordell's account. Here are the steps Sandy followed:

STEP 1 ▶ Record the account heading.

Sandy opened the account by recording the customer's name, address, and account number at the top of the account form.

STEP 2 ▶ Record charge sales in the Debit column.

Sandy entered the date in the Date column. Since the charge sale on May 1 was the first transaction in the account, she recorded the year (19--), month (May), and day (1). Sandy will not record the year or month in that account again until the year or month changes or she goes on to a new page.

Sandy also recorded the number of the invoice (1924) in the Item column to show that merchandise was sold. She recorded the number of the invoice in the account so that if there were to be any question about the transaction, she could refer back to the original invoice.

Debits increase customer accounts.

T I P

Next, Sandy recorded the amount of the charge sale ($213.45) in the *Debit column* of the account. Since there was no balance in the account on May 1, she entered the same amount into the Balance column.

When Sandy recorded the charge sale on May 12, however, she *added* the amount ($150.89) to the old balance in the account ($213.45) and recorded the new balance ($364.34) in the Balance column. Sandy recorded the other charge sale in the same way.

STEP 3 ▶ Record payments received in the Credit column.

Sandy recorded the day (25) in the Date column and amount of the first cash payment received ($175.00) in the *Credit column* of the account. She wrote the word *Cash* in the Item column to show that it was a cash receipt. She then *subtracted* the payment from the old balance ($364.34) and entered the new balance ($189.34) in the Balance column. Sandy recorded each payment received in the same way.

Credits decrease customer accounts.

T I P

Notice that every time Sandy recorded an amount in the Debit or Credit column, she also entered the new balance the customer owed into the Balance column. Notice also that Sandy always (1) added debits to the old balance and (2) subtracted credits from the old balance to find the new balance.

STEP 4 ▶ Prove the balance.

Total debits - Total credits = Account balance

T I P

At the end of the month, Sandy checked the balance in the account to make sure that it was correct. She footed the Debit and Credit columns to get the totals for the month. Sandy subtracted the total credits from the total debits.

Total debits	$ 548.50
Less: Total credits	- 350.00
Final balance	$ 198.50

Notice that Sandy proved the balance in small figures in the Items column of Randolph Vordell's account. If the total debits had been equal to the total credits, the account balance would have been zero. She would have written the zero balance in the Balance column as 0.00 or drawn a line through the Balance column as shown:

In that case, Sandy would only have footed the Debit and Credit columns. She would not have written the totals in the Items column (as shown in Illustration 39A, page 340). Also, if there had been only one amount in a column, Sandy would not have needed to foot that column.

Calculator Tips

Many record keepers use calculators to find the running balances in customer accounts. If Sandy Temple used a calculator to find the running balances in Randolph Vordell's account, here is how she would do it:

STEP 1 ▶ *Add the sale on account for May 1 to the sale on account for May 12.*

Press these keys in order:

| 2 | 1 | 3 | . | 4 | 5 | + | 1 | 5 | 0 | . | 8 | 9 | = |

The answer, 364.34, will appear in the display. This is the balance Sandy would enter into the Balance column of the customer's account.

STEP 2 ▶ *Subtract the cash received on May 25.*

Without clearing the calculator, press these keys in order:

| − | 1 | 7 | 5 | . | 0 | 0 | = |

The balance for May 25, 189.34, will appear in the display.

STEP 3 ▶ *Add the amount sold on account on May 28.*

Without clearing the calculator, press these keys in order:

| + | 1 | 8 | 4 | . | 1 | 6 | = |

The balance for May 28, 373.50, will appear in the display.

STEP 4 ▶ *Subtract the cash received on May 31.*

Without clearing the calculator, press these keys in order:

| − | 1 | 7 | 5 | • | 0 | 0 | = |

The balance for May 31, 198.50, will appear in the display.

*B*UILDING YOUR BUSINESS VOCABULARY

On a sheet of paper, write the headings **Statement Number** and **Words**. Next, choose the words that match the statements. Write each word you choose next to the statement number it matches. Be careful; not all the words listed should be used.

Statements	Words
1. Record of charge customer's purchases and payments	account balance
	accounts receivable account
2. Total debits minus total credits	
3. An increase in a customer account	accounts receivable clerk
4. A decrease in a customer account	
5. Part payment of the amount due	authorization
6. Has debit, credit, and balance columns	credit
7. The balance found after each entry is made	debit
8. An employee who keeps records for charge customers	payment on account
	running balance
	subtotal
	three-column account

PROBLEM SOLVING MODEL FOR: *Keeping Records for Charge Customers*

STEP 1 ▶ *Record the account heading.*

STEP 2 ▶ *Record charge sales in the Debit column.*

STEP 3 ▶ *Record payments received in the Credit column.*

STEP 4 ▶ *Prove the balance.*

PROBLEM | **39-1** ▶ You are an accounts receivable clerk for the Playtime Toy Store. It is your job to keep the accounts for charge customers. The data for each customer shown was taken from copies of sales slips and from the record of payments received from the charge customers.

AUTOMATED

Directions

a. Open a three-column account for each charge customer listed by writing the customer's name, address, and account number at the top of an account form.
b. Record in each customer account the charge sales made and the payments received.
c. Find the new balance after each debit or credit is recorded.
d. At the end of the month, foot the Debit and Credit columns of each account. Prove the balance of each account by subtracting the total credits from the total debits. Write your proofs on the debit side of the accounts.

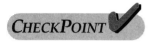

39-1 (1)
Balance = $166.46

Account #1 Customer's name   Thomas Venn
             Address   1715 High Street, Anchorage, AK 99501-3120
             Account number   2091

Feb.   2 Sold merchandise on credit to Thomas Venn for $134.50; invoice #130.
        8 Sold merchandise on credit to Thomas Venn for $225.20; invoice #189.
       18 Received a check from Thomas Venn for $150.00 in payment on account.
       26 Received a check from Thomas Venn for $150.00 in payment on account.
       27 Sold merchandise on credit to Thomas Venn for $106.76; invoice #373.

39-1 (2)
Balance = $53.25

Account #2 Customer's name   Katie Hurst
             Address   4118 Barrow Street, Anchorage, AK 99503-1201
             Account number   2092

Feb.   3 Sold merchandise on credit to Katie Hurst for $201.85; invoice #137.
        8 Sold merchandise on credit to Katie Hurst for $315.80; invoice #193.
       21 Received a check from Katie Hurst for $450.00 in payment on account.
       23 Sold merchandise on credit to Katie Hurst for $235.60; invoice #309.
       28 Received a check from Katie Hurst for $250.00 in payment on account.

Account #3 Customer's name Andres Medina
            Address   15 King Street, Anchorage, AK 99502-7283
            Account number   2093

Feb.   5 Sold merchandise on credit to Andres Medina for $96.50;
          invoice #156.
      12 Sold merchandise on credit to Andres Medina for $163.80;
          invoice #221.
      18 Received a check from Andres Medina for $180.00 in payment
          on account.
      25 Sold merchandise on credit to Andres Medina for $212.75;
          invoice #341.
      28 Received a check from Andres Medina for $175.00 in payment
          on account.

Account #4 Customer's name Nicole Renee
            Address   2107 Norvall Street, Anchorage, AK 99507-4605
            Account number   2094

Feb.   1 Sold merchandise on credit to Nicole Renee for $397.75;
          invoice #115.
       8 Received a check from Nicole Renee for $350.00 in payment on
          account.
      15 Sold merchandise on credit to Nicole Renee for $287.50;
          invoice #256.
      21 Received a check from Nicole Renee for $250.00 in payment on
          account.
      26 Sold merchandise on credit to Nicole Renee for $419.65;
          invoice #362.

Account #5 Customer's name Sidney Blume
            Address   635 Wool Boulevard, Anchorage, AK 99516-5975
            Account number   2095

Feb.   3 Sold merchandise on credit to Sidney Blume for $806.15; invoice
          #134.
       9 Sold merchandise on credit to Sidney Blume for $485.90; invoice
          #198.
      15 Received a check from Sidney Blume for $800.00 in payment on
          account.
      24 Sold merchandise on credit to Sidney Blume for $576.70; invoice
          #326.

Account #6 Customer's name   Garry Ryan
Address   965 Lariat Street, Anchorage, AK 99504-6758
Account number   2096

Feb.   4   Sold merchandise on credit to Garry Ryan for $75.60; invoice #151.
   6   Sold merchandise on credit to Garry Ryan for $87.50; invoice #163.
   10   Sold merchandise on credit to Garry Ryan for $96.25; invoice #210.
   24   Received a check from Garry Ryan for $100.00 in payment on account.
   28   Received a check from Garry Ryan for $100.00 in payment on account.

Account #7 Customer's name   Mary Tremont
Address   6589 Lakeshore Drive, Anchorage, AK 99502-2162
Account number   2097

Feb.   7   Sold merchandise on credit to Mary Tremont for $45.90; invoice #172.
   9   Sold merchandise on credit to Mary Tremont for $78.85; invoice #199.
   20   Received a check from Mary Tremont for $75.00 in payment on account.
   22   Sold merchandise on credit to Mary Tremont for $108.00; invoice #307.
   27   Received a check from Mary Tremont for $157.75 as full payment of the amount due.

Account #8 Customer's name   Reed Perry
Address   145 Story Avenue, Anchorage, AK 99502-7683
Account number   2098

Feb.   7   Sold merchandise on credit to Reed Perry for $215.85; invoice #173.
   12   Sold merchandise on credit to Reed Perry for $324.70; invoice #223.
   25   Received a check from Reed Perry for $500.00 in payment on account.
   26   Sold merchandise on credit to Reed Perry for $317.40; invoice #367.
   28   Received a check from Reed Perry for $350.00 in payment on account.

Problem 39-2 may be found in the Working Papers.

APPLIED MATH PREVIEW

Copy and complete these problems.

1. $301.14	2. $ 119.75	3. $ 2,078.35	4. $ 3,109.74
71.87	100.88	+ 2,008.67	+ 1,078.21
137.09	9.32	a. _____	a. _____
222.56	38.63		
8.91	201.77	- 125.88	- 205.70
172.64	76.28	b.	b.
+ 31.52	+ 186.67		

BUSINESS TERM PREVIEW

• **Credit memo** •

GOAL

To learn how to record merchandise returned by charge customers.

𝒰NDERSTANDING THE JOB

KEY *Terms*

Credit memo.
Shows that a charge customer has returned merchandise and owes less money.

CR = credit

TIP

You have learned that sales clerks give credit slips when customers return goods bought with bank credit cards. When customers buy with store credit cards or have accounts with a store, sales clerks usually give them a form called a credit memorandum or **credit memo**.

A credit memo is shown in Illustration 40A on page 349. A credit memo shows that the customer owes less money than before. The retailer will keep a copy of the credit memo so that the amount of the return can be recorded in the customer's account.

Many department stores that use point-of-sale (POS) terminals do not use special credit memorandum forms. Instead, the terminals print the credit to the customer account on a regular sales slip, like the one in Illustration 40B on page 349. The amount may be shown on the sales slip as a negative number with the letters *CR* printed beside it. The letters *CR* show that the amount is to be recorded in the Credit column of the customer account.

You have learned that you record a payment from a charge customer in the Credit column of the customer's account to show that the customer owes less. Since a return of merchandise also means that the customer owes less, it is also recorded in the Credit column.

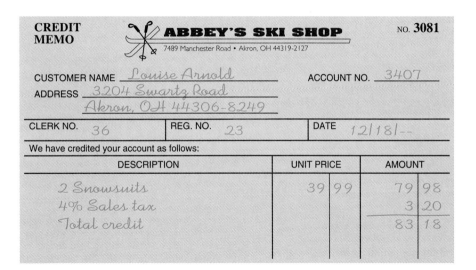

CREDIT MEMO — ABBEY'S SKI SHOP
7489 Manchester Road • Akron, OH 44319-2127
NO. **3081**

CUSTOMER NAME _Louise Arnold_ ACCOUNT NO. _3407_
ADDRESS _3204 Swartz Road_
Akron, OH 44306-8249

| CLERK NO. | 36 | REG. NO. | 23 | DATE | 12/18/-- |

We have credited your account as follows:

DESCRIPTION	UNIT PRICE	AMOUNT
2 Snowsuits	39 99	79 98
4% Sales tax		3 20
Total credit		83 18

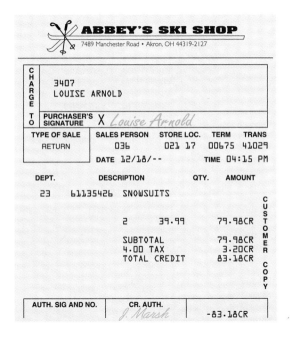

Remember: Charge sales are recorded in the Debit column, while cash received and merchandise returned are recorded in the Credit column. (See Illustration 40C.)

NAME				ACCOUNT NO.	
ADDRESS					
DATE	ITEM		DEBIT	CREDIT	BALANCE

Charge sales are recorded in this column. Debits increase the balance of a customer's account.

Payments and returns are recorded in this column. Credits decrease the balance of a customer's account.

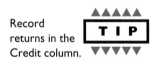

Record returns in the Credit column.

Bill Nozaki, a salesclerk at Abbey's Ski Shop, opened a charge account for Louise Arnold. The following charge sales, returns, and payments were made during December:

Inv. = invoice

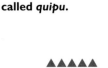

Dec. 8 Sold merchandise on credit to Louise Arnold for $220.67; Inv. #228.

11 Received a check from Louise Arnold for $50.00 in payment on account.

18 Issued Credit Memo #3081 to Louise Arnold for $83.18 for merchandise returned. (See Illustration 40A, page 351.)

21 Sold merchandise on credit to Louise Arnold for $72.90; Inv. #589.

Illustration 40D shows how Bill recorded these transactions in the accounts receivable account for Louise Arnold.

Illustration 40D
Accounts receivable account

NAME	*Louise Arnold*			ACCOUNT NO.	*3407*
ADDRESS	*3204 Swartz Road, Akron, OH 44306-8249*				

DATE		ITEM	DEBIT	CREDIT	BALANCE
19-- Dec.	8	*Inv. #228*	2 2 0 67		2 2 0 67
	11	*Cash*		5 0 00	1 7 0 67
	18	*Cr. Memo #3081* 293.57		8 3 18	8 7 49
	21	*Inv. #589* 133.18	7 2 90		1 6 0 39
		160.39	2 9 3 57	1 3 3 18	

Here is how Bill did it:

STEP 1 ▶ *Record the account heading.*

Bill opened the account by recording Louise Arnold's name, address, and account number at the top of the account form.

STEP 2 ▶ *Record charge sales in the Debit column.*

Charge sales are recorded in the debit column.

Bill entered the date in the Date column. Since the charge sale on December 8 was the first transaction in the account, he recorded the year (19--), month (December), and day (8). Bill did not record the year or month in that account again during December since neither the year nor month changed and no new page was required.

Bill also recorded "Inv. #228" in the Item column to provide a reference to the original sales invoice. Were there to be any question about the charge sale later, the original invoice could be examined.

Next, Bill recorded the amount of the charge sale ($220.67) in the *Debit column* of the account. Since there was no balance in the account on December 8, he entered the same amount in the Balance column.

STEP 3 ▶ *Record payments received in the Credit column.*

Subtract credits.

Bill recorded the day (11) in the Date column and amount of the cash payment received ($50.00) in the *Credit column* of the account. He wrote the word *Cash* in the Item column to show that it was a cash receipt. He then *subtracted* the payment from the old balance ($220.67) and entered the new balance ($170.67) in the Balance column.

STEP 4 ▶ *Record the merchandise returned in the Credit column.*

Payments and returns are recorded in the credit column.

Bill recorded the day (18) in the Date column and amount of the return ($83.18) in the *Credit column* of the account. He wrote "Credit Memo #3081" in the Item column to show that it was a return of merchandise and to provide a reference to the original credit memo in case there should be any question about the transaction later. He then *subtracted* the amount of the return from the old balance ($170.67) and entered the new balance ($87.49) in the Balance column.

STEP 5 ▶ *Record the other charge sale.*

Add debits.

Bill recorded the other charge sale made on December 21 in the Debit column. Since there was a balance this time ($87.49), he *added* the charge sale ($72.90) to that balance and entered the total ($160.39) in the Balance column.

STEP 6 ▶ *Prove the balance.*

At the end of the month, Bill checked the balance in the account to make sure that it was correct. He started with the opening balance at the beginning of the month. He then footed the Debit and Credit columns to get the totals for the month. Bill added the total debits to the opening balance and subtracted the total credits.

Opening balance	$ 0.00
Plus: Total debits	+ 293.57
Total	$ 293.57
Less: Total credits	- 133.18
Final balance	$ 160.39

BUILDING YOUR BUSINESS VOCABULARY

On a sheet of paper, write the headings **Statement Number** and **Words**. Next, choose the words that match the statements. Write each word you choose next to the statement number it matches. Be careful; not all the words listed should be used.

Statements	Words
1. The column used to record a charge sale in a customer account	account balance
	accounts receivable
2. The column used to record a payment or a return in a customer account	account
	credit
3. Part payment of the amount due	credit memo
4. Total debits minus total credits	debit
5. Record of charge customer's purchases and payments	payment on account
	running balance
6. A form that shows that a charge customer has returned merchandise and owes less money	sales returns
	subtotal
7. The balance found after each entry is made	

PROBLEM SOLVING MODEL FOR: *Handling Sales and Returns*

STEP 1 ▶ *Record the account heading.*

STEP 2 ▶ *Record charge sales in the Debit column.*

STEP 3 ▶ *Record payments received in the Credit column.*

STEP 4 ▶ *Record the merchandise returned in the Credit column.*

STEP 5 ▶ *Record the other charge sales.*

STEP 6 ▶ *Prove the balance.*

PROBLEM | **40-1** ▶ You are employed in the bookkeeping department of the Troy Department Store. Your job is to keep the accounts for charge customers.

Directions

a. Open an account for each charge customer by writing the customer's name, address, and account number at the top of an account form.
b. Record in each customer's account the charge sales made, the payments received, and the merchandise returned.
c. Prove the balance of each account by footing the columns and subtracting the total credits from the total debits.

Account #1 Customer's name   Susan Rovelar
Address   3829 Davis Avenue, Pittsburgh, PA 15212-8346
Account number   6841

40-1 (1)
Balance = $34.25

March 1 Sold merchandise on credit to Susan Rovelar for $156.78; Inv. #101.
3 Sold merchandise on credit to Susan Rovelar for $288.81; Inv. #132.
9 Issued Credit Memo #15 to Susan Rovelar for $12.29 for merchandise returned.
15 Received a check from Susan Rovelar for $300.00 in payment on account.
21 Sold merchandise on credit to Susan Rovelar for $73.45; Inv. #259.
28 Issued Credit Memo #27 to Susan Rovelar for $22.50 for merchandise returned.
31 Received a check from Susan Rovelar for $150.00 in payment on account.

Account #2 Customer's name   Paul Singletary
Address   1425 Botkin Street, Pittsburgh, PA 15214-1146
Account number   6842

40-1 (2)
Balance = $115.46

March 2 Sold merchandise on credit to Paul Singletary for $88.97; Inv. #115.
5 Sold merchandise on credit to Paul Singletary for $47.85; Inv. #159.
7 Issued Credit Memo #12 to Paul Singletary for $27.80 for merchandise returned.
19 Received a check from Paul Singletary for $75.00 in payment on account.

23 Received a check from Paul Singletary for $25.00 in payment on account.

24 Sold merchandise on credit to Paul Singletary for $125.65; Inv. #295.

30 Issued Credit Memo #32 to Paul Singletary for $19.21 for merchandise returned.

Account #3 Customer's name   Richard Quigley
          Address   289 Delaware Avenue, Pittsburgh, PA 15221-6736
          Account number   6843

March 3 Sold merchandise on credit to Richard Quigley for $39.99; Inv. #135.

5 Sold merchandise on credit to Richard Quigley for $29.50; Inv. #154.

8 Issued Credit Memo #14 to Richard Quigley for $12.45 for merchandise returned.

19 Received a check from Richard Quigley for $50.00 in payment on account.

23 Sold merchandise on credit to Richard Quigley for $127.55; Inv. #287.

27 Issued Credit Memo #22 to Richard Quigley for $28.90 for merchandise returned.

30 Received a check from Richard Quigley for $75.00 in payment on account.

Account #4 Customer's name   Edith Mackey
          Address   2489 Glass Run Road, Pittsburgh, PA 15236-7091
          Account number   6844

March 5 Sold merchandise on credit to Edith Mackey for $448.73; Inv. #149.

7 Sold merchandise on credit to Edith Mackey for $225.65; Inv. #179.

19 Received a check from Edith Mackey for $650.00 in payment on account.

20 Sold merchandise on credit to Edith Mackey for $175.66; Inv. #251.

23 Issued Credit Memo #20 to Edith Mackey for $18.25 for merchandise returned.

29 Received a check from Edith Mackey for $175.00 in payment on account.

31 Sold merchandise on credit to Edith Mackey for $128.50; Inv. #499.

Account #5 Customer's name   Trevor Pfieffer
               Address   7451 Main Street, Pittsburgh, PA 15224-5582
               Account number   6845

March 1 Sold merchandise on credit to Trevor Pfieffer for $189.89; Inv. #111.

      3 Sold merchandise on credit to Trevor Pfieffer for $147.88; Inv. #138.

      6 Issued Credit Memo #9 to Trevor Pfieffer for $9.60 for merchandise returned.

    17 Received a check from Trevor Pfieffer for $165.00 in payment on account.

    28 Received a check from Trevor Pfieffer for $150.00 in payment on account.

    29 Sold merchandise on credit to Trevor Pfieffer for $96.30; Inv. #472.

    31 Issued Credit Memo #34 to Trevor Pfieffer for $32.76 for merchandise returned.

Account #6 Customer's name   Constance Udall
               Address   6512 Locust Street, Pittsburgh, PA 15221-8657
               Account number   6846

March 6 Sold merchandise on credit to Constance Udall for $94.50; Inv. #163.

      9 Sold merchandise on credit to Constance Udall for $141.89; Inv. #189.

    12 Issued Credit Memo #17 to Constance Udall for $12.68 for merchandise returned.

    24 Received a check from Constance Udall for $145.00 in payment on account.

    25 Sold merchandise on credit to Constance Udall for $114.20; Inv. #310.

    28 Issued Credit Memo #29 to Constance Udall for $43.30 for merchandise returned.

    30 Sold merchandise on credit to Constance Udall for $31.15; Inv. #481.

Account #7 Customer's name   Kim Hunter
               Address   8445 Ridge Road, Pittsburgh, PA 15236-3428
               Account number   6847

March 5 Sold merchandise on credit to Kim Hunter for $251.67; Inv. #142.

      9 Issued Credit Memo #16 to Kim Hunter for $28.90 for merchandise returned.

    12 Sold merchandise on credit to Kim Hunter for $568.50; Inv. #197.

22 Received a check from Kim Hunter for $575.00 in payment on account.
26 Received a check from Kim Hunter for $200.00 in payment on account.
28 Sold merchandise on credit to Kim Hunter for $82.25; Inv. #416.
31 Issued Credit Memo #37 to Kim Hunter for $7.85 for merchandise returned.

Account #8   Customer's name   Jeremy Blakeman
              Address   2445 Sequoia Drive, Pittsburgh, PA 15241-9466
              Account number   6848

March 2 Sold merchandise on credit to Jeremy Blakeman for $56.12; Inv. #121.
      4 Issued Credit Memo #5 to Jeremy Blakeman for $5.90 for merchandise returned.
      6 Sold merchandise on credit to Jeremy Blakeman for $310.88; Inv. #174.
    14 Issued Credit Memo #19 to Jeremy Blakeman for $32.70 for merchandise returned.
    19 Received a check from Jeremy Blakeman for $300.00 in payment on account.
    25 Sold merchandise on credit to Jeremy Blakeman for $125.50; Inv. #314.
    30 Sold merchandise on credit to Jeremy Blakeman for $38.42; Inv. #480.

Problem 40-2 may be found in the Working Papers.

JOB 41 ▶ PREPARING CUSTOMER STATEMENTS

APPLIED MATH PREVIEW

Copy and complete these problems. Try to solve all problems mentally.

1.	50 + 25 =	6.	50 - 20 =
2.	25 + 40 =	7.	48 - 18 =
3.	35 + 15 =	8.	68 - 24 =
4.	135 + 25 =	9.	132 - 16 =
5.	162 + 18 =	10.	156 - 23 =

BUSINESS TERMS PREVIEW

- Billing clerks • Customer statement • Cycle billing •
- Previous balance •

GOAL

To learn how to prepare customer statements.

UNDERSTANDING THE JOB

KEY Terms

Customer statement. A monthly report of customer transactions.

You have learned how to keep records of the amounts owed by charge customers in forms called accounts. Retailers usually send each charge customer a monthly report showing all the transactions recorded in the customer's account during the month. This report is called a **customer statement**, or simply a statement. The customer statement:

1. Allows customers to check their own records against the store's records.
2. Reminds customers of the amounts they owe.

Customer statements are usually prepared and mailed at the end of each month. However, stores with thousands of customers will spread out this work over the month. They divide their customers into groups, and prepare and mail a portion of the customer statements on different days of the month. For example, if your last name begins with the letter *A*, you might receive your customer statement at the beginning of the month. Customers with last names beginning with the letter *K* might receive customer statements in the middle of the month, and so forth. This method of preparing and mailing customer statements is called **cycle billing**.

Accounts receivable clerks may prepare the customer statements or bills. Or, specialized employees may prepare the customer statements. Employees who spend most of their time preparing customer statements are called **billing clerks**.

SAMPLE PROBLEM

You are employed in the accounts receivable department of the Salas Department Store. The store sends customer statements to each charge customer at the end of every month. Statements were sent to all charge customers at the end of March. It is now the end of April. You are asked to prepare a customer statement for April for Amanda Beatty. The customer account is shown in Illustration 41A on page 359 along with the statement you will prepare. Here is how you prepare the statement:

STEP 1 ▶ *Record the statement heading.*

Date the statement as of the last day of the month, April 30. Copy the customer's name, address, and account number from the account heading.

STEP 2 ▶ *Record the date and previous balance.*

Record the date, April 1, on the line for the **previous balance** on the customer statement.

K E Y | **Terms**

Previous balance. Balance of account at the end of last month.

Find the amount of the previous balance by looking at the last balance for March ($45.23) in the customer's account. Record this balance in the Balance column on the line for the previous balance. This was the ending account balance shown in the customer statement for March. This balance becomes the opening balance in the customer statement for April.

NAME		Amanda Beatty		ACCOUNT NO.	3549	
ADDRESS		31298 Bird Road, Miami, FL 33165-9337				

DATE		ITEM	DEBIT	CREDIT	BALANCE
19-- March	4	Inv. #2119	1 4 5 23		1 4 5 23
	14	Cash		1 0 0 00	4 5 23
April	5	Inv. #2314	2 0 8 99		2 5 4 22
	18	Credit Memo #392		8 89	2 4 5 33
	25	Cash		2 0 0 00	4 5 33
	30	Inv. #3197	6 8 19		1 1 3 52

Sala5 DEPARTMENT STORE
23145 Collins Avenue, Miami, Fl 33160-7823

CUSTOMER STATEMENT

TO: Amanda Beatty
31298 Bird Road
Miami, FL 33165-9337

April 30, 19 --

ACCOUNT NO. 3549

DATE		ITEM	DEBIT	CREDIT	BALANCE
19-- April	1	PREVIOUS BALANCE			45 23
	5	Inv. #2314	208 99		254 22
	18	Credit Memo #392		8 89	245 33
	25	Cash		200 00	45 33
	30	Inv. #3197	68 19		113 52

LAST AMOUNT IN THIS COLUMN IS THE BALANCE DUE

STEP 3 ▶ **Copy the entries for the month.**

After recording the opening balance of $45.23, copy all the entries in the account for April, starting with April 5. The last amount in the Balance column, $113.52, is the balance due at the end of April.

BUILDING YOUR BUSINESS VOCABULARY

On a sheet of paper, write the headings **Statement Number** and **Words**. Next, choose the words that match the statements. Write each word you choose next to the statement number it matches. Be careful; not all the words listed should be used.

Statements	Words
1. The balance of the account at the end of last month	billing clerks
	credit
2. The column used to record a charge sale in a customer account	credit memo
	customer statement
3. A monthly report listing all transactions in a customer account during the month	cycle billing
	debit
4. A form which shows that a charge customer has returned merchandise and owes less money	previous balance
	running balance
	subtotal
5. The column used to record a payment or a return in a customer account	transaction
6. Billing groups of customers at different times during the month	
7. The balance found after each entry is made	
8. Employees who spend most of their time preparing customer statements	

PROBLEM SOLVING MODEL FOR: *Preparing Customer Statements*

STEP 1 ▶ **Record the statement heading.**

STEP 2 ▶ **Record the date and previous balance.**

STEP 3 ▶ **Copy the entries for the month.**

*A*PPLICATION PROBLEM

PROBLEM | 41-1 ▶ You work in the accounting department of Rebard's, a department store in Decatur, Illinois. Your job is to prepare customer statements for charge customers. Customer statements were sent to all charge customers at the end of June. It is now the end of July.

Directions

Prepare customer statements for July for the following customer accounts. Date all statements July 31. Remember to start each statement with the previous balance.

Account #1

CheckPoint ✓

41-1 (1)
Balance due = $251.52

NAME		Tamara Barker			ACCOUNT NO.		1288
ADDRESS		2132 Fairview Avenue, S., Decatur, IL 62521-9337					

DATE		ITEM	DEBIT	CREDIT	BALANCE
19-- June	4	Inv. #3208	6 3 2 81		6 3 2 81
	14	Cash		2 8 0 00	3 5 2 81
July	8	Inv. #3223	9 3 15		4 4 5 96
	18	Credit Memo #225		5 6 16	3 8 9 80
	25	Cash		2 5 0 00	1 3 9 80
	31	Inv. #3231	1 1 1 72		2 5 1 52

Account #2

NAME		Adam Carpenter			ACCOUNT NO.		1289
ADDRESS		3764 Monroe Street, N., Decatur, IL 62526-1377					

DATE		ITEM	DEBIT	CREDIT	BALANCE
19-- June	5	Inv. #3211	3 6 5 61		3 6 5 61
	15	Cash		1 2 5 00	2 4 0 61
July	6	Inv. #3217	1 1 3 41		3 5 4 02
	17	Credit Memo #223		3 2 07	3 2 1 95
	23	Cash		2 0 0 00	1 2 1 95
	27	Inv. #3224	2 0 3 27		3 2 5 22

Account #3

NAME		Chet Underwood			ACCOUNT NO.		1290
ADDRESS		4312 Main Street, N., Decatur, IL 62526-6593					

DATE		ITEM	DEBIT	CREDIT	BALANCE
19-- June	6	Inv. #3213	1 5 0 5 15		1 5 0 5 15
	14	Cash		3 5 0 00	1 1 5 5 15
July	6	Inv. #3218	2 7 93		1 1 8 3 08
	19	Credit Memo #226		7 3 47	1 1 0 9 61
	25	Cash		3 5 0 00	7 5 9 61
	29	Inv. #3228	4 2 27		8 0 1 88

Account #4

NAME		Robert Bock					ACCOUNT NO.			1291		
ADDRESS		2129 Webster Street, S., Decatur, IL 62521-3165										

DATE		ITEM	DEBIT			CREDIT			BALANCE		
19-- June	6	Inv. #3214	7 2 8	82					7 2 8	82
	12	Cash				3 0 0	00		4 2 8	82
July	7	Inv. #3219	1 1	54					4 4 0	36
	16	Credit Memo #222				1 2	35		4 2 8	01
	27	Cash				2 5 0	00		1 7 8	01
	30	Inv. #3229	1 0 1	11					2 7 9	12

Account #5

NAME		Robyn Carver					ACCOUNT NO.			1292		
ADDRESS		4163 Oakland Avenue, N., Decatur, IL 62526-2878										

DATE		ITEM	DEBIT			CREDIT			BALANCE		
19-- June	7	Inv. #3215	1 9 2	66					1 9 2	66
	12	Cash				1 0 0	00		9 2	66
July	5	Inv. #3216	7 7	15					1 6 9	81
	19	Credit Memo #227				6	23		1 6 3	58
	27	Cash				1 3 0	00		3 3	58
	28	Inv. #3226	1 0 1	27					1 3 4	85

Account #6

NAME		Ronald Werner					ACCOUNT NO.			1293		
ADDRESS		4167 Charles Street, N., Decatur, IL 62526-4459										

DATE		ITEM	DEBIT			CREDIT			BALANCE		
19-- June	4	Inv. #3209	5 3 3	71					5 3 3	71
	11	Cash				2 2 5	00		3 0 8	71
July	7	Inv. #3220	2 2 1	15					5 2 9	86
	15	Credit Memo #221				3 3	84		4 9 6	02
	22	Cash				3 5 0	00		1 4 6	02
	28	Inv. #3227	1 0 2	22					2 4 8	24

Account #7

NAME	Kay Wilson			ACCOUNT NO.	1294
ADDRESS	3476 College Street, N., Decatur, IL 62526-9199				

DATE		ITEM	DEBIT	CREDIT	BALANCE
19-- June	5	Inv. #3212	2 8 4 42		2 8 4 42
	13	Cash		1 2 5 00	1 5 9 42
July	7	Inv. #3221	3 0 3 91		4 6 3 33
	17	Credit Memo #224		1 8 45	4 4 4 88
	26	Cash		2 2 5 00	2 1 9 88
	30	Inv. #3230	1 1 3 02		3 3 2 90

Account #8

NAME	Karla Frieden			ACCOUNT NO.	1295
ADDRESS	4618 Broadway Street, S., Decatur, IL 62521-4152				

DATE		ITEM	DEBIT	CREDIT	BALANCE
19-- June	4	Inv. #3210	1 2 4 1 07		1 2 4 1 07
	13	Cash		4 5 0 00	7 9 1 07
July	7	Inv. #3222	2 3 12		8 1 4 19
	20	Credit Memo #228		5 7 47	7 5 6 72
	24	Cash		4 5 0 00	3 0 6 72
	27	Inv. #3225	9 3 1 16		1 2 3 7 88

Reinforcement Activities

CHAPTER 8

DISCUSSION

Bermian's Department Store does not send out all of its customer statements at the end of the month. Instead, it uses the plan shown below:

Customer's Last Name Begins With	Working Day Statement Sent	Customer's Last Name Begins With	Working Day Statement Sent
A	1	L	15
B	2	M	16
C	3	N	17
D	4	O	18
E	5	P, Q	19
F	8	R	22
G	9	S	23
H	10	T, U	24
I, J	11	V	25
K	12	W, X, Y, Z	26

Explain how this plan helps the store.

PROFESSIONAL BUSINESS ETHICS

You are an accounts receivable clerk. Part of your job is to open the mail and make a list of the checks that come in from customers. One of the checks that you received today is from Kevin Walsh, as indicated by the printed name and address on the check. However you discover that Mr. Walsh, in error, wrote in the word *Cash* following the words *Pay to the order of*. You realize that anyone can use this check, which is in the amount of $2,000. What should you do with this check? What should you not do with this check?

1. Look at the customer account and customer statement shown below. The customer account is correct. However, the customer statement has several errors in it. List and describe each error you find in the customer statement.
2. Suppose that the incorrect customer statement was accidentally sent to the customer before it was corrected. Suppose also that you find the errors before the customer calls or writes. Prepare a corrected customer statement to send to the customer.
3. Write a letter of apology to the customer for the errors found in the customer statement.

NAME Sharon Long   **ACCOUNT NO.** 39822

ADDRESS 1956 Arlington Avenue, Baltimore, MD 21227-2933

DATE		ITEM	DEBIT	CREDIT	BALANCE
19-- Sept.	3	Inv. #7812	234 28		234 28
	5	Inv. #7934	88 79		323 07
	14	Cash		250 00	73 07
	15	Credit Memo #23		18 98	54 09
	30	Inv. #8567	195 49		249 58

YOUNGMAN'S, INC. 2398 Wallbrook Avenue, San Antonio, TX 78237-8823   **CUSTOMER STATEMENT**

TO: Sharon Long
1956 Arlington Avenue
Baltimore, MD 21227-2933

September 30, 19 --

ACCOUNT NO. 39822

DATE		ITEM	DEBIT	CREDIT	BALANCE
19-- Sept.	1	PREVIOUS BALANCE			0 00
	5	Inv. #7934	188 79		332 07
	14	Cash		250 00	82 07
	15	Credit Memo #23	18 98		101 05
	30	Inv. #8567	195 49		296 54

LAST AMOUNT IN THIS COLUMN IS THE BALANCE DUE ⟶

One of the advantages of being a large business is that a firm can have **specialization of labor**. When labor is specialized, employees have a limited range of tasks to do or work for which they are responsible. For example, a very small firm may have one record keeper to keep all the records for the firm. A larger business may have cash clerks, sales clerks, accounts receivable clerks, and other employees who keep records for only one part of the business. An even larger business may have accounts receivable clerks and billing clerks who work with only part of the firm's customers. For example, one accounts receivable clerk may be responsible only for customers whose last names begin with A through E. Another accounts receivable clerk may be responsible only for customers whose last names begin with F through J, and so on through the alphabet.

1. How might specialization of labor make employees more efficient?
2. How might specialization of labor make it easier for firms to train employees?
3. How might specialization of labor make it easier for firms to find new employees?
4. What disadvantages might specialization of labor hold for employees?

REVIEWING WHAT YOU HAVE LEARNED

On a sheet of paper, write the headings **Statement Number** and **Words**. Next, choose the words that best complete the statements. Write each word you choose next to the statement number it completes. Be careful; not all the words listed should be used. Some words may be used more than once.

Statements	Words
1. Many large department stores use _____ terminals to record each sale.	account
	added
2. Charge sales are recorded in the _____ column of a customer's account.	credit
	credit memo
3. Merchandise returns are recorded in the _____ column of a customer's account.	cycle billing
	debit
4. Cash payments are recorded in the _____ column of a customer's account.	decrease
	increase
5. Debits _____ the balance of customer accounts.	POS
	specialization of labor
6. Credits _____ the balance of customer accounts.	subtracted
7. Debits are always _____ to the balance of a customer's account.	
8. Credits are always _____ from the balance of a customer's account.	

9. A plan to mail customer statements to groups of customers at different times during the month is called _____ .

10. Making employees responsible for a limited range of work is called _____ .

MASTERY PROBLEM

AUTOMATED

You are an accounts receivable clerk for Preston's, Inc. Your job is to keep accounts for charge customers and prepare customer statements at the end of each month.

Directions

a. Copy the following data onto a three-column account for each charge customer.

NAME	Tad Meadows		ACCOUNT NO.	3109
ADDRESS	4809 Hoyt Street, Chattanooga, TN 37411-8879			

DATE		ITEM	DEBIT	CREDIT	BALANCE
19-- April	6	Inv. #2811	3 5 1 89		3 5 1 89
	15	Inv. #2945	1 3 6 19		4 8 8 08

NAME	Anne O'Hara		ACCOUNT NO.	3183
ADDRESS	4516 Vine Street, Chattanooga, TN 37404-2617			

DATE		ITEM	DEBIT	CREDIT	BALANCE
19-- April	3	Inv. #2536	1 0 7 82		1 0 7 82
	12	Inv. #2794	4 2 1 64		5 2 9 46

b. Record the following charge sales, payments, and merchandise returns for May in the customer accounts.

May 2 Sold merchandise on account to Tad Meadows for $219.78; Invoice #3061.

3 Sold merchandise on account to Anne O'Hara for $322.19; Invoice #3255.

5 Sold merchandise on account to Tad Meadows for $107.87; Invoice #3416.

6 Issued Credit Memo #125 for $45.90 to Tad Meadows for merchandise returned.

7   Received a check from Tad Meadows for $750.00 in payment on account.
10 Sold merchandise on account to Anne O'Hara for $418.62; Invoice #3739.
12 Issued Credit Memo #131 for $23.19 to Anne O'Hara for merchandise returned.
14 Sold merchandise on account to Tad Meadows for $156.45; Invoice #3887.
18 Received a check from Anne O'Hara for $1,200.00 in payment on account.
19 Received a check from Tad Meadows for $75.00 in payment on account.
23 Sold merchandise on account to Anne O'Hara for $381.15; Invoice #3982.
25 Received a check from Anne O'Hara for $300.00 in payment on account.
28 Sold merchandise on account to Tad Meadows for $178.47; Invoice #4174.
31 Received a check from Tad Meadows for $150.00 in payment on account.

c. Prepare customer statements for May for the two accounts.

(c)
Tad Meadows
Balance due = $129.75

This activity may be found in the Working Papers.

CHAPTER 9

Record Keeping for Accounts Receivable Clerks

*W*holesalers are businesses that sell in large quantities to retailers. The wholesaler gets orders for merchandise from the retailer by mail, by telephone, or through the wholesaler's salesperson. Most wholesalers first record all merchandise ordered by the retailer on a special form called a sales order. Also, because most merchandise sold in a wholesale business is sold on credit, wholesalers must keep records of how much each customer owes. This bookkeeping is done in accounts receivable records.

In Chapter 9, you will learn how to prepare sales invoices from sales orders and how to keep accounts receivable records. You will learn how to use a sales journal, a cash receipts journal, and a sales returns and allowances journal.

JOB 42 ▶ PREPARING SALES INVOICES

APPLIED MATH PREVIEW

Copy and complete these problems.

1.	10 × $238.90 =	7.	50 × $ 7.50 =
2.	10 × $ 18.75 =	8.	25 × $36.20 =
3.	100 × $ 9.15 =	9.	20 × $18.50 =
4.	100 × $ 0.45 =	10.	150 × $24.10 =
5.	1,000 × $ 6.27 =	11.	125 × $16.40 =
6.	1,000 × $ 21.97 =	12.	120 × $12.60 =

BUSINESS TERMS PREVIEW

• **Due date** • **Sales invoice** • **Sales order** •
• **Terms** • **Wholesaler** •

GOALS

1. To learn how sales orders are used in business.
2. To learn how to prepare sales invoices from sales orders.
3. To learn how to find the due dates of invoices from the terms of the sale.

You have learned how to prepare sales slips for a retail store where merchandise is sold directly to the consumer. Retailers get the merchandise they sell from **wholesalers**. In this job, you will learn about the sales records of a wholesale business.

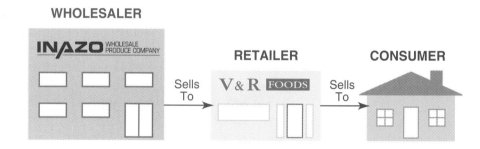

Illustration 42A
Wholesalers, retailers,
and consumers

Sales order copies to:

1. credit dept.
2. stock dept.
3. billing dept.

Sales invoice copies to:

1. customer
2. shipping dept.
3. accounting dept.

When you make a sale in a retail store, you prepare a sales slip. In a wholesale business, two forms may be prepared. The first form is a **sales order**. The second form is a **sales invoice**, or bill.

Wholesalers usually sell their goods on credit. Therefore, after the sales order is completed, it is sent to the credit department. The credit department checks to see if the customer is a good credit risk. If the credit department decides the customer is not a good credit risk, the customer will be asked to pay cash or the order will be canceled.

If the credit department decides the customer is a good credit risk, a copy of the sales order is sent to the stock department. The stock department checks to see if the merchandise ordered is on hand. If it is, the sales order will be sent to the billing department where the sales invoice will be prepared.

The information for the sales invoice is copied from the sales order. Usually, at least three copies of the sales invoice are prepared. The original is mailed to the customer when the order is shipped. The second copy is sent to the shipping department to be used to select and ship the merchandise. The third copy is sent to the accounting department so that they will know how much the customer owes.

You are employed by the Inazo Wholesale Produce Company. It is part of your job to complete sales invoices from completed sales order forms. V & R Foods, a retailer of grocery products, ordered 100 bags of potatoes and 50 crates of tomatoes. Illustration 42B shows the completed sales order form.

Illustration 42B Sales order

Sales orders show no extensions or totals.

SALES ORDER

INAZO WHOLESALE PRODUCE COMPANY
4233 Gervais Street • Columbia, SC 29204-5071 • 555-3285

SOLD TO	V & R Foods 13467 Walker Street Houston, TX 77064-2981	OUR ORDER NO.	4389
		DATE	May 1, 19--
		CUSTOMER ORDER NO.	34199A
TERMS	30 days	SHIP VIA	Truck

QUANTITY	STOCK NO.	DESCRIPTION	UNIT PRICE
100 bags	P1928	Potatoes	3 | 49
50 crates	T8891	Tomatoes	6 | 29

Notice the following information recorded on the sales order:

1. *Our order number.* Sales order forms are usually numbered in consecutive order. The number used for V & R Foods order was 4389. The next sales order form will be numbered 4390.
2. *The date.* The date (May 1, 19--) shows when the order was received.
3. *The customer's order number.* The customer's order number, 34199A, is the number the customer, V & R Foods, assigned to the order for its records. It is important to record this number because V & R Foods will use this order number when calling or writing about the merchandise ordered.
4. *The customer's name and address.* The customer's name and address shows where the merchandise and the invoice are to be sent.
5. *The terms.* The **terms** of the sale are 30 days. This means that the customer should pay for the merchandise within 30 days from

K E Y *Terms*

Terms. Length of time customer has to pay a bill.

the date of the invoice. If the invoice is dated May 1, payment will be due 30 days later (May 31).

6. *Method of shipment.* V & R Foods wanted the merchandise shipped by truck. This fact is shown on the sales order with the words "ship via truck."

7. *The merchandise ordered.* The quantity, stock number, description, and unit price of the merchandise are recorded on the sales order. Notice that no extensions or totals are shown. You will show the extensions and the total on the sales invoice when the customer is billed.

The sales invoice you would prepare from the sales order for V & R Foods is shown in Illustration 42C. Like sales orders, sales invoices are also usually numbered in consecutive order. The invoice for V & R Foods is numbered 2279.

Here are the steps to follow to prepare the sales invoice from the sales order:

STEP 1 ▶ *Copy the information from the sales order.*

Copy the same information that was recorded on the sales order form onto the sales invoice.

STEP 2 ▶ *Extend and total the invoice.*

Find the extensions by multiplying the quantity times the unit price for each item. Record the extensions in the Amount column. Draw a single ruling and add the extensions. Record the total and write the words "Total invoice" in the Description column.

It is important to check the figures on the invoice for accuracy. Any error in the total means that you are asking the customer to pay an incorrect amount.

Illustration 42C   Sales invoice

Sales invoices show extensions and totals.

▲▲▲▲▲
T I P
▼▼▼▼▼

SALES INVOICE

INAZO WHOLESALE PRODUCE COMPANY
4233 Gervais Street • Columbia, SC 29204-5071 • 555-3285

SOLD TO	V & R Foods 13467 Walker Street Houston, TX 77064-2981		INVOICE NO.	2279
			DATE	May 1, 19--
			OUR ORDER NO.	4389
			CUSTOMER ORDER NO.	34199A
TERMS	30 days		SHIP VIA	Truck

QUANTITY	STOCK NO.	DESCRIPTION	UNIT PRICE	AMOUNT
100 bags	P1928	Potatoes	3 49	349 00
50 crates	T8891	Tomatoes	6 29	314 50
		Total invoice		663 50

Large companies use computers for electronic billing systems. Computers process and print invoices at rapid speeds. The computers use the data on the invoices to update customer accounts and stock records.

Finding Due Dates

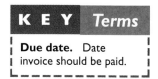

The terms of the sale to V & R Foods are 30 days. This means that the customer has 30 days from the date of the invoice to pay the bill. The date that this invoice should be paid, the **due date**, is May 31.

$$\underset{\text{(Date of Invoice)}}{\text{May 1}} \quad + \quad \underset{\text{(Terms)}}{\text{30 days}} = \underset{\text{(Due Date)}}{\text{May 31}}$$

It is not always this easy to find the due date. For example, if an invoice is dated May 11 and the terms are 30 days, the due date would be June 10. This due date is found this way:

1. Find the number of days left in the month in which the invoice is dated. Since this invoice is dated May 11 and there are 31 days in May, there will be 20 days left in the month of May.

   31   (days in May)
   - 11   (date of invoice, May 11)
   20   (days from May 11 to May 31)

2. Add the number of days in the following month or months until the total equals the terms of the invoice. Since you found that there are 20 days left in May, you need 10 days more in the next month (June) to get a total of 30 days.

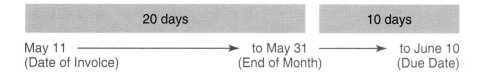

20 days		10 days

May 11   ⟶   to May 31   ⟶   to June 10
(Date of Involce)   (End of Month)   (Due Date)

May 11 to May 31	20 days
Needed to reach 30 days	+ 10 days (to June 10)
Total according to terms	30 days

To find the correct due date, you must know the exact number of days in each month. If you are not sure of the days in each month, the following rhyme may help you:

Thirty days hath September,
April, June, and November.
All the rest have thirty-one
Except February alone
To which we twenty-eight assign,
But leap year gives it twenty-nine.

Now test yourself and see if you agree with the due dates in the following example:

Date of Invoice	Terms of Invoice	Due Date
July 9	15 days	July 24
August 21	15 days	September 5
March 25	30 days	April 24
November 26	30 days	December 26
August 20	60 days	October 19
June 26	60 days	August 25

BUILDING YOUR BUSINESS VOCABULARY

On a sheet of paper, write the headings **Statement Number** and **Words**. Next, choose the words that match the statements. Write each word you choose next to the statement number it matches. Be careful; not all the words listed should be used.

Statements	Words
1. The date by which an invoice should be paid	accounts receivable
2. The price for one unit	accounts
3. Quantity times the unit price	charges
4. A business that sells in large quantities to retailers	due date
5. A bill	extension
6. The length of time the customer has to pay a bill, such as 30 days	retailer
7. Accounts for charge customers	sales invoice
8. A form on which a customer's request for merchandise is first recorded	sales order
9. A business that sells directly to the consumer	terms
	transaction
	unit price
	wholesaler

PROBLEM SOLVING MODEL FOR: *Preparing Sales Invoices*

STEP 1 ▶ *Copy the information from the sales order.*

STEP 2 ▶ *Extend and total the invoice.*

*A*PPLICATION PROBLEMS

PROBLEM 42-1 ▶ **Directions**

Find the due date of each invoice.

CHECKPOINT ✔

42-1
(a) July 26
(c) Sept. 14

	Date of Invoice	Terms of Invoice	Due Date		Date of Invoice	Terms of Invoice	Due Date
a.	July 16	10 days	___	i.	Feb. 12	15 days	___
b.	Nov. 9	20 days	___	j.	May 25	20 days	___
c.	Aug. 15	30 days	___	k.	July 27	30 days	___
d.	Dec. 8	30 days	___	l.	Nov. 23	30 days	___
e.	March 22	30 days	___	m.	Jan. 16	30 days	___
f.	Oct. 14	60 days	___	n.	March 3	75 days	___
g.	June 7	60 days	___	o.	May 19	90 days	___
h.	April 29	90 days	___	p.	Sept. 11	90 days	___

PROBLEM 42-2 ▶ You are employed by CompuMail, Inc., a wholesaler of computer software and hardware. It is part of your job to prepare sales invoices from copies of sales orders.

Directions

CHECKPOINT ✔

42-2 (Sale No. 1)
Invoice total = $33.85

The information for the sales that follow was taken from the sales orders. Prepare a sales invoice for each sale. Date each invoice May 4. Terms allowed each customer are 30 days. All merchandise is to be shipped by truck. Start numbering invoices with 8021.

Sale #1
Sold to: Don's Office Supply, Inc.
6155 Idaho Avenue
St. Paul, MN 55117-2819
Our order no. 833
Customer's order no. 2514
1 ea. Sampler Pak, #M312 @ $9.95
2 ea. Label Pak, #M404 @ $11.95

Sale #2
Sold to: Computer Needs, Inc.
8321 Cervantes Road
Pensacola, FL 32505-7437
Our order no. 834
Customer's order no. 3-971
10 ea. Computer Tool Kit, #M539 @ $17.95
8 ea. Locking Disk File, #M123 @ $8.95
5 ea. Printer Stand, #M662 @ $11.95

Sale #3
Sold to: Martins on the Square
91 Washington Square
Wilmington, DE 19802-2584
Our order no. 835
Customer's order no. 5-902
12 ea. Premium Pak, #M242 @ $18.95
6 ea. Keyboard Carrel, #3165 @ $21.95

Sale #4
Sold to: ComputerEase Company
1422-A Homer Avenue
New Haven, CT 06518-1752
Our order no. 836
Customer's order no. 8335
8 ea. File Clerk Pak, #3713 @ $31.95
5 ea. Retriever Program, #4322 @ $47.95

Sale #5

Sold to: Best Supply Company
          88527 Massachusetts Avenue
          Indianapolis, IN 46227-3908

Our order no. 837
Customer's order no. 714
3 $\frac{1}{3}$ dz. Disk Head Kit, #A799 @ $17.95
10 ea. Basics of Basic, #2718 @ $54.95
5 ea. C Compiler, #2799 @ $49.95

Sale #6

Sold to: Bea's Compuland
          52946 Glenside Avenue
          Baton Rouge, LA 70808-5626

Our order no. 838
Customer's order no. 2257
$10\frac{1}{2}$ dz. Reference Set, #4318 @ $52.95
12 ea. Glare Screen, #3723 @ $16.95
8 ea. Dust Cover, #2901 @ $6.95

You may find it easier to multiply by some fractions if you change them to decimals. For example: $1/2 = 0.50$, $1/4 = 0.25$, $3/4 = 0.75$, $1 1/2 = 1.50$, and $2 1/4 = 2.25$.

APPLIED MATH PREVIEW

Copy and complete these problems.

1. $1/2 \times \$ 8.68 =$
2. $1/3 \times \$ 7.53 =$
3. $1/4 \times \$20.48 =$
4. $2/3 \times \$ 2.31 =$
5. $3/4 \times \$ 9.68 =$
6. $3 1/2 \times \$ 6.48 =$
7. $3 1/3 \times \$ 8.76 =$
8. $2 1/4 \times \$14.08 =$
9. $1 2/3 \times \$21.33 =$
10. $4 3/4 \times \$ 9.92 =$

BUSINESS TERMS PREVIEW

• **Accounts receivable ledger** • **Schedule of accounts receivable** •

GOALS

1. To learn how to keep accounts receivable records for a wholesale business.
2. To learn how to prepare a schedule of accounts receivable.

UNDERSTANDING THE JOB

KEY *Terms*

Accounts receivable ledger. A group of customer accounts.

Since most merchandise sold in a wholesale business is sold on credit, wholesalers must keep records of how much each customer owes. This is done by keeping a separate account for each customer in the same way you learned to keep accounts for retail charge customers in Chapter 8. The customer accounts are usually kept together in an **accounts receivable ledger**.

In a manual system, a loose-leaf binder or a set of ledger cards may be used for the ledger. Customer accounts may be put in alphabetical order by customer name or numerical order by customer account number. New accounts can be added easily.

Many companies use computers for their accounts receivable records. When computers are used, the accounts receivable ledger may be stored on disks.

Remember that when you keep accounts for customers, all sales to customers are recorded in the Debit column of the account. All cash received from the customer and merchandise returned are recorded in the Credit column of the account.

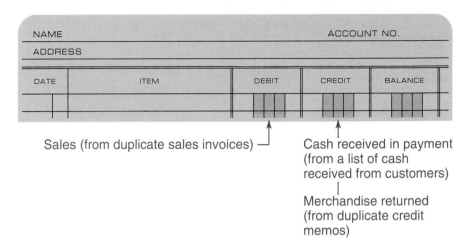

| NAME | | | | ACCOUNT NO. |
| DATE | ITEM | DEBIT | CREDIT | BALANCE |

Sales (from duplicate sales invoices) ⌐

Cash received in payment
(from a list of cash
received from customers)

Merchandise returned
(from duplicate credit
memos)

SAMPLE PROBLEM

You work as an accounts receivable clerk in the accounting department of the Herrera Wholesale Company. You record data in customer accounts from duplicate sales invoices, duplicate credit memos, and a list of cash collected.

Here is a list of the duplicate sales invoices:

Date	Invoice Number	Customer	Amount
Nov. 7	101	Deitz & Kaufman	$2,125.00
8	102	J & R Distributors, Inc.	5,732.56
10	103	Eiko Kimura, Inc.	1,987.43
22	104	J & R Distributors, Inc.	9,114.19
26	105	Deitz & Kaufman	3,208.90

Here is a list of the duplicate credit memos issued for merchandise returned:

Date	Credit Memo No.	Customer	Amount
Nov. 10	81	Deitz & Kaufman	$125.00
14	82	Eiko Kimura, Inc.	380.00

Here is a list of the cash received from customers:

Date	Customer	Amount
Nov. 17	Deitz & Kaufman	$2,000.00
18	J & R Distributors, Inc.	5,732.56
20	Eiko Kimura, Inc.	1,607.43

Illustration 43A shows how the customer accounts would look after the sales, merchandise returns, and cash receipts were recorded. Notice how the final balances were checked.

Illustration 43A
Customer accounts

NAME	Deitz & Kaufman		ACCOUNT NO.	109
ADDRESS	5198 Oak Street, Eugene, OR 97405-9971		TERMS	10 days

DATE		ITEM		DEBIT	CREDIT	BALANCE
19-- Nov.	7	Invoice #101		2 1 2 5 00		2 1 2 5 00
	10	Credit Memo #81			1 2 5 00	2 0 0 0 00
	17	Cash	5,333.90		2 0 0 0 00	————
	26	Invoice #105	2,125.00	3 2 0 8 90		3 2 0 8 90
			3,208.90	5 3 3 3 90	2 1 2 5 00	

NAME	J & R Distributors, Inc.		ACCOUNT NO.	110
ADDRESS	3215 Clark Street, Eugene, OR 97402-7734		TERMS	10 days

DATE		ITEM		DEBIT	CREDIT	BALANCE
19-- Nov.	8	Invoice #102		5 7 3 2 56		5 7 3 2 56
	18	Cash	14,846.75		5 7 3 2 56	————
	22	Invoice #104	5,732.56	9 1 1 4 19		9 1 1 4 19
			9,114.19	14 8 4 6 75		

NAME	Eiko Kimura, Inc.		ACCOUNT NO.	111
ADDRESS	5628 Olive Street, Eugene, OR 97405-2712		TERMS	10 days

DATE		ITEM		DEBIT	CREDIT	BALANCE
19-- Nov.	10	Invoice #103		1 9 8 7 43		1 9 8 7 43
	14	Credit Memo #82			3 8 0 00	1 6 0 7 43
	20	Cash			1 6 0 7 43	————
					1 9 8 7 43	

Remember: *Debits* are always *added* to the old balance to find the new balance. *Credits* are always *subtracted* from the old balance to find the new balance.

In the Sample Problem, there are only three customers. In a real business, there would be many more customers. A separate account would be kept for each customer.

At the end of the month, your employer asks you for a list of customers and the amount each customer owes. This list is called a **schedule of accounts receivable**. The schedule of accounts receivable you would prepare is shown in Illustration 43B.

Illustration 43B
Schedule of accounts
receivable

Herrera Wholesale Company		
Schedule of Accounts Receivable		
November 30, 19--		
Deitz & Kaufman		3 2 0 8 90
J & R Distributors, Inc.		9 1 1 4 19
Total		12 3 2 3 09

KEY Terms

Schedule of accounts receivable. A list of customers who owe money.

These are the steps you would follow to prepare the schedule of accounts receivable:

STEP 1 ▶ Record the heading.

The heading you record for the schedule of accounts receivable must answer these questions:

WHO?　　Herrera Wholesale Company
WHAT?　 Schedule of Accounts Receivable
WHEN?　November 30, 19--

STEP 2 ▶ List the accounts with balances due.

The name and the balance due for each customer are listed in the schedule. If no account numbers are shown on the schedule, accounts are usually listed in alphabetical order. Notice that the Eiko Kimura, Inc., account was not listed because this account had no balance due.

STEP 3 ▶ Find the total.

Rule and foot the money column. Verify your work by re-adding the amounts. Then write the total again and double rule the money column. The total of $12,323.09 is the total amount due from all customers on November 30.

ℬUILDING YOUR BUSINESS VOCABULARY

On a sheet of paper, write the headings **Statement Number** and **Words**. Next, choose the words that match the statements. Write each word you choose next to the statement number it matches. Be careful; not all the words listed should be used.

Statements	Words
1. The length of time the customer has to pay a bill, such as 20 days	accounts receivable ledger
2. The date by which an invoice should be paid	credit memo
	due date
3. A business that sells directly to the consumer	menu
	retailer
4. A form on which a customer's request for merchandise is first recorded	sales order
	schedule of accounts
5. A form which shows that a customer has returned merchandise and owes less money	receivable
	terms
6. A group of customer accounts	wholesaler
7. A list of customers who owe money	

PROBLEM SOLVING MODEL FOR: *Preparing a Schedule of Accounts Receivable*

S T E P 1 ▶ *Record the heading.*

S T E P 2 ▶ *List the accounts with balances due.*

S T E P 3 ▶ *Find the total.*

☝PPLICATION PROBLEMS

PROBLEM | **43-1** ▶ You are employed in the accounting department of Lake Wholesalers Company. Your job is to take care of the accounts receivable records.

Directions

a. Open an account for each of the following customers. The terms for all customers are 20 days.

Mercer, Inc., 62004 Berrent Street, Houston, TX 77003-2418, Acct. #208

Pine Brothers, Inc., 6 Market Square, Houston, TX 77029-3307, Acct. #209

Slattery Stores, 2217 Rancho Verde Drive, Houston, TX 77078-4356, Acct. #210

b. Record the following transactions in the order in which they occurred:

List of Duplicate Sales Invoices

Date	Invoice Number	Customer	Amount
June 3	894	Pine Brothers, Inc.	$424.00
4	895	Slattery Stores	912.00
8	896	Mercer, Inc. ✓	685.00
10	897	Mercer, Inc.	239.00
13	898	Slattery Stores	353.00
22	899	Pine Brothers, Inc. ✓	178.00
25	900	Pine Brothers, Inc.	203.00

List of Duplicate Credit Memos

Date	Credit Memo No.	Customer	Amount
June 15	512	Pine Brothers, Inc.	$118.00
18	513	Slattery Stores	76.00

CHECKPOINT ✔

43-1
Mercer balance = $0.00

List of Cash Received

Date	Customer	Amount
June 17	Mercer, Inc.	$450.00
20	Pine Brothers, Inc.	306.00
22	Mercer, Inc.	200.00
23	Slattery Stores	836.00
28	Mercer, Inc.	274.00

c. To check the final balance of each account, foot the Debit and Credit columns at the end of the month. Subtract the total credits from the total debits. Show your math in the Item column.

d. Prepare a schedule of accounts receivable on June 30.

PROBLEM 43-2 ▶ You are an accounts receivable clerk for the Abbott Wholesale Company. Your job is to keep the records of charge customers.

AUTOMATED

Directions

a. Open an account for each of the following customers. The terms for all customers are 20 days.

Harmon & Sons, 4221 Lindell Avenue, Eugene, OR 97402-5324, Acct. #834

Martin & Jones, 18 Polka Street, Eugene, OR 97404-7222, Acct. #835

Ruther Company, 152992 Jefferson Avenue, Eugene, OR 97401-1918, Acct. #836

b. Record the following transactions in the order in which they occurred:

List of Duplicate Sales Invoices

Date	Invoice Number	Customer	Amount
May 1	709	Ruther Company	$643.15
3	710	Harmon & Sons	286.40
7	711	Martin & Jones	380.50
10	712	Martin & Jones	505.25
11	713	Harmon & Sons	112.00
13	714	Ruther Company	437.85
23	715	Martin & Jones	73.75

List of Duplicate Credit Memos

Date	Credit Memo No.	Customer	Amount
May 20	242	Martin & Jones	$162.45
27	243	Ruther Company	48.90

CHECKPOINT

43-2
Martin & Jones balance = $73.75

List of Cash Received

Date	Customer	Amount
May 21	Ruther Company	$643.15
23	Harmon & Sons	286.40
27	Martin & Jones	218.45
30	Martin & Jones	504.85
31	Harmon & Sons	112.00

c. To check the final balance of each account, foot the Debit and Credit columns at the end of the month. Subtract the total credits from the total debits. Show your math in the Item column.

d. Prepare a schedule of accounts receivable on May 31.

Problem 43-3 may be found in the Working Papers.

APPLIED MATH PREVIEW

Find the due dates of these invoices.

	Date of Invoice	Terms		Date of Invoice	Terms
1.	March 8	15 days	6.	July 19	60 days
2.	June 22	15 days	7.	December 12	60 days
3.	January 17	20 days	8.	September 1	90 days
4.	April 3	30 days	9.	July 13	90 days
5.	November 17	30 days	10.	March 22	90 days

BUSINESS TERMS PREVIEW

• **Journalize** • **Post** • **Posting references** • **Sales journal** •

GOALS

1. To learn how to record sales in a sales journal.
2. To learn how to post to customer accounts from a sales journal.

*U*NDERSTANDING THE JOB

KEY *Terms*

Sales journal. Record of charge sales.

So far, you have learned to record the totals of sales invoices directly in customer accounts as debits. This method is used in many businesses. However, some businesses record sales invoices first in a separate record called a **sales journal**, like the one shown in Illustration 44A (page 385).

Here are the steps that you would follow to make the entry in the sales journal:

STEP 1 ► *Copy the date.*

Copy the date, March 1, from the duplicate sales invoice.

STEP 2 ► *Copy the customer's name.*

Copy the customer's name, Duveno Market Company, into the Customer's Name column.

STEP 3 ► *Copy the invoice number.*

Write the invoice number, 7168, in the Invoice No. column.

Illustration 44A
Recording sales invoices
in a sales journal

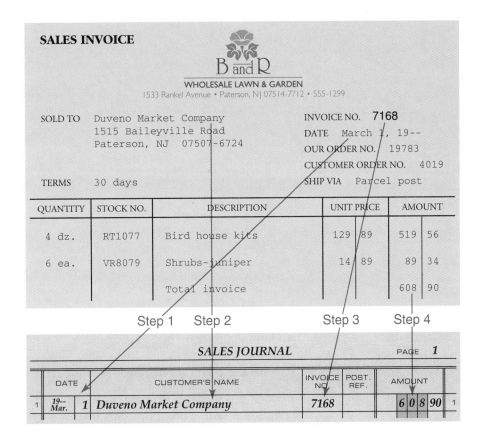

SALES INVOICE

B and R
WHOLESALE LAWN & GARDEN
1533 Rankel Avenue • Paterson, NJ 07514-7712 • 555-1299

SOLD TO   Duveno Market Company
            1515 Baileyville Road
            Paterson, NJ 07507-6724

INVOICE NO. **7168**
DATE March 1, 19--
OUR ORDER NO. 19783
CUSTOMER ORDER NO. 4019

TERMS   30 days   SHIP VIA Parcel post

QUANTITY	STOCK NO.	DESCRIPTION	UNIT PRICE	AMOUNT
4 dz.	RT1077	Bird house kits	129 89	519 56
6 ea.	VR8079	Shrubs-juniper	14 89	89 34
		Total invoice		608 90

Step 1   Step 2   Step 3   Step 4

SALES JOURNAL   PAGE **1**

	DATE		CUSTOMER'S NAME	INVOICE NO.	POST. REF.	AMOUNT	
1	19-- Mar.	1	*Duveno Market Company*	*7168*		6 0 8 90	1

STEP **4** ▶ *Copy the amount.*

Write the invoice amount, $608.90, in the Amount column.

After you have recorded the sales invoice in the sales journal, you then record the sales invoice in the customer account to show how much the customer owes. To do this, you must transfer, or **post**, data from the sales journal to the customer accounts. Postings should be made daily to keep the accounts up-to-date.

This means that two records are used to record sales on account. The first record is the sales journal, where you first record sales invoices. The second record is the accounts receivable ledger, to which you post from the sales journal. You must post carefully so that the correct amount is transferred from the sales journal to the customer account. Also, you must be sure that the amount is posted to the correct customer account.

Illustration 44B on page 386 shows an entry in a sales journal posted to a customer account. Here are the six steps you would follow to make this posting:

K E Y *Terms*

Post. To transfer data from one record to another.

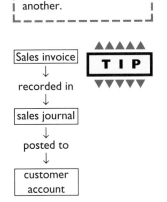

Sales invoice
↓
recorded in
↓
sales journal
↓
posted to
↓
customer account

T I P

STEP **1** ▶ *Copy the date.*

Copy the date, March 1, from the sales journal into the Date column of the customer account.

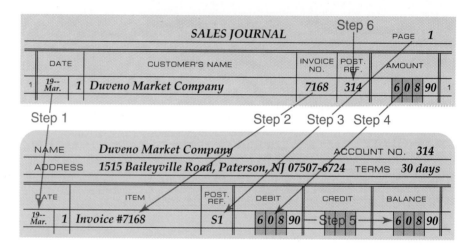

	DATE		CUSTOMER'S NAME	INVOICE NO.	POST. REF.	AMOUNT	
1	19-- Mar.	1	Duveno Market Company	7168	314	6 0 8 90	1

SALES JOURNAL — Step 6 — PAGE **1**

Step 1   Step 2   Step 3   Step 4

NAME   **Duveno Market Company**   ACCOUNT NO. **314**
ADDRESS   **1515 Baileyville Road, Paterson, NJ 07507-6724**   TERMS   **30 days**

DATE		ITEM	POST. REF.	DEBIT	CREDIT	BALANCE
19-- Mar.	1	Invoice #7168	S1	6 0 8 90	— Step 5 — ➤	6 0 8 90

K E Y   Terms

Posting references.
Abbreviations which
show where entries
were posted from.

STEP 2 ▶ **Copy the invoice number.**

Copy the invoice number, 7168, into the Item column of the customer
account. The invoice number will help you find the invoice if any
question comes up about the sale.

STEP 3 ▶ **Record the posting reference in the customer account.**

Record the **posting reference**, S1, in the Post. Ref. column of the customer account. The abbreviation, S1, shows that the entry was posted from page *1* of the sales journal. When you post from the second
page of the sales journal, you will use S2.

STEP 4 ▶ **Post the amount.**

Write the amount, $608.90, in the Debit column of the account
because all sales are recorded in the Debit column.

I N T E R V I E W

AGUS ZUNAEDI

Agus Zunaedi is a
citizen of Indonesia,
where he is the Head
of Curriculum Planning
for the Central Training
and Education Depart-
ment of Pertamina. He
took a leave to study in
the United States for a
master's degree in
business education at
New   Hampshire
College.

Before attaining his current position, Agus

worked in several jobs in Indonesia after receiving his
undergraduate degree. One job required door-to-
door work and a lot of tallying, an important record
keeping task. His next major job was with the
Pertamina Company, a state-owned oil and gas
mining company. Here he worked with many forms,
including employee applications and evaluation forms.
He was also responsible for managing a budget and
six workers.

Agus says that there are three keys to his
success: the right educational background, proper
experience, and motivation to do well. A fourth can
be added: the ability to work accurately with
whatever records go with a job.

STEP 5 ▶ Find the new balance.

Find the new balance and record it in the Balance column. Since the amount posted in the Debit column is the only amount in the account, the new balance is the same as the debit amount.

STEP 6 ▶ Enter the account number in the sales journal.

Put the account number in the Post. Ref. column of the sales journal to show that the entry has been posted to the customer account. If you are interrupted while you are posting, the account numbers will let you know where you left off.

***S*AMPLE PROBLEM**

You are the accounts receivable clerk for B & R Wholesale Lawn & Garden. The duplicate sales invoices show these sales for the month:

Mar. 1 Sold merchandise to Duveno Market Company for $608.90. (Start with Invoice #7168.)
5 Sold merchandise to Revis Goods, Inc., for $3,120.00.
16 Sold merchandise to Sheng & Yi for $2,530.00.
17 Sold merchandise to Revis Goods, Inc., for $1,715.00.
25 Sold merchandise to Revis Goods, Inc., for $1,950.00.
30 Sold merchandise to Duveno Market Company for $3,310.00.

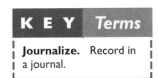

KEY *Terms*

Journalize. Record in a journal.

Illustration 44C (pages 388 and 389) shows how these sales would be recorded in the sales journal and posted to the customer accounts.

Here are the steps that you would follow:

STEP 1 ▶ Record the sales in the sales journal.

Record the sales in the sales journal using the data from the duplicate sales invoices. Recording data in a journal is called **journalizing**.

STEP **2** ▶ **Post to the customer accounts.**

At the end of each day, post the amounts in the sales journal to the customer accounts in the accounts receivable ledger. Enter the account number in the Post. Ref. column of the sales journal as you complete each posting.

STEP **3** ▶ **Total the sales journal.**

At the end of the month, rule and foot the Amount column of the sales journal. Re-add the column before writing the final total. Draw a double ruling under the final total. Write the word *Total* in the Customer's Name column. Date the total as the last day of the month.

Illustration 44C Sales journal and accounts receivable ledger

SALES JOURNAL — PAGE 1

	DATE		CUSTOMER'S NAME	INVOICE NO.	POST. REF.	AMOUNT	
1	19-- Mar.	1	Duveno Market Company	7168	314	6 0 8 90	1
2		5	Revis Goods, Inc.	7169	315	3 1 2 0 00	2
3		16	Sheng & Yi	7170	316	2 5 3 0 00	3
4		17	Revis Goods, Inc.	7171	315	1 7 1 5 00	4
5		25	Revis Goods, Inc.	7172	315	1 9 5 0 00	5
6		30	Duveno Market Company	7173	314	3 3 1 0 00	6
7		31	Total			13 2 3 3 90 / 13 2 3 3 90	7

NAME *Duveno Market Company*   **ACCOUNT NO. 314**
ADDRESS *1515 Baileyville Road, Paterson, NJ 07507-6724* **TERMS** *30 days*

DATE		ITEM	POST. REF.	DEBIT	CREDIT	BALANCE
19-- Mar.	1	Invoice #7168	S1	6 0 8 90		6 0 8 90
	30	Invoice #7173	S1	3 3 1 0 00		3 9 1 8 90
				3 9 1 8 90		

NAME *Revis Goods, Inc.*   **ACCOUNT NO. 315**
ADDRESS *21089 Rugnel Blvd., Paterson, NJ 07503-1145*   **TERMS** *30 days*

DATE		ITEM	POST. REF.	DEBIT	CREDIT	BALANCE
19-- Mar.	5	Invoice #7169	S1	3 1 2 0 00		3 1 2 0 00
	17	Invoice #7171	S1	1 7 1 5 00		4 8 3 5 00
	25	Invoice #7172	S1	1 9 5 0 00		6 7 8 5 00
				6 7 8 5 00		

| NAME | Sheng & Yi | | | | | ACCOUNT NO. | 316 |
| ADDRESS | 5101 Kurchel Ave., Paterson, NJ 07514-3315 | | | | | TERMS | 30 days |

DATE	ITEM	POST. REF.	DEBIT	CREDIT	BALANCE
19-- Mar. 16	Invoice #7170	S1	2 5 3 0 00		2 5 3 0 00

Illustration 44C   Sales journal and accounts receivable ledger (continued)

BUILDING YOUR BUSINESS VOCABULARY

On a sheet of paper, write the headings **Statement Number** and **Words**. Next, choose the words that match the statements. Write each word you choose next to the statement number it matches. Be careful; not all the words listed should be used.

Statements	Words
1. To record in a journal	accounts receivable
2. A business that sells in large quantities to retailers	ledger
	credit
3. A group of customer accounts	debit
4. A bill	journalize
5. To transfer data from one record to another	post
	posting references
6. A record of all charge sales	retailer
7. A list of customers who owe money	sales invoice
8. Abbreviations, such as S1, which show where entries were posted from	sales journal
	schedule of accounts
9. The column used to record a charge sale in a customer account	receivable
	wholesaler

PROBLEM SOLVING MODEL FOR: *Recording in the Sales Journal*

STEP 1 ▶ *Record the sales in the sales journal.*

STEP 2 ▶ *Post to the customer accounts.*

STEP 3 ▶ *Total the sales journal.*

APPLICATION PROBLEMS

AUTOMATED

PROBLEM **44-1** ▶ You are employed by ViaTech Wholesale Company as an accounts receivable clerk. Part of your job is to record sales in the sales journal and post to the customer accounts.

Directions

a. Open an account for each customer. The terms for all customers are 30 days.

CHECKPOINT ✓

44-1
Sales journal total =
$3,271.00

Jiminez & Rica, Inc., 19 Taylor Ave., Racine, WI 53402-1146, Acct. #101

Soy & Ross, 33607 Cornhusker Hwy., Lincoln, NE 68506-3438, Acct. #102

Stein & Sons, 524 Owen Street, Toledo, OH 43602-7909, Acct. #103

Use
Illustration
44C (page 388-
389) as a guide.
▲▲▲▲▲
T I P
▼▼▼▼▼

b. Record the following sales in a sales journal. Number the journal page 1.

May 3 Sold merchandise to Soy & Ross for $330.00. (Start with Invoice #231.)
  7 Sold merchandise to Stein & Sons for $613.00.
  19 Sold merchandise to Jiminez & Rica, Inc., for $1,143.00.
  22 Sold merchandise to Stein & Sons for $256.00.
  25 Sold merchandise to Soy & Ross for $526.00.
  27 Sold merchandise to Jiminez & Rica, Inc., for $403.00.

Post daily to
customer
accounts.
▲▲▲▲▲
T I P
▼▼▼▼▼

c. Post daily from the sales journal to the customer accounts. Do not forget to enter an account number in the sales journal and the posting reference S1 in the accounts as you post.
d. Foot, total, and rule the sales journal for the month.
e. Check the balance in each customer account by footing the Debit column.

AUTOMATED

PROBLEM **44-2** ▶ You work as an accounts receivable clerk for Rivera Wholesale Distributors, Inc.

Directions

CHECKPOINT ✓

44-2
Sales journal total =
$2,963.23

a. Open an account for each customer. The terms for all customers are 30 days.

Lester's, 481 Beachview Road, Tampa, FL 33624-5061, Acct. #301
Pretty Things, Inc., 12322 Tampania Pky., Tampa, FL 33615-4188, Acct. #302
Sandy's Dress Shop, 12317 Lee Road, Tampa, FL 33612-2278, Acct. #303

b. Record the following sales in a sales journal. Number the journal page 5.

Oct. 2 Sold merchandise to Lester's for $638.00. (Start with Invoice #721.)
11 Sold merchandise to Pretty Things, Inc., for $352.35.
16 Sold merchandise to Sandy's Dress Shop for $478.15.
21 Sold merchandise to Pretty Things, Inc., for $267.45.
24 Sold merchandise to Sandy's Dress Shop for $715.00.
28 Sold merchandise to Lester's for $512.28.

c. Post daily from the sales journal to the customer accounts. Do not forget to enter an account number in the sales journal and the posting reference S5 in the accounts as you post.
d. Foot, total, and rule the sales journal for the month.
e. Check the balance in each customer account by footing the Debit column.

Problems 44-3, 44-4, and 44-5 may be found in the Working Papers.

APPLIED MATH PREVIEW

Find the due dates of these invoices.

	Date of Invoice	Terms		Date of Invoice	Terms
1.	April 7	15 days	6.	October 5	60 days
2.	December 19	30 days	7.	November 14	60 days
3.	February 13	15 days	8.	July 1	90 days
4.	May 12	30 days	9.	October 19	90 days
5.	January 11	30 days	10.	March 3	90 days

BUSINESS TERM PREVIEW

• **Cash receipts journal** •

GOALS

1. To learn how to record cash received from customers in a cash receipts journal.
2. To learn how to post to customer accounts from a cash receipts journal.

$\mathscr{U}$NDERSTANDING THE JOB

KEY *Terms*

Cash receipts journal.
A record of cash received.

You have just learned to enter sales in a record called a sales journal. A sales journal is a record of all charge sales. It is used to record sales that have been charged by customers. These sales are posted to the customer accounts. In this case, *posted* means that the data are transferred from the sales journal to the customer accounts. Charge sales increase the amounts that customers owe.

On or before the due dates shown on their invoices, the customers will pay for the charge sales. When the payments are received, they are recorded in a record called the **cash receipts journal**.

You will now learn how to record cash received from customers in the cash receipts journal. Entries recorded in the cash receipts journal are posted to the customer accounts. In this case, *posted* means that the data are transferred from the cash receipts journal to the customer accounts. Cash receipts from charge customers decrease the amounts that customers owe. The amounts are recorded as credits. Postings are made daily to keep the accounts up-to-date.

SAMPLE PROBLEM

The customer accounts in Illustration 45A show the sales made by the Fingar Wholesale Company during March. The terms show that customers should pay their bills within 45 days. Since the sales were made in March, payments for these sales should begin to be received by Fingar Wholesale Company during April.

Illustration 45A
Customer accounts

NAME	E & L Deliveries			ACCOUNT NO.	208
ADDRESS	9525 Ash Ave., NW, Lawton, OK 73505-8839			TERMS	45 days

DATE	ITEM	POST. REF.	DEBIT	CREDIT	BALANCE
19-- Mar. 3	Invoice #451	S1	893 21		893 21
23	Invoice #455	S1	453 09		1346 30

NAME	Arrow Traders, Inc.			ACCOUNT NO.	209
ADDRESS	8544 Oak Ave., NW, Lawton, OK 73505-3389			TERMS	45 days

DATE	ITEM	POST. REF.	DEBIT	CREDIT	BALANCE
19-- Mar. 6	Invoice #452	S1	338 78		338 78
15	Invoice #454	S1	732 11		1070 89
24	Invoice #456	S1	634 12		1705 01

NAME	Grandell Discount Mart, Inc.			ACCOUNT NO.	210
ADDRESS	7623 Hoover Ave., NW, Lawton, OK 73505-6672		TERMS	45 days

DATE	ITEM	POST. REF.	DEBIT	CREDIT	BALANCE
19-- Mar. 8	Invoice #453	S1	702 17		702 17

The following is a record of the money collected during April:

Apr. 17 Received a check for $893.21 from E & L Deliveries for the invoice of March 3.

20 Received a check for $338.78 from Arrow Traders, Inc., for the invoice of March 6.

22 Received a check for $702.17 from Grandell Discount Mart, Inc., for the invoice of March 8.

29 Received a check for $732.11 from Arrow Traders, Inc., for the invoice of March 15.

30 Received a check for $300.00 from E & L Deliveries in payment on account.

Illustration 45B shows how these cash receipts were recorded in the cash receipts journal and posted to the customer accounts.

Illustration 45B Cash receipts journal and accounts receivable ledger

Post from the cash receipts journal daily. ▲▲▲▲▲ **TIP** ▼▼▼▼▼

CASH RECEIPTS JOURNAL — PAGE 1

	DATE	RECEIVED FROM	FOR	POST. REF.	AMOUNT	
1	19-- Apr. 17	E & L Deliveries	Invoice, 3/3	208	8 9 3 21	1
2	20	Arrow Traders, Inc.	Invoice, 3/6	209	3 3 8 78	2
3	22	Grandell Disc't Mart	Invoice, 3/8	210	7 0 2 17	3
4	29	Arrow Traders, Inc.	Invoice, 3/15	209	7 3 2 11	4
5	30	E & L Deliveries	On account	208	3 0 0 00	5
6	30	Total			2 9 6 6 27	6

ACCOUNTS RECEIVABLE LEDGER

Post from the cash receipts journal to the Credit column of customer accounts. ▲▲▲▲▲ **TIP** ▼▼▼▼▼

NAME **E & L Deliveries**   ACCOUNT NO. **208**
ADDRESS **9525 Ash Ave., NW, Lawton, OK 73505-8839**   TERMS **45 days**

DATE	ITEM	POST. REF.	DEBIT	CREDIT	BALANCE
19-- Mar. 3	Invoice #451	S1	8 9 3 21		8 9 3 21
23	Invoice #455	S1	4 5 3 09		1 3 4 6 30
Apr. 17	Cash 1,346.30	CR1		8 9 3 21	4 5 3 09
30	Cash 1,193.21	CR1		3 0 0 00	1 5 3 09
			153.09	1 3 4 6 30	1 1 9 3 21

Subtract credits. ▲▲▲▲▲ **TIP** ▼▼▼▼▼

CR1 = cash receipts journal page 1. ▲▲▲▲▲ **TIP** ▼▼▼▼▼

NAME **Arrow Traders, Inc.**   ACCOUNT NO. **209**
ADDRESS **8544 Oak Ave., NW, Lawton, OK 73505-3389**   TERMS **45 days**

DATE	ITEM	POST. REF.	DEBIT	CREDIT	BALANCE
19-- Mar. 6	Invoice #452	S1	3 3 8 78		3 3 8 78
15	Invoice #454	S1	7 3 2 11		1 0 7 0 89
24	Invoice #456	S1	6 3 4 12		1 7 0 5 01
Apr. 20	Cash 1,705.01	CR1		3 3 8 78	1 3 6 6 23
29	Cash 1,070.89	CR1		7 3 2 11	6 3 4 12
			634.12	1 7 0 5 01	1 0 7 0 89

			NAME	*Grandell Discount Mart, Inc.*		ACCOUNT NO. **210**		
			ADDRESS	*7623 Hoover Ave., NW, Lawton, OK 73505-6672*	TERMS	**45 days**		

DATE		ITEM	POST. REF.	DEBIT	CREDIT	BALANCE
19-- Mar.	8	*Invoice #453*	S1	7 0 2 17		7 0 2 17
Apr.	22	*Cash*	CR1		7 0 2 17	

Here are the steps to follow:

STEP 1 ▶ **Record the receipts in the cash receipts journal.**

As money is received from each customer, record the date, the customer's name, an explanation, and the amount in the cash receipts journal. For example, in Illustration 45B (pages 394-395), the first entry shows that on April 17 a payment was received from E & L Deliveries for the invoice dated March 3 for $893.21.

STEP 2 ▶ **Post to the customer accounts.**

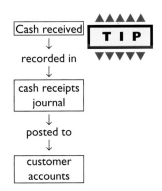

Cash received
↓
recorded in
↓
cash receipts
journal
↓
posted to
↓
customer
accounts

▲▲▲▲▲
TIP
▼▼▼▼▼

At the end of each day, post from the cash receipts journal to the customer accounts in the accounts receivable ledger. The $893.21 received from E & L Deliveries on April 17 was posted as a credit to the customer account. Credits are subtracted from the account balance to show that the customer owes less than before. The $893.21 credit was subtracted from the old balance of $1,346.30 to get a new balance of $453.09.

As each posting is made, enter the posting reference CR1 in the customer account. The posting reference CR1 shows that the entry was posted from page *1* of the *c*ash *r*eceipts journal. Enter an account number in the Post. Ref. column of the cash receipts journal to show that the posting has been made.

STEP 3 ▶ **Total the cash receipts journal.**

After you finish posting for the month, total the Amount column of the cash receipts journal. The total is the amount of cash collected from all customers for the month. The cash receipts journal in Illustration 45B (pages 394-395) shows that $2,966.27 was collected from customers during April. Notice that the total was first written as a footing and then re-added before the final total was written. After recording the final total, double rule the Amount column and write the word *Total* in the Received From column. Date the total as the last day of the month.

STEP 4 ▶ *Check the account balances.*

Total debits
- Total credits
Final balance

Check the balance in each customer account by footing the Debit and Credit columns. Subtract the total credits from the total debits. The answer should agree with the final balance shown in the account. Notice how the math is done in the accounts in Illustration 45B (pages 394-395).

𝓑UILDING YOUR BUSINESS VOCABULARY

On a sheet of paper, write the headings **Statement Number** and **Words**. Next, choose the words that match the statements. Write each word you choose next to the statement number it matches. Be careful; not all the words listed should be used.

Statements	Words
1. To transfer data from one record to another	accounts receivable ledger
2. Abbreviations, such as CR1, which show where entries were posted from	cash receipts journal
3. To record in a journal	credit
4. A business that sells in large quantities to retailers	debit
5. The date by which an invoice should be paid	due date
6. A record of all cash received	duplicate
7. A group of customer accounts	journalize
8. The column in which increases in a customer account are recorded	post
9. The column in which decreases in a customer account are recorded	posting references
	retailer
	wholesaler

PROBLEM SOLVING MODEL FOR: *Using a Cash Receipts Journal*

STEP 1 ▶ *Record the receipts in the cash receipts journal.*

STEP 2 ▶ *Post to the customer accounts.*

STEP 3 ▶ *Total the cash receipts journal.*

STEP 4 ▶ *Check the account balances.*

PPLICATION PROBLEMS

PROBLEM | 45-1 ▶ You work for Sheng & Chi, Inc., as an accounts receivable clerk.

Directions

a. Copy the following customer accounts, which show the sales recorded in March.

45-1
Cash receipts journal total
= $3,125.00

NAME	Burroughs Associates, Inc.			ACCOUNT NO. 826		
ADDRESS	1049 Commercial Street, Portland, ME 04102-1037			TERMS	30 days	
DATE	ITEM	POST. REF.	DEBIT	CREDIT	BALANCE	
19-- Mar. 11	Invoice #423	S5	1 1 2 2 00		1 1 2 2 00	

NAME	T. Moreno & Company			ACCOUNT NO. 827		
ADDRESS	178 Tide View Road, Portland, ME 04110-9171			TERMS	30 days	
DATE	ITEM	POST. REF.	DEBIT	CREDIT	BALANCE	
19-- Mar. 4	Invoice #421	S5	5 1 2 00		5 1 2 00	
21	Invoice #425	S5	2 3 5 00		7 4 7 00	

NAME	Newton and Figge			ACCOUNT NO. 828		
ADDRESS	2708 York Street, Portland, ME 04102-1885			TERMS	30 days	
DATE	ITEM	POST. REF.	DEBIT	CREDIT	BALANCE	
19-- Mar. 8	Invoice #422	S5	3 3 7 00		3 3 7 00	
19	Invoice #424	S5	9 1 9 00		1 2 5 6 00	

b. Record the following cash receipts in a cash receipts journal. Number the journal page 5.

Apr. 3 Received a check for $512.00 from T. Moreno & Company for the invoice of March 4.

6 Received a check for $337.00 from Newton and Figge for the invoice of March 8.

10 Received a check for $1,122.00 from Burroughs Associates, Inc., for the invoice of March 11.

18 Received a check for $919.00 from Newton and Figge for the invoice of March 19.

20 Received a check for $235.00 from T. Moreno & Company for the invoice of March 21.

c. Post daily from the cash receipts journal to the Credit column of the customer accounts. Enter the posting reference CR5 in the

accounts and an account number in the cash receipts journal as
you post.

d. Foot, total, and rule the Amount column of the cash receipts journal.

e. Check the balance in each customer account by footing the Debit
and Credit columns. Subtract the total credits from the total debits. The answer should agree with the final balance shown in the
account.

PROBLEM | **45-2** ▶ You are employed as an accounts receivable clerk by Bemer's, Inc.

Directions

a. Copy the following customer accounts, which show the sales
recorded in June.

45-2
Cash receipts journal total
= $2,214.00

NAME	Jason Brothers, Inc.				ACCOUNT NO. 381	
ADDRESS	36311 Jefferson St., Roanoke, VA 24014-2513				TERMS 45 days	
DATE	ITEM	POST. REF.	DEBIT	CREDIT	BALANCE	
19-- June 6	Invoice #783	S1	5 4 0 00		5 4 0 00	

NAME	McCracken's				ACCOUNT NO. 382	
ADDRESS	28 Wakefield Road, Roanoke, VA 24019-7727				TERMS 45 days	
DATE	ITEM	POST. REF.	DEBIT	CREDIT	BALANCE	
19-- June 3	Invoice #781	S1	2 8 5 00		2 8 5 00	
21	Invoice #785	S1	7 3 0 00		1 0 1 5 00	

NAME	Stewart Markets				ACCOUNT NO. 383	
ADDRESS	17 Colonial Ave., Roanoke, VA 24017-3013				TERMS 45 days	
DATE	ITEM	POST. REF.	DEBIT	CREDIT	BALANCE	
19-- June 4	Invoice #782	S1	6 3 2 00		6 3 2 00	
14	Invoice #784	S1	3 7 7 00		1 0 0 9 00	
25	Invoice #786	S1	5 8 0 00		1 5 8 9 00	

b. Record the following cash receipts in a cash receipts journal.
Number the journal page 1.

July   17   Received a check for $285.00 from McCracken's for the invoice
of June 3.

19   Received a check for $632.00 from Stewart Markets for the
invoice of June 4.

21   Received a check for $540.00 from Jason Brothers, Inc., for the
invoice of June 6.

27 Received a check for $377.00 from Stewart Markets for the invoice of June 14.

28 Received a check for $250.00 from McCracken's in payment on account.

29 Received a check for $130.00 from Stewart Markets in payment on account.

c. Post daily from the cash receipts journal to the Credit column of the customer accounts. Enter the posting reference CR1 in the accounts and an account number in the cash receipts journal as you post.

d. Foot, total, and rule the Amount column of the cash receipts journal.

e. Check the balance in each customer account by footing the Debit and Credit columns. Subtract the total credits from the total debits. The answer should agree with the final balance shown in the account.

Problems 45-3 and 45-4 may be found in the Working Papers.

JOB 46 ▶ USING SALES AND CASH RECEIPTS JOURNALS

APPLIED MATH PREVIEW

Copy and complete these problems.

1.	$ 25.00 + $50.00 =	2.	$ 48.00 - $20.00 =
	110.00 + 75.00 =		76.00 - 12.00 =
	54.80 + 18.20 =		80.00 - 48.00 =
	38.40 + 68.10 =		150.00 - 75.00 =
	23.60 + 71.50 =		240.00 - 14.00 = ____

GOALS

To practice using the

1. sales journal.
2. cash receipts journal.
3. accounts receivable ledger.

𝒰NDERSTANDING THE JOB

You have learned how to use three records to record transactions with customers who buy merchandise on credit. The three records are

1. The *sales journal,* in which you record all sales invoices.
2. The *cash receipts journal,* in which you record all cash received from customers.
3. The *accounts receivable ledger,* in which you keep the customer accounts. Debits in the customer accounts are posted from the sales journal. Credits in these accounts are posted from the cash receipts journal.

Look at Illustration 46A.

Illustration 46A   How sales invoices and cash receipts are recorded

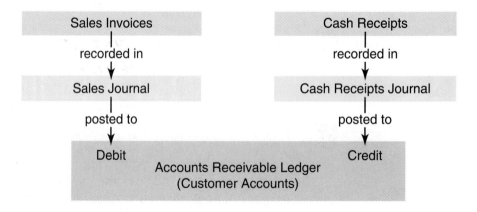

Posting must follow the order of the dates.

TIP

In this job, you will use all three records. You will be posting from both the sales journal and the cash receipts journal to the customer accounts. Remember: *postings are made each day and must follow the order of the dates.*

SAMPLE PROBLEM

You are an accounts receivable clerk for Transon Lumber Products, Inc. During April you recorded the following transactions:

Apr. 6 Sold merchandise to Aldor, Inc. for $1,500.00 (Invoice #458).
     16 Received a check for $1,500.00 from Aldor, Inc. for the invoice of April 6.
     18 Sold merchandise to Aldor, Inc. for $2,000.00 (Invoice #459).
     28 Received a check for $2,000.00 from Aldor, Inc. for the invoice of April 18.
     29 Sold merchandise to Aldor, Inc. for $1,200.00 (Invoice #460).

Illustration 46B (page 402) shows how you recorded these entries in both journals and posted to the customer account.

Here are the steps you took:

STEP 1 ▶ *Record the transactions in the proper journals.*

When you received a sales invoice or a check, you decided in which journal you should record it. You recorded all sales invoices in the sales journal and all checks received in the cash receipts journal.

STEP 2 ▶ *Post daily to the customer accounts.*

After you entered each transaction in the proper journal, you posted the transaction to the customer account. It is important to post daily to customer accounts so that customer balances are up-to-date.

STEP 3 ▸ **Foot, total, and rule each journal.**

At the end of the month, you footed, totaled, and ruled the sales and cash receipts journals.

STEP 4 ▸ **Check the account balances.**

At the end of the month, you verified the balances in the customer account by footing the Debit and Credit columns. You subtracted the total credits from the total debits and compared that amount to the balance in the account. You showed your math in the Item column of the account.

Illustration 46B   Posting from the sales journal and the cash receipts journal

SALES JOURNAL   PAGE **1**

	DATE		CUSTOMER'S NAME	INVOICE NO.	POST. REF.	AMOUNT	
1	*19--* *Apr.*	6	*Aldor, Inc.*	**458**	**101**	1 5 0 0 00	1
2		18	*Aldor, Inc.*	**459**	**101**	2 0 0 0 00	2
3		29	*Aldor, Inc.*	**460**	**101**	1 2 0 0 00	3
4		30	*Total*			4 7 0 0 00	4

CASH RECEIPTS JOURNAL   PAGE **1**

	DATE		RECEIVED FROM	FOR	POST. REF.	AMOUNT	
1	*19--* *Apr.*	16	*Aldor, Inc.*	*Invoice, 4/6*	**101**	1 5 0 0 00	1
2		28	*Aldor, Inc.*	*Invoice, 4/18*	**101**	2 0 0 0 00	2
3		30	*Total*			3 5 0 0 00	3

NAME   *Aldor, Inc.*   ACCOUNT NO. **101**

ADDRESS   *1427 Krisland Lane, Cincinnati, OH 45227-7736*   TERMS **10 days**

DATE		ITEM		POST. REF.	DEBIT	CREDIT	BALANCE
19-- *Apr.*	6	*Invoice #458*		**S1**	1 5 0 0 00		1 5 0 0 00
	16	*Cash*		**CR1**		1 5 0 0 00	—
	18	*Invoice #459*		**S1**	2 0 0 0 00		2 0 0 0 00
	28	*Cash*	*4,700.00*	**CR1**		2 0 0 0 00	—
	29	*Invoice #460*	*3,500.00*	**S1**	1 2 0 0 00		1 2 0 0 00
			1,200.00		4 7 0 0 00	3 5 0 0 00	

On a sheet of paper, write the headings **Statement Number** and **Words**. Next, choose the words that match the statements. Write each word you choose next to the statement number it matches. Be careful; not all the words listed should be used.

Statements	Words
1. A list of customers who owe money	accounts receivable
2. A group of customer accounts	ledger
3. To transfer data from one record to another	credit
	credit memo
4. A record of all charge sales	debit
5. The date by which an invoice should be paid	due date
	journalize
6. The column used to record a charge sale in a customer account	post
	sales invoice
7. The column used to record a cash receipt in a customer account	sales journal
	sales order
8. To record in a journal	schedule of accounts
9. The length of time the customer has to pay a bill, such as 10 days	receivable
	terms
10. A form which shows that the balance of an account has been reduced because merchandise was returned	

PROBLEM SOLVING MODEL FOR: *Using Sales and Cash Receipts Journals*

STEP 1 ▶ *Record the transactions in the proper journals.*

STEP 2 ▶ *Post daily to the customer accounts.*

STEP 3 ▶ *Foot, total, and rule each journal.*

STEP 4 ▶ *Check the account balances.*

APPLICATION PROBLEMS

PROBLEM 46-1 ▶ You are employed in the accounting department of Greyson Wholesalers, Inc. to handle accounts receivable records.

AUTOMATED

Directions

a Open an account for each of the customers on page 404. The terms for all customers are 10 days.

Horvath's, 29 Rose Avenue, Pasadena, CA 99103-3518, Acct. #301
Oberle & Company, 351 Farmlife Road, Miami, FL 33189-1202, Acct. #302
Vanity Shop, 2288 Dwight Street, Springfield, MA 01106-7355, Acct. #303

CHECKPOINT ✔

46-1
Sales journal total =
$3,978.70

b. Record the following sales and cash receipts in the proper journals. As you read each transaction, decide if it should be recorded in the sales journal or in the cash receipts journal. Use page 1 for both journals. Post to the customer accounts as soon as you have recorded each transaction.

Oct. 3 Sold merchandise to Horvath's for $382.40. Since this is a sale, it must be recorded in the sales journal. (Start with Invoice #501.)

7 Sold merchandise to Oberle & Company for $432.20.

10 Sold merchandise to Horvath's for $628.80.

13 Received a check for $382.40 from Horvath's for the invoice of October 3. Since this is a cash receipt, it must be entered in the cash receipts journal.

15 Sold merchandise to Vanity Shop for $507.40.

17 Received a check for $432.20 from Oberle & Company for the invoice of October 7.

20 Received a check for $628.80 from Horvath's for the invoice of October 10.

22 Sold merchandise to Vanity Shop for $965.65.

25 Received a check for $507.40 from Vanity Shop for the invoice of October 15.

28 Sold merchandise to Oberle & Company for $387.90.

30 Sold merchandise to Vanity Shop for $674.35.

c. Foot, total, and rule the sales and the cash receipts journals.
d. Check the balance at the end of the month in each account. Show all footings.
e. Prepare a schedule of accounts receivable on October 31. If necessary, refer back to Illustration 43B (page 380) as a guide.

PROBLEM 46-2 ▶ You are an accounts receivable clerk for Newton Interstate Distributors, Inc.

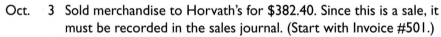

AUTOMATED

Directions

a. Open an account for each of the following customers. The terms for all customers are 10 days.

Kyle's Goods, Inc., 9929 Vinewood Street, Detroit, MI 48214-1188, Acct. #801
Peppe's, 49 Wolfe Street, Little Rock, AR 72204-5003, Acct. #802
Marine Needs, Inc., 312 Bay Drive, Annapolis, MD 21401-6239, Acct. #803

b. Record the following transactions using a sales journal and a cash receipts journal. Use page 7 for both journals. Post to the customer accounts as soon as you have recorded each transaction.

Apr. 1 Sold merchandise to Kyle's Goods, Inc. for $673.20. (Start with Invoice #401.)
5 Sold merchandise to Peppe's for $817.85.
9 Sold merchandise to Kyle's Goods, Inc. for $394.80.
11 Received a check for $673.20 from Kyle's Goods, Inc. for the invoice of April 1.
14 Sold merchandise to Marine Needs, Inc. for $1,202.00.
15 Received a check for $817.85 from Peppe's for the invoice of April 5.
19 Received a check for $394.80 from Kyle's Goods, Inc. for the invoice of April 9.
22 Sold merchandise to Peppe's for $519.45.
24 Received a check for $1,202.00 from Marine Needs, Inc. for the invoice of April 14.
26 Sold merchandise to Marine Needs, Inc. for $723.65.
29 Sold merchandise to Peppe's for $466.15.

c. Foot, total, and rule the sales and cash receipts journals.
d. Check the balance at the end of the month in each account. Show all footings.
e. Prepare a schedule of accounts receivable on April 30.

Problem 46-3 may be found in the Working Papers.

BUSINESS TERMS PREVIEW

• **Allowance** • **Overcharge** • **Sales returns and allowances journal** •

GOALS

1. To learn how to record credit memos in a sales returns and allowances journal.
2. To practice posting from the sales journal, the sales returns and allowances journal, and the cash receipts journal to the accounts receivable ledger.

𝒰NDERSTANDING THE JOB

KEY *Terms*

Allowance. A price reduction.

Overcharge. A price on the invoice is more than it should be.

Sales returns and allowances journal. Record of all duplicate credit memos.

An allowance is given to:
1. reduce the price.
2. correct an overcharge.

Credit memos are issued for:
1. returns.
2. allowances.

You have learned that when a credit customer returns merchandise, the seller prepares a form called a credit memo. (See Illustration 47A.) Occasionally, the customer may want to keep damaged merchandise if the wholesaler will reduce the price. Reducing the price for damaged merchandise is called giving an **allowance**. An allowance may also be given to correct an **overcharge** on a sales invoice. When an allowance is given, a credit memo is issued for the amount of the allowance. So, credit memos may be issued for two reasons:

1. To show that a customer owes less money because merchandise was *returned*.
2. To show that a customer owes less money because an *allowance* was given.

Two copies of the credit memo are prepared. In a wholesale business, the original is sent to the customer to show that a record has been made of the return or allowance. The duplicate is kept by the wholesaler, and the information on it is recorded in a **sales returns and allowances journal**. The entry recorded in the sales returns and allowances journal is posted to the customer account in the accounts receivable ledger. The amount of the credit memo is recorded in the *Credit* column. Postings are made daily.

Illustration 47A   Credit memo for an allowance

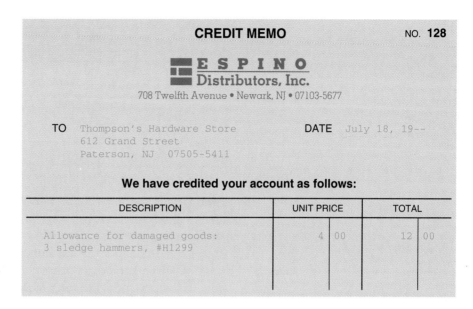

CREDIT MEMO   NO. **128**

ESPINO
Distributors, Inc.
708 Twelfth Avenue • Newark, NJ • 07103-5677

TO   Thompson's Hardware Store   **DATE**   July 18, 19--
     612 Grand Street
     Paterson, NJ 07505-5411

We have credited your account as follows:

DESCRIPTION	UNIT PRICE	TOTAL
Allowance for damaged goods: 3 sledge hammers, #H1299	4 00	12 00

ＳAMPLE PROBLEM

You are an accounts receivable clerk for Espino Distributors, Inc. The customer accounts in Illustration 47B (pages 407-408) show the sales made by the company during July.

Illustration 47B
Customer accounts

NAME	*Thompson's Hardware Store*					ACCOUNT NO.	*221*	
ADDRESS	*612 Grand Street, Paterson, NJ 07505-5411*					TERMS	*30 days*	

DATE		ITEM	POST. REF.	DEBIT	CREDIT	BALANCE
19-- July	7	*Invoice #382*	*S1*	3 1 0 00		3 1 0 00
	15	*Invoice #384*	*S1*	7 4 0 00		1 0 5 0 00

| NAME | *Susan's Tool Market* | | | | ACCOUNT NO. | **222** |
| ADDRESS | *4089 Birch Street, Toms River, NJ 08753-8262* | | | | TERMS | *30 days* |

DATE		ITEM	POST. REF.	DEBIT	CREDIT	BALANCE
19-- July	*4*	*Invoice #381*	*S1*	8 8 0 00		8 8 0 00
	14	*Invoice #383*	*S1*	5 5 0 00		1 4 3 0 00

The following sales returns and allowances were made during the month:

July 18 Issued Credit Memo #128 for $12.00 to Thompson's Hardware Store as an allowance for damaged merchandise. (The credit memo is shown in Illustration 47A on page 407.)

19 Issued Credit Memo #129 for $50.00 to Susan's Tool Market as an allowance to correct an overcharge on the invoice of July 14.

21 Issued Credit Memo #130 for $75.00 to Thompson's Hardware Store for merchandise returned.

After you recorded these transactions, the sales returns and allowances journal and customer accounts looked as shown in Illustration 47C.

			SALES RETURNS AND ALLOWANCES JOURNAL			PAGE	**1**	
	DATE		CUSTOMER'S NAME	CREDIT MEMO NO.	POST. REF.	AMOUNT		
1	*19-- July*	*18*	*Thompson's Hardware Store*	*128*	*221*	1 2 00		1
2		*19*	*Susan's Tool Market*	*129*	*222*	5 0 00		2
3		*21*	*Thompson's Hardware Store*	*130*	*221*	7 5 00		3
4		*31*	*Total*			1 3 7 00		4

| NAME | *Thompson's Hardware Store* | | | | ACCOUNT NO. | **221** |
| ADDRESS | *612 Grand Street, Paterson, NJ 07505-5411* | | | | TERMS | *30 days* |

DATE		ITEM	POST. REF.	DEBIT	CREDIT	BALANCE
19-- July	*7*	*Invoice #382*	*S1*	3 1 0 00		3 1 0 00
	15	*Invoice #384*	*S1*	7 4 0 00		1 0 5 0 00
	18	*Credit Memo #128*	*SR1*		1 2 00	1 0 3 8 00
	21	*Credit Memo #130*	*SR1*		7 5 00	9 6 3 00

Illustration 47C   Sales
returns and allowances
journal and customer
accounts (continued)

NAME	Susan's Tool Market		ACCOUNT NO.	222			
ADDRESS	4089 Birch Street, Toms River, NJ 08753-8262		TERMS	30 days			

DATE		ITEM	POST. REF.	DEBIT	CREDIT	BALANCE
19-- July	4	Invoice #381	S1	8 8 0 00		8 8 0 00
	14	Invoice #383	S1	5 5 0 00		1 4 3 0 00
	19	Credit Memo #129	SR1		5 0 00	1 3 8 0 00

Here are the steps to follow to record the transactions:

STEP 1 ▶ **Record the credit memos in the sales returns and allowances journal.**

Record returns and allowances in the sales returns and allowances journal from the data you find on the duplicate credit memos.

STEP 2 ▶ **Post to the customer accounts.**

After you record the returns and allowances in the journal, post the entries to the customer accounts. Each amount should be posted to the Credit column of the customer account. Subtract to find the new balance.

You can see how this is done by looking at the Thompson's Hardware Store account in Illustration 47C (on page 408). On June 18, the store received an allowance of $12.00 for damaged merchandise. The amount was posted to the Credit column of the account. The $12.00 was then subtracted from the old balance of $1,050.00 to get the new balance of $1,038.00.

As you post each transaction, enter the posting reference SR1 in the customer account. The posting reference SR1 shows that the entry was posted from page 1 of the sales returns and allowances journal. Also, enter an account number in the sales returns and allowances journal to show that the posting has been made.

STEP 3 ▶ **Total the sales returns and allowances journal.**

After you finish all the postings for the month, add the amounts in the sales returns and allowances journal. The journal in Illustration 47C (page 408) shows that the total returns and allowances for June were $137.00. This total was footed and re-added before the final total was written. Date the final total as the last day of the month, and write the word *Total* in the Customer's Name column.

Handling Customer Payments

When customers return goods or receive an allowance on goods, they do not owe as much as before. Thus, they pay the amount of the invoice less the amount of the credit memo. For example, Susan's Tool Market purchased $550.00 on July 14 (Invoice #383). On July 19, it was issued Credit Memo #129 for $50.00. This means that the company owed only $550.00 - $50.00, or $500.00, as the balance on Invoice #383.

When you received the $500.00 payment for this invoice, you recorded it in the cash receipts journal in this way:

	DATE		RECEIVED FROM	FOR	POST REF.	AMOUNT	
				CASH RECEIPTS JOURNAL		PAGE 1	
1	19-- Aug.	23	*Susan's Tool Market*	*Bal. Inv., 7/14*	222	5 0 0 00	1

Notice that the reason for the receipt was shown as "Bal. Inv., 7/14." This means that the receipt was for the balance of the invoice dated July 14.

You are now using four records to keep track of transactions with customers to whom merchandise is sold on credit. The four records are

1. The *sales journal*, in which you record all the duplicate sales invoices.
2. The *cash receipts journal*, in which you record all collections from customers.
3. The *sales returns and allowances journal*, in which you record all the duplicate credit memos.
4. The *accounts receivable ledger*, in which you keep the customer accounts.

The debits in the customer accounts are posted from the sales journal. The credits in these accounts are posted from the cash receipts journal and from the sales returns and allowances journal. When you use all of these books, it is important to remember to post in the order of the dates of the transactions.

Look at Illustration 47D.

Illustration 47D
Recording sales invoices, cash receipts, and credit memos

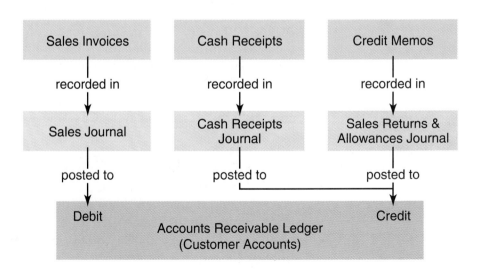

On a sheet of paper, write the headings **Statement Number** and **Words**. Next, choose the words that match the statements. Write each word you choose next to the statement number it matches. Be careful; not all the words listed should be used.

Statements	Words
1. To transfer data from one record to another	allowance
2. A record of all cash received	cash receipts journal
3. The column used to record a charge sale in a customer account	credit
4. The column used to record a receipt, return, or allowance in a customer account	credit memo
5. A bill	debit
6. A record in which you record credit memos	original
7. A form that shows that the balance of an account has been reduced because of a return or allowance	overcharge
8. A reduction in price given for damaged merchandise or to correct an overcharge	post
9. When the price on a sales invoice is more than it should be	sales invoice
	sales returns and allowances journal

PROBLEM SOLVING MODEL FOR: *Using a Sales Returns and Allowances Journal*

STEP 1 ▶ *Record the credit memos in the sales returns and allowances journal.*

STEP 2 ▶ *Post to the customer accounts.*

STEP 3 ▶ *Total the sales returns and allowances journal.*

APPLICATION PROBLEMS

PROBLEM **47-1** ▶ You are employed in the accounting department of Prusacki Wholesale Company.

Directions

a. Copy the following customer accounts. Include the amounts already posted.

NAME	Busse Handiware					ACCOUNT NO. 281	
ADDRESS	48 Iroquois Avenue, N., Tucson, AZ 85716-1686				TERMS	30 days	

DATE		ITEM	POST. REF.	DEBIT	CREDIT	BALANCE
19-- Dec.	3	Invoice #382	S1	3 0 7 00		3 0 7 00
	10	Invoice #385	S1	2 4 1 00		5 4 8 00

NAME	Lin's Discount Hardware					ACCOUNT NO. 282	
ADDRESS	982 Yuma Drive, Tucson, AZ 85710-5009				TERMS	30 days	

DATE		ITEM	POST. REF.	DEBIT	CREDIT	BALANCE
19-- Dec.	7	Invoice #384	S1	1 2 9 00		1 2 9 00
	11	Invoice #386	S1	4 3 6 00		5 6 5 00

NAME	Tomaselli Bros., Inc.					ACCOUNT NO. 283	
ADDRESS	231 Pompano Road, Tucson, AZ 85730-6714				TERMS	30 days	

DATE		ITEM	POST. REF.	DEBIT	CREDIT	BALANCE
19-- Dec.	5	Invoice #383	S1	2 7 8 00		2 7 8 00
	15	Invoice #387	S1	4 6 0 00		7 3 8 00

b. Use a sales returns and allowances journal to record the following data taken from the credit memos issued during the month. Number the journal page 1.

Date	Customer's Name	Credit Memo No.	Amount
Dec. 12	Busse Handiware	256	$35.00
14	Lin's Discount Hardware	257	50.00
17	Tomaselli Bros., Inc.	258	85.00
20	Lin's Discount Hardware	259	15.00
23	Tomaselli Bros., Inc.	260	70.00

CHECKPOINT

47-1 (e)
Busse Handiware ending
balance = $513.00

c. Post from the sales returns and allowances journal to the customer accounts. Enter the posting reference SR1 in the accounts and an account number in the sales returns and allowances journal as you post.

d. Foot, total, and rule the sales returns and allowances journal.

e. Check the balance at the end of the month in each account. Show all footings in each account.

You are the assistant bookkeeper for the Husain Merchandising Company.

Directions

a. Copy the following customer accounts. Include the amounts already posted.

NAME	Bernsin's			ACCOUNT NO.	**1021**
ADDRESS	35 Richmond Drive, Biloxi, MS 39531-2084			TERMS	**30 days**

DATE	ITEM	POST. REF.	DEBIT	CREDIT	BALANCE
19-- May 4	Invoice #428	S5	8 0 1 00		8 0 1 00
16	Invoice #432	S5	3 6 6 00		1 1 6 7 00

NAME	Maggie O'Day's Shoppe			ACCOUNT NO.	**1022**
ADDRESS	1045 12th Avenue, Biloxi, MS 39530-6641			TERMS	**30 days**

DATE	ITEM	POST. REF.	DEBIT	CREDIT	BALANCE
19-- May 8	Invoice #430	S5	6 3 4 00		6 3 4 00
19	Invoice #433	S5	5 7 7 00		1 2 1 1 00

NAME	The Waltermire Company			ACCOUNT NO.	**1023**
ADDRESS	14 Beach Boulevard, Biloxi, MS 39532-3203			TERMS	**30 days**

DATE	ITEM	POST. REF.	DEBIT	CREDIT	BALANCE
19-- May 7	Invoice #429	S5	5 3 5 00		5 3 5 00
13	Invoice #431	S5	1 1 0 00		6 4 5 00

b. Use a sales returns and allowances journal to record the following data taken from the credit memos issued during the month. Number the journal page 5.

Date	Customer's Name	Credit Memo No.	Amount
May 17	Bernsin's	134	$80.00
18	The Waltermire Company	135	35.00
20	Maggie O'Day's Shoppe	136	70.00
24	The Waltermire Company	137	55.00
27	Bernsin's	138	42.00

CHECKPOINT ✓

47-2 (d)
Journal total = $282.00

c. Post from the sales returns and allowances journal to the customer accounts. Use the posting reference SR5.
d. Foot, total, and rule the sales returns and allowances journal.
e. Check the balance at the end of the month in each account. Show all footings in each account.

You are employed by the Aztec Wholesale Company. It is part of your job to handle the accounts for customers.

Directions

a. Copy the following customer accounts. Include the amounts already posted.

NAME	Creative Choices, Inc.				ACCOUNT NO.	2201	
ADDRESS	5572 Mercy Drive, Orlando, FL 32811-8357			TERMS	30 days		

DATE		ITEM	POST. REF.	DEBIT	CREDIT	BALANCE
19-- Feb.	8	Invoice #957	S9	5 5 3 85		5 5 3 85
	16	Invoice #959	S9	2 1 7 40		7 7 1 25

NAME	Levy's Art Supplies				ACCOUNT NO.	2202	
ADDRESS	617 State Road 120, Orlando, FL 32803-1177			TERMS	30 days		

DATE		ITEM	POST. REF.	DEBIT	CREDIT	BALANCE
19-- Feb.	2	Invoice #955	S9	4 3 8 20		4 3 8 20
	19	Invoice #960	S9	7 5 3 85		1 1 9 2 05

NAME	L. Plarski & Sons				ACCOUNT NO.	2203	
ADDRESS	12486 Raleigh Street, Orlando, FL 32819-4306			TERMS	30 days		

DATE		ITEM	POST. REF.	DEBIT	CREDIT	BALANCE
19-- Feb.	5	Invoice #956	S9	1 7 8 45		1 7 8 45
	12	Invoice #958	S9	4 0 9 15		5 8 7 60

b. Use a sales returns and allowances journal to record the following data taken from the credit memos issued during the month. Number the journal page 9.

Date	Customer's Name	Credit Memo No.	Amount
Feb. 20	Levy's Art Supplies	1027	$43.35
21	L. Plarski & Sons	1028	24.60
23	Creative Choices, Inc.	1029	86.15
25	Levy's Art Supplies	1030	61.70
26	Creative Choices, Inc.	1031	14.25

CHECKPOINT ✔

47-3 (e)
L. Plarski & Sons ending balance = $563.00

c. Post from the sales returns and allowances journal to the customer accounts. Use the posting reference SR9.
d. Foot, total, and rule the sales returns and allowances journal.
e. Check the balance at the end of the month in each account. Show all footings in each account.

Problems 47-4, 47-5, and 47-6 may be found in the Working Papers.

CHAPTER

9

Reinforcement
Activities

DISCUSSION

You are the supervisor of a group of order clerks. The clerks take orders over the phone and use a computer program to record each order.

Your manager wants to pay higher wages to clerks who produce more than other workers. Your manager has asked you to suggest a way to measure the productivity of each of your order clerks. That is, your manager wants you to find a way to measure how much each clerk produces.

You decide to ask your order clerks for ideas. One clerk feels that the number of hours each clerk spends working is a good measure of productivity. Another feels that the number of orders completed should be used as the measure. Still another feels that productivity should be measured by how "hard" each clerk works.

List one advantage and one disadvantage for each of the three ideas.

CRITICAL THINKING

You are an order clerk for Towsom Merchandise, Inc. Towsom's customers order merchandise by phone using a catalog that the company has sent them. The catalog contains a description and the stock number for each item of merchandise the company sells. Your job is to take customer orders over the telephone and enter the data into a computer.

Answer the questions listed below. Keep in mind that you may be the only person from Towsom Merchandise, Inc., that the customer ever meets or talks to. How the customer feels about the company may depend on what you say and do. Also keep in mind that you should not waste time idly chatting with a customer over the telephone. Other customers may be waiting to call in orders.

1. What would you say when you first answered the telephone?
2. If the customer said, "I'd like to order some merchandise," what would you ask the customer?
3. What would you say when you finish taking the order?

APPLIED COMMUNICATIONS

Raul is a new order clerk with Towsom Merchandise, Inc., the same company as in the Critical Thinking exercise. You are his supervisor and are responsible for training him in his new job. Write what you would say to Raul to explain why

1. He should not chew gum or eat food while talking with customers.
2. He should be as pleasant to customers as possible.
3. He must be accurate when recording orders from customers.

RECORD KEEPING CAREERS

Order clerks who take orders over the telephone are important to the business for which they work. They must have certain skills and knowledge to do their work well. What are two special skills or areas of knowledge that order clerks should have to succeed at their work?

GLOBAL BUSINESS—FOREIGN CURRENCY

Lu Chang is an accounts receivable clerk for a book wholesaler with many international customers. The payments that he receives are sometimes in U.S. dollars and sometimes in foreign currencies. If the payment is in a foreign currency, such as Japanese yen, Lu must convert the yen into U.S. dollars before he records the payment in the cash receipts journal.

To convert the yen, Lu must know the exchange rate, or the value of yen in relation to the U.S. dollar. Lu can find the exchange rate in many daily newspapers or by calling a bank. The following list of exchange rates is taken from a newspaper. Because rates can change daily, the current exchange rates could be quite different from the ones shown here.

Country	Currency	U.S. Dollar Equivalent
Australia	dollar	.7303
Canada	dollar	.7908
Germany	deutsche mark	.6757
Japan	yen	.0090
Mexico	new peso	.323154
Peru	new sol	.7931
South Africa	rand	.2519

The numbers in this table are based on one unit of each foreign currency. To use this table, take the amount of the payment in foreign currency—for example, 1,204.5 yen—and multiply by the U.S. $ equivalent:

1,204.5 yen x .0090 = $10.8405, rounded to $10.84

A Foreign Currency Activity can be found in the Working Papers.

On a sheet of paper, write the headings **Statement Number** and **Words**. Next, choose the words that best complete the statements. Write each word you choose next to the statement number it completes. Be careful; not all the words listed should be used. Some words may be used more than once.

Statements	Words
1. To find out if there is enough merchandise to fill an order, a copy of a sales order is sent to the _____ department.	accounts receivable ledger
2. When the seller gives you 30 days to pay for the goods you bought, the 30 days are known as the _____ .	allowance
3. You should post _____ to charge customer accounts so that the account balances are kept up-to-date.	April 1
4. At the end of the period, the accounts receivable clerk prepares a list of all charge customers who have balances in their accounts. This list is called (a, an) _____ .	credit
	daily
	debit
	extension
	March 31
5. A customer may want to keep damaged merchandise if the wholesaler will give (a, an) _____ .	schedule of accounts receivable
6. The amount of a sale on account is posted to the _____ column of the customer's account.	stock
7. The amount of a cash receipt is posted to the _____ column of the customer's account.	terms
8. The amount of a return of merchandise is posted to the _____ column of the customer's account.	weekly
9. When you multiply the unit price by the quantity, you are finding the _____ .	

AUTOMATED

You are employed by Comtech Trading Company, a wholesale computer equipment firm. Part of your job is to prepare sales invoices from copies of sales orders. You also record sales invoices in a sales journal.

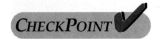
CHECKPOINT ✔

(a)
Marsh Computer Store
invoice total = $2,487.25

Directions

a. The data from the sales that follow were taken from sales orders. Prepare a sales invoice for each sale. Date each invoice January 15. Terms for each customer are 30 days. All merchandise is to be shipped by parcel post.

Sale #1

Sold To: Marsh Computer Store
          3408 Delaware Street
          Mobile, AL 36604-1983
Our Order No. 701
Customer Order No. 307988
15 Dot matrix printers, #DM144
@ $119.89
50 Diskette caddies, #DC108
@ $3.78
10 1200 BPS modems, #M0120
@ $49.99

Sale #2

Sold To: Keys Technology, Inc.
          9183 Bell Road
          Montgomery, AL 36116-7348
Our Order No. 702
Customer Order No. 3078-45
10 Tape backup units, #TB110
@ $329.89
25 Serial boards, #SB960
@ $24.88
30 Memory boards, #MB300
@ $149.99

Sale #3

Sold To: Computer Barn
          6319 Goode Street
          Montgomery, AL 36105-3366
Our Order No. 703
Customer Order No. A781
25 Star computers, #C286
@ $1,799.80
15 Milan hard drives, #HD40
@ $268.90
15 Star floppy drives, #FD36
@ $59.99

Sale #4

Sold To: Coastal Computers, Inc.
          6891 Lake Drive
          Mobile, AL 36613-3361
Our Order No. 704
Customer Order No. 10444
20 VGA boards, #VB233
@ $169.79
15 Color monitors, #VT137
@ $148.90
10 Mouse kits, #MK991
@ $39.59

b. Record the sales invoices in a sales journal. Number the journal page 1. Do not foot the journal since other sales invoices must be recorded for January.

REVIEWING YOUR BUSINESS VOCABULARY

This activity may be found in the Working Papers.

COMPREHENSIVE PROJECT 3

Comprehensive Project 3 has been designed to reinforce major concepts of this and previous chapters. The Comprehensive Project is found in the Working Papers.

The Video Center is a store that rents and sells videotapes to the public and to businesses. This business simulation requires students to use the skills and procedures presented in the first semester of record keeping. Students get hands-on experience working with realistic business documents such as sales slips, petty cash vouchers, bank deposit slips, sales journal, cash receipts journal, checks, and more. This simulation is available from the publisher in either manual or automated versions. Students will perform the following activities as they simulate on-the-job training at The Video Center.

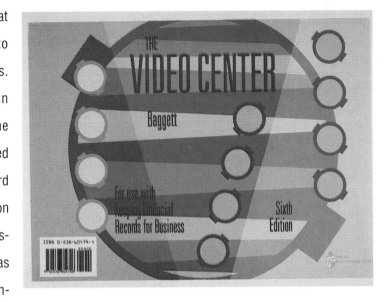

Activities in the Video Center

1. Completing source documents for cash and for charge rentals, sales, and returns.
2. Completing and recording petty cash vouchers.
3. Proving cash.
4. Recording transactions in a cash receipts journal, sales journal, and sales returns and allowances journal from source documents.
5. Counting cash.
6. Making a bank deposit.
7. Writing checks and check stubs.
8. Posting to the accounts receivable ledger from the cash receipts journal, from the sales journal, and from the sales returns and allowances journal.
9. Completing customer statements.
10. Making a schedule of accounts receivable.
11. Analyzing a budget.

A BUSINESS SIMULATION A BUSINESS SIMULATION A BUSINESS SIMULATION A BUSINESS SIMULATION A BUSINESS SIMULATION A BUSINESS SIMULATION

419

C H A P T E R

10

Record Keeping for Stock Record Clerks

$\mathcal{M}$ost stores have a large selection of merchandise. Have you ever wondered how business people

1. Keep a record of the merchandise they have on hand?
2. Know which merchandise sells fast and should be reordered?
3. Know which merchandise moves slowly and should be reduced in price for a quick sale?

Successful businesses are able to answer these questions by keeping accurate records of their merchandise.

In Chapter 10, you will learn how to keep, use, and check a stock record. You will also learn how to prepare a purchase requisition and an open order report. A Calculator Tip will be given for verifying the ending balance on a stock record.

J O B 48 ► KEEPING STOCK RECORDS

APPLIED MATH PREVIEW

Copy and complete these problems. Pay close attention to + and - signs.

1. + 93	2. + 54	3. + 75	4. + 2,310
+ 120	+ 82	+ 105	+ 1,540
- 48	+ 77	+ 1,124	- 1,306
- 75	- 46	- 73	- 945
+ 130	- 37	- 401	+ 1,157
- 108	- 55	- 86	- 2,001
- 27	+ 518	- 97	- 45
- 6	- 275	+ 1,441	+ 431
+ 96	+ 155	- 299	+ 909
- 68	- 103	- 716	+ 1,247

BUSINESS TERMS PREVIEW

• **Balance** • **Issue** • **Logging on** • **Maximum** • **Menu bar** •
• **Minimum** • **Option** • **Passwords** • **Periodic inventory** •
• **Perpetual inventory system** • **Stock** • **Stock record** •
• **Stock record clerk** •

1. To learn how to record the receipt and issuance of merchandise on a stock record.
2. To learn how to use the information on a stock record.

𝒰NDERSTANDING THE JOB

As you know, merchandise is also called **stock**. It is stored in a stock-room.

Businesses are able to keep accurate records of their stock by using a form called a **stock record**. A stock record shows stock received, stock issued, and how much there is on hand for any one item of stock. A stock record is shown in Illustration 48A.

Illustration 48A   Stock record

STOCK RECORD

ITEM _Footballs_   MAXIMUM _160_

STOCK NO. ___1110___   MINIMUM _65_

UNIT _Each_

DATE		QUANTITY RECEIVED	QUANTITY ISSUED	BALANCE
19--AUG.	1	140		140
	5		30	110
	12		40	70
	16	55		125

The balance changes after each entry

MULTICULTURAL INSIGHT

Around 630 B.C., an important contribution to record keeping was made in Greece in Europe. The Greeks invented coined money, making it easier to assign values to transactions. An example of Greek financial records is the Zenon papyri (transactions recorded on papyrus). These records date back to 256 B.C. when Egypt was a Greek province. The papyri are named after Zenon who was an Egyptian manager.

You are employed as a **stock record clerk** by the Lucci Sports Equipment Company. This company only sells wholesale. This means that it sells only to retail stores and not to the general public. You work in the stockroom where all the merchandise is stored. You are handed some stock records that were filled in by another clerk, Cheryl Larson. Each record is for a different item of equipment, such as footballs, baseball gloves, or hockey sticks. Each item in the stockroom must have its own record. The first record you look at is shown in Illustration 48A on page 421.

Here are the steps Larson followed to complete the record:

STEP 1 ▶ *Complete the heading.*

Larson first filled in the heading. Next to the word *Item* she wrote Footballs, since this record will be used only to keep track of footballs.

Each item is given a stock number to identify it. In the space for Stock No., Larson recorded 1110, the number assigned to footballs.

Unit refers to the measure in which items are sold. Those sold individually, including footballs, have the word *Each* recorded as the unit. Some items are sold by the dozen (12). Some are sold by the gross (12 dozen or 144). Each record must show what the unit of measure is.

The word **maximum** means the most that should ever be on hand. Your employer thinks that you will never need more than 160 footballs on hand, so 160 was recorded next to the word *Maximum*.

Minimum refers to the least that should ever be on hand. You always want to have on hand the merchandise your customers need. Your employer thinks that at least 65 footballs should be in stock, so 65 was entered next to the word *Minimum*.

STEP 2 ▶ *Record the merchandise received and issued.*

On August 1, 140 footballs were received in the stockroom. Larson entered Aug. 1 on the first line of the Date column. Then she wrote 140 in the Quantity Received column. Since there was no previous **balance**, the amount on hand was also 140. Larson wrote 140 in the Balance column.

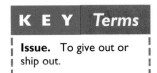

KEY *Terms*

Issue. To give out or
ship out.

On August 5, 30 footballs were shipped out, or **issued**. Since the month was still August, only the new day, 5, was written in the Date column. The amount issued, 30, was entered in the Quantity Issued column. Cheryl then figured the new balance this way:

Previous balance	140
Less: Quantity issued	- 30
Equals: New balance	110

Larson entered 110 in the Balance column below the old balance of 140.

The entry on August 12 was handled in the same way as the entry on August 5.

On August 16, 55 footballs were received. Larson entered 55 in the Quantity Received column. This time, she figured the new balance a little differently:

Previous balance	70
Plus: Quantity received	+ 55
Equals: New balance	125

She entered 125 in the Balance column to complete her recording.

Remember: Every time you receive or issue merchandise, the balance changes. When you receive, the balance increases; when you issue, the balance decreases. Be sure to check carefully each addition or subtraction before you enter it in the Balance column.

There is a special name given to a system in which the new balance is found after each entry. It is called a **perpetual inventory system**. In a perpetual inventory system, the new or running balance is calculated after each receipt or issuance of stock. Thus, the balance will always be up-to-date.

One problem with a perpetual inventory system is that the longer it is kept, the more errors there are in the stock balances in the system. There are a number of reasons why the stock balances in a perpetual inventory system can be wrong:

KEY *Terms*

Perpetual inventory
system. Running
balance is kept for each
item of stock.

Periodic inventory.
Actual count of stock
on hand.

1. The wrong amount of stock may have been entered when a sale or receipt of merchandise was recorded.
2. The wrong amount may have been sent to a customer, and the customer may not have notified the company of the error.
3. Some stock may have been damaged in the stockroom and removed from the shelves.
4. Some stock may have been stolen.
5. Some stock may have been placed on the wrong shelves.

To correct the balances in a perpetual inventory system, most companies take an actual count of the stock on hand at least once each year. This actual count is called a **periodic inventory**. A periodic inventory is also referred to as a physical inventory.

The stock balances from the periodic inventory are then compared to the balances on the stock records. When differences are found, the balances on the stock records are corrected. It is very important to every business to have an accurate list of each stock item and the balance of that item on hand.

SAMPLE PROBLEM 2

Cheryl Larson has worked at Lucci Sports Equipment for the month of August. On September 1, her stock record for footballs is full, so she must start a new record. The new record is shown in Illustration 48B on page 425.

Here are the steps Larson followed in preparing the new record:

STEP 1 ▶ *Complete the heading.*

Larson filled in the heading by copying all of the information from the heading of the August record.

STEP 2 ▶ *Record the balance on hand.*

The August record showed that there were 125 footballs on hand after the last entry. Larson wrote Sept. 1 in the Date column and 125 in the Balance column of the new record. Notice that the amount, 125, was written *only* in the Balance column. This is always done when a balance is carried forward from a previous record. No additional footballs were purchased on September 1, so no amount was entered in the Quantity Received column on September 1.

STEP 3 ▶ *Record the merchandise received and issued.*

Larson recorded the receipt and issuance of stock as she did in Sample Problem 1.

If you study the stock record in Illustration 48B (page 425), you will find valuable information on it. For example, you can add the amounts on September 17 (60) and September 22 (40) from the Quantity Issued column to get a total of 100. This tells you that 100 footballs were sold in September. If you total the Quantity Received column, you find that 30 + 50 = 80 footballs were purchased in September.

STOCK RECORD

ITEM ___Footballs___   MAXIMUM ___160___

STOCK NO. ___1110___   MINIMUM ___65___

UNIT ___Each___

DATE		QUANTITY RECEIVED	QUANTITY ISSUED	BALANCE
19-- SEPT.	1			125
	7	30		155
	17		60	95
	22		40	55
	27	50		105

You can also see why the company decided to make a purchase in late September. The balance went down to 55, which is below minimum. Notice also the day of the highest number of footballs on hand, September 7. All the information that you record helps your business to make good decisions about buying and selling.

USING THE COMPUTER

Many businesses use computers to keep stock records. When you keep stock records using a computer, you follow many of the same steps used in a manual system. For example, if Cheryl Larson were to use a computer in her job, here are the steps that she might follow to keep records of footballs:

STEP 1 ▶ *Log on to the computer.*

KEY Terms

Passwords. Secret words that let you use the terminal.

Logging on. Identifying yourself as an authorized user.

Menu bar. List of choices or options.

Larson enters her employee number, her password, and the date in order to log on to the computer. **Passwords** are secret words that are given to each clerk. Only persons who have a password can use the computer. This prevents unauthorized persons from using the computer. When Larson keys her employee number, password, and the date, she is **logging on** to the computer. Log-on procedures are those steps you take to identify yourself to the computer as an authorized user.

After logging on and selecting Inventory, a **menu bar** appears on the screen. The Items option is selected from the menu bar and appears as shown in Illustration 48C on page 426.

STEP 2 ▶ *Choose an option from the menu.*

KEY Terms

Option. A choice from a menu.

The Items menu shows two choices or **options**. Cheryl wants to create a stock record for footballs. So, she chooses Option 2, Maintain Inventory. In this example, the Maintain Inventory option is used to add, change, or delete inventory items.

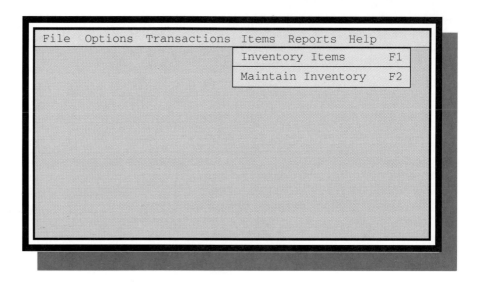

STEP 3 ▶ *Enter the stock number.*

The computer asks Larson to key the stock number of the record she wants to add. Cheryl keys 1110.

STEP 4 ▶ *Enter the description.*

The description is the name of the item. So, Cheryl enters the word *Footballs*.

STEP 5 ▶ *Enter the unit of measure.*

The unit of measure defines how the footballs are ordered. The word *Each* is keyed here.

STEP 6 ▶ *Enter the reorder point.*

The reorder point is the minimum number of footballs in stock when the new order is placed. Cheryl keys 65 for this line.

STEP 7 ▶ *Enter the retail price.*

Cheryl must go to the bill for the footballs to find the retail price. She checks and it is $50.00, so that is what she keys. The screen appears as shown in Illustration 48D.

Illustration 48D Stock record

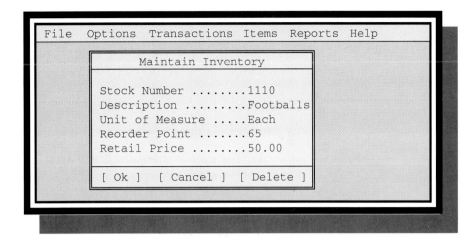

Illustration 48D Stock record

```
 File   Options  Transactions  Items  Reports  Help

              Maintain Inventory

        Stock Number .......1110
        Description ........Footballs
        Unit of Measure .....Each
        Reorder Point .......65
        Retail Price ........50.00

           [ Ok ]   [ Cancel ]   [ Delete ]
```

BUILDING YOUR BUSINESS VOCABULARY

On a sheet of paper, write the headings **Statement Number** and **Words**. Next, choose the words that match the statements. Write each word you choose next to the statement number it matches. Be careful; not all the words listed should be used.

Statements	Words
1. The least	balance
2. To give out or ship out	gross
3. 12 dozen or 144	issue
4. A worker who keeps track of goods received and issued	logging on
	maximum
5. The amount of stock on hand	menu bar
6. A record of each item in the stockroom	minimum
7. Merchandise	option
8. A choice from a menu	password
9. A system in which a running balance is kept of each item in stock	periodic inventory
	perpetual inventory system
10. Actual count of stock on hand	stock
	stock record
	stock record clerk

Use the Problem Solving Model as a reminder when you are working on the Application Problems or studying for a test.

▲▲▲▲▲
TIP
▼▼▼▼▼

PROBLEM SOLVING MODEL FOR: *Preparing a New Stock Record*

STEP 1 ▶ *Complete the heading.*

STEP 2 ▶ *Record the balance on hand.*

STEP 3 ▶ *Record the merchandise received and issued.*

PROBLEM | **48-1** ▷ You are the stock record clerk for Polanski Skate Company.

Directions

a. Enter the following information at the top of a stock record:

1. The item is men's figure skates.
2. The stock number is 3.
3. The unit is pair.
4. The maximum is 250.
5. The minimum is 50.

b. Record the following:

Nov.   1 The balance on hand is **67**. (Enter 67 only in the Balance column.)
     3 Received 175 pairs of men's figure skates.
     8 Issued 83 pairs of men's figure skates.
    10 Issued 112 pairs of men's figure skates.
    12 Received 210 pairs of men's figure skates.
    16 Issued 76 pairs of men's figure skates.
    19 Issued 59 pairs of men's figure skates.
    22 Issued 73 pairs of men's figure skates.
    27 Received 211 pairs of men's figure skates.
    30 Issued 59 pairs of men's figure skates.

CHECKPOINT ✔

48-1
Final balance = 201

c. Answer the following questions:

1. On what date did you have the largest quantity of men's figure skates?
2. On what date did you have the smallest quantity?
3. On what dates did you go above maximum?
4. On what dates did you go below minimum?
5. How many pairs of men's figure skates were received during November?
6. How many pairs of men's figure skates were sold during November?

PROBLEM | **48-2** ▷ You are the stock record clerk for Polanski Skate Company.

Directions

a. Open a stock record for each of the following items. Enter all information listed in this table. Sort the stock records numerically.

Item	Stock No.	Unit	Maximum	Minimum	Balance on Dec. 1
Men's figure skates	3	Pair	250	50	201
Women's figure skates	2	Pair	275	75	90
Children's figure skates	4	Pair	175	60	72
Adult hockey skates	1	Pair	300	70	67
Children's hockey skates	6	Pair	100	20	96
Double runner skates	5	Pair	150	40	46

b. Record the following in the order in which they are shown:

Dec. 2 Received 200 pairs of women's figure skates.
      2 Issued 42 pairs of children's hockey skates.
      2 Received 19 pairs of children's figure skates.
      7 Received 203 pairs of adult hockey skates.
      7 Issued 37 pairs of children's hockey skates.
      7 Received 65 pairs of double runner skates.
      10 Issued 72 pairs of men's figure skates.
      10 Issued 76 pairs of women's figure skates.
      10 Received 35 pairs of double runner skates.
      15 Issued 83 pairs of men's figure skates.
      15 Received 55 pairs of children's hockey skates.
      17 Issued 29 pairs of children's figure skates.
      17 Issued 83 pairs of women's figure skates.
      17 Issued 31 pairs of adult hockey skates.
      20 Received 30 pairs of children's hockey skates.
      20 Issued 18 pairs of children's figure skates.
      20 Received 190 pairs of men's figure skates.
      20 Issued 42 pairs of double runner skates.
      21 Issued 47 pairs of adult hockey skates.
      21 Issued 54 pairs of women's figure skates.
      21 Received 9 pairs of double runner skates.
      26 Issued 38 pairs of children's hockey skates.
      26 Issued 62 pairs of men's figure skates.
      26 Received 150 pairs of women's figure skates.
      29 Received 84 pairs of children's figure skates.
      29 Issued 77 pairs of adult hockey skates.

CHECKPOINT

48-2
Stock No. 3 final balance = 174

c. Foot the Quantity Received and Quantity Issued columns of each record.

d. Answer the following questions. (Remember that each item has a different maximum and minimum.)
   1. Which items were below the minimum during December?
   2. Which items were above the maximum during December?
   3. Which item sold the most during December?
   4. Which item sold the least during December?

Problem 48-3 may be found in the Working Papers.

APPLIED MATH PREVIEW

Copy and complete these problems. Pay close attention to + and - signs.
Notice that each problem needs two answers.

1.	60	2.	174	3.	1,400	4.	8,347
	+ 154		+ 853		+ 4,210		+ 11,204
	- 107		- 796		- 3,875		- 17,169

BUSINESS TERM PREVIEW

• Chaining •

GOALS

1. To learn a new way to check stock records.
2. To practice keeping stock records.

𝒰NDERSTANDING THE JOB

Stock record clerks must be accurate when they record new balances on stock records. If you worked carefully on Job 48, you always checked your addition or subtraction before you entered each new balance. To check your addition, you should add the numbers again in the opposite direction. For example, suppose that you added 70 + 55 and got 125. To check the addition, 55 + 70 = 125. To check your subtraction, you should add the answer you got to the number you subtracted. For example, 140 - 30 = 110. To check the subtraction, 110 + 30 = 140.

In this job, you will learn another method to check the accuracy of your math, for you may one day be in charge of a large supply of stock.

SAMPLE PROBLEM

You are a stock record clerk for Cindy's Sock Shop. Refer to Illustration 49A. To check the accuracy of the May 31 final balance of 32 pairs of socks, follow these 4 steps:

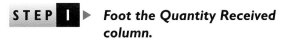

STEP 1 ▶ **Foot the Quantity Received column.**

Add the numbers in the Quantity Received column. The total is 82. Write this total under the line on which the last amount was recorded. You have now footed the column.

STEP 2 ▶ **Foot the Quantity Issued column.**

Add the numbers in the Quantity Issued column. The total is 110. Write this total on the same line as you wrote the footing of the Quantity Received column.

Illustration 49A   Stock record

STOCK RECORD

ITEM _Socks_   MAXIMUM _75_

STOCK NO. _KH43_   MINIMUM _25_

UNIT _Pair_

DATE		QUANTITY RECEIVED	QUANTITY ISSUED	BALANCE
19-- MAY	1			60
	5		15	45
	7		25	20
	15	50		70
	16		42	28
	22	15		43
	27		28	15
	31	17		32
		82	110	

STEP 3 ▸ *Find the ending balance.*

On another sheet of paper, write the amount of the opening balance, 60, shown on the stock record. Add the total Quantity Received (from Step 1) to this balance. Then, from this total, subtract the total Quantity Issued (from Step 2). This difference will give you the ending balance.

Opening balance	60
Add: Total quantity received	+ 82
Total	142
Less: Total quantity issued	- 110
Ending balance	32

STEP 4 ▸ *Verify the ending balance.*

Compare your calculation from Step 3 with the ending balance on the stock record. In this case, 32 = 32. This tells you that your work is correct. You have verified it.

What if the two figures do not agree? First, go back through the four steps. If you find that the two balances still do not agree, there is a math error on the stock record. You must now check each calculation on the stock record.

Look at Illustration 49B. It is the same record from Illustration 49A (on page 431) but with an error made on May 16. A line was

Illustration 49B
Corrected stock record

STOCK RECORD

ITEM _Socks_   MAXIMUM _75_

STOCK NO. _KH43_   MINIMUM _25_

UNIT _Pair_

DATE		QUANTITY RECEIVED	QUANTITY ISSUED	BALANCE
19-- MAY	1			60
	5		15	45 ✓
	7		25	20 ✓
	15	50		70 ✓
	16		42	28 / 38
	22	15		43 / 53
	27		28	15 / 25
	31	17		32 / 42
		82	110	

Check (✓) each correct balance

Correct each incorrect balance

drawn through the incorrect balance of 38, and the correct figure of 28 was written above it. Since the May 16 balance was incorrect, all remaining balances had to be changed.

If you want to avoid this extra work, be careful and check your math before you record each new balance.

A calculator can be an aid in verifying the ending balance on a stock record in two ways. First, you can use it, as you already know, to add the Quantity Received and Quantity Issued columns.

There is also another way to use the calculator. If there is an error, your calculator can aid you in rapid correction. Suppose you were checking the stock record in Illustration 49A (on page 431). By hand, you are doing this: 60 - 15 = 45; 45 - 25 = 20; 20 + 50 = 70; 70 - 42 = 28; and so forth. With a calculator, you do not have to enter each new balance again. You just keep adding or subtracting. Here's how:

STEP 1 ▶ *Enter the opening balance.*

Enter the opening balance by pressing these keys:

| 6 | 0 |

STEP 2 ▶ *Subtract the first issuance.*

Subtract the first issuance by pressing these keys:

| – | 1 | 5 |

The balance of 45 will appear in the display. Check it off on your stock record.

STEP 3 ▶ *Enter the remaining issuances and receipts.*

Do not clear your answer. Do not re-enter 45. Simply press these keys to enter the next issuance:

| – | 2 | 5 |

A new balance of 20 will appear in the display. Check it off.
Add the receipt on May 15 by pressing these keys:

| + | 5 | 0 |

A balance of 70 will appear in the display. Check it off.

Subtract 42, the next issuance, by pressing these keys:

$$\boxed{-}\ \boxed{4}\ \boxed{2}$$

A balance of 28 will appear in the display.

STEP 4 ▶ *Continue to the end.*

You are using the idea of **chaining** on a calculator. Chaining means that you can continue adding or subtracting without clearing and re-entering your previous answer. It saves a lot of time and chance of error.

UILDING YOUR BUSINESS VOCABULARY

On a sheet of paper, write the headings **Statement Number** and **Words**. Next, choose the words that match the statements. Write each word you choose next to the statement number it matches. Be careful; not all the words listed should be used.

Statements	Words
1. To check for accuracy	balance
2. The most	chaining
3. A list of choices or options	foot
4. The amount of stock on hand	issue
5. To add a column and record the total	maximum
6. A record of each item in the stockroom	menu bar
7. Continuous calculation without clearing	minimum
8. A system in which a running balance is kept of each item in stock	perpetual inventory system
	stock record
	verify

PROBLEM SOLVING MODEL FOR: *Checking Stock Records*

STEP 1 ▶ *Foot the Quantity Received column.*

STEP 2 ▶ *Foot the Quantity Issued column.*

STEP 3 ▶ *Find the ending balance.*

STEP 4 ▶ *Verify the ending balance.*

𝓐PPLICATION PROBLEMS

PROBLEM | **49-1** ▶ You are a stock record clerk for Ace Supply Company.

49-1

The first record is correct.

Directions

a. Follow the four steps in the Sample Problem to check the accuracy of the following stock records. If the ending balances are correct, you are finished with this problem. If not, then continue with part "b."

DATE	QUANTITY RECEIVED	QUANTITY ISSUED	BALANCE
19-- JUNE 1			96
3	21		117
6	15		132
7		19	113
12		36	77
15	29		106
18		15	91
22		12	79
27	42		121
30		37	84

DATE	QUANTITY RECEIVED	QUANTITY ISSUED	BALANCE
19-- JUNE 1			59
6		19	40
8	38		78
12	54		132
15		26	106
17		29	87
19	41		128
22	22		150
26		37	113
30		18	95

b. Go back through the four steps. If the balances still do not agree, check each daily balance on each stock record. If a balance is incorrect, draw a line through it and write the correct figure above it. (Use Illustration 49B on page 432 as an example.)

PROBLEM | **49-2** ▶ You are a stock record clerk for Ace Supply Company.

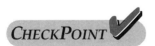

49-2

First record's correct balance = 146

Directions

a. Follow the four steps in the Sample Problem to check the accuracy of the stock records on page 436. If the ending balances are correct, you are finished with this problem. If not, then continue with part "b."

b. Go back through the four steps. If the balances still do not agree, check each daily balance on each stock record. If a balance is incorrect, draw a line through it and write the correct figure above it. (Use Illustration 49B on page 432 as an example.)

DATE		QUANTITY RECEIVED	QUANTITY ISSUED	BALANCE
19-- MAY	1			207
	7		99	108
	9	57		165
	14	44		209
	15		37	172
	17		86	86
	27	130		216
	29		59	167
	30	31		198
	31		42	156

DATE		QUANTITY RECEIVED	QUANTITY ISSUED	BALANCE
19-- MAY	1			107
	3		42	65
	8	39		94
	10		27	67
	12	41		108
	17		33	75
	20		21	54
	22	85		139
	28	45		184
	31		109	75

PROBLEM **49-3** ▶ You are a stock record clerk for the Bright Lamp Company.

Directions

a. Open a separate stock record for each of the four items listed in the following table:

Item	Stock No.	Unit	Maximum	Minimum	Balance May 1
Desk lamps	DL 141	Each	200	50	61
Floor lamps	FL 063	Each	175	30	74
Hanging lamps	HL 119	Each	125	20	23
Table lamps	TL 003	Pair	250	40	46

b. Record the following in the order in which they are shown:

May 2 Received 130 desk lamps.
2 Received 60 hanging lamps.
5 Issued 51 floor lamps.
5 Received 195 pairs of table lamps.
5 Issued 59 desk lamps.
8 Issued 57 hanging lamps.
8 Received 150 floor lamps.
8 Issued 67 pairs of table lamps.
12 Received 95 hanging lamps.
12 Issued 43 desk lamps.

May 17 Received 40 pairs of table lamps.
17 Issued 36 floor lamps.
17 Issued 83 hanging lamps.
22 Issued 79 pairs of table lamps.
22 Issued 29 floor lamps.
25 Received 90 desk lamps.
25 Issued 51 pairs of table lamps.
29 Received 50 hanging lamps.
29 Issued 47 floor lamps.
29 Issued 73 desk lamps.

c. Check the accuracy of the ending balance on each record with the method you used in Problems 49-1 and 49-2. If the balance is incorrect, make the necessary corrections on each record.

JOB **50** ▶ PREPARING PURCHASE REQUISITIONS AND OPEN ORDER REPORTS

APPLIED MATH PREVIEW

Copy and complete the following problems.

1. 175	2. 250	3. 1,050	4. 975
- 96	- 83	- 827	- 246

5. 800	6. 750	7. 1,275	8. 2,185
- 111	- 169	- 297	- 996

BUSINESS TERMS PREVIEW

- Open order • **Open order report** • **Purchase requisition** •
- **Purchasing agent** •

GOALS

1. To learn how to complete a purchase requisition.
2. To learn how to prepare an open order report.

UNDERSTANDING THE JOB

KEY Terms

Purchasing agent. The buyer for a business.

Purchase requisition. A form telling the purchasing agent to place an order.

So far, you have learned to record information on stock records and to check the accuracy of your work. However, there is more to a stock record clerk's position. You must let the person who buys stock know when more stock is needed. This person has the job title of **purchasing agent** or buyer.

To be able to tell the purchasing agent when to buy, you must watch carefully three numbers on the stock records:

1. The balance
2. The maximum
3. The minimum

When the balance gets close to the minimum, it is time to order. To find out how much to order, subtract the balance from the maximum. Then, tell the purchasing agent to place an order by preparing a **purchase requisition**. Sample Problem 1 will show you how to prepare a purchase requisition.

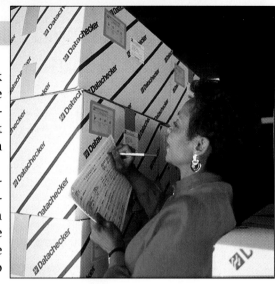

Sarah Jackson is a stock record clerk for the LaPete Shoe Store. Illustration 50A shows a stock record that she has been working on.

After finding the balance of 55, Jackson compared it to the minimum of 50. Because the balance was getting close to the minimum, she decided to request more merchandise.

To find out how much to request, she subtracted the balance from the maximum.

Maximum	125
Balance	- 55
Amount to Request	70

Illustration 50A Stock record

STOCK RECORD

ITEM _Tennis shoes_   MAXIMUM _125_

STOCK NO. _T14_   MINIMUM _50_

UNIT _Pair_

DATE	QUANTITY RECEIVED	QUANTITY ISSUED	BALANCE
19-- MAR. 1			107
9		52	55

— When the balance nears the minimum, it is time to prepare a purchase requisition.

The amount of 70 is the most that she should request, since she does not want to go above the maximum. Jackson then prepared the purchase requisition shown in Illustration 50B (page 439) in five steps.

PURCHASE REQUISITION

FOR DEPARTMENT _Shoes_   NO. _1_

NOTIFY _Sarah Jackson_ ON DELIVERY   DATE _March 9, 19--_

                                            DATE WANTED _March 19, 19--_

QUANTITY	DESCRIPTION	REMARKS
70 pairs	Tennis shoes, T14	Assorted colors

ORDER FROM _____   APPROVED BY _____

STEP 1 ▶ Record the name of the department.

Next to the words *For Department*, Jackson wrote Shoes to show that the merchandise is needed for the Shoe Department.

STEP 2 ▶ Record the name of the stock clerk who needs the stock.

Jackson wrote her own name next to the word *Notify*. Because she is the person requesting the stock, she should be notified when it arrives.

STEP 3 ▶ Number the requisition.

Since this is the first requisition prepared by Jackson, it is numbered 1. The next will be numbered 2, and so forth.

STEP 4 ▶ Record the dates.

Two dates must be recorded on a purchase requisition. The first is the date on which the requisition was prepared, March 9, 19--. Jackson recorded March 9, 19--, by the word *Date*.

The second date is when the stock is needed. Jackson wants the new shoes by March 19, 19--, so she recorded this date in the Date Wanted space.

STEP 5 ▶ Record the merchandise details.

Jackson must let the purchasing agent know exactly what she needs. In the Quantity column, she wrote 70 pairs, the amount calculated from the stock record. (It is possible that the purchasing agent will order a different quantity to get a better price, but it is Jackson's duty to request up to the maximum.)

In the Description column, she recorded what was needed—tennis shoes, (stock number) T 14. Since she wants a variety of colors, she wrote Assorted colors in the Remarks column.

The spaces at the bottom, Order From and Approved By, are used by the purchasing agent. Jackson sends the original purchase requisition to that agent after making a copy for her records. From the copies of all the purchase requisitions that she keeps, she prepares an **open order report**. This form lists all of the requisitions that she has prepared and when they are filled. In Sample Problem 2, you will see how this report is prepared.

𝒮AMPLE PROBLEM 2

Jackson issued five purchase requisitions during March. Illustration 50C on page 441 shows the open order report that Jackson prepared in two steps.

STEP 1 ▸ *Fill in the first three columns from copies of the purchase requisitions.*

The information for the first three columns of the open order report is filled in when the requisitions are made out. All of the information is contained on the requisitions. The requisitions are recorded in numerical order.

STEP 2 ▸ *Fill in the last two columns when the merchandise is received.*

The date of receipt and any information about the order are filled in when the merchandise is received.

Look at the remark for Purchase Requisition 1 in Illustration 50C (page 441). While 70 pairs were requested, only 68 were received. The stock record clerk, Jackson, must notify the purchasing agent immediately. Perhaps the purchasing agent ordered only 68, so there is no problem. But if 70 were ordered, then the purchasing agent must ask the seller why only 68 were sent.

The remark for Purchase Requisition 2 is None, indicating that what was requested was received. Jackson need take no action about properly filled orders. However, she must notify the purchasing

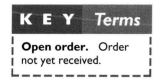
agent about Purchase Requisition 4, since 2 of the cartons were damaged.

Notice also that Purchase Requisitions 3 and 5 are not yet received. They are **open orders**, or orders not yet received. Jackson can tell which orders are still out by looking at the open order report.

Illustration 50C   Open order report

OPEN ORDER REPORT

DATE OF REQUISITION	PURCHASE REQUISITION NO.	DATE WANTED	DATE RECEIVED	REMARKS
19-- MAR. 9	1	Mar. 19	Mar. 17	Only 68 pairs
12	2	Mar. 20	Mar. 19	None
17	3	Mar. 25		
22	4	Mar. 30	Mar. 30	2 cartons damaged
29	5	Apr. 8		

ℬUILDING YOUR BUSINESS VOCABULARY

On a sheet of paper, write the headings **Statement Number** and **Words**. Next, choose the words that match the statements. Write each word you choose next to the statement number it matches. Be careful; not all the words listed should be used.

Statements	Words
1. A record of each item in the stockroom	chaining
2. Check for accuracy	foot
3. A form telling the purchasing agent to place an order	issue
	open order
4. A list of filled and unfilled purchase requisitions	open order report
	perpetual inventory
5. Continuous calculation without clearing	system
6. A system in which a running balance is kept of each item in stock	purchase requisition
	purchasing agent
7. An order not yet received	stock record
8. The buyer for a business	verify

PROBLEM SOLVING MODEL FOR: *Preparing Purchase Requisitions*

> **STEP 1** ▶ *Record the name of the department.*
>
> **STEP 2** ▶ *Record the name of the stock clerk who needs the stock.*
>
> **STEP 3** ▶ *Number the requisition.*
>
> **STEP 4** ▶ *Record the dates.*
>
> **STEP 5** ▶ *Record the merchandise details.*

PROBLEM SOLVING MODEL FOR: *Preparing Open Order Reports*

> **STEP 1** ▶ *Fill in the first three columns from copies of the purchase requisitions.*
>
> **STEP 2** ▶ *Fill in the last two columns when the merchandise is received.*

𝒜PPLICATION PROBLEMS

| PROBLEM | **50-1** ▶ You are a stock record clerk for Fong Auto Supply Company.

Directions

Complete the following table:

50-1 (1)
Amount needed = 659

Item No.	Balance, May 1	Maximum	Amount needed to bring the balance up to maximum
1	791	1,450	
2	137	900	
3	294	750	
4	1,188	1,875	
5	304	475	
6	177	650	
7	96	700	
8	947	2,150	

Maximum
- Balance

Amount
Needed

You are a stock record clerk for the Drummond Toy Store.

Directions

a. For each of the items listed, find the amount that you must order to bring the balance up to maximum. (To do this, subtract the June 1 balance from the maximum.)

Description	Unit of Measure	Maximum	Date Wanted	Balance on June 1	Amount to be Ordered
Stuffed animal, #A 6	Each	275	June 15	22	
Electric train, #T 4	Set	190	June 20	72	
Jigsaw puzzle, #P 7	Each	500	June 24	103	
Rocking horse, #H 9	Each	150	June 27	64	

b. Prepare a purchase requisition for each item that needs to be ordered in part "a." You work for Department B. Start with purchase requisition no. 62. Date all requisitions June 6, 19--. (Use Illustration 50B on page 439 as an example.)

c. Record each of the four requisitions on an open order report. (Use Illustration 50C on page 441 as an example.)

d. Enter the following information about stock received on the open order report.

Purchase Requisition No.	Date Received	Remarks
62	June 14	None
63	June 19	Only 115 received
65	June 28	One doesn't rock

Problems 50-3 and 50-4 may be found in the Working Papers.

CHAPTER 10

Reinforcement Activities

DISCUSSION

You work for a ski shop as a stock record clerk. Kendall Parker has just begun to work with you. He is a stock record clerk, also. Kendall does not understand why the stock records need to have maximum and minimum amounts recorded. He has asked you to explain. What would you say to him?

PROFESSIONAL BUSINESS ETHICS

You are working as a stock record clerk for a wholesaler of television sets. You keep a perpetual inventory record. Once a month you go to the stockroom to count the sets on hand. The purpose of manually counting is to see if the number of sets in the stockroom matches what is supposed to be there.

You notice over a three-month period that your records are always off. You seem to have three or four less sets in stock than are on the records. One evening, you happen to notice a good friend taking a set home. Two days later, you notice it again and conclude that your friend is stealing television sets. You mention it to that friend, who offers to split the money with you on the sale of the stolen sets if you don't say anything about it.

Write what you would do in this situation.

APPLIED COMMUNICATIONS

Part of your job is preparing an open order report. You record purchase requisitions when they are made out. You then fill in the last two columns of the report when merchandise is received. Look at Illustration 50C (page 441) to see your finished work.

When merchandise received is damaged, you must notify the purchasing agent. Purchase Requisition 4, which was for 12 cartons of socks, included 2 damaged cartons. Write the body of the note that you would send to the purchasing agent to indicate what is damaged. Be sure to include all details about the shipment that are found in the open order report in Illustration 50C (on page 441). Be as brief as possible.

(on page 441)

RECORD KEEPING CAREERS

You read the following ad found in your local newspaper:

Inventory Clerks

Earn extra cash during our semi-annual store-wide inventory. Immediate part-time positions (day, evening, and weekend schedules) are available for individuals to conduct our inventory (that is, organize, count and check prices of merchandise). Potential for regular placement. Please apply in person, Monday through Saturday, 10 AM to 6 PM. No experience necessary.

Answer the following questions:

1. Is this an entry-level job? Explain your answer.
2. How do you go about applying for this job?
3. Is the job a temporary one or a permanent one? Explain your answer.

REVIEWING WHAT YOU HAVE LEARNED

On a sheet of paper, write the headings **Statement Number** and **Words**. Next, choose the words that best complete the statements. Write each word you choose next to the statement number it completes. Be careful; not all the words listed should be used.

Statements	Words
1. A record of each item in the stockroom is called (a, an) _____ .	balance
2. The form used to tell the purchasing agent to place an order is the _____ .	issue
3. The lowest amount of stock that should be on hand is the _____ .	maximum
4. A list of filled and unfilled purchase requisitions is the _____ .	menu bar
5. When an order received contains goods that are damaged, the person to notify is the _____ .	merchandise
6. The amount of stock on hand is the _____ .	minimum
7. Another name for stock is _____ .	open order report
	option
	perpetual inventory system
	purchase requisition
	purchasing agent
	stock record
	verify

Statements	Words

8. The highest amount of stock that should be on hand is the _____ .

9. When you keep a running balance of each item of stock you are using a(an) _____ .

AUTOMATED

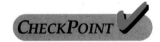

(g)
Final balance = 165

You are the stock record clerk for Farrel's Tire Company.

Directions

a. Open a stock record for Hi-Grade Radial Tires with the following information: stock number, 27; maximum, 175; minimum, 50; balance on June 1, 57. The unit of count is each.

b. Prepare a purchase requisition on June 1 to bring the balance up to maximum. Your department is Department 2. You want the tires in 3 days. The purchase requisition number is 37.

c. Enter the purchase requisition on an open order report.

d. Record receipt of the order of tires on June 4 on the open order report. Only 115 were received.

e. Enter the receipt of 115 tires on the stock record.

f. Record the remaining receipts and issues of tires for June on your stock record.

June   5 Issued 36 tires.
       10 Issued 49 tires.
       12 Received 81 tires.
       15 Issued 27 tires.
       17 Received 20 tires.
       19 Issued 29 tires.
       22 Issued 57 tires.
       28 Received 90 tires.

g. Verify the balance of tires by footing the Quantity Received and Quantity Issued columns.

This activity may be found in the Working Papers.

Record Keeping for Purchase Order Clerks

$\mathcal{Y}$ou surely have made wise purchases whenever you have checked out information and prices on the same product from different companies. Think about how you might select a backpack for hiking. You do not buy one at the first store that you visit. You "shop around" at many stores.

A purchasing agent also shops around and notes costs from various vendors on a price quotation record. When merchandise is ready to be ordered, the purchasing agent will ask for a purchase order to be prepared. Receiving reports and purchase invoices are forms that are also part of the purchasing cycle.

In Chapter 11, you will learn how to prepare a price quotation record, a purchase order, and a receiving report. You will also learn how to check and file purchase invoices. A Calculator Tip will be given for checking extensions and totals on purchase invoices.

JOB **51** ▶ PREPARING PRICE QUOTATION RECORDS

APPLIED MATH PREVIEW

Copy and complete these problems.

1. $715 \times \$ 7.05 =$
2. $1,475 \times \$ 6.27 =$
3. $2,690 \times \$15.85 =$
4. $5,144 \times \$29.50 =$
5. $4,077 \times \$ 47.95 =$
6. $3,615 \times \$ 17.92 =$
7. $4,711 \times \$ 51.10 =$
8. $518 \times \$107.60 =$

BUSINESS TERMS PREVIEW

• Price quotation record • Purchase order clerk •

GOALS

1. To learn how to keep records of prices that different companies charge for the same item.
2. To learn how to choose the best price for the same item.

UNDERSTANDING THE JOB

KEY	Terms

Purchase order clerk.
Assists purchasing agent.

Price quotation record. Record of vendors, information, and prices relating to one stock item.

In Chapter 10, you learned how to compare the balance on a stock record with its minimum amount. You also learned that when the balance neared the minimum (or went below it), it was time to prepare a purchase requisition. The purchase requisition is used to notify the purchasing agent that more merchandise is needed.

In this chapter, you will learn the duties of the **purchase order clerk**, a clerk who assists the purchasing agent in his or her duties. In this job, you will learn how to keep records that help the purchasing agent make wise purchases.

A purchasing agent gets information and prices from several vendors, or sellers. The purchase order clerk records the information and prices on a form called a **price quotation record**, like the ones shown in Illustration 51A on pages 449-450. In this job, you will learn how to prepare price quotation records from which the purchasing agent can make wise purchases.

SAMPLE PROBLEM

You are a purchase order clerk for the LaBrie Shoe Store. On June 1, you are asked by the purchasing agent to open a separate price quotation record for each item in the following table:

Firm Name and Address	Stock No.	Item	Unit	Price	Terms
P. Duffy Company	HT 4	High-top sneakers	Dozen		
116 Harvard Road			Pair	$312.50	60 days
Boxborough, MA 01451-0116	LC 3	Low-court sneakers	Pair	22.99	60 days
S. Mangaroo Company	LC 3	Low-court sneakers	Pair	$ 24.99	30 days
4706 Pioneer Avenue					
Cheyenne, WY 82001-4706					
N. Roush Company	HT 4	High-top sneakers	Dozen		
504 Grand Avenue			Pair	$319.75	45 days
Elgin, IL 60120-0504	LC 3	Low-court sneakers	Pair	23.59	45 days

Firm Name and Address	Stock No.	Item	Unit	Price	Terms
O. Thomas Company 7210 Florence Place S. Tulsa, OK 74136-7210	HT 4	High-top sneakers	Dozen Pair	$309.70	20 days

Since you are given prices for two different items, HT 4 and LC 3, you will open two price quotation records. Illustration 51A (below and on page 450) shows how the completed records will look. Here are the steps you would follow in preparing the price quotation records:

STEP 1 ▶ Complete the headings.

Fill in three items in the heading of each record: the item, the stock number, and the unit of count.

STEP 2 ▶ Record the date, firm name and address, price, terms, and any additional information.

In the columns provided, record the date (June 1), the name and address of each company, the price, the terms, and any additional information that might be provided.

Notice the P. Duffy Company is on both records. This is because P. Duffy Company sells both kinds of sneakers.

From each record, the purchasing agent can answer such questions as who offers the lowest price and who offers the longest terms. For high-top sneakers, O. Thomas Company offers the lowest price.

Illustration 51A Completed price quotation records

PRICE QUOTATION RECORD

STOCK NO. _HT 4_

ITEM _High-top sneakers_

UNIT _Dozen pair_

DATE		FIRM AND ADDRESS	PRICE		TERMS	ADDITIONAL INFORMATION
19-- JUNE	1	P. Duffy Company 116 Harvard Road Boxborough, MA 01451-0116	312	50	60 days	
	1	N. Roush Company 504 Grand Avenue Elgin, IL 60120-0504	319	75	45 days	
	1	O. Thomas Company 7210 Florence Place S. Tulsa, OK 74136-7210	309	70	20 days	

PRICE QUOTATION RECORD

ITEM _Low-court sneakers_

STOCK NO. _LC 3_

UNIT _Pair_

DATE		FIRM AND ADDRESS	PRICE		TERMS	ADDITIONAL INFORMATION
19-- JUNE	1	P. Duffy Company				
		116 Harvard Road				
		Boxborough, MA 01451-0116	22	99	60 days	
	1	S. Mangaroo Company				
		4706 Pioneer Avenue				
		Cheyenne, WY 82001-4706	24	99	30 days	
	1	N. Roush Company				
		504 Grand Avenue				
		Elgin, IL 60120-0504	23	59	45 days	

Illustration 51A Completed price quotation records (continued)

P. Duffy Company offers the longest terms. What the records do not show are such things as quality of sneakers and service by the company. Thus, the purchasing agent will not always choose the lowest price. Terms, quality, and service must be considered. You know from your own experience that there are many reasons to buy from one store rather than another.

USING THE COMPUTER

As you can see, keeping price quotation records manually takes a lot of work. When a new price quotation is received from a vendor, the correct price quotation record must be found in the filing system. Then, the new quotation must be added to the record. This will usually mean recopying the vendor's name and address as well as the terms. This work is much easier when using a computer.

For example, suppose a new quotation is received from S. Mangaroo Company for low-court sneakers. The price is $24.79 per pair for stock number LC 3. The purchase order clerk will enter the vendor's name into the computer to bring up the vendor's record. When the clerk does this, the computer will search its files for the vendor's record and automatically show the vendor's address beneath the name. (See Illustration 51B, page 451.) The clerk will check the address to see that the correct record is on the screen.

Illustration 51B
Bringing the record up
on the screen

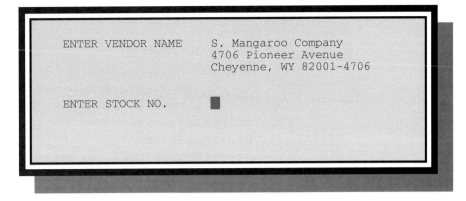

```
ENTER VENDOR NAME      S. Mangaroo Company
                       4706 Pioneer Avenue
                       Cheyenne, WY 82001-4706


ENTER STOCK NO.        ■
```

The clerk will then enter the stock number, LC 3. When this is done, the last quotation made by S. Mangaroo Company for low-court sneakers will appear on the screen. (See Illustration 51C.)

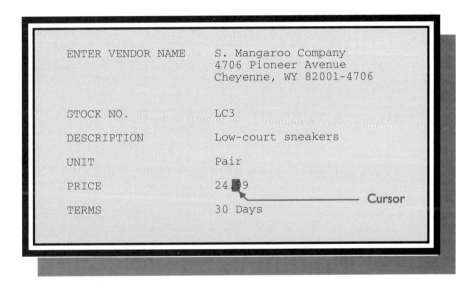

```
ENTER VENDOR NAME      S. Mangaroo Company
                       4706 Pioneer Avenue
                       Cheyenne, WY 82001-4706


STOCK NO.              LC3

DESCRIPTION            Low-court sneakers

UNIT                   Pair

PRICE                  24.99 ————————— Cursor

TERMS                  30 Days
```

All the clerk has to do now is to move the cursor down to the price line which shows $24.99. The clerk simply types in $24.79 over the old price and the price is changed. As you can see, the computer lets you keep accurate and up-to-date records of price quotations easily.

BUILDING YOUR BUSINESS VOCABULARY

On a sheet of paper, write the headings **Statement Number** and **Words**. Next, choose the words that match the statements. Write each word you choose next to the statement number it matches. Be careful; not all the words listed should be used.

Statements	Words
1. Seller	minimum
2. The buyer for a business	open order report
3. A record of each item of stock	price quotation record
4. Assists the purchasing agent	purchase order clerk
5. A request to the buyer to place an order	purchase requisition
6. The length of time a customer has to pay a bill, such as 30 days	purchasing agent
	stock record
7. Record of vendors, information, and prices relating to one stock item	stock record clerk
	terms
8. The least	vendor

PROBLEM SOLVING MODEL FOR: *Preparing Price Quotation Records*
....

STEP 1 ▶ *Complete the headings.*

STEP 2 ▶ *Record the date, firm name and address, price, terms, and any additional information.*

APPLICATION PROBLEMS

PROBLEM **51-1** ▶ You are a purchase order clerk for the Macalister Appliance Store.

Directions

a. Open a price quotation record for each item listed in the table below and on page 453. You will need five records. Fill in the records with the information from the table. Use April 1 as the date. Remember, each record is used to record information about all the companies that sell that one item.

Firm Name and Address	Stock No.	Item	Unit	Price	Terms
P. Webby Company	TR 5	Toasters	Ea.	$ 24.95	60 days
3712 Anderson Road	MW 1	Microwave ovens	Ea.	218.95	60 days
Duluth, MN 55811-3712					
A & R Company	CM 3	Coffee makers	Ea.	$ 21.10	45 days
102 Kalmia Avenue	CO 4	Electric can openers	Ea.	9.95	45 days
Boulder, CO 80302-0102	BL 9	Blenders	Ea.	39.90	45 days
W. W. Baxter Company	MW 1	Microwave ovens	Ea.	$265.10	30 days
416 South Broadway	CM 3	Coffee makers	Ea.	19.55	30 days
Sikeston, MO 63801-0416	BL 9	Blenders	Ea.	36.15	30 days

Firm Name and Address	Stock No.	Item	Unit	Price	Terms
R. Aiello Company 12 Summit Road Mountain Home, AR 72653-0012	TR 5 CO 4	Toasters Electric can openers	Ea. Ea.	$ 26.95 15.25	60 days 60 days
K. Solomon Company 3 Melrose Avenue Batavia, NY 14020-0030	MW 1 BL 9	Microwave ovens Blenders	Ea. Ea.	$249.90 41.40	20 days 20 days
M. Delacroix Company Wilson Road Luray, VA 22835-1036	CO 4 TR 5 CM 3	Electric can openers Toasters Coffee makers	Ea. Ea. Ea.	$ 11.50 25.50 17.95	90 days 90 days 90 days

CHECKPOINT ✔

51-1 (b. 1)
W. W. Baxter Company

b. Answer the following questions:

1. Which firm sells blenders at the lowest price?
2. Which firm sells toasters at the lowest price?
3. Which firm offers the longest terms on coffee makers?

PROBLEM **51-2** ▶ You are a purchase order clerk for Jefferson's Auto Parts Store.

Directions

a. Open a price quotation record for each item listed in the table below and on page 454. You will need six records. Fill in the information from the table. Use August 1 as the date. Remember, each record is used to record information about all the companies that sell that one item.

Firm Name and Address	Stock No.	Item	Unit	Price	Terms
J. Gomez Company 15 Garry Avenue W. Santa Ana, CA 92907-0150	BA 6 TR 3 OF 7	Batteries Tires Oil filters	Ea. Ea. Dz.	$ 75.50 49.50 108.00	30 days 30 days 30 days
Auto Novelties Company 9117 Dolph Street, S.W. Portland, OR 97223-9117	FD 8 BP 4	Fuzzy dice Bumper stickers	Pr. Gr.	$ 7.50 72.00	20 days 20 days
Abdul-Hassan Company 5166 13th Avenue New York, NY 10031-5166	TR 3 OF 7 JU 2	Tires Oil filters Jumper cables	Ea. Dz. Pr.	$ 54.50 117.50 14.95	90 days 90 days 90 days
Rupprecht Company 1503 Arlington Street Ames, IA 50010-1503	BA 6 JU 2	Batteries Jumper cables	Ea. Pr.	$ 72.95 12.10	45 days 45 days
Bernie's Auto Parts 86 Mountain Street Murdo, SD 57559-0086	OF 7 FD 8 BP 4	Oil filters Fuzzy dice Bumper stickers	Dz. Pr. Gr.	$120.00 7.95 84.00	15 days 15 days 15 days

Firm Name and Address	Stock No.	Item	Unit	Price	Terms
R. Stigler Company	TR 3	Tires	Ea.	$ 52.10	60 days
5613 Oliver Street	BA 6	Batteries	Ea.	81.95	60 days
Ft. Wayne, IN 46806-5613	JU 2	Jumper cables	Pr.	10.90	60 days

51-2 (b. 1)
J. Gomez Company

b. Answer the following questions:

1. Which firm sells tires at the lowest price?
2. Which firm sells oil filters at the lowest price?
3. Which firm sells jumper cables at the lowest price?
4. Which firm offers the longest terms on batteries?

Problem 51-3 may be found in the Working Papers.

JOB 52 ▶ PREPARING PURCHASE ORDERS

APPLIED MATH PREVIEW

Copy and complete the following problems.

1.   319 × $ 8.76 =
2. 4,045 × $15.29 =
3.   218 × $ 0.45 =
4. 5,345 × $ 0.51 =
5. 9,006 × $17.09 =
6. 5,900 × $27.60 =
7. 6,120 × $ 5.17½ =
8. 2,576 × $ 3.09¼ =

BUSINESS TERMS PREVIEW

• Prenumbered • Purchase order • Reorder level • Triplicate •

GOAL

To learn how to prepare purchase orders.

𝒰NDERSTANDING THE JOB

You have learned that a stock record clerk prepares

1. Stock records, which tell when more merchandise is needed.
2. Purchase requisitions, which tell the purchasing agent that more merchandise is needed.

You have also learned that a purchase order clerk prepares

3. Price quotation records, which help the purchasing agent choose the best vendor.

When merchandise is ordered, the purchasing agent will ask the purchase order clerk to prepare a **purchase order**. Purchase order forms are usually **prenumbered**, or numbered in advance. They are also usually prepared in three copies, which is called in **triplicate**. Illustration 52A (on page 456) shows where each copy goes.

K E Y Terms

Purchase order. A form used to order merchandise.

Prenumbered. Numbered in advance.

Triplicate. Three copies.

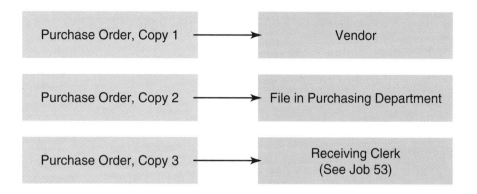

Purchase Order, Copy 1	→	Vendor
Purchase Order, Copy 2	→	File in Purchasing Department
Purchase Order, Copy 3	→	Receiving Clerk (See Job 53)

SAMPLE PROBLEM

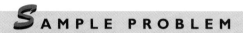

MULTICULTURAL INSIGHT

By around 1000 B.C., the Chinese had developed one of the most complex accounting systems in the world. They used a system of currency and had a central bank. The Office of the Superintendent of Records produced for the government lists of receipts and payments, maps, totals of the number of workers in each occupation, kinds and quantities of production tools, and estimates of natural resources.

You are a purchase order clerk for LaBrie Shoe Store. On June 5, you are asked by the purchasing agent, Ray Chan, to prepare a purchase order for the following items from N. Roush Company:

36 pair Low-court sneakers, Stock No. LC 3
3 dozen pair High-top sneakers, Stock No. HT 4

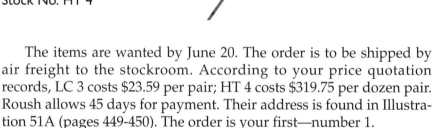

The items are wanted by June 20. The order is to be shipped by air freight to the stockroom. According to your price quotation records, LC 3 costs $23.59 per pair; HT 4 costs $319.75 per dozen pair. Roush allows 45 days for payment. Their address is found in Illustration 51A (pages 449-450). The order is your first—number 1.

Illustration 52B (page 457) shows the purchase order that was completed in three steps.

STEP 1 ▶ *Complete the top part of the form.*

Copy the name, address, and terms from the price quotation records. Then, fill in the order number, date of the order, ship via, ship to, and date wanted. Make sure that all blanks are filled in.

STEP 2 ▶ *Complete the bottom part of the form.*

Fill in the quantity, description (including stock number), and unit price of each item. The unit prices will come from the price quotation records. The quantity can be each, dozen, pair, dozen pair, gross, or some other unit of count.

LABRIE SHOE STORE

1610 Upland Avenue
Chester, PA 19013-1610

PURCHASE ORDER

MARK OUR ORDER NO. ON ALL INVOICES, PACKAGES, AND SHIPPING PAPERS.

ORDER NO. _1_

DATE _June 5, 19--_

SHIP VIA _Air freight_

TO _N. Roush Company_
504 Grand Avenue
Elgin, IL 60120-0504

SHIP TO _Stockroom_

DATE WANTED _June 20, 19--_

TERMS _45 days_

QUANTITY	DESCRIPTION	UNIT PRICE	
36 pair	Low-court sneakers, stock no. LC 3	23	59
3 dz. pair	High-top sneakers, stock no. HT 4	319	75

BY _Ray Chan_
PURCHASING AGENT

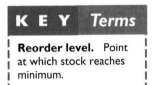

STEP 3 ▶ *Request the purchasing agent's signature.*

Give the purchase order to Ray Chan, the purchasing agent, for his signature. Usually, you would give a batch of purchase orders at one time for him to sign. Once signed, the triplicate copies are separated and sent where they need to go.

USING THE COMPUTER

KEY Terms

Reorder level. Point at which stock reaches minimum.

If a computer is used, purchase orders can be prepared automatically when stock levels become low. The computer searches the stock records for any item that has reached its **reorder level**. The reorder level is reached when an item falls to or below its minimum amount.

For example, the computer searches the stock records and finds that item LC 3 has fallen below the minimum and must be reordered. This information is shown in Illustration 52C (page 458).

The computer subtracts the balance (47) from the maximum (200). The difference (153) is the amount that will be ordered. If price quotation records are also computerized, the computer may select the vendor if the purchasing agent has indicated the preferred vendor in advance.

By combining data from the stock record with data from the price quotation record, the computer generates a purchase order. Illustration 52D (page 458) shows the purchase order prepared by the computer system.

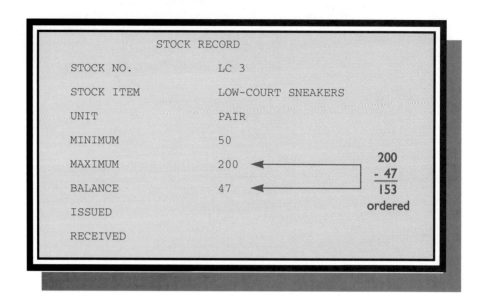

```
                    STOCK RECORD

        STOCK NO.          LC 3

        STOCK ITEM         LOW-COURT SNEAKERS

        UNIT               PAIR

        MINIMUM            50

        MAXIMUM            200          ←        200
                                                - 47
        BALANCE            47           ←        153
                                                 ordered
        ISSUED

        RECEIVED
```

LABRIE SHOE STORE
1610 Upland Avenue
Chester, PA 19013-1610

PURCHASE ORDER

**MARK OUR ORDER NO. ON ALL INVOICES,
PACKAGES, AND SHIPPING PAPERS.**

TO
P. DUFFY COMPANY
116 HARVARD ROAD
BOXBOROUGH, MA 01451-0116

ORDER NO.   2
DATE   JUNE 15, 19--
SHIP VIA   TRUCK
SHIP TO   STOCKROOM
DATE WANTED   JUNE 30, 19--
TERMS   60 DAYS

QUANTITY	DESCRIPTION	UNIT PRICE
153 PAIR	LOW-COURT SNEAKERS, STOCK NO. LC 3	22.99

BY _Ray Chan_
PURCHASING AGENT

Illustration 52D   Purchase order prepared by computer

𝓑UILDING YOUR BUSINESS VOCABULARY

On a sheet of paper, write the headings **Statement Number** and **Words**. Next, choose the words that match the statements. Write each word you choose next to the statement number it matches. Be careful; not all the words listed should be used.

Statements	Words
	prenumbered
1. Assists the purchasing agent	price quotation record
2. Record of vendors, information, and	purchase order
prices relating to one stock item	purchase order clerk
3. Numbered in advance	purchase requisition
4. Seller	purchasing agent
5. Point at which stock reaches minimum	reorder level
6. The buyer for a business	stock record clerk
7. A form used to order merchandise	terms
8. A request to the buyer to place an order	triplicate
9. Three copies	vendor

PROBLEM SOLVING MODEL FOR: *Preparing Purchase Orders*

STEP 1 ▶ *Complete the top part of the form.*

STEP 2 ▶ *Complete the bottom part of the form.*

STEP 3 ▶ *Request the purchasing agent's signature.*

APPLICATION PROBLEMS

PROBLEM **52-1** ▶ You are a purchase order clerk for Midstate Motel, 419 South Street, Santee, SC 29142-0419. It is your job to help the purchasing agent prepare purchase orders.

CheckPoint ✔

52-1
There should be two items of merchandise entered on each purchase order.

Directions

Prepare purchase orders from the following information. Fill in all spaces except the purchasing agent's signature. All merchandise is to be shipped by truck to the stockroom.

Purchase Order No. 55
Date: March 7
Date Wanted: March 17
To: Phillips Company
1210 Mint Avenue
High Point, NC 27260-1210
Terms: 30 days
30 ea. Bedspreads—Stock No. B5 @ $15.99
30 ea. Pillows—Stock No. P6 @ $5.99

Purchase Order No. 56
Date: March 9
Date Wanted: March 19
To: Southern Motel Suppliers
6110 St. Mary's Road
Columbus, GA 31906-6110
Terms: 45 days
20 ea. Side chairs—Stock No. SC 5 @ $29.95
3 dz. Lamp shades—Stock No. LS 7 @ $107.88

Purchase Order No. 57
Date: March 17
Date Wanted: March 27
To: Davidson Company
5103 Murphy Road
Nashville, TN 37209-5103
Terms: 60 days
10 dz. Towels—Stock No. T6 @ $58.80
10 dz. Wash cloths—Stock No. W8 @ $23.88

PROBLEM **52-2** ▶ You are a purchase order clerk for Jane's Formal Wear, RFD 191, Abilene, KS 67410-0191. You help the purchasing agent prepare purchase orders.

Directions

52-2
There should be two items
of merchandise entered on
each purchase order.

Prepare purchase orders from the following information. Fill in all spaces except the purchasing agent's signature. All merchandise is to be shipped by air freight to the stockroom.

Purchase Order No. 116
Date: July 8
Date Wanted: July 15
To: C. Omar Company
31 Stone Street
Plaistow, NH 03865-0031
Terms: 60 days
45 ea. White jackets—Stock No. WJ 7 @ $75.50
4 dz. Bow ties—Stock No. BT 12 @ $59.88

Purchase Order No. 117
Date: July 12
Date Wanted: July 19
To: R. Mikluk
57 14th Street, W.
Juneau, AK 99801-5714
Terms: 45 days
36 ea. Black jackets—Stock No. BJ 8 @ $71.99
2 gr. Invitations—Stock No. IN 4 @ $24.00

Purchase Order No. 118
Date: July 17
Date Wanted: July 24
To: P. Chiravara Company
124 Canada Street
Presque Isle, ME 04769-0124
Terms: 20 days
30 dz. pr. Black shoes—Stock No. B 17 @ $513.00
50 ea. Cummerbunds—Stock No. CB 3 @ $5.85

Problem 52-3 may be found in the Working Papers.

JOB **53** ► PREPARING RECEIVING REPORTS

BUSINESS TERMS PREVIEW

• **Backordered** • **Discontinued** • **Over** • **Packing slip** •
• **Receiving clerk** • **Receiving report** • **Short** •

GOALS

1. To learn how to compare stock received to stock ordered.
2. To learn how to prepare receiving reports.

UNDERSTANDING THE JOB

KEY Terms

Receiving clerk.
Receives goods and compares with goods ordered.

Receiving report.
Form that shows goods ordered and received.

You have learned that one copy of each purchase order is sent to the receiving department. The receiving department records are kept by a **receiving clerk**. It is the job of the receiving clerk to compare what was ordered with what was actually received. The form used to show this comparison is the **receiving report**, which is shown in Illustration 53C on page 464.

Sample Problem 1 describes how to prepare a receiving report in a manual system. Sample Problem 2 shows how to prepare a receiving report in a computer system.

Manual System

Lena Morrison is a receiving clerk for LaBrie Shoe Store. Her job is to compare goods received with the purchase order and prepare a receiving report. Here is how she does her job:

STEP **1** ▶ *Compare the stock received with the packing slip.*

K E Y Terms

Packing slip. Form which describes contents of a shipment.

Lena opens the cartons received and unpacks the merchandise. Included with the cartons is a **packing slip**. The packing slip describes the contents of the shipment. A packing slip that Lena received is shown in Illustration 53A. Lena will compare the stock received with what is printed on the packing slip.

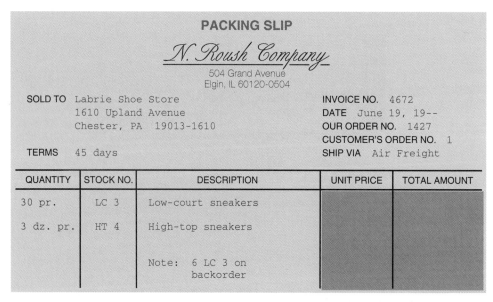

PACKING SLIP

N. Roush Company

504 Grand Avenue
Elgin, IL 60120-0504

SOLD TO	Labrie Shoe Store 1610 Upland Avenue Chester, PA 19013-1610	INVOICE NO. 4672 DATE June 19, 19-- OUR ORDER NO. 1427 CUSTOMER'S ORDER NO. 1
TERMS	45 days	SHIP VIA Air Freight

QUANTITY	STOCK NO.	DESCRIPTION	UNIT PRICE	TOTAL AMOUNT
30 pr.	LC 3	Low-court sneakers		
3 dz. pr.	HT 4	High-top sneakers		
		Note: 6 LC 3 on backorder		

Illustration 53A   Packing slip

Lena first compares the quantity received with the quantity listed on the packing slip. She counts 30 pairs of low-court sneakers, which agrees with the packing slip. She also compares stock numbers and finds that LC 3 is on both the cartons and the packing slip. Lena also inspects the condition of the sneakers and finds them undamaged. Since that stock item was in good condition and in the quantity listed, Lena places a check mark on the packing slip next to "30 pr."

If Lena finds damaged stock or errors in the shipment, she notes the errors or the damage on the packing slip. For example, when she examines the stock, she finds that 3 pairs of high-top sneakers are damaged and cannot be put in the stockroom. So, she writes "3 pairs, damaged" on the packing slip. Of the 36 (3 dozen) pairs ordered, only 33 are in good condition.

Notice that the Unit Price and Total Amount columns on the packing slip are blackened out. The receiving clerk deals only with quantity, not with price.

Notice also that 6 LC 3 are on **backorder**. Backorder means that the vendor is temporarily out of stock on that item. The stock will be sent as soon as possible. If the goods ordered are never to be sold again by the vendor, they are called **discontinued** goods. Lena will record information about backordered and discontinued goods in Step 3.

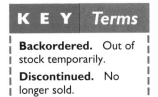
STEP 2 ▶ *Compare the packing slip with the purchase order.*

Lena compares the checked packing slip with the purchase order (Illustration 53B). She finds that 36 pairs of LC 3 were ordered. The packing slip shows that 30 pairs of LC 3 were received and 6 are on backorder, so LC 3 checks out. She finds that 3 dozen pairs (36) of HT 4 were ordered and were received, though 3 are damaged. No goods are **short** (less than ordered) or **over** (more than ordered). She is now ready to prepare a receiving report.

Illustration 53B
Completed purchase order

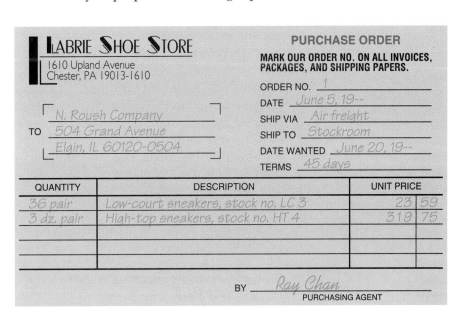

	LABRIE SHOE STORE	PURCHASE ORDER

LABRIE SHOE STORE
1610 Upland Avenue
Chester, PA 19013-1610

PURCHASE ORDER
MARK OUR ORDER NO. ON ALL INVOICES, PACKAGES, AND SHIPPING PAPERS.

ORDER NO. *1*
DATE *June 5, 19--*
SHIP VIA *Air freight*
SHIP TO *Stockroom*
DATE WANTED *June 20, 19--*
TERMS *45 days*

TO *N. Roush Company*
504 Grand Avenue
Elgin, IL 60120-0504

QUANTITY	DESCRIPTION	UNIT PRICE
36 pair	Low-court sneakers, stock no. LC 3	23 59
3 dz. pair	High-top sneakers, stock no. HT 4	319 75

BY *Ray Chan*
PURCHASING AGENT

STEP 3 ▶ *Prepare the receiving report.*

The receiving report that Lena prepares is shown in Illustration 53C (page 464).

On the report, Lena writes in the date on which the shipment was received and fills in the vendor name and number. She also fills

LABRIE SHOE STORE
1610 Upland Avenue
Chester, PA 19013-1610

RECEIVING REPORT

Date Received ___June 21,___ 19 __--__

Vendor Name ___N. Roush Company___   Vendor No. ___714___

Our Purchase Order No. ___1___   Vendor Invoice No. ___4672___

Item No.	Item Description	Unit	Quantity Ordered	Quantity Received	Remarks
LC 3	Low-court sneakers	Pr.	36	30	6 backordered
HT 4	High-top sneakers	Dz. Pr.	3	33 pr.	3 pr. damaged

Receiving Clerk ___L. Morrison___

Illustration 53C   Completed receiving report

in the purchase order number used by the purchasing department and the vendor's invoice number that she found on the packing slip.

Lena copies the item numbers, descriptions, units, and quantities ordered from the purchase order. She then lists the quantities actually received. Since only 30 pairs of item LC 3 were received, Lena records only 30 in the Quantity Received column. She writes "6 backordered" in the Remarks column to explain the difference between the Quantity Ordered and Quantity Received columns.

She then records the undamaged pairs of HT 4 that were received. Of the 3 dozen (36) pairs ordered, only 33 can be placed into stock, so she enters "33 pr." in the Quantity Received column. Lena also writes "3 pr. damaged" in the Remarks column. Finally, she signs the receiving report to indicate that it is she who has prepared it.

STEP 4 ▶ *Send copies of the receiving report to the accounting clerk and the stock record clerk.*

Lena sends two copies of the receiving report. One goes to the accounting department so that they can pay the vendor. The second goes to the stock record clerk who can then update two records:

1. The stock records, by adding the amounts received to the balance on hand.
2. The open order report, by recording an order now filled.

In some companies, a copy of the purchase order is used as the receiving report. The receiving clerk places a check mark on the purchase order next to each item that has been received in the quantity ordered and in good condition. If there are any differences (such as damage, backorder, over, or short), the clerk writes these remarks next to the quantity ordered on the purchase order. Copies of the purchase order are then sent to the accounting clerk and the stock record clerk.

$\mathcal{S}$AMPLE PROBLEM 2

Computer System

In many companies, the receiving report is prepared using a computer. When the computer is used, the same steps are followed as in a manual system, but much of the work is done automatically. If Lena used a computer, here is how she would record the shipment of the two types of sneakers:

STEP 1 ▶ *Compare the stock received with the packing slip.*

Even though she is using a computer, Lena must still examine the stock received and compare it with the packing slip. In other words, Step 1 will remain unchanged when using a computer.

STEP 2 ▶ *Compare the packing slip with the purchase order.*

Step 2 also remains unchanged when using a computer. The packing slip and the purchase order must be compared to see if what was received was what the company ordered.

STEP 3 ▶ *Prepare the receiving report.*

It is at this point that the computer becomes a timesaver. Instead of copying data by hand onto a receiving report, Lena brings up the receiving report form on the screen of her computer. Illustration 53D (page 466) shows this report.

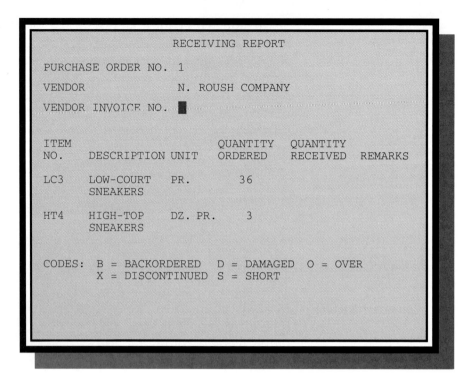

```
                    RECEIVING REPORT

PURCHASE ORDER NO.  1

VENDOR                N. ROUSH COMPANY

VENDOR INVOICE NO.  █


ITEM                         QUANTITY   QUANTITY
NO.    DESCRIPTION UNIT      ORDERED    RECEIVED  REMARKS

LC3    LOW-COURT   PR.          36
       SNEAKERS

HT4    HIGH-TOP    DZ. PR.       3
       SNEAKERS


CODES:  B = BACKORDERED   D = DAMAGED  O = OVER
        X = DISCONTINUED  S = SHORT
```

Lena keys the purchase order number, 1, and the computer automatically fills in the facts about the purchase order. These facts were stored in the computer files when the purchase order was prepared.

The cursor, next to Vendor Invoice No., is asking Lena to enter the vendor invoice number, so she keys 4672, as shown in Illustration 53E. The cursor then moves to the Quantity Received column, asking Lena to key the amount of stock that was received. There were 36 pairs of LC3 ordered, but since only 30 were received, Lena keys in 30.

The cursor moves under the Remarks column. Lena uses the codes at the bottom of the screen and keys in 6B to show that six pairs are on backorder.

She then enters the quantity received for HT4, 33 pr., and records 3PRD for three pairs damaged in the Remarks column. Illustration 53E shows a completed receiving report.

The computer will print the receiving report if asked to do so. Copies do not need to be sent to the accounting clerk and the stock record clerk since each can bring it up on his or her own screen.

As you can see, the computer makes the job of the receiving clerk much easier. The work of the stock record clerk is also reduced. The computer will automatically update the stock records and the open order report. However, you must be careful when entering data into a computer, for a wrong entry will make several different records incorrect.

```
                         RECEIVING REPORT

PURCHASE ORDER NO.  1

VENDOR               N. ROUSH COMPANY

VENDOR INVOICE NO.  4672


ITEM                          QUANTITY   QUANTITY
NO.     DESCRIPTION UNIT      ORDERED    RECEIVED   REMARKS

LC3     LOW-COURT   PR.          36         30        6B
        SNEAKERS

HT4     HIGH-TOP    DZ. PR.       3       33 PR.     3PRD
        SNEAKERS


CODES:  B = BACKORDERED   D = DAMAGED   O = OVER
        X = DISCONTINUED  S = SHORT
```

BUILDING YOUR BUSINESS VOCABULARY

On a sheet of paper, write the headings **Statement Number** and **Words**. Next, choose the words that match the statements. Write each word you choose next to the statement number it matches. Be careful; not all the words listed should be used.

Statements	Words
1. Three copies	backordered
2. Form that shows goods ordered and received	discontinued
	over
3. No longer sold	packing slip
4. Less than ordered	prenumbered
5. Receives goods and compares with goods ordered	receiving clerk
	receiving report
6. Out of stock temporarily	reorder level
7. More than ordered	short
8. Point at which stock reaches minimum	terms
9. Form which describes contents of a shipment	triplicate

PROBLEM SOLVING MODEL FOR: *Receiving Goods and Preparing Receiving Reports—Manual System*

STEP 1 ▶ *Compare the stock received with the packing slip.*

STEP 2 ▶ *Compare the packing slip with the purchase order.*

STEP 3 ▶ *Prepare the receiving report.*

STEP 4 ▶ *Send copies of the receiving report to the accounting clerk and the stock record clerk.*

APPLICATION PROBLEMS

PROBLEM 53-1 ▶ In the table that follows, stock ordered appears in the left column. Stock received appears in the right column.

Directions

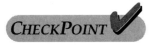

CHECKPOINT ✔

53-1
There should be 4 check marks in the Agree column.

On a sheet of paper, write the numbers 1 through 10 and two column headings, Agree and Disagree. If the information about stock ordered agrees with the information about stock received, place a check mark in the Agree column. If the information about stock ordered and stock received disagrees, place a check mark in the Disagree column.

	Ordered		Received	
1.	36	LC575	36	LC575
2.	175	RB82	173	RB82
3.	198	LLA15	198	LLA15
4.	217	CY27	271	CY27
5.	57	M3766	57	M3676
6.	43	G182	43	G182
7.	15 dz.	RP599	15 dz.	RP599
8.	18	J2077	18	J2076
9.	2 gr.	RZ1388	2 gr.	RZ1338
10.	106 pr.	BN4399	105 pr.	BN4399

PROBLEM 53-2 ▶ You are the shipping clerk for West Card Shop. Your job is to check shipments of stock received and prepare receiving reports.

Directions

Prepare a receiving report from the information that follows. Use Illustration 53C (page 464) as a model.

You have received today, August 8, a shipment of merchandise from N. Charles Company, Vendor No. 63. The purchase order number for this shipment is 3712; the vendor's invoice number is 2041.

The packing slip sent with the shipment lists the following:

Qty.	Unit	Item No.	Description
250	Each	BC 06	Birthday cards
145	Rolls	WP 19	Wrapping paper
6	Dozen	SA 12	Stuffed animals
20	Pounds	PN 24	Peanuts

When you examine the shipment, you discover that 4 rolls of wrapping paper are damaged and cannot be placed in inventory. You also find a note telling you that 25 birthday cards are on backorder.

Purchase Order No. 3712 lists the following order:

Qty.	Unit	Item No.	Description
275	Each	BC 06	Birthday cards
145	Rolls	WP 19	Wrapping paper
6	Dozen	SA 12	Stuffed animals
20	Pounds	PN 24	Peanuts

CHECKPOINT

53-2 (d)
Two items need to be entered in the Remarks column.

a. On the top part of the receiving report, enter the date received, vendor name and number, our purchase order number, and the vendor invoice number.

b. Fill in the Item No., Item Description, Unit, and Quantity Ordered columns using information from the purchase order.

c. Fill in the Quantity Received column from the information given on the packing slip. Remember to enter only stock that has actually been received in good condition.

d. Explain any differences between the amounts in the Quantity Ordered and Quantity Received columns. Use the Remarks column.

e. Sign your name as receiving clerk.

PROBLEM | **53-3** ▶ You are the receiving clerk for A-One Health Spa. Your job is to check shipments of stock received and prepare receiving reports.

Directions

CHECKPOINT

53-3
Four items need to be entered in the Remarks column.

Prepare a receiving report from the information that follows. Use Illustration 53C (page 464) as a model. Follow steps *a.* through *e.* listed in Problem 53-2.

You have received today, October 9, a shipment of merchandise from McMurray Company, Vendor No. 471. The purchase order number for this shipment is 1047; the vendor's invoice number is 3166.

The packing slip sent with the shipment lists the following:

Qty.	Unit	Item No.	Description
30	Each	TL 07	Towels
5	Dozen	LB 15	Light bulbs
50	Each	LK 21	Locks
0	Each	SB 09	Storage baskets

When you examine the shipment, you discover that three towels are damaged and cannot be placed in inventory. You also find a note telling you that 10 locks are on backorder. A second note tells you that SB 09 storage baskets are no longer available.

Purchase Order No. 1047 lists the following order:

Qty.	Unit	Item No.	Description
30	Each	TL 07	Towels
6	Dozen	LB 15	Light bulbs
60	Each	LK 21	Locks
50	Each	SB 09	Storage baskets

No reason was given for the 1 dozen missing light bulbs.

Problem 53-4 may be found in the Working Papers.

CHECKING AND FILING PURCHASE INVOICES

APPLIED MATH PREVIEW

Copy and complete the following problems. Round your answers to the nearest whole cent.

1. $3,714 \times \$27.65 =$
2. $5,181 \times \$9.97 =$
3. $4,377 \times \$0.09 =$
4. $3,124 \times \$0.55 =$
5. $5,170 \times \$1.24^{1}/_2 =$
6. $1,600 \times \$0.17^{1}/_4 =$
7. $950 \times \$1.09^{1}/_4 =$
8. $16^{1}/_2 \times \$1.035 =$

BUSINESS TERMS PREVIEW

• **Cash discount** • **Purchase invoice** • **Vouch** •

GOALS

1. To learn how to check purchase invoices.
2. To learn how to figure a cash discount.
3. To learn how to file purchase invoices by due date.

UNDERSTANDING THE JOB

KEY Terms

Purchase invoice.
What buyer calls bill from vendor.

You have learned in Job 52 that a purchase order is sent by a purchasing agent to a vendor. After shipping the merchandise ordered, the vendor sends a bill to the buyer. The vendor calls this bill a sales invoice. The buyer calls this bill a **purchase invoice**.

A clerk in the accounting department will need to check the accuracy of the math on the invoice before it is paid. The clerk will then need to file the invoice by its due date, which is the date by which it must be paid. By using this filing process, invoices can be pulled from the file and paid when they are due.

As you learned in Job 42, invoices have terms of sale, which tell when an invoice is due. An example of terms is 60 days (also expressed as n/60), which means that the invoice must be paid by 60 days after its date. Thus, the invoice in Illustration 54A (page 473) dated August 9 with terms of 60 days is due by October 8. (You can review how to figure the due date in Job 42.) The clerk will file the invoice under the date of October 5 or 6 to be sure that payment reaches the seller by the due date of October 8.

KEY *Terms*

Cash discount. Small discount given for early payment.

Sometimes, the seller will want to give the buyer a reason to pay the invoice earlier than its due date. In such cases, the seller will offer the buyer a **cash discount**. A cash discount is a small discount given for early payment of an invoice. Cash discounts are usually 1 percent, 2 percent, or 3 percent.

If terms include a cash discount, they are written in this form: 2/10, n/60. This expression means that a 2 percent discount will be given for payment within 10 days of the date of the invoice, or the full amount of the invoice must be paid by 60 days after its date.

▲▲▲▲▲
TIP
▼▼▼▼▼

2/10, n/60 means a 2% cash discount if paid within 10 days; full amount due within 60 days.

If the invoice in Illustration 54A (page 473) had terms of 2/10, n/60, then payment by 10 days after August 9, which is August 19, would entitle the buyer to a 2 percent discount. The discount would be figured as follows:

Corrected amount of invoice	$4,209.80
Rate of cash discount	x .02
Amount of cash discount	$ 84.20

The amount to be paid within the discount period would not be the full amount of $4,209.80, but $84.20 less.

Corrected amount of invoice	$4,209.80
Less: amount of cash discount	- 84.20
Amount to be paid	$4,125.60

𝒮AMPLE PROBLEM

Kay Reed is an accounting clerk at the LaBrie Shoe Store. She receives the invoice shown in Illustration 54A (page 473).

These are the steps Kay followed to check and file this invoice:

STEP 1 ▶ *Compare the invoice with the purchase order.*

Reed compared the invoice with the purchase order to see if the quantities, stock numbers, descriptions, and unit prices agreed. If they did not agree, she would have notified the purchasing agent.

STEP 2 ▶ *Compare the invoice with the receiving report.*

Reed compared the quantities listed on the invoice with the receiving report to see if the quantities agreed. If they did not agree, she would have notified the purchasing agent.

P. Duffy Company

116 Harvard Road
Boxborough, MA 01451-0116

SOLD TO Labrie Shoe Store
1610 Upland Avenue
Chester, PA 19013-1610

TERMS 60 days

INVOICE NO. 217
DATE August 9, 19--
OUR ORDER NO. 1473
CUSTOMER'S ORDER NO. 19
SHIP VIA Truck

QUANTITY	STOCK NO.	DESCRIPTION	UNIT PRICE	TOTAL AMOUNT
12 dz. pr.	HT 4	High-top sneakers	312 50	3,750 00
20 pr.	LC 3	Low-court sneakers	22 99	459 80 ~~469 80~~
		Total invoice *Approved Kay Reed*		4,209 80 ~~4,219 80~~

Illustration 54A   Approved purchase invoice

STEP 3 ▶ **Check the extensions.**

The invoice shows that 12 x $312.50 = $3,750.00. Reed used her calculator to check the extension. She found that it was correct.

She then checked the second extension. The product of 20 x $22.99 is $459.80, not $469.80. Reed crossed out the wrong extension, $469.80, and entered the correct extension, $459.80, just above it.

STEP 4 ▶ **Check the total.**

After Reed checked both extensions and corrected the second one, she added them in order to check the total of $4,219.80. Because of the error in the second extension, she needed to correct the total to $4,209.80. She did so by crossing out the incorrect total and writing in the correct total above it.

STEP 5 ▶ **Approve the invoice for payment.**

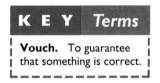

K E Y   Terms

Vouch. To guarantee that something is correct.

After correcting the invoice, Reed wrote the word *Approved* and signed her name. Her signature means that the invoice can be paid when it is due. Reed **vouched** the invoice, which means that she guaranteed its correctness.

STEP 6 ▶ **File the invoice for payment.**

The invoice will then be filed for payment. Labrie Shoe Store follows the practice of filing by a date three days before the due date in order to pay it on time. Since the due date is October 8, it will be filed under October 5.

If there were a cash discount available, the invoice would be filed by a date three days before the last date for discount. Thus, if terms were 2/10 for a discount, it would be filed for payment three days before August 19, which is August 16.

If Reed used a computer to check an invoice, she would select the invoice approval option from the menu. She would key the information from the purchase invoice. The computer would automatically check this information against the purchase order and the receiving report records. In the case of any differences, the computer would indicate a problem. Reed would then notify the purchasing agent. The computer would then check and correct extensions and the total, and display them on the screen. Reed would approve and sign the invoice as in a manual system.

Calculator Tips

A calculator can be useful in verifying purchase invoices. Both extensions and the total can be checked. Here's how to check the invoice shown in Illustration 54A (page 473) with a calculator:

STEP 1 ▶ *Find the first extension.*

Enter the first quantity by pressing these keys:

| 1 | 2 |

Next, multiply by the first unit price by pressing these keys:

| x | 3 | 1 | 2 | • | 5 |

Now, store the extension, 3,750, in memory by pressing the M+ key.

STEP 2 ▶ *Find the second extension.*

Enter the second quantity by pressing these keys:

| 2 | 0 |

Next, multiply by the second unit price by pressing these keys:

| x | 2 | 2 | • | 9 | 9 |

Store the extension, 459.8, in memory by pressing the M+ key. Correct the incorrect extension on the invoice at this point.

STEP 3 ▶ *Check the total on the invoice.*

Press the MR/C or MR key. This will display the total in the memory, 4,209.8, or $4,209.80. Correct the incorrect total on the invoice.

Press the MR/C or MC key to clear the memory. Now, press the C key. This will clear your calculator for the next operation.

On a sheet of paper, write the headings **Statement Number** and **Words**. Next, choose the words that match the statements. Write each word you choose next to the statement number it matches. Be careful; not all the words listed should be used.

Statements	Words
1. Record of vendors, information, and prices relating to one stock item	cash discount
	extension
2. Assists the purchasing agent	issue
3. A form used to order merchandise	menu
4. Quantity times unit price	prenumbered
5. Seller	price quotation record
6. Length of time a customer has to pay a bill	purchase invoice
	purchase order
7. To guarantee that something is correct	purchase order clerk
8. What the vendor calls the bill to the buyer	sales invoice
	terms
9. What the buyer calls the bill from the vendor	vendor
	vouch
10. Numbered in advance	
11. A reduction in price for early payment of an invoice	

PROBLEM SOLVING MODEL FOR: *Checking and Filing Purchase Invoices*

STEP 1 ▶ *Compare the invoice with the purchase order.*

STEP 2 ▶ *Compare the invoice with the receiving report.*

STEP 3 ▶ *Check the extensions.*

STEP 4 ▶ *Check the total.*

STEP 5 ▶ *Approve the invoice for payment.*

STEP 6 ▶ *File the invoice for payment.*

| | PROBLEM | 54-1 ▶ | A group of extensions follows. Your job is to check the extensions. |

Directions

CHECKPOINT ✔

54-1
There are 4 incorrect
extensions.

On a sheet of paper, write the numbers 1 through 10 and two column headings, Correct and Incorrect. If the extension is correct, place a check mark in the Correct column. If it is not correct, calculate the correct extension and write the correct amount in the Incorrect column.

1.	425	x $16.12 = $	6,851.00
2.	371	x $ 9.08 = $	3,368.68
3.	17	x $ 0.39 = $	6.53
4.	109	x $ 2.16 = $	253.44
5.	57	x $ 1.97 = $	112.29
6.	317	x $10.95 = $	3,471.15
7.	1,004	x $ 1.89 = $	1,897.65
8.	271 1/2	x $ 0.52 = $	141.18
9.	191	x $19.87 = $	3,795.17
10.	2,137	x $ 8.17 =	$174,592.90

| | PROBLEM | 54-2 ▶ | You are responsible for figuring the amount to be paid for invoices. Round your answers to the nearest cent. |

Directions

CHECKPOINT ✔

54-2 (2)
Amount to be Paid = $3,430

Copy and complete the following table by:

a. Calculating the amount of cash discount, if one is offered.
b. Figuring the amount to be paid.

	Amount of Invoice	Terms	Cash Discount	Amount to be Paid
1.	$2,000.00	n/30		
2.	$3,500.00	2/10, n/30		
3.	$4,600.00	n/60		
4.	$ 750.00	2/10, n/60		
5.	$ 455.00	3/10, n/30		
6.	$ 845.00	n/90		
7.	$ 555.75	1/10, n/60		
8.	$2,575.40	n/45		
9.	$3,324.05	2/10, n/30		
10.	$ 575.95	3/20, n/60		

| | PROBLEM | 54-3 ▶ | You are working in the accounting department of Acme Luggage Company. Your job is to check purchase invoices. You have received the following invoices and have already compared them with purchase orders and receiving reports. |

54-3 (1)
All correct; due date: April 16; filing date: April 13

Directions

a. Copy the following partial invoices. Check each extension and each total. If you find an error, draw a line through the incorrect amount and write the correct amount above it. Remember, if an extension is incorrect, the total will also need to be corrected.

b. After making the necessary corrections, write the word *Approved* on each invoice and sign your name.

c. Indicate the due date and the date under which you would file to pay each invoice. Assume that invoices should be filed by a date three days before they are due.

Invoice #1 (Date: March 17, 19--; Terms: n/30)

QUANTITY	STOCK NO.	DESCRIPTION	UNIT PRICE		TOTAL AMOUNT	
40 ea.	DB 9	Duffel bags	37	16	1,486	40
37 ea.	GB 9	Garment bags	42	89	1,586	93
		Total invoice			3,073	33

Invoice #2 (Date: May 30, 19--; Terms: 30 days)

QUANTITY	STOCK NO.	DESCRIPTION	UNIT PRICE		TOTAL AMOUNT	
45 ea.	PT 4	Packing trunks	99	75	4,488	75
9 dz.	TK 14	Travel kits	104	70	942	30
		Total invoice			5,331	05

Invoice #3 (Date: July 7, 19--; Terms: n/60)

QUANTITY	STOCK NO.	DESCRIPTION	UNIT PRICE		TOTAL AMOUNT	
37 ea.	FL 14	Foot lockers	64	15	2,373	55
19 ea.	ST 01	Shoulder totes	42	25	802	75
52 ea.	BP 16	Backpacks	29	98	1,585	96
		Total invoice			4,762	26

Invoice #4 (Date: April 10, 19--; Terms: 60 days)

QUANTITY	STOCK NO.	DESCRIPTION	UNIT PRICE		TOTAL AMOUNT	
31 ea.	BC 8	Beauty cases	79	55	2,466	05
15 ea.	WC 6	Weekend cases	86	90	1,303	50
19 ea.	PC 4	Pullman cases	51	45	977	55
		Total invoice			4,747	10

Invoice #5 (Date: October 14, 19--; Terms: 90 days)

QUANTITY	STOCK NO.	DESCRIPTION	UNIT PRICE		TOTAL AMOUNT	
28 ea.	SC 12	Suitcases	72	94	2,042	32
40 ea.	EB 19	Executive bags	86	12	3,444	80
		Total invoice			5,487	12

Invoice #6 (Date: August 22, 19--; Terms: n/90)

QUANTITY	STOCK NO.	DESCRIPTION	UNIT PRICE		TOTAL AMOUNT	
21 ea.	TC 4	Travel cases	117	27	2,426	67
19 ea.	WC 11	Wardrobe cases	93	20	1,770	80
50 ea.	AC 10	Attache cases	71	62	3,581	00
		Total invoice			7,778	47

CHAPTER 11

Reinforcement
Activities

DISCUSSION

You and Otto Schuler work together as receiving clerks. Otto cannot understand why it is necessary to use both the packing slip and the purchase order before preparing a receiving report. He has asked you to explain. What would you say to him?

CRITICAL THINKING

You are a receiving clerk. Your supervisor has complained to you recently that too many damaged goods are being found in the inventory. You know that you are not responsible for these because you carefully unpack each shipment and look for damage. If goods are damaged, you put them aside for return. You report only undamaged goods on your receiving report.

However, there is a new worker in the department. You watch him unpack goods and discover that he counts them, but does not inspect them for damage. You decide to talk to him directly. Write two reasons that you would give him for inspecting shipments for damage.

APPLIED COMMUNICATIONS

You are the purchasing agent for your school store. You wish to obtain a price quotation for a school sweatshirt. Prepare a letter that you would write to a vendor to obtain a price quotation. Include the following in your letter:

a. A description of the item in detail (such as color, size, material, and so forth)
b. A request for the price
c. A request for terms
d. A request for information about discounts if a large quantity is purchased

Your letter should not be more than one page in length.

RECORD KEEPING CAREERS

KEY **Terms**

Clerk. Person who keeps records as a major part of his or her work.

A **clerk** is defined in most dictionaries as a person who is employed to keep records as the major part of his or her daily work. The reason that different clerks have different titles is that they keep different kinds of records.

1. What record does a stock record clerk keep?
2. What record does a purchase order clerk keep?
3. What record does a receiving clerk keep?

Sometimes you can tell the title of the clerk if you know the record kept.

4. What title would be given to a clerk who keeps payroll records?
5. What title would be given to a clerk who keeps records of accounts receivable?

However, a clerk sometimes keeps so many records that a more general title is given. The title "general clerk" is often used for this person.

6. If a general clerk were in charge of all of the activities discussed in this chapter, list all of the records that he or she might keep.

REVIEWING WHAT YOU HAVE LEARNED

On a sheet of paper, write the headings **Statement Number** and **Words**. Next, choose the words that best complete the statements. Write each word you choose next to the statement number it completes. Be careful; not all the words listed should be used.

Statements	Words
1. The form used to order merchandise is the _____ .	backordered
2. Goods that are out of stock temporarily are said to be _____ .	cash discount
3. The form that shows goods ordered and received is the _____ .	discontinued
4. Goods no longer sold by a vendor are said to be _____ .	packing slip
5. A record of vendors, information, and prices relating to one item is a _____ .	price quotation record
6. The form that describes the contents of a shipment is the _____ .	purchase invoice
7. The point at which stock reaches its minimum level is the _____ .	purchase order
8. The term that means to guarantee that something is correct is _____ .	receiving report
9. A _____ is a reduction in the amount of an invoice for early payment.	reorder level
	vendor
	vouch

You work for Connie's Home Appliances, located at 3509 A Avenue, Columbus, OH 43207-3509. Because you are the only clerk in the business, you perform a variety of jobs.

Directions

(d)
The invoice is incorrect.

a. You are acting as a purchase order clerk. You have requested price quotations from three companies for food processors, item no. FP 7. The quotations are as follows:

Vendor No.	Co. Name and Address	Unit	Price	Terms
167	J & N Company 6317 Frank Avenue Flint, MI 48507-6317	Ea.	$49.95	60 days
192	Pete's Kitchen Goods 21 Indian Drive Hobbs, NM 88240-0021	Ea.	$52.75	30 days
413	Southeast Food Equipment Company 191 7th Avenue Dothan, AL 36301-1917	Ea.	$51.99	45 days

Prepare a price quotation record and enter this information. The date is July 9, 19--.

b. It is now July 12, 19--. You have the authority to select the vendor who offered the lowest price. Do so and prepare Purchase Order No. 419 for 75 food processors. You want the goods in 20 days, shipped by truck to your stockroom.

c. You are now acting as a receiving clerk. The goods ordered arrive on July 31, 19--. The packing slip that accompanies the goods indicates the following:

65 FP 7 food processors; 10 backordered

You count the goods and find 65 present. All are in good condition. Prepare a receiving report. Remember to include under Quantity Received only those goods actually received. The vendor invoice number is 1897.

d. You are now acting as accounting clerk. Copy the following partial invoice. Check the invoice and guarantee it for payment.

QUANTITY	STOCK NO.	DESCRIPTION	UNIT PRICE	TOTAL AMOUNT
65 ea.	FP 7	Food processors	49 95	3,264 75

This activity may be found in the Working Papers.

CHAPTER 12

Record Keeping for Accounts Payable Clerks

*W*holesalers purchase merchandise in large quantities from manufacturers and other suppliers. Because most merchandise purchased by a wholesale business is bought on credit, wholesalers must keep records of how much they owe each vendor.

In Chapter 12, you will learn how to keep accounts payable records. You will also learn how to use a purchases journal, a cash payments journal, and a purchases returns and allowances journal.

JOB 55 ▶ KEEPING CREDITOR ACCOUNTS

APPLIED MATH PREVIEW

Copy and complete these problems. Pay close attention to the + and - signs.

1. + 377	2. + 685	3. + 4,177	4. + 1,414
- 218	+ 724	- 3,987	+ 987
+ 104	- 319	- 104	+ 3,621
- 196	- 508	+ 2,166	+ 473
+ 355	- 97	+ 1,045	- 1,476
- 127	+ 206	+ 919	- 2,990

BUSINESS TERMS PREVIEW

- Accounts payable ledger - Creditors - Purchase on account -
- Schedule of accounts payable -

GOALS

1. To learn how to keep a record of the amounts owed to creditors.
2. To learn how to prepare a schedule of accounts payable.

K E Y *Terms*

Creditors. People or businesses to whom money is owed.

Accounts payable ledger. Group of creditor accounts.

Purchase on account. Buying merchandise on credit.

You have learned to keep accounts for customers. In this job, you will learn to keep accounts for **creditors**. Creditors are people or businesses to whom your company owes money. A group of creditor accounts is called the **accounts payable ledger**.

When your company buys merchandise from another company on credit, this is called a **purchase on account**. The company from which you buy merchandise on credit is the creditor. When merchandise is purchased on credit, the record keeper must do the following:

1. Open a separate account for each creditor from whom merchandise is purchased.
2. Keep the accounts in a separate book called the accounts payable ledger.
3. Record information in the accounts using the rules shown in Illustration 55A.

Illustration 55A
Rules for recording in a creditor account

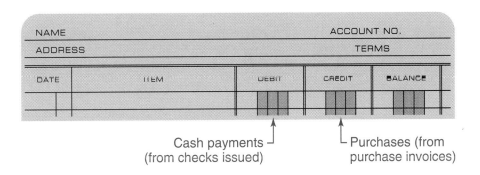

NAME				ACCOUNT NO.	
ADDRESS				TERMS	
DATE	ITEM	DEBIT	CREDIT	BALANCE	

Cash payments ⌐ (from checks issued)   └ Purchases (from purchase invoices)

When using accounts for creditors, all purchases are recorded in the Credit column of the account. Credits increase the balance of the creditor account. All cash payments are recorded in the Debit column of the account. Debits decrease the balance of a creditor account.

Illustration 55B shows how BW Supply Company's creditor account (number 2116) would look after recording a purchase for $710.00 on May 3, Invoice No. 112. Terms of the purchase were 20 days.

Illustration 55B
Recording a purchase in a creditor account

NAME	*BW Supply Company*				ACCOUNT NO. *2116*	
ADDRESS	*1773 Warfel Ave., Erie, PA 16503-1294*				TERMS *20 days*	
DATE	ITEM		DEBIT	CREDIT	BALANCE	
19-- May 3	*Invoice #112*			710 00	710 00	

Notice the following about the recording shown in Illustration 55B:

1. The heading shows the name and address of the creditor, as well as the account number and terms of sale.

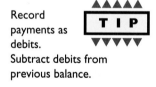

Record
purchases as **T I P**
credits.
Add credits to previous
balance.

2. The date of the invoice, May 3, was recorded in the Date column.
3. The invoice number, 112, was entered in the Item column.
4. The amount of the purchase invoice, $710.00, was entered in the Credit column. Amounts owed to creditors are always entered in the Credit column of a creditor account.
5. The amount of the credit, $710.00, was added to the previous balance, $0.00, to find the new balance of $710.00. Credits are always added to the previous balance to find the new balance of a creditor account. The new balance was recorded in the Balance column.

Illustration 55C shows how BW Supply Company's creditor account would look after recording a cash payment of $710.00 on May 23, check no. 132.

Illustration 55C
Recording a cash
payment in a creditor
account

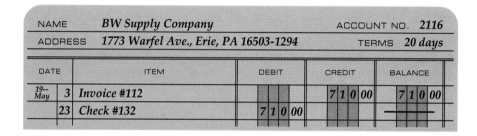

NAME	**BW Supply Company**		ACCOUNT NO.		**2116**
ADDRESS	**1773 Warfel Ave., Erie, PA 16503-1294**		TERMS		**20 days**

DATE		ITEM	DEBIT	CREDIT	BALANCE
19-- May	3	*Invoice #112*		7 1 0 00	7 1 0 00
	23	*Check #132*	7 1 0 00		—

Notice the following about the recording shown in Illustration 55C:

1. The date of the payment, May 23, was entered in the Date column. Only the number 23 was entered, since the year and month were already there and did not change.
2. The check number, 132, was written in the Item column.
3. The amount of the payment, $710.00, was entered in the Debit column. Payments to creditors are always entered in the Debit column of a creditor account.
4. The amount of the debit, $710.00, was subtracted from the previous balance, $710.00, to find the new balance of $0.00. Debits are always subtracted from the previous balance to find the new balance of a creditor account. The new balance was entered as a line drawn through the Balance column.

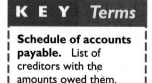

Record
payments as **T I P**
debits.
Subtract debits from
previous balance.

The account now shows all of the dealings with BW Supply Company in May. No money is owed to that company as of May 23. Since the debits and credits are equal, the balance is zero.

A company will have many creditor accounts in the accounts payable ledger. These accounts may be kept in a loose-leaf binder, on a floppy disk, or on a hard drive. Whether there are 2 or 1,000 creditor accounts, a list of what all creditors are owed must be prepared monthly. This list is called a **schedule of accounts payable**. A schedule that goes along with the Sample Problem is shown in Illustration 55E on page 487.

K E Y   Terms

**Schedule of accounts
payable.** List of
creditors with the
amounts owed them.

You are an accounts payable clerk for P. O'Shea Construction Company. Your company purchased materials and other items from three companies:

Creditor	Address	Account No.	Terms
J. Mason Company	124 Evans Avenue Reno, NV 89501-3036	2101	15 days
L. Nieves Company	147 Evans Avenue Reno, NV 89501-3036	2102	20 days
R. Quintero Company	5117 Pacific Street Reno, NV 89501-9001	2103	30 days

During March, your company made the following purchases and payments. Illustration 55D (page 486) shows how you recorded them in the creditor accounts.

Mar. 3 Received Purchase Invoice No. 137 from L. Nieves Company for $765.00.

4 Received Purchase Invoice No. 297 from R. Quintero Company for $995.00.

5 Received Purchase Invoice No. 505 from J. Mason Company for $865.00.

7 Received Purchase Invoice No. 509 from J. Mason Company for $410.00.

20 Issued Check No. 271 to J. Mason Company in payment of the invoice dated March 5.

22 Issued Check No. 272 to J. Mason Company in payment of the invoice dated March 7.

23 Issued Check No. 273 to L. Nieves Company in payment of the invoice dated March 3.

28 Received Purchase Invoice No. 317 from R. Quintero Company for $316.00.

31 Received Purchase Invoice No. 159 from L. Nieves Company for $805.00.

Notice the pencil footings in the three accounts to prove the final balances. Only columns with at least two numbers were footed. This is why the L. Nieves Company Debit column was not footed.

Illustration 55D
Creditor accounts in an
accounts payable ledger

NAME		J. Mason Company			ACCOUNT NO.	2101
ADDRESS		124 Evans Ave., Reno, NV 89501-3036			TERMS	15 days

DATE		ITEM	DEBIT	CREDIT	BALANCE
19-- Mar.	5	Invoice #505		865 00	865 00
	7	Invoice #509		410 00	1 275 00
	20	Check #271	865 00		410 00
	22	Check #272	410 00		
			1 275 00	1 275 00	

NAME		L. Nieves Company			ACCOUNT NO.	2102
ADDRESS		147 Evans Ave., Reno, NV 89501-3036			TERMS	20 days

DATE		ITEM		DEBIT	CREDIT	BALANCE
19-- Mar.	3	Invoice #137			765 00	765 00
	23	Check #273	1,570.00	765 00		
	31	Invoice #159	-765.00		805 00	805 00
			805.00		1 570 00	

NAME		R. Quintero Company			ACCOUNT NO.	2103
ADDRESS		5117 Pacific St., Reno, NV 89501-9001			TERMS	30 days

DATE		ITEM	DEBIT	CREDIT	BALANCE
19-- Mar.	4	Invoice #297		995 00	995 00
	28	Invoice #317		316 00	1 311 00
				1 311 00	

To prove the final balance of the L. Nieves Company account, the following math was done:

Total Credits	$1,570.00
Less: Total debits	- 765.00
Final balance	$ 805.00

Illustration 55E (page 487) shows the schedule of accounts payable you prepared for P. O'Shea Construction Company. It was prepared in three steps:

STEP 1 ▶ *Record the heading.*

The standard three-line heading was entered to answer the questions Who?, What?, and When? The schedule is prepared as of the last day of the month.

STEP 2 ▶ *List the creditor names and balances.*

List only accounts with balances.

T I P

Each creditor account with a balance was entered. Notice that since the J. Mason Company account had a zero balance, it was left out of the schedule. Accounts are listed in alphabetical order, as they appear in the accounts payable ledger.

Illustration 55E
Schedule of accounts payable

P. O'Shea Construction Company		
Schedule of Accounts Payable		
March 31, 19--		
L. Nieves Company		8 0 5 00
R. Quintero Company	1 3 1 1 00	
Total	2 1 1 6 00	2 1 1 6 00

STEP 3 ▶ *Find the total.*

The money column was ruled and footed. The footed total, after being checked by re-adding, was entered again as a final total. The word *Total* was written under the creditor names, and a double ruling was drawn under the money column.

ℬUILDING YOUR BUSINESS VOCABULARY

On a sheet of paper, write the headings **Statement Number** and **Words**. Next, choose the words that match the statements. Write each word you choose next to the statement number it matches. Be careful; not all the words listed should be used.

Statements	Words
1. The column used to record an increase in a creditor account	accounts payable ledger
2. Buying merchandise on credit	accounts receivable account
3. A group of creditor accounts	accounts receivable ledger
4. A record of a charge customer's purchases and payments	credit
5. A list of creditors with the amounts owed to them	creditors
6. The column used to record a decrease in a creditor account	debit
	purchase on account
7. People or businesses to whom money is owed	schedule of accounts payable
	three-column account

PROBLEM SOLVING MODEL FOR: *Preparing a Schedule of Accounts Payable*

STEP 1 ▶ **Record the heading.**

STEP 2 ▶ **List the creditor names and balances.**

STEP 3 ▶ **Find the total.**

🅐PPLICATION PROBLEMS

PROBLEM **55-1** ▶ You are employed by the Huston Appliance Company as an accounts payable clerk. Your job is to record purchase invoices and checks written to pay these invoices in creditor accounts.

Directions

a. Open a creditor account for P. Carlock Company, 99 North Street, Jackson, MS 39201-4846, Account Number 2361. Terms of purchase are 20 days.

b. Record the following items in the P. Carlock Company account. Remember to find the new balance after each debit or credit is recorded.

55-1 (c)
Final balance = $1,994.60

June	4	Received Purchase Invoice No. 506 for $7,142.20.
	9	Received Purchase Invoice No. 509 for $2,116.80.
	17	Received Purchase Invoice No. 527 for $975.50.
	24	Issued Check No. 277 in payment of the invoice dated June 4.
	27	Received Purchase Invoice No. 546 for $1,019.10.
	29	Issued Check No. 291 in payment of the invoice dated June 9.

c. Prove the balance at the end of the month. Show all footings in the account.

PROBLEM **55-2** ▶ You are employed by the Wendell Vacuum Cleaner Company as an accounts payable clerk. Your job is to record purchase invoices and checks written to pay these invoices in creditor accounts.

AUTOMATED

Directions

a. Open a creditor account for W. Baez Company, 557 Munoz Rivera, Hato Rey, PR 00919-0557, Account Number 2270. Terms of purchase are 10 days.

b. Record the following items in the W. Baez Company account. Remember to find the new balance after entering each amount.

55-2 (c)
Final balance = $3,220.01

Oct.   3   Received Purchase Invoice No. 809 for $963.84.

        8   Received Purchase Invoice No. 821 for $1,604.37.

     13   Issued Check No. 411 in payment of the invoice dated October 3.

     15   Received Purchase Invoice No. 837 for $1,047.82.

     18   Issued Check No. 417 in payment of the invoice dated October 8.

     26   Received Purchase Invoice No. 856 for $2,172.19.

c. Prove the balance at the end of the month. Show all footings in the account.

PROBLEM **55-3** ▶ You are employed by the M. Arend Company as an accounts payable clerk. Your job is to record purchase invoices and checks written to pay these invoices in creditor accounts.

AUTOMATED

Directions

a. Open accounts for the following creditors:

Creditor	Address	Account No.	Terms
J. Cernak Company	502 SE Long Street Topeka, KS 66607-8054	2101	10 days
D. Hahn Company	491 Morton Avenue Des Moines, IA 50313-7120	2102	20 days
F. Schwartz Company	612 Colonial Avenue Waterbury, CT 06708-4208	2103	15 days

b. Record the following information in the creditor accounts. Remember to find the new balance after entering each amount.

55-3 (d)
Total = $1,029.97

Aug.   3   Received Purchase Invoice No. 112 from J. Cernak Company for $310.85.

       5   Received Purchase Invoice No. 511 from D. Hahn Company for $511.81.

       8   Received Purchase Invoice No. 701 from F. Schwartz Company for $408.19.

     11   Received Purchase Invoice No. 705 from F. Schwartz Company for $511.12.

     13   Issued Check No. 104 to J. Cernak Company in payment of the invoice dated August 3.

     17   Received Purchase Invoice No. 119 from J. Cernak Company for $416.47.

     18   Received Purchase Invoice No. 721 from F. Schwartz Company for $317.81.

     19   Received Purchase Invoice No. 514 from D. Hahn Company for $712.16.

     23   Issued Check No. 119 to F. Schwartz Company in payment of the invoice dated August 8.

25 Issued Check No. 121 to D. Hahn Company in payment of the invoice dated August 5.

26 Issued Check No. 124 to F. Schwartz Company in payment of the invoice dated August 11.

27 Issued Check No. 126 to J. Cernak Company in payment of the invoice dated August 17.

c. Prove the balances at the end of the month. Show all footings in the accounts.

d. Prepare a schedule of accounts payable as of August 31.

Problem 55-4 may be found in the Working Papers.

USING A PURCHASES JOURNAL AND AN ACCOUNTS PAYABLE LEDGER

APPLIED MATH PREVIEW

Find the due date of these invoices.

Date of Invoice	Terms	Date of Invoice	Terms
1. July 23	10 days	5. August 6	15 days
2. May 9	20 days	6. June 12	45 days
3. March 16	30 days	7. October 3	60 days
4. April 8	60 days	8. November 13	30 days

BUSINESS TERM PREVIEW

• **Purchases journal** •

GOALS

1. To learn how to record purchase invoices in a purchases journal.
2. To learn how to post from the purchases journal to the accounts payable ledger.
3. To learn how purchase invoices are filed.

ᴜNDERSTANDING THE JOB

KEY *Terms*

Purchases journal.
A record of purchases on account.

You have learned how to record amounts due to creditors directly from the purchase invoices into the accounts payable ledger. Many accounts payable clerks do not record directly into the creditor accounts. Instead, they first enter purchase invoices in a special record called a **purchases journal**. The purchases journal lists all purchases from creditors by date. Illustration 56A on page 492 shows how data from a purchase invoice are recorded in a purchases journal.

Here are the steps you would follow to make the entry in the purchases journal shown in Illustration 56A (page 492):

STEP 1 ▶ *Copy the date of entry.*

Entry date goes in Date column.

TIP

Copy the date of entry (date of approval) in the Date column. This will usually be a date *after* the date of the invoice, since a few days are needed to check and approve an invoice.

STEP 2 ▶ *Copy the creditor's name.*

Copy the name on the top of the invoice, D. Phillips Company, into the Creditor's Name column.

Illustration 56A
Recording a purchase
invoice in a purchases
journal

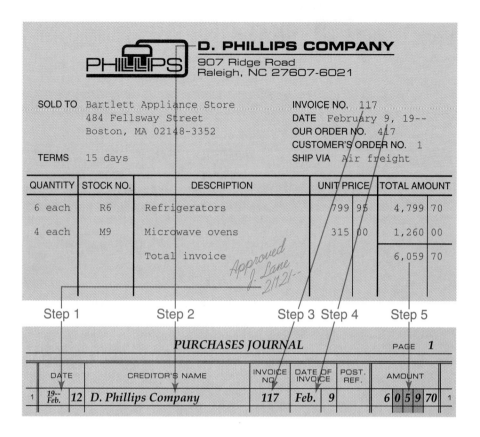

D. PHILLIPS COMPANY
907 Ridge Road
Raleigh, NC 27607-6021

SOLD TO	Bartlett Appliance Store	INVOICE NO. 117
	484 Fellsway Street	DATE February 9, 19--
	Boston, MA 02148-3352	OUR ORDER NO. 417
		CUSTOMER'S ORDER NO. 1
TERMS	15 days	SHIP VIA Air freight

QUANTITY	STOCK NO.	DESCRIPTION	UNIT PRICE	TOTAL AMOUNT
6 each	R6	Refrigerators	799 95	4,799 70
4 each	M9	Microwave ovens	315 00	1,260 00
		Total invoice		6,059 70

*Approved
J. Lane
2/12/--*

Step 1   Step 2   Step 3 Step 4   Step 5

PURCHASES JOURNAL   PAGE **1**

	DATE	CREDITOR'S NAME	INVOICE NO.	DATE OF INVOICE	POST. REF.	AMOUNT	
1	19-- Feb. 12	*D. Phillips Company*	*117*	*Feb. 9*		6 0 5 9 70	1

STEP 3 ▶ *Copy the invoice number.*

Write the invoice number, 117, in the Invoice No. column.

STEP 4 ▶ *Copy the date of invoice.*

Write the date of the invoice, February 9, in the Date of Invoice column. Of the two dates entered in the purchases journal, February 9 and February 12, the 9th is the more important date. Since the terms are 15 days, the due date is 15 days after February 9, or February 24.

STEP 5 ▶ *Copy the amount.*

The total amount of the invoice, $6,059.70, is written in the Amount column.

Recording in the purchases journal is only part of the process. A record still needs to be made in the creditor accounts in the accounts payable ledger. To do this, you must post from the purchases journal to the creditor accounts.

Posting must be done with great care and accuracy. The correct amounts must be posted to the correct accounts. Illustration 56B (page 493) shows how the purchase already recorded in the purchases journal is posted to the D. Phillips Company account. Here are the steps followed:

STEP 1 ▶ **Copy the date.**

Be very careful here. The *date of invoice* is the date that is written in the Date column of the creditor account. February 9 is the date written in the account.

STEP 2 ▶ **Copy the invoice number.**

Write the invoice number, 117, in the Item column.

STEP 3 ▶ **Record the posting reference in the creditor account.**

The posting reference is P1. P stands for *purchases* journal; 1 stands for page *1*. A posting from the second page of the purchases journal would be written as P2. Enter P1 in the Post. Ref. column of the D. Phillips Company account.

STEP 4 ▶ **Post the amount.**

Write the amount, $6,059.70, in the Credit column of the account, since all purchases are recorded in the Credit column.

<table>
<tr><td rowspan="6">Date of invoice is recorded in Date column of creditor account.
Post purchases to the Credit column of a creditor account.
Add credits to previous balance.</td><td>▲▲▲▲▲▲
T I P
▼▼▼▼▼</td></tr>
</table>

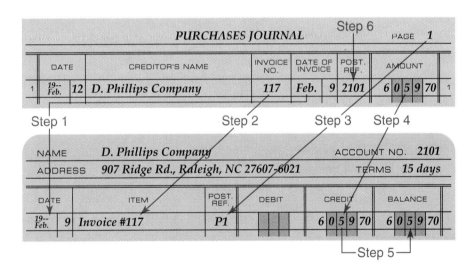

Illustration 56B   Posting from purchases journal to creditor account

STEP 5 ▶ **Find the new balance.**

Find the new balance of the account and record it in the Balance column. Since there was no previous balance, the balance is $6,059.70.

STEP 6 ▶ **Enter an account number in the purchases journal.**

Put the number of the creditor account, 2101, in the Post. Ref. column of the purchases journal to show that the entry has been posted to the creditor account.

You are the accounts payable clerk for the S & R Wholesale Company. Your purchase invoices show these purchases for the month:

Apr.   4 Received Purchase Invoice No. 106 from Z. Baxter Company, dated April 3, for $1,075.10.

7 Received Purchase Invoice No. 219 from T. Stevens Company, dated April 4, for $963.85.

13 Received Purchase Invoice No. 123 from Z. Baxter Company, dated April 11, for $805.91.

21 Received Purchase Invoice No. 229 from T. Stevens Company, dated April 18, for $1,417.90.

27 Received Purchase Invoice No. 245 from T. Stevens Company, dated April 25, for $601.12.

Illustration 56C (below and on page 495) shows how these purchases would be recorded in the purchases journal and posted to the creditor accounts. The creditor accounts on page 495 show the terms for each creditor. Here are the steps that you would follow:

STEP 1 ▶ *Record the purchases in the purchases journal.*

Record the purchases in the purchases journal, using the data from the purchase invoices.

Illustration 56C   Purchases journal and accounts payable ledger

PURCHASES JOURNAL   PAGE 7

	DATE		CREDITOR'S NAME	INVOICE NO.	DATE OF INVOICE		POST. REF.	AMOUNT	
1	19-- Apr.	4	Z. Baxter Company	106	Apr.	3	101	1 0 7 5 10	1
2		7	T. Stevens Company	219		4	102	9 6 3 85	2
3		13	Z. Baxter Company	123		11	101	8 0 5 91	3
4		21	T. Stevens Company	229		18	102	1 4 1 7 90	4
5		27	T. Stevens Company	245		25	102	6 0 1 12	5
6		30	Total					4 8 6 3 88 / 4 8 6 3 88	6

Illustration 56C
Purchases journal and
accounts payable ledger
(continued)

ACCOUNTS PAYABLE LEDGER

NAME	Z. Baxter Company				ACCOUNT NO.		101	
ADDRESS	14 Edwards St., Mobile AL 36610-5233				TERMS		10 days	

DATE		ITEM	POST. REF.	DEBIT	CREDIT	BALANCE
19-- Apr.	3	Invoice #106	P7		1075 10	1075 10
	11	Invoice #123	P7		805 91	1881 01
					1881 01	

NAME	T. Stevens Company				ACCOUNT NO.		102	
ADDRESS	297 Edwards St., Mobile, AL 36610-3119				TERMS		25 days	

DATE		ITEM	POST. REF.	DEBIT	CREDIT	BALANCE
19-- Apr.	4	Invoice #219	P7		963 85	963 85
	18	Invoice #229	P7		1417 90	2381 75
	25	Invoice #245	P7		601 12	2982 87
					2982 87	

STEP 2 ▶ *File the invoices.*

Once an invoice has been recorded in the purchases journal, it is ready for filing. There are many different ways to file purchase invoices. As you learned in Job 54, some clerks file purchase invoices two or three days before the due date. Another common method is to file them according to the dates they are due. When filing according to due date, 31 folders would be used—one for each day of the month. Illustration 56D (page 496) shows this type of filing system.

Invoices are usually filed by due date.

Using this system, Z. Baxter Invoice No. 106 would be filed under the 13 folder, since April 3 (date of invoice) plus 10 days (terms) equals April 13 (due date). T. Stevens Invoice No. 219 would be filed under 29. (April 4 plus 25 days equals April 29.) This system lets the accounts payable clerk pay invoices on the due date.

STEP 3 ▶ *Post to the creditor accounts.*

At the end of each day, post the amounts in the purchases journal to the creditor accounts in the accounts payable ledger. Notice P7 was entered in the Post. Ref. column, since page 7 of the purchases journal was used. The account number was entered in the purchases journal after each posting. New account balances were calculated after each posting.

Post daily to creditor accounts.

STEP 4 ▶ *Total the purchases journal.*

At the end of the month, rule and foot the Amount column of the purchases journal. Re-add the column before writing the final total. Draw

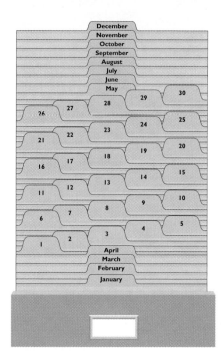

a double ruling under the final total. Write the word Total in the Creditor's Name column. Date the total as of the last day of the month.

STEP 5 ▶ *Prove the account balances and prepare a schedule of accounts payable.*

Each account was footed to prove its balance, and then a schedule of accounts payable was prepared for S & R Wholesale Company. (See Illustration 56E, page 497.)

INTERVIEW

CAROLYN M. MOORE

A native of St. Louis, Missouri, Carolyn Moore attended Hazelwood High School and took business courses such as keyboarding, office practice, computer programming, and bookkeeping. She also was an officer in the Junior Achievement Program.

While in high school, Carolyn found that she really liked bookkeeping and decided that she would seek further education to enter the business world. When she was graduated from Hazelwood High, Carolyn was admitted to Southern Illinois University in the accounting program.

Carolyn paid for some of her college costs by putting her knowledge of record keeping to work right away. She participated in an internship program at the Ralston Purina Company in St. Louis. In her first summer, she was assigned to the Accounts Receivable Department where she did data entry work. In her second summer, her work included checking the credit ratings of certain types of customers to ensure that they would be likely to pay their bills.

Carolyn will be graduated with a bachelor's degree in accounting and wants to start her career with a public accounting firm in the area. She feels that this experience will give her the foundation she needs to start her own accounting firm in a few years.

S & R Wholesale Company					
Schedule of Accounts Payable					
April 30, 19--					
Z. Baxter Company	1	8	8	1	01
T. Stevens Company	2	9	8	2	87
Total	4	8	6	3	88

*B*UILDING YOUR BUSINESS VOCABULARY

On a sheet of paper, write the headings **Statement Number** and **Words**. Next, choose the words that match the statements. Write each word you choose next to the statement number it matches. Be careful; not all the words listed should be used.

Statements	Words
1. The column used to record an increase in a creditor account	accounts payable ledger
2. People or businesses to whom money is owed	accounts receivable ledger
3. A group of customer accounts	credit
4. Buying merchandise on credit	creditors
5. A record of purchases on account	debit
6. A list of creditors with the amounts owed to them	purchase on account
7. The account column in which payments to creditors are recorded	purchases journal
8. A group of creditor accounts	schedule of accounts payable
	schedule of accounts receivable
	terms

PROBLEM SOLVING MODEL FOR: *Using a Purchases Journal and an Accounts Payable Ledger*

STEP 1 ▶ *Record the purchases in the purchases journal.*

STEP 2 ▶ *File the invoices.*

STEP 3 ▶ *Post to the creditor accounts.*

STEP 4 ▶ *Total the purchases journal.*

STEP 5 ▶ *Prove the account balances and prepare a schedule of accounts payable.*

*A*PPLICATION PROBLEMS

PROBLEM | **56-1** ▶ You are employed as an accounts payable clerk at J & R Lumber Company. Your job is to record approved purchase invoices in the purchases journal.

AUTOMATED

Directions

a. Open a purchases journal for March. Number the journal page 1.

b. Record the following approved purchase invoices in the purchases journal:

Mar. 3 Received Purchase Invoice No. 137 from T. Allen Company, dated March 1, for $747.16.

6 Received Purchase Invoice No. 701 from S. Uniak Company, dated March 2, for $916.32.

9 Received Purchase Invoice No. 142 from T. Allen Company, dated March 6, for $1,610.93.

12 Received Purchase Invoice No. 603 from J. McClellan Company, dated March 9, for $104.17.

CHECKPOINT ✔

56-1 (e)
Total = $6,206.42

15 Received Purchase Invoice No. 155 from T. Allen Company, dated March 11, for $397.82.

17 Received Purchase Invoice No. 706 from S. Uniak Company, dated March 14, for $1,121.05.

22 Received Purchase Invoice No. 813 from A. Poindexter Company, dated March 19, for $711.18.

30 Received Purchase Invoice No. 717 from S. Uniak Company, dated March 27, for $597.79.

c. Total the Amount column of the purchases journal.

d. Verify the footing of the purchases journal by re-adding.

e. Record the final total in the Amount column of the purchases journal. Double rule the journal, and write the date and the word *Total* in the proper places.

PROBLEM | **56-2** ▶ You are employed as an accounts payable clerk by R. Guillaume Company. Your job is to record approved purchase invoices in the purchases journal and post to the creditor accounts in the accounts payable ledger.

AUTOMATED

Directions

a. Open a purchases journal for July. Number the journal page 1.

b. Open ledger accounts for the creditors below and on page 499:

Creditor	Address	Account No.	Terms
C. Brooks Company	162 Kenneth Street Detroit, MI 48203-0162	101	10 days

Creditor	Address	Account No.	Terms
W. Navarro Company	1328 SW Douglas Street Portland, OR 97219-3208	102	30 days
N. Salazar Company	3117 Hartford Avenue Providence, RI 02919-3117	103	20 days

CHECKPOINT

56-2 (f)
Total = $4,928.99

c. Record the following approved purchase invoices in the purchases journal. Post daily from the purchases journal to the Credit column of the creditor accounts. Do not forget to enter P1 as a posting reference in the accounts and an account number as a posting reference in the journal.

July   5 Received Purchase Invoice No. 917 from W. Navarro Company, dated July 1, for $439.17.

        8 Received Purchase Invoice No. 308 from C. Brooks Company, dated July 6, for $2,104.19.

   11 Received Purchase Invoice No. 417 from N. Salazar Company, dated July 8, for $147.65.

   17 Received Purchase Invoice No. 320 from C. Brooks Company, dated July 15, for $711.02.

   22 Received Purchase Invoice No. 946 from W. Navarro Company, dated July 19, for $731.04.

   26 Received Purchase Invoice No. 329 from C. Brooks Company, dated July 23, for $618.34.

   30 Received Purchase Invoice No. 477 from N. Salazar Company, dated July 27, for $177.58.

d. Total the Amount column of the purchases journal.
e. Verify the footing of the purchases journal by re-adding.
f. Record the final total in the Amount column of the purchases journal. Double rule the journal, and write the date and the word *Total* in the proper places.
g. Prove the account balances at the end of the month by footing the Credit column in each creditor account.
h. Prepare a schedule of accounts payable as of July 31. Use Illustration 56E (page 497) as a guide.

Problem 56-3 may be found in the Working Papers.

JOB 57 ▶ Using a Cash Payments Journal and an Accounts Payable Ledger

APPLIED MATH PREVIEW

Copy and complete these problems. Pay close attention to the + and - signs.

1. +511	2. +4,176	3. +$411.25	4. +$1,471.08
- 317	+2,093	- 37.95	+ 1,396.12
+209	-1,277	+ 206.10	- 1,471.08
- 167	-1,094	- 199.40	+ 2,099.16
+410	- 472	+ 146.81	- 1,396.12
- 377	+ 389	- 209.94	- 2,099.16

BUSINESS TERM PREVIEW

• Cash payments journal •

GOALS

1. To learn how to record payments to creditors in a cash payments journal.
2. To learn how to post from the cash payments journal to the accounts payable ledger.

UNDERSTANDING THE JOB

KEY Terms

Cash payments journal. A record of cash payments.

You have learned how to record approved purchase invoices in the purchases journal. You have also learned how to post from the purchases journal to the creditor accounts in the accounts payable ledger. In this job, you will learn how to record payments made to creditors in a **cash payments journal**. The cash payments journal lists all cash payments by date. The data for entries in the cash payments journal come from check stubs. Illustration 57A (page 501) shows how data from a check stub are recorded in a cash payments journal.

Illustration 57A
Recording a check stub in
a cash payments journal

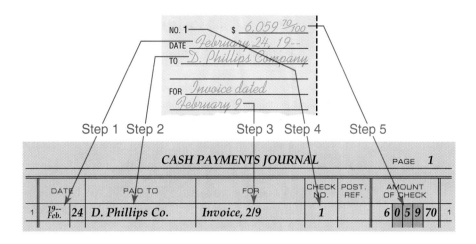

Here are the steps you would follow to make the entry in the cash payments journal shown in Illustration 57A:

STEP 1 ▸ **Copy the date of the check.**

Copy the date, February 24, in the Date column.

STEP 2 ▸ **Copy the creditor's name.**

Write the name, D. Phillips Co., in the Paid To column. You should abbreviate as needed to fit data in the space provided.

STEP 3 ▸ **Copy the invoice date.**

Write the words *Invoice, 2/9* in the For column to show which invoice was paid with this check.

STEP 4 ▸ **Copy the check number.**

Write the number of the check, 1, in the Check No. column.

STEP 5 ▸ **Enter the amount.**

Copy the amount of the check, $6,059.70, in the Amount of Check column of the cash payments journal.

After recording the check in the cash payments journal, you must post to the D. Phillips Company account in the accounts payable ledger. Illustration 57B (page 502) shows how this posting is done. Here are the steps followed:

STEP 1 ▸ **Copy the date.**

Enter the day, 24, in the Date column of the account. The year and month do not need to be repeated.

STEP 2 ▶ **Enter the check number.**

Write *Check #1* in the Item column.

STEP 3 ▶ **Record the posting reference in the creditor account.**

Enter CP1 for *Cash Payments Journal, page 1* in the Post. Ref. column of the account.

STEP 4 ▶ **Post the amount.**

Write the amount, $6,059.70, in the Debit column of the account, since all payments are recorded in the Debit column.

STEP 5 ▶ **Find the new balance.**

▲▲▲▲▲
T I P
▼▼▼▼▼

Post payments to the Debit column of a creditor account. Subtract a debit from the previous balance.

Find the new balance of the account and enter it in the Balance column. Since the amount was recorded in the Debit column, *subtract* it from the previous balance to find the new balance. The zero balance in the account is calculated as follows:

Previous balance	$ 6,059.70
Debit on February 24	- 6,059.70
New balance	$ 00.00

STEP 6 ▶ **Enter an account number in the cash payments journal.**

Enter the account number, 2101, in the Post. Ref. column of the cash payments journal to show that the entry has been posted to the creditor account.

Illustration 57B   Posting from cash payments journal to creditor account

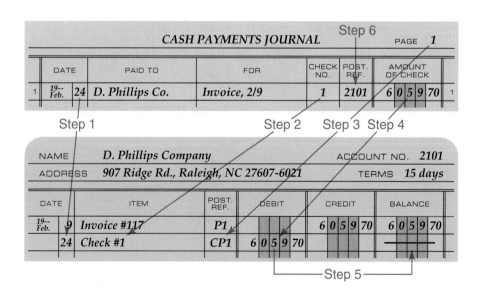

You are the accounts payable clerk for S & R Wholesale Company. The creditor accounts in your accounts payable ledger already contain postings from the purchases journal. You make the following cash payments during April:

Apr. 13 Issued Check No. 57 to Z. Baxter Company for $1,075.10 in payment of the invoice dated April 3.

21 Issued Check No. 58 to Z. Baxter Company for $805.91 in payment of the invoice dated April 11.

29 Issued Check No. 59 to T. Stevens Company for $963.85 in payment of the invoice dated April 4.

Illustration 57C (page 504) shows how these cash payments would be recorded in the cash payments journal and posted to the creditor accounts. Here are the steps you would follow:

STEP 1 ▶ *Record the cash payments in the cash payments journal.*

Record the payments in the cash payments journal, using the data from the check stubs.

STEP 2 ▶ *File the paid invoices.*

Pull the purchase invoices paid from the due date folders and file them under each creditor's name.

STEP 3 ▶ *Post to the creditor accounts.*

Post daily to creditor accounts.

At the end of each day, post the amounts in the cash payments journal to the creditor accounts in the accounts payable ledger. Notice CP6 in the Post. Ref. column, since page 6 of the cash payments journal was used. An account number was entered in the cash payments journal after each posting. New account balances were calculated after each posting.

STEP 4 ▶ *Total the cash payments journal.*

At the end of the month, rule and foot the Amount of Check column of the cash payments journal. Re-add the column before writing the final total. Draw a double ruling under the final total. Write the word *Total* in the Paid To column. Date the total as of the last day of the month.

STEP 5 ▸ *Prove the account balances and prepare a schedule of accounts payable.*

Each account was footed to prove its balance, and then a schedule of accounts payable was prepared. Since only T. Stevens Company has a balance other than zero, the schedule is not shown here.

Illustration 57C   Cash payments journal and accounts payable ledger

CASH PAYMENTS JOURNAL PAGE **6**

	DATE		PAID TO	FOR	CHECK NO.	POST. REF.	AMOUNT OF CHECK	
1	19-- Apr.	13	Z. Baxter Co.	Invoice, 4/3	57	101	1 0 7 5 10	1
2		21	Z. Baxter Co.	Invoice, 4/11	58	101	8 0 5 91	2
3		29	T. Stevens Co.	Invoice, 4/4	59	102	9 6 3 85	3
4		30	Total				2 8 4 4 86	4

ACCOUNTS PAYABLE LEDGER

NAME   **Z. Baxter Company**   ACCOUNT NO.   **101**
ADDRESS   **14 Edwards St., Mobile, AL 36610-5233**   TERMS   **10 days**

DATE		ITEM	POST. REF.	DEBIT	CREDIT	BALANCE
19-- Apr.	3	Invoice #106	P7		1 0 7 5 10	1 0 7 5 10
	11	Invoice #123	P7		8 0 5 91	1 8 8 1 01
	13	Check #57	CP6	1 0 7 5 10		8 0 5 91
	21	Check #8	CP6	8 0 5 91		——
				1 8 8 1 01	1 8 8 1 01	

NAME   **T. Stevens Company**   ACCOUNT NO.   **102**
ADDRESS   **297 Edwards St., Mobile, AL 36610-5119**   TERMS   **25 days**

DATE		ITEM		POST. REF.	DEBIT	CREDIT	BALANCE
19-- Apr.	4	Invoice #219		P7		9 6 3 85	9 6 3 85
	18	Invoice #229		P7		1 4 1 7 90	2 3 8 1 75
	25	Invoice #245	2,982.87	P7		6 0 1 12	2 9 8 2 87
	29	Check #59	-963.85	CP6	9 6 3 85		2 0 1 9 02
			2,019.02			2 9 8 2 87	

BUILDING YOUR BUSINESS VOCABULARY

On a sheet of paper, write the headings **Statement Number** and **Words**. Next, choose the words that match the statements. Write each word you choose next to the statement number it matches. Be careful; not all the words listed should be used.

Statements	Words
1. A group of creditor accounts	accounts payable ledger
2. A record of cash payments	cash payments journal
3. To transfer data from one record to another	cash receipts journal
	creditors
4. A record of all cash received	post
5. A record of purchases on account	purchase on account
6. A list of creditors with the amounts owed to them	purchases journal
	sales journal
7. Buying merchandise on credit	schedule of accounts payable
8. People or businesses to whom money is owed	schedule of accounts receivable

PROBLEM SOLVING MODEL FOR: *Using a Cash Payments Journal and an Accounts Payable Ledger*

STEP 1 ▶ *Record the cash payments in the cash payments journal.*

STEP 2 ▶ *File the paid invoices.*

STEP 3 ▶ *Post to the creditor accounts.*

STEP 4 ▶ *Total the cash payments journal.*

STEP 5 ▶ *Prove the account balances and prepare a schedule of accounts payable.*

APPLICATION PROBLEMS

PROBLEM 57-1 ▶ You are employed as an accounts payable clerk at Wilson Wholesale Company. Your job is to record cash payments in a cash payments journal.

Directions

a. Open a cash payments journal. Number the journal page 1.
b. Record the following data taken from the check stubs for October:

Oct. 12 Issued Check No. 1 for $712.90 to J. Normandin Company in payment of the invoice dated October 2.

19 Issued Check No. 2 for $611.75 to K. Bohan Company in payment of the invoice dated October 4.

22 Issued Check No. 3 for $477.12 to B. Smith Company in payment of the invoice dated October 7.

26 Issued Check No. 4 for $1,161.35 to J. Poisson Company in payment of the invoice dated October 6.

28 Issued Check No. 5 for $1,024.10 to S. Rosen Company in payment of the invoice dated October 8.

29 Issued Check No. 6 for $977.18 to K. Conway Company in payment of the invoice dated October 19.

30 Issued Check No. 7 for $439.63 to A. Partridge Company in payment of the invoice dated October 5.

CHECKPOINT

57-1 (c)
Total = $5,404.03

c. Find the total cash paid for the month by footing the Amount of Check column. Check your footing, write the final total, double rule the column, write the word *Total* in the Paid To column, and enter the date.

PROBLEM 57-2 ▶ You are an accounts payable clerk for Digennero Computer Company. Your job is to keep the accounts payable records.

Directions

a. Open a cash payments journal for June. Number the journal page 1.
b. Copy the creditor accounts below and on page 507. Include the amounts that have already been posted.

NAME	J. Asbury Company					ACCOUNT NO.	610
ADDRESS	106 Hills Rd., Sioux Falls, SD 57103-2469					TERMS	20 days

DATE		ITEM	POST. REF.	DEBIT	CREDIT	BALANCE
19-- June	3	Invoice #47	P1		4 0 1 10	4 0 1 10
	9	Invoice #51	P1		3 9 6 85	7 9 7 95
	20	Invoice #56	P1		5 1 8 17	1 3 1 6 12

NAME	M. Durocher Company					ACCOUNT NO.	611
ADDRESS	66 Lawn Ave., St. Louis, MO 63144-8216					TERMS	10 days

DATE		ITEM	POST. REF.	DEBIT	CREDIT	BALANCE
19-- June	11	Invoice #614	P1		1 0 2 6 19	1 0 2 6 19
	14	Invoice #619	P1		4 1 8 02	1 4 4 4 21

| NAME | S. Gatlin Company | | ACCOUNT NO. | 612 | | | |
| ADDRESS | 1240 Custer Ave., Billings, MT 59101-3227 | | | TERMS | 15 days | | |

DATE		ITEM	POST. REF.	DEBIT	CREDIT	BALANCE
19-- June	4	Invoice #301	P1		8 1 7 11	8 1 7 11
	10	Invoice #310	P1		2 9 1 73	1 1 0 8 84
	18	Invoice #327	P1		5 1 5 27	1 6 2 4 11

c. Record the following data taken from the check stubs for June. Post daily from the cash payments journal to the creditor accounts. Do not forget to record CP1 and account numbers in the proper Post. Ref. columns.

June 19 Issued Check No. 1 for $817.11 to S. Gatlin Company in payment of the invoice dated June 4.

21 Issued Check No. 2 for $1,026.19 to M. Durocher Company in payment of the invoice dated June 11.

23 Issued Check No. 3 for $401.10 to J. Asbury Company in payment of the invoice dated June 3.

24 Issued Check No. 4 for $418.02 to M. Durocher Company in payment of the invoice dated June 14.

25 Issued Check No. 5 for $291.73 to S. Gatlin Company in payment of the invoice dated June 10.

29 Issued Check No. 6 for $396.85 to J. Asbury Company in payment of the invoice dated June 9.

CHECKPOINT ✔

57-2 (f)
Total = $1,033.44

d. Find the total cash paid for the month by footing the Amount of Check column in the cash payments journal. Check your footing, write the final total, double rule the column, write the word *Total* in the Paid To column, and enter the date.

e. Prove the balance at the end of the month in each creditor account. Show all footings.

f. Prepare a schedule of accounts payable as of June 30.

PROBLEM | **57-3** ▶ You are an accounts payable clerk for Ricard Chemical Company. Your job is to keep the accounts payable records.

Directions

a. Open a cash payments journal for January. Number the journal page 1.

b. Copy the creditor accounts on page 508. Include the amounts that have already been posted.

c. Record the data on page 508 taken from the check stubs for January. Post daily from the cash payments journal to the creditor accounts. Record the proper posting reference marks.

NAME	R. Crowley Company			ACCOUNT NO.	151	
ADDRESS	957 Elm St., Birmingham, AL 35206-1716			TERMS	20 days	

DATE	ITEM	POST. REF.	DEBIT	CREDIT	BALANCE
19-- Jan. 5	Invoice #68	P1		372 80	372 80
8	Invoice #74	P1		577 16	949 96
10	Invoice #81	P1		412 20	1362 16

NAME	C. Dowling Company			ACCOUNT NO.	152	
ADDRESS	88 Seale Ave., Palo Alto, CA 94301-2203			TERMS	15 days	

DATE	ITEM	POST. REF.	DEBIT	CREDIT	BALANCE
19-- Jan. 3	Invoice #94	P1		906 37	906 37
9	Invoice #99	P1		695 70	1602 07
17	Invoice #117	P1		599 85	2201 92

NAME	S. Marquis Company			ACCOUNT NO.	153	
ADDRESS	376 Maple Ave., Lexington, KY 40508-7370			TERMS	10 days	

DATE	ITEM	POST. REF.	DEBIT	CREDIT	BALANCE
19-- Jan. 13	Invoice #312	P1		756 35	756 35
16	Invoice #319	P1		801 12	1557 47
22	Invoice #327	P1		437 65	1995 12

Jan. 18 Issued Check No. 1 for $906.37 to C. Dowling Company in payment of the invoice dated January 3.

23 Issued Check No. 2 for $756.35 to S. Marquis Company in payment of the invoice dated January 13.

24 Issued Check No. 3 for $695.70 to C. Dowling Company in payment of the invoice dated January 9.

25 Issued Check No. 4 for $372.80 to R. Crowley Company in payment of the invoice dated January 5.

26 Issued Check No. 5 for $801.12 to S. Marquis Company in payment of the invoice dated January 16.

28 Issued Check No. 6 for $577.16 to R. Crowley Company in payment of the invoice dated January 8.

30 Issued Check No. 7 for $412.20 to R. Crowley Company in payment of the invoice dated January 10.

CHECKPOINT

57-3 (d)
Total = 4,521.70

d. Find the total cash paid for the month by footing the Amount of Check column in the cash payments journal. Check your footing, write the final total, double rule the column, write the word *Total* in the Paid To column, and enter the date.

e. Prove the balance at the end of the month in each creditor account. Show all footings.

f. Prepare a schedule of accounts payable as of January 31.

USING A PURCHASES JOURNAL, A CASH PAYMENTS JOURNAL, AND AN ACCOUNTS PAYABLE LEDGER

APPLIED MATH PREVIEW

Copy and complete these problems.

1. $ 3,771.27	2. $ 5,136.90	3. $ 7,299.04
- 1,639.81	+ 1,039.06	- 6,301.99
- 1,045.12	+ 795.18	- 712.77
+ 2,776.18	- 4,172.12	+ 5,096.88

GOALS

1. To practice using the purchases journal, the cash payments journal, and the accounts payable ledger.
2. To learn how accounts payable records are kept with a computer.

UNDERSTANDING THE JOB

You have learned to use three records to enter transactions with creditors from whom you buy merchandise on credit. The three records are

1. The *purchases journal*, in which you record all approved invoices.
2. The *cash payments journal*, in which you record all cash payments to creditors.
3. The *accounts payable ledger*, in which you keep the creditor accounts. Credits to these creditor accounts are posted from the purchases journal. Debits to these accounts are posted from the cash payments journal.

Illustration 58A shows the flow of data for these three records.

In this job, you will use all three records. You will be posting from both the purchases journal and the cash payments journal to the creditor accounts. *Remember:* Postings must be made each day.

Illustration 58A How purchase invoices and cash payments are recorded

Check Stubs	Approved Purchase Invoices
recorded in	recorded in
Cash Payments Journal	Purchases Journal
posted to	posted to
Debit	Credit

Accounts Payable Ledger
(Creditor Accounts)

SAMPLE PROBLEM

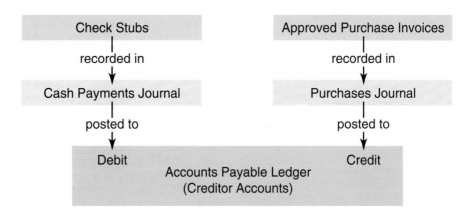

You are an accounts payable clerk for Walzer Company. During June, you recorded the following transactions:

June 5 Received Purchase Invoice No. 477 from P. Parker Company, dated June 3, for $463.89.

   9 Received Purchase Invoice No. 482 from P. Parker Company, dated June 6, for $704.60.

13 Issued Check No. 1 for $463.89 to P. Parker Company in payment of the invoice dated June 3.

16 Issued Check No. 2 for $704.60 to P. Parker Company in payment of the invoice dated June 6.

27 Received Purchase Invoice No. 499 from P. Parker Company, dated June 24, for $615.95.

Illustration 58B (page 511) shows how you recorded these transactions in the two journals and then posted to the creditor account. Here are the steps that you followed:

STEP 1 ▶ *Record the transactions in the proper journals.*

When you received an approved purchase invoice or a check stub, you decided in which journal you should record it. You recorded the purchase invoices in the purchases journal and the check stubs in the cash payments journal.

STEP 2 ▶ **Post daily to the creditor account(s).**

After you recorded each transaction in the proper journal, you posted each transaction to the creditor account. It is important to post daily so that creditor account balances are up-to-date. Post in the order of the transactions.

Post in the order of transactions.

▲▲▲▲▲
T I P
▼▼▼▼▼

STEP 3 ▶ **Total and rule each journal.**

At the end of the month, you footed, totaled, and ruled the purchases and cash payments journals.

STEP 4 ▶ **Check the account balance(s).**

At the end of the month, you verified the running balance of the account by footing the Debit and Credit columns. You subtracted the Debit total from the Credit total and compared that amount to the balance in the account.

Illustration 58B
Recording purchases and
cash payments in two
journals and a creditor
account

PURCHASES JOURNAL — PAGE 1

	DATE		CREDITOR'S NAME	INVOICE NO.	DATE OF INVOICE	POST. REF.	AMOUNT	
1	19-- June	5	P. Parker Company	477	June 3	550	4 6 3 89	1
2		9	P. Parker Company	482	6	550	7 0 4 60	2
3		27	P. Parker Company	499	24	550	6 1 5 95	3
4		30	Total				1 7 8 4 44	4

CASH PAYMENTS JOURNAL — PAGE 1

	DATE		PAID TO	FOR	CHECK NO.	POST. REF.	AMOUNT OF CHECK	
1	19-- June	13	P. Parker Co.	Invoice, 6/3	1	550	4 6 3 89	1
2		16	P. Parker Co.	Invoice, 6/6	2	550	7 0 4 60	2
3		30	Total				1 1 6 8 49	3

NAME **P. Parker Company** — ACCOUNT NO. **550**

ADDRESS **1013 Henson St., Las Vegas, NV 89107-6793** — TERMS **10 days**

DATE		ITEM		POST. REF.	DEBIT	CREDIT	BALANCE
19-- June	3	Invoice #477		P1		4 6 3 89	4 6 3 89
	6	Invoice #482		P1		7 0 4 60	1 1 6 8 49
	13	Check #1		CP1	4 6 3 89		7 0 4 60
	16	Check #2	1,784.44	CP1	7 0 4 60		———
	24	Invoice #499	-1,168.49	P1		6 1 5 95	6 1 5 95
			615.95		1 1 6 8 49	1 7 8 4 44	

STEP 5 ▶ *Prepare a schedule of accounts payable.*

You did not prepare a schedule of accounts payable in this problem because there is only one creditor account. You would usually do this as your final step.

*U*SING THE COMPUTER

The computer can be a useful tool to assist the accounts payable clerk in his or her job. Illustration 58C shows a purchases menu.

The clerk would have already used menu item 1, APPROVE PURCHASE INVOICES, before recording an invoice in the creditor accounts. In order to record in the creditor accounts, the clerk will use menu item 2, POST PURCHASE INVOICES. The computer will then post automatically to the correct creditor account.

Illustration 58C
Purchases menu

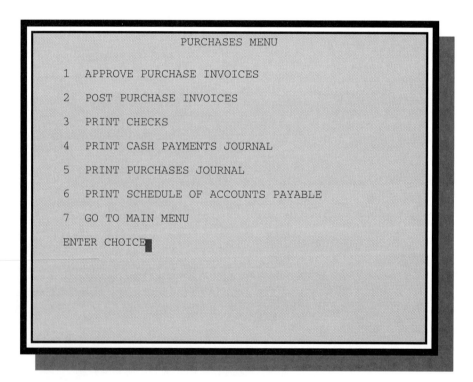

```
                        PURCHASES MENU


        1   APPROVE PURCHASE INVOICES

        2   POST PURCHASE INVOICES

        3   PRINT CHECKS

        4   PRINT CASH PAYMENTS JOURNAL

        5   PRINT PURCHASES JOURNAL

        6   PRINT SCHEDULE OF ACCOUNTS PAYABLE

        7   GO TO MAIN MENU

        ENTER CHOICE
```

In a computerized, or automated, accounts payable system, journals are not prepared directly. If a journal is needed, the computer will print the data from the purchase invoices or the check stubs by date. Using menu items 4 and 5 can get this job done.

No additional work is needed to prepare a schedule of accounts payable. The computer will respond to menu item 6, PRINT SCHEDULE OF ACCOUNTS PAYABLE, by printing out the schedule.

A computer can also print checks to pay invoices. By selecting menu item 3, PRINT CHECKS, and inserting check forms into the printer, a check such as the one shown in Illustration 58D will be prepared. The check is a voucher check, since it has the explanation of the check attached.

Accuracy in entering data is vital when a computer is used to process accounts payable. A single error in entering an invoice quantity, for example, will cause errors in every other menu item. The creditor account, journals, check, and schedule of accounts payable will all be incorrect.

Illustration 58D Check to creditor printed by computer

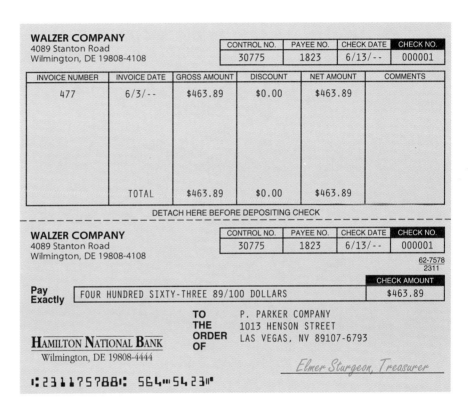

WALZER COMPANY
4089 Stanton Road
Wilmington, DE 19808-4108

	CONTROL NO.	PAYEE NO.	CHECK DATE	CHECK NO.
	30775	1823	6/13/--	000001

INVOICE NUMBER	INVOICE DATE	GROSS AMOUNT	DISCOUNT	NET AMOUNT	COMMENTS
477	6/3/--	$463.89	$0.00	$463.89	
	TOTAL	$463.89	$0.00	$463.89	

DETACH HERE BEFORE DEPOSITING CHECK

WALZER COMPANY
4089 Stanton Road
Wilmington, DE 19808-4108

	CONTROL NO.	PAYEE NO.	CHECK DATE	CHECK NO.
	30775	1823	6/13/--	000001

62-7578
2311

	CHECK AMOUNT
Pay Exactly FOUR HUNDRED SIXTY-THREE 89/100 DOLLARS	$463.89

TO THE ORDER OF
P. PARKER COMPANY
1013 HENSON STREET
LAS VEGAS, NV 89107-6793

HAMILTON NATIONAL BANK
Wilmington, DE 19808-4444

Elmer Sturgeon, Treasurer

⑆231175788⑆ 564⑈5423⑈

BUILDING YOUR BUSINESS VOCABULARY

On a sheet of paper, write the headings **Statement Number** and **Words**. Next, choose the words that match the statements. Write each word you choose next to the statement number it matches. Be careful; not all the words listed should be used.

Statements	Words
1. The column used to record an increase in a creditor account	accounts payable ledger
	accounts receivable ledger
2. A list of programs	
3. A group of creditor accounts	cash payments journal
4. A check with a special stub attached	credit
5. The column used to record a decrease in a creditor account	creditors
	debit
6. A record of cash payments	menu
7. People or businesses to whom money is owed	post
	purchases journal
8. A record of purchases on account	voucher check

PROBLEM SOLVING MODEL FOR: *Using a Purchases Journal, a Cash Payments Journal, and an Accounts Payable Ledger*

STEP 1 ▶ *Record the transactions in the proper journals.*

STEP 2 ▶ *Post daily to the creditor account(s).*

STEP 3 ▶ *Total and rule each journal.*

STEP 4 ▶ *Check the account balance(s).*

STEP 5 ▶ *Prepare a schedule of accounts payable.*

APPLICATION PROBLEMS

PROBLEM 58-1 ▶ You are an accounts payable clerk for the Wadleigh Tool Company.

Directions

a. Open a purchases journal and a cash payments journal for September. Number each journal page 1.
b. Record the following transactions. You must decide if each transaction is to be recorded in the purchases journal or the cash payments journal.

Sept. 5 Received Purchase Invoice No. 517, dated September 4, from J. Winger Company, for $906.45.

10 Received Purchase Invoice No. 519, dated September 9, from J. Winger Company, for $711.80.

13 Received Purchase Invoice No. 972, dated September 12, from W. Bellerive Company, for $375.85.

CHECKPOINT ✔

58-1 (c)
Purchases journal total =
$3,826.50

14 Issued Check No. 1 for $906.45 to J. Winger Company in payment of the invoice dated September 4.

19 Issued Check No. 2 for $711.80 to J. Winger Company in payment of the invoice dated September 9.

22 Received Purchase Invoice No. 136, dated September 20, from S. Veilleux Company, for $581.70.

25 Received Purchase Invoice No. 979, dated September 23, from W. Bellerive Company, for $209.60.

27 Issued Check No. 3 for $375.85 to W. Bellerive Company in payment of the invoice dated September 12.

29 Received Purchase Invoice No. 144, dated September 27, from S. Veilleux Company, for $1,041.10.

30 Issued Check No. 4 for $581.70 to S. Veilleux Company in payment of the invoice dated September 20.

c. Foot, total, and rule the journals.

PROBLEM **58-2** ▶ You are an accounts payable clerk for Rigby Storage Company.

AUTOMATED

Directions

a. Open a purchases journal and a cash payments journal for May. Number each journal page 1.

b. Open accounts for the following creditors:

Creditor	Address	Account No.	Terms
P. Choates Company	496 Morton Avenue Des Moines, IA 50313-7121	800	10 days
L. Eliot Company	375 NE Long Street Topeka, KS 66607-8055	801	20 days
S. Parzuch Company	59 Ridge Road Richmond, VA 23229-7582	802	15 days

c. Record the following transactions. You must decide if each transaction is to be recorded in the purchases journal or the cash payments journal. Post daily to the creditor accounts.

May 5 Received Purchase Invoice No. 55, dated May 3, from P. Choates Company, for $311.76.

7 Received Purchase Invoice No. 97, dated May 5, from S. Parzuch Company, for $585.12.

12 Received Purchase Invoice No. 105, dated May 9, from L. Eliot Company, for $721.05.

13 Issued Check No. 1 for $311.76 to P. Choates Company in payment of the invoice dated May 3.

18 Received Purchase Invoice No. 59, dated May 17, from P. Choates Company, for $1,041.95.

19 Received Purchase Invoice No. 112, dated May 18, from S. Parzuch Company, for $1,277.19.

20 Issued Check No. 2 for $585.12 to S. Parzuch Company in payment of the invoice dated May 5.

23 Received Purchase Invoice No. 137, dated May 21, from L. Eliot Company, for $971.37.

27 Issued Check No. 3 for $1,041.95 to P. Choates Company in payment of the invoice dated May 17.

29 Issued Check No. 4 for $721.05 to L. Eliot Company in payment of the invoice dated May 9.

31 Received Purchase Invoice No. 141, dated May 30, from S. Parzuch Company, for $609.27.

CHECKPOINT

58-2 (f)
Total = $2,857.83

d. Foot, total, and rule the journals.

e. Prove the balance at the end of the month in each account. Show all footings.

f. Prepare a schedule of accounts payable as of May 31.

PROBLEM **58-3** ▶ You are an accounts payable clerk for Marshall Software Company.

AUTOMATED

Directions

a. Open a purchases journal and a cash payments journal for June. Number each journal page 1.

b. Open accounts for the following creditors:

Creditor	Address	Account No.	Terms
N. Boyle Company	16 Circle Drive Cleveland, OH 44106-2902	722	20 days
O. Newfield Company	746 Oakwood Drive Charlotte, NC 28205-3746	723	10 days
R. Van Meer Company	333 Maple Street Charleston, SC 29406-1333	724	15 days

c. Record the following transactions. You must decide if each transaction is to be recorded in the purchases journal or the cash payments journal. Post daily to the creditor accounts.

June   4 Received Purchase Invoice No. 94, dated June 2, from O. Newfield Company, for $811.36.

5 Received Purchase Invoice No. 361, dated June 3, from N. Boyle Company, for $392.07.

8 Received Purchase Invoice No. 365, dated June 5, from N. Boyle Company, for $516.11.

11 Received Purchase Invoice No. 99, dated June 9, from O. Newfield Company, for $1,027.95.

12 Issued Check No. 1 for $811.36 to O. Newfield Company in payment of the invoice dated June 2.

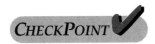

58-3 (f)
Total = $1,113.62

15 Received Purchase Invoice No. 411, dated June 11, from R. Van Meer Company, for $879.31.

19 Issued Check No. 2 for $1,027.95 to O. Newfield Company in payment of the invoice dated June 9.

23 Issued Check No. 3 for $392.07 to N. Boyle Company in payment of the invoice dated June 3.

25 Received Purchase Invoice No. 435, dated June 24, from R. Van Meer Company, for $413.67.

25 Issued Check No. 4 for $516.11 to N. Boyle Company in payment of the invoice dated June 5.

26 Issued Check No. 5 for $879.31 to R. Van Meer Company in payment of the invoice dated June 11.

29 Received Purchase Invoice No. 113, dated June 28, from O. Newfield Company, for $699.95.

d. Foot, total, and rule the journals.
e. Prove the balance at the end of the month in each account. Show all footings.
f. Prepare a schedule of accounts payable as of June 30.

Problem 58-4 may be found in the Working Papers.

JOB **59** ► USING A PURCHASES RETURNS AND ALLOWANCES JOURNAL AND AN ACCOUNTS PAYABLE LEDGER

APPLIED MATH PREVIEW

Copy and complete the following problems.

1. $ 6,179.44	2. $ 599.74	3. $ 1,577.26
- 1,496.89	- 46.87	+ 2,014.91
- 3,199.05	- 39.95	- 103.80
+ 2,172.18	- 19.83	- 1,577.26

BUSINESS TERMS PREVIEW

• **Debit memo** • **Purchases returns and allowances journal** •

GOALS

1. To learn how to record credit memos received from creditors in a purchases returns and allowances journal.
2. To learn how to post from the purchases returns and allowances journal to the accounts payable ledger.
3. To learn how to file credit memos.

𝒰NDERSTANDING THE JOB

KEY Terms

Debit memo. A form used by the buyer to notify a creditor of a return or an allowance.

▲▲▲▲▲
TIP
▼▼▼▼▼

Debit a creditor account for returns and allowances.

You have learned that purchase invoices are recorded in a purchases journal and posted to the Credit column of a creditor account. You have also learned that cash payments are recorded in a cash payments journal and posted to the Debit column of a creditor account. A third transaction with a creditor results from a return of merchandise or an incorrect charge or shortage on an invoice.

When you return merchandise or request an allowance because of an overcharge or a shortage, you may notify the creditor in writing. To do this, you may use a form called a **debit memo** to notify the creditor. Illustration 59A (page 519) shows a debit memo issued by the buyer (Bartlett Appliance Store) to the creditor (D. Phillips Company).

The form is called a debit memo because it tells the creditor that his or her account will be debited. Returns and allowances are recorded in the Debit column of a creditor account.

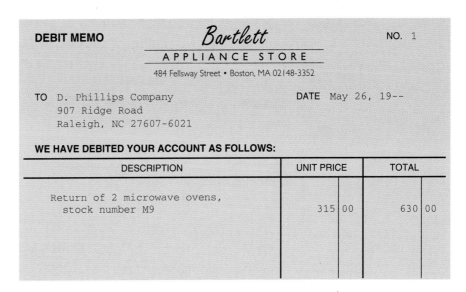

The following transcribes the content of the debit memo illustration:

DEBIT MEMO

Bartlett

APPLIANCE STORE

484 Fellsway Street • Boston, MA 02148-3352

NO. 1

TO D. Phillips Company
    907 Ridge Road
    Raleigh, NC 27607-6021

DATE May 26, 19--

WE HAVE DEBITED YOUR ACCOUNT AS FOLLOWS:

DESCRIPTION	UNIT PRICE	TOTAL
Return of 2 microwave ovens, stock number M9	315 00	630 00

Illustration 59B shows all of the transactions that affect a creditor account. Notice in Illustration 59B that returns and allowances are recorded from either a debit memo or a credit memo.

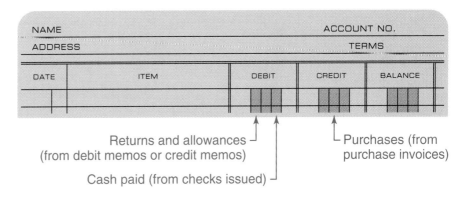

NAME				ACCOUNT NO.	
ADDRESS				TERMS	
DATE	ITEM	DEBIT	CREDIT	BALANCE	

Returns and allowances ┘
(from debit memos or credit memos)

└ Purchases (from purchase invoices)

Cash paid (from checks issued) ┘

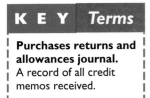

TIP

Debit memo prepared by buyer.
Credit memo prepared by seller.

K E Y Terms

Purchases returns and allowances journal.
A record of all credit memos received.

You learned about credit memos in Job 47. A debit memo is issued by the buyer; the credit memo is issued by the seller after receiving the debit memo. Most buyers do not record a return or an allowance until after receiving the credit memo from the seller. Illustration 59C shows the credit memo that Bartlett Appliance Store received from D. Phillips Company in response to its debit memo.

Bartlett Appliance Store will record this credit memo in a **purchases returns and allowances journal**. This journal is used to record all credit memos received. Illustration 59C shows how the credit memo is recorded. Here are the steps you would follow to make the entry in the purchases returns and allowances journal:

STEP 1 ▶ *Copy the date of the credit memo.*

Copy the date, May 31, in the Date column.

STEP 2 ▶ Copy the creditor's name.

Enter the name, D. Phillips Company, in the Creditor's Name column.

STEP 3 ▶ Copy the credit memo number.

Enter the credit memo number, 17, in the Credit Memo No. column.

STEP 4 ▶ Enter the amount.

Enter the total amount, $630.00, in the Amount column of the purchases returns and allowances journal.

Illustration 59C
Recording a credit memo
in a purchases returns
and allowances journal

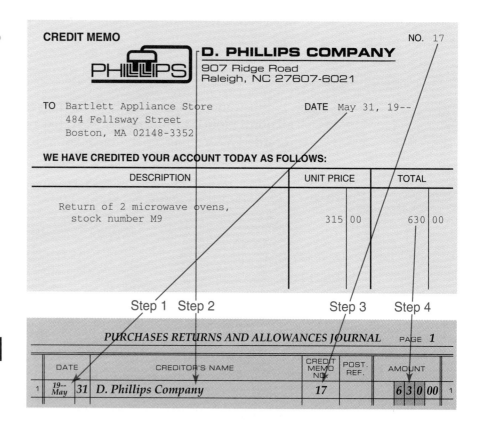

Credit
memos are
for
1. Returns
2. Overcharges
3. Shortages

After recording the credit memo in the purchases returns and allowances journal, you must now post to the D. Phillips account in the accounts payable ledger. Illustration 59D on page 521 shows how this posting is done.

Here are the steps followed:

STEP 1 ▶ Copy the date.

Enter the day, 31, in the Date column.

STEP 2 ▶ Enter the credit memo number.

Write "Credit Memo #17" in the Item column.

STEP 3 ▶ **Record the posting reference in the creditor account.**

Enter PR1 for *Purchases Returns and Allowances* Journal, page *1* in the Post. Ref. column of the account.

STEP 4 ▶ **Post the amount.**

Write the amount, $630.00, in the Debit column, since all credit memos are recorded in the Debit column.

STEP 5 ▶ **Find the new balance.**

Find the new balance by subtracting the debit amount, $630.00, from the previous balance, $6,300.00. Enter the difference, $5,670.00, in the Balance column.

STEP 6 ▶ **Enter an account number in the purchases returns and allowances journal.**

▲▲▲▲▲
Post credit
memos to
the Debit
T I P
▼▼▼▼▼
column of a creditor account.
Subtract debits from
previous balance.

Write the account number, 2101, in the Post. Ref. column of the journal to show that the posting is complete.

Illustration 59D Posting from purchases returns and allowances journal to creditor account

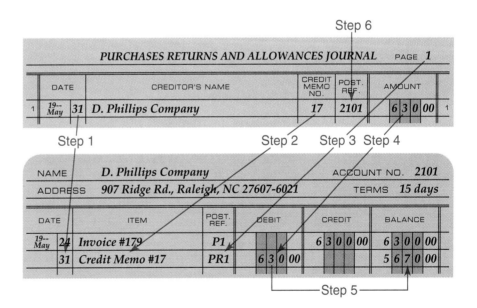

Step 6

PURCHASES RETURNS AND ALLOWANCES JOURNAL   PAGE *1*

	DATE		CREDITOR'S NAME	CREDIT MEMO NO.	POST. REF.	AMOUNT	
1	*19-- May*	*31*	*D. Phillips Company*	*17*	*2101*	*6 3 0 00*	1

Step 1   Step 2   Step 3 Step 4

NAME	*D. Phillips Company*		ACCOUNT NO.	*2101*
ADDRESS	*907 Ridge Rd., Raleigh, NC 27607-6021*		TERMS	*15 days*

DATE		ITEM	POST. REF.	DEBIT	CREDIT	BALANCE
19-- May	*24*	*Invoice #179*	*P1*		*6 3 0 0 00*	*6 3 0 0 00*
	31	*Credit Memo #17*	*PR1*	*6 3 0 00*		*5 6 7 0 00*

Step 5

SAMPLE PROBLEM

You are the accounts payable clerk for Milburn Supply Company. The creditor accounts in your accounts payable ledger already contain postings from the purchases journal. You receive the following credit memos during May:

May 16 Received Credit Memo No. 46 for $35.00 from C. Wallace Company to correct an overcharge.

17 Received Credit Memo No. 27 for $175.50 from S. Atwell Company for a shortage in the shipment of goods.

19 Received Credit Memo No. 51 for $95.10 from C. Wallace Company for damaged merchandise returned.

Illustration 59E below and on page 523 shows how these credit memos are recorded in the purchases returns and allowances journal and posted to the creditor accounts. Here are the steps you would follow:

STEP 1 ▶ **Record the credit memos in the purchases returns and allowances journal.**

Record the data from the credit memos in the purchases returns and allowances journal.

STEP 2 ▶ **File the credit memos.**

You have learned that purchase invoices are filed according to due date. A credit memo should be attached to the purchase invoice for which it was received. Credit Memo No. 27, for example, should be attached to Purchase Invoice No. 406.

Illustration 59E
Purchases returns and allowances journal and accounts payable ledger

PURCHASES RETURNS AND ALLOWANCES JOURNAL   PAGE 1

	DATE		CREDITOR'S NAME	CREDIT MEMO NO.	POST. REF.	AMOUNT	
1	19-- May	16	C. Wallace Company	46	991	3 5 00	1
2		17	S. Atwell Company	27	990	1 7 5 50	2
3		19	C. Wallace Company	51	991	9 5 10	3
4		31	Total			3 0 5 60	4

Illustration 59E
Purchases returns and
allowances journal and
accounts payable ledger
(continued)

Accounts Payable Ledger

NAME	S. Atwell Company		ACCOUNT NO.	990		
ADDRESS	379 Spruce Ave., Wilmington, DE 19804-0379			TERMS	20 days	

DATE		ITEM	POST. REF.	DEBIT	CREDIT	BALANCE
19-- May	12	Invoice #406	P1		595 00	595 00
	17	Credit Memo #27	PR1	175 50		419 50

NAME	C. Wallace Company		ACCOUNT NO.	991		
ADDRESS	1873 Grange St., Racine, WI 53405-9084			TERMS	30 days	

DATE		ITEM		POST. REF.	DEBIT	CREDIT	BALANCE
19-- May	13	Invoice #51		P1		635 00	635 00
	16	Invoice #55		P1		415 00	1050 00
	16	Cr. Memo #46	1,050.00	PR1	35 00		1015 00
	19	Cr. Memo #51 - 130.10		PR1	95 10		919 90
			919.90		130 10	1050 00	

On June 1, when Invoice No. 406 is due, it will be removed from the file folder with Credit Memo No. 27 attached. The clerk who writes the check to pay the invoice will see that $175.50 should be subtracted from $595.00 and will write a check for the difference, $419.50.

STEP 3 ▶ **Post to the creditor accounts.**

At the end of each day, post from the purchases returns and allowances journal to the creditor accounts. Notice PR1 in the Post. Ref. column of the accounts and the account numbers in the journal Post. Ref. column. New account balances were calculated after each posting.

STEP 4 ▶ **Total the purchases returns and allowances journal.**

At the end of the month, rule and foot the Amount column of the journal. Re-add the column before writing in the final total. Draw a double ruling under the final total. Write the word *Total* and the last day of the month, 31, in the correct places.

STEP 5 ▶ **Prove the account balances and prepare a schedule of accounts payable.**

Each account was footed to prove its balance. A schedule of accounts payable was prepared as of May 31. (See Illustration 59F.)

Milburn Supply Company					
Schedule of Accounts Payable					
May 31, 19--					
S. Atwell Company		4	1	9	50
C. Wallace Company		9	1	9	90
Total	1	3	3	9	40

You are now using four records to keep track of transactions with creditors from whom merchandise is bought. They are

1. The *purchases journal*, in which you record approved purchase invoices.
2. The *cash payments journal*, in which you record checks written to creditors.
3. The *purchases returns and allowances journal*, in which you record credit memos received from creditors.
4. The *accounts payable ledger*, in which you keep the creditor accounts.

The debits in the creditor accounts are posted from the cash payments journal and from the purchases returns and allowances journal. The credits in the creditor accounts are posted from the purchases journal. When you use all of the records, it is important to remember to post in the order of the dates of the transactions.

Illustration 59G shows the source documents, the journals, and the postings for creditors.

Illustration 59G
Recording check stubs,
credit memos, and
purchase invoices

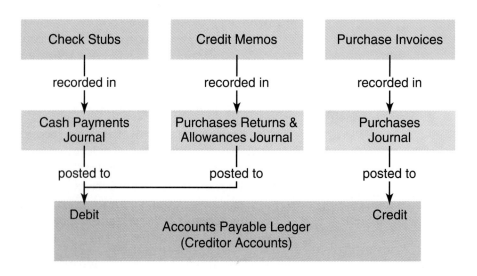

BUILDING YOUR BUSINESS VOCABULARY

On a sheet of paper, write the headings **Statement Number** and **Words**. Next, choose the words that match the statements. Write each word you choose next to the statement number it matches. Be careful; not all the words listed should be used.

Statements	Words
1. A record of cash payments	accounts payable ledger
2. A form used by the seller to show that the balance of an account has been reduced because of a return or an allowance	cash payments journal
	credit
	credit memo
3. A group of creditor accounts	creditors
4. A form used by the buyer to notify a creditor of a return or an allowance	debit
	debit memo
5. A record of all credit memos received	purchase invoice
6. A record of purchases on account	purchases journal
7. A list of creditors with the amounts owed to them	purchases returns and allowances journal
8. People or businesses to whom money is owed	schedule of accounts payable

PROBLEM SOLVING MODEL FOR: *Using a Purchases Returns and Allowances Journal and an Accounts Payable Ledger*

STEP 1 ▶ *Record the credit memos in the purchases returns and allowances journal.*

STEP 2 ▶ *File the credit memos.*

STEP 3 ▶ *Post to the creditor accounts.*

STEP 4 ▶ *Total the purchases returns and allowances journal.*

STEP 5 ▶ *Prove the account balances and prepare a schedule of accounts payable.*

APPLICATION PROBLEMS

PROBLEM 59-1 ▶ You are employed as an accounts payable clerk at the Cambridge Company.

Directions

a. Open a purchases returns and allowances journal for August. Number the journal page 5.

b. Copy the following creditor accounts. Include the amounts that have already been posted.

NAME **A. Chandler Company**   ACCOUNT NO. **501**
ADDRESS **1594 Lewis St., Charleston, WV 25301-9008**   TERMS **30 days**

DATE		ITEM	POST. REF.	DEBIT	CREDIT	BALANCE
19-- Aug.	5	Invoice #1710	P9		6 1 1 75	6 1 1 75
	10	Invoice #1713	P9		9 0 4 15	1 5 1 5 90

NAME **S. Hynes Company**   ACCOUNT NO. **502**
ADDRESS **94 Rogers Ave., Fort Smith, AR 72901-1210**   TERMS **45 days**

DATE		ITEM	POST. REF.	DEBIT	CREDIT	BALANCE
19-- Aug.	8	Invoice #2104	P9		5 8 5 63	5 8 5 63
	12	Invoice #2172	P9		8 1 0 95	1 3 9 6 58

NAME **N. Tougas Company**   ACCOUNT NO. **503**
ADDRESS **81 Bird Rd., Miami, FL 33146-4931**   TERMS **60 days**

DATE		ITEM	POST. REF.	DEBIT	CREDIT	BALANCE
19-- Aug.	3	Invoice #591	P9		4 1 2 87	4 1 2 87
	7	Invoice #599	P9		7 3 9 81	1 1 5 2 68

c. Enter the following credit memos in the purchases returns and allowances journal. Post daily to the creditor accounts.

Aug.   8   Received Credit Memo No. 55 for $35.00 from N. Tougas Company for a shortage in the shipment of goods.

     11   Received Credit Memo No. 106 for $18.75 from A. Chandler Company for damaged merchandise returned.

     13   Received Credit Memo No. 27 for $29.60 from S. Hynes Company to correct an overcharge.

     14   Received Credit Memo No. 58 for $19.75 from N. Tougas Company for damaged merchandise returned.

     17   Received Credit Memo No. 117 for $31.45 from A. Chandler Company to correct an overcharge.

     18   Received Credit Memo No. 30 for $45.00 from S. Hynes Company for a shortage in the shipment of goods.

CHECKPOINT

59-1 (e)
Total = $3,885.61

d. Foot, total, and rule the purchases returns and allowances journal. Enter the date and the word *Total*.

e. Check the balance of each creditor account, and prepare a schedule of accounts payable as of August 31.

PROBLEM	59-2 ▶	You are employed as an accounts payable clerk at the Morgan Toy Store.

Directions

a. Open a purchases returns and allowances journal for December. Number the journal page 8.

b. Copy the following creditor accounts. Include the amounts that have already been posted.

NAME	T. Dupuis Company				ACCOUNT NO.	**471**	
ADDRESS	103 Kenmore Ave., Joliet, IL 60433-4920				TERMS	**30 days**	

DATE		ITEM	POST. REF.	DEBIT	CREDIT	BALANCE
19-- Dec.	2	Invoice #771	P12		4 9 0 25	4 9 0 25
	9	Invoice #789	P12		6 1 3 46	1 1 0 3 71

NAME	L. Fayette Company				ACCOUNT NO.	**472**	
ADDRESS	15 Cherry St., South Bend, IN 46625-0015				TERMS	**45 days**	

DATE		ITEM	POST. REF.	DEBIT	CREDIT	BALANCE
19-- Dec.	3	Invoice #512	P12		7 1 2 37	7 1 2 37
	8	Invoice #522	P12		2 6 5 48	9 7 7 85

NAME	M. Lannone Company				ACCOUNT NO.	**473**	
ADDRESS	99 Beech St., Pueblo, CO 81003-5011				TERMS	**90 days**	

DATE		ITEM	POST. REF.	DEBIT	CREDIT	BALANCE
19-- Dec.	10	Invoice #719	P12		1 1 2 0 45	1 1 2 0 45
	12	Invoice #726	P12		9 1 3 76	2 0 3 4 21

c. Enter the following credit memos in the purchases returns and allowances journal. Post daily to the creditor accounts.

Dec. 9 Received Credit Memo No. 74 for $42.10 from L. Fayette Company for a shortage in the shipment of goods.

10 Received Credit Memo No. 14 for $57.50 from T. Dupuis Company to correct an overcharge.

12 Received Credit Memo No. 76 for $265.48 from L. Fayette Company for damaged merchandise returned.

15 Received Credit Memo No. 112 for $31.10 from M. Lannone Company for damaged merchandise returned.

16 Received Credit Memo No. 17 for $74.30 from T. Dupuis Company for a shortage in the shipment of goods.

19 Received Credit Memo No. 114 for $36.80 from M. Lannone Company to correct an overcharge.

59-2 (e)
Total = $3,608.49

d. Foot, total, and rule the purchases returns and allowances journal.
e. Check the balance of each creditor account, and prepare a schedule of accounts payable.

Problem 59-3 may be found in the Working Papers.

12

Reinforcement
Activities

You are one of two accounts payable clerks at Bethorn Wholesale Company. You noticed in checking through your journals that you owed A. Taylor Company $900.00 and had received a credit memo for $70.00. Yet, when it came time to pay A. Taylor Company, a check was written for $900.00. Your co-worker is responsible for posting from the journals to the creditor accounts. The $70.00 credit memo had never been posted, even though the Post. Ref. column of the journal showed the A. Taylor Company account number. When you asked your co-worker about this, here is the answer you received: "I always write the account number when I record the transaction in the journal. It saves time."

What would you say to your co-worker to explain why the procedure followed is wrong?

PROFESSIONAL BUSINESS ETHICS

You are an accounts payable clerk. Another accounts payable clerk works alongside you. The other clerk is not a friend, but just a co-worker. You notice unusual attendance habits by the other clerk. The clerk is 5 to 10 minutes late each morning, 5 to 10 minutes late returning from lunch every day, and leaves work about 10 minutes early each afternoon.

Your company is small, so employees fill out time slips by hand every Friday for the week. You just happen to notice that your co-worker filled out this week's form for a full 40 hours. No lateness was recorded.
You wonder what, if anything, you should do about this situation. Write some of the possible things that you might do. Then, write what you would do.

APPLIED COMMUNICATIONS

You are the accounts payable clerk for Waltham Company. You recently received a shipment of 10 clock-radios, Stock No. CR 12, @ $45.95 each, from T. Melrose Company. One of the 10 is damaged, so you want to return the item and ask for a credit memo from T. Melrose Company. Your company does not use debit memos, so a letter is needed. Write a letter to T. Melrose Company asking for the credit memo. Keep your letter to one page.

The following ad appears in the newspaper:

Accounts Payable

Organized and detail-oriented individual needed to handle all invoicing and check writing responsibilities for a multi-company structure. For this position, you must be hard working and willing to work with our computerized system.

1. What four characteristics must the person who applies for this position possess?
2. Will the person who does this job record in journals? Explain.
3. What do you think is meant by a multicompany structure?
4. Is this job an entry-level job? Explain.

GLOBAL BUSINESS: INTERNATIONAL WEIGHTS AND MEASURES

As an accounts payable clerk for a large hardware wholesaler, you see many purchase invoices from vendors in other countries. The weights and measures of those items are usually given in the metric system, which is used by most industrial countries other than the United States. The metric system is based on a decimal system that is similar to one we use for U.S. currency.

Your company's stock records, however, use the U.S. system of weights and measures. Your boss has asked you to convert the metric quantities shown on the purchase invoices. You use the following table and round to the nearest whole number.

To Change	To	Multiply By
kilograms	pounds	2.205
meters	inches	39.37
centimeters	inches	0.39
millimeters	inches	0.039
liter (dry)	quarts (dry)	0.908
liter (liquid)	quarts (liquid)	1.057

To convert, take the metric weight or measure and multiply by the number shown. For example, 50 kilograms x 2.205 = 110.25 pounds, rounded to 110 pounds.

An International Weights and Measures Activity can be found in the Working Papers.

On a sheet of paper, write the headings **Statement Number** and **Words**. Next, choose the words that best complete the statements. Write each word you choose next to the statement number it completes. Be careful; not all the words listed should be used.

Statements	Words
1. Credit memos are recorded in the _____ .	accounts payable ledger
2. Posting from any journal to creditor accounts is done _____ .	balance
	cash payments journal
3. On a schedule of accounts payable, the _____ of a creditor account is listed.	creditors
	daily
4. To record checks written to creditors, use the _____ .	debit memo
	due date
5. Credit memos should be attached to the related _____ .	purchase invoice
	purchase on account
6. Creditor accounts are found in the _____ .	purchases journal
7. Approved purchase invoices are filed by their _____ .	purchases returns and allowances journal
8. A form that can be used to request a reduction in your account from a creditor is the _____ .	schedule of accounts payable
9. When you buy merchandise from a creditor with 30 days to pay, you are making (a, an) _____ .	

You are employed as an accounts payable clerk for the W. Joyce Company.

Directions

a. Open a purchases journal, a cash payments journal, and a purchases returns and allowances journal. Number each journal page 1.

b. Open accounts for creditors as follows:

Creditor	Address	Account No.	Terms
E. Cronin Company	613 Division Street Baltimore, MD 21207-1613	2101	10 days
K. Delorme Company	276 Emerson Street Erie, PA 16502-3186	2102	20 days
R. Watley Company	12357 Bell Road Scottsdale, AZ 85351-2570	2103	15 days

c. Record the following transactions. You must decide in which of the three journals to record each transaction. As soon as you have recorded in the journal, post *immediately* to the creditor account.

June   3   Received Purchase Invoice No. 109, dated June 1, from K. Delorme Company, for $410.90.

           5   Received Purchase Invoice No. 46, dated June 3, from E. Cronin Company, for $475.50.

           6   Received Purchase Invoice No. 97, dated June 5, from R. Watley Company, for $1,277.40.

           7   Received Credit Memo No. 12 for $18.00 from E. Cronin Company for damaged merchandise returned on Invoice No. 46.

           9   Received Purchase Invoice No. 114, dated June 7, from K. Delorme Company, for $595.60.

        10   Received Credit Memo No. 13 for $151.35 from R. Watley Company for damaged merchandise returned on Invoice No. 97.

        11   Received Credit Memo No. 36 for $19.05 from K. Delorme Company to correct an overcharge on Invoice No. 114.

        13   Issued Check No. 1 for $457.50 to E. Cronin Company in payment of the balance of the invoice dated June 3.

        20   Issued Check No. 2 for $1,126.05 to R. Watley Company in payment of the balance of the invoice dated June 5.

        20   Received Purchase Invoice No. 57, dated June 18, from E. Cronin Company, for $912.87.

        21   Issued Check No. 3 for $410.90 to K. Delorme Company in payment of the invoice dated June 1.

        22   Received Credit Memo No. 15 for $13.95 from E. Cronin Company for a shortage in the shipment of goods on Invoice No. 57.

        26   Received Purchase Invoice No. 105, dated June 24, from R. Watley Company, for $811.75.

        27   Issued Check No. 4 for $576.55 to K. Delorme Company in payment of the balance of the invoice dated June 7.

        28   Issued Check No. 5 for $898.92 to E. Cronin Company in payment of the balance of the invoice dated June 18.

        30   Received Purchase Invoice No. 112, dated June 29, from R. Watley Company, for $295.10.

        30   Received Purchase Invoice No. 151, dated June 30, from K. Delorme Company, for $1,045.10.

CHECKPOINT ✔

(f)
Total = $2,151.95

d. Foot, total and rule the journals.
e. Prove the last balance in each account. Show all footings in the accounts.
f. Prepare a schedule of accounts payable as of June 30.

This activity may be found in the Working Papers.

COMPREHENSIVE PROJECT 4

Comprehensive Project 4 has been designed to reinforce major concepts of this and previous chapters. The Comprehensive Project is found in the Working Papers.

C H A P T E R

13

Record Keeping for Small Businesses

*I*f you were someday to own and operate a small business, such as a computer repair shop, you would receive money from your customers for repairing their computers. You would also have expenses. Expenses include such things as rent for the building in which your shop is located, the telephone bill, the electric bill, truck gas and repairs, and parts and supplies.

In Chapter 13, you will learn how to record income in a cash receipts journal and expenses in a cash payments journal. You will also learn about posting from both journals to a general ledger and about preparing a trial balance.

JOB **60** ▶ ## RECORDING INCOME IN A CASH RECEIPTS JOURNAL

APPLIED MATH PREVIEW

Copy and complete the following problems.

1. $ 1,517.50	2. $ 3,127.85	3. $ 4,075.50	4. $ 2,117.19
209.95	1,129.75	2,195.45	101.67
1,635.71	377.15	3,160.10	3,292.92
412.99	87.95	8,177.99	6,483.83
+ 1,037.16	+ 5,081.21	+ 4,059.86	+ 5,754.01

BUSINESS TERMS PREVIEW

• **Double-entry system** • **Income** • **Merchandising business** •
• **Service business** •

GOALS

1. To learn how a service business earns income.
2. To learn how to record this income in a cash receipts journal.

$\mathcal{U}$NDERSTANDING THE JOB

<table>
<tr><td>

K E Y Terms

Income. Money received.

Merchandising business. One that sells a product.

Service business. One in which a service for a customer is performed.

</td>
<td>

If you owned your own small business, such as a computer repair shop, the money that you would receive is called **income**. If your small business sold a product, such as computers, you would own a **merchandising business**. But, since your business only repairs computers, it is called a **service business**. In this job, you will learn how to record income for a service business.

In Job 45, you learned how to record cash received for sales of merchandise using a cash receipts journal. In this job, you will learn how to record cash received for services that you perform. You will record cash received for services in a cash receipts journal, also.

Illustration 60A shows a completed cash receipts journal for a service business.

</td>
</tr>
</table>

Illustration 60A A cash receipts journal for a service business

CASH RECEIPTS JOURNAL   PAGE 1

	DATE		ACCOUNT TITLE	DOC. NO.	POST. REF.	INCOME CREDIT		CASH DEBIT	BANK DEPOSITS	
						WOOD FENCE	METAL FENCE			
1	19--Mar.	1	√	T1	√	2 9 5 00	2 3 0 00	5 2 5 00	5 2 5 00	1
2		8	√	T8	√		3 6 5 00	3 6 5 00	3 6 5 00	2
3		15	√	T15	√		1 0 4 5 00	1 0 4 5 00		3
4		17	√	T17	√	9 7 5 00		9 7 5 00	2 0 2 0 00	4
5		29	√	T29	√	7 1 5 00	3 2 0 00	1 0 3 5 00	1 0 3 5 00	5
6		31	Totals			1 9 8 5 00	1 9 6 0 00	3 9 4 5 00	3 9 4 5 00	6

$\mathcal{S}$AMPLE PROBLEM

Bill Auclair owns and operates Bill's Fence Company. The company installs and repairs wood and metal fences. Bill prepares an invoice for each customer and keeps a duplicate for his records. Payment is made by each customer at the time the service is performed; that is, when the fence is put up.

Bill separates income from wood fences and income from metal fences in order to know how much is received from each type of fence. Entries are recorded for each type of income in the cash receipts journal.

At the end of each day, Bill separates his duplicate invoices. He puts the invoices from the sales of wood fences into one stack. He puts the invoices from the sales of metal fences into another stack. Bill uses a calculator with a printer. He adds the amounts in the stack of invoices for wood fences, and then adds the amounts in the stack of invoices for metal fences. On March 1, Bill makes the following calculations while adding the amounts of the duplicate invoices:

Income From	Amount	Income From	Amount
Wood fence	$100.00	Metal fence	$125.00
Wood fence	195.00	Metal fence	105.00
Totals	$295.00		$230.00

The printout or tape from the calculator will be Bill's source document for the journal entry. On the calculator tape, he writes *T* (for *tape*) and *1* (for March *1*, the date of the sales). Bill also writes the words *Wood fence* next to the total of wood fence sales and the words *Metal fence* next to the total of metal fence sales. See Illustration 60B.

Illustration 60B
Calculator tape for
March 1

```
T1
                    100.00+
                    195.00+
Wood fence          295.00*+


                    125.00+
                    105.00+
Metal fence         230.00*+
```

Total sales for March are listed below:

Date	Income From	Amount
March 1	Wood fence	$ 295.00
	Metal fence	230.00
8	Metal fence	365.00
15	Metal fence	1,045.00
17	Wood fence	975.00
29	Wood fence	715.00
	Metal fence	320.00

Bank deposits were made on March 1, 8, 17, and 29.

Here is how the income was recorded in the cash receipts journal:

STEP 1 ▶ *Enter the first calculator tape in the journal.*

From the calculator tape, the date, tape number, and amount were recorded.

Special amount columns are provided for all accounts in this transaction. Therefore, a check mark is placed in the Account Title column to show that no account title needs to be written. A check mark is also placed in the Post. Ref. column. The check mark in the Post. Ref. column will be explained in Job 61.

To enter the amounts in the correct columns, examine the calculator tape to determine the type of income. Because two types of fences were installed on March 1, both Income Credit columns were used. *Income is always recorded as a credit.*

The first total on Tape T1 is marked *Wood fence.* The first total, $295.00, was entered in the Wood Fence column under Income Credit. The second total on Tape T1 is marked *Metal fence.* The second total, $230.00, was entered in the Metal Fence column.

The journal being used is part of a **double-entry system**. In a double-entry system, every transaction has at least one debit and one credit. For Tape T1, the individual amounts of the sales were entered in the Income Credit columns. The total of $295.00 + $230.00, or $525.00, was entered again in (extended into) the Cash Debit column. *Cash received is always recorded as a debit.* In a double-entry system, debits must always equal credits.

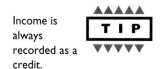

Income is always recorded as a credit.

KEY Terms

Double-entry system. Each transaction has at least one debit and one credit.

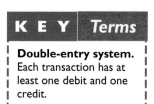

Cash received is always recorded as a debit.

STEP 2 ▶ *Enter the bank deposits.*

Bill Auclair deposits all of the money that he receives in his checking account at the bank. He goes to the bank every few days to make a deposit. Each time a deposit is made, he records the amount of the deposit in the Bank Deposits column of the cash receipts journal. The March 1 receipts of $525.00 were deposited on that same day, so $525.00 was entered in the Bank Deposits column.

STEP 3 ▶ *Record the remaining calculator tapes and bank deposits in the journal.*

The income on March 8, $365.00, was from a metal fence, so it was entered in the journal in the Metal Fence column under Income Credit and in the Cash Debit column. A bank deposit was made on that date, so $365.00 was entered in the Bank Deposits column.

Notice that no bank deposit was made on March 15, but one was made on March 17 for the total of the receipts from March 15 and 17. So, the amounts of $1,045.00 on March 15 and $975.00 on March 17 were added to get a total of $2,020.00, which was entered in the Bank Deposits column on March 17.

STEP 4 ▶ *Total and rule the journal.*

Rule and foot all four money columns. Check the totals as shown on page 538:

1. Since debits must equal credits, add the two Income Credit column totals, Wood Fence and Metal Fence. The total of these columns should equal the Cash Debit column total.

Income, Wood Fence	$ 1,985.00
Income, Metal Fence	+ 1,960.00
Cash Debit	$ 3,945.00

2. Since all cash received was deposited in the bank, the total of the Cash Debit column should equal the total of the Bank Deposits column.

After the footings have been checked, enter the final totals and double rule each money column. Date the totals as of the last day of the month, and write the word *Totals* in the Account Title column.

BUILDING YOUR BUSINESS VOCABULARY

On a sheet of paper, write the headings **Statement Number** and **Words**. Next, choose the words that match the statements. Write each word you choose next to the statement number it matches. Be careful; not all the words listed should be used.

Statements	Words
1. How income is always recorded	cash receipts journal
2. Money received from the sale of merchandise or services	credit
	debit
3. A record of income received	double-entry system
4. A business that sells a product	extended
5. A system in which every transaction has at least one debit and one credit	income
	invoice
6. A business in which a service for customers is performed	merchandising business
	post
7. How cash received is always recorded	service business
8. Entered again in a second column	

PROBLEM SOLVING MODEL FOR: *Recording Income in a Cash Receipts Journal*

> **STEP 1** ▶ *Enter the first calculator tape in the journal.*
>
> **STEP 2** ▶ *Enter the bank deposits.*
>
> **STEP 3** ▶ *Record the remaining calculator tapes and bank deposits in the journal.*
>
> **STEP 4** ▶ *Total and rule the journal.*

PPLICATION PROBLEMS

PROBLEM **60-1** ▶ You are the record keeper for Wanda Stern, who owns and operates Wanda's Fence Company. Your job is to record income in the cash receipts journal. Wanda's income is earned by installing wood and metal fences.

AUTOMATED

Directions

a. Set up a cash receipts journal identical to the one shown in Illustration 60A (on page 547). Number the journal page 1.

b. Record in the cash receipts journal the following information taken from calculator tapes made by adding the duplicate invoices:

June   3 Received $655.00 for installing a wood fence, T3.

5 Received $385.00 for installing a metal fence, T5.

5 Deposited all money received from June 3 to 5 in the bank. The deposit amounted to $1,040.00. Enter this amount in the Bank Deposits column on the same line with T5.

11 Received $1,450.00: $945.00 for a wood fence and $505.00 for a metal fence, T11.

14 Received $2,110.00: $1,010.00 for wood fences and $1,100.00 for metal fences, T14.

14 Deposited all money received from June 11 to 14 in the bank. The deposit amounted to $3,560.00.

18 Received $585.75 for installing a wood fence, T18.

19 Received $1,035.50 for installing metal fences, T19.

19 Deposited all cash received from June 18 to 19 in the bank. The deposit amounted to $1,621.25.

25 Received $1,645.50: $510.75 for wood fences and $1,134.75 for metal fences, T25.

27 Received $971.85: $311.65 for a wood fence and $660.20 for a metal fence, T27.

27 Deposited all money received from June 25 to 27 in the bank. The deposit amounted to $2,617.35.

CHECKPOINT ✔

60-1 (d)
Cash Debit total =
$8,838.60

c. Rule and foot all money columns. Check the footings to be sure that the sum of the Income Credit column totals equals the total of the Cash Debit column. Check also to be sure that the total of the Cash Debit column equals the total of the Bank Deposits column.

d. Enter the final totals and double rule the money columns. Date the totals as of the last day of June, and write the word *Totals* in the proper place.

PROBLEM **60-2** ▶ You are employed by Wilma's Window Company, a business owned and operated by Wilma Paine. Wilma earns income by repairing broken windows and broken screens. It is part of your job to transfer

AUTOMATED

information from calculator tapes, made by adding duplicate sales invoices, into the cash receipts journal.

Directions

a. Open a cash receipts journal with the following headings. Number the journal page 1.

				INCOME CREDIT			
DATE	ACCOUNT TITLE	DOC. NO.	POST. REF.	WINDOWS	SCREENS	CASH DEBIT	BANK DEPOSITS

CASH RECEIPTS JOURNAL PAGE

b. Record in the cash receipts journal the following information taken from calculator tapes:

July 5 Received $17.50 for a window repair, T5.
　　 7 Received $31.10 for a window repair, T7.
　　 8 Received $9.75 for a screen repair, T8.
　　 8 Deposited all money received from July 5 to 8 in the bank. The deposit amounted to $58.35. Enter this amount in the Bank Deposits column on the same line as T8.
　　 12 Received $57.50: $46.75 for a window repair and $10.75 for a screen repair, T12.
　　 14 Received $83.45: $61.10 for a window repair and $22.35 for a screen repair, T14.
　　 15 Received $106.35: $47.25 for a window repair and $59.10 for a screen repair, T15.
　　 15 Deposited all money received from July 12 to 15 in the bank. The deposit amounted to $247.30.
　　 22 Received $94.15 for a window repair, T22.
　　 25 Received $31.75 for a window repair, T25.
　　 27 Received $45.20: $36.10 for a window repair and $9.10 for a screen repair, T27.
　　 27 Deposited all money received from July 22 to 27 in the bank. The deposit amounted to $171.10.

CHECKPOINT

60-2 (d)
Bank Deposits total = $476.75

c. Rule and foot all money columns. Check the footings to be sure that the sum of the Income Credit column totals equals the total of the Cash Debit column. Check also to be sure that the total of the Cash Debit column equals the total of the Bank Deposits column.

d. Enter the final totals and double rule the money columns. Date the totals as of the last day of July, and write the word *Totals* in the proper place.

Problem 60-3 may be found in the Working Papers.

RECORDING INCOME IN THE GENERAL LEDGER

APPLIED MATH PREVIEW

Copy and complete these problems.

1. $ 6,157.45	2. $ 47.95	3. $ 512.85	4. $ 4.55
704.19	209.21	417.90	2,177.16
371.45	1,377.18	1,046.37	308.12
218.09	659.27	9.15	119.04
+ 4,177.63	+ 2,047.76	+ 87.12	+ 2,173.62

BUSINESS TERMS PREVIEW

- Four-column ledger account • General ledger •
- Memorandum column •

GOALS

1. To learn how to post from a cash receipts journal to the general ledger.
2. To learn how to use four-column general ledger accounts.

𝒰NDERSTANDING THE JOB

KEY Terms

General ledger. A group of accounts other than customer and creditor accounts.

Four-column ledger account. A general ledger account with two balance columns.

In earlier jobs, you learned how to post from a journal to a ledger. For example, in Job 45, you posted from a cash receipts journal to customer accounts in an accounts receivable ledger.

In this job, you will learn again how to post from the cash receipts journal. However, you will be posting to a **general ledger**. A general ledger is the place where all accounts, other than those for customers and creditors, are kept.

You will also learn how to use a **four-column ledger account** in this job. Illustration 61A shows this form of account.

Illustration 61A   A four-column general ledger account

GENERAL LEDGER

ACCOUNT					BALANCE	
DATE	ITEM	POST. REF.	DEBIT	CREDIT	DEBIT	CREDIT

The first two money columns, Debit and Credit, are used in the usual way. But, while customer and creditor accounts have only one balance column, general ledger accounts have two balance columns. This is because a general ledger account can have either a debit balance or a credit balance. You will see how all of these columns are used in the Sample Problem.

SAMPLE PROBLEM

Bill Auclair's cash receipts journal and general ledger are shown in Illustration 61B (on pages 543 and 544). Here are the steps followed in posting from the cash receipts journal to the general ledger:

STEP 1 ▶ **Enter the date in the accounts.**

Date totals as of the last day of the month.

The date of the totals in the cash receipts journal is March 31. That date is entered in the Date column of each account as it is posted. Totals are always posted as of the last day of the month.

STEP 2 ▶ **Enter the posting reference in the accounts.**

Enter CR1 in the accounts.

The reference, CR1, for *c*ash *r*eceipts journal, page *1*, is entered in the Post. Ref. column of each account as it is posted.

STEP 3 ▶ **Post the totals of the journal columns to the accounts.**

Post only totals. Column headings tell where and how to post. Do not post the total of the Bank Deposits column.

To save time, only the totals of the debit and credit journal columns will be posted. The column headings in the cash receipts journal tell you where and how to post. Go to the account titled "Income, Wood Fence," and enter a *credit* of $1,985.00. Go to the account titled "Income, Metal Fence," and enter a *credit* of $1,960.00. These are both posted as credits because the column heading in the cash receipts journal is "Income Credit."

Next, go to the Cash account. The column heading in the cash receipts journal is Cash Debit. So, enter a *debit* of $3,945.00 in the Cash account.

The total of the Bank Deposits column is *not posted*. Its purpose is to help the owner of the business remember important information, such as when money was deposited in the bank. For this reason, it is called a **memorandum column**. *You never post from a memorandum column.*

STEP 4 ▶ **Figure the new balances in each account.**

After you post the total to a ledger account, figure the new balance.

All three accounts began with a zero balance, so the new balance is the same as the first amount entered. In the Cash account, since you entered a debit of $3,945.00, the balance is also a debit of $3,945.00. In each income account, you entered a credit. The balance of each income account is also a credit for that amount.

STEP 5 ▶ **Enter the posting references in the cash receipts journal.**

Enter the account number in parentheses under each journal column.

The number of each account is entered in parentheses under each column total as soon as the account has been posted and the new balance figured. Writing the number shows that the posting is complete. Since the Cash account is Account Number 110, 110 is entered as (110) under the Cash Debit column total. Since the Income, Wood Fence account is Account Number 410, 410 is entered as (410) under the Income Credit, Wood Fence column. For Income Credit, Metal Fence, (420) is entered.

Illustration 61B   Posting from the cash receipts journal to the general ledger

CASH RECEIPTS JOURNAL — PAGE 1

	DATE	ACCOUNT TITLE	DOC. NO.	POST. REF.	INCOME CREDIT WOOD FENCE	INCOME CREDIT METAL FENCE	CASH DEBIT	BANK DEPOSITS	
1	19-- Mar. 1	√	T1	√	2 95 00	2 30 00	5 25 00	5 25 00	1
2	8	√	T8	√		3 65 00	3 65 00	3 65 00	2
3	15	√	T15	√		10 45 00	10 45 00		3
4	17	√	T17	√	9 75 00		9 75 00	20 20 00	4
5	29	√	T29	√	7 15 00	3 20 00	10 35 00	10 35 00	5
6	31	Totals			19 85 00	19 60 00	39 45 00	39 45 00	6
7					(410)	(420)	(110)	(√)	7

ACCOUNT Cash — ACCOUNT NO. 110

DATE	ITEM	POST. REF.	DEBIT	CREDIT	BALANCE DEBIT	BALANCE CREDIT
19-- Mar. 31		CR1	3 9 4 5 00		3 9 4 5 00	

ACCOUNT Income, Wood Fence — ACCOUNT NO. 410

DATE	ITEM	POST. REF.	DEBIT	CREDIT	BALANCE DEBIT	BALANCE CREDIT
19-- Mar. 31		CR1		1 9 8 5 00		1 9 8 5 00

Illustration 61B   Posting
from the cash receipts
journal to the general
ledger (continued)

ACCOUNT		*Income, Metal Fence*				ACCOUNT NO.	*420*	

DATE	ITEM	POST. REF.	DEBIT	CREDIT	BALANCE	
					DEBIT	CREDIT
19-- Mar. 31		CR1		1 9 6 0 00		1 9 6 0 00

STEP 6 ▶ *See that check marks were entered for amounts not posted; add any necessary for memorandum column(s).*

A check
mark means
"do not post."

Check marks were already entered in the Post. Ref. column on each date, except on the Totals line. These check marks show that the individual amounts on March 1, 8, 15, 17, and 29 are not to be posted; they are posted as part of the March 31 total.

Now, enter a check mark under the Bank Deposits column total. This check mark is entered because a memorandum column total is not posted.

Illustration 61C (below and on page 545) shows how the balance columns of the general ledger accounts work. In this illustration, you see how postings for April's totals are made. For the Cash account, a debit of $6,150.00 is entered on April 30. To find the new balance, add the new debit to the old debit balance:

Add a new
debit to a
debit balance.

Previous debit balance	$ 3,945.00
New debit	+ 6,150.00
New debit balance	$10,095.00

For the Income, Wood Fence account, $3,150.00 is entered on April 30. To find the new balance, add the new credit to the old credit balance:

Add a new
credit to a
credit balance.

Previous credit balance	$ 1,985.00
New credit	+ 3,150.00
New credit balance	$ 5,135.00

Notice in Illustration 61C (below and on page 545) that the posting reference CR2 is entered in the accounts. Page 2 of the cash receipts journal was used in April.

Illustration 61C
General ledger accounts
with balances for two
months

					CASH RECEIPTS JOURNAL			PAGE 2	
	DATE	ACCOUNT TITLE	DOC. NO.	POST. REF.	INCOME CREDIT		CASH DEBIT	BANK DEPOSITS	
					WOOD FENCE	METAL FENCE			
6	30	Totals			3 1 5 0 00	3 0 0 0 00	6 1 5 0 00	6 1 5 0 00	6
7					(4 1 0)	(4 2 0)	(1 1 0)	(√)	7

Illustration 61C
General ledger accounts
with balances for two
months (continued)

ACCOUNT	*Cash*				ACCOUNT NO.	*110*	

DATE	ITEM	POST. REF.	DEBIT	CREDIT	BALANCE	
					DEBIT	CREDIT
19-- Mar. 31		CR1	3 9 4 5 00		3 9 4 5 00	
Apr. 30		CR2	6 1 5 0 00		10 0 9 5 00	

ACCOUNT	*Income, Wood Fence*				ACCOUNT NO.	*410*	

DATE	ITEM	POST. REF.	DEBIT	CREDIT	BALANCE	
					DEBIT	CREDIT
19-- Mar. 31		CR1		1 9 8 5 00		1 9 8 5 00
Apr. 30		CR2		3 1 5 0 00		5 1 3 5 00

ACCOUNT	*Income, Metal Fence*				ACCOUNT NO.	*420*	

DATE	ITEM	POST. REF.	DEBIT	CREDIT	BALANCE	
					DEBIT	CREDIT
19-- Mar. 31		CR1		1 9 6 0 00		1 9 6 0 00
Apr. 30		CR2		3 0 0 0 00		4 9 6 0 00

*B*UILDING YOUR BUSINESS VOCABULARY

On a sheet of paper, write the headings **Statement Number** and **Words**. Next, choose the words that match the statements. Write each word you choose next to the statement number it matches. Be careful; not all the words listed should be used.

Statements	Words
1. A group of customer accounts	accounts payable ledger
2. A group of accounts other than customer and creditor accounts	accounts receivable ledger
3. A general ledger account with two balance columns	double-entry system extend
4. A group of creditor accounts	four-column ledger account
5. Money received from the sale of merchandise or services	general ledger
6. A type of column used to remember information	income memorandum column
7. To transfer data from one record to another	post
8. A system in which every transaction has at least one debit and one credit	three-column account

PROBLEM SOLVING MODEL FOR: *Recording Income in the General Ledger*

STEP 1 ▶ **Enter the date in the accounts.**

STEP 2 ▶ **Enter the posting reference in the accounts.**

STEP 3 ▶ **Post the totals of the journal columns to the accounts.**

STEP 4 ▶ **Figure the new balances in each account.**

STEP 5 ▶ **Enter the posting references in the cash receipts journal.**

STEP 6 ▶ **See that check marks were entered for amounts not posted; add any necessary for memorandum column(s).**

APPLICATION PROBLEMS

PROBLEM | 61-1 ▶ You are the record keeper for Jeanne Lombardi, a consultant and financial manager.

Directions

a. Copy the following cash receipts journal for May, 19--:

	DATE		ACCOUNT TITLE	DOC. NO.	POST. REF.	INCOME CREDIT		CASH DEBIT	BANK DEPOSITS	
						CONSULTING	MANAGEMENT			
1	19-- May	3	√	T3	√	4 0 0 00		4 0 0 00		1
2		6	√	T6	√		7 0 0 00	7 0 0 00		2
3		7	√	T7	√	3 5 0 00		3 5 0 00	1 4 5 0 00	3
4		15	√	T15	√	5 0 0 00	6 5 0 00	1 1 5 0 00		4
5		18	√	T18	√	3 3 0 00	1 5 0 00	4 8 0 00	1 6 3 0 00	5

CASH RECEIPTS JOURNAL   PAGE **1**

b. Open the following general ledger accounts. (Allow three lines for each account.)

Cash	#110
Income, Consulting	#410
Income, Management	#420

c. Rule the money columns in the cash receipts journal and foot the columns.

d. Check the footings to see if total debits equal total credits. Also, check to see that the Cash Debit and Bank Deposits column totals are equal.

e. Write the final totals and double rule the money columns. Enter the date and the word *Totals* in the proper places.

f. Post the totals to the general ledger accounts. Be sure to include posting references in the accounts and in the journal.

g. Insert a check mark in the proper place.

CHECKPOINT

61-1 (e)
Cash Debit total =
$3,080.00

PROBLEM **61-2** ▶ You are the record keeper for Move and Groove, a water ski instruction and rental shop.

Directions

a. Copy the following cash receipts journal for June, 19--:

CASH RECEIPTS JOURNAL — PAGE 4

	DATE	ACCOUNT TITLE	DOC. NO.	POST. REF.	INCOME CREDIT LESSONS	INCOME CREDIT RENTALS	CASH DEBIT	BANK DEPOSITS	
1	19-- June 3	√	T3	√	75 00		75 00		1
2	5	√	T5	√		45 00	45 00	120 00	2
3	16	√	T16	√	80 00		80 00		3
4	18	√	T18	√		125 00	125 00	205 00	4
5	27	√	T27	√	350 00		350 00	350 00	5

b. Copy the following general ledger accounts. They show the postings for the past three months. (Allow five lines for each account.)

ACCOUNT **Cash**   ACCOUNT NO. **110**

DATE	ITEM	POST. REF.	DEBIT	CREDIT	BALANCE DEBIT	BALANCE CREDIT
19-- Mar. 31		CR1	805 00		805 00	
Apr. 30		CR2	710 00		1515 00	
May 31		CR3	745 00		2260 00	

ACCOUNT **Income, Lessons**   ACCOUNT NO. **410**

DATE	ITEM	POST. REF.	DEBIT	CREDIT	BALANCE DEBIT	BALANCE CREDIT
19-- Mar. 31		CR1		520 00		520 00
Apr. 30		CR2		470 00		990 00
May 31		CR3		390 00		1380 00

ACCOUNT	*Income, Rentals*						ACCOUNT NO.	*420*	
DATE	ITEM	POST. REF.	DEBIT	CREDIT	BALANCE				
					DEBIT		CREDIT		
19-- Mar. 31		CR1		2 8 5 00			2 8 5 00		
Apr. 30		CR2		2 4 0 00			5 2 5 00		
May 31		CR3		3 5 5 00			8 8 0 00		

c. Rule the money columns in the cash receipts journal and foot the columns.

d. Check the footings to see if total debits equal total credits. Also, check to see that the Cash Debit and Bank Deposits column totals are equal.

CHECKPOINT ✔

61-2 (f)
Cash account final balance = $2,935.00

e. Write the final totals and double rule the money columns. Enter the date and the word *Totals* in the proper places.

f. Post the totals to the general ledger accounts. Include all posting references. Calculate new account balances.

g. Insert a check mark in the proper place.

Problem 61-3 may be found in the Working Papers.

JOB 62 ► USING A CASH RECEIPTS JOURNAL AND A GENERAL LEDGER

APPLIED MATH PREVIEW

Copy and complete these problems. In each problem, crossfoot and then add down. Find the grand totals.

1. 44 + 53 + 27 + 91 =	2. $ 7.56 + $ 8.12 + $ 5.95 + $11.75 =
37 + 36 + 19 + 81 =	19.12 + 0.56 + 11.16 + 31.09 =
29 + 42 + 35 + 55 =	31.15 + 9.71 + 2.75 + 45.04 =
66 + 57 + 21 + 29 =	18.06 + 12.10 + 6.99 + 11.55 =
18 + 69 + 76 + 32 =	19.11 + 75.80 + 31.04 + 72.09 =
+ + + =	+ + + =

GOALS

1. To practice recording in a cash receipts journal and posting to the general ledger.
2. To use a cash receipts journal with three income columns.

UNDERSTANDING THE JOB

In Jobs 60 and 61, you learned how to record income in a cash receipts journal and in the general ledger. In this job, you will have the chance to practice both of these skills. You will use a cash receipts journal with a Cash Debit column and three Income Credit columns, as well as the Bank Deposits column.

SAMPLE PROBLEM

Ellen Powell owns and operates a travel agency. She earns income from tours, air fares, and train fares. You are her record keeper. You record her income in a cash receipts journal with three income columns. You also post to her general ledger accounts.

Her transactions for May, 19--, are as follows:

May   2 Received $745.60 for a tour, T2.
         4 Received $475.15 for air fare, T4.
         4 Deposited all cash received from May 2 to 4.
     14 Received $1,505.37: $942.12 for air fare and $563.25 for train fare, T14.
     16 Received $755.00 for a tour, T16.
     16 Deposited all cash received from May 14 to 16.
     24 Received $135.00 for train fare and $517.86 for air fare, T24.
     25 Received $637.50 for a tour and $812.44 for air fare, T25.
     28 Received $375.50 for train fare, $1,044.65 for air fare, and $2,175.00 for a tour, T28.
     28 Deposited all cash received from May 24 to 28.

Illustration 62A (page 551) shows how these transactions are recorded in the cash receipts journal and posted to the general ledger. Here are the steps that are followed:

STEP 1 ▶ ***Open the cash receipts journal and the general ledger accounts.***

Open a cash receipts journal with three Income Credit columns, a Cash Debit column, and a Bank Deposits column.

Open four general ledger accounts. The Cash account is always first.

STEP 2 ▶ ***Journalize each transaction.***

Record each transaction in the cash receipts journal. Look carefully at the data that are given. On May 14, you are given the amounts for cash debit ($1,505.37), air fare ($942.12), and train fare ($563.25).

On May 24, however, you are given the amounts for train fare ($135.00) and air fare ($517.86), but not for cash debit. To find the amount for cash debit, add the two Income Credit column amounts:

▲▲▲▲▲
TIP
▼▼▼▼▼

Extend total credit amounts to the Cash Debit column.

Income Credit, Train Fares	$ 135.00
Income Credit, Air Fares	+ 517.86
Cash Debit	$ 652.86

Enter a check mark in the Post. Ref. column for each daily transaction, since only totals are posted.

STEP 3 ▶ ***Record the bank deposits in the Bank Deposits column.***

The first deposit is made on May 4. It is the sum of the cash debits on May 2 and 4. Add $745.60 + $475.15 to get $1,220.75, the first bank deposit.

STEP 4 ▶ ***Rule and foot the cash receipts journal, and check the totals.***

On the last day of the month, the columns are ruled, footed, and checked. Totals are checked by crossfooting total debits with total credits to see if they are equal, as shown on page 551.

Debits =
Credits

Income Credit, Tours	$ 4,313.10
Income Credit, Air Fares	3,792.22
Income Credit, Train Fares	+ 1,073.75
Cash Debit	$ 9,179.07

Illustration 62A   Cash receipts journal and general ledger

CASH RECEIPTS JOURNAL   PAGE 1

	DATE		ACCOUNT TITLE	DOC. NO.	POST. REF.	INCOME CREDIT — TOURS	INCOME CREDIT — AIR FARES	INCOME CREDIT — TRAIN FARES	CASH DEBIT	BANK DEPOSITS	
1	19-- May	2	√	T2	√	7 4 5 60			7 4 5 60		1
2		4	√	T4	√		4 7 5 15		4 7 5 15	1 2 2 0 75	2
3		14	√	T14	√		9 4 2 12	5 6 3 25	1 5 0 5 37		3
4		16	√	T16	√	7 5 5 00			7 5 5 00	2 2 6 0 37	4
5		24	√	T24	√		5 1 7 86	1 3 5 00	6 5 2 86		5
6		25	√	T25	√	6 3 7 50	8 1 2 44		1 4 4 9 94		6
7		28	√	T28	√	2 1 7 5 00	1 0 4 4 65	3 7 5 50	3 5 9 5 15	5 6 9 7 95	7
8		31	Totals			4 3 1 3 10	3 7 9 2 22	1 0 7 3 75	9 1 7 9 07	9 1 7 9 07	8
9						(4 1 0)	(4 2 0)	(4 3 0)	(1 1 0)	(√)	9

General Ledger

ACCOUNT Cash							ACCOUNT NO. 110	
DATE	ITEM	POST. REF.	DEBIT	CREDIT	BALANCE DEBIT		BALANCE CREDIT	
19-- May 31		CR1	9 1 7 9 07		9 1 7 9 07			

ACCOUNT Income, Tours							ACCOUNT NO. 410	
DATE	ITEM	POST. REF.	DEBIT	CREDIT	BALANCE DEBIT		BALANCE CREDIT	
19-- May 31		CR1		4 3 1 3 10			4 3 1 3 10	

ACCOUNT Income, Air Fares							ACCOUNT NO. 420	
DATE	ITEM	POST. REF.	DEBIT	CREDIT	BALANCE DEBIT		BALANCE CREDIT	
19-- May 31		CR1		3 7 9 2 22			3 7 9 2 22	

ACCOUNT Income, Train Fares							ACCOUNT NO. 430	
DATE	ITEM	POST. REF.	DEBIT	CREDIT	BALANCE DEBIT		BALANCE CREDIT	
19-- May 31		CR1		1 0 7 3 75			1 0 7 3 75	

The Cash Debit column total and the Bank Deposits column total are also compared. They should be equal. If the totals do not agree, re-add the columns. If they still are not equal,

1. Recheck each entry to make sure that the debits and the credits are equal.
2. Recheck your addition for each bank deposit.

STEP 5 ▶ *Write in final totals and double rule the columns.*

Date your totals as of the last day of the month, and write the word *Totals* in the Account Title column. Double rule all five money columns.

STEP 6 ▶ *Post to the general ledger accounts.*

Enter the date (May 31) and posting reference (CR1) in each account. Enter the amount in each account. The column heading of the journal will indicate the name of the account and if it is a debit or a credit. Income accounts are always credited. The Cash account is always debited for cash received.

▲▲▲▲▲
T I P
▼▼▼▼▼

Credit income accounts. Debit the Cash account for cash received.

Enter the balance in each account. Income accounts will have a credit balance. The Cash account will have a debit balance.

Enter the account number in parentheses under each total in the cash receipts journal, except for the Bank Deposits column total.

STEP 7 ▶ *See that check marks were entered in the journal for items not posted; add any necessary for memorandum column(s).*

Enter a check mark under the Bank Deposits column total since the total of a memorandum column is not posted.

𝓑UILDING YOUR BUSINESS VOCABULARY

On a sheet of paper, write the headings **Statement Number** and **Words**. Next, choose the words that match the statements. Write each word you choose next to the statement number it matches. Be careful; not all the words listed should be used.

Statements	Words
1. The side of an account on which income is recorded	credit
	debit
2. A general ledger account with two balance columns	extended
	four-column ledger account
3. The side of an account on which cash received is recorded	general ledger
4. A type of column used to remember information	income
	journalize
5. Entered again in a second column	memorandum column
6. A group of accounts other than customer and creditor accounts	post
	posting references
7. To record in a journal	
8. Symbols, such as CR1, that show from where an entry was posted	

PROBLEM SOLVING MODEL FOR: *Using a Cash Receipts Journal and a General Ledger*

STEP 1 ▶ **Open the cash receipts journal and the general ledger accounts.**

STEP 2 ▶ **Journalize each transaction.**

STEP 3 ▶ **Record the bank deposits in the Bank Deposits column.**

STEP 4 ▶ **Rule and foot the cash receipts journal, and check the totals.**

STEP 5 ▶ **Write in final totals and double rule the columns.**

STEP 6 ▶ **Post to the general ledger accounts.**

STEP 7 ▶ **See that check marks were entered in the journal for items not posted; add any necessary for memorandum column(s).**

APPLICATION PROBLEMS

PROBLEM **62-1** ▶ You are the record keeper for Andrew Chang, who owns a ticket agency. Andrew separates income into three types: theater tickets, baseball tickets, and concert tickets. Your job is to journalize and post his income transactions.

AUTOMATED

Directions

a. Open a cash receipts journal with the following headings. Number the journal page 1.

					INCOME CREDIT				
DATE	ACCOUNT TITLE	DOC. NO.	POST. REF.	THEATER	BASEBALL	CONCERTS	CASH DEBIT	BANK DEPOSITS

CASH RECEIPTS JOURNAL — PAGE

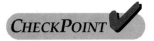

62-1 (f)
Bank Deposits total =
$2,467.10

b. Open the following general ledger accounts. The accounts have no previous balances. (Allow three lines for each account.)

Cash	#110
Income, Theater	#410
Income, Baseball	#420
Income, Concerts	#430

c. Record the following information for July in the cash receipts journal:

July 3 Received $195.50 for theater tickets, T3.
 5 Received $57.75 for baseball tickets, T5.
 5 Deposited all cash received from July 3 to 5.
 10 Received $127.60 for concert tickets, T10.
 11 Received $217.40: $106.35 for concert tickets and $111.05 for theater tickets, T11.
 11 Deposited all cash received from July 10 to 11.
 15 Received $316.95: $210.90 for theater tickets and $106.05 for baseball tickets, T15.
 17 Received $296.10: $45.60 for baseball tickets and $250.50 for theater tickets, T17.
 18 Received $217.40 for concert tickets, T18.
 18 Deposited all cash received from July 15 to 18.
 22 Received $103.90 for theater tickets and $75.55 for baseball tickets, T22.
 23 Received $64.10 for baseball tickets and $104.95 for concert tickets, T23.
 23 Deposited all cash received from July 22 to 23.
 28 Received $45.10 for baseball tickets, $95.80 for concert tickets, and $131.10 for theater tickets, T28.
 29 Received $417.90: $104.30 for concert tickets, $96.85 for baseball tickets, and $216.75 for theater tickets, T29.
 29 Deposited all cash received from July 28 to 29.

d. Rule and foot all money columns in the cash receipts journal.
e. Check the footings to see if total debits equal total credits. Also, see if the totals of the Cash Debit and Bank Deposits columns agree.
f. Write in final totals and draw a double ruling.
g. Post the totals to the ledger accounts. Be sure to include all posting references and check marks.

PROBLEM | **62-2** ▶ You are the record keeper for Ellen Powell, who runs a travel agency. (See Sample Problem, page 549.) You record her income and post to the general ledger.

AUTOMATED

Directions

a. Open a cash receipts journal identical to the one used in the Sample Problem (Illustration 62A, page 551). Number the journal page 2.
b. Copy the ledger accounts shown in Illustration 62A. (Allow three lines for each account.)
c. Record the following information for June in the cash receipts journal:

CHECKPOINT ✔

62-2 (g)
Cash account final balance = $22,050.78

June	2	Received $974.10 for a tour, T2.
	4	Received $645.70 for air fare, T4.
	4	Deposited all cash received from June 2 to 4.
	7	Received $1,710.36: $775.40 for a tour and $934.96 for air fare, T7.
	9	Received $882.40: $511.24 for air fare and $371.16 for train fare, T9.
	10	Received $197.55 for train fare, T10.
	10	Deposited all cash received from June 7 to 10.
	15	Received $408.17 for air fare and $795.99 for a tour, T15.
	16	Received $511.76 for air fare and $204.75 for train fare, T16.
	17	Received $625.94: $108.10 for train fare and $517.84 for air fare, T17.
	17	Deposited all cash received from June 15 to 17.
	21	Received $508.10 for air fare, $795.05 for a tour, and $199.99 for train fare, T21.
	22	Received $1,755.95 for a tour, T22.
	22	Deposited all cash received from June 21 to 22.
	28	Received $2,655.90: $1,045.00 for a tour, $496.86 for air fare, and $1,114.04 for train fare, T28.
	28	Deposited all cash received on June 28.

d. Rule and foot all money columns in the cash receipts journal.
e. Check the footings to see if total debits equal total credits. Also, see if the totals of the Cash Debit and Bank Deposits columns agree.
f. Write in final totals and draw a double ruling.
g. Post the totals to the ledger accounts. Calculate new balances after each posting. Be sure to include all posting references and check marks.

Problem 62-3 may be found in the Working Papers.

USING A CASH PAYMENTS JOURNAL

APPLIED MATH PREVIEW

Copy and complete the following problems.

1. $ 4,671.45	2. $ 7,142.19	3. $ 6,177.09	4. $ 6,244.18
2,179.84	5,017.36	5,834.11	8,280.92
5,011.36	1,457.21	2,621.17	1,415.15
+ 4,277.19	+ 9,368.02	+ 3,117.09	+ 3,637.34

BUSINESS TERMS PREVIEW

• Drawing • Expenses • General columns • Special columns •

GOALS

1. To learn about the expenses of a service business.
2. To learn how to record these expenses in a cash payments journal.
3. To learn how to record personal expenses in a cash payments journal.

𝒰NDERSTANDING THE JOB

KEY Terms

Expenses. Costs of operating a business.

Drawing. Money taken out of a business by the owner.

In Job 60, you learned how to record income earned by a service business. To operate your own business, you will also have **expenses**. Expenses are the costs of operating a business. Expenses include such things as rent for the building, the telephone bill, the electric bill, truck gas and repairs, and parts and supplies.

In addition to these business expenses, most owners of a business take or withdraw money from the business for their personal living expenses. These personal expenses include rent, food, clothing, and other personal expenses. To show the amount withdrawn for personal use, a separate account is used in the general ledger. The account used is called the owner's **drawing** account. If the owner's name is Bill Auclair, the account would be called "Bill Auclair, Drawing."

In this job, you will learn how to record both types of expenses in a journal that you were introduced to in Job 57, the cash payments journal.

Illustration 63A (on page 557) shows a completed cash payments journal for a service business.

Bill Auclair owns and operates Bill's Fence Company. (See Job 60.) Bill uses a checkbook to pay all expenses. He uses the check stubs as the source documents for entries in the cash payments journal.

CASH PAYMENTS JOURNAL

PAGE **1**

	DATE		ACCOUNT TITLE	CHECK NO.	POST. REF.	GENERAL DEBIT	BILL AUCLAIR, DRAWING DEBIT	SUPPLIES EXPENSE DEBIT	CASH CREDIT	
1	19-- Mar.	1	Rent Expense	101		9 5 0 00			9 5 0 00	1
2		4	√	102	√		1 5 0 00		1 5 0 00	2
3		12	√	103	√			7 1 0 00	7 1 0 00	3
4		17	√	104	√			2 4 5 00	2 4 5 00	4
5		22	Telephone Expense	105		1 3 5 00			1 3 5 00	5
6		30	√	106	√		3 0 0 00		3 0 0 00	6
7		31	Totals			1 0 8 5 00	4 5 0 00	9 5 5 00	2 4 9 0 00	7

Illustration 63A A cash payments journal for a service business

Bill's cash payments for March, 19--, are as follows:

Mar. 1 Issued Check No. 101 for $950.00 to Nash Realty for March rent.

4 Issued Check No. 102 for $150.00 to Bill Auclair for personal use.

12 Issued Check No. 103 for $710.00 to Briggs Company for supplies.

17 Issued Check No. 104 for $245.00 to Russell Company for supplies.

22 Issued Check No. 105 for $135.00 to County Telephone for the telephone bill for March.

30 Issued Check No. 106 for $300.00 to Central Bank for Bill Auclair's personal car payment.

Here is how the expenses were recorded in the cash payments journal:

Enter each check stub in the journal.

From each check stub, record the date, check number, and amount.

To enter the amounts in the correct column, examine each check stub to see what it was paid for. Then remember the meaning of the double-entry system: each transaction has at least one debit and one credit.

1. Enter the amount first in one of the debit columns.
2. Enter the amount of every check stub again in the Cash Credit column. *Cash paid out is always recorded as a credit.*

The cash payments journal in Illustration 63A (page 557) has three debit columns: General Debit; Bill Auclair, Drawing Debit; and Supplies Expense Debit. Columns such as Bill Auclair, Drawing Debit and Supplies Expense Debit are called **special columns**. Special columns in a journal are used for only one type of item. Every time there is a personal expense, such as for Check No. 102 and No. 106, the amount will be entered in the Bill Auclair, Drawing column. Every time there is a supplies expense, such as for Check No. 103 and No. 104, the amount will be entered in the Supplies Expense Debit column. A check mark is placed in the Account Title column to show that no account title needs to be written. A check mark is also placed in the Post. Ref. column. The check mark in the Post. Ref. column will be explained in Job 64.

The names of special columns will vary from company to company. Each company will set up a special column for an expense that is paid often. The Cash Credit column is also a special column.

Now, look at how Check No. 101 is extended. There is no special column for rent expense, so the General Debit column must be used. Since there will be many different kinds of other items, the name of the expense, Rent Expense, is written in the Account Title column. The Post. Ref. column is left blank. The amount is then recorded in the General Debit column. Columns like the General Debit column are called **general columns**, since they are used for many different types of items. When recording in a journal with special columns and general columns, use the general columns when there is no special column for your amount.

Look at how Check No. 105 was recorded. There is no special column for telephone expense. The General Debit column was used. The name of the expense, Telephone Expense, was written in the Account Title column, the Post. Ref. column was left blank, and the amount was entered in the General Debit column.

Whether you extend to a special column or to the general column in the cash payments journal, *an expense is always recorded as a debit.*

Sidebar

▲▲▲▲▲
T I P
▼▼▼▼▼

In a double-entry system, each transaction has at least one debit and one credit. Cash paid out is always recorded as a credit.

K E Y   Terms

Special columns. Columns in a journal used for only one type of item.

K E Y   Terms

General columns. Columns in a journal used for items that have no special column.

▲▲▲▲▲

T I P
▼▼▼▼▼

Expense is always recorded as a debit.

Rule and foot the money columns.

Rule and foot all four money columns. Check the totals to see if debits equal credits as shown on page 559:

General Debit	$1,085.00
Bill Auclair, Drawing Debit	450.00
Supplies Expense Debit	+ 955.00
Cash Credit	$2,490.00

After the footings have been checked, enter the final totals and draw a double ruling under each money column. Date the totals as of the last day of the month, and write the word *Totals* in the Account Title column.

BUILDING YOUR BUSINESS VOCABULARY

On a sheet of paper, write the headings **Statement Number** and **Words**. Next, choose the words that match the statements. Write each word you choose next to the statement number it matches. Be careful; not all the words listed should be used.

Statements	Words
1. A record of income received	cash payments journal
2. Money taken out of the business by the owner	cash receipts journal
	credit
3. A column in a journal used for only one type of item	debit
	double-entry system
4. How an expense is always recorded	drawing
5. A record of expenses paid	expenses
6. Columns in a journal used for items that have no special column	general columns
	general ledger
7. Costs of operating a business	special column
8. How cash paid out is always recorded	

PROBLEM SOLVING MODEL FOR: *Recording Expenses in a Cash Payments Journal*

STEP 1 ▶ *Enter each check stub in the journal.*

STEP 2 ▶ *Rule and foot the money columns.*

APPLICATION PROBLEMS

PROBLEM **63-1** ▶ You work in the office of Alex Carney, a lawyer. Part of your job is to record cash payments in a cash payments journal.

Directions

a. Open a cash payments journal with the same headings as in Illustration 63A (page 557), but label the Drawing Debit column "Alex Carney, Drawing." Number the journal page 1.

b. Record the following cash payments in the cash payments journal:

CHECKPOINT ✔

63-1 (c)
Cash Credit total =
$3,165.00

Oct. 3 Issued Check No. 101 for $550.00 to City Stationery Company for office supplies.

7 Issued Check No. 102 for $125.00 to Alex Carney for personal use.

10 Issued Check No. 103 for $95.00 to Main Street Supply Company for mailing supplies.

12 Issued Check No. 104 for $900.00 to Prime Realty for office rent. (Use the account Rent Expense.)

17 Issued Check No. 105 for $145.00 to City Telephone Company for the phone bill. (Use the account Telephone Expense.)

19 Issued Check No. 106 for $350.00 to Alex Carney for personal use.

26 Issued Check No. 107 for $250.00 to City Stationery Company for office supplies.

29 Issued Check No. 108 for $750.00 to Prime Realty for Alex Carney's home rent.

c. Total and rule the journal. Remember to check your totals to be sure that debits equal credits before entering final totals.

PROBLEM **63-2** ▶ You work for Jennie Cartwright, a self-employed plumber. Part of your job is to record cash payments in a cash payments journal.

AUTOMATED

Directions

a. Open a cash payments journal with the following column headings. Number the journal page 42.

					CASH PAYMENTS JOURNAL			PAGE
DATE	ACCOUNT TITLE	CHECK NO.	POST. REF.	GENERAL DEBIT	PLUMBING SUPPLIES EXPENSE DEBIT	TRUCK EXPENSE DEBIT	CASH CREDIT	

b. Record the cash payments below and on page 561 in the cash payments journal:

CHECKPOINT ✔

63-2 (c)
Cash Credit total =
$2,055.00

Mar. 2 Issued Check No. 1001 for $165.00 to Neptune Company for plumbing supplies.

6 Issued Check No. 1002 for $75.00 to Kay's Garage for truck repairs.

11 Issued Check No. 1003 for $135.00 to Kendall Auto Parts for a truck battery.

14 Issued Check No. 1004 for $200.00 to Jennie Cartwright for personal use. (Use the account J. Cartwright, Drawing.)

17 Issued Check No. 1005 for $175.00 to Acme Tire Company for a new tire for the truck.

20 Issued Check No. 1006 for $675.00 to Neptune Company for plumbing supplies.

22 Issued Check No. 1007 for $355.00 to Lincoln Insurance Company for insurance expense.

28 Issued Check No. 1008 for $275.00 to R & S Supply Company for plumbing supplies.

c. Total and rule the journal. Remember to check your totals to be sure that debits equal credits before entering final totals.

PROBLEM **63-3** ▶ You work in the office of Larry Hodgkiss, a printer. Part of your job is to record cash payments in a cash payments journal.

AUTOMATED

Directions

a. Open a cash payments journal with the following headings. Number the journal page 3.

	CASH PAYMENTS JOURNAL							PAGE
DATE	ACCOUNT TITLE	CHECK NO.	POST. REF.	GENERAL DEBIT	LARRY HODGKISS, DRAWING DEBIT	PRINTING SUPPLIES EXPENSE DEBIT	CASH CREDIT	

b. Record the following cash payments in the cash payments journal:

CHECKPOINT ✔

63-3 (c)
General Debit total = $1,080.00

May 3 Issued Check No. 49 for $175.00 to Larry Hodgkiss for personal use.

7 Issued Check No. 50 for $395.00 to Best Ink Company for printing supplies.

10 Issued Check No. 51 for $250.00 to Wilson Bank for Larry Hodgkiss' car payment.

16 Issued Check No. 52 for $955.00 to James Realty for office rent.

18 Issued Check No. 53 for $425.00 to Best Ink Company for printing supplies.

22 Issued Check No. 54 for $350.00 to Granite Phone Company for Larry Hodgkiss' home phone bill.

27 Issued Check No. 55 for $125.00 to Lee's Garage for truck repair.

29 Issued Check No. 56 for $755.00 to C & J Paper Company for printing paper.

c. Total and rule the journal.

APPLIED MATH PREVIEW

Copy and complete the following problems.

1. $ 5,327.16	2. $ 3,627.08	3. $ 57.25	4. $ 206.19
1,099.19	45.27	5,083.11	1,127.35
6.34	599.94	416.12	391.08
975.12	8,064.12	1,935.10	2,077.17
+ 2,777.89	+ 3,152.06	+ 46.12	+ 9.19

GOAL

To learn how to post from the cash payments journal to the general ledger.

UNDERSTANDING THE JOB

In Job 61, you learned how to post from the cash receipts journal to the general ledger. The total cash received was posted to the debit side of the Cash account, and the total amounts of each type of income were posted to the credit side of each income account.

In this job, you will learn how to post from the cash payments journal to the general ledger.

SAMPLE PROBLEM

Bill Auclair's cash payments journal from Job 63 is shown in Illustration 64A on page 564. Also shown are some general ledger accounts on page 564. These accounts include an amount which has been posted from the cash receipts journal to the Cash account.

Here are the steps followed to journalize and post the cash payments journal to these accounts:

STEP 1 ▶ *Journalize each transaction.*

Record each transaction in the journal as you learned to do in Job 63.

STEP 2 ▶ *Record check marks where necessary.*

Make sure that a check mark was put in the Post. Ref. column of the journal for those items that do not require daily posting. Transactions that are recorded in special columns will not be posted daily. They will be posted at the end of the month as part of column totals. There should be check marks for March 4, 12, 17, and 30 in the Post. Ref. column.

STEP 3 ▶ *Complete the daily postings.*

Post individual amounts from general columns. Date individual items on the date of entry.

Only entries in the General Debit column are posted daily. On March 1, the $950.00 that was recorded in the General Debit column was posted to the Rent Expense account in the general ledger. The posting was done in these steps:

a. Enter the date, March 1, in the Date column of the Rent Expense account.
b. Enter the posting reference, CP1 (for *c*ash *p*ayments journal, page *1*), in the Post. Ref. column of the Rent Expense account.
c. Enter the amount, $950.00, in the Debit column of the Rent Expense account.
d. Figure the new balance of the Rent Expense account. Since there was no previous balance, the new balance is a debit of $950.00.
e. Enter the number of the Rent Expense account, 520, in the Post. Ref. column of the cash payments journal.

The debit to the Telephone Expense account on March 22 was posted in the same way.

STEP 4 ▶ *Rule, foot, and check the totals.*

On the last day of the month, rule, foot, and check the totals of the cash payments journal as you learned to do in Job 63.

STEP 5 ▶ *Post the totals of the special columns to the accounts.*

Post the totals of the three special columns to the general ledger accounts. The column headings tell you where and how to post.

Post the total of the Cash Credit column by following these steps:

Date totals as of the last day of the month.

a. Enter the date, 31, in the Date column of the Cash account.
b. Enter the post reference, CP1, in the Post. Ref. column of the Cash account.
c. Enter the amount, $2,490.00, in the Credit column of the Cash account.
d. Figure the new balance of the Cash account. The Cash account has a previous debit balance. Subtract the credit entered from the

CASH PAYMENTS JOURNAL

PAGE **1**

	DATE		ACCOUNT TITLE	CHECK NO.	POST. REF.	GENERAL DEBIT	BILL AUCLAIR, DRAWING DEBIT	SUPPLIES EXPENSE DEBIT	CASH CREDIT	
1	19-- Mar.	1	Rent Expense	101	520	9 5 0 00			9 5 0 00	1
2		4	√	102	√		1 5 0 00		1 5 0 00	2
3		12	√	103	√			7 1 0 00	7 1 0 00	3
4		17	√	104	√			2 4 5 00	2 4 5 00	4
5		22	Telephone Expense	105	530	1 3 5 00			1 3 5 00	5
6		30	√	106	√		3 0 0 00		3 0 0 00	6
7		31	Totals			1 0 8 5 00	4 5 0 00	9 5 5 00	2 4 9 0 00	7
						(√)	(3 2 0)	(5 1 0)	(1 1 0)	

General Ledger

| ACCOUNT | Cash | | | | | ACCOUNT NO. | **110** |

DATE	ITEM	POST. REF.	DEBIT	CREDIT	BALANCE DEBIT	BALANCE CREDIT
19-- Mar. 31		CR1	3 9 4 5 00		3 9 4 5 00	
31		CP1		2 4 9 0 00	1 4 5 5 00	

| ACCOUNT | Bill Auclair, Drawing | | | | | ACCOUNT NO. | **320** |

DATE	ITEM	POST. REF.	DEBIT	CREDIT	BALANCE DEBIT	BALANCE CREDIT
19-- Mar. 31		CP1	4 5 0 00		4 5 0 00	

| ACCOUNT | Supplies Expense | | | | | ACCOUNT NO. | **510** |

DATE	ITEM	POST. REF.	DEBIT	CREDIT	BALANCE DEBIT	BALANCE CREDIT
19-- Mar. 31		CP1	9 5 5 00		9 5 5 00	

| ACCOUNT | Rent Expense | | | | | ACCOUNT NO. | **520** |

DATE	ITEM	POST. REF.	DEBIT	CREDIT	BALANCE DEBIT	BALANCE CREDIT
19-- Mar. 1		CP1	9 5 0 00		9 5 0 00	

| ACCOUNT | Telephone Expense | | | | | ACCOUNT NO. | **530** |

DATE	ITEM	POST. REF.	DEBIT	CREDIT	BALANCE DEBIT	BALANCE CREDIT
19-- Mar. 22		CP1	1 3 5 00		1 3 5 00	

Subtract a credit from a debit balance.

TIP

debit balance and enter the difference. You still have a debit balance, though it is a smaller one. Here is how it is calculated:

Previous debit balance	$ 3,945.00
Credit	- 2,490.00
New debit balance	$ 1,455.00

e. Enter (110) under the total of the Cash Credit column of the cash payments journal.

Following the same steps used to post to the Cash account, post the totals of the Supplies Expense Debit column ($955.00) and the Bill Auclair, Drawing Debit column ($450.00) to the proper accounts in the general ledger.

Do not post totals of general columns.

TIP

Notice that the total of the General Debit column was not posted. A check mark (✔) was entered under the total to show that the total should not be posted. Since this column is not a special column, the total was not posted.

Add a debit to a debit balance.

TIP

Illustration 64B shows how an expense account balance column is used. The March 1 debit balance of $950.00 and the April 1 debit of $950.00 were added to get the new balance of $1,900.00.

Illustration 64B   Adding a debit to a debit balance

ACCOUNT	*Rent Expense*					ACCOUNT NO.	*520*	
						BALANCE		
DATE	ITEM	POST. REF.	DEBIT	CREDIT		DEBIT	CREDIT	
19-- Mar. 1		CP1	950 00			950 00		
Apr. 1		CP2	950 00			1900 00		

BUILDING YOUR BUSINESS VOCABULARY

On a sheet of paper, write the headings **Statement Number** and **Words**. Next, choose the words that match the statements. Write each word you choose next to the statement number it matches. Be careful; not all the words listed should be used.

Statements	Words
1. Columns in a journal used for items that have no special column	accounts payable ledger
	credit
2. Costs of operating a business	debit
3. A general ledger account with two balance columns	drawing
	expenses
4. The balance of an expense account	four-column ledger
5. The balance of an income account	account
6. Money received from the sale of merchandise or services	general columns
	general ledger
7. A column in a journal used for only one type of item	income
	memorandum column
8. Money taken out of the business by the owner	special column

PROBLEM SOLVING MODEL FOR: *Recording Expenses in the General Ledger*

STEP 1 ▶ *Journalize each transaction.*

STEP 2 ▶ *Record check marks where necessary.*

STEP 3 ▶ *Complete the daily postings.*

STEP 4 ▶ *Rule, foot, and check the totals.*

STEP 5 ▶ *Post the totals of the special columns to the accounts.*

APPLICATION PROBLEMS

PROBLEM 64-1 ▶ You are the record keeper for Ellen Katz, the owner of a tree service company.

Directions

a. Copy the cash payments journal for July, 19--, that follows:

	DATE		ACCOUNT TITLE	CHECK NO.	POST. REF.	GENERAL DEBIT	ELLEN KATZ, DRAWING DEBIT	TRUCK EXPENSE DEBIT	CASH CREDIT	
1	19-- July	5	√	101	√			6 5 0 00	6 5 0 00	1
2		12	√	102	√		2 0 0 00		2 0 0 00	2
3		17	Insurance Expense	103		2 0 5 00			2 0 5 00	3
4		27	√	104	√			9 5 00	9 5 00	4
5		28	√	105	√		3 5 0 00		3 5 0 00	5
6		30	Office Expense	106		5 7 5 00			5 7 5 00	6

CASH PAYMENTS JOURNAL   PAGE **1**

b. Open the following general ledger accounts. (Allow three lines for each account.)

Cash	#110
Ellen Katz, Drawing	#320
Truck Expense	#510
Insurance Expense	#520
Office Expense	#530

c. Enter a debit of $2,550.00 in the Cash account. Date the entry July 31. Write CR1 in the Post. Ref. column. Extend $2,550.00 to the Balance Debit column.

d. Post the individual items from the General Debit column to the general ledger accounts. Enter the correct posting references for each item in the journal and accounts.

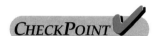
CHECKPOINT

64-1 (g)
Cash Credit total = $2,075.00

e. Rule the money columns in the cash payments journal and foot the columns.

f. Check the footings to see if total debits equal total credits.

g. Write the final totals and double rule the money columns. Enter the date and the word *Totals* in the proper places.

h. Post the totals to the general ledger accounts. Be sure to include posting references in the accounts and in the journal. Calculate the new balance of the Cash account.

i. Enter a check mark under the General Debit column total.

PROBLEM **64-2** ▶ You are the record keeper for Ken Watson, who owns and operates a lawn service.

Directions

a. Copy the cash payments journal for May, 19--, that follows:

CASH PAYMENTS JOURNAL   PAGE   2

	DATE		ACCOUNT TITLE	CHECK NO.	POST. REF.	GENERAL DEBIT	KEN WATSON, DRAWING DEBIT	SUPPLIES EXPENSE DEBIT	CASH CREDIT	
1	19-- May	1	Rent Expense	107		8 7 5 50			8 7 5 50	1
2		5	√	108	√		5 2 5 00		5 2 5 00	2
3		9	√	109	√			6 1 1 37	6 1 1 37	3
4		12	Truck Expense	110		3 6 7 92			3 6 7 92	4
5		17	√	111	√			1 0 4 6 12	1 0 4 6 12	5
6		27	√	112	√		3 5 0 00		3 5 0 00	6

b. Copy the general ledger accounts that follow. They show postings for the previous month. (Allow five lines for each account.)

c. Post the individual items from the General Debit column to the general ledger accounts. Enter the correct posting references for each item in the journal and accounts.

ACCOUNT *Cash* ACCOUNT NO. *110*

DATE	ITEM	POST. REF.	DEBIT	CREDIT	BALANCE DEBIT	BALANCE CREDIT
19-- Apr. 30		CR1	5 1 9 2 07		5 1 9 2 07	
30		CP1		3 7 7 2 64	1 4 1 9 43	
May 31		CR2	6 0 1 7 90		7 4 3 7 33	

ACCOUNT *Ken Watson, Drawing* ACCOUNT NO. *320*

DATE	ITEM	POST. REF.	DEBIT	CREDIT	BALANCE DEBIT	BALANCE CREDIT
19-- Apr. 30		CP1	7 7 5 00		7 7 5 00	

ACCOUNT *Supplies Expense* ACCOUNT NO. *510*

DATE	ITEM	POST. REF.	DEBIT	CREDIT	BALANCE DEBIT	BALANCE CREDIT
19-- Apr. 30		CP1	1 6 1 1 05		1 6 1 1 05	

ACCOUNT *Rent Expense* ACCOUNT NO. *520*

DATE	ITEM	POST. REF.	DEBIT	CREDIT	BALANCE DEBIT	BALANCE CREDIT
19-- Apr. 1		CP1	8 7 5 50		8 7 5 50	

ACCOUNT *Truck Expense* ACCOUNT NO. *530*

DATE	ITEM	POST. REF.	DEBIT	CREDIT	BALANCE DEBIT	BALANCE CREDIT
19-- Apr. 15		CP1	5 1 1 09		5 1 1 09	

d. Rule the money columns in the cash payments journal and foot the columns.

e. Check the footings to see if total debits equal total credits.

f. Write the final totals and double rule the money columns. Enter the date and the word *Totals* in the proper places.

g. Post the totals to the general ledger accounts. Be sure to include posting references in the accounts and in the journal. Calculate new balances in all accounts.

h. Enter a check mark under the General Debit column total.

Problem 64-3 may be found in the Working Papers.

CHECKPOINT

64-2 (g)
Cash account final balance =
$3,661.42

JOB **65** ▶ USING A CASH PAYMENTS JOURNAL AND A GENERAL LEDGER

APPLIED MATH PREVIEW

Copy and complete these problems. In each problem, crossfoot and then add down. Find the grand totals.

1. 63 + 16 + 41 + 32 =
   21 + 45 + 26 + 10 =
   30 + 74 + 50 + 75 =
   72 + 86 + 74 + 38 =
   84 + 13 + 99 + 92 =
   ___ + ___ + ___ + ___ = ___

2. $ 4.27 + $15.41 + $59.16 + $37.06 =
   15.99 + 22.90 +   5.99 + 59.10 =
   14.76 + 37.10 + 17.44 + 91.04 =
   73.85 + 12.11 + 51.82 +   8.32 =
   10.11 +   6.95 + 36.18 + 51.09 =
   ___ + ___ + ___ + ___ = ___

GOAL

To practice recording in a cash payments journal and posting to the general ledger.

UNDERSTANDING THE JOB

In Jobs 63 and 64, you learned how to record expenses in a cash payments journal and in the general ledger. In this job, you will have a chance to practice both of these skills.

SAMPLE PROBLEM

Ed Iles owns and operates a ticket agency. You are his record keeper. You record his expenses in the cash payments journal and post to the general ledger accounts. The journal has special columns for Computer Expense and Van Expense. His transactions for March, 19--, are as follows:

Mar. 1 Issued Check No. 101 for $745.37 to DJ Computers for computer supplies.

5 Issued Check No. 102 for $145.86 to Ajax Garage for van repairs.

9 Issued Check No. 103 for $537.50 to West Realty for Ed Iles' home rent.

12 Issued Check No. 104 for $177.84 to Computown for computer supplies.

15 Issued Check No. 105 for $975.00 to West Realty for business rent.

22 Issued Check No. 106 for $350.00 to Ed Iles for personal expenses.

27 Issued Check No. 107 for $611.82 to Main Motors for van maintenance and repairs.

Illustration 65A on page 571 shows how these transactions would be recorded in the cash payments journal and posted to the general ledger. Here are the steps that are followed:

STEP 1 ▶ Set up the cash payments journal and the general ledger accounts.

Set up a cash payments journal with a Cash Credit column, two special columns for expenses, and a General Debit column.

Set up five ledger accounts. The Cash account will already have a debit balance from the March 31 posting from the cash receipts journal.

STEP 2 ▶ Journalize each transaction.

Record each transaction in the journal. Be sure to use the Cash Credit column and one debit column for each check written. When the General Debit column is used, remember to write in both the name of the account and the amount. Also, remember to place check marks in the Account Title and Post. Ref. columns for entries made in special columns.

STEP 3 ▶ Post the entries in the General Debit column.

Enter the date, CP1, and amount in the ledger accounts, and calculate the new balance. Enter the account number in the Post. Ref. column of the journal.

STEP 4 ▶ Rule and foot the cash payments journal, and check the totals.

On the last day of the month, rule, foot, and total the money columns. Check the totals by comparing total debits with total credits to see if they are equal.

Debits = Credits

TIP

General Debit	$1,862.50
Computer Expense Debit	923.21
Van Expense Debit	+ 757.68
Cash Credit	$3,543.39

CASH PAYMENTS JOURNAL

PAGE **1**

	DATE		ACCOUNT TITLE	CHECK NO.	POST. REF.	GENERAL DEBIT	COMPUTER EXPENSE DEBIT	VAN EXPENSE DEBIT	CASH CREDIT	
1	19-- Mar.	1	√	101	√		7 4 5 37		7 4 5 37	1
2		5	√	102	√			1 4 5 86	1 4 5 86	2
3		9	Ed Iles, Drawing	103	320	5 3 7 50			5 3 7 50	3
4		12	√	104	√		1 7 7 84		1 7 7 84	4
5		15	Rent Expense	105	530	9 7 5 00			9 7 5 00	5
6		22	Ed Iles, Drawing	106	320	3 5 0 00			3 5 0 00	6
7		27	√	107	√			6 1 1 82	6 1 1 82	7
8		31	Totals			1 8 6 2 50	9 2 3 21	7 5 7 68	3 5 4 3 39	8
9						(√)	(5 1 0)	(5 2 0)	(1 1 0)	9

General Ledger

ACCOUNT   **Cash**   ACCOUNT NO. **110**

DATE	ITEM	POST. REF.	DEBIT	CREDIT	BALANCE DEBIT	BALANCE CREDIT
19-- Mar. 31		CR1	4 1 3 7 91		4 1 3 7 91	
31		CP1		3 5 4 3 39	5 9 4 52	

ACCOUNT   **Ed Iles, Drawing**   ACCOUNT NO. **320**

DATE	ITEM	POST. REF.	DEBIT	CREDIT	BALANCE DEBIT	BALANCE CREDIT
19-- Mar. 9		CP1	5 3 7 50		5 3 7 50	
22		CP1	3 5 0 00		8 8 7 50	

ACCOUNT   **Computer Expense**   ACCOUNT NO. **510**

DATE	ITEM	POST. REF.	DEBIT	CREDIT	BALANCE DEBIT	BALANCE CREDIT
19-- Mar. 31		CP1	9 2 3 21		9 2 3 21	

ACCOUNT   **Van Expense**   ACCOUNT NO. **520**

DATE	ITEM	POST. REF.	DEBIT	CREDIT	BALANCE DEBIT	BALANCE CREDIT
19-- Mar. 31		CP1	7 5 7 68		7 5 7 68	

ACCOUNT   **Rent Expense**   ACCOUNT NO. **530**

DATE	ITEM	POST. REF.	DEBIT	CREDIT	BALANCE DEBIT	BALANCE CREDIT
19-- Mar. 15		CP1	9 7 5 00		9 7 5 00	

If debits do not equal credits, re-add your column totals. If they still are not equal, check each entry to see that you recorded equal debits and credits.

STEP 5 ▶ *Write in final totals and double rule the money columns.*

Date your totals as of the last day of the month, and write the word *Totals* in the Account Title column. Double rule all four money columns.

STEP 6 ▶ *Post the column totals to the general ledger accounts.*

▲▲▲▲▲
T I P
▼▼▼▼▼

Credit the Cash account for cash paid out. Debit expense accounts.

Enter March 31, CP1, and the column total in the ledger accounts. The Cash account is always credited for cash paid out. Expense accounts are always debited. Calculate the new balance of each account. Enter the account number in parentheses under each total that you post. Place a check mark under the total that is not posted—General Debit.

*B*UILDING YOUR BUSINESS VOCABULARY

On a sheet of paper, write the headings **Statement Number** and **Words**. Next, choose the words that match the statements. Write each word you choose next to the statement number it matches. Be careful; not all the words listed should be used.

Statements	Words
1. A business in which a service for customers is performed	cash payments journal
2. Columns in a journal used for items that have no special column	cash receipts journal
3. A record of expenses paid	drawing
4. Costs of operating a business	expenses
5. Money taken out of the business by the owner	general columns
6. Money received from the sale of merchandise or services	general ledger
7. A group of accounts other than customer or creditor accounts	income
8. A column in a journal used for only one type of item	merchandising business
	service business
	special column

PROBLEM SOLVING MODEL FOR: *Using a Cash Payments Journal and a General Ledger*

STEP 1 ▶ **Set up the cash payments journal and the general ledger accounts.**

STEP 2 ▶ **Journalize each transaction.**

STEP 3 ▶ **Post the entries in the General Debit column.**

STEP 4 ▶ **Rule and foot the cash payments journal, and check the totals.**

STEP 5 ▶ **Write in final totals and double rule the money columns.**

STEP 6 ▶ **Post the column totals to the general ledger accounts.**

$\mathscr{A}$PPLICATION PROBLEMS

PROBLEM **65-1** ▶ You are the record keeper for Walter Evans, who owns and operates a television repair shop. Your job is to journalize and post his expense transactions.

AUTOMATED

Directions

a. Open a cash payments journal with the following headings. Number the journal page 1.

		CASH PAYMENTS JOURNAL					PAGE
DATE	ACCOUNT TITLE	CHECK NO.	POST. REF.	GENERAL DEBIT	TRUCK EXPENSE DEBIT	SUPPLIES EXPENSE DEBIT	CASH CREDIT

b. Open the following general ledger accounts. (Allow three lines for each account.)

Cash	#110
Walter Evans, Drawing	#320
Truck Expense	#510
Supplies Expense	#520
Rent Expense	#530

c. Enter a debit of $11,624.19 in the Cash account. Date the entry June 30. Write CR1 in the Post. Ref. column. Extend $11,624.19 to the Balance Debit column.

d. Record the following transactions for June in the cash payments journal. (Enter check marks in the Post. Ref. column for those entries in special columns.)

June 1 Issued Check No. 101 for $614.76 to Carson Supply Company for supplies.

3 Issued Check No. 102 for $250.00 to Walter Evans for personal expenses.

7 Issued Check No. 103 for $65.70 to Irene's Garage for truck maintenance.

9 Issued Check No. 104 for $436.09 to Winwood Supply Company for supplies.

12 Issued Check No. 105 for $416.35 to A & S Auto Company for truck tires.

15 Issued Check No. 106 for $1,040.00 to Lebel Realty Company for business rent.

19 Issued Check No. 107 for $850.00 to Lebel Realty Company for Walter Evans' home rent.

21 Issued Check No. 108 for $527.16 to Carson Supply Company for supplies.

24 Issued Check No. 109 for $361.04 to Irene's Garage for truck repairs.

27 Issued Check No. 110 for $127.16 to Midwest Telephone Company for Walter Evans' home phone bill.

29 Issued Check No. 111 for $1,126.12 to Winwood Supply Company for supplies.

CHECKPOINT

65-1 (h)
Cash Credit total =
$5,814.38

e. Post daily from the General Debit column, and enter the correct posting references in the journal and ledger.
f. Rule and foot all money columns in the cash payments journal.
g. Check the footings to be sure that total debits equal total credits.
h. Write the final totals and double rule the money columns.
i. Post the totals to the general ledger accounts. Be sure to include all posting references and check marks.

PROBLEM | 65-2 ▶ You are the record keeper for Ed Iles, who owns a ticket agency. (See Sample Problem, pages 569–572.) Your job is to journalize and post his expense transactions.

AUTOMATED

Directions

a. Open a cash payments journal identical to the one used in the Sample Problem (Illustration 65A, page 571). Number your journal page 2.
b. Copy the ledger accounts shown in Illustration 65A on page 571. (Allow five lines for each account.)
c. Record an April 30 debit in the Cash account for $6,047.91. Use CR2 as the posting reference.

d. Record the following transactions for April in the cash payments journal. (Enter check marks in the Post. Ref. column for those entries in special columns.)

Apr.   2 Issued Check No. 108 for $612.09 to DJ Computers for computer supplies.
       3 Issued Check No. 109 for $199.06 to Ajax Garage for van repairs.
       9 Issued Check No. 110 for $537.50 to West Realty for Ed Iles' home rent.
      12 Issued Check No. 111 for $1,036.15 to Computown for computer supplies.
      15 Issued Check No. 112 for $975.00 to West Realty for business rent.
      17 Issued Check No. 113 for $511.04 to DJ Computers for computer supplies.
      20 Issued Check No. 114 for $96.34 to Ajax Garage for van repairs and maintenance.
      22 Issued Check No. 115 for $300.00 to Ed Iles for personal expenses.
      25 Issued Check No. 116 for $477.99 to Computown for computer supplies.
      27 Issued Check No. 117 for $117.71 to State Telephone Company for Ed Iles' home phone bill.
      28 Issued Check No. 118 for $245.00 to Main Motors for new tires for the van.

CHECKPOINT

65-2 (i)
Cash account final balance =
$1,534.55

e. Post daily from the General Debit column, and enter the correct posting references in the journal and ledger.
f. Rule and foot all money columns in the cash payments journal.
g. Check the footings to be sure that total debits equal total credits.
h. Write the final totals and double rule the money columns.
i. Post the totals to the general ledger accounts. Be sure to include all posting references and check marks.

Problem 65-3 may be found in the Working Papers.

JOB **66** ▶ PREPARING A TRIAL BALANCE

APPLIED MATH PREVIEW

Copy and complete the following problems.

1. $ 7,147.16	2. $ 3,172.04	3. $ 75.12	4. $ 511.17
9,024.71	4,066.19	6,014.16	2,230.15
377.50	5,122.11	371.08	3,189.27
196.25	477.06	51.14	424.60
5,172.09	305.41	4,709.96	955.48
+ 47.65	+ 2,771.19	+ 8,521.79	+ 1,767.39

BUSINESS TERMS PREVIEW

• **Normal balance** • **Slide** • **Transposition** • **Trial balance** •

GOAL

To learn how to prepare a trial balance.

𝒰NDERSTANDING THE JOB

It is easy to understand how a record keeper—who may have to record hundreds of transactions in a day—may make mistakes. To catch possible mistakes, the record keeper regularly checks the journals and ledgers. You have learned how to check the footings of a journal to prove that debits equal credits. In this job, you will learn how to check the balances of general ledger accounts to prove that debits equal credits. If you have posted correctly to the general ledger, the total of all debits in the general ledger will equal the total of all credits in the general ledger. The form used to show this proof is called the **trial balance**. The word *trial* is used because the trial balance is a test, or trial, of the accuracy of the general ledger. You are testing to see if total debits equal the total credits. The word *balance* is used because only the balance of each account is listed.

Illustration 66B on page 578 shows a completed trial balance.

KEY Terms

Trial balance. A form used to prove that debits equal credits in the ledger.

SAMPLE PROBLEM

Bill Auclair's general ledger accounts for Bill's Fence Company are shown in Illustration 66A, below and on page 578. These include all of his income transactions that you posted in Job 61 and his expense transactions that you posted in Job 64. You now need to prepare a trial balance to check the accuracy of your postings. The trial balance will show you if you have posted equal debits and credits.

Illustration 66A
General ledger with income and expense accounts

General Ledger

ACCOUNT **Cash**   ACCOUNT NO. **110**

DATE	ITEM	POST. REF.	DEBIT	CREDIT	BALANCE DEBIT	BALANCE CREDIT
19-- Mar. 31		CR1	3 9 4 5 00		3 9 4 5 00	
31		CP1		2 4 9 0 00	1 4 5 5 00	

ACCOUNT **Bill Auclair, Drawing**   ACCOUNT NO. **320**

DATE	ITEM	POST. REF.	DEBIT	CREDIT	BALANCE DEBIT	BALANCE CREDIT
19-- Mar. 31		CP1	4 5 0 00		4 5 0 00	

ACCOUNT **Income, Wood Fence**   ACCOUNT NO. **410**

DATE	ITEM	POST. REF.	DEBIT	CREDIT	BALANCE DEBIT	BALANCE CREDIT
19-- Mar. 31		CR1		1 9 8 5 00		1 9 8 5 00

ACCOUNT **Income, Metal Fence**   ACCOUNT NO. **420**

DATE	ITEM	POST. REF.	DEBIT	CREDIT	BALANCE DEBIT	BALANCE CREDIT
19-- Mar. 31		CR1		1 9 6 0 00		1 9 6 0 00

Illustration 66A
General ledger with
income and expense
accounts (continued)

ACCOUNT	Supplies Expense				ACCOUNT NO.	510	
DATE	ITEM	POST. REF.	DEBIT	CREDIT	BALANCE		
					DEBIT	CREDIT	
19-- Mar. 31		CP1	9 5 5 00		9 5 5 00		

ACCOUNT	Rent Expense				ACCOUNT NO.	520	
DATE	ITEM	POST. REF.	DEBIT	CREDIT	BALANCE		
					DEBIT	CREDIT	
19-- Mar. 1		CP1	9 5 0 00		9 5 0 00		

ACCOUNT	Telephone Expense				ACCOUNT NO.	530	
DATE	ITEM	POST. REF.	DEBIT	CREDIT	BALANCE		
					DEBIT	CREDIT	
19-- Mar. 22		CP1	1 3 5 00		1 3 5 00		

Here are the steps you would follow to prepare the trial balance shown in Illustration 66B:

STEP 1 ▶ *Enter the heading.*

Every business summary has a three-line heading, answering these questions: WHO?, WHAT?, and WHEN?

WHO?   Bill's Fence Company
WHAT? Trial Balance
WHEN? March 31, 19--

A trial balance is always dated as of the last day of the period.

Bill's Fence Company		
Trial Balance		
March 31, 19--		
ACCOUNT TITLE	DEBIT	CREDIT
Cash	1 4 5 5 00	
Bill Auclair, Drawing	4 5 0 00	
Income, Wood Fence		1 9 8 5 00
Income, Metal Fence		1 9 6 0 00
Supplies Expense	9 5 5 00	
Rent Expense	9 5 0 00	
Telephone Expense	1 3 5 00	
Totals	3 9 4 5 00	3 9 4 5 00

STEP 2 ▶ *Enter the account titles.*

Do not include accounts with zero balances.

Write the names of all accounts in the general ledger in the order they appear in the ledger. Thus, write *Cash* first and *Telephone Expense* last. Do not include any accounts with a zero balance. Check that an account has a balance before you list it on the trial balance.

STEP 3 ▶ *Enter the amounts.*

Enter debit balances in the Debit column. Enter credit balances in the Credit column.

Copy the balances from the accounts to the trial balance. The balance to be copied is the last amount in the Balance column of each account. For the Cash account, you will be copying $1,455.00.

Enter the balance of accounts with debit balances in the Debit column of the trial balance. The balances of the cash, drawing, and expense accounts are debit balances.

Enter the balance of accounts with credit balances in the Credit column of the trial balance. The balances of income accounts are credit balances.

STEP 4 ▶ *Rule and foot the money columns.*

Draw a single rule and foot the Debit and Credit columns. If the totals are the same, you have done your work correctly. If the totals are not the same, there is an error. To find the error, work in reverse:

1. Foot the columns again; this time add them from the bottom up. If they still do not agree, go to #2.
2. Check to see if the correct amounts were copied to the trial balance from the general ledger accounts. Also, be sure that you entered the amounts in the correct column—Debit or Credit.

Look for these common errors: **transpositions** (for example, 83 for 38), **slides** (for example, 10 for 100), and balances that are not normal. The **normal balance** of each account is the side of the account (debit or credit) where the balance is usually found. For example, the cash, drawing, and expense accounts normally have debit balances. Income accounts normally have credit balances.

If the columns still do not balance, go to #3.

3. Check the math in each account to see if the balances calculated are correct. If the columns do not balance after this step, go to #4.
4. Check the posting from the journals to the accounts. Were all amounts posted? Were they posted to the correct columns in the correct accounts? If the columns still do not balance, go to #5.
5. Check your journals. Were they footed accurately? If you still have not found the error, go to #6.
6. Check each entry in the journal to see if you entered equal debits and credits.

K E Y Terms

Transposition. A reversal of digits in a number.

Slide. Entering an amount a column or more off.

Normal balance. Where the balance of an account is usually found.

Normal balance of cash and drawing accounts is debit. Normal balance of income accounts is credit. Normal balance of expense accounts is debit.

STEP 5 ▶ *Enter the totals and double rule the money columns.*

When your footings are equal, enter the final totals and double rule the columns. Write the word *Totals* directly under the last account title.

USING THE COMPUTER

If you are doing manual record keeping, you will prepare your trial balance from general ledger accounts. If you are using a computer and you want a trial balance prepared, you ask the computer to prepare one. Illustration 66C shows the trial balance for Bill's Fence Company prepared by the computer system.

```
                        Bill's Fence Company
                           Trial Balance
                             03/31/--
------------------------------------------------------------------------
Acct.               Account
Number              Title                      Debit        Credit
------------------------------------------------------------------------

110                 Cash                      1455.00
320                 Bill Auclair, Drawing      450.00
410                 Income, Wood Fence                      1985.00
420                 Income, Metal Fence                     1960.00
510                 Supplies Expense           955.00
520                 Rent Expense               950.00
530                 Telephone Expense          135.00
                                             ------------   ------------
                    Totals                    3945.00       3945.00
                                             ============   ============
```

Illustration 66C   Trial balance prepared by computer system

BUILDING YOUR BUSINESS VOCABULARY

On a sheet of paper, write the headings **Statement Number** and **Words**. Next, choose the words that match the statements. Write each word you choose next to the statement number it matches. Be careful; not all the words listed should be used.

Statements	Words
1. Costs of operating a business	cash payments journal
2. Entering an amount a column or more off, such as 10 for 1,000	cash receipts journal
	credit
3. A record of expenses paid	debit
4. A system in which every transaction has at least one debit and one credit	double-entry system
	expenses
5. The side of an account where the balance is usually found	income
	normal balance
6. A reversal of digits in a number, such as 67 for 76	slide
	transposition
7. A form used to prove that debits equal credits in the ledger	trial balance
8. Money received from the sale of merchandise or services	

PROBLEM SOLVING MODEL FOR: *Preparing a Trial Balance*

STEP 1 ▶ *Enter the heading.*

STEP 2 ▶ *Enter the account titles.*

STEP 3 ▶ *Enter the amounts.*

STEP 4 ▶ *Rule and foot the money columns.*

STEP 5 ▶ *Enter the totals and double rule the money columns.*

*A*PPLICATION PROBLEMS

PROBLEM 66-1 ▶ You work for Richard Coleman, owner of Rich's Auto Repair Shop. Richard's accounts as of July 31 are as follows:

ACCOUNT	*Cash*				ACCOUNT NO.	*110*

DATE	ITEM	POST. REF.	DEBIT	CREDIT	BALANCE DEBIT	BALANCE CREDIT
19-- July 31		CR1	10 4 3 9 28		10 4 3 9 28	
31		CP1		7 9 0 4 21	2 5 3 5 07	

| ACCOUNT | Richard Coleman, Drawing | | | | | ACCOUNT NO. | 320 |

| DATE | | ITEM | POST. REF. | DEBIT | CREDIT | BALANCE | |
						DEBIT	CREDIT
19-- July	31		CP1	1 4 7 5 00		1 4 7 5 00	

| ACCOUNT | Income, Truck Repairs | | | | | ACCOUNT NO. | 410 |

| DATE | | ITEM | POST. REF. | DEBIT | CREDIT | BALANCE | |
						DEBIT	CREDIT
19-- July	31		CR1		4 2 6 5 19		4 2 6 5 19

| ACCOUNT | Income, Car Repairs | | | | | ACCOUNT NO. | 420 |

| DATE | | ITEM | POST. REF. | DEBIT | CREDIT | BALANCE | |
						DEBIT	CREDIT
19-- July	31		CR1		6 1 7 4 09		6 1 7 4 09

| ACCOUNT | Supplies Expense | | | | | ACCOUNT NO. | 510 |

| DATE | | ITEM | POST. REF. | DEBIT | CREDIT | BALANCE | |
						DEBIT	CREDIT
19-- July	31		CP1	5 1 7 2 09		5 1 7 2 09	

CHECKPOINT ✔

66-1
Total debits= $10,439.28

| ACCOUNT | Rent Expense | | | | | ACCOUNT NO. | 520 |

| DATE | | ITEM | POST. REF. | DEBIT | CREDIT | BALANCE | |
						DEBIT	CREDIT
19-- July	1		CP1	9 4 0 00		9 4 0 00	

| ACCOUNT | Telephone Expense | | | | | ACCOUNT NO. | 530 |

| DATE | | ITEM | POST. REF. | DEBIT | CREDIT | BALANCE | |
						DEBIT	CREDIT
19-- July	30		CP1	3 1 7 12		3 1 7 12	

Directions

Prepare a trial balance as of July 31, 19--.

PROBLEM **66-2** ▶ You work for Lori Stokes, owner of Lori's Painting Company. Lori's accounts as of June 30 are shown on pages 583–584.

ACCOUNT Cash   ACCOUNT NO. 110

DATE		ITEM	POST. REF.	DEBIT	CREDIT	BALANCE DEBIT	BALANCE CREDIT
19-- May	31		CR1	9 7 3 4 11		9 7 3 4 11	
	31		CP1		8 4 3 3 71	1 3 0 0 40	
June	30		CR2	15 3 9 0 23			
	30		CP2		9 5 5 5 99		

ACCOUNT Lori Stokes, Drawing   ACCOUNT NO. 320

DATE		ITEM	POST. REF.	DEBIT	CREDIT	BALANCE DEBIT	BALANCE CREDIT
19-- May	12		CP1	4 7 5 00		4 7 5 00	
June	6		CP2	3 8 1 16			
	19		CP2	2 9 9 05			

ACCOUNT Income, Home Painting   ACCOUNT NO. 410

DATE		ITEM	POST. REF.	DEBIT	CREDIT	BALANCE DEBIT	BALANCE CREDIT
19-- May	31		CR1		3 5 7 7 09		3 5 7 7 09
June	30		CR2		6 0 1 2 17		

CheckPoint

66-2 (c)
Total credits= $25,124.34

ACCOUNT Income, Business Painting   ACCOUNT NO. 420

DATE		ITEM	POST. REF.	DEBIT	CREDIT	BALANCE DEBIT	BALANCE CREDIT
19-- May	31		CR1		6 1 5 7 02		6 1 5 7 02
June	30		CR2		9 3 7 8 06		

ACCOUNT Supplies Expense   ACCOUNT NO. 510

DATE		ITEM	POST. REF.	DEBIT	CREDIT	BALANCE DEBIT	BALANCE CREDIT
19-- May	31		CP1	4 1 7 2 09		4 1 7 2 09	
June	30		CP2	5 3 6 1 15			

ACCOUNT Truck Expense   ACCOUNT NO. 520

DATE		ITEM	POST. REF.	DEBIT	CREDIT	BALANCE DEBIT	BALANCE CREDIT
19-- May	31		CP1	2 1 7 6 12		2 1 7 6 12	
June	30		CP2	1 9 0 4 13			

ACCOUNT	*Insurance Expense*					ACCOUNT NO.	**530**	
DATE	ITEM	POST. REF.	DEBIT	CREDIT	BALANCE			
					DEBIT		CREDIT	
19-- May 10		CP1	4 1 0 50		4 1 0 50			
June 6		CP2	4 1 0 50					

ACCOUNT	*Rent Expense*					ACCOUNT NO.	**540**	
DATE	ITEM	POST. REF.	DEBIT	CREDIT	BALANCE			
					DEBIT		CREDIT	
19-- May 1		CP1	1 2 0 0 00		1 2 0 0 00			
June 1		CP2	1 2 0 0 00					

Directions

a. Copy the accounts.
b. Enter the missing balances in the accounts.
c. Prepare a trial balance as of June 30, 19--.

PROBLEM | **66-3** ▶ You work for Scotch Welding Company. The November 30 account balances are listed below:

CHECKPOINT ✔

66-3
Total debits = $25,623.31

Account Title	Balance
Cash	$ 2,667.36
Joan Scotch, Drawing	1,031.95
Income, Welding	14,172.06
Income, Finishing	10,147.15
Income, Repairs	1,304.10
Supplies Expense	11,501.19
Van Expense	7,179.21
Insurance Expense	595.00
Rent Expense	2,177.50
Telephone Expense	471.10

Directions

Prepare a trial balance as of November 30, 19--.

Chapter 13 Record Keeping for Small Businesses

PROBLEM | **66-4** ▶ You work for Bestlawn Lawn Care Company. The February 28 account balances are listed below:

```
--------------------------------------------------------------------
    Account Title                                    Balance
--------------------------------------------------------------------

    Cash                                            $3,241.88
    Sid Ames, Drawing                                  525.10
    Income, Seeding                                  4,173.19
    Income, Fertilizing                              6,011.97
    Income, Shrub Care                               4,295.81
    Supplies Expense                                 6,912.12
    Truck Expense                                    2,047.17
    Insurance Expense                                  411.04
    Rent Expense                                       945.50
    Telephone Expense                                  398.16
```

CHECKPOINT ✔

66-4
Total credits = $14,480.97

Directions

Prepare a trial balance as of February 28, 19--.

Reinforcement
Activities

DISCUSSION

You are a record keeper at Whittier Trucking Company. You record entries in the cash receipts and cash payments journals, while your assistant does the posting. Your assistant is very confused about posting references. He asks you these questions:

1. Why am I entering a number on some lines and a check mark on other lines in the Post. Ref. column of the journals?
2. Why am I entering a number below some journal totals and a check mark below others?
3. Can you give me some simple rules to tell me when to use a number and when to use a check mark?

How would you answer his questions?

CRITICAL THINKING

Your company has been using a cash payments journal with a single money column. To save time posting, a journal with special columns will now be used. Your job is to decide which three special columns should be chosen. You count the debits to the different expense accounts over the past year. Here is what you find:

Account Title	Number of Debits
Rent Expense	12
Supplies Expense	42
Telephone Expense	31
Truck Expense	57
Insurance Expense	5

Using this information, write which special columns you would use and explain why you chose them.

You are the head record keeper in your firm. A new assistant has just been hired. In the past, your assistants have had difficulty understanding how to use source documents. In order to avoid this problem with the new assistant, you plan to write a note to explain the following:

1. What a source document is.
2. How calculator tapes, check stubs, and bank deposit slips are used as source documents for the cash journals.

Write the note to the new assistant to explain these items. Keep your note to half a sheet of paper.

A *full-charge record keeper* handles the general ledger. An *assistant record keeper* handles the other ledgers. Using these definitions, answer the following questions:

1. What ledgers would be kept by the assistant record keeper?
2. How would the full-charge record keeper check his or her ledger?
3. How would the assistant record keeper check his or her ledger?
4. Who would post to the income and expense accounts?
5. Who would use a double-entry system?
6. Who would keep the customer or creditor accounts?

On a sheet of paper, write the headings **Statement Number** and **Words**. Next, choose the words that best complete the statements. Write each word you choose next to the statement number it completes. Be careful; not all the words listed should be used.

Statements	Words
1. To prove that debits and credits in the general ledger are equal, prepare (a, an) _____ .	double-entry system drawing expenses
2. An expense is always recorded as a debit because that is its _____ .	extended four-column ledger account
3. The costs of operating a business are its _____ .	general columns general ledger
4. Accounts, other than those for creditors and customers, are found in the _____ .	income memorandum column
5. Individual amounts are posted from _____ in a journal.	merchandising business

Statements	Words
6. A general ledger account with two balance columns is (a, an) _____ .	normal balance
7. Only the total is posted from (a, an) _____ in a journal.	post
8. Paying the owner's home phone bill is classified as _____ .	service business
9. A repair business is an example of (a, an) _____ .	slide
10. You always make equal debits and credits in (a, an) _____ .	special column
11. The Bank Deposits column is an example of (a, an) _____ .	trial balance
12. The money earned from the sale of services or merchandise is the _____ of a business.	
13. A department store is an example of (a, an) _____ .	

MASTERY PROBLEM

AUTOMATED

You are a record keeper for Mona Wellman, owner and operator of Mona's Money Saver Travel Agency. Your job is to record income and expenses in the cash receipts and cash payments journals. You then post to the general ledger and prepare a trial balance.

Directions

a. Open a cash receipts journal with Income Credit columns for Tours, Train Fares, and Air Fares. Number the journal page 1.

b. Open a cash payments journal with special columns for Telephone Expense and Computer Expense. Number the journal page 1.

c. Open 8 general ledger accounts as follows:

Account Title	Number
Cash	110
Mona Wellman, Drawing	320
Income, Tours	410
Income, Train Fares	420
Income, Air Fares	430
Telephone Expense	510
Computer Expense	520
Rent Expense	530

d. Record the transactions below and on page 589 in the correct journal:

March 1 Received $475.50 for train fare, T1.
2 Received $1,965.10 for a tour, T2.

4 Received $1,655.80: $397.60 for air fare and $1,258.20 for a tour, T4.

4 Deposited all cash received from March 1 to 4.

5 Issued Check No. 101 for $1,027.91 to Ace Computer Supply Company for computer supplies.

5 Issued Check No. 102 for $1,200.00 to Magnet Realty for March rent.

9 Received $906.45 for a tour and $199.00 for train fare, T9.

10 Received $104.70 for train fare and $417.76 for air fare, T10.

10 Issued Check No. 103 for $310.70 to State Telephone Company for phone calls to date.

11 Received $935.99 for a tour and $675.40 for air fare, T11.

11 Deposited all cash received from March 9 to 11.

14 Issued Check No. 104 for $200.00 to Mona Wellman for personal expenses.

16 Received $602.99 for air fare, T16.

19 Issued Check No. 105 for $991.03 to Carl's Computer Company for computer software.

20 Issued Check No. 106 for $377.91 to State Telephone Company for phone calls to date.

20 Received $1,043.61: $247.63 for train fare and the balance for a tour, T20,

20 Deposited all cash received from March 16 to 20.

24 Issued Check No. 107 for $1,177.62 to Ace Computer Supply Company for computer supplies.

26 Received $757.50 for a tour, $645.93 for air fare, and $199.99 for train fare, T26.

29 Issued Check No. 108 for $975.00 to Magnet Realty for Mona Wellman's home rent.

29 Received $573.16 for air fare and $1,017.90 for a tour, T29.

29 Deposited all cash received from March 26 to 29.

(h)
Total = $12,176.78

e. Enter check marks in the Post. Ref. column of the cash payments journal for entries in special columns. Post individual amounts from the cash payments journal.

f. Foot, total, and rule both journals.

g. Make all postings of totals to the general ledger accounts. Post the cash receipts journal first. Enter check marks for totals not posted.

h. Prepare a trial balance as of March 31, 19--.

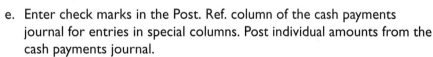

REVIEWING YOUR BUSINESS VOCABULARY

This activity may be found in the Working Papers.

Financial Statements for Small Businesses

*E*very business has a value to its owner and to potential buyers. This value is what the business is worth. As a business operates, its value changes. A net income makes the value of a business go up. A net loss makes the value of a business go down.

In Chapter 14, you will learn how to calculate net income or loss, prepare an income statement, and compute taxes. You will also learn how to prepare a capital statement, a balance sheet, and a six-column work sheet.

JOB 67 ▶ PREPARING AN INCOME STATEMENT

APPLIED MATH PREVIEW

Copy and complete these problems.

1. $ 6,177.14	2. $ 501.14	3. $ 3,760.50	5. $ 31,247.12
3,024.19	377.26	- 2,915.10	- 19,973.21
746.03	1,045.19		
129.51	2,786.49		
511.18	7,104.93	4. $ 15,109.10	6. $ 46,311.04
+ 3,014.55	+ 415.72	- 13,965.08	- 39,794.28

BUSINESS TERMS PREVIEW

• Financial statements • Income statement • Net income •
• Net loss • Revenue •

GOALS

1. To learn how to calculate net income for a service business.
2. To learn how to prepare an income statement.

You have learned that income is money received from selling merchandise or performing services. You have also learned that expenses are the costs of operating a business. When expenses are subtracted from income, the difference is your earnings—your **net income**.

For example, if during one month you received $3,500.00 from your customers for repairs that you made and you spent $1,400.00 for expenses, your net income would be $2,100.00.

Income from repairs	$ 3,500.00
Less expenses	- 1,400.00
Net income	$ 2,100.00

The $2,100.00 is your earnings for the month. Your earnings may change from month to month as your income and expenses increase or decrease.

If your expenses are greater than your income, you have a **net loss**. For example, if your income is $1,700.00 and your expenses are $1,900.00, you have a net loss of $200.00.

Expenses	$ 1,900.00
Less income	- 1,700.00
Net loss	$ 200.00

Business people use **financial statements** to summarize the results of a business. One financial statement is the **income statement**. The income statement shows income, expenses, and net income or net loss for a certain period of time. In this job, you will learn how to prepare an income statement.

$\mathcal{S}$AMPLE PROBLEM

Kathleen Conway operates her own clock repair shop, called Keep 'Em Tickin'. She keeps separate records of income from repairs of clocks and repairs of watches.

During the month of April, she received $750.00 from clock repairs and $1,570.00 from watch repairs.

She paid the following business expenses during April: rent, $750.00; insurance, $45.00; supplies, $150.00; truck, $135.00; telephone, $120.00; and electricity, $170.00.

Illustration 67A shows Kathleen's income statement for April to summarize this information. Here are the steps to follow to prepare the income statement:

STEP 1 ▸ **Enter the heading.**

The heading answers the three questions that start most business forms:

> WHO? Keep 'Em Tickin'
> WHAT? Income Statement
> WHEN? For the Month Ended April 30, 19--

Notice that the WHO? is the name of the business, not the name of the owner. The WHEN? is for a period of time, not just one day. If the income statement were for a full calendar year, the third line would read "For the Year Ended December 31, 19--."

STEP 2 ▸ **Record the income.**

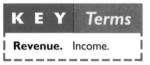

K E Y Terms

Revenue. Income.

On income statements, the word **revenue** is often used in place of the word *income*. The words mean the same. So, write the word *Revenue:* on the first line. Indent the next two lines and write the types of income: *Clock repairs* and *Watch repairs*. Enter the amount of each type of income in the first money column. Draw a single line, add the two amounts, and enter the total one line below in the second money column. Write the words *Total income* on the line with the total. Notice that dollar signs are not written because money columns are used.

Illustration 67A Income statement

Keep 'Em Tickin'		
Income Statement		
For the Month Ended April 30, 19--		
Revenue:		
Clock repairs	7 5 0 00	
Watch repairs	1 5 7 0 00	
Total income		2 3 2 0 00
Expenses:		
Rent	7 5 0 00	
Insurance	4 5 00	
Supplies	1 5 0 00	
Truck	1 3 5 00	
Telephone	1 2 0 00	
Electricity	1 7 0 00	
Total expenses		1 3 7 0 00
Net income		9 5 0 00

STEP 3 ▶ Record the expenses.

Write the word *Expenses:* on the next line. Then, indent and write the name of each expense on the next several lines. Record each amount in the first money column. Draw a single line, add the amounts, and enter the total one line below in the second money column. Write the words *Total expenses* on the line with the total.

STEP 4 ▶ Enter the net income or net loss.

Rule a single line under the amount of total expenses. Subtract the total expenses from the total income. Enter the difference on the next line in the second money column. If total income is more than total expenses, write the words *Net income* on the line with the difference. In this example, there is a net income, calculated as follows:

Total income	$ 2,320.00
Less total expenses	- 1,370.00
Net income	$ 950.00

If total expenses are greater than total income, there is a net loss. A net loss would be entered by writing the words *Net loss* and entering the amount of the net loss in parentheses. For example, a loss of $400.00 would be entered as (400.00).

Draw a double ruling under the last amount to show that the income statement is complete.

INTERVIEW

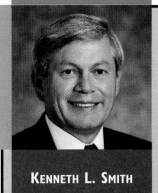

KENNETH L. SMITH

Ken Smith, a member of the Wasco tribe, is Chief Executive Officer/ Secretary-Treasurer (CEO/S-T) for The Confederated Tribes of the Warm Springs Reservation of Oregon. The Confederated Tribes of Warm Springs is one of the largest employers in central Oregon, with about 1,200 employees. The tribes' revenues of about $80 million per year come from timber sales, their Kah-Nee-Ta Resort, an apparel factory, three radio stations, a wood-substitute manufacturing plant, and a hydro electric power plant.

Ken grew up on the Warm Springs Reservation. Ken earned a business administration degree from the University of Oregon and then went to work as an accountant for his tribe. After several promotions, he became general manager. Ken's accounting background helped him to understand business operations and analyze the key issues involved in important decisions.

Ken then served as the Assistant Secretary for Indian Affairs in the United States Department of the Interior. He was responsible for 15,000 employees and a billion dollar budget. Ken's accounting and record keeping skills helped him prepare government budgets. Ken also developed innovative programs to help tribes start businesses on reservations throughout the United States.

After completing his government service, Ken became the CEO/S-T for The Confederated Tribes of Warm Springs. He also serves on various boards of directors, such as the U.S. National Bank of Oregon and U.S. West Communications of Oregon. Ken's hard work and knowledge of accounting have given him valuable advantages in his business career and his work for the government.

Many small businesses with computers use programs that will prepare financial statements automatically. The computer program will pull income and expense account data that has been stored in the computer and print it out as an income statement. Illustration 67B shows how the income statement in Illustration 67A (page 592) might appear if prepared by the computer.

Illustration 67B Income statement prepared by computer

```
                        Keep 'Em Tickin'
                        Income Statement
                   For Period Ended 04/30/--

      Operating Revenue
      -----------------------------------------------------------

         Income, Clock Repairs                    750.00
         Income, Watch Repairs                   1570.00

         Total Operating Revenue                 2320.00

      Operating Expenses
      -----------------------------------------------------------

         Rent Expense                             750.00
         Insurance Expense                         45.00
         Supplies Expense                         150.00
         Truck Expense                            135.00
         Telephone Expense                        120.00
         Electricity Expense                      170.00

         Total Operating Expenses                1370.00

      Net Income                                  950.00
```

BUILDING YOUR BUSINESS VOCABULARY

On a sheet of paper, write the headings **Statement Number** and **Words**. Next, choose the words that match the statements. Write each word you choose next to the statement number it matches. Be careful; not all the words listed should be used.

Statements	Words
1. Costs of operating a business	expenses
2. Summaries of the results of a business	financial statements
3. Another word for income	income statement
4. When income is greater than expenses	invoice
5. A form that shows income, expenses, and net income or net loss	net income
	net loss
6. When expenses are greater than income	revenue
	withdrawals

PROBLEM SOLVING MODEL FOR: *Preparing an Income Statement*

> **STEP 1** ▶ **Enter the heading.**
>
> **STEP 2** ▶ **Record the income.**
>
> **STEP 3** ▶ **Record the expenses.**
>
> **STEP 4** ▶ **Enter the net income or net loss.**

*A*PPLICATION PROBLEMS

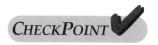 PROBLEM | **67-1** ▶ Dr. Matt Goldberg owns and operates Dr. Matt's Animal House, an animal hospital. He records income received from animal care and income received from animal surgery separately.

Directions

CHECKPOINT ✔

67-1
Net income = $10,276.00

Prepare an income statement for the month ended March 31, 19--, from the following information:

During March, he received $11,745.00 from animal care and $9,306.00 from animal surgery.

He paid these business expenses during March: rent, $3,500.00; electricity, $575.00; telephone, $275.00; insurance, $235.00; and supplies, $6,190.00.

 PROBLEM | **67-2** ▶ Judy Prescott is a locksmith who owns and operates Prescott Lock & Key Services. She records income received from lock repairs and income received from key making separately.

Directions

AUTOMATED

CHECKPOINT ✔

67-2
Net income = $3,738.58

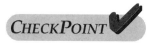

Prepare an income statement for the month ended July 31, 19--, from the following information:

During July, she received $7,136.10 from lock repairs and $1,475.50 from key making.

She paid these business expenses during July: advertising, $247.00; electricity, $79.50; locks and supplies, $2,947.65; rent, $1,045.00; truck, $271.25; telephone, $147.62; and insurance, $135.00.

PROBLEM **67-3** ▶ Tom Crowley owns and operates a word processing service called Jiffy Papers. Tom records income received from preparing paperwork for students and for businesses separately.

AUTOMATED

67-3
Net loss = ($756.08)

Directions

Prepare an income statement for the month ended October 31, 19--, from the following information:

During October, he received $2,120.00 from student paperwork and $3,240.00 from business paperwork.

He paid these business expenses during October: supplies, $4,255.90; rent, $755.00; electricity, $155.10; telephone, $137.22; advertising, $245.00; auto, $375.10; and miscellaneous, $192.76.

JOB 68 ▶ USING THE INCOME STATEMENT TO COMPUTE TAXES

UNDERSTANDING THE JOB

In Job 67, you learned that business people prepare a financial statement called an income statement. The income statement shows income, expenses, and net income or net loss.

You will also learn in later jobs that people who work for others pay two kinds of taxes to the federal government's Internal Revenue Service (IRS). These taxes are income tax and social security tax. If you work for an employer, these taxes are deducted from your pay. The employer then sends them to the IRS for you. However, if you are self-employed, you must figure out your own taxes and send them to the IRS. Both taxes are figured using the net income shown on your income statement.

Self-Employment Taxes

KEY *Terms*

Self-employment tax. Social security tax for self-employed people.

The social security taxes paid by business owners are called **self-employment taxes**. The amount of self-employment tax an owner must pay is found by multiplying the owner's net income by the self-employment tax rate. The rate of self-employment tax is set by Congress and is changed often. In this text, a rate of 14% on the first $50,000.00 of net income will be used. This means that once the self-employment taxes on the first $50,000.00 of the owner's net income have been paid, no more self-employment taxes are paid that year.

For example, if you have a net income of $40,000.00, your self-employment tax would be found this way:

$$\$40,000.00 \times 0.14 = \$5,600.00 \quad \text{self-employment tax}$$

If your net income is $50,000.00, your self-employment tax would be:

$$\$50,000.00 \times 0.14 = \$7,000.00 \quad \text{self-employment tax}$$

If your net income is over $50,000.00, the tax is still $7,000.00.

Income Taxes

Business owners must also pay **income taxes** on their net income. The amount of income taxes paid depends on many factors. In this job, you will be given the amounts of income tax that the owner must pay.

Estimated Taxes

A business owner never knows the *exact* amount of income taxes or self-employment taxes that must be paid until the end of the year. That is true because the owner does not know the exact amount of net income until the income statement is prepared at the end of the year. However, the IRS requires owners to **estimate** their net income and send parts of the income and self-employment taxes to them on April 15, June 15, September 15, and January 15. The estimated tax payments made on these dates are called **estimated taxes**.

By April 15 of the next year, the owner must report the net income earned on an income tax return sent to the IRS. On this return, the owner can correct the estimates made and settle up any difference with the IRS.

SAMPLE PROBLEM

Fred Cogrove owns and operates Fred's Motel. At the beginning of the year, Fred estimated that his income tax and self-employment tax due for the year would be $8,800.00. He sent in the estimated taxes in four equal payments during the year.

At the end of the year, Fred's income statement for the year showed a net income of $30,000.00. Here is how Fred would figure what his actual taxes should be for the year and what he must pay the IRS:

S T E P 1 ▶ *Compute the actual income tax.*

Fred's income tax would be found by looking up his net income in a government table provided by the IRS. The amount of income tax Fred found in the table for his net income was $4,800.00.

S T E P 2 ▶ *Compute the actual self-employment tax.*

Fred would multiply his net income by 14% to get the amount of self-employment tax.

$$\$30,000.00 \times 0.14 = \$4,200.00$$

S T E P 3 ▶ *Figure the total taxes due.*

Since self-employed people must pay both income tax and self-employment tax, Fred would add the answers from Steps 1 and 2 to get the total taxes due.

Income tax	$ 4,800.00
Self-employment tax	+ 4,200.00
Total taxes due	$ 9,000.00

S T E P 4 ▶ *Settle up with the IRS.*

Fred would compare the total taxes due with the estimated taxes paid. If the total taxes due are greater than the estimated taxes paid, he has a **balance due**. He must then pay this balance. He will send a check for the balance with his tax return. Fred has a balance due of $200.00, calculated as follows:

Total taxes due	$ 9,000.00
Estimated taxes paid	- 8,800.00
Balance due	$ 200.00

If the estimated taxes paid were greater than the total taxes due, Fred would receive a **refund**. He would send in his tax return and request that the difference be returned to him. For example, if Fred paid estimated taxes of $7,000.00 but his total taxes due were only $6,700.00, his refund is calculated as follows:

Estimated taxes paid	$ 7,000.00
Total taxes due	- 6,700.00
Refund	$ 300.00

You can also tell the IRS to keep that difference as part of next year's estimated taxes paid.

Maintaining Records for a Tax Audit

The Internal Revenue Service **audits**, or verifies the tax returns of certain individuals and companies each year. The reasons that the IRS selects certain income tax returns to audit change from time to time.

If your income tax return is selected for audit, it is important that you have records to back up the data you entered on the return you sent to the IRS. For small businesses, these records include source documents, such as sales invoices and check stubs. They also include record keeping forms, such as cash receipts and payments journals, and financial statements.

Usually the IRS does not audit your income tax return in the year you sent it in. You are more likely to be audited for returns you submitted three or four years ago. Most accountants recommend that you keep your source documents, record keeping forms, and financial statements for at least five years. Many businesses keep these records for a much longer time.

BUILDING YOUR BUSINESS VOCABULARY

On a sheet of paper, write the headings **Statement Number** and **Words**. Next, choose the words that match the statements. Write each word you choose next to the statement number it matches. Be careful; not all the words listed should be used.

Statements	Words
1. A careful guess	audit
2. Social security tax for self-employed people	balance due
	estimate
3. A form that shows income, expenses, and net income or net loss	estimated tax
	expenses
4. When expenses are greater than income	financial statements
5. When estimated taxes paid are greater than total taxes due	income
	income statement
6. When total taxes due are greater than estimated taxes paid	income tax
	net income
7. When income is greater than expenses	net loss
8. A tax on net income	refund
9. Estimated amounts of income tax and self-employment tax paid during the year	self-employment tax
10. To verify or check for accuracy and completeness	

PROBLEM SOLVING MODEL FOR: *Using the Income Statement to Compute Taxes*

> **STEP 1** ▶ *Compute the actual income tax.*
>
> **STEP 2** ▶ *Compute the actual self-employment tax.*
>
> **STEP 3** ▶ *Figure the total taxes due.*
>
> **STEP 4** ▶ *Settle up with the IRS.*

APPLICATION PROBLEMS

PROBLEM 68-1 ▶ **Directions**

Copy and complete the table that follows in this way:

a. Calculate the self-employment tax on each net income by using a rate of 14% and a maximum of $50,000.00. Enter your answer in Column A.
b. Add the income tax on each line to your answer in Column A. Enter this total in Column B.
c. Compare the total taxes due that you have entered in Column B with the estimated taxes paid listed on each line. Enter the difference in Column C.
d. Label the difference that you entered in Column C as either a *balance due* or a *refund*. Enter the words *balance due* or *refund* in Column D.

Line 1 is filled in for you as an example. (Watch out for the $50,000.00 limit.)

Net Income × .14 = income

		A		B		C	D
	Net Income	Self-Employment Tax	Income Tax	Total Taxes Due	Estimated Taxes Paid	Difference	Balance Due or Refund
1.	$ 20,000.00	$ 2,800.00	$ 3,200.00	$ 6,000.00	$ 5,800.00	$ 200.00	balance due
2.	$ 40,000.00	$_____	$ 8,000.00	$_____	$13,200.00	$_____	_____
3.	$ 50,000.00	$_____	$12,500.00	$_____	$19,700.00	$_____	_____
4.	$ 35,000.00	$_____	$ 7,100.00	$_____	$12,300.00	$_____	_____
5.	$ 15,000.00	$_____	$ 2,250.00	$_____	$ 4,870.00	$_____	_____
6.	$ 18,500.00	$_____	$ 3,100.00	$_____	$ 5,630.00	$_____	_____
7.	$ 60,000.00	$_____	$16,000.00	$_____	$23,500.00	$_____	_____
8.	$100,000.00	$_____	$31,500.00	$_____	$43,750.00	$_____	_____

Directions

Complete the following table by using directions *a.* through *d.* given in Problem 1.

	A Self-Employment Tax		B	Estimated Taxes Paid	C Difference	D Balance Due or Refund
Net Income		Income Tax	Total Taxes Due			
1. $ 42,000.00	$_____	$ 8,100.00	$_____	$13,700.00	$_____	_____
2. $ 53,500.00	$_____	$13,200.00	$_____	$20,100.00	$_____	_____
3. $ 17,500.00	$_____	$ 3,075.00	$_____	$ 5,510.00	$_____	_____
4. $ 12,700.00	$_____	$ 1,905.00	$_____	$ 4,630.00	$_____	_____
5. $ 49,000.00	$_____	$12,450.00	$_____	$19,250.00	$_____	_____
6. $ 37,400.00	$_____	$ 7,650.00	$_____	$12,650.00	$_____	_____
7. $170,000.00	$_____	$59,500.00	$_____	$66,600.00	$_____	_____
8. $200,000.00	$_____	$70,000.00	$_____	$77,250.00	$_____	_____

CHECKPOINT

68-2 (1b)
Total Taxes Due
= $13,980.00

Amy Starr owns and operates Starr Racquet Club. She keeps separate records of income received from renting tennis courts and from giving tennis lessons.

Directions

CHECKPOINT

68-3 (d)
Difference = $303.14

a. Prepare an income statement for the year ended December 31, 19--, from the following information:

During the year, she received $27,650.00 from tennis court rentals and $19,475.00 from tennis lessons.

She paid the following expenses during the year: advertising, $525.15; electricity, $1,795.45; rent, $8,375.00; insurance, $796.25; office, $1,095.40; supplies, $3,725.75; telephone, $887.60; and miscellaneous, $1,375.40.

b. Calculate her self-employment tax, using a rate of 14% of net income.
c. If her income taxes are $5,600.00, find the total taxes due.
d. If estimated taxes that she paid during the year are $9,900.00, find the difference between estimated taxes paid and total taxes due.
e. Label the difference you calculated in *d.* as either balance due or refund.

Problem 68-4 may be found in the Working Papers.

BUSINESS TERMS PREVIEW

- Capital • Capital statement • Net decrease in capital •
- Net increase in capital • Withdrawal •

GOALS

1. To learn how capital changes.
2. To learn how to prepare a capital statement.

𝒰NDERSTANDING THE JOB

KEY *Terms*

Capital. The worth of a business.

Net income increases capital.
Net loss decreases capital.
Withdrawals decrease capital.

KEY *Terms*

Withdrawal. Cash or other items of value taken for the owner's use.

Capital statement. A form that shows changes in capital over a period of time.

Every business has a value to its owner and to potential buyers. This value is what the business is worth. The name given to the worth of a business is **capital**.

As a business operates, capital changes. Capital can increase or it can decrease. A net income will cause capital to increase. Net income makes the value of a business go up. A net loss will cause capital to decrease. A net loss makes the value of a business go down.

You learned in earlier jobs that owners of businesses may take cash, or other items of value, from their businesses for their own use. These **withdrawals** will cause capital to decrease. Withdrawals make the value of a business go down.

You have also learned how to prepare one kind of financial statement—the income statement. In this job, you will learn how to prepare another financial statement—the **capital statement**. A capital statement shows the changes in capital over a period of time. You will find net income, net loss, and withdrawals on a capital statement, since these are the items that cause a change in the value of a business.

Kathleen Conway, owner of the Keep 'Em Tickin' clock repair shop, began the month of April with capital of $100,000.00. During April, she earned net income of $950.00. (See Illustration 69A, below.) During April, she withdrew $700.00. Your job is to prepare her capital statement for April.

Illustration 69A shows Kathleen's capital statement for April. Here are the steps you would follow to prepare it:

STEP 1 ▶ Enter the heading.

As usual, the capital statement has a three-line heading.

WHO? Keep 'Em Tickin'
WHAT? Capital Statement
WHEN? For the Month Ended April 30, 19--

Like the income statement, the capital statement covers a period of time, so the WHEN? reads "For the Month Ended..." For a twelve-month period, it would read "For the Year Ended..."

STEP 2 ▶ Record the beginning amount of capital.

Write "Capital, April 1, 19--" on the first line. Enter the amount of capital on April 1 in the second money column. Dollar signs are not needed.

Illustration 69A Capital statement

Keep 'Em Tickin'				
Capital Statement				
For the Month Ended April 30, 19--				
Capital, April 1, 19--				100 0 0 0 00
Net income		9 5 0 00		
Less: withdrawals		7 0 0 00		
Net increase in capital				2 5 0 00
Capital, April 30, 19--				100 2 5 0 00

STEP 3 ▶ *Record the net income or net loss.*

Write the words "Net income" on the next line. Enter the amount of net income in the first money column.

The net income amount comes from the income statement. Look at the final amount in Illustration 67A (page 592), and you will find $950.00. Whenever a record keeper prepares both an income statement and a capital statement, the income statement must be done first. The reason for this is that you need the net income figure to prepare the capital statement.

If there was a net loss instead of a net income, the words *Net loss* would be written instead and the amount would be entered in parentheses.

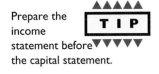

TIP

Prepare the income statement before the capital statement.

STEP 4 ▶ *Record the withdrawals.*

Since withdrawals decrease capital, they will be subtracted from the amount of net income. Write "Less: withdrawals" on the next line. The word *Less* tells you to subtract. Enter the amount in the first money column.

STEP 5 ▶ *Figure the change in capital.*

Draw a single rule and subtract the amount of withdrawals from the amount of net income to find the change in capital. If the owner had more net income than she or he withdrew, the capital would increase. This is the case for Kathleen. She had a **net increase in capital**, calculated as follows:

Net income	$ 950.00
Less: withdrawals	- 700.00
Net increase in capital	$ 250.00

Kathleen earned a net income of $950.00, but she chose to remove $700.00 of it from the business. The value of her business, the capital, increased by $250.00. The amount of $250.00 is entered in the second money column. "Net increase in capital" is written on the fourth line.

Some business owners withdraw more than they earn. When this happens, you have a **net decrease in capital**. If you have a net income of $950.00, but withdraw $1,150.00, the net decrease in capital is calculated as follows:

Net income	$ 950.00
Less: withdrawals	- 1,150.00
Net decrease in capital	($ 200.00)

The amount of $200.00 is entered in parentheses in the second money column, and "Net decrease in capital" is written on the fourth line.

Rule a single line under the amount of net increase in capital. Add the net increase in capital to the beginning amount of capital to get the ending amount of capital.

Capital, April 1, 19--	$100,000.00
Net increase in capital	+ 250.00
Capital, April 30, 19--	$100,250.00

Enter the total in the second money column and double rule the column. Write "Capital, April 30, 19--" on the fifth line.

If there were a net decrease in capital, it would be subtracted from the beginning amount of capital. For example, if you began with capital of $75,000.00 and had a net decrease in capital of $200.00, you would calculate the ending amount of capital as follows:

Capital, April 1, 19--	$75,000.00
Net decrease in capital	- 200.00
Capital, April 30, 19--	$74,800.00

You would still write "Capital, April 30, 19--" on the fifth line. You would enter the new amount of capital in the second money column and double rule the column.

Illustration 69B shows a computer-generated capital statement. All financial statements can be prepared by a computer by selecting the proper menu key.

Illustration 69B   Capital statement prepared by computer

```
                        Keep 'Em Tickin'
                        Capital Statement
                     For Period Ended 04/30/--


   Kathleen Conway, Capital (Beg. of Period)      100,000.00

   Net Income                              950.00
   Less:  Withdrawals                      700.00

   Net Increase in Capital                             250.00

   Kathleen Conway, Capital (End of Period)        100,250.00
```

BUILDING YOUR BUSINESS VOCABULARY

On a sheet of paper, write the headings **Statement Number** and **Words**. Next, choose the words that match the statements. Write each word you choose next to the statement number it matches. Be careful; not all the words listed should be used.

Statements	Words
1. When cash or other items of value of a business are taken for the owner's use	balance due
2. The worth of a business	capital
3. Summaries of the results of a business	capital statement
4. When net income is greater than withdrawals	estimate
5. A form that shows income, expenses, and net income or net loss	financial statements
6. A form that shows changes in capital over a period of time	income statement
7. When withdrawals are greater than net income	net decrease in capital
8. A careful guess	net increase in capital
	revenue
	withdrawal

PROBLEM SOLVING MODEL FOR: *Preparing a Capital Statement*

STEP 1 ▶ *Enter the heading.*

STEP 2 ▶ *Record the beginning amount of capital.*

STEP 3 ▶ *Record the net income or net loss.*

STEP 4 ▶ *Record the withdrawals.*

STEP 5 ▶ *Figure the change in capital.*

STEP 6 ▶ *Find the ending amount of capital.*

PPLICATION PROBLEMS

PROBLEM 69-1 ▶ Carl Lambert, owner of Carl's Service Station, begins the month of March, 19--, with capital of $75,000.00. During March, he earns net income of $2,500.00. During March, he withdraws $1,450.00 from the business.

CHECKPOINT ✓

69-1
Ending amount of capital = $76,050.00

Directions

Using the information given, prepare a capital statement for Carl's Service Station for the month ended March 31, 19--.

PROBLEM 69-2 ▶ Kari Primo, owner of Kari's Home Decorating Service, begins the month of October, 19--, with capital of $96,350.75. During October, she earns net income of $17,345.30. During October, she withdraws $13,142.95 from the business.

AUTOMATED

CHECKPOINT ✓

69-2
Ending amount of capital = $100,553.10

Directions

Using the information given, prepare a capital statement for Kari's Home Decorating Service for the month ended October 31, 19--.

PROBLEM 69-3 ▶ Paula James owns and operates Paula's Child Care Service. She begins the month of May, 19--, with capital of $32,104.63. During May, she earns net income of $3,155.00. During May, she withdraws $4,275.14 from the business.

AUTOMATED

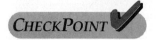

CHECKPOINT ✓

69-3
Ending amount of capital = $30,984.49

Directions

Using the information given, prepare a capital statement for Paula's Child Care Service for the month ended May 31, 19--.

Problem 69-4 may be found in the Working Papers.

APPLIED MATH PREVIEW

Find the missing amount on each line.

1. $ _____ = $17,500.00 + $ 40,000.00
2. $ 75,000.00 = $45,000.00 + $ _____
3. $ 95,000.00 = $ _____ + $ 60,000.00
4. $ 17,475.40 = $ 4,378.15 + $ _____
5. $ _____ = $19,207.35 + $ 31,436.95
6. $196,411.05 = $ _____ + $104,127.99

BUSINESS TERMS PREVIEW

- Accounting equation • Assets • Balance sheet • Liabilities •

GOALS

1. To learn the fundamental equation of accounting.
2. To learn how to prepare a balance sheet.

𝒰NDERSTANDING THE JOB

KEY Terms

Assets. Things owned that have money value.

Liabilities. Amounts owed to creditors.

When one person owns a business, the items that are owned are known as the **assets** of that business. Assets are things owned that have money value. Examples of business assets are cash, supplies, equipment, land, and buildings.

Some of the assets that you own will be fully paid for. Some of the assets may not be fully paid for. For example, you may have borrowed money to buy a building. Or, you may owe money for equipment that you purchased on credit. Amounts owed to creditors are called **liabilities**. Examples of liabilities are accounts payable and sales tax payable. A liability always includes the word *payable* in its title.

If a business has assets of $10,000.00 and liabilities of $3,000.00, the business is actually worth the difference, $7,000.00:

Assets -
Liabilities =
Capital.

△△△△△
TIP
▽▽▽▽▽

Assets	-	Liabilities	=	Capital
$10,000.00	-	$3,000.00	=	$7,000.00

One way to prove your math is to add the capital to the liabilities. The total should equal the assets, as shown on page 610:

$$\begin{array}{lcccc}
\text{Assets} & = & \text{Liabilities} & + & \text{Capital} \\
\$10{,}000.00 & = & \$3{,}000.00 & + & \$7{,}000.00
\end{array}$$

Balance
sheet shows
that accounting
equation is in balance.

▲▲▲▲▲
TIP
▼▼▼▼▼

The statement Assets = Liabilities + Capital is called the **accounting equation**. An equation shows that the amounts on each side of the equals sign are equal, or in balance. In the accounting equation, that means that the total amount of assets must equal the total amount of liabilities and capital for a business.

In this job, you will learn how to prepare another type of financial statement—the **balance sheet**. A balance sheet shows the assets, liabilities, and capital of a business. To be correct, the balance sheet must show that the assets of a business are equal to its liabilities and capital. So, the balance sheet shows the accounting equation for a business.

SAMPLE PROBLEM

Kathleen Conway, owner of Keep 'Em Tickin', finds that the business has the following asset, liability, and capital balances on April 30, 19--:

Cash	$ 13,700.00
Supplies	4,750.00
Equipment	68,000.00
Truck	25,500.00
Accounts payable	11,700.00
Kathleen Conway capital	100,250.00

Your job is to prepare the balance sheet for the business as of April 30.

Illustration 70A shows Kathleen's balance sheet. Here are the steps to follow to prepare it:

STEP **1** ▶ **Enter the heading.**

The heading again answers three questions:

WHO? Keep 'Em Tickin'
WHAT? Balance Sheet
WHEN? April 30, 19--

Notice that the balance sheet is prepared as of a single date. It does not cover a period of time as the income and capital statements do. A balance sheet tells you balances on that date.

Illustration 70A
Balance sheet

Keep 'Em Tickin'										
Balance Sheet										
April 30, 19--										
Assets										
Cash	13	7	0	0	00					
Supplies	4	7	5	0	00					
Equipment	68	0	0	0	00					
Truck	25	5	0	0	00					
Total assets						111	9	5	0	00
Liabilities										
Accounts payable						11	7	0	0	00
Capital										
Kathleen Conway, capital						100	2	5	0	00
Total liabilities and capital						111	9	5	0	00

STEP **2** ▶ **Prepare the Assets section.**

Write the word *Assets* on the first line. Center it and underline it. Then, list each asset at the left margin. Enter the amount of each asset in the first money column.

Draw a single ruling under the last asset amount. Add the amounts, and enter the total one line down in the second money column. Write the words *Total assets* at the left margin, on the line with $111,950.00. Draw a double ruling under the total.

Kathleen has only four assets. Whether a business has four assets or twenty assets, the organization of the Assets section will be the same.

STEP **3** ▶ **Prepare the Liabilities section.**

Write the word *Liabilities* on the next line. Center it and underline it. Then, list each liability at the left margin. Kathleen has only one liability, Accounts payable. Enter the amount in the second money column.

If there were more than one liability, the Liabilities section would be set up in the same way as the Assets section. Illustration 70B (page 612) shows how this would look.

Liabilities																
Accounts payable					15	7	2	0	00							
Sales tax payable						3	1	4	5	00						
Total liabilities											18	8	6	5	00	

STEP 4 ▶ **Prepare the Capital section.**

Write the word *Capital* on the next line. Center it and underline it. Write "Kathleen Conway, capital" on the following line at the left margin. Enter the amount of capital, $100,250.00, in the second money column.

Prepare the
capital
statement
before the balance sheet.

▲▲▲▲▲
TIP
▼▼▼▼▼

The amount may be familiar to you. You will find it in Illustration 69A (page 604). It is the ending amount of capital from the capital statement. When you are preparing financial statements, you must prepare the capital statement before you prepare the balance sheet. You need that ending capital figure for the balance sheet.

STEP 5 ▶ **Complete the balance sheet.**

Draw a single ruling under the amount of capital. Add the amount of total liabilities ($11,700.00) to the amount of capital ($100,250.00). The total should equal the total of the assets ($111,950.00). Since it does, you have proven that the accounting equation is in balance.

$$\text{Assets} \quad = \text{Liabilities} \; + \; \text{Capital}$$
$$\$111{,}950.00 = \;\; \$11{,}700.00 \quad + \quad \$100{,}250.00$$

Draw a double ruling under the total. Write "Total liabilities and capital" on the line with the total.

Illustration 70C shows how a computer-generated balance sheet would look. The menu key for balance sheet would display this form on the screen.

Illustration 70C
Balance sheet prepared
by computer

```
                        Keep 'Em Tickin'
                         Balance Sheet
                           04/30/--

    A s s e t s
    ------------
    Cash                                    13700.00
    Supplies                                 4750.00
    Equipment                               68000.00
    Truck                                   25500.00
                                           ----------
    Total Assets                                          111950.00
                                                         ===========
    L i a b i l i t i e s
    ----------------------
    Accounts Payable                        11700.00
                                           ----------
    Total Liabilities                                      11700.00

    C a p i t a l
    --------------
    Kathleen Conway, Capital               100250.00
                                           ----------
    Total Capital                                         100250.00

    Total Liabilities & Capital                           111950.00
                                                         ===========
```

On a sheet of paper, write the headings **Statement Number** and **Words**. Next, choose the words that match the statements. Write each word you choose next to the statement number it matches. Be careful; not all the words listed should be used.

Statements	Words
1. A form that shows income, expenses, and net income or net loss	accounting equation
	assets
2. Things owned that have money value	balance sheet
3. Summaries of the results of a business	capital
4. A form that shows that assets equal liabilities plus capital	capital statement
	financial statements
5. Assets equal liabilities plus capital	income statement
6. A form that shows changes in capital over a period of time	liabilities
	net income
7. Amounts owed to creditors	withdrawal
8. The worth of a business	

PROBLEM SOLVING MODEL FOR: *Preparing a Balance Sheet*

STEP 1 ▶ *Enter the heading.*

STEP 2 ▶ *Prepare the Assets section.*

STEP 3 ▶ *Prepare the Liabilities section.*

STEP 4 ▶ *Prepare the Capital section.*

STEP 5 ▶ *Complete the balance sheet.*

APPLICATION PROBLEMS

PROBLEM **70-1** ▶ Nelsa Sanchez has the following assets, liabilities, and capital on July 31, 19--:

Cash	$ 2,134.78
Office supplies	1,279.65
Store supplies	3,017.19
Office equipment	11,047.30
Store equipment	19,145.10
Truck	11,500.00
Accounts payable	17,950.00
Nelsa Sanchez, capital	30,174.02

CHECKPOINT ✓

70-1
Total assets = $48,124.02

Directions

Prepare a balance sheet as of July 31, 19--, for Nelsa's business, Sanchez Computer Service.

PROBLEM 70-2 ▶ Marcia Wilkes owns and operates Marcia's Preschool. Her assets, liabilities, and capital on November 30, 19--, are as follows:

Cash	$ 9,164.36
Supplies	2,177.12
Furniture	11,024.19
Equipment	21,750.00
Accounts payable	14,175.60
Marcia Wilkes, capital	29,940.07

CHECKPOINT ✔

70-2
Total assets = $44,115.67

Directions

Prepare her balance sheet as of November 30, 19--.

PROBLEM 70-3 ▶ Pavel Sulu owns and operates Sulu's Amusement Park. His assets, liabilities, and capital on October 31, 19--, are as follows:

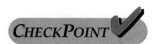

Cash	$ 1,907.21
Supplies	2,135.09
Adult ride equipment	27,145.00
Children's ride equipment	16,090.00
Arcade games	4,175.50
Truck	17,195.00
Accounts payable	22,745.10
Sales tax payable	1,396.05
Pavel Sulu, capital	44,506.65

CHECKPOINT ✔

70-3
Total liabilities = $24,141.15

Directions

Prepare his balance sheet as of October 31, 19--.

Problem 70-4 may be found in the Working Papers.

JOB 71 ▶ PREPARING A SIX-COLUMN WORK SHEET

APPLIED MATH PREVIEW

Copy and complete these problems.

1. $4,716.19	2. $ 5,171.12	3. $14,175.50	5. $ 21,190.64
308.12	45,000.00	- 4,097.12	- 17,204.83
1,204.47	31,750.00		
391.17	625.75		
3,177.49	401.97	4. $ 13,199.64	6. $ 36,595.09
+ 496.72	+ 2,177.63	- 11,102.77	- 22,177.64

BUSINESS TERM PREVIEW

- **Work sheet** -

GOALS

1. To learn how to prepare a six-column work sheet.
2. To learn how to prepare financial statements from a work sheet.

UNDERSTANDING THE JOB

You have learned how to prepare three financial statements in this chapter: the income statement, the capital statement, and the balance sheet. This is the order in which the statements should be prepared. Illustration 71A (page 616) shows the relationship among the statements.

Illustration 71A shows that income and expense information is used to prepare the income statement. The answer to the income statement, net income or net loss, is used on the capital statement. Beginning capital and withdrawals information is used to prepare the capital statement. The answer to the capital statement, ending capital, is used on the balance sheet. Assets and liabilities information is used to prepare the balance sheet.

The titles listed on the financial statements are actually *names of accounts* found in the general ledger. General ledger account titles and balances are used to prepare the statements.

The fastest way to prepare all financial statements from information in the accounts is to use a form called a **work sheet**. A work sheet is not a formal financial statement. It is a form on which you summarize all the information you need for the financial statements.

KEY Terms

Work sheet. A form used to summarize information for financial statements.

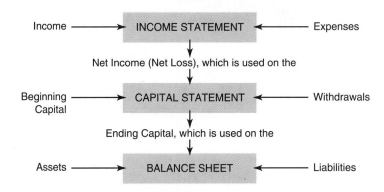

Illustration 71A   How the financial statements are related

Income ⟶ INCOME STATEMENT ⟵ Expenses

Net Income (Net Loss), which is used on the ↓

Beginning Capital ⟶ CAPITAL STATEMENT ⟵ Withdrawals

Ending Capital, which is used on the ↓

Assets ⟶ BALANCE SHEET ⟵ Liabilities

Illustration 71B on page 617 shows a completed work sheet. Sample Problem 1 shows you how it was prepared. Sample Problem 2 shows you how financial statements are prepared from the work sheet.

SAMPLE PROBLEM 1

Kathleen Conway's general ledger account balances for Keep 'Em Tickin' as of April 30, 19--, follow:

Acct. No.	Account Title	Balance Debit	Balance Credit
110	Cash	$13,700.00	
120	Supplies	4,750.00	
130	Equipment	68,000.00	
140	Truck	25,500.00	
210	Accounts Payable		$ 11,700.00
310	Kathleen Conway, Capital		100,000.00
320	Kathleen Conway, Drawing	700.00	
410	Income, Clock Repairs		750.00
420	Income, Watch Repairs		1,570.00
510	Rent Expense	750.00	
520	Insurance Expense	45.00	
530	Supplies Expense	150.00	
540	Truck Expense	135.00	
550	Telephone Expense	120.00	
560	Electricity Expense	170.00	

Keep 'Em Tickin'
Work Sheet
For the Month Ended April 30, 19--

| | | TRIAL BALANCE | | INCOME STATEMENT | | BALANCE SHEET | |
ACCOUNT TITLE	ACCT. NO.	DEBIT	CREDIT	DEBIT	CREDIT	DEBIT	CREDIT
Cash	110	1,595.00				1,595.00	
Supplies	120	475.00				475.00	
Equipment	130	6,800.00				6,800.00	
Truck	140	2,550.00				2,550.00	
Accounts Payable	210		1,170.00				1,170.00
Kathleen Conway, Capital	310		10,000.00				10,000.00
Kathleen Conway, Drawing	320	700.00				700.00	
Income, Clock Repairs	410		750.00		750.00		
Income, Watch Repairs	420		1,570.00		1,570.00		
Rent Expense	510	750.00		750.00			
Insurance Expense	520	45.00		45.00			
Supplies Expense	530	150.00		150.00			
Truck Expense	540	135.00		135.00			
Telephone Expense	550	120.00		120.00			
Electricity Expense	560	170.00		170.00			
Totals		13,490.00	13,490.00	1,370.00	2,320.00	12,120.00	11,170.00
Net Income				950.00			950.00
				2,320.00	2,320.00	12,120.00	12,120.00

Illustration 71B (page 617) shows how these account balances were used to prepare a work sheet. Here are the steps to follow:

STEP 1 ▶ **Enter the heading.**

The heading should again answer:

WHO? Keep 'Em Tickin'
WHAT? Work Sheet
WHEN? For the Month Ended April 30, 19--

STEP 2 ▶ **Prepare a trial balance on the work sheet.**

Enter all account titles in the Account Title column. Enter all account numbers in the Acct. No. column. Enter account balances in the Debit or Credit columns of the trial balance. What you are doing is preparing the trial balance on the work sheet.

Draw a single ruling under the Trial Balance columns. Foot each column. When your Debit and Credit totals are equal, write in final totals and double rule under the totals. Write the word *Totals* in the Account Title column. Do not continue to Step 3 until your trial balance is in balance. Illustration 71C shows the completed trial balance.

Illustration 71C
Completed trial balance

	ACCOUNT TITLE	ACCT. NO.	TRIAL BALANCE DEBIT	TRIAL BALANCE CREDIT
1	*Cash*	110	13 7 0 0 00	
2	*Supplies*	120	4 7 5 0 00	
3	*Equipment*	130	68 0 0 0 00	
4	*Truck*	140	25 5 0 0 00	
5	*Accounts Payable*	210		11 7 0 0 00
6	*Kathleen Conway, Capital*	310		100 0 0 0 00
7	*Kathleen Conway, Drawing*	320	7 0 0 00	
8	*Income, Clock Repairs*	410		7 5 0 00
9	*Income, Watch Repairs*	420		1 5 7 0 00
10	*Rent Expense*	510	7 5 0 00	
11	*Insurance Expense*	520	4 5 00	
12	*Supplies Expense*	530	1 5 0 00	
13	*Truck Expense*	540	1 3 5 00	
14	*Telephone Expense*	550	1 2 0 00	
15	*Electricity Expense*	560	1 7 0 00	
16	*Totals*		114 0 2 0 00	114 0 2 0 00
17				
18				

STEP 3 ▶ **Extend asset, liability, capital, and drawing account balances to the Balance Sheet columns.**

Extend the accounts that belong on the balance sheet and the capital statement to the Balance Sheet columns:

Extend balance sheet and capital statement accounts to the Balance Sheet columns.
Extend assets and drawing to the Balance Sheet Debit column.
Extend liabilities and capital to the Balance Sheet Credit column.

Assets—Cash, Supplies, Equipment, Truck
Liabilities—Accounts Payable
Capital—Kathleen Conway, Capital
Drawing—Kathleen Conway, Drawing

To extend an amount, copy that amount a second time. *Extend a debit as a debit.* Thus, the amount of Cash, $13,700.00, is extended to the Balance Sheet Debit column. The balances of the Supplies, Equipment, Truck, and Kathleen Conway, Drawing accounts are all extended to the Balance Sheet Debit column.

Extend a credit as a credit. The balances of the Accounts Payable and Kathleen Conway, Capital accounts are extended to the Balance Sheet Credit column.

Illustration 71D shows the extensions to the Balance Sheet columns.

	ACCOUNT TITLE	ACCT. NO.	TRIAL BALANCE		BALANCE SHEET		
			DEBIT	CREDIT	DEBIT	CREDIT	
1	Cash	110	13 700 00		13 700 00		1
2	Supplies	120	4 750 00		4 750 00		2
3	Equipment	130	68 000 00		68 000 00		3
4	Truck	140	25 500 00		25 500 00		4
5	Accounts Payable	210		11 700 00		11 700 00	5
6	Kathleen Conway, Capital	310		100 000 00		100 000 00	6
7	Kathleen Conway, Drawing	320	700 00		700 00		7

Illustration 71D Extending amounts to the Balance Sheet columns

STEP 4 ▶ *Extend income and expense account balances to the Income Statement columns.*

Extend income statement accounts to the Income Statement columns.
Extend income accounts to the Income Statement Credit column.
Extend expense accounts to the Income Statement Debit column.

Extend the accounts that belong on the income statement to the Income Statement columns. Extend both income accounts and all six expense accounts to the Income Statement columns.

Extend a credit as a credit. Thus, both income accounts are extended to the Income Statement Credit column.

Extend a debit as a debit. Thus, all expense accounts are extended to the Income Statement Debit column.

Illustration 71E on page 620 shows the extensions to the Income Statement columns.

STEP 5 ▶ *Foot the Income Statement and Balance Sheet columns.*

Draw a single ruling under all four columns to which you have extended amounts. Foot all four columns.

	ACCOUNT TITLE	ACCT. NO.	TRIAL BALANCE DEBIT	TRIAL BALANCE CREDIT	INCOME STATEMENT DEBIT	INCOME STATEMENT CREDIT
8	*Income, Clock Repairs*	410		7 5 0 00		7 5 0 00
9	*Income, Watch Repairs*	420		1 5 7 0 00		1 5 7 0 00
10	*Rent Expense*	510	7 5 0 00		7 5 0 00	
11	*Insurance Expense*	520	4 5 00		4 5 00	
12	*Supplies Expense*	530	1 5 0 00		1 5 0 00	
13	*Truck Expense*	540	1 3 5 00		1 3 5 00	
14	*Telephone Expense*	550	1 2 0 00		1 2 0 00	
15	*Electricity Expense*	560	1 7 0 00		1 7 0 00	

**Illustration 71F
Contents of the four
financial statement
columns**

INCOME STATEMENT DEBIT	INCOME STATEMENT CREDIT	BALANCE SHEET DEBIT	BALANCE SHEET CREDIT	
				1
EXPENSES	INCOME	ASSETS	LIABILITIES	2
		DRAWING	CAPITAL	3

STEP 6 ▶ Calculate net income or net loss.

Think about what each of the four columns contains. Illustration 71F summarizes the contents of each column.

To find net income or net loss, you subtract expenses from income. Using the work sheet, subtract the total of the Income Statement Debit column (expenses) from the total of the Income Statement Credit column (income). The difference is net income or net loss.

Income
Statement
Credit - Income
Statement Debit = Net
Income or Net Loss

▲▲▲▲▲
TIP
▼▼▼▼▼

Income Statement, Credit	$ 2,320.00
Income Statement, Debit	- 1,370.00
Net Income	$ 950.00

Since income (Credit) is larger than expenses (Debit), you have a net income. If the total expenses were larger, you would have a net loss.

STEP 7 ▶ Check the amount of net income (or net loss).

To check your answer for net income, subtract the Balance Sheet Credit column from the Balance Sheet Debit column. The answer should be the same as in Step 6 if you have done all of your extensions and additions correctly.

Balance
Sheet
Debit -
Balance Sheet Credit = Net
Income

▲▲▲▲▲
TIP
▼▼▼▼▼

Balance Sheet Debit	$ 112,650.00
Balance Sheet Credit	- 111,700.00
Net Income	$ 950.00

STEP 8 ▶ Complete the work sheet.

You have five more steps to follow to complete the work sheet.

1. Record the totals of the Income Statement and Balance Sheet columns as final totals.
2. Enter the amount of net income twice: in the Income Statement column with the smaller total (Debit) and in the Balance Sheet column with the smaller total (Credit).
3. Draw a single ruling under the four financial statement columns again. Foot one more time. You should have two pairs of equal totals.
4. Write in the four final totals and double rule the four columns.
5. Write the words *Net Income* in the Account Title column on the line where you recorded $950.00 twice.

Illustration 71G shows the steps to complete a work sheet.

	ACCOUNT TITLE	3 INCOME STATEMENT DEBIT	4 INCOME STATEMENT CREDIT	5 BALANCE SHEET DEBIT	6 BALANCE SHEET CREDIT	
16		1 3 7 0 00 / 1 3 7 0 00	2 3 2 0 00 / 2 3 2 0 00	112 6 5 0 00 / 112 6 5 0 00	111 7 0 0 00 / 111 7 0 0 00	16
17	*Net Income*	9 5 0 00			9 5 0 00	17
18		2 3 2 0 00 / 2 3 2 0 00	2 3 2 0 00 / 2 3 2 0 00	112 6 5 0 00 / 112 6 5 0 00	112 6 5 0 00 / 112 6 5 0 00	18

Illustration 71G   Completing a work sheet

SAMPLE PROBLEM 2

Kathleen Conway will now prepare her financial statements from the work sheet. Here are the steps she follows:

STEP 1 ▶ Prepare the income statement.

To prepare the income statement from the work sheet, Kathleen will use all of the information in the Income Statement columns. Illustration 71H on page 622 shows how the information is taken from the Income Statement columns and placed on the income statement.

Illustration 71H
Transferring information
from the work sheet to
the income statement

	ACCOUNT TITLE	ACCT. NO.	INCOME STATEMENT	
			DEBIT	CREDIT
1	Cash	110		
2	Supplies	120		
3	Equipment	130		
4	Truck	140		
5	Accounts Payable	210		
6	Kathleen Conway, Capital	310		
7	Kathleen Conway, Drawing	320		
8	Income, Clock Repairs	410		7 5 0 00
9	Income, Watch Repairs	420		1 5 7 0 00
10	Rent Expense	510	7 5 0 00	
11	Insurance Expense	520	4 5 00	
12	Supplies Expense	530	1 5 0 00	
13	Truck Expense	540	1 3 5 00	
14	Telephone Expense	550	1 2 0 00	
15	Electricity Expense	560	1 7 0 00	
16	Totals		1 3 7 0 00	2 3 2 0 00
17	Net Income		9 5 0 00	
18			2 3 2 0 00	2 3 2 0 00

Keep 'Em Tickin'		
Income Statement		
For the Month Ended April 30, 19--		
Revenue:		
Clock repairs	7 5 0 00	
Watch repairs	1 5 7 0 00	
Total income		2 3 2 0 00
Expenses:		
Rent expense	7 5 0 00	
Insurance expense	4 5 00	
Supplies expense	1 5 0 00	
Truck expense	1 3 5 00	
Telephone expense	1 2 0 00	
Electricity expense	1 7 0 00	
Total expenses		1 3 7 0 00
Net income		9 5 0 00

STEP 2 ▶ *Prepare the capital statement.*

To prepare the capital statement from the work sheet, Kathleen will use three figures: beginning capital, net income, and withdrawals. Illustration 71I on page 623 shows where these figures are found on the work sheet and how they are transferred to the capital statement.

Notice that the Kathleen Conway, Drawing account is used for the withdrawals figure.

STEP 3 ▶ **Prepare the balance sheet.**

To prepare the balance sheet from the work sheet, Kathleen will use the asset and liability accounts from the Balance Sheet columns.

Use ending capital from capital statement for balance sheet.

▲▲▲▲▲ **T I P** ▼▼▼▼▼

The capital amount to be used on the balance sheet is *not* found on the work sheet. It is the final figure on her capital statement—the ending capital. (See Illustration 71I.) Illustration 71J shows how information is transferred from the Balance Sheet columns to the balance sheet.

Illustration 71I
Transferring information from the work sheet to the capital statement

	ACCOUNT TITLE	ACCT. NO.	5 BALANCE SHEET DEBIT	6 BALANCE SHEET CREDIT	
1	Cash	110	13 7 0 0 00		1
2	Supplies	120	4 7 5 0 00		2
3	Equipment	130	68 0 0 0 00		3
4	Truck	140	25 5 0 0 00		4
5	Accounts Payable	210		11 7 0 0 00	5
6	Kathleen Conway, Capital	310		100 0 0 0 00	6
7	Kathleen Conway, Drawing	320	7 0 0 00		7
8	Income, Clock Repairs	410			8
9	Income, Watch Repairs	420			9
10	Rent Expense	510			10
11	Insurance Expense	520			11
12	Supplies Expense	530			12
13	Truck Expense	540			13
14	Telephone Expense	550			14
15	Electricity Expense	560			15
16	Totals		112 6 5 0 00	111 7 0 0 00	16
17	Net Income			9 5 0 00	17
18			112 6 5 0 00	112 6 5 0 00	18

Keep 'Em Tickin'
Capital Statement
For the Month Ended April 30, 19--

Capital, April 1, 19--		100 0 0 0 00
Net income	9 5 0 00	
Less: withdrawals	7 0 0 00	
Net increase in capital		2 5 0 00
Capital, April 30, 19--		100 2 5 0 00

Illustration 71J
Transferring information
from the work sheet to
the balance sheet

	ACCOUNT TITLE	ACCT. NO.	BALANCE SHEET	
			DEBIT	CREDIT
1	Cash	110	13 7 0 0 00	
2	Supplies	120	4 7 5 0 00	
3	Equipment	130	68 0 0 0 00	
4	Truck	140	25 5 0 0 00	
5	Accounts Payable	210		11 7 0 0 00
6	Kathleen Conway, Capital	310		100 0 0 0 00
7	Kathleen Conway, Drawing	320	7 0 0 00	
8	Income, Clock Repairs	410		
9	Income, Watch Repairs	420		
10	Rent Expense	510		
11	Insurance Expense	520		
12	Supplies Expense	530		
13	Truck Expense	540		
14	Telephone Expense	550		
15	Electricity Expense	560		
16	Totals		112 6 5 0 00	111 7 0 0 00
17	Net Income			9 5 0 00
18			112 6 5 0 00	112 6 5 0 00

Keep 'Em Tickin'		
Balance Sheet		
April 30, 19--		
Assets		
Cash	13 7 0 0 00	
Supplies	4 7 5 0 00	
Equipment	68 0 0 0 00	
Truck	25 5 0 0 00	
Total assets		111 9 5 0 00
Liabilities		
Accounts payable		11 7 0 0 00
Capital		
Kathleen Conway, capital		100 2 5 0 00
Total liabilities and capital		111 9 5 0 00

BUILDING YOUR BUSINESS VOCABULARY

On a sheet of paper, write the headings **Statement Number** and **Words**. Next, choose the words that match the statements. Write each word you choose next to the statement number it matches. Be careful; not all the words listed should be used.

Statements	Words
1. Entered again in a second column	accounting equation
2. Assets equal liabilities plus capital	assets
3. A form used to summarize information	balance sheet
for financial statements	capital
4. Things owned with money value	capital statement
5. Amounts owed to creditors	extended
6. When income is greater than expenses	income statement
7. A form that shows changes in capital over	liabilities
a period of time	net income
8. A form that shows income, expenses,	net loss
and net income or net loss	work sheet

PROBLEM SOLVING MODEL FOR: *Preparing a Six-Column Work Sheet*

STEP 1 ▶ *Enter the heading.*

STEP 2 ▶ *Prepare a trial balance on the work sheet.*

STEP 3 ▶ *Extend asset, liability, capital, and drawing account balances to the Balance Sheet columns.*

STEP 4 ▶ *Extend income and expense account balances to the Income Statement columns.*

STEP 5 ▶ *Foot the Income Statement and Balance Sheet columns.*

STEP 6 ▶ *Calculate net income or net loss.*

STEP 7 ▶ *Check the amount of net income (or net loss).*

STEP 8 ▶ *Complete the work sheet.*

APPLICATION PROBLEMS

PROBLEM | **71-1** ▶ You work for Rob Bellman, owner of Rob the Roofer, a roof repair firm. Rob's account balances on January 31, 19--, are as shown on page 626:

71-1

Net Income = $725.00

Acct. No.	Account Title	Balance Debit	Credit
110	Cash	$1,700.00	
120	Supplies	500.00	
130	Equipment	12,500.00	
140	Truck	15,000.00	
210	Accounts Payable		$ 9,600.00
310	Rob Bellman, Capital		19,875.00
320	Rob Bellman, Drawing	500.00	
410	Income, Repairs		3,150.00
510	Supplies Expense	950.00	
520	Truck Expense	450.00	
530	Rent Expense	900.00	
540	Insurance Expense	50.00	
550	Miscellaneous Expense	75.00	

Directions

Prepare a work sheet for the month ended January 31, 19--.

PROBLEM **71-2** ▶ You work for Maria Ricci, owner of Maria's Travel Agency. Maria's account balances on March 31, 19--, are as follows:

71-2

Net Income = $1,759.90

Acct. No.	Account Title	Balance Debit	Credit
110	Cash	$ 3,155.90	
120	Office Supplies	2,175.15	
130	Computer Supplies	997.60	
140	Office Equipment	13,500.00	
150	Computer Equipment	21,750.00	
210	Accounts Payable		$15,650.00
220	Sales Tax Payable		950.00
310	Maria Ricci, Capital		24,458.75
320	Maria Ricci, Drawing	1,240.00	
410	Income, Air Fare		4,775.00
420	Income, Tours		3,495.40
510	Computer Expense	4,110.90	
520	Rent Expense	1,210.00	
530	Utilities Expense	975.50	
540	Miscellaneous Expense	214.10	

Directions

Prepare a work sheet for the month ended March 31, 19--.

PROBLEM **71-3** ▶ **Directions**

Use the completed work sheet from Problem 71-2 to

CHECKPOINT ✔

71-3 (b)

Ending amount of capital = $24,978.65

a. Prepare an income statement for the month ended March 31, 19--.
b. Prepare a capital statement for the month ended March 31, 19--.
c. Prepare a balance sheet as of March 31, 19--.

Problem 71-4 may be found in the Working Papers.

CHAPTER 14

Reinforcement Activities

DISCUSSION

1. Your work sheet shows a net income of $500.00.
   a. If the Income Statement Debit total is $7,000.00, what is the Income Statement Credit total?
   b. If the Balance Sheet Credit total is $25,000.00, what is the Balance Sheet Debit total?
2. Your work sheet shows a net income of $900.00.
   a. If the Income Statement Credit total is $7,900.00, what is the Income Statement Debit total?
   b. If the Balance Sheet Debit total is $37,400.00, what is the Balance Sheet Credit total?

CRITICAL THINKING

You have learned many times throughout this textbook how important neatness and accuracy are to a record keeper. They are really important when doing a work sheet because so many different types of errors are possible.

List five different types of errors that can be made on a work sheet.

APPLIED COMMUNICATIONS

You are on your first record keeping job as a general ledger clerk. You record in the cash journal, post to the general ledger, and prepare a six-column work sheet. Write a short letter to your record keeping teacher to tell him or her some of the things you learned in class that you think have helped you on the job. Remind your teacher of who you are in your letter. Keep the letter to 100 words or less.

Bring to class 10 want ads for office and record keeping jobs. Find them in your local newspaper. List the titles of those jobs in which

1. Accuracy is required.
2. Keyboarding/typewriting is required.
3. Previous experience is required.
4. A high school education is required.
5. Use of computers is required.
6. Knowledge of record keeping is required or desired.

REVIEWING WHAT YOU HAVE LEARNED

On a sheet of paper, write the headings **Statement Number** and **Words**. Next, choose the words that best complete the statements. Write each word you choose next to the statement number it completes. Be careful; not all the words listed should be used.

Statements	Words
1. If your withdrawals are higher than your net income, you have (a, an) _____ .	assets
2. The first financial statement to prepare is the _____ .	balance due
	balance sheet
3. A careful guess is (a, an) _____ .	capital
4. To show that debits equal credits in your general ledger accounts, prepare (a, an) _____ .	capital statement
	estimate
	extended
5. The accounting equation is assets equal _____ plus capital.	income statement
6. Items with money value owned by a business are its _____ .	liabilities
	net decrease in capital
7. If your estimated taxes are $600.00 and your total tax due is $650.00, you have (a, an) _____ of $50.00.	net income
	net increase in capital
	refund
8. On a work sheet, amounts are _____ from the trial balance columns to the other columns.	revenue
	trial balance
9. The difference between the Income Statement columns on the work sheet is the amount of _____ .	work sheet
10. Both beginning and ending capital balances are found on the _____ .	
11. Before preparing your financial statements, it is handy to prepare (a, an) _____ .	

MASTERY PROBLEM

You are a record keeper for Rita's Health Club. Rita Walsh, the owner, separates income into two types: membership dues and rentals of equipment, towels, lockers, and so forth.

AUTOMATED

Rita's account balances as of December 31, 19--, follow:

Acct. No.	Account Title	Balance
110	Cash	$ 4,371.16
120	Supplies	1,779.24
130	Tanning Equipment	15,100.00
140	Athletic Equipment	47,375.00
150	Automobile	21,750.00
210	Accounts Payable	19,210.00
220	Sales Tax Payable	4,100.00
310	Rita Walsh, Capital	51,627.59
320	Rita Walsh, Drawing	12,500.00
410	Income, Membership	33,950.00
420	Income, Rentals	45,175.50
510	Rent Expense	9,000.00
520	Repairs Expense	5,167.09
530	Heat and Light Expense	7,275.46
540	Telephone Expense	1,510.90
550	Insurance Expense	2,175.00
560	Cleaning Expense	9,378.64
570	Supplies Expense	11,755.17
580	Miscellaneous Expense	4,925.43

Directions

a. Prepare a work sheet for the year ended December 31, 19--. You will need to use your knowledge of normal balance rules to do your trial balance.
b. Prepare an income statement for the year ended December 31, 19--.
c. Prepare a capital statement for the year ended December 31, 19--. Date your beginning capital January 1, 19--.
d. Prepare a balance sheet as of December 31, 19--.
e. Calculate the refund or balance due on Rita's taxes from the following information:

CHECKPOINT

(d)
Total assets = $90,375.40

Estimated tax payments made	$9,950.00
Income tax	$5,690.00
Self-employment tax	net income x 14%

REVIEWING YOUR BUSINESS VOCABULARY

This activity may be found in the Working Papers.

COMPREHENSIVE PROJECT 5

Comprehensive Project 5 has been designed to reinforce major concepts of this and previous chapters. The Comprehensive Project is found in the Working Papers.

Olympic Cyclery is a wholesale merchandising operation that sells racing bicycles and accessories to retail outlets. This business simulation requires students to use the skills and procedures presented in the second semester of record keeping. Students get hands-on experience preparing and verifying sales invoices, recording in special journals from source documents, posting from special journals, opening and updating stock records, preparing purchasing source documents, preparing financial statements, and more. This simulation is available from the publisher in either manual or automated versions. Students will perform the following activities as they simulate on-the-job training at Olympic Cyclery.

Activities in Olympic Cyclery
1. Preparing sales invoices, credit memorandums, and customer statements.
2. Preparing purchase requisitions, price quotation records, and purchase orders.
3. Preparing receiving reports and debit memorandums.
4. Checking purchase invoices.
5. Opening and updating stock records.
6. Reconciling the bank statement with the checkbook.
7. Preparing checks for monthly expenses and for creditor accounts.
8. Endorsing and depositing customer checks.
9. Using and posting from a sales journal, a sales returns and allowances journal, a cash receipts journal, a purchases journal, a purchases returns and allowances journal, and a cash payments journal.
10. Preparing a schedule of accounts receivable, a schedule of accounts payable, a work sheet, an income statement, a capital statement, and a balance sheet.

CHAPTER 15

Record Keeping for Payroll Clerks: Computing Gross Pay

*T*here are many wage plans used to pay workers. Some workers are paid for each hour they work. Others are paid for a fixed number of hours per week. Still others are paid for the number of pieces of work they finish. Many salespeople are paid a percentage of what they sell.

In Chapter 15, you will learn how to handle time cards, compute weekly wages including overtime wages, and use a payroll register. You will also learn how to compute salaries, commissions, and piece-work pay. A Calculator Tip will be given for finding regular pay, overtime pay, and gross pay.

J O B 72 ▶ HANDLING TIME CARDS

APPLIED MATH PREVIEW

Copy and complete these problems.

1.	2.	3.	4.	5.
4	$2\frac{1}{2}$	$19\frac{1}{4}$	$8\frac{1}{2}$	$7\frac{1}{4}$
5	$4\frac{1}{2}$	$8\frac{1}{2}$	$15\frac{3}{4}$	$4\frac{3}{4}$
$9\frac{1}{2}$	$7\frac{1}{4}$	4	$12\frac{1}{2}$	$3\frac{3}{4}$
$2\frac{1}{2}$	$5\frac{1}{4}$	$6\frac{1}{4}$	7	$12\frac{1}{2}$
$+ 7\frac{1}{2}$	$+ 8\frac{1}{2}$	$+ 1\frac{1}{4}$	$+ 17\frac{1}{4}$	$+ 9\frac{1}{4}$

BUSINESS TERMS PREVIEW

• Badge • Badge reader • In rack • Out rack • Punching in •
• Punching out • Time card • Time clock •

GOALS

1. To learn how to read a time card.
2. To learn how to find the number of hours an employee worked in a week.

631

UNDERSTANDING THE JOB

Some businesses use **time clocks** to keep accurate records of the hours each employee works.

Each employee is given a **time card**, like the one shown in Illustration 72A. Near the time clock, two racks are provided to hold the time cards—an **Out rack** and an **In rack**. Each employee's card is numbered. At the beginning of each week, the payroll clerk arranges the time cards in numerical order in the *Out* rack.

Illustration 72A shows the time card for Roberta Latham. Each morning when she arrives, Roberta goes to the *Out* rack and removes her card. She inserts the card in the opening in the time clock. The time clock stamps the time on her card. This is called *clocking in* or **punching in**. Look at the In column for Monday on Roberta's time card. Notice that the clock has stamped her card for 8:00 a.m. This means that she punched in at 8:00 a.m. on Monday.

Illustration 72A   Time card

Name	Roberta Latham				No.	112	

Week Ending   March 22, 19--

DAY	IN	OUT	IN	OUT	IN	OUT	TOTAL
M	8:00	12:00	1:00	5:00			
T	7:50	12:03	1:00	5:00			
W	7:54	12:04	12:57	5:06			
TH	7:58	12:02	12:58	5:03			
F	8:04	12:07	1:02	5:05			

TOTAL HOURS WORKED

	HOURS	RATE	WAGES
REGULAR			
OVERTIME			
TOTAL			

After clocking in, Roberta takes the time card out of the time clock and puts it in the *In* rack. This shows that she has clocked in for the day's work.

At lunch time, Roberta goes to the In rack, removes her card, and inserts it into the clock. The clock prints 12:00 in the first Out column for Monday. This is called *clocking out* or **punching out**. Roberta then puts the card in the Out rack to show that she has gone out for lunch.

When she returns from lunch, Roberta repeats the steps she went through in the morning. She clocks in and puts her time card in the In rack. Roberta clocked in at 1:00 p.m. When Roberta goes home, she clocks out and puts her time card in the Out rack.

Notice that Roberta used her time card four times on Monday. This procedure is repeated daily for the rest of the week.

The other In and Out columns on the time card are used for special situations. For example, an employee may leave to eat dinner and return to work later. Also, an employee may have a dentist appointment or have to run an urgent errand in the afternoon. If the employee returns to work before the day is finished, the other In and Out columns are used.

Roberta's employer has these rules for working hours:

1. The employees must start working at 8:00 a.m., go to lunch at 12:00 noon, return by 1:00 p.m., and work until 5:00 p.m.
2. If workers come to work late, their time will be counted from the next quarter hour according to Schedule #1. Notice that in the morning, employees are given a four-minute leeway (up to 8:04) to clock in. Employees are also given a four-minute leeway to clock in after lunch (up to 1:04).

Schedule #1

Morning		Afternoon	
Punches In	Paid From	Punches In	Paid From
8:01- 8:04	8:00	1:01-1:04	1:00
8:05- 8:15	8:15	1:05-1:15	1:15
8:16- 8:30	8:30	1:16-1:30	1:30
8:31- 8:45	8:45	1:31-1:45	1:45
8:46- 9:00	9:00	1:46-2:00	2:00
9:01- 9:15	9:15	2:01-2:15	2:15
9:16- 9:30	9:30	2:16-2:30	2:30
9:31- 9:45	9:45	2:31-2:45	2:45
9:46-10:00	10:00	2:46-3:00	3:00
And so on			

While companies usually give workers a few minutes leeway for clocking in, they lose a great deal of money when their machines are idle or when workers must wait for latecomers. Leeway is provided for occasional lateness. Continued lateness is a cause for dismissal.

3. If workers must leave early, they will be paid for the time worked through the last quarter of an hour according to Schedule #2:

Schedule #2

Morning Punches Out	Paid To	Afternoon Punches Out	Paid To
9:45- 9:59	9:45	2:45-2:59	2:45
10:00-10:14	10:00	3:00-3:14	3:00
10:15-10:29	10:15	3:15-3:29	3:15
10:30-10:44	10:30	3:30-3:44	3:30
10:45-10:59	10:45	3:45-3:59	3:45
11:00-11:14	11:00	4:00-4:14	4:00
11:15-11:29	11:15	4:15-4:29	4:15
11:30-11:44	11:30	4:30-4:44	4:30
11:45-11:59	11:45	4:45-4:59	4:45
And so on			

The payroll clerk figured Roberta's time and recorded her hours on the time card shown in Illustration 72B using the foregoing rules for counting time worked.

Illustration 72B Time card showing total hours worked

Name Roberta Latham No. 112

Week Ending March 22, 19--

DAY	IN	OUT	IN	OUT	IN	OUT	TOTAL
M	8:00	12:00	1:00	5:00			8
T	7:50	12:03	1:00	5:00			8
W	7:54	12:04	12:57	5:06			8
TH	7:58	12:02	12:58	5:03			8
F	8:04	12:07	1:02	5:05			8

TOTAL HOURS WORKED			40

	HOURS	RATE	WAGES
REGULAR			
OVERTIME			
TOTAL			

This is how the payroll clerk figured the time that Roberta worked:

Monday: Since Roberta did not arrive late or leave early on Monday, the payroll clerk found that she worked 8 hours:

From 8:00 a.m. to 12:00 noon = 4 hours (12:00 - 8:00 = 4 hours)
From 1:00 p.m. to 5:00 p.m. = 4 hours (5:00 - 1:00 = 4 hours)

The payroll clerk added the two amounts together and wrote 8 in the Total column for Monday on Roberta's time card.

Tuesday: Roberta came to work at 7:50 a.m. However, since she does not start work until 8:00, her time is counted from 8:00 a.m. Roberta clocked out at 12:03 for lunch. However, since Roberta is paid to work only to 12:00, her time was counted to 12:00. In a large company, many people will wait in line to clock out. It may take a few minutes to reach the time clock.

The payroll clerk figured that Roberta worked 8 hours on Tuesday. Check Roberta's total hours worked each day to see if you agree with the total hours recorded by the payroll clerk.

Notice that on Friday, Roberta clocked in at 8:04. Since 4 minutes are allowed for lateness, she was given 8 hours for the day.

Time cards must be an accurate record of the hours employees work. The record will be used to compute the employees' wages. Also, time cards may be used to prove that employers are meeting government regulations for hours of work and minimum pay.

Most firms have supervisors check the time cards of the employees they supervise. If the supervisors find no errors on the time cards, they sign or initial them and send them to the payroll department.

Using Computers to Record Time Worked

Many businesses now use computers to keep track of employee hours. These firms do not use time cards. Instead, each employee may be given a special coded card or **badge**. On the badge, each employee number is printed in MICR or in another form that the computer can read.

When employees report to and leave work, they insert their badges into a **badge reader**. The badge reader reads the employee number and records the time that each badge was inserted into the machine. The badge reader is connected to a computer.

The computer figures the total hours worked for each employee automatically, using the data recorded by the badge reader. At the end of the week, the computer prints out a list showing the hours each employee worked during the week. The supervisor for each department checks the list for errors. If there are none, the supervisor approves the list by signing it.

K E Y *Terms*

Badge. A special employee card that is read by a badge reader.

Badge reader. A machine that reads employee badges and records the time.

You are the payroll clerk for Mercandis Roth, Inc. The rules for counting time at your company are

1. There is a five-day workweek starting on Monday and ending on Friday.
2. All employees must start work at 8:00 a.m., leave for lunch at 12:00 noon, return at 1:00 p.m., and work until 5:00 p.m.
3. When employees arrive late, their time is counted from the next quarter hour using Schedule #1 on page 633.
4. Employees who leave early are paid for the time worked through the last quarter hour completed using Schedule #2 on page 634.

You use these rules to find the hours worked by employees during the week of October 14, 19--. Illustration 72C (page 637) shows how you completed the first time card.

Here are the steps you would follow to find the hours worked by Aldo Rich for the week ending October 14, 19--:

STEP 1 ▶ *Compute the total hours worked each day.*

For each day, find the hours worked until lunchtime. Then find the hours worked during the afternoon. Add the two amounts together to get the total hours worked for the day.

Monday
Aldo punched in at 7:56 a.m., but is paid from 8:00 a.m. He also left for lunch at 12:01 p.m., but is only paid until 12:00 noon. To find the hours worked Monday morning, subtract the time that Aldo started work (8:00) from the time he stopped work for lunch (12:00):

$$12:00 - 8:00 = 4 \text{ hours}$$

Aldo punched in at 12:57 p.m., but is paid from 1:00 p.m. He punched out at 5:03 p.m., but is paid only until 5:00 p.m. To find the hours worked Monday afternoon, subtract the time that Aldo began work after lunch (1:00) from the time he stopped work (5:00):

$$5:00 - 1:00 = 4 \text{ hours}$$

The total number of hours Aldo worked Monday is 4 + 4 = 8 hours.

Name	Aldo Rich			No. 26			

Week Ending   October 14, 19--

DAY	IN	OUT	IN	OUT	IN	OUT	TOTAL
M	7:56	12:01	12:57	5:03			8
T	9:49	12:04	12:55	5:08			6
W	8:09	12:02	1:48	5:05			6 3/4
TH	7:57	11:09	1:03	5:04			7
F	9:19	12:03	12:54	4:35			6

TOTAL HOURS WORKED   33 3/4

	HOURS	RATE	WAGES
REGULAR			
OVERTIME			
TOTAL			

Tuesday

On Tuesday morning, Aldo punched in late, at 9:49 a.m. According to Schedule #1, he should be paid from 10:00 a.m. Although he left at 12:04, he is paid only to 12:00 noon. His time for the morning is:

$$12:00 - 10:00 = 2 \text{ hours}$$

On Tuesday afternoon, Aldo worked a normal 4 hours. Although he punched in at 12:55, he is only paid from 1:00 p.m. Although he punched out at 5:08, he is only paid to 5:00 p.m. His time for the afternoon is:

$$5:00 - 1:00 = 4 \text{ hours}$$

Aldo worked 2 + 4 , or 6 hours on Tuesday.

Wednesday

On Wednesday morning, Aldo punched in late, at 8:09 a.m. According to Schedule #1, he should be paid from 8:15 a.m. Although he punched out for lunch at 12:02, he is only paid to 12:00 noon. His time for the morning is:

$$12:00 - 8:15 = 3 \text{ hours and 45 minutes, or } 3\,{}^{3}/_{4} \text{ hours}$$

On Wednesday afternoon, Aldo punched in late, returning from lunch at 1:48 p.m. According to Schedule #1, he should be paid from 2:00 p.m. Although he punched out at 5:05, he should be paid only to 5:00 p.m. His time for the afternoon is:

$$5:00 - 2:00 = 3 \text{ hours}$$

Aldo worked $3\,^3/_4 + 3$, or $6\,^3/_4$ hours on Wednesday.

Thursday
On Thursday morning, Aldo should be paid from 8:00 a.m. He punched out early for lunch, at 11:09. According to Schedule #2, he should be paid until 11:00. His time for the morning is:

$$11:00 - 8:00 = 3 \text{ hours}$$

On Thursday afternoon, Aldo punched in at 1:03 p.m., but according to Schedule #1, should be paid from 1:00 p.m. because of the four-minute leeway. He punched out at 5:04 but should only be paid until 5:00 p.m. His time for the afternoon is:

$$5:00 - 1:00 = 4 \text{ hours}$$

Aldo worked $3 + 4$, or 7 hours on Thursday.

Friday
Aldo reported late for work, at 9:19 a.m. According to Schedule #1, he should be paid starting at 9:30 a.m. Although he left at 12:03 for lunch, he should be paid only to 12:00 noon. His time for the morning is:

$$12:00 - 9:30 = 2 \text{ hours and 30 minutes, or } 2\,^1/_2 \text{ hours}$$

Aldo punched in after lunch at 12:54, but should be paid starting at 1:00 p.m. He punched out early in the afternoon, at 4:35. According to Schedule #2, he should be paid until 4:30 p.m. His time for the afternoon is:

$$4:30 - 1:00 = 3 \text{ hours and 30 minutes, or } 3\,^1/_2 \text{ hours}$$

Aldo worked $2\,^1/_2 + 3\,^1/_2$, or 6 hours on Friday.

STEP 2 ▶ *Enter the total hours worked each day in the proper column on the time card.*

As soon as you find the total hours worked on Monday (8 hours), record 8 in the Total column for Monday. In the same way, enter the total hours worked for every day of the week.

STEP 3 ▶ *Total the hours for the week.*

When you finish entering each daily total, add them to find the total for the week. Enter the weekly total (33³/₄ hours) on the Total Hours Worked line of the time card. You will learn how to finish the rest of the card in the next job.

ℬUILDING YOUR BUSINESS VOCABULARY

On a sheet of paper, write the headings **Statement Number** and **Words**. Next, choose the words that match the statements. Write each word you choose next to the statement number it matches. Be careful; not all the words listed should be used.

Statements	Words
1. A record of the hours worked by an employee	badge
2. A machine that records a worker's time in and out on a time card	badge reader
	employee
	employer
3. Having the time printed on your time card when you arrive at work	in rack
4. Having the time printed on your time card when you leave work	out rack
5. A business that hires people	punching in
6. A machine that reads special employee badges and records the time	punching out
	terms
7. Where you place your time card when you start work	time card
8. Where you place your time card when you leave work	time clock
9. A special employee card that is read by a badge reader	

PROBLEM SOLVING MODEL FOR: *Handling Time Cards*
....

STEP 1 ▶ *Compute the total hours worked each day.*

STEP 2 ▶ *Enter the total hours worked each day in the proper column on the time card.*

STEP 3 ▶ *Total the hours for the week.*

APPLICATION PROBLEM

PROBLEM | **72-1** ▶ You are a payroll clerk at Garrel-Whitacker Products, Inc. The rules in your office are

1. Operating hours: Employees start work at 8:00 a.m., leave for lunch at 12:00 noon, return by 1:00 p.m., and work until 5:00 p.m.
2. When employees arrive late, their time is counted from the next quarter hour. (Use Schedule #1 on page 633.)
3. When employees leave early, they are paid for the time they worked through the last quarter hour. (Use Schedule #2 on page 634.)

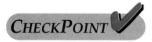

CHECKPOINT

72-1
(#1)
Total hours worked = 40
(#2)
Total hours worked = 37 ½

Directions

a. For each time card, compute the number of hours the employee worked for each day and enter the number in the Total column.
b. Find each employee's total number of hours worked for the week and enter that number on the Total Hours Worked line.

Card #1

DAY	IN	OUT	IN	OUT	IN	OUT	TOTAL
M	8:00	12:01	1:00	5:01			
T	7:58	12:02	1:02	5:03			
W	7:55	12:04	12:55	5:00			
TH	8:03	12:01	1:00	5:02			
F	7:57	12:00	1:03	5:01			
TOTAL HOURS WORKED							

Card #2

DAY	IN	OUT	IN	OUT	IN	OUT	TOTAL
M	8:06	12:02	12:59	5:01			
T	7:55	11:56	12:58	5:02			
W	7:58	12:01	12:56	5:00			
TH	8:01	12:00	1:01	3:02			
F	7:55	12:02	12:57	5:05			
TOTAL HOURS WORKED							

Card #3

DAY	IN	OUT	IN	OUT	IN	OUT	TOTAL
M	8:01	12:02	2:02	5:02			
T	7:57	12:01	1:01	4:30			
W	7:55	12:02	12:56	4:50			
TH	7:58	12:01	12:55	5:01			
F	7:59	12:01	1:03	5:05			
TOTAL HOURS WORKED							

Card #4

DAY	IN	OUT	IN	OUT	IN	OUT	TOTAL
M	7:55	11:08	12:58	5:01			
T	9:08	12:02	12:58	5:01			
W	7:59	12:02	12:59	4:41			
TH	8:27	12:01	12:58	5:02			
F	8:03	12:02	12:59	5:01			
TOTAL HOURS WORKED							

Card #5

DAY	IN	OUT	IN	OUT	IN	OUT	TOTAL
M	7:56	10:48	1:01	5:02			
T	8:00	12:00	12:59	3:57			
W	7:55	12:02	12:56	5:02			
TH	8:01	12:02	1:00	4:35			
F	7:58	12:01	12:55	5:02			
TOTAL HOURS WORKED							

Card #6

DAY	IN	OUT	IN	OUT	IN	OUT	TOTAL
M	9:14	12:01	1:00	5:02			
T	9:01	12:02	12:58	5:01			
W	7:58	12:00	1:00	5:03			
TH	9:17	12:02	12:57	5:01			
F	8:01	12:01	12:59	5:03			
TOTAL HOURS WORKED							

Card #7

DAY	IN	OUT	IN	OUT	IN	OUT	TOTAL
M	7:58	12:02	1:58	5:02			
T	8:35	12:01	12:57	5:01			
W	7:59	12:00	1:04	5:02			
TH	8:01	11:25	12:59	5:01			
F	7:59	12:01	12:58	2:50			
TOTAL HOURS WORKED							

Card #8

DAY	IN	OUT	IN	OUT	IN	OUT	TOTAL
M	7:58	12:02	12:58	5:03			
T	8:02	12:00	1:03	4:05			
W	7:55	12:02	12:56	4:48			
TH	8:02	12:01	12:58	5:02			
F	7:59	11:55	1:01	5:03			
TOTAL HOURS WORKED							

APPLIED MATH PREVIEW

Copy and complete these problems.

1.	2.	3.	4.	5.
$8\frac{1}{2}$	$2\frac{1}{4}$	$5\frac{3}{4}$	$\$8.70$	$\$12.40$
$5\frac{1}{2}$	$14\frac{1}{2}$	$2\frac{1}{4}$	$\times\ 37\frac{1}{2}$	$\times\ 38\frac{1}{4}$
$12\frac{1}{4}$	$9\frac{1}{4}$	$8\frac{3}{4}$		
7	$4\frac{3}{4}$	$7\frac{3}{4}$		
$+\ 3\frac{1}{4}$	$+\ 6\frac{1}{2}$	$+\ 1\frac{1}{2}$		

BUSINESS TERMS PREVIEW

- Commission pay • Gross pay • Hourly pay •
- Piecework pay • Weekly pay •

GOAL

To learn how to compute the weekly wages of employees.

UNDERSTANDING THE JOB

KEY Terms

Hourly pay. Pay workers for each hour they work.

Weekly pay. Pay workers for a fixed number of hours per week.

Piecework pay. Pay workers for each piece of work finished.

Commission pay. Pay workers a percentage of what they sell.

You now know how to find the total hours worked by an employee. However, this is only the first step in computing a worker's wages. To find a worker's earnings, the payroll clerk must know the wage plan the employer uses to pay the employee.

There are many wage plans used to pay workers. Some workers are paid for each hour they work. These workers are paid on an **hourly pay** plan. Others are paid for a fixed number of hours per week. These workers are paid on a **weekly pay** plan. Still others are paid for the number of pieces of work they finish. These workers are paid on a **piecework pay** plan. Many salespeople are paid a percentage of what they sell. They are paid on a **commission pay** plan.

In this job, you will learn how to compute wages on an hourly basis.

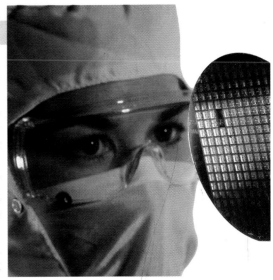

You are still the payroll clerk for Mercandis Roth, Inc., from Job 72. Cheri Lange has been hired to work for the company at the rate of $8.50 per hour. You use the same rules for counting time as shown in Schedule #1 and Schedule #2 in Job 72.

Cheri's completed time card for the week ending July 12, 19--, is shown in Illustration 73A. These are the steps you would follow to find the total pay earned by Cheri for the week:

STEP 1 ▶ ***Enter the hours worked for each day on the time card.***

Compute the hours worked for each day and enter each amount in the Total column of the time card.

Illustration 73A
Completed time card for
Cheri Lange

Name ___Cheri Lange___ No. _23_

Week Ending ___July 12, 19--___

DAY	IN	OUT	IN	OUT	IN	OUT	TOTAL
M	8:00	12:01	12:58	5:02			8
T	7:57	12:02	1:00	5:01			8
W	8:02	12:02	12:59	5:03			8
TH	7:56	11:37	12:57	5:02			7½
F	8:55	12:02	12:58	5:01			7

TOTAL HOURS WORKED			38½

	HOURS	RATE	WAGES
REGULAR	38½	8.50	327.25
OVERTIME			
TOTAL	38½		327.25

STEP 2 ▶ *Find the total hours for the week.*

Add the total hours worked each day and enter the total ($38\frac{1}{2}$ hours) on the Total Hours Worked line of the time card. Also record the total weekly hours in the Regular Hours box at the bottom of the card.

STEP 3 ▶ *Enter the rate per hour.*

Cheri is paid $8.50 an hour. Enter this amount in the Regular Rate box at the bottom of the time card.

STEP 4 ▶ *Compute the weekly wages.*

Find Cheri's total weekly wages, or **gross pay**, for the week by multiplying the hourly rate by the total hours worked:

$$\$8.50 \times 38\frac{1}{2} = \$327.25$$

Enter the gross pay amount in the Regular Wages box of the time card.

KEY | Terms

Gross pay. Total wages.

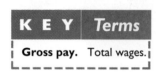

Hourly rate x Hours worked = Gross pay

T I P

BUILDING YOUR BUSINESS VOCABULARY

On a sheet of paper, write the headings **Statement Number** and **Words**. Next, choose the words that match the statements. Write each word you choose next to the statement number it matches. Be careful; not all the words listed should be used.

Statements	Words
1. A wage plan that pays workers for each piece of work finished	badge
2. A wage plan that pays workers for each hour they work	badge reader
3. A wage plan that pays workers a percentage of what they sell	commission pay
4. A record of the hours worked by an employee	gross pay
5. A machine that records a worker's time in and out on a time card	hourly pay
6. Having the time printed on your time card when you arrive at work	piecework pay
	punching in
	punching out
	time card
	time clock
	weekly pay

Statements	Words

7. A machine that reads special employee badges and records the time
8. A special employee card that is read by a badge reader
9. Total wages
10. A wage plan that pays workers for a fixed number of hours per week.

PROBLEM SOLVING MODEL FOR: *Computing Hourly Wages*

STEP 1 ▶ *Enter the hours worked for each day on the time card.*

STEP 2 ▶ *Find the total hours for the week.*

STEP 3 ▶ *Enter the rate per hour.*

STEP 4 ▶ *Compute the weekly wages.*

APPLICATION PROBLEMS

PROBLEM | **73-1** ▶ You are the payroll clerk for Neibuhr Medical Clinic.

Directions

Find the gross pay for each worker.

CHECKPOINT ✔

73-1 (1)
Gross Pay = $420.00

Name of Worker	Hours Worked	Rate Per Hour	Gross Pay
1. Trish Avila	40	10 50	
2. Aaron Klein	37	7 25	
3. Elise Brown	38	11 70	
4. Brent Chen	37 ¹/₂	8 60	
5. Rita Oreno	38 ¹/₄	7 80	
6. Frank Knabe	35 ¹/₂	10 60	
7. Genille Lewis	39 ¹/₄	8 80	
8. Brad Inacher	34 ¹/₂	9 40	

PROBLEM | **73-2** ▶ You are the payroll clerk for Galileo Distributors, Inc.

Directions

Find the gross pay for each worker.

CHECKPOINT ✔

73-2 (1)
Gross Pay = $297.25

Name of Worker	Hours Worked	Rate Per Hour		Gross Pay
1. Genise Pamisano	$36\frac{1}{4}$	8	20	
2. Harold Benson	$38\frac{1}{2}$	6	90	
3. Anne Riley	$39\frac{1}{4}$	12	40	
4. Regis Washington	$36\frac{1}{2}$	10	28	
5. Nancy Wellhausen	$35\frac{1}{4}$	8	85	
6. Clyde Maag	$37\frac{1}{2}$	7	74	
7. Darlene Yamoto	$36\frac{1}{4}$	9	76	
8. Thomas Blocher	$33\frac{1}{2}$	12	68	

PROBLEM **73-3** ▶ You are the payroll clerk for Watson Motor Company.

Directions

CHECKPOINT ✔

73-3 (No. 12)
Total Wages = $380.00

Complete the following time cards by finding the hours worked each day, the total hours worked for the week, and the gross pay for each worker. Use Schedules #1 and #2 from Job 72 to figure the hours worked each day.

Name ___Yuki Sage___ No. _12_

Week Ending ___February 12, 19--___

DAY	IN	OUT	IN	OUT	IN	OUT	TOTAL
M	8:01	12:01	12:58	5:02			
T	7:58	12:02	1:01	5:00			
W	7:56	12:03	12:57	5:04			
TH	7:59	12:00	1:02	5:01			
F	8:03	12:01	12:57	5:03			

TOTAL HOURS WORKED

	HOURS	RATE	WAGES
REGULAR		9.50	
OVERTIME			
TOTAL			

Name ___Orlando Thomas___ No. _13_

Week Ending ___February 12, 19--___

DAY	IN	OUT	IN	OUT	IN	OUT	TOTAL
M	7:56	12:02	1:01	4:08			
T	8:02	12:02	12:58	5:02			
W	7:56	12:01	1:44	5:01			
TH	8:01	12:03	12:57	5:03			
F	7:59	12:03	12:59	4:48			

TOTAL HOURS WORKED

	HOURS	RATE	WAGES
REGULAR		10.70	
OVERTIME			
TOTAL			

Name	Norma Morales				No. 14	

Week Ending February 12, 19--

DAY	IN	OUT	IN	OUT	IN	OUT	TOTAL
M	8:02	12:02	1:15	5:02			
T	7:59	12:02	12:58	5:01			
W	8:01	12:03	12:56	4:14			
TH	7:56	12:02	12:59	5:02			
F	8:00	12:03	1:00	5:02			

TOTAL HOURS WORKED

	HOURS	RATE	WAGES
REGULAR		12.80	
OVERTIME			
TOTAL			

Name	Victor Blumenthal				No. 15	

Week Ending February 12, 19--

DAY	IN	OUT	IN	OUT	IN	OUT	TOTAL
M	7:58	12:01	12:59	5:01			
T	8:01	12:03	2:14	5:02			
W	7:56	12:02	12:58	5:01			
TH	7:59	12:03	12:56	5:04			
F	8:23	12:02	12:58	5:02			

TOTAL HOURS WORKED

	HOURS	RATE	WAGES
REGULAR		8.76	
OVERTIME			
TOTAL			

APPLIED MATH PREVIEW

Copy and complete these problems.

1.	$8\frac{1}{4}$	2.	$10\frac{1}{2}$	3.	$5\frac{1}{4}$	4.	$15.12
	$6\frac{1}{2}$		$3\frac{1}{4}$		$7\frac{3}{4}$		$\times\ 37\frac{1}{2}$
	$4\frac{1}{4}$		$12\frac{1}{2}$		$8\frac{1}{2}$		
	$7\frac{1}{2}$		$5\frac{1}{4}$		$2\frac{1}{2}$	5.	$12.88
	$+\ 2\frac{1}{4}$		$+\ 11\frac{1}{4}$		$+\ 12\frac{1}{2}$		$\times\ 35\frac{1}{4}$

BUSINESS TERM PREVIEW

• **Payroll register** •

GOAL

To learn how to record time card data in a payroll register.

UNDERSTANDING THE JOB

After hours and wages have been recorded on time cards, payroll clerks may post the data at the end of the week to a **payroll register**.

SAMPLE PROBLEM

KEY *Terms*

Payroll register.
Record of wages earned by employees.

You are a payroll clerk for Marcy Brothers, Inc. At the end of the week, you took all the time cards and computed the hours and wages for each employee. Illustration 74A shows two cards that you completed. Illustration 74B shows how the payroll register looked after you posted the data from the time cards to the payroll register.

Here are the steps you took to record time card data in the payroll register:

STEP 1 ▶ *Enter the data from each time card.*

Notice that the hours worked each day by each employee have been entered. Some payroll clerks do not enter the hours for each day in the payroll register. They enter only the weekly total for each employee.

STEP 2 ▶ *Total and rule the Gross Pay column.*

After the data from each time card have been entered, you ruled and footed the Gross Pay column of the register. You then re-added the column and recorded the final total. You drew a double ruling under the final total and wrote the word *Total* in the Name of Employee column. You will use a new page in the payroll register for each week.

Illustration 74A   Completed time cards

Name	Francine Vinalla					No. 16

Week Ending   March 24, 19--

DAY	IN	OUT	IN	OUT	IN	OUT	TOTAL
M	8:02	12:01	12:58	5:04			8
T	7:59	12:02	1:01	5:02			8
W	7:56	12:04	12:57	5:01			8
TH	8:01	12:00	1:02	5:03			8
F	7:58	12:01	12:57	5:04			8
TOTAL HOURS WORKED							40

	HOURS	RATE	WAGES
REGULAR	40	11.50	460.00
OVERTIME			
TOTAL	40		460.00

Name	Enrico Robards					No. 17

Week Ending   March 24, 19--

DAY	IN	OUT	IN	OUT	IN	OUT	TOTAL
M	7:57	12:01	1:01	5:03			8
T	7:58	12:02	12:57	5:02			8
W	7:57	12:01	12:59	5:01			8
TH	8:01	12:02	12:58	4:03			7
F	7:59	12:03	12:59	5:03			8
TOTAL HOURS WORKED							39

	HOURS	RATE	WAGES
REGULAR	39	9.70	378.00
OVERTIME			
TOTAL	39	9.70	378.00

Illustration 74B   Payroll register with entries

					PAYROLL REGISTER				WEEK ENDING	*March 24, 19--*

| | CARD NO. | NAME OF EMPLOYEE | HOURS WORKED | | | | | TOTAL HOURS WORKED | PAY PER HOUR | GROSS PAY | |
			M	T	W	TH	F				
1	16	*Francine Vinalla*	8	8	8	8	8	40	11 50	460 00	1
2	17	*Enrico Robards*	8	8	8	7	8	39	9 70	378 30	2
3		*Total*								838 30	3

If Marcy Brothers, Inc., used a computer to maintain payroll records, your job would be somewhat different. If a badge system were used to record employee time, the computer would compute employee time and create the payroll register automatically. There would be no need to keep time cards, compute time cards, or record time card data in a payroll register.

If time cards were used along with a computer, you would still have to find the total hours worked for each employee. Then, you would log on to your computer by keying your employee number, password, and the date.

After you logged on, the computer screen might look like this:

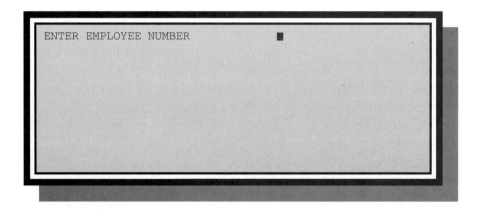

```
ENTER EMPLOYEE NUMBER                    ■
```

The computer is asking you to enter the number of the first employee. You would key the employee number from the first time card (Francine Vinalla's card). The screen would then change to

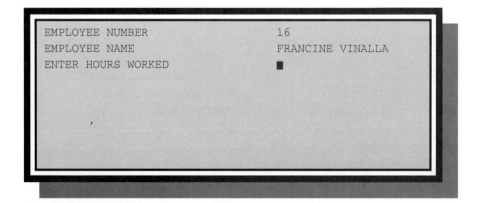

```
EMPLOYEE NUMBER                          16
EMPLOYEE NAME                            FRANCINE VINALLA
ENTER HOURS WORKED                       ■
```

Notice that when you keyed in the employee number, the computer checked its files and displayed Francine Vinalla's name on the screen. This saved you from having to key the name, and it also let you check to make sure that you keyed the correct number.

The computer is now asking you to key the number of hours that Vinalla worked. You would check the card and key 40. You would not have to enter the employee's rate of pay. This information would already be in the computer's files. The computer would automatically figure the total weekly wages and then ask you for the next employee number.

So, the only items that you must enter for each time card are the employee number and the total hours worked. The computer does the rest.

BUILDING YOUR BUSINESS VOCABULARY

On a sheet of paper, write the headings **Statement Number** and **Words**. Next, choose the words that match the statements. Write each word you choose next to the statement number it matches. Be careful; not all the words listed should be used.

Statements	Words
1. To transfer data from one record to another	data
	gross pay
2. A wage plan that pays a worker so much for each piece of work completed	hourly pay
	payroll register
3. Information	piecework pay
4. A record of wages earned by employees	post
5. A wage plan that pays a worker so much for each hour worked	punching in
	punching out
6. A machine that records a worker's time in and out on a time card	time clock
	weekly pay
7. Having the time printed on your time card when you arrive at work	
8. Total wages	

PROBLEM SOLVING MODEL FOR: *Using a Payroll Register*

STEP 1 ▶	*Enter the data from each time card.*
STEP 2 ▶	*Total and rule the Gross Pay column.*

APPLICATION PROBLEMS

PROBLEM **74-1** ▶ You are the payroll clerk for R & R Auto Racing Equipment, Inc.

Directions

a. Copy the data for the week ending August 24, 19--, into a payroll register.

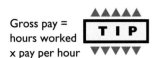

CHECKPOINT ✓

74-1 (d)
Total Gross Pay =
$2,139.00

Card No.	Name of Employee	Hours Worked					Pay Per Hour
		M	T	W	TH	F	
1	Todd Bauer	7	8	8	8	7	$ 8.50
2	Rita Levin	7 ¹/₂	8	7	8	7 ¹/₂	9.40
3	Meng Chen	8	6 ¹/₄	8	7	8	11.20
4	Rose Bianco	6 ¹/₂	7	8	7	8	7.80
5	Lewis Peters	7 ¹/₄	8	6 ¹/₂	7 ¹/₂	8	9.20
6	Diane Aud	8	7 ¹/₂	7	7 ¹/₂	8	10.90

Gross pay =
hours worked **TIP**
x pay per hour

b. Find and enter the total hours worked for each employee in the Total Hours Worked column of the payroll register.
c. Find and enter the gross pay for each employee in the Gross Pay column of the register.
d. Find the total wages for the week (total of the Gross Pay column).

PROBLEM **74-2** ▶ You are the payroll clerk for Diamond Graduation Supplies Company.

Directions

a. Copy the data for the week ending April 12, 19--, into a payroll register.

CHECKPOINT ✓

74-2 (d)
Total Gross Pay =
$2,165.20

Card No.	Name of Employee	Hours Worked					Pay Per Hour
		M	T	W	TH	F	
1	Ralph Batten	6	7	7	7 ¹/₂	7 ¹/₄	$ 7.80
2	Nancy Houseman	8	6 ¹/₂	8	7 ¹/₂	8	8.70
3	Fred Thomas	7	7	6 ¹/₂	7 ¹/₄	7 ¹/₄	12.30
4	Venessa Brock	7 ¹/₂	8	7	6 ¹/₄	6 ¹/₂	8.40
5	Larry Barnes	7 ¹/₂	7 ¹/₄	7 ¹/₂	8 ¹/₂	6	9.80
6	Dennis Meeks	8	8	7 ¹/₂	6 ¹/₂	7 ¹/₄	12.80

b. Find and enter the total hours worked for each employee in the Total Hours Worked column of the payroll register.
c. Find and enter the gross pay for each employee in the Gross Pay column of the register.
d. Find the total wages for the week (Total of the Gross Pay column).

Problem 74-3 may be found in the Working Papers.

APPLIED MATH PREVIEW

Copy and complete these problems.

	1.	2.	3.	
	$9\frac{1}{2}$	$8\frac{1}{4}$	$11\frac{1}{2}$	4. $\$10.90 \times 1\frac{1}{2} =$
	$12\frac{1}{4}$	$14\frac{1}{2}$	$5\frac{3}{4}$	5. $\$ 8.60 \times 1\frac{1}{2} =$
	$7\frac{3}{4}$	$6\frac{3}{4}$	$13\frac{1}{2}$	6. $\$15.35 \times 1\frac{1}{2} =$
	$3\frac{1}{2}$	$2\frac{1}{2}$	$2\frac{3}{4}$	7. $\$12.74 \times 1\frac{1}{2} =$
	$+ 10\frac{1}{4}$	$+ 5\frac{3}{4}$	$+ 7\frac{1}{4}$	8. $\$11.55 \times 1\frac{1}{2} =$
				9. $\$ 7.85 \times 1\frac{1}{2} =$

BUSINESS TERMS PREVIEW

- Overtime • **Overtime rate of pay** • **Regular time** •
- **Regular time rate of pay** •

GOALS

1. To learn what overtime means.
2. To learn how to compute the overtime rate.
3. To learn how to compute gross pay including overtime.

𝒰NDERSTANDING THE JOB

K E Y *Terms*

Regular time rate of pay. Rate of pay for first 40 hours in a week.

Overtime rate of pay. Rate of pay for any hours beyond 40 hours in a week.

Regular time. First 40 hours of work in a week.

Overtime. Time worked beyond 40 hours in a week.

Overtime rate = regular rate x $1\frac{1}{2}$

▲▲▲▲▲
T I P
▼▼▼▼▼

Federal and state laws or union agreements may require that employers pay employees extra if they work more than a certain number of hours in a week. For example, employees may be paid a **regular time rate of pay** for working 40 hours in a week. If they work more than 40 hours in a week, they must be paid an **overtime rate of pay**. In that case, the first 40 hours of the week are called **regular time** and the hours beyond 40 are called **overtime**.

For many workers, the overtime rate that they are paid is $1\frac{1}{2}$ (1.5) times the regular rate. This means that if they are paid $6.00 for each regular hour, they will be paid $9.00 for each overtime hour they work:

$6.00 (regular time rate of pay) x 1.5 = $9.00 (overtime rate of pay)

Some businesses pay overtime if employees work more than a certain number of hours in a day. For example, employees may be paid overtime if they work more than 8 hours in one day. In this job, you will learn how to compute overtime only for employees who work more than 40 hours in one week.

Employees are paid overtime only if the extra time that they work is authorized by their employers. Employees cannot simply stay on after their normal day in order to earn overtime pay without the approval of their employers.

Figuring overtime hours is much like figuring regular time hours. The same schedules you have already used for punching in and punching out are followed.

SAMPLE PROBLEM

You are the payroll clerk for Ambrose Greeting Card Company. Tony Canata is hired at a regular hourly rate of $10.80. Overtime at Ambrose is paid at 1½ times the regular hourly rate. Illustration 75A shows Tony's completed time card at the end of his first week.

Illustration 75A
Completed time card showing overtime

| Name | Anthony Canata | | | | No. | 36 | |

Week Ending   February 15, 19--

DAY	IN	OUT	IN	OUT	IN	OUT	TOTAL
M	7:58	12:02	12:56	5:02			8
T	7:57	12:03	12:59	6:03			9
W	7:55	12:01	12:57	6:01			9
TH	7:59	12:00	1:02	5:01			8
F	8:01	12:02	12:58	6:04			9

| TOTAL HOURS WORKED | | | 43 |

	HOURS	RATE	WAGES
REGULAR	40	10.80	432.00
OVERTIME	3	16.20	48.60
TOTAL	43		480.60

Here are the steps to follow to find Tony's gross pay:

STEP 1 ▶ *Find the total hours worked each day.*

Find the total hours worked each day and record the amounts in the Total column of the time card.

STEP 2 ▶ *Find the total hours worked for the week.*

Add the hours worked each day to find the total hours worked for the week. Enter this amount on the Total Hours Worked line of the time card.

STEP 3 ▶ *Find the total overtime hours.*

If the total hours worked for the week is more than 40, you must find the number of overtime hours the employee worked. To do this, subtract 40 hours (the total number of regular hours) from the total hours worked:

▲▲▲▲▲▲
Total hours
- Regular   **T I P**
hours =
▼▼▼▼▼
Overtime hours

$$\begin{array}{rl} 43 & \text{(total hours worked in week)} \\ -\ 40 & \text{(total regular hours)} \\ \hline 3 & \text{(total overtime hours)} \end{array}$$

Enter the number of regular hours (40) in the box for regular hours. Enter the number of overtime hours (3) in the box for overtime hours. Enter the total number of hours (43) in the box for total hours worked.

STEP 4 ▶ *Find the amount of regular pay.*

Enter Tony's regular hourly rate of pay ($10.80) in the Regular Rate box of the time card. Then multiply the regular rate by the number of regular hours (40) to find Tony's regular pay:

▲▲▲▲▲
Regular rate
x Regular   **T I P**
hours = Regular ▼▼▼▼▼
pay

$$\begin{array}{rl} \$\ 10.80 & \text{(regular rate)} \\ \underline{\times\quad 40} & \text{(regular hours)} \\ \$432.00 & \text{(regular pay)} \end{array}$$

Enter the amount of regular pay ($432.00) in the Regular Wages box of the time card.

STEP 5 ▶ *Find the overtime rate of pay.*

Multiply the regular rate of pay ($10.80) by 1.5 to find the overtime rate of pay:

$10.80 x 1.5 = $16.20 (overtime rate of pay)

Enter the overtime rate of pay in the Overtime Rate box on the time card.

STEP 6 ▶ *Find the amount of overtime pay.*

Multiply the overtime rate of pay ($16.20) by the number of overtime hours (3) to find the amount of overtime pay:

$16.20   (overtime rate)
x   3   (overtime hours)
$48.60   (overtime pay)

Enter the amount of overtime pay in the Overtime Wages box of the time card.

Do not round off overtime rates of pay.

TIP

Sometimes the overtime rate of pay does not come out evenly. For example, if Tony's regular rate of pay had been $10.85, his overtime rate of pay would have been $10.85 x 1.5 = $16.275. When this happens, do not round off the overtime rate of pay. You may round off to the nearest cent only after you have multiplied the number of overtime hours by the overtime rate:

$16.275   (overtime rate)
x   3   (overtime hours)
$48.825, or $48.83 (overtime pay)

STEP 7 ▶ *Find the gross pay.*

Find Tony's gross pay for the week by adding the amount of regular pay and the amount of overtime pay:

$432.00   (regular pay)
+ 48.60   (overtime pay)
$480.60   (gross pay)

Calculator Tips

Many record keepers use calculators to find regular pay, overtime pay, and gross pay. If you wanted to use a calculator to find these amounts for Tony Canata, here is how you would do it:

STEP 1 ▶ *Multiply the regular time hours by the regular rate of pay.*

Press these keys in order:

| 4 | 0 | x | 1 | 0 | . | 8 | = |

The answer, 432.00, will appear in the display. This is Tony's regular time pay. Enter this in the box for regular wages on the time card.

STEP 2 ▶ *Add regular time pay to memory.*

Press the M+ key to add regular pay ($432.00) to memory.

STEP 3 ▶ *Find the overtime rate of pay.*

Multiply the regular rate of pay, $10.80, by 1.5. Press these keys in order:

| 1 | 0 | • | 8 | x | 1 | • | 5 | = |

The answer, 16.20, will appear in the display. This is Tony's overtime rate of pay. Enter this in the box for overtime rate on the time card.

STEP 4 ▶ *Find the amount of overtime pay.*

Now, without clearing the calculator, multiply the overtime rate by the number of overtime hours (3). Press these keys in order:

| x | 3 | = |

The answer, 48.60, will appear in the display. Enter this amount in the box for overtime wages on the time card.

STEP 5 ▶ *Add the amount of overtime pay to memory.*

Without clearing the calculator, press the M+ key.

STEP 6 ▶ *Display the amount of gross pay.*

Without clearing memory, press the MR key or the MR/C key *once*. The amount of gross pay, 480.60, will appear in the display. Enter this amount in the box for total wages on the time card.

Now clear memory for the next problem by pressing the MC key or the MR/C key again.

ℬUILDING YOUR BUSINESS VOCABULARY

On a sheet of paper, write the headings **Statement Number** and **Words**. Next, choose the words that match the statements. Write each word you choose next to the statement number it matches. Be careful; not all the words listed should be used.

Statements	Words
1. Time worked beyond 40 hours in a week	badge reader
2. The first 40 hours worked in a week	gross pay
3. A record of wages earned by employees	overtime
4. The rate of pay for the first 40 hours in a week	overtime rate of pay
	payroll register
5. The rate of pay for any hours beyond 40 hours in a week	piecework pay
	regular time
6. Total wages	regular time rate of pay
7. A machine that records a worker's time in and out on a time card	time clock

PROBLEM SOLVING MODEL FOR: *Computing Gross Pay Including Overtime*
....

STEP 1 ▶ *Find the total hours worked each day.*

STEP 2 ▶ *Find the total hours worked for the week.*

STEP 3 ▶ *Find the total overtime hours.*

STEP 4 ▶ *Find the amount of regular pay.*

STEP 5 ▶ *Find the overtime rate of pay.*

STEP 6 ▶ *Find the amount of overtime pay.*

STEP 7 ▶ *Find the gross pay.*

APPLICATION PROBLEMS

PROBLEM | 75-1 ▶ You are the payroll clerk for Molinaro Seafood Distributors, Inc. The company pays an overtime rate of $1\frac{1}{2}$ times the regular rate for all hours worked by an employee beyond 40 hours in one week.

Do not round off overtime rates.

▲▲▲▲▲
TIP
▼▼▼▼▼

Directions

a. Copy and complete the following table. The first employee's wages have been computed for you as an example.

Card No.	Total Hours Worked	Regular Time Rate	Regular Hours	Overtime Hours	Regular Time Pay	Overtime Rate	Overtime Pay	Gross Pay
1	45	8 20	40	5	328 00	12 30	61 50	389 50
2	41	7 60						
3	48	9 30						
4	52	12 40						
5	46	8 80						
6	50	6 50						
7	44	8 25						
8	49	9 37						
9	43	10 15						
10	41	12 27						

CHECKPOINT

75-1 (c)
Total of Gross Pay column
= $4,538.09

b. Foot these columns: Regular Time Pay, Overtime Pay, Gross Pay.
c. Check the totals by crossfooting. The totals of the Regular Time Pay and Overtime Pay columns together should equal the total of the Gross Pay column.

PROBLEM | **75-2** ▶ You are the payroll clerk for Evers All-Terrain Vehicle Supply Company. The company pays an overtime rate of $1\frac{1}{2}$ times the regular rate for all hours worked by an employee beyond 40 hours in one week.

Directions

a. Copy and complete the following table. Remember not to round off overtime rates of pay.

Card No.	Total Hours Worked	Regular Time Rate	Regular Hours	Overtime Hours	Regular Time Pay	Overtime Rate	Overtime Pay	Gross Pay
1	44	7 60						
2	48	9 75						
3	51	10 65						
4	47	6 97						
5	44	9 83						
6	45 1/4	7 30						
7	49 1/2	8 20						
8	43 1/2	11 60						
9	41 1/2	12 70						
10	46 1/4	12 90						

CHECKPOINT

75-2 (c)
Total of Gross Pay column
= $4,755.26

b. Foot these columns: Regular Time Pay, Overtime Pay, Gross Pay.
c. Check the totals by crossfooting. The totals of the Regular Time Pay and Overtime Pay columns together should equal the total of the Gross Pay column.

Problem 75-3 may be found in the Working Papers.

APPLIED MATH PREVIEW

Copy and complete the following problems. Do not round your answers.

1. $9\frac{1}{4}$
   $8\frac{1}{2}$
   $6\frac{3}{4}$
   $4\frac{1}{4}$
   $+ 12\frac{3}{4}$

2. $\$ 8.90 \times 1\frac{1}{2} =$
3. $\$ 6.40 \times 1\frac{1}{2} =$
4. $\$12.26 \times 1\frac{1}{2} =$
5. $\$13.25 \times 1\frac{1}{2} =$
6. $\$11.45 \times 1\frac{1}{2} =$
7. $\$10.85 \times 1\frac{1}{2} =$

GOAL

To learn how to record overtime pay in a payroll register.

𝒰NDERSTANDING THE JOB

In this job, you will use a payroll register with columns for regular time pay and overtime pay. The payroll register is shown in Illustrations 76B and 76C on page 662.

𝒮AMPLE PROBLEM

You are the payroll clerk for the Port Jervis Music Company. The company pays overtime for all hours worked beyond 40 hours in one week.

Elizabeth Friend is hired by the company at an hourly rate of $12.50. Illustration 76A shows her completed time card for the week ending August 12, 19--.

Here are the steps to follow to record the data from Elizabeth's time card into the payroll register shown in Illustrations 76B and 76C (page 662):

| Name | Elizabeth Friend | | | | No. | 24 |

Week Ending August 12, 19--

DAY	IN	OUT	IN	OUT	IN	OUT	TOTAL
M	7:58	12:01	12:59	5:01			8
T	7:57	12:02	12:57	5:02	5:58	8:01	10
W	7:58	12:03	12:58	5:02			8
TH	7:55	12:02	12:57	6:01			9
F	7:59	12:00	1:01	5:02			8
TOTAL HOURS WORKED							43

	HOURS	RATE	WAGES
REGULAR	40	12.50	500.00
OVERTIME	3	18.75	56.25
TOTAL	43		556.25

STEP 1 ▶ Enter the hours worked daily and the total hours for the week.

Using the data shown on Elizabeth's time card, record the hours she worked each day and the total hours she worked in the week in the proper columns of the payroll register.

Notice that Elizabeth returned to work on Tuesday evening and worked two hours in addition to the eight hours she had worked during the regular day. Her total hours worked on Tuesday were:

$$12:00 - 8:00 = 4 \text{ hours in the morning}$$
$$5:00 - 1:00 = 4 \text{ hours in the afternoon}$$
$$8:00 - 6:00 = \underline{2} \text{ hours in the evening}$$
$$10 \text{ hours total for Tuesday}$$

Notice also that Elizabeth worked until 6:00 p.m. on Thursday. This meant that she worked a total of 9 hours on Thursday. Because she worked more hours on Tuesday and Thursday, her total hours for the week were 43, or 40 regular time hours and 3 overtime hours.

STEP 2 ▶ Enter the regular time pay.

Look at the bottom section of the time card. Copy the regular hours (40), the regular time rate ($12.50), and the regular time pay ($500.00) in the columns for regular pay in the payroll register.

STEP 3 ▶ **Enter the overtime wages.**

Look at the bottom section of the time card. Copy the overtime hours (3), the overtime rate ($18.75), and the overtime pay ($56.25) in the columns for overtime pay in the payroll register.

STEP 4 ▶ **Enter the gross pay for the week.**

The bottom section of the time card shows $556.25 as Elizabeth's gross pay for the week. Enter this figure in the Gross Pay column of the payroll register.

STEP 5 ▶ **Foot, rule, and verify the payroll register.**

After you have entered the wages for all employees, foot the Regular Pay Amount column, Overtime Pay Amount column, and Gross Pay column. Verify the register by crossfooting these columns:

Regular Pay	$1,648.02
Overtime Pay	105.15
Gross Pay	$1,753.17

Since the crossfooted total for gross pay agrees with the total gross pay in your payroll register, double rule the three columns to show that you are finished.

Illustration 76B   Completed payroll register (left page)

	CARD NO.	NAME OF EMPLOYEE	HOURS WORKED					
			M	T	W	TH	F	
1	1	Elizabeth Friend	8	10	8	9	8	1
2	2	Shane Giraldi	8	8½	8	9	8	2
3	3	Yolanda Dunlap	8	7½	8½	10	8	3
4	4	Jerry Velhoff	8	7	8	8	7	4

PAYROLL REGISTER

Illustration 76C   Completed payroll register (right page)

PAYROLL REGISTER   WEEK ENDING *August 12, 19--*

	TOTAL HOURS WORKED	REGULAR PAY			OVERTIME PAY			GROSS PAY	
		HRS.	RATE	AMOUNT	HRS.	RATE	AMOUNT		
1	43	40	12 50	5 0 0 00	3	18 75	5 6 25	5 5 6 25	1
2	41½	40	8 60	3 4 4 00	1½	12 90	1 9 35	3 6 3 35	2
3	42	40	9 85	3 9 4 00	2	14 775	2 9 55	4 2 3 55	3
4	38	38	10 79	4 1 0 02				4 1 0 02	4
5				1 6 4 8 02 1 6 4 8 02			1 0 5 15 1 0 5 15	1 7 5 3 17 1 7 5 3 17	5

BUILDING YOUR BUSINESS VOCABULARY

On a sheet of paper, write the headings **Statement Number** and **Words**. Next, choose the words that match the statements. Write each word you choose next to the statement number it matches. Be careful; not all the words listed should be used.

Statements	Words
1. A record of wages earned by employees	employee
2. A wage plan that pays workers for each unit of work finished	employer
	gross pay
3. Time worked beyond 40 hours a week	overtime
4. The first 40 hours worked in a week	overtime rate of pay
5. A business that hires people	payroll register
6. The rate of pay for the first 40 hours in a week	piecework pay
	regular time
7. The rate of pay for any hours beyond 40 hours in a week	regular time rate of pay
8. Total wages	time clock

PROBLEM SOLVING MODEL FOR: *Recording Overtime Wages in the Payroll Register*

> **STEP 1** ▶ *Enter the hours worked daily and the total hours for the week.*
>
> **STEP 2** ▶ *Enter the regular time pay.*
>
> **STEP 3** ▶ *Enter the overtime wages.*
>
> **STEP 4** ▶ *Enter the gross pay for the week.*
>
> **STEP 5** ▶ *Foot, rule, and verify the payroll register.*

APPLICATION PROBLEMS

PROBLEM **76-1** ▶ You are the payroll clerk for the Arven Drilling Company. The company pays overtime ($1\frac{1}{2}$ times the regular hourly rate) for all hours worked beyond 40 hours in one week.

Directions

a. Copy the following data for the week ending February 15, 19--, into a payroll register.

| Card No. | Name of Employee | \multicolumn{5}{c|}{Hours Worked} | Pay Per Hour |
		M	T	W	TH	F	
1	Denise Chen	8	8	8	10	8	$11.50
2	Earl Dittmer	8	9	8	11	8	8.80
3	Francine Stein	7	8	9	8	8	10.25
4	Garry Reade	8	9	9	10	8	7.65
5	Hillary Vadalabene	7	8	7	8	7 1/2	12.80

CHECKPOINT

76-1 (g)
Total Gross Pay =
$2,141.20

b. Find the total hours worked by each employee, and enter the figures in the Total Hours Worked column of the payroll register.

c. Find the regular time hours and pay for each employee, and enter the figures in the Regular Pay columns of the payroll register.

d. Find the overtime hours and pay for each employee, and enter the figures in the Overtime Pay columns of the payroll register.

e. Find the gross pay for each employee, and enter the figures in the Gross Pay column of the payroll register.

f. Rule and foot the two Amount columns and the Gross Pay column.

g. Check your answers by crossfooting. The sum of the totals of the Amount columns should equal the total of the Gross Pay column.

h. Enter the final totals and double rule the columns.

PROBLEM 76-2 ▶ You are the payroll clerk for the Renee Paper Company. The company pays overtime (1¹/₂ times the regular hourly rate) for all hours worked beyond 40 hours in one week.

Directions

a. Copy the following data for the week ending October 24, 19--, into a payroll register.

| Card No. | Name of Employee | \multicolumn{5}{c|}{Hours Worked} | Pay Per Hour |
		M	T	W	TH	F	
1	Carole Rivera	8	8	9	10	8	$ 7.90
2	Dan Vieth	8	7	9	10	8	12.40
3	Edward Broome	7	7 1/2	8	8 1/2	7	10.75
4	Frank Carlione	8 1/2	8 1/2	9	10 1/2	8	8.50
5	Gretchen Stern	8	9 1/4	9 1/2	9 1/2	8	11.25

CHECKPOINT

76-2 (g)
Total Gross Pay =
$2,212.35

b. Complete the payroll register by following steps b. through h. of Problem 76-1.

PROBLEM 76-3 ▶ You are the payroll clerk for Borlin Printing Company. The company pays overtime (1¹/₂ times the regular hourly rate) for all hours worked beyond 40 hours in one week.

The following four time cards are for the week ending May 18, 19--. Each card shows the regular hourly rate for the employee.

Julia Huang — No. 17

Name Julia Huang No. 17

Week Ending May 18, 19--

DAY	IN	OUT	IN	OUT	IN	OUT	TOTAL
M	7:58	12:01	12:58	5:01			
T	7:59	12:02	12:57	5:02	5:57	8:02	
W	7:58	12:02	12:59	5:03			
TH	8:01	12:00	1:01	6:02			
F	8:00	12:02	12:57	5:03			

TOTAL HOURS WORKED

	HOURS	RATE	WAGES
REGULAR		10.40	
OVERTIME			
TOTAL			

James Riddle — No. 18

Name James Riddle No. 18

Week Ending May 18, 19--

DAY	IN	OUT	IN	OUT	IN	OUT	TOTAL
M	7:59	12:01	12:57	5:02			
T	8:01	12:02	1:01	5:01			
W	7:59	12:01	12:59	6:02			
TH	7:57	12:02	1:01	5:01			
F	7:58	12:01	12:57	5:02	5:58	7:31	

TOTAL HOURS WORKED

	HOURS	RATE	WAGES
REGULAR		9.70	
OVERTIME			
TOTAL			

Edith Runge — No. 19

Name Edith Runge No. 19

Week Ending May 18, 19--

DAY	IN	OUT	IN	OUT	IN	OUT	TOTAL
M	7:59	12:02	12:58	5:01			
T	7:58	12:01	12:56	6:03			
W	8:01	12:02	12:57	5:02			
TH	7:58	12:01	12:58	5:34			
F	7:59	12:01	12:59	5:16			

TOTAL HOURS WORKED

	HOURS	RATE	WAGES
REGULAR		12.85	
OVERTIME			
TOTAL			

Howard Schmidt — No. 20

Name Howard Schmidt No. 20

Week Ending May 18, 19--

DAY	IN	OUT	IN	OUT	IN	OUT	TOTAL
M	7:57	12:02	1:01	5:31			
T	8:01	12:01	12:56	5:02			
W	7:56	12:02	1:00	5:03			
TH	7:59	12:01	12:59	5:01	5:57	7:35	
F	7:58	12:02	12:57	5:32			

TOTAL HOURS WORKED

	HOURS	RATE	WAGES
REGULAR		10.65	
OVERTIME			
TOTAL			

Directions

CHECKPOINT ✔

76-3 (c)
Total Overtime Pay =
$156.85

a. Complete each time card. Use Illustration 76A (page 661) as an example.
b. Enter the data from each card in a payroll register.
c. Complete the payroll register. Use Illustrations 76B and 76C (both on page 662) as an example.

JOB ▸ 77 ▸ COMPUTING SALARIES AND COMMISSIONS

APPLIED MATH PREVIEW

Copy and complete these problems.

1. $34,000 × 0.02 =
2. $23,500 × 0.03 =
3. $45,670 × 0.05 =
4. $18,789 × 0.04 =
5. $28,108 × 0.06 =
6. $112,239 × 0.04 =
7. $ 89,124 × 0.01 =
8. $ 72,231 × 0.03 =
9. $ 13,208 × 0.08 =
10. $ 11,307 × 0.07 =

BUSINESS TERMS PREVIEW

- **Commissions** • **Graduated commission** • **Rate of commission** •
  • **Salary** • **Salary plus commission** • **Straight commission** •

GOALS

1. To learn how to compute commissions.
2. To learn how to compute commissions when the rate of commission increases as sales increase.
3. To learn how to compute gross pay when the employee is paid a salary plus commission.
4. To learn how to complete a payroll register for employees who are paid on a commission pay plan.

UNDERSTANDING THE JOB

Employers offer many pay plans to workers in addition to the hourly pay plan. Two types of pay plans, salaries and commissions, are used often in the business world.

Salaries

KEY Terms

Salary. A fixed amount of pay for a time period.

Many workers, especially office workers, managers, and professional workers, are paid a fixed amount of income, or **salary**, each week or each month. For example, an office worker may be paid $350 a week and work 37½ or 40 hours during the week. A manager may be paid $600 a week in salary but be expected to work as long as is needed during the week to get the work done.

Salaried workers may not have to use time clocks. However, they are expected to be at work for the full amount of time for which they are paid. If some salaried employees work beyond their normal hours, they may be paid overtime. For example, clerical workers and secretaries are usually paid overtime. However, supervisors and managers are not usually paid for any hours they spend beyond the normal work week.

Straight Commission

Many sales workers are paid on the basis of how much they sell. The more they sell, the more they make. For example, Jane Eiler, a salesperson, is paid 5% on all sales she makes during the week. Jane's earnings are called **commissions**. The 5% is called the **rate of commission**.

Jane is paid on a **straight commission** pay plan. This means that her total sales for the week are multiplied by the commission rate to find her total commissions. For example, Jane sold $10,000 last week. Her total commissions would be found this way:

$10,000   Total sales
x   0.05   Commission rate
$500.00   Total commissions

Since Jane is only paid commissions, her total commissions of $500 are also her gross pay for the week.

Salary Plus Commission

Many workers, especially managers and professional workers, are paid a fixed amount of income, or salary, each week or each month for their work. For example, a manager may be paid $500 a week in salary.

Some salespeople are paid a **salary plus commission** on their sales. For example, Jose Flores is paid a weekly salary of $400 plus a commission of 2% on all sales he makes in a week. Last week Jose sold $8,000.00. His gross pay would be found in two steps:

Step 1 $ 8,000   Total sales   Step 2 $ 400.00   Weekly salary
         x   0.02   Commission rate   + 160.00   Total commissions
         $160.00   Total commissions $ 560.00   Gross pay

Graduated Commission

Some companies try to encourage their workers to sell more by raising the commission rates as the amount of goods sold increases in a week. For example, Johnson and Bell, Inc., pays its workers commissions according to this schedule:

Total Weekly Sales	Commission Rate
$1 - $10,000	5%
$10,001 - $20,000	8%
$20,001 and over	10%

This pay plan is called a **graduated commission** pay plan. If you worked for Johnson and Bell, Inc., and sold $25,000.00 worth of goods last week, here is how your gross pay would be found:

$10,000 x 0.05 = $ 500.00   Commission on $1 - $10,000
$10,000 x 0.08 = $ 800.00   Commission on $10,001 - $20,000
$ 5,000 x 0.10 = $ 500.00   Commission on $20,001 and over
$25,000 $ 1,800.00   Total commissions or gross pay

With total sales of $25,000.00, you would earn $1,800.00 in commissions.

You maintain the payroll register for salespeople for Vanek Party Supply Company. Vanek pays each of their salespersons a weekly salary plus 2% commission on all sales made in one week.

Last week, the following five salespeople were paid these salaries and made these total sales:

No.	Salesperson	Total Sales	Weekly Salary
1	Arias Rodriquez	$27,000.00	$400.00
2	Becky Ryan	29,100.00	350.00
3	Stanley Szrbo	32,230.00	375.00
4	Tabatha Torina	33,138.00	475.00
5	Charles Wolper	34,345.00	425.00

Illustration 77A shows the payroll register you completed for the week ending May 28, 19--. Notice that the payroll register for those paid on commission is somewhat different from those paid on an hourly pay plan. There are no columns for hours worked. There are columns for total weekly sales, commission, and weekly salary.

| | PAYROLL REGISTER | | | | WEEK ENDING | May 28, 19-- |

NO.	NAME OF SALESPERSON	TOTAL WEEKLY SALES	COMMISSION	WEEKLY SALARY	GROSS PAY
1	Arias Rodriquez	27 0 0 0 00	5 4 0 00	4 0 0 00	9 4 0 00
2	Becky Ryan	29 1 0 0 00	5 8 2 00	3 5 0 00	9 3 2 00
3	Stanley Szrbo	32 2 3 0 00	6 4 4 60	3 7 5 00	1 0 1 9 60
4	Tabatha Torina	33 1 3 8 00	6 6 2 76	4 7 5 00	1 1 3 7 76
5	Charles Wolper	34 3 4 5 00	6 8 6 90	4 2 5 00	1 1 1 1 90
	Totals	155 8 1 3 00	3 1 1 6 26	2 0 2 5 00	5 1 4 1 26
		155 8 1 3 00	3 1 1 6 26	2 0 2 5 00	5 1 4 1 26

Illustration 77A   Payroll register for salespeople on commission

Here is how you did your work:

STEP **1** ▶ *Enter the date and the employee numbers, names, total weekly sales, and weekly salaries.*

You entered the date on the Week Ending line. Then you entered the number, name, total weekly sales, and weekly salary of each salesperson in the correct columns of the payroll register.

STEP 2 ▶ ***Find and enter the commission for each salesperson.***

You found the commission for Arias Rodriquez this way:

$27,000.00	Total weekly sales
x 0.02	Commission rate
$ 540.00	Total commissions

You entered the amount of his commission in the Commission column of the payroll register. You then followed the same procedures for each of the other salespeople.

STEP 3 ▶ ***Find the gross pay for each salesperson.***

You then added the commission and weekly salary for each salesperson and entered the total in the Gross Pay column of the payroll register.

STEP 4 ▶ ***Foot, crossfoot, and rule the payroll register.***

You footed each of the money columns in the register. Then you verified your work by crossfooting these totals:

$ 3,116.26	Total commissions
+ 2,025.00	Total weekly salaries
$ 5,141.26	Gross pay

Since the crossfooted total, $5,141.26, agreed with the total of the Gross Pay column, you entered the final totals and double ruled the money columns.

ℬUILDING YOUR BUSINESS VOCABULARY

On a sheet of paper, write the headings **Statement Number** and **Words**. Next, choose the words that match the statements. Write each word you choose next to the statement number it matches. Be careful; not all the words listed should be used.

Statements	Words
1. A pay plan based on how much is sold	commissions
2. The commission percent	graduated commission
3. Total sales multiplied by the commission rate	hourly pay
	overtime
4. A fixed amount of pay	rate of commission
5. A fixed amount of pay plus the amount of commission	salary
	salary plus commission
6. When the rate of commission increases as the amount of sales increases	straight commission

STEP 1 ▶	*Enter the date and the employee numbers, names, total weekly sales, and weekly salaries.*
STEP 2 ▶	*Find and enter the commission for each salesperson.*
STEP 3 ▶	*Find the gross pay for each salesperson.*
STEP 4 ▶	*Foot, crossfoot, and rule the payroll register.*

*A*PPLICATION PROBLEMS

PROBLEM | **77-1** ▶

You are the payroll clerk for W & W Distributors, Inc. The company pays its salespersons a 3% straight commission on all sales made in one week.

Directions

CHECKPOINT ✔

77-1 (b)
Total of Commission
column = $7,073.85

a. Complete the pay chart for the week ending September 17, 19--, by finding the total commission, or gross pay, for each worker.
b. Find the total sales and the total commissions paid for the week by the company.
c. Verify your work by multiplying the total of the Total Sales column by the rate of commission. This amount should agree with the total of the Gross Pay column.

Weekly Pay Chart		
Salesperson	Total Sales	Commission (Gross Pay)
Carmen Benite	$30,000	
Blake Bloomingdale	12,000	
Dennis Carter	28,900	
Gino Ferraro	19,250	
Sally Veblen	24,500	
Jasmine Wilson	28,270	
Parker Yates	16,873	
Alice Yoder	22,589	
Tammy Yvonnes	31,876	
William Zane	21,537	
Totals		

PROBLEM 77-2 ▶ You are the payroll clerk for Ribkins Toy Sales, Inc. The company pays its salespersons a weekly salary plus a 2% commission on all sales made in one week.

Directions

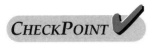

CHECKPOINT

77-2 (b)
Total of Gross Pay column
= $11,431.82

a. Complete the pay chart for the week ended December 2, 19--, by finding the total commission and gross pay for each worker.
b. Find the totals of all the money columns.
c. Verify your work by crossfooting the totals of the Commission, Weekly Salary, and Gross Pay columns.

Weekly Pay Chart				
Salesperson	Total Sales	Commission	Weekly Salary	Gross Pay
Earl Romine	$25,000		$400.00	
Amy Westerhold	34,000		375.00	
Les Pai	47,350		285.00	
Midori Hayashi	23,780		357.00	
Chip Trent	52,876		470.00	
Zelda Raimkin	32,427		450.00	
Patrick Zopolo	18,893		500.00	
Vana Williams	48,380		525.00	
Gregory Rasmussen	42,128		515.00	
Jill Smith	33,457		389.00	
Totals				

PROBLEM 77-3 ▶ You are the payroll clerk for Bronson Company. The company pays its salespeople using the following graduated commission pay plan:

Total Weekly Sales	Commission Rate
$1 - $5,000	2%
$5,001 - $10,000	4%
$10,001 and over	6%

CHECKPOINT

77-3 (a)
Oscar Baker's commission
= $600.00

Directions

a. Complete the pay chart for the week ended April 23, 19--, by finding the total commission, or gross pay, for each worker.
b. Find the total sales and the total commissions paid for the week by the company.

Weekly Pay Chart		
Salesperson	Total Sales	Commission (Gross Pay)
Oscar Baker	$15,000	
Olivia Bonice	11,000	
Rodney Chase	7,560	
Mia Henderson	21,160	
Joshua Pinkerton	13,500	
Keith Prentice	17,140	
Carla Pryor	21,567	
Quincy Romono	7,472	
Patricia Small	21,514	
Earlene Stover	11,873	
Totals		

PROBLEM **77-4** ▶ You are the payroll clerk who maintains the payroll register for all salespeople for Bigelow Iron Products, Inc. The company pays a weekly salary plus a 2% commission on total weekly sales to each salesperson.

Directions

77-4 (a)
Oliver Tunnel's gross pay
= $750.00

a. Enter these data for the week ending June 14, 19--, into a payroll register with the same headings as in Illustration 77A (page 668).

No.	Salesperson	Total Sales	Weekly Salary
1	Oliver Tunnel	$17,500.00	$400.00
2	Sheila Turnbull	19,400.00	450.00
3	Reginald Tyler	21,630.00	475.00
4	Vera Tyson	24,356.00	480.00
5	Tomasina Ulgood	25,198.00	420.00

b. Foot each of the money columns.
c. Verify your work by crossfooting the Commission, Weekly Salary, and Gross Pay columns.
d. Enter the final totals and double rule the register.

APPLIED MATH PREVIEW

Copy and complete these problems.

1. 400 × $ .20 =	6. 500 × $1.23 =
2. 350 × $ .45 =	7. 420 × $2.35 =
3. 615 × $ .26 =	8. 598 × $3.21 =
4. 129 × $ .78 =	9. 200 × $ .23 $\frac{1}{2}$ =
5. 327 × $ .24 =	10. 120 × $ .15 $\frac{1}{4}$ =

BUSINESS TERMS PREVIEW

- Graduated piecework pay • Piecerate • Straight piecework pay •

GOALS

1. To learn how to compute an employee's gross pay when the employee is paid on a piecework pay plan.
2. To learn how to compute piecework pay when the rate for each piece increases as the number of pieces increases.
3. To learn how to complete a payroll register for piecework employees.

𝒰NDERSTANDING THE JOB

Some employees are paid an amount for each unit or piece of work that they complete and that is accepted. For example, Richard Lee is paid $.75 for each table lamp he assembles correctly. During the work day, another employee inspects each of the lamps he assembles to make sure that they have been completed correctly. Richard is not paid for any lamps that have been improperly assembled.

Straight Piecework

Since Richard is paid the same amount for each unit or piece of work he completes properly, he is paid on a **straight piecework pay** plan. The $.75 he receives for each properly assembled table lamp is called the **piecerate**. If Richard assembled 400 table lamps properly in one week, his gross pay would be found this way:

400	Pieces
× $.75	Piecerate
$300.00	Gross pay

KEY Terms

Straight piecework pay. Same pay for each piece.

Piecerate. The rate paid for each piece.

Graduated Piecework

To encourage employees to produce more products, many employers increase the piecerate as the number of accepted units of work increases.

For example, the Atlantic Clothing Company pays its employees using the following piecerate schedule:

Number of Accepted Units in One Week	Piecerate
1 - 400	$.30
401 - 800	.40
801 - 1,200	.50
1,201 and over	.60

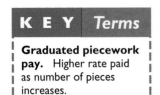

KEY *Terms*

Graduated piecework pay. Higher rate paid as number of pieces increases.

This pay plan is called a **graduated piecework pay** plan. If you worked for Atlantic Clothing Company and completed 1,300 pieces last week, here is how you would find your gross pay:

400 x $.30 = $120.00	Pay for 1 - 400 pieces
400 x $.40 = 160.00	Pay for 401 - 800 pieces
400 x $.50 = 200.00	Pay for 801 - 1,200 pieces
100 x $.60 = 60.00	Pay for 1,201 and over pieces
1,300 $540.00	Gross pay

If you completed 1,300 pieces, you would earn $540.00 in gross pay.

SAMPLE PROBLEM

You are the payroll clerk for Donevetti Industries. Donevetti pays its factory employees a straight piecerate for each accepted unit of work they complete. Since some work is more difficult than other work, different piecerates are paid. Last week, six factory employees completed these pieces:

No.	Employee Name	M	T	W	TH	F	Piecerate
1	Roland Allen	17	18	16	17	16	$2.80
2	Roberta Clark	18	19	19	18	19	2.82
3	Raymond Derby	17	19	20	18	17	2.82
4	Rosalind Eto	22	23	24	22	21	2.91
5	Ronald Fuentes	21	21	22	20	20	2.95
6	Rae Grindell	20	20	21	22	24	2.98½

No. of Pieces Completed

Illustration 78A shows the payroll register you completed for the week ending July 15, 19--. Notice that the payroll register for a piecework pay plan is different from the one used for an hourly pay plan. The columns for hours worked are replaced by columns for pieces completed. Also, the column for pay per hour is replaced by one for piecerate.

Illustration 78A   Payroll register for piecerate employees

PAYROLL REGISTER   WEEK ENDING *July 15, 19--*

	NO.	NAME OF EMPLOYEE	PIECES COMPLETED					TOTAL NO. OF PIECES	PIECERATE	GROSS PAY	
			M	T	W	TH	F				
1	1	Roland Allen	17	18	16	17	16	84	2 80	2 3 5 20	1
2	2	Roberta Clark	18	19	19	18	19	93	2 82	2 6 2 26	2
3	3	Raymond Derby	17	19	20	18	17	91	2 82	2 5 6 62	3
4	4	Rosalind Eto	22	23	24	22	21	112	2 91	3 2 5 92	4
5	5	Ronald Fuentes	21	21	22	20	20	104	2 95	3 0 6 80	5
6	6	Rae Grindell	20	20	21	22	24	107	2 98½	3 1 9 40	6
		Total						591 591		1 7 0 6 20 1 7 0 6 20	7

Here is how you did your work:

STEP 1 ▶ *Enter the date and the employee numbers, names, daily number of pieces completed, and piecerate.*

You entered the date on the Week Ending line. Then you entered the number, name, daily number of pieces completed, and piecerate for each factory employee in the proper columns of the payroll register.

STEP 2 ▶ *Find and enter the total number of pieces completed in the week.*

You added the completed units of work for each employee and entered these amounts in the Total No. of Pieces column of the payroll register.

STEP 3 ▶ *Find the gross pay for each employee.*

You found and entered the gross pay for each employee in the Gross Pay column of the payroll register. For example, you found the gross pay for Roland Allen this way:

84	Total number of pieces
x $2.80	Piecerate
$235.20	Gross pay

Sometimes the piecerate contains a fraction. For example, Rae Grindell's piecerate is 2.98^1/_2$, or $2.985. Do not round off piecerates that contain less than one cent. Round off only the final gross pay:

107	Total number of pieces
x $2.985	Piecerate
$319.395, or $319.40	Gross pay

STEP 4 ▶ *Foot and rule the payroll register.*

You footed the Total No. of Pieces and the Gross Pay columns in the register. After you re-added the columns, you entered the final totals and double ruled the columns.

*B*UILDING YOUR BUSINESS VOCABULARY

On a sheet of paper, write the headings **Statement Number** and **Words**. Next, choose the words that match the statements. Write each word you choose next to the statement number it matches. Be careful; not all the words listed should be used.

Statements	Words
1. A pay plan based on how much is sold	commission pay
2. A pay plan which pays the same amount for each unit of work completed	graduated commission
3. A pay plan which increases the amount paid as the units of work completed increase	graduated piecework pay
4. The percent of commission paid	hourly pay
5. The rate paid for each piece completed	overtime
6. Total sales multiplied by the commission rate	piecerate
7. A fixed amount of pay	rate of commission
8. A fixed amount of pay plus the amount of commission	salary
9. When the rate of commission increases as the amount of sales increases	salary plus commission
	straight commission
	straight piecework pay

STEP 1 ▶ *Enter the date and the employee numbers, names, daily number of pieces completed, and piecerate.*

STEP 2 ▶ *Find and enter the total number of pieces completed in the week.*

STEP 3 ▶ *Find the gross pay for each employee.*

STEP 4 ▶ *Foot and rule the payroll register.*

🚀PPLICATION PROBLEMS

| PROBLEM | **78-1** ▶ You are a payroll clerk for Austin Bicycle Company. The company pays its factory employees $.78 for each unit of work completed properly.

78-1 (1)
Gross Pay = $423.54

Directions

a. Find the total number of pieces completed by each employee.
b. Find the gross pay for each employee.

Employee	\multicolumn{5}{c}{No. of Pieces Completed}	Total Pieces	Gross Pay
	M	T	W	TH	F		
1	110	112	105	115	101	____	$____
2	98	89	97	101	99	____	____
3	121	118	117	121	122	____	____
4	89	91	90	89	88	____	____
5	103	105	106	107	105	____	____
6	88	89	87	82	83	____	____

| PROBLEM | **78-2** ▶ You are a payroll clerk for Blume Electronics, Inc. Blume Electronics, Inc., pays its assembly-line employees according to the following graduated piecerate schedule:

Number of Accepted Units in One Week	Piecerate
1 - 300	$.45
301 - 500	.60
501 - 600	.75
601 and over	.90

Directions

a. Find the total number of pieces completed by each employee.
b. Find the gross pay for each employee.

| | No. of Pieces Completed | | | | | Total | Gross |
Employee	M	T	W	TH	F	Pieces	Pay
1	80	90	110	90	100	____	$____
2	71	82	79	78	75	____	____
3	112	114	111	113	115	____	____
4	121	119	118	121	122	____	____
5	89	95	98	92	94	____	____
6	101	99	97	102	103	____	____

PROBLEM 78-3 ▶ You are the payroll clerk for Southern Copy Manufacturing Company. The company pays its factory employees a straight piecerate for each completed and accepted piece of work.

Directions

a. Copy the following information for the week ended March 22, 19--, into a payroll register with the same headings as in Illustration 78A (page 675).

| No. | Employee Name | No. of Pieces Completed | | | | | Piecerate |
		M	T	W	TH	F	
1	Thad Corolla	60	70	65	72	75	$1.50
2	Ria Vitale	62	73	61	68	76	1.50
3	James Rolla	55	58	56	59	60	1.50
4	Gina Bolina	42	41	40	43	44	1.75
5	David Rutman	40	42	39	40	41	1.75
6	Esther Kaufman	32	32	34	35	33	1.85

b. Find the total number of pieces completed and the gross pay for each employee.
c. Foot and rule the Total No. of Pieces and Gross Pay columns of the payroll register.

Problem 78-4 may be found in the Working Papers.

Reinforcement Activities

DISCUSSION

1. Why do you think supervisors should check time cards or a list of the times and hours each employee worked before an employee is paid? Give two reasons why you think checking is necessary.
2. Why do you think business firms should have a late schedule? Give two reasons why you think a late schedule is needed.

PROFESSIONAL BUSINESS ETHICS

You are a payroll clerk for Biddle Sales Company. Tom James, who works in the billing department at Biddle, is a friend of yours. He calls you on the phone and asks you how much Rita Toomey, who also works in the billing department, is paid an hour.

What should you tell Tom? Write down what you would say. Do not use more than half a sheet of paper.

APPLIED COMMUNICATIONS

You are the supervisor of five accounts receivable clerks who work in the accounting department of a large wholesaling firm. One employee, Robin Jarrett, has been late for the first three mornings of this week. Robin has punched in at 8:04 a.m., 8:05 a.m., and 8:09 a.m. on Monday, Tuesday, and Wednesday, respectively.

When you talk to Robin about the late arrivals, she says, "I've only been a few minutes late. Give me a break! It doesn't hurt anybody."

As her supervisor, what would you say to Robin? Write what you would say on no more than one sheet of paper.

K E Y *Terms*

Flextime. A plan that allows employees to vary the time they arrive and leave work.

Some firms make it possible for employees to have a say about when they arrive and leave work. Employees may be able to schedule times to arrive and leave that are earlier or later than usual. These work plans are called **flextime** plans. Flextime permits employees to vary their arrival and departure times to suit their needs. For example, some firms may allow employees responsible for picking up or dropping off their children at school to leave and arrive at times which make this possible.

1. What are two other reasons why employees may wish to vary the time they arrive and leave work?
2. Why do you think employers decide to offer flextime plans?

GLOBAL BUSINESS: INTERNATIONAL MAIL

You are a record keeper for a financial services company that has clients around the world. You often must send correspondence or your company's newsletters to foreign countries.

There are three categories of international mail:

1. LC mail (initials for the French *lettres* and *cartes postales*—meaning "letters" and "post cards"). LC mail consists mainly of letters and post cards. These items are mailed at the letter rate of postage. This service is airmail delivery.
2. AO mail (initials for the French *Autres Objets*—meaning "other things"). AO mail usually consists of printed materials such as books, periodicals, newsletters, and braille publications. This service is usually by ship and is slower than airmail.
3. CP mail (initials for the French *par Colis Postal*—meaning "by parcel post"). CP mail is the equivalent of parcel post in the U.S. Parcel post is used for items such as merchandise. It is the only class of mail that can be insured. This service is also usually by ship and, again, is slower than airmail.

If required, there are also special delivery services offered.

1. Express Mail offers a faster delivery than regular airmail, but costs more.
2. International Priority Airmail is intended for bulk items.
3. Registered mail is for items that require a proof of delivery be returned to the sender.

An International Mail Activity can be found in the Working Papers.

On a sheet of paper, write the headings **Statement Number** and **Words**. Next, choose the words that best complete the statements. Write each word you choose next to the statement number it completes. Be careful; not all the words listed should be used.

Statements	Words
1. A device that records the time when a worker reports to work or leaves work on a time card is called (a, an) _____ .	badge reader
	commission pay
	flextime
2. A record of the hours worked by a single employee is called (a, an) _____ .	gross pay
	one and one-half
3. An employee who processes payroll data for a business is called (a, an) _____ .	overtime
	payroll clerk
4. Regular pay plus overtime pay is called _____ .	payroll register
	piecework pay
5. A wage plan that pays an employee by the number of items completed or produced is called (a, an) _____ plan.	punching in
	punching out
	time card
6. A wage plan that pays an employee a percentage of the total amount the employee sells is called (a, an) _____ plan.	time clock
7. The number of hours you work beyond 40 hours a week is called _____ .	
8. A record of wages paid to a group of employees is called (a, an) _____ .	
9. The overtime rate of pay is _____ times the regular time rate of pay.	
10. Having the time printed on your time card when you leave work is called _____ .	
11. A plan that allows employees to vary the time they arrive and leave work is called _____ .	

(4)
Total Wages = $399.26

You are the payroll clerk for Lavelle Window Corporation. The following four time cards are for the week ending April 14, 19--. Each card shows the regular hourly rate for the employee.

Directions

a. Complete each time card. Use the work schedules found in Job 72 on pages 633 and 634.

b. Enter the data for each time card in the payroll register.

c. Complete the payroll register for the week.

Card 1

Name	Rita Vosburgh			No.	1	

Week Ending April 14, 19--

DAY	IN	OUT	IN	OUT	IN	OUT	TOTAL
M	7:59	12:01	12:58	5:01			
T	8:02	12:00	12:57	4:02			
W	7:56	11:32	12:59	5:02			
TH	7:57	12:03	12:56	5:03			
F	7:59	12:01	1:58	5:01			

TOTAL HOURS WORKED

	HOURS	RATE	WAGES
REGULAR		11.50	
OVERTIME			
TOTAL			

Card 2

Name	Victor Voluchi			No.	2	

Week Ending April 14, 19--

DAY	IN	OUT	IN	OUT	IN	OUT	TOTAL
M	7:59	12:02	12:58	6:01			
T	7:57	12:03	12:57	5:02			
W	7:59	12:01	12:59	5:01			
TH	7:57	12:02	12:58	5:03	5:58	8:02	
F	7:56	12:03	12:56	5:00			

TOTAL HOURS WORKED

	HOURS	RATE	WAGES
REGULAR		10.20	
OVERTIME			
TOTAL			

Card 3

Name	Reno Caragine			No.	3	

Week Ending April 14, 19--

DAY	IN	OUT	IN	OUT	IN	OUT	TOTAL
M	7:57	12:02	1:01	5:00	5:28	7:01	
T	7:58	12:01	12:59	5:02	5:58	8:01	
W	8:01	12:00	12:58	5:03	5:58	8:02	
TH	8:00	12:01	12:59	6:00			
F	7:57	12:02	12:58	5:01			

TOTAL HOURS WORKED

	HOURS	RATE	WAGES
REGULAR		12.80	
OVERTIME			
TOTAL			

Card 4

Name	Olga Timovich			No.	4	

Week Ending April 14, 19--

DAY	IN	OUT	IN	OUT	IN	OUT	TOTAL
M	7:57	12:02	12:57	5:01			
T	8:01	12:01	12:59	6:32			
W	8:00	12:02	1:00	5:02			
TH	7:56	12:01	12:58	5:03			
F	7:57	12:02	12:57	5:02			

TOTAL HOURS WORKED

	HOURS	RATE	WAGES
REGULAR		9.45	
OVERTIME			
TOTAL			

REVIEWING YOUR BUSINESS VOCABULARY

This activity may be found in the Working Papers.

CHAPTER

16

Record Keeping for Payroll Clerks: Computing Net Pay

*E*mployers pay wages to their workers. Employers also make deductions from the wages of their workers. The deductions are for federal withholding tax, social security tax, any state or city income taxes, and other special reasons, such as health insurance.

In Chapter 16, you will learn how to find social security and withholding taxes. You will learn how to use a payroll register and an employee earnings record. You will also learn about the Wage and Tax Statement (W-2 form). A Calculator Tip will be given for finding the amount of social security (FICA) tax and an employee's net pay.

JOB 79 ▶ COMPUTING SOCIAL SECURITY TAXES

Before multiplying one number

TIP

by a percent, change the percent to a decimal. For example, before multiplying $478.00 by 8%, change 8% to a decimal. You can do this by moving the decimal two places to the left and dropping the percent sign: 8% = 0.08.

APPLIED MATH PREVIEW

Copy and complete each problem. Round your answers to the nearest cent.

1. $227.00	2. $344.80	3. $ 463.75	4. $ 581.97
x 0.08	x 0.08	x 0.0715	x 0.0751

5. $307.00 x 8% =   6. $424.89 x 8% =

BUSINESS TERMS PREVIEW

- **Deductions** • **Federal Insurance Contributions Act (FICA)** •
- **FICA tax** • **Net pay** • **Social Security Act** •
- **Social security number** •

GOALS

1. To learn about social security.
2. To learn how to figure deductions for social security.

UNDERSTANDING THE JOB

KEY Terms

Social Security Act. Law that allows qualified persons to receive monthly payments from the federal government.

FICA. Federal Insurance Contributions Act.

FICA Tax. Tax collected to pay for social security program.

Deductions. Amounts subtracted from wages.

Social security number. An account number in the social security system.

In 1935, Congress passed the **Social Security Act**. This law allows people to receive monthly payments from the federal government if they qualify. Since 1935, there have been many changes in the law that have increased the amount people receive. There have also been changes as to the kinds of people who can qualify for benefits.

In general, workers may retire at 62 years of age and receive benefits. Benefits may also be received by widows and widowers, dependent children, and permanently disabled workers. Since 1966, the law has also provided medical care (called *Medicare*) for persons over 65 years of age.

Another law, the **Federal Insurance Contributions Act (FICA)**, was passed by Congress to cover the cost of the social security program. Under this law, the government gets the money to pay social security benefits by collecting taxes from employers and employees. The employee's **FICA tax** is collected as a **deduction** from the employee's wages. The employer must contribute the same amount as is deducted from the employee's wages.

The tax rate is a certain percent of the employee's wages. This tax is deducted each payday until the worker's wages reach a certain amount for the year. Both the rate and the amount are set by Congress and can be changed by Congress at any time. They are changed often. But even though the rate and the amount change, the method of computing the FICA tax is the same.

In this chapter, you will use a FICA tax rate of *8%*. The maximum amount of wages taxable for the year will be *$50,000.00*. The FICA tax will be deducted from the worker's wages until the worker has contributed $4,000.00 ($50,000.00 x 8%) to FICA.

Since the employer must match the amount contributed by the employee, the employer's FICA tax rate used will also be *8%*. On certain dates, the employer sends the FICA tax money collected from the employer's and the employees' contributions to the government. For example, if a total of $300.00 has been collected from all of the employees, the employer must match this $300.00 and send $600.00 to the government.

The federal government keeps an individual record for each worker. The record shows the wages earned and all the taxes collected for that worker. This record is started when the government is notified that a person has become a member of the social security system.

Everyone must have a **social security number**. You can get an application for a social security number at any social security office or your local post office. Most students already have a social security number like the one shown on the card in Illustration 79A on page 685. Their parents had to get them a number for income tax reasons.

Since both your name and social security number are needed for an employer's payroll records, your card must be shown to an employer when you are hired. The employer sends in a report of the name, social security number, gross pay, and social security deduction for each employee. When the government receives this information, the employee's record is updated.

Illustration 79A Social security card

$\mathcal{S}$AMPLE PROBLEM

Ray Hirsch is employed by Benson Furniture Company. He earned $475.00 last week. Here are the steps to find how much will be deducted from his wages for social security and the amount he will actually take home, or **net pay**:

STEP 1 ▶ *Multiply the gross pay by the FICA, or social security, rate.*

Multiply Ray's gross pay ($475.00) by the FICA rate (8%). To multiply a number by a percent, first change the percent to a decimal. To change 8% to a decimal, drop the percent sign and move the decimal point two places to the left.

$$8\% = 0.08$$

Now multiply the gross pay ($475.00) by the FICA rate (0.08).

$475.00	(gross pay)
x 0.08	(8% changed to a decimal)
$ 38.00	(social security deduction)

STEP 2 ▶ *Deduct the social security tax from gross pay to find net pay.*

$475.00   (gross pay)
- 38.00   (social security deduction)
$437.00   (net pay)

TIPS

Many payroll clerks use a calculator to find the amount of FICA tax and an employee's net pay. This is how they might do it to find Ray Hirsch's FICA tax and net pay:

STEP 1 ▶ *Enter gross pay into memory.*

First enter Ray's gross pay into memory by pressing these keys in order:

| 4 | 7 | 5 | M+ |

Do not clear the display. Leave the amount of gross pay in the display.

STEP 2 ▶ *Find the amount of FICA tax.*

Multiply Ray's gross pay ($475.00) by the FICA rate (8%) by pressing these keys in order:

| x | • | 0 | 8 | = |

The amount of the FICA tax, $38.00, will appear in the display.

STEP 3 ▶ *Find the amount of net pay.*

Subtract the FICA tax from gross pay by pressing these keys in order:

| MR | – | 3 | 8 | = |

The amount of net pay, $437.00, will appear in the display. You should now clear the display and memory to prepare for the next problem.

BUILDING YOUR BUSINESS VOCABULARY

On a sheet of paper, write the headings **Statement Number** and **Words**. Next, choose the words that match the statements. Write each word you choose next to the statement number it matches. Be careful; not all the words listed should be used.

Statements	Words
1. Tax collected to pay for social security	commissions
2. A machine that records a worker's time in and out	deductions
	Federal Insurance Contributions Act (FICA)
3. Gross pay less deductions, or take-home pay	
4. Time worked beyond 40 hours a week	FICA tax
5. Amounts subtracted from your wages	net pay
6. A record of wages earned by employees	overtime
7. Law passed by Congress to cover the cost of the social security program	payroll register
	piecework pay
8. A wage plan that pays workers for each unit of work finished	Social Security Act
	social security number
9. An account number in the social security system	time clock
10. Law that allows qualified persons to receive monthly payments from the federal government.	

PROBLEM SOLVING MODEL FOR: *Computing Social Security Taxes*

STEP 1 ▶ *Multiply the gross pay by the FICA, or social security, rate.*

STEP 2 ▶ *Deduct the social security tax from gross pay to find net pay.*

APPLICATION PROBLEM

PROBLEM   **79-1** ▶ You are the payroll clerk for Tolance Books, Inc.

Directions

CHECKPOINT ✓

79-1
Total net pay = $2,123.36

a. Copy the following table:

Week Ending March 6, 19--						
Name of Employee	Gross Pay		FICA Tax		Net Pay	
L. Arroyo	259	00				
W. Borland	408	00				
P. Coblitz	288	00				
N. Dubarr	513	00				
S. Ellery	378	00				
T. Feng	462	00				
Totals						

b. Find the net pay for each employee using 8% as the FICA tax rate. Enter the FICA tax and net pay for each worker in the proper columns.

c. Foot the columns. Check your work by adding the totals of the Net Pay and FICA Tax columns. The total should equal the total of the Gross Pay column. If your work is correct, enter the final totals.

PROBLEM | **79-2** ▶ You are the payroll clerk for the Laidlaw Company.

Directions

79-2
Total net pay = $2,307.40

a. Copy the following table:

Week Ending April 24, 19--			
Name of Employee	Gross Pay	FICA Tax	Net Pay
T. Garello	378 38		
E. Hua	451 24		
N. Isenberg	301 88		
A. Jones	557 28		
K. Kellog	345 67		
M. Leiber	473 59		
Totals			

b. Find the net pay for each employee using 8% as the FICA tax rate. Enter the FICA tax and net pay for each worker in the proper columns.

c. Foot the columns. Check your work by adding the totals of the Net Pay and FICA Tax columns. The total should equal the total of the Gross Pay column. If your work is correct, enter the final totals.

Problem 79-3 may be found in the Working Papers.

USING THE SOCIAL SECURITY TAX TABLE

APPLIED MATH PREVIEW

Copy and complete each problem. Round your answers to the nearest cent.

1. $489.58	2. $276.94	3. $ 508.31	4. $ 562.77
x 0.08	x 0.08	x 0.0751	x 0.0751

BUSINESS TERM PREVIEW

• **Take-home pay** •

GOAL

To learn how to use a table to find the social security (FICA) tax deduction.

*U*NDERSTANDING THE JOB

In the previous job, you learned how to compute the deduction for social security by multiplication. Payroll clerks who must manually compute the deduction for many workers need a fast and easy way to do it. These workers may use a social security tax table.

A table for social security tax deductions can be found in a booklet issued by the Internal Revenue Service called the *Employer's Tax Guide*. New tables are published every time the tax rate changes but the method of using the tax table remains the same.

Part of a social security tax table for an 8% FICA tax rate is shown in Illustration 80A (page 690). Use this table to solve the problems in this job.

KEY Terms

Take-home pay. Net pay.

You are the payroll clerk for the Felster & Eades Paper Company. Your duties include calculating net pay, or **take-home pay**, for each employee for the week ending May 12. The first time card for the week shows that Robin Moody has earned gross pay of $401.89. The social security tax table shows that the social security tax deduction from Robin Moody's wages should be $32.15. Here is how you would find the tax using the table:

STEP 1 ▶ *Find where the employee's wages fall within the Wages section of the table.*

When you look at the table, you will find the word *Wages* above two columns. The figures in the column headed "At least" are the ones you look at first to locate an amount that the employee's actual wages are *close to but not less than.* Then you look at the amount in the second column headed "But less than." The employee's wages should fall somewhere between the amounts in these two columns.

For example, when you look for the amount of Robin Moody's wages in the table, you will find that it falls between $401.82 and $401.94. It is close to but not less than $401.82, the amount on the second line of the "At least" column. It is also less than $401.94, the amount on the second line of the "But less than" column.

Illustration 80A Partial social security tax table

Partial Social Security Tax Table
8% Employee Tax Deduction

Wages		Tax to be withheld	Wages		Tax to be withheld
At least	But less than		At least	But less than	
$401.69	$401.82	$32.14	$410.69	$410.82	$32.86
401.82	401.94	32.15	410.82	410.94	32.87
401.94	402.07	32.16	410.94	411.07	32.88
402.07	402.19	32.17	411.07	411.19	32.89
402.19	402.32	32.18	411.19	411.32	32.90
$402.32	$402.44	$32.19	$411.32	$411.44	$32.91
402.44	402.57	32.20	411.44	411.57	32.92
402.57	402.69	32.21	411.57	411.69	32.93
402.69	402.82	32.22	411.69	411.82	32.94
402.82	402.94	32.23	411.82	411.94	32.95

Find the amount of FICA tax in the "Tax to be withheld" column.

Once you locate the correct line in the table, look at the amount shown in the next column headed "Tax to be withheld." You will see $32.15. This is the amount of FICA tax to be withheld from Robin Moody's wages.

You can see that any wages that fall between $401.82 and $401.94 will have the same FICA tax of $32.15. If you multiplied $401.82 by 8%, you would get an answer of $32.15. If you multiplied $401.93 by 8%, your answer would be rounded off to $32.15. In fact, you would get the same answer of $32.15 if you multiplied any number that is at least $401.82 but less than $401.94 by 8%. The rounded off amount would only change to $32.16 when you multiplied $401.94 by 8%. That is why the columns are headed "At least" and "But less than."

If you had to find the tax on $402.07, would you choose $32.16 or $32.17? You should choose $32.17. Notice that even though $402.07 is shown in the second column, the column is headed "But less than." That means it does not include $402.07. You must go to the next line and look at the "At least" column where you also see $402.07. This column includes $402.07, so the tax is $32.17.

To help you learn to use the social security tax table, the table in Illustration 80B shows wages with the correct FICA tax deductions. Look at the social security tax table and see if you find the same amount of tax for each wage amount. Place a ruler underneath the proper wage amount to prevent your eyes from shifting to the wrong line in the table.

Illustration 80B Using a table to find social security taxes

Time Card No.	Wages		Social Security Tax (FICA Tax) From Table	
1	401	98	32	16
2	402	79	32	22
3	411	47	32	92
4	401	82	32	15
5	411	69	32	94
6	410	72	32	86
7	402	82	32	23
8	410	93	32	87
9	402	41	32	19
10	411	20	32	90

Using a Computer to Find FICA Taxes

If a computer is used to handle payroll, all employee and employer payroll tax data are stored on disks. The record keeper does not use the FICA table. The record keeper also does not have to multiply the employee's weekly wage by the FICA rate. The computer will automatically

1. Check the total FICA taxes paid by the employee to make sure that the total FICA taxes paid so far this year do not exceed the maximum. (If the FICA rate is 8% and the maximum wages are $50,000.00, $4,000.00 is the most FICA taxes an employee must pay in one year.)
2. Multiply the weekly wages by the FICA tax rate.

This saves payroll clerks a great deal of time, and it also makes the payroll more accurate.

*B*UILDING YOUR BUSINESS VOCABULARY

On a sheet of paper, write the headings **Statement Number** and **Words**. Next, choose the words that match the statements. Write each word you choose next to the statement number it matches. Be careful; not all the words listed should be used.

Statements	Words
1. Tax collected for social security	commission pay
2. A fixed amount of pay	deductions
3. Net pay	FICA tax
4. Amounts subtracted from your wages	Federal Insurance Contributions Act (FICA)
5. Law which allows qualified persons to receive monthly payments from the federal government	gross pay
6. A pay plan based on how much is sold	salary
	Social Security Act
	take-home pay

PROBLEM SOLVING MODEL FOR: *Using the Social Security Tax Table*

> **STEP 1** ▶ *Find where the employee's wages fall within the Wages section of the table.*

> **STEP 2** ▶ *Find the amount of FICA tax in the "Tax to be withheld" column.*

PROBLEM 80-1 ▶ You are the payroll clerk for Rita Voroff Designs, Inc.

Directions

Copy and complete the following table. Find the social security tax for each wage using the social security tax table in Illustration 80A (page 690).

CHECKPOINT ✔

80-1 (1)
FICA tax amount = $32.94

Time Card No.	Wages		Social Security Tax (FICA Tax) From Table
1	411	69	
2	401	69	
3	410	70	
4	402	41	
5	410	95	
6	401	99	
7	411	58	
8	402	31	
9	402	05	
10	411	03	

PROBLEM 80-2 ▶ You are the payroll clerk for the Rolla Cycle Shop.

Directions

Copy and complete the following table. Find the social security tax for each wage using the social security tax table in Illustration 80A (page 690).

CHECKPOINT ✔

80-2 (1)
FICA tax amount = $32.94

Time Card No.	Wages		Social Security Tax (FICA Tax) From Table
1	411	81	
2	410	71	
3	402	37	
4	401	98	
5	411	00	
6	402	18	
7	410	87	
8	402	09	
9	401	89	
10	402	93	

Problem 80-3 may be found in the Working Papers.

FINDING WITHHOLDING TAXES

APPLIED MATH PREVIEW

Copy and complete each problem. Round your answers to the nearest cent.

1. $568.73	2. $299.36	3. $809.26	4. $1,207.56
- 64.00	- 35.00	x 0.08	x 0.08

BUSINESS TERMS PREVIEW

- Biweekly • Semimonthly • W-4 form • Withholding allowances •
- Withholding tax •

GOALS

1. To learn about withholding taxes.
2. To learn how to use a withholding tax table.

UNDERSTANDING THE JOB

To pay for the expenses of operating the federal government, people earning more than a certain amount of income must pay a federal income tax. In general, a person who earns more than someone else will pay a larger tax. Our tax system is based upon the ability of people to pay the tax.

Federal income taxes used to be paid once a year. To make paying the tax easier, the government passed a withholding tax law. This law requires employers to deduct money for federal income tax from the wages of their employees each payday. Because the tax is withheld from employee wages, it is often called a **withholding tax**.

The amount that must be deducted can be found in the *Employer's Tax Guide*, published by the Internal Revenue Service. The tax guide has tables for finding the federal withholding tax and the social security tax. There are separate tables for making deductions from wages that are paid daily, weekly, **biweekly** (every two weeks), **semimonthly** (twice a month), and monthly to both single and married workers. Since businesses use different pay periods, they need tables for these different pay periods.

In Illustration 81C on pages 697 and 698, you will find an example of a withholding tax table for married persons for a weekly pay

KEY Terms

Withholding tax. Income tax deducted from wages each payday.

Biweekly. Every two weeks.

Semimonthly. Twice a month.

period. Once you understand how to use this table, you should be able to use the tables for other pay periods, for single workers, or for any changes that the government may make to withholding amounts.

At the top of the table, you will notice column headings that read from 0 to 10. These figures show the number of **withholding allowances** a worker expects to claim in figuring income tax at the end of the year. A withholding allowance is a deduction a worker may claim for the support of another person, such as a child or spouse.

In general, a single worker has one allowance—himself or herself. A married worker with no children has two allowances, one for the husband and one for the wife. A married worker with two children can claim four allowances—one for the husband, one for the wife, and one for each of the two children. A worker who is single and who supports a widowed mother may claim two allowances—one for the worker and one for the mother.

Sometimes a worker may claim no allowances because that worker is claimed as an allowance by someone else. For example, a wife may claim her husband as an allowance. So, he would claim no allowance for himself.

When you are hired, your employer will ask you to fill out a **W-4 form**. The W-4 form tells the employer how many allowances a worker claims. A completed W-4 form is shown in Illustration 81A.

MULTICULTURAL
INSIGHT

The United States has many different kinds of people and cultures. In addition to a large population of Caucasians from various European backgrounds, there are also large groups of people with African, Asian, and Hispanic backgrounds. The original residents of North America, the Native Americans, make up another cultural group. It is no surprise, then, that the work force also has many different kinds of people who understand and appreciate cultures from around the world. American businesses can use the knowledge and talents of their diverse work force to expand global trade.

Form **W-4** Department of the Treasury Internal Revenue Service	**Employee's Withholding Allowance Certificate** ► For Privacy Act and Paperwork Reduction Act Notice, see reverse.	OMB No. 1545-0010
1 Type or print your first name and middle initial Olive R.	Last name Berrios	**2** Your social security number 386-92-9748

1 Type or print your first name and middle initial: Olive R. Last name: Berrios **2** Your social security number: 386-92-9748

Home address (number and street or rural route)
3892 Newton Street

City or town, state, and ZIP code
Allentown, PA 18104-3892

3 Marital Status: ☐ Single ☒ Married ☐ Married, but withhold at higher Single rate.
Note: *If married, but legally separated, or spouse is a nonresident alien, check the Single box*

4 Total number of allowances you are claiming (from line G above or from the Worksheets on back if they apply) . . . . . **4** | 4

5 Additional amount, if any, you want deducted from each pay . . . . **5** | $ -0-

6 I claim exemption from withholding and I certify that I meet ALL of the following conditions for exemption:
• Last year I had a right to a refund of **ALL** Federal income tax withheld because I had **NO** tax liability; **AND**
• This year I expect a refund of **ALL** Federal income tax withheld because I expect to have **NO** tax liability; **AND**
• This year if my income exceeds $500 and includes nonwage income, another person cannot claim me as a dependent.
If you meet all of the above conditions, enter the year effective and "EXEMPT" here . . . . ► **6** | 19

7 Are you a full-time student? (**Note:** *Full-time students are not automatically exempt.*) . . . . **7** ☐ Yes ☒ No

Under penalties of perjury, I certify that I am entitled to the number of withholding allowances claimed on this certificate or entitled to claim exempt status.

Employee's signature ► *Olive R. Berrios*   Date ► March 22   , 19 --

8 Employer's name and address (**Employer:** Complete 8 and 10 **only if sending to IRS**)
Ralis Plastics Corporation
2135 River Road, Allentown, PA 18104-2135

9 Office code (optional)

10 Employer identification number
87-8629483

Illustration 81A W-4 form

$\mathcal{S}$ AMPLE PROBLEM

You are the payroll clerk for Centrix Telephone Company. Olive Berrios, whose W-4 form is shown in Illustration 81A, claims 4 allowances and has a gross pay of $507.80. Here are the steps that you would follow to find her withholding tax deduction:

STEP 1 ▶ **Locate the wages in the wages section of the withholding tax table.**

Look at the withholding tax table in Illustration 81C on pages 697and 698. Find the columns headed "At least" and "But less than." Read down these columns until you come to the amounts within which Berrios's wages of $507.80 fall. You will find that her wages fall between the amounts $500.00 and $510.00 in the table.

STEP 2 ▶ **Find the withholding tax deduction in the correct allowance column.**

Berrios has claimed 4 allowances. Once you have found the correct wages line, read across the table until the column for 4 allowances is reached. Use a ruler to keep your eyes from straying to the wrong line. You will find an amount of $43.00. This tells you that you must deduct $43.00 from Berrios's wages for federal withholding tax.

To help you learn to use the table, Illustration 81B shows some wages and their correct withholding tax amounts. Look at Illustration 81C and see if you can find the same answers.

Illustration 81B   Using the federal income tax withholding table

Time Card No.	Number of Allowances	Wages		Federal Withholding Tax	
1	1	235	00	20	00
2	2	370	00	35	00
3	5	1,038	00	141	00
4	0	436	85	56	00
5	8	731	73	55	00

MARRIED Persons–WEEKLY Payroll Period

And the wages are–		And the number of withholding allowances claimed is–										
At least	But less than	0	1	2	3	4	5	6	7	8	9	10
		The amount of income tax to be withheld shall be–										
$0	$65	$0	$0	$0	$0	$0	$0	$0	$0	$0	$0	$0
65	70	1	0	0	0	0	0	0	0	0	0	0
70	75	2	0	0	0	0	0	0	0	0	0	0
75	80	2	0	0	0	0	0	0	0	0	0	0
80	85	3	0	0	0	0	0	0	0	0	0	0
85	90	4	0	0	0	0	0	0	0	0	0	0
90	95	5	0	0	0	0	0	0	0	0	0	0
95	100	5	0	0	0	0	0	0	0	0	0	0
100	105	6	0	0	0	0	0	0	0	0	0	0
105	110	7	1	0	0	0	0	0	0	0	0	0
110	115	8	2	0	0	0	0	0	0	0	0	0
115	120	8	3	0	0	0	0	0	0	0	0	0
120	125	9	3	0	0	0	0	0	0	0	0	0
125	130	10	4	0	0	0	0	0	0	0	0	0
130	135	11	5	0	0	0	0	0	0	0	0	0
135	140	11	6	0	0	0	0	0	0	0	0	0
140	145	12	6	1	0	0	0	0	0	0	0	0
145	150	13	7	1	0	0	0	0	0	0	0	0
150	155	14	8	2	0	0	0	0	0	0	0	0
155	160	14	9	3	0	0	0	0	0	0	0	0
160	165	15	9	4	0	0	0	0	0	0	0	0
165	170	16	10	4	0	0	0	0	0	0	0	0
170	175	17	11	5	0	0	0	0	0	0	0	0
175	180	17	12	6	0	0	0	0	0	0	0	0
180	185	18	12	7	1	0	0	0	0	0	0	0
185	190	19	13	7	2	0	0	0	0	0	0	0
190	195	20	14	8	2	0	0	0	0	0	0	0
195	200	20	15	9	3	0	0	0	0	0	0	0
200	210	22	16	10	4	0	0	0	0	0	0	0
210	220	23	17	11	6	0	0	0	0	0	0	0
220	230	25	19	13	7	1	0	0	0	0	0	0
230	240	26	20	14	9	3	0	0	0	0	0	0
240	250	28	22	16	10	4	0	0	0	0	0	0
250	260	29	23	17	12	6	0	0	0	0	0	0
260	270	31	25	19	13	7	2	0	0	0	0	0
270	280	32	26	20	15	9	3	0	0	0	0	0
280	290	34	28	22	16	10	5	0	0	0	0	0
290	300	35	29	23	18	12	6	0	0	0	0	0
300	310	37	31	25	19	13	8	2	0	0	0	0
310	320	38	32	26	21	15	9	3	0	0	0	0
320	330	40	34	28	22	16	11	5	0	0	0	0
330	340	41	35	29	24	18	12	6	1	0	0	0
340	350	43	37	31	25	19	14	8	2	0	0	0
350	360	44	38	32	27	21	15	9	4	0	0	0
360	370	46	40	34	28	22	17	11	5	0	0	0
370	380	47	41	35	30	24	18	12	7	1	0	0
380	390	49	43	37	31	25	20	14	8	2	0	0
390	400	50	44	38	33	27	21	15	10	4	0	0
400	410	52	46	40	34	28	23	17	11	5	0	0
410	420	53	47	41	36	30	24	18	13	7	1	0
420	430	55	49	43	37	31	26	20	14	8	3	0
430	440	56	50	44	39	33	27	21	16	10	4	0
440	450	58	52	46	40	34	29	23	17	11	6	0
450	460	59	53	47	42	36	30	24	19	13	7	1
460	470	61	55	49	43	37	32	26	20	14	9	3
470	480	62	56	50	45	39	33	27	22	16	10	4
480	490	64	58	52	46	40	35	29	23	17	12	6
490	500	65	59	53	48	42	36	30	25	19	13	7
500	510	67	61	55	49	43	38	32	26	20	15	9
510	520	68	62	56	51	45	39	33	28	22	16	10
520	530	70	64	58	52	46	41	35	29	23	18	12
530	540	71	65	59	54	48	42	36	31	25	19	13
540	550	73	67	61	55	49	44	38	32	26	21	15
550	560	74	68	62	57	51	45	39	34	28	22	16
560	570	76	70	64	58	52	47	41	35	29	24	18
570	580	77	71	65	60	54	48	42	37	31	25	19
580	590	79	73	67	61	55	50	44	38	32	27	21
590	600	80	74	68	63	57	51	45	40	34	28	22
600	610	82	76	70	64	58	53	47	41	35	30	24
610	620	83	77	71	66	60	54	48	43	37	31	25

MARRIED Persons–WEEKLY Payroll Period

And the wages are–		And the number of withholding allowances claimed is–										
At least	But less than	0	1	2	3	4	5	6	7	8	9	10
		The amount of income tax to be withheld shall be–										
$620	$630	$85	$79	$73	$67	$61	$56	$50	$44	$38	$33	$27
630	640	86	80	74	69	63	57	51	46	40	34	28
640	650	88	82	76	70	64	59	53	47	41	36	30
650	660	89	83	77	72	66	60	54	49	43	37	31
660	670	92	85	79	73	67	62	56	50	44	39	33
670	680	94	86	80	75	69	63	57	52	46	40	34
680	690	97	88	82	76	70	65	59	53	47	42	36
690	700	100	89	83	78	72	66	60	55	49	43	37
700	710	103	92	85	79	73	68	62	56	50	45	39
710	720	106	95	86	81	75	69	63	58	52	46	40
720	730	108	98	88	82	76	71	65	59	53	48	42
730	740	111	100	90	84	78	72	66	61	55	49	43
740	750	114	103	92	85	79	74	68	62	56	51	45
750	760	117	106	95	87	81	75	69	64	58	52	46
760	770	120	109	98	88	82	77	71	65	59	54	48
770	780	122	112	101	90	84	78	72	67	61	55	49
780	790	125	114	104	93	85	80	74	68	62	57	51
790	800	128	117	106	96	87	81	75	70	64	58	52
800	810	131	120	109	98	88	83	77	71	65	60	54
810	820	134	123	112	101	91	84	78	73	67	61	55
820	830	136	126	115	104	93	86	80	74	68	63	57
830	840	139	128	118	107	96	87	81	76	70	64	58
840	850	142	131	120	110	99	89	83	77	71	66	60
850	860	145	134	123	112	102	91	84	79	73	67	61
860	870	148	137	126	115	105	94	86	80	74	69	63
870	880	150	140	129	118	107	97	87	82	76	70	64
880	890	153	142	132	121	110	99	89	83	77	72	66
890	900	156	145	134	124	113	102	91	85	79	73	67
900	910	159	148	137	126	116	105	94	86	80	75	69
910	920	162	151	140	129	119	108	97	88	82	76	70
920	930	164	154	143	132	121	111	100	89	83	78	72
930	940	167	156	146	135	124	113	103	92	85	79	73
940	950	170	159	148	138	127	116	105	95	86	81	75
950	960	173	162	151	140	130	119	108	97	88	82	76
960	970	176	165	154	143	133	122	111	100	89	84	78
970	980	178	168	157	146	135	125	114	103	92	85	79
980	990	181	170	160	149	138	127	117	106	95	87	81
990	1,000	184	173	162	152	141	130	119	109	98	88	82
1,000	1,010	187	176	165	154	144	133	122	111	101	90	84
1,010	1,020	190	179	168	157	147	136	125	114	103	93	85
1,020	1,030	192	182	171	160	149	139	128	117	106	95	87
1,030	1,040	195	184	174	163	152	141	131	120	109	98	88
1,040	1,050	198	187	176	166	155	144	133	123	112	101	90
1,050	1,060	201	190	179	168	158	147	136	125	115	104	93
1,060	1,070	204	193	182	171	161	150	139	128	117	107	96
1,070	1,080	206	196	185	174	163	153	142	131	120	109	99
1,080	1,090	209	198	188	177	166	155	145	134	123	112	102
1,090	1,100	212	201	190	180	169	158	147	137	126	115	104
1,100	1,110	215	204	193	182	172	161	150	139	129	118	107
1,110	1,120	218	207	196	185	175	164	153	142	131	121	110
1,120	1,130	220	210	199	188	177	167	156	145	134	123	113
1,130	1,140	223	212	202	191	180	169	159	148	137	126	116
1,140	1,150	226	215	204	194	183	172	161	151	140	129	118
1,150	1,160	229	218	207	196	186	175	164	153	143	132	121
1,160	1,170	232	221	210	199	189	178	167	156	145	135	124
1,170	1,180	234	224	213	202	191	181	170	159	148	137	127
1,180	1,190	237	226	216	205	194	183	173	162	151	140	130
1,190	1,200	240	229	218	208	197	186	175	165	154	143	132
1,200	1,210	243	232	221	210	200	189	178	167	157	146	135
1,210	1,220	246	235	224	213	203	192	181	170	159	149	138
1,220	1,230	248	238	227	216	205	195	184	173	162	151	141
1,230	1,240	251	240	230	219	208	197	187	176	165	154	144
1,240	1,250	254	243	232	222	211	200	189	179	168	157	146
1,250	1,260	257	246	235	224	214	203	192	181	171	160	149
1,260	1,270	260	249	238	227	217	206	195	184	173	163	152
1,270	1,280	262	252	241	230	219	209	198	187	176	165	155

Using the Computer for Withholding Taxes

If a computer is used for payroll, the payroll clerk does not need to look up and record each employee's federal withholding tax. The computer stores the federal withholding tax tables in its memory and automatically looks up and records each employee's withholding tax. This saves the payroll office a great deal of work and also makes the calculations more accurate.

```
Period Ended  03/04/--          Employee No.    1078
Name          Everett Landon    Social Sec. No. 334-87-1029


                  Totals This Period      Totals Year-to-Date

Total Pay            $389.89                 $3,509.01
Fed. With.             43.00                    387.00
FICA Tax               31.19                    280.71
Net Pay              $315.70                 $2,841.30
```

Illustration 81D   The top part of a paycheck printed by a computer showing the withholding tax for the week and the total paid for the year

BUILDING YOUR BUSINESS VOCABULARY

On a sheet of paper, write the headings **Statement Number** and **Words**. Next, choose the words that match the statements. Write each word you choose next to the statement number it matches. Be careful; not all the words listed should be used.

Statements	Words
1. An income tax deducted from a worker's wages each payday	biweekly
2. Time worked beyond 40 hours a week	commission
3. Gross pay less deductions	deductions
4. Twice a month	FICA tax
5. A deduction a worker may claim for the support of another person	net pay
6. Amounts subtracted from wages	overtime
7. A form which shows how many withholding allowances a worker claims	regular time pay
8. Every two weeks	semimonthly
9. A tax collected to pay for social security	W-4 form
	withholding allowance
	withholding tax

PROBLEM SOLVING MODEL FOR: *Finding Withholding Taxes*

STEP 1 ▶ **Locate the wages in the wages section of the withholding tax table.**

STEP 2 ▶ **Find the withholding tax deduction in the correct allowance column.**

*A*PPLICATION PROBLEMS

PROBLEM **81-1** ▶ You work as a payroll clerk for Integrated Systems Corporation.

Directions

Copy and complete the following table. Find the federal withholding tax for each wage amount using the withholding tax table found in Illustration 81C (pages 697–698).

CHECKPOINT

81-1 (1)
Withholding amount =
$26.00

Time Card No.	Number of Allowances	Wages		Federal Withholding Tax	
1	2	310	00		
2	6	578	00		
3	0	489	17		
4	1	1,040	89		
5	7	839	27		
6	3	628	51		
7	1	293	15		
8	4	764	63		
9	0	1,128	85		
10	3	375	45		

PROBLEM **81-2** ▶ You are the payroll clerk for Jolor Alloy Company.

Directions

Copy and complete the following table. Find the federal withholding tax for each wage amount using the withholding tax table found in Illustration 81C (pages 697–698).

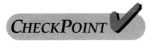
Time Card No.	Number of Allowances	Wages		Federal Withholding Tax	
1	4	1,272	37		
2	6	271	39		
3	1	516	07		
4	0	463	91		
5	7	361	20		
6	3	609	75		
7	5	834	51		
8	0	708	64		
9	1	372	34		
10	2	1,011	26		

PROBLEM **81-3** ▶ You are a payroll clerk for Sea Trailers, Inc.

Directions

Copy and complete the following table. Find the social security tax and the federal withholding tax for each wage amount. Use the social security tax table found in Illustration 80A on page 690 in Job 80. Use the withholding tax table found in Illustration 81C on pages 697–698 in this job. Remember that the withholding tax is based on the gross pay, or total wages.

Time Card No.	Number of Allowances	Wages		FICA Tax		Federal Withholding Tax	
1	1	401	80				
2	0	411	90				
3	5	402	02				
4	9	410	95				
5	3	401	91				
6	2	411	01				

JOB **82** ▶ PREPARING THE PAYROLL

GOALS

1. To learn how to find a worker's take-home pay after making social security and withholding tax deductions.
2. To learn how to enter the information in a payroll register.

UNDERSTANDING THE JOB

In the previous chapter, you learned to record payroll data, including gross pay, in a payroll register. In the last two jobs, you learned how to find the amounts for social security and federal withholding taxes. In this job, you will learn how to record all these data in a payroll register.

SAMPLE PROBLEM

You work as a payroll clerk for Lasalle Glass Company. You just completed the payroll register shown in Illustrations 82A and 82B on pages 703 and 704. Here are the steps you followed to record the payroll data in the payroll register:

STEP 1 ▶ *Enter the time card data.*

STEP 1 ▶ *Enter the time card data.*

From the time cards, you filled in the columns for card number, name of employee, hours worked, wage rates, wage amounts, and gross pay.

STEP 2 ▶ *Enter the number of allowances.*

In the No. of Allow. column, you entered the number of allowances the employee claimed on the W-4 form.

STEP 3 ▶ *Enter the social security tax deduction.*

You found the social security tax deduction (FICA tax) for each employee by multiplying the gross pay by 8%, the FICA tax rate used in this chapter. You entered the amount in the FICA Tax column.

STEP 4 ▶ *Enter the federal withholding tax deduction.*

You found the federal withholding tax deduction for each employee by using the table in Illustration 81C on pages 697–698 in Job 81. You entered the amount in the federal withholding tax (Fed. With.) column.

STEP 5 ▶ *Enter the total deductions for each employee.*

You added the amounts in the FICA Tax and Fed. With. tax columns together for each employee and entered the total deductions in the total deductions (Total Ded.) column.

For example, in Illustration 82B (page 704), Michelle Levy's total deductions were found this way:

Social security (FICA) tax	$ 32.64
Federal withholding tax	+ 46.00
Total deductions	$ 78.64

You entered the amount of Levy's total deductions, $78.64, in the Total Ded. column.

Illustration 82A   Payroll register (left page)

PAYROLL REGISTER

	TIME CARD NO.	NAME OF EMPLOYEE	NO. OF ALLOW.	HOURS WORKED					TOTAL HOURS WORKED	REGULAR PAY			
				M	T	W	TH	F		HRS.	RATE	AMOUNT	
1	1	Michelle Levy	1	8	8	8	8	8	40	40	10 20	4 0 8 00	1
2	2	Roberto Lopez	3	8	8	8	10	8	42	40	8 50	3 4 0 00	2
3		Totals										7 4 8 00 / 7 4 8 00	3

STEP **6** ▶ *Find the net pay, or take-home pay, for each employee.*

You found net pay by subtracting the total deductions from the gross pay. You entered the amount of net pay in the Net Pay column. For example, in Illustration 82B, Levy's net pay was found this way:

Gross pay	$408.00
Less: Total deductions	- 78.64
Net pay	$329.36

STEP **7** ▶ *Foot each money column and check the totals.*

You ruled and footed all the money columns. You checked the total of the Gross Pay column by adding the total of the Regular Pay column to the total of the Overtime Pay column.

Regular pay	$748.00
Overtime pay	+ 25.50
Gross pay	$773.50

The total of the Total Ded. column was checked this way:

Total FICA tax	$ 61.88
Total federal withholding tax	+ 74.00
Total deductions	$135.88

The total of the Net Pay column was checked as follows:

Gross pay	$ 773.50
Total deductions	- 135.88
Total net pay	$ 637.62

STEP **8** ▶ *Record the final totals and double rule the money columns.*

After checking the totals by crossfooting, you recorded the final totals. Then, you double ruled the money columns, as shown in Illustrations 82A (page 703) and 82B.

Illustration 82B   Payroll register (right page)

		PAYROLL REGISTER					WEEK ENDING	*April 6, 19--*	

| | OVERTIME PAY | | | GROSS PAY | DEDUCTIONS | | | | NET PAY | |
	HRS.	RATE	AMOUNT		FICA TAX	FED. WITH.	TOTAL DED.			
1				4 0 8 00	3 2 64	4 6 00	7 8 64		3 2 9 36	1
2	2	12 75	2 5 50	3 6 5 50	2 9 24	2 8 00	5 7 24		3 0 8 26	2
3			2 5 50 / 2 5 50	7 7 3 50 / 7 7 3 50	6 1 88 / 6 1 88	7 4 00 / 7 4 00	1 3 5 88 / 1 3 5 88		6 3 7 62 / 6 3 7 62	3

On a sheet of paper, write the headings **Statement Number** and **Words**. Next, choose the words that match the statements. Write each word you choose next to the statement number it matches. Be careful; not all the words listed should be used.

Statements	Words
1. The amount left after deductions; take-home pay	biweekly
	FICA tax
2. Twice a month	net pay
3. Social security tax	overtime
4. Every two weeks	semimonthly
5. A deduction a worker may claim for the support of another person	total wages
	W-4 form
6. An income tax deducted from a worker's wages each payday	withholding allowance
	withholding tax
7. A form which shows how many withholding allowances a worker claims	

PROBLEM SOLVING MODEL FOR: *Preparing the Payroll*

STEP 1 ▶	*Enter the time card data.*
STEP 2 ▶	*Enter the number of allowances.*
STEP 3 ▶	*Enter the social security tax deduction.*
STEP 4 ▶	*Enter the federal withholding tax deduction.*
STEP 5 ▶	*Enter the total deductions for each employee.*
STEP 6 ▶	*Find the net pay, or take-home pay, for each employee.*
STEP 7 ▶	*Foot each money column and check the totals.*
STEP 8 ▶	*Record the final totals and double rule the money columns.*

APPLICATION PROBLEMS

PROBLEM 82-1 ▶ You are employed as a payroll clerk by Yanaka Major Leagues, Inc.

Directions

a. Copy and complete the following table. Find the social security tax using an 8% FICA tax rate. Find the federal withholding tax using the income tax withholding table shown in Illustration 81C on pages 697–698 in Job 81.

CHECKPOINT ✔

82-1 (b)
Total net pay = $1,899.86

Time Card No.	No. of Allow.	Total Wages	Social Security (FICA) Tax	Federal With. Tax	Total Deductions	Net Pay
1	1	289 78				
2	5	402 78				
3	0	473 59				
4	4	511 38				
5	3	634 27				
	Totals					

b. Foot each money column and check your totals.

PROBLEM 82-2 ▶ You are the payroll clerk for Herbst Appliance Company.

Directions

a. Prepare a payroll register with the same column headings as shown in Illustrations 82A and 82B (pages 703 and 704).
b. Enter the following information for the week ending October 18, 19--, in the payroll register:

CHECKPOINT ✔

82-2 (d)
Total net pay = $1,895.79

Time Card No.	Name of Employee	No. of Allow.	Hours Worked M	T	W	TH	F	Wages Per Hour
1	T. Howard	1	8	8	8	8	8	$ 8.80
2	V. Hyslip	0	7 1/2	8 1/4	8 1/2	8	8	13.50
3	B. Ivany	3	8	9	8 1/4	8 3/4	9	9.57
4	C. Johnsen	2	8	8 1/2	9 1/2	8	7 1/2	12.45
5	D. Keller	8	10	9 1/2	10	9 1/2	10 1/2	8.25

c. Complete the payroll register. Use a FICA tax rate of 8% and the income tax withholding table shown in Illustration 81C on pages 697–698 in Job 81.
d. Foot each money column and check your totals.

PROBLEM 82-3 ▶ You are the payroll clerk for Chiang's Tour Company.

Directions

a. Prepare a payroll register with the same column headings as shown in Illustrations 82A and 82B (pages 703 and 704).
b. Enter the following information for the week ending June 24, 19--, in the payroll register:

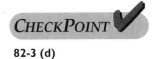

CHECKPOINT

82-3 (d)
Total net pay = $1,631.74

Time Card No.	Name of Employee	No. of Allow.	Hours Worked M	T	W	TH	F	Wages Per Hour
1	D. Toussant	1	8 1/2	8	8 1/2	8 1/2	8	$ 7.80
2	L. Tunile	0	8	10 1/4	8 1/2	8	7	10.10
3	S. Tyler	6	8	8	9 1/4	8	10 1/2	10.65
4	O. Underwood	3	7 1/2	8	7 1/2	7	7 1/2	8.95
5	Y. Vander	1	8	8 1/2	8	7 1/2	8 1/2	9.70

c. Complete the payroll register. Use a FICA tax rate of 8% and the income tax withholding table shown in Illustration 81C on pages 697–698 in Job 81.
d. Foot each money column and check your totals.

APPLIED MATH PREVIEW

Copy and complete these problems.

1. $ 287.91
   712.83
   567.34
   907.78
   297.08
   + 674.98

2. Crossfoot and then add down:

   16 + 83 + 40 + 62 =
   65 + 20 + 56 + 49 =
   28 + 15 + 29 + 48 =
   87 + 17 + 54 + 42 =
   201 + 307 + 74 + 3 =

BUSINESS TERMS PREVIEW

• Employee earnings record • FWT • Quarter •

GOAL

To learn how to keep a record of each employee's earnings and deductions.

𝒰NDERSTANDING THE JOB

K E Y *Terms*

Employee earnings record. A record of an employee's earnings and deductions.

Quarter. 13 weeks or ¼ of a year.

You have learned how social security and federal withholding taxes are deducted from an employee's wages. Employers must pay the money deducted to the federal government at certain times during the year. Employers must also give federal and state agencies information about the earnings and deductions of each employee. To have this information ready when it is needed, payroll clerks keep an **employee earnings record** for each employee, like the one shown in Illustration 83B on page 710.

The information for the top part of the record is recorded when the employee is hired. At the end of each week, the payroll clerk enters data from the payroll register into the employee earnings record. The employee earnings record is totaled and summarized at the end of thirteen weeks, or each **quarter**.

SAMPLE PROBLEM

Keiko Saburo is the payroll clerk for Rand Insurance Company. The payroll register for the week ending January 4 is shown in Illustration 83A.

Illustration 83B (page 710) shows an employee earnings record for Ari Shaheen. Look at the entry for the week ending January 4. Notice how these data were taken from the payroll register shown in Illustration 83A.

Keiko Saburo followed these steps to complete the employee earnings record:

STEP 1 ▶ **Record the data on the top part of the record when the employee is hired.**

Ari Shaheen was hired at a salary of $387.20 a week (40 hours). Keiko recorded this information on the employee earnings record. Ari Shaheen was also asked a number of personal questions. His answers were entered on the top part of his employee earnings record.

PAYROLL REGISTER   WEEK ENDING *January 4, 19--*

| | TIME CARD NO. | NAME OF EMPLOYEE | GROSS PAY | DEDUCTIONS | | | NET PAY | |
				FICA TAX	FED. WITH.	TOTAL DED.		
1	102	*Ari Shaheen*	3 8 7 20	3 0 98	3 1 00	6 1 98	3 2 5 22	1
2	103	*Sally Skelly*	5 2 8 92	4 2 31	5 8 00	1 0 0 31	4 2 8 61	2
3	104	*Todd Skinner*	4 7 6 31	3 8 10	6 2 00	1 0 0 10	3 7 6 21	3
4	105	*Vi Stein*	6 1 0 42	4 8 83	7 1 00	1 1 9 83	4 9 0 59	4
5		*Totals*	2 0 0 2 85	1 6 0 22	2 2 2 00	3 8 2 22	1 6 2 0 63	5

Illustration 83A   Partial payroll register

STEP 2 ▶ **Post data from the payroll register to the employee earnings record each payday.**

For each employee, the amount of gross pay, FICA tax, and federal withholding tax is posted from the payroll register to the employee earnings record each payday. Compare Illustration 83A to Illustration 83B (page 710). Notice how the information for Ari Shaheen in the payroll register was copied to the employee earnings record for the week ending January 4.

At the end of the second week, January 11, the information was again posted to the employee earnings record from the payroll register. Notice that the gross pay on January 11 differs from the gross pay on January 4. During that week, Ari worked more than 40 hours (42 hours) and received overtime wages for the two hours worked beyond 40 hours.

Illustration 83B
Employee earnings
record

EMPLOYEE EARNINGS RECORD

Name: Ari Shaheen
Address: 25 Woodley Road, Rockford, IL 61111-0025
Date of Birth: 2 / 23 / --
Job Title: Secretary
Wage Rate $ 387.20
Date Hired: 5 / 17 / --

Time Card No.: 102
Social Security No.: 352-82-1872
No. of Allowances: 3
Single _____ Married ✓
Department: Investments (8)
Wage Plan: Weekly Salary
Termination Date: ____ / ____ / ____

FIRST QUARTER

Week Ending		Gross Pay	FICA Tax	Fed. With. Tax
1	19-- Jan. 4	387 20	30 98	31 00
2	11	416 24	33 30	36 00
3	18	387 20	30 98	31 00
4	25	387 20	30 98	31 00
5	Feb. 1	445 28	35 62	40 00
6	8	387 20	30 98	31 00
7	15	387 20	30 98	31 00
8	22	387 20	30 98	31 00
9	Mar. 1	387 20	30 98	31 00
10	8	416 24	33 30	36 00
11	15	387 20	30 98	31 00
12	22	387 20	30 98	31 00
13	29	387 20	30 98	31 00
	Totals	5149 76	412 02	422 00

SUMMARY

Quarters		Gross Pay	FICA Tax	Fed. With. Tax
First		5149 76	412 02	422 00
Second				
Third				
Fourth				
Yearly Total				

STEP 3 ▶ *Total each money column at the end of the quarter.*

At the end of the 13 weeks, or quarter, Keiko footed the amount columns of the employee earnings record. After checking the footings, Keiko entered the final totals. The employee earnings record in Illustration 83B shows data about Ari's earnings and deductions for the first quarter of the year.

At the end of each quarter, the totals for the quarter are recorded in the Summary section of the employee earnings record. At the end of the year, the totals for each quarter are added together to find the totals for the year. The amounts are recorded on the Yearly Total line at the bottom of the card. Illustration 83C shows the completed Summary section of Ari Shaheen's employee earnings record at the end of the year.

Illustration 83C
Completed Summary
section of employee
earnings record

Totals																	
SUMMARY																	
Quarters	Gross Pay					FICA Tax				Fed. With. Tax							
First		5	1	4	9	76		4	1	2	02		4	2	2	00
Second		5	0	3	3	60		4	0	2	74		4	0	3	00
Third		5	0	6	2	·64		4	0	5	06		4	0	8	00
Fourth		5	0	3	3	60		4	0	2	74		4	0	3	00
Yearly Total	20	2	7	9	60		1	6	2	2	56		1	6	3	6	00

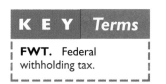

In a computerized payroll system, an employee earnings record is also kept. A printout of Ari Shaheen's employee earnings data produced by a computer at the end of the first quarter is shown in Illustration 83D. You will learn more about computerized payroll systems in Job 84.

Notice that to save space, federal withholding taxes are abbreviated to Federal W/H. Some reports use **FWT**.

```
                        Rand Insurance Company
                           Payroll Report
                              03/29/--
-------------------------------------------------------------------------------
                                       Current   Quarterly  Yearly
-------------------------------------------------------------------------------
     102-Ari Shaheen          Gross Pay      387.20    5149.76  5149.76
     25 Woodley Road          Federal W/H     31.00     422.00   422.00
     Rockford, Il 61111-0025  State W/H
     352-82-1872              FICA W/H        30.98     412.02   412.02
     W/H Allow   3   Married  Medicare
     Department  8            Deduction  1
     Pay Periods             Deduction  2
     Reg. Hrs.                Deduction  3
     O.T. Hrs.                Net Pay        325.22
     Extra Pay
     Salary        387.20
```

Illustration 83D   Printout of employee earnings record

While some of the data in the employee earnings record must be entered by record keepers, much of the data are kept current automatically by the computer.

BUILDING YOUR BUSINESS VOCABULARY

On a sheet of paper, write the headings **Statement Number** and **Words**. Next, choose the words that match the statements. Write each word you choose next to the statement number it matches. Be careful; not all the words listed should be used.

Statements	Words
1. A record of an employee's earnings and deductions	biweekly
	deductions
2. ¼ year or 13 weeks	employee earnings record
3. A deduction a worker may claim for the support of another person	FICA tax
4. Every two weeks	FWT
5. Social security tax	gross pay
6. The amount of wages left after deductions	net pay
7. Amounts subtracted from your wages	quarter
8. A fixed amount of pay	salary
9. Federal withholding tax	semimonthly
	withholding allowance

PROBLEM SOLVING MODEL FOR: *Keeping an Employee Earnings Record*

STEP 1 ▶ **Record the data on the top part of the record when the employee is hired.**

STEP 2 ▶ **Post data from the payroll register to the employee earnings record each payday.**

STEP 3 ▶ **Total each money column at the end of the quarter.**

STEP 4 ▶ **Record the totals for each quarter in the Summary section.**

APPLICATION PROBLEMS

PROBLEM **83-1** ▶ You are a payroll clerk for Ferral Graphics Company.

Directions

a. Open separate employee earnings records for the following people.

83-1

Rhonda Lorey's total gross
pay = $1,640.00

Use Illustration 83B (page 710) as a guide. You will need four records.

1. Rhonda Lorey lives at 1425 Kyle Street, San Antonio, TX 78224-1425. She is married and claims 3 allowances. Her date of birth is August 21, 19--. Her social security number is 361-72-7615. She is employed in the art department as a designer. She was hired at a weekly salary of $410.00 on January 2 and was given Time Card No. 1.
2. Roger Monet lives at 3145 Iowa Street, San Antonio, TX 78203-3145. He is married and claims 2 allowances. His date of birth is May 12, 19--. His social security number is 322-87-5612. He is employed in the production department as a keyboard operator. He was hired at an hourly rate of $9.87 on January 2 and was given Time Card No. 2.
3. Edith Nunnes lives at 2871 Kendalia Avenue, San Antonio, TX 78224-2871. She is single and claims 1 allowance. Her date of birth is November 15, 19--. Her social security number is 472-81-4578. She is employed in the editorial office as an office manager. She was hired at a weekly salary of $485.00 on January 2 and was given Time Card No. 3.
4. Wallies O'Hare lives at 623 Mclane Street, San Antonio, TX 78212-0623. He is single and claims 1 allowance. His date of birth is June 16, 19--. His social security number is 507-67-8263. He is employed in the sales department as a sales manager. He was hired at a weekly salary of $540.00 on January 2 and was given Time Card No. 4.

b. The pages of the payroll register that follow show data for the first four weeks of the first quarter. Post the data in the payroll register to the proper employee earnings records.
c. Foot each column on the employee earnings records to show the totals for the month of January.

PAYROLL REGISTER   WEEK ENDING *January 7, 19--*

	TIME CARD NO.	NAME OF EMPLOYEE	GROSS PAY	DEDUCTIONS FICA TAX	DEDUCTIONS FED. WITH.	DEDUCTIONS TOTAL DED.	NET PAY	
1	1	Rhonda Lorey	4 1 0 00	3 2 80	3 6 00	6 8 80	3 4 1 20	1
2	2	Roger Monet	3 9 4 80	3 1 58	3 8 00	6 9 58	3 2 5 22	2
3	3	Edith Nunnes	4 8 5 00	3 8 80	7 3 00	1 1 1 80	3 7 3 20	3
4	4	Wallies O'Hare	5 4 0 00	4 3 20	9 0 00	1 3 3 20	4 0 6 80	4
5		Totals	1 8 2 9 80 / 1 8 2 9 80	1 4 6 38 / 1 4 6 38	2 3 7 00 / 2 3 7 00	3 8 3 38 / 3 8 3 38	1 4 4 6 42 / 1 4 4 6 42	5

CHECKPOINT

PAYROLL REGISTER — WEEK ENDING January 14, 19--

	TIME CARD NO.	NAME OF EMPLOYEE	GROSS PAY	DEDUCTIONS — FICA TAX	DEDUCTIONS — FED. WITH.	DEDUCTIONS — TOTAL DED.	NET PAY	
1	1	Rhonda Lorey	410 00	32 80	36 00	68 80	341 20	1
2	2	Roger Monet	439 22	35 14	44 00	79 14	360 08	2
3	3	Edith Nunnes	485 00	38 80	73 00	111 80	373 20	3
4	4	Wallies O'Hare	540 00	43 20	90 00	133 20	406 80	4
5		Totals	1874 22	149 94	243 00	392 94	1481 28	5

PAYROLL REGISTER — WEEK ENDING January 21, 19--

	TIME CARD NO.	NAME OF EMPLOYEE	GROSS PAY	DEDUCTIONS — FICA TAX	DEDUCTIONS — FED. WITH.	DEDUCTIONS — TOTAL DED.	NET PAY	
1	1	Rhonda Lorey	410 00	32 80	36 00	68 80	341 20	1
2	2	Roger Monet	394 80	31 58	38 00	69 58	325 22	2
3	3	Edith Nunnes	485 00	38 80	73 00	111 80	373 20	3
4	4	Wallies O'Hare	540 00	43 20	90 00	133 20	406 80	4
5		Totals	1829 80	146 38	237 00	383 38	1446 42	5

PAYROLL REGISTER — WEEK ENDING January 28, 19--

	TIME CARD NO.	NAME OF EMPLOYEE	GROSS PAY	DEDUCTIONS — FICA TAX	DEDUCTIONS — FED. WITH.	DEDUCTIONS — TOTAL DED.	NET PAY	
1	1	Rhonda Lorey	410 00	32 80	36 00	68 80	341 20	1
2	2	Roger Monet	468 83	37 51	49 00	86 51	382 32	2
3	3	Edith Nunnes	485 00	38 80	73 00	111 80	373 20	3
4	4	Wallies O'Hare	540 00	43 20	90 00	133 20	406 80	4
5		Totals	1903 83	152 31	248 00	400 31	1503 52	5

PROBLEM 83-2 ▶ You continue to work as the payroll clerk for Ferral Graphics Company.

Directions

CHECKPOINT ✔

83-2 (b)
Roger Monet's total FICA
tax = $271.61

a. Record the data from the pages of the payroll register shown on page 715 into the same employee earnings records you used in Application Problem 83-1.

b. Foot each column on the employee earnings records to show the totals for the quarter thus far.

Problem 83-3 may be found in the Working Papers.

PAYROLL REGISTER — WEEK ENDING February 4, 19--

	TIME CARD NO.	NAME OF EMPLOYEE	GROSS PAY	DEDUCTIONS FICA TAX	DEDUCTIONS FED. WITH.	DEDUCTIONS TOTAL DED.	NET PAY	
1	1	Rhonda Lorey	471 50	37 72	45 00	82 72	388 78	1
2	2	Roger Monet	394 80	31 58	38 00	69 58	325 22	2
3	3	Edith Nunnes	485 00	38 80	73 00	111 80	373 20	3
4	4	Wallies O'Hare	540 00	43 20	90 00	133 20	406 80	4
5		Totals	1891 30	151 30	246 00	397 30	1494 00	5

PAYROLL REGISTER — WEEK ENDING February 11, 19--

	TIME CARD NO.	NAME OF EMPLOYEE	GROSS PAY	DEDUCTIONS FICA TAX	DEDUCTIONS FED. WITH.	DEDUCTIONS TOTAL DED.	NET PAY	
1	1	Rhonda Lorey	486 88	38 95	46 00	84 95	401 93	1
2	2	Roger Monet	483 63	38 69	52 00	90 69	392 94	2
3	3	Edith Nunnes	485 00	38 80	73 00	111 80	373 20	3
4	4	Wallies O'Hare	540 00	43 20	90 00	133 20	406 80	4
5		Totals	1995 51	159 64	261 00	420 64	1574 87	5

PAYROLL REGISTER — WEEK ENDING February 18, 19--

	TIME CARD NO.	NAME OF EMPLOYEE	GROSS PAY	DEDUCTIONS FICA TAX	DEDUCTIONS FED. WITH.	DEDUCTIONS TOTAL DED.	NET PAY	
1	1	Rhonda Lorey	410 00	32 80	36 00	68 80	341 20	1
2	2	Roger Monet	394 80	31 58	38 00	69 58	325 22	2
3	3	Edith Nunnes	485 00	38 80	73 00	111 80	373 20	3
4	4	Wallies O'Hare	540 00	43 20	90 00	133 20	406 80	4
5		Totals	1829 80	146 38	237 00	383 38	1446 42	5

PAYROLL REGISTER — WEEK ENDING February 25, 19--

	TIME CARD NO.	NAME OF EMPLOYEE	GROSS PAY	DEDUCTIONS FICA TAX	DEDUCTIONS FED. WITH.	DEDUCTIONS TOTAL DED.	NET PAY	
1	1	Rhonda Lorey	456 13	36 49	42 00	78 49	377 64	1
2	2	Roger Monet	424 41	33 95	43 00	76 95	347 46	2
3	3	Edith Nunnes	485 00	38 80	73 00	111 80	373 20	3
4	4	Wallies O'Hare	540 00	43 20	90 00	133 20	406 80	4
5		Totals	1905 54	152 44	248 00	400 44	1505 10	5

BUSINESS TERMS PREVIEW

• Wage and Tax Statement • W-2 form •

GOALS

1. To learn why the Wage and Tax Statement (W-2 form) is prepared.
2. To learn how a W-2 form is prepared.

UNDERSTANDING THE JOB

KEY Terms

Wage and Tax Statement. W-2 form.

W-2 form. A record of total wages and deductions for a year.

You have learned that the employee earnings records are used to provide employees and government agencies with information when needed. In this job, you will learn to use the records to give the government and employees a record of total wages and deductions for the year. This record is called a **Wage and Tax Statement** or **W-2** form. An example of this form is shown in Illustration 84B on page 718.

The W-2 form must be filed by the employer within one month after the close of each year (that is, by January 31 of the following year). The data for this form can be taken from the employee earnings record. The data needed are in the Summary section of the employee earnings record. Look at Illustration 84A. Notice that the total wages, total social security tax, and total federal withholding tax for the year can be found easily.

The payroll clerk prepares four copies of the W-2 form for each employee. One copy is sent to the Social Security Administration. The Social Security Administration records the employee's FICA data and sends the FICA and income tax data to the Internal Revenue Service. One copy is kept by the employer for the files. Two copies are given to each employee. The employee attaches one of the copies to the federal income tax return and keeps the other copy.

If the employee works in a city or state which has an income tax, the payroll clerk prepares six copies of the form. The additional copies are for the state and city and for the employee to attach to the state or local income tax return. Items 24 through 29 of the W-2 form are filled out for state and local governments.

As an employee, you should always compare all the data on the W-2 forms with your records of weekly earnings and deductions. If they do not agree, the payroll clerk should be notified so that corrections can be made immediately.

SAMPLE PROBLEM

Roland Moore owns a computer consulting firm at 2313 School Street, St. Joseph, MO 64503-2313, and employs two workers. His employer federal identification number is 67-8162735. His employer state identification number is 1766-8653.

Illustration 84A shows the Summary section of the employee earnings record of one of the firm's employees, Lisa M. Goldmeir, who lives at 4810 Glenside Drive, St. Joseph, MO 64505-4810. Lisa is married and earns $414.40 for a 40-hour week. Her social security number is 389-62-1070.

Illustration 84A
Summary section of employee earnings record

Totals														
SUMMARY														
Quarters	Gross Pay					FICA Tax					Fed. With. Tax			
First		5	3	8	7	20		4	3	0	95		6	1	1	00
Second		5	3	8	7	20		4	3	0	95		6	1	1	00
Third		5	4	3	3	52		4	3	4	66		6	1	9	00
Fourth		5	3	8	7	20		4	3	0	95		6	1	1	00
Yearly Total	21	5	9	5	12	1	7	2	7	51	2	4	5	2	00

Illustration 84B (page 718) shows the W-2 form that the payroll clerk prepared at the end of the year. Notice that boxes 24 through 29 have been left blank since Missouri has no state income tax and St. Joseph has no local income tax. Other boxes that did not apply to Lisa were also left blank.

Here are the steps that the payroll clerk followed to complete the form:

STEP 1 ▶ *Record the employer's name, address, and federal and state identification numbers.*

The employer's name, address, and identification numbers were entered in Boxes 2, 3, and 4, as shown in Illustration 84B.

1 Control number	22222	For Official Use Only ▶ OMB No. 1545-0008						

2 Employer's name, address, and ZIP code	**6** Statutory employee ☐ Deceased ☐ Pension plan ☐ Legal rep. ☐ 942 emp. ☐ Subtotal ☐ Deferred compensation ☐ Void ☐
Computer Helper, Inc. 2313 School Street St. Joseph, MO 64503-2313	**7** Allocated tips · · · · · · · · · · · **8** Advance EIC payment
	9 Federal income tax withheld 2,452.00 · · · · **10** Wages, tips, other compensation 21,595.12

3 Employer's identification number 67-8162735	4 Employer's state I.D. number 1766-8653	11 Social security tax withheld 1,727.51	12 Social security wages 21,595.12
5 Employee's social security number 389-62-1070		13 Social security tips	14 Medicare wages and tips
19a Employee's name (first, middle initial, last) Lisa M. Goldmeir		15 Medicare tax withheld	16 Nonqualified plans
4810 Glenside Drive St. Joseph, MO 64505-4810		17 See Instrs. for Form W-2	18 Other
19b Employee's address and ZIP code			

20	21	22 Dependent care benefits	23 Benefits included in Box 10
24 State income tax	25 State wages, tips, etc. · 26 Name of state	27 Local income tax · 28 Local wages, tips, etc. · 29 Name of locality

Copy A For Social Security Administration   Department of the Treasury—Internal Revenue Service

Form **W-2 Wage and Tax Statement**

Illustration 84B   Completed W-2 form

STEP 2 ▶ *Record the employee's social security number, name, and address.*

These data were copied from Lisa's employee earnings record and entered in Boxes 5 and 19 of the W-2 form.

STEP 3 ▶ *Record the total wages, social security tax, and federal withholding tax.*

These data were copied from the Summary section of the employee earnings record (Illustration 84A on page 717), which shows the total wages, social security tax, and federal withholding tax for the year. The information was entered in Boxes 9, 10, 11, and 12 as shown in Illustration 84B.

Using the Computer

In a computerized payroll system, W-2 forms are prepared automatically when the payroll clerk orders the computer to do so. In one computerized system, the payroll clerk does this by selecting W-2 statements from the payroll reports menu like the one shown in Illustration 84C. The payroll clerk must first load the computer printer with blank W-2 forms.

Other Payroll Forms

At the end of each quarter, employers are required to file a Form 941, or the Employer's Quarterly Federal Tax Return. This form is shown in Illustration 84E on page 720. The form shows the total wages earned by all employees, total federal income taxes withheld, and total FICA taxes collected from both the employee and the employer.

Illustration 84C Payroll menu

The amounts deducted for federal income taxes and for FICA taxes must then be paid to the federal government. This is done by depositing the funds at a bank using Form 8109, the Federal Tax Deposit Coupon. This form is shown in Illustration 84D.

Illustration 84D Federal Tax Deposit Coupon

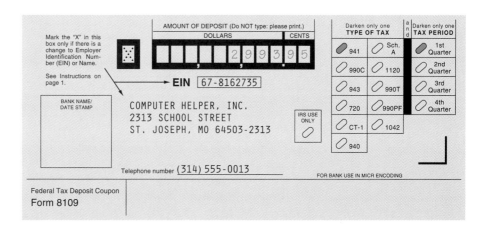

Form **941**

Department of the Treasury
Internal Revenue Service

41141

Employer's Quarterly Federal Tax Return

► See Circular E for more information concerning employment tax returns.

Please type or print.

Your name, address, employer identification number, and calendar quarter of return. (If not correct, please change.)

If address is different from prior return, check here ►

Name (as distinguished from trade name)	Date quarter ended	OMB No. 1545-0029
Computer Helper, Inc.	March 31, 19--	T
Trade name, if any	Employer identification number	FF
	67-8162735	FD
Address (number and street)	City, state, and ZIP code	FP
2313 School Street, St. Joseph, MO 64503-2313		I
		T

```
1 1 1 1 1 1 1 1 1 1 1   2   3 3 3 3 3 3   4 4 4
[boxes]
5 5 5    6    7    8 8 8 8 8   9 9 9   10 10 10 10 10 10 10 10 10 10
```

IRS Use

If you do not have to file returns in the future, check here . ► ☐   Date final wages paid . . ► March 31, 19--

If you are a seasonal employer, see **Seasonal employers** on page 2 and check here . . ► ☐

1	Number of employees (except household) employed in the pay period that includes March 12th ►	**1**	
2	Total wages and tips subject to withholding, plus other compensation . . . . . . ►	**2**	$10,912 20
3	Total income tax withheld from wages, tips, pensions, annuities, sick pay, gambling, etc. . ►	**3**	1,248 00
4	Adjustment of withheld income tax for preceding quarters of calendar year (see instructions) . ►	**4**	0 00
5	Adjusted total of income tax withheld (line 3 as adjusted by line 4—see instructions) . . .	**5**	1,248 00
6a	Taxable social security wages **(Complete line 7)** $ 10,912 20 x 13.0% (.13) =	**6a**	1,418 59
b	Taxable social security tips $ 0 00 x 13.0% (.13) =	**6b**	0 00
7	Taxable Medicare wages and tips . . . . $ 10,912 20 x 3.0% (.03) =	**7**	327 37
8	Total social security and Medicare taxes (add lines 6a, 6b, and 7)	**8**	1,745 96
9	Adjustment of social security and Medicare taxes (see instructions for required explanation) .	**9**	0 00
10	Adjusted total of social security and Medicare taxes (line 8 as adjusted by line 9—see instructions) . ►	**10**	1,745 96
11	Backup withholding (see instructions)	**11**	0 00
12	Adjustment of backup withholding tax for preceding quarters of calendar year	**12**	0 00
13	Adjusted total of backup withholding (line 11 as adjusted by line 12)	**13**	0 00
14	**Total taxes** (add lines 5, 10, and 13)	**14**	2,993 96
15	Advance earned income credit (EIC) payments made to employees, if any . . . . . ►	**15**	0 00
16	Net taxes (subtract line 15 from line 14). **This should equal line IV below** (plus line IV of Schedule A (Form 941) if you have treated backup withholding as a separate liability) . . .	**16**	2,993 96
17	**Total deposits for quarter,** including overpayment applied from a prior quarter, from your records ►	**17**	2,993 96
18	**Balance due** (subtract line 17 from line 16). This should be less than $500. Pay to Internal Revenue Service . . ►	**18**	0 00

19 Overpayment, if line 17 is more than line 16, enter excess here ► $ _____ and check if to be:

☐ Applied to next return **OR** ☐ Refunded.

Record of Federal Tax Liability (You must complete if line 16 is $500 or more and Schedule B is not attached.) See instructions before checking these boxes.

If you made deposits using the 95% rule, check here ► ☐   If you are a first time 3-banking-day depositor, check here . . ► ☐

DO NOT Show Federal Tax Deposits Here

Date wages paid	Show tax liability here, **not deposits.** The IRS gets deposit data from FTD coupons.						
	First month of quarter		Second month of quarter		Third month of quarter		
1st through 3rd	A		I		Q		
4th through 7th	B		J		R		
8th through 11th	C		K		S		
12th through 15th	D		L		T		
16th through 19th	E		M		U		
20th through 22nd	F		N		V		
23rd through 25th	G		O		W		
26th through the last	H		P		X		
Total liability for month	I	921.20	II	921.20	III	1,151.56	
IV Total for quarter (add lines **I, II,** and **III**). **This should equal line 16 above** . . . . . . ►						2,993.96	

Sign Here

Under penalties of perjury, I declare that I have examined this return, including accompanying schedules and statements, and to the best of my knowledge and belief, it is true, correct, and complete.

Signature ► *Roland Moore*   Print Your Name and Title ► Roland Moore President   Date ► 4/28/--

Illustration 84E   Employer's Quarterly Federal Tax Return

On a sheet of paper, write the headings **Statement Number** and **Words**. Next, choose the words that match the statements. Write each word you choose next to the statement number it matches. Be careful; not all the words listed should be used.

Statements	Words
1. An income tax deducted from a worker's wages each payday	biweekly
2. A form which shows how many withholding allowances a worker claims	FWT
3. Twice a month	menu
4. 1/4 year or 13 weeks	net pay
5. A statement showing the total wages and deductions for an employee for a year	quarter
6. FICA tax	semimonthly
7. A list of computer programs	social security tax
8. Gross pay less deductions	W-2 form (Wage and Tax Statement)
	W-4 form
	withholding tax

PROBLEM SOLVING MODEL FOR: *Preparing the Wage and Tax Statement (W-2 Form)*

STEP 1 ▶ *Record the employer's name, address, and federal and state identification numbers.*

STEP 2 ▶ *Record the employee's social security number, name, and address.*

STEP 3 ▶ *Record the total wages, social security tax, and federal withholding tax.*

APPLICATION PROBLEMS

PROBLEM 84-1 ▶ You are the payroll clerk for Rivas Excavating Company located at 1421 Coval Street, Florissant, MO 63031-1421. The employer's federal identification number is 82-2970816. The employer's state identification number is 6291-4357. Florissant does not have a state or local income tax.

The names, addresses, social security numbers, and Summary sections for three employees follow:

Employee #1   Evelyn A. Wooks
212 Foller Street
Florissant, MO 63031-0212
Social security #378-98-7561

Totals														

SUMMARY												
Quarters	**Gross Pay**					**FICA Tax**				**Fed. With. Tax**		
First	5	8	4	4	80	4	6	7	61	6	7	6	00
Second	5	8	4	4	80	4	6	7	61	6	7	6	00
Third	5	8	4	4	80	4	6	7	61	6	7	6	00
Fourth	5	8	4	4	80	4	6	7	61	6	7	6	00
Yearly Total													

Employee #2 Reed E. Sanford
2179 Montley Avenue
Florissant, MO 63031-2179
Social security #410-54-8273

Totals														

SUMMARY												
Quarters	**Gross Pay**					**FICA Tax**				**Fed. With. Tax**		
First	4	5	2	4	00	3	6	1	92	4	8	1	00
Second	4	5	2	4	00	3	6	1	92	4	8	1	00
Third	4	7	8	4	52	3	8	2	72	5	2	0	00
Fourth	4	7	8	4	52	3	8	2	72	5	2	0	00
Yearly Total													

Employee #3 Dana V. Rodriguez
897 Ranson Drive
Florissant, MO 63031-0897
Social security #397-61-1452

Totals														

SUMMARY												
Quarters	**Gross Pay**					**FICA Tax**				**Fed. With. Tax**		
First	5	0	7	0	00	4	0	5	60	5	7	2	00
Second	5	0	7	0	00	4	0	5	60	5	7	2	00
Third	5	0	7	0	00	4	0	5	60	5	7	2	00
Fourth	5	2	0	0	00	4	1	6	00	5	9	8	00
Yearly Total													

CHECKPOINT

84-1 (a)
Employee #1 gross pay =
$23,379.20

Directions

a. Copy and complete each Summary section by totaling the columns.
b. Prepare W-2 forms for each employee. Use Illustration 84B (page 718) as an example.

PROBLEM **84-2** ▶ You are the payroll clerk for the A & D Auto Company located at 3197 Castleton Avenue, St. Charles, MO 63303-3197. The employer's federal identification number is 28-8675933. The employer's state identification number is 6735-9173. St. Charles does not have a state or local income tax.

The names, addresses, social security numbers, and Summary sections for three employees follow:

Employee #1   Evan R. Wakely
               2863 Razul Drive
               St. Charles, MO 63303-2863
               Social security #289-65-2867

Totals																	

SUMMARY																	
Quarters		Gross Pay						FICA Tax						Fed. With. Tax			
First		4	0	5	6	00		3	2	4	48			4	1	6	00
Second		4	2	1	8	20		3	3	7	42			4	3	9	00
Third		4	2	1	8	20		3	3	7	42			4	3	9	00
Fourth		4	2	6	4	00		3	4	1	12			4	4	2	00
Yearly Total																	

Employee #2   Doreen R. Brown
               776 Spagrow Street
               St. Charles, MO 63303-0776
               Social security #533-42-5241

Totals																	

SUMMARY																	
Quarters		Gross Pay						FICA Tax						Fed. With. Tax			
First		5	9	8	0	00		4	7	8	40			7	1	5	00
Second		5	9	8	0	00		4	7	8	40			7	1	5	00
Third		5	9	8	0	00		4	7	8	40			7	1	5	00
Fourth		5	9	8	0	00		4	7	8	40			7	1	5	00
Yearly Total																	

Employee #3   Vince L. Gibrelli
               365 North Bunson Avenue
               St. Charles, MO 63303-0365
               Social security #329-55-9787

Totals																	

SUMMARY																	
Quarters		Gross Pay						FICA Tax						Fed. With. Tax			
First		5	5	9	0	00		4	4	7	20			6	5	0	00
Second		5	5	9	0	00		4	4	7	20			6	5	0	00
Third		5	5	9	0	00		4	4	7	20			6	5	0	00
Fourth		5	5	9	0	00		4	4	7	20			6	5	0	00
Yearly Total																	

CHECKPOINT

84-2 (a)
Employee #2 FICA tax =
$1,913.60

Directions

a. Copy and complete each Summary section by totaling the columns.

b. Prepare W-2 forms for each employee. Use Illustration 84B (page 718) as an example.

JOB 85 ▶ HANDLING OTHER DEDUCTIONS

APPLIED MATH PREVIEW

Copy and complete these problems.

1. $ 8,907.52
   15,816.91
   20,549.08
   17,050.69
   39,468.20
   1,395.87
   24,634.76
   +   83.45

2. Crossfoot and then add down:

   29 + 49 + 60 + 89 =

   68 + 98 + 18 + 30 =

   70 + 106 + 504 + 16 =

   302 + 603 + 720 + 437 =

   130 + 870 + 365 + 908 =

BUSINESS TERM PREVIEW

• Pegboard •

GOALS

1. To learn about wage deductions other than social security and federal withholding taxes.
2. To learn how to record these deductions in a payroll register.

UNDERSTANDING THE JOB

You have learned that deductions are made from a worker's wages for federal withholding tax and social security tax. You may have wondered why the column in the payroll register is headed "Fed. With." for federal withholding tax instead of just "Withholding Tax." The reason is that some states and cities also require employers to withhold money for state and city income taxes.

To separate the federal from other withholding taxes, one column is headed "Fed. With." for federal withholding tax and the others are headed "State Withholding Tax" and "City Withholding Tax." Separate withholding tax tables are published by the state and city income tax departments for use by the payroll clerk in computing the amounts to be deducted. You use these withholding tax tables the same way you use federal withholding tax tables.

Some employers make other deductions from wages with the approval of the worker. Examples of other deductions include union dues, United States savings bonds, health insurance, life insurance, or private pension plans. The deductions may be made each payday or on certain paydays. The payroll clerk must be careful to make these deductions according to the plan agreed on by the worker and the organization to which the money is to be sent.

Most payroll registers have columns for social security and federal withholding tax deductions. They also usually have two or three columns with no headings. The payroll clerk fills in the headings needed for other deductions.

To learn how to use these other columns, you will complete problems that include monthly deductions for union dues and health insurance.

SAMPLE PROBLEM

Jane Chen is the payroll clerk for the Lippold Company. The company is located in a state with no state income tax. The following shows the payroll data for Vince DiMato, an employee at the company, for the week ending August 26, 19--:

Regular pay	$346.00	
Overtime pay	38.93	
Gross pay		$384.93
Less:		
Social security tax	$ 30.79	
Federal withholding tax	43.00	
Union dues	17.00	
Health insurance	41.17	
Total deductions		131.96
Net pay		$252.97

Illustration 85A   Payroll register (left page)

PAYROLL REGISTER

TIME CARD NO.	NAME OF EMPLOYEE	NO. OF ALLOW.	TOTAL HOURS WORKED	REGULAR PAY			OVERTIME PAY			
				HRS.	RATE	AMOUNT	HRS.	RATE	AMOUNT	
1	Vince DiMato	2	43	40	8 65	3 4 6 00	3	12 975	3 8 93	1

STEP 1 ▶ *Record the payroll data in the payroll register.*

Illustrations 85A (page 725) and 85B show how Chen entered these data in the payroll register.

STEP 2 ▶ *Foot, verify, and rule the payroll register.*

Chen would enter the data for other employees in the same way. After all the data have been entered, she would foot, verify, and rule the money columns just as you have learned to do before. When all data have been recorded in the payroll register, Chen will post some of the data to the employee earnings records.

Using Pegboards to Prepare the Payroll

To speed up the process of preparing the payroll manually, some small businesses use **pegboards**, like the one shown in Illustration 85C on page 727. These are specially designed writing boards which will allow you to, all at once

1. Record data in a payroll book.
2. Record data on the employee earnings record.
3. Write a paycheck for the employee.

Pegboards allow you to line up the columns on the three forms so that the data are entered in the correct place on all three forms at once. Carbon paper is used between the forms so that the data are written only once. They are called pegboards because pegs are located along the sides of the board. These pegs allow you to line up the forms correctly.

Since the information is written only once and not recopied, errors that may be made in recopying are eliminated.

Using Computers to Prepare the Payroll

Today, many businesses, even small businesses, use computers to keep and prepare payroll records. If a computerized payroll system is used, the paycheck, employee earnings record, and payroll register will be prepared automatically by the computer.

Illustration 85B   Payroll register (right page)

PAYROLL REGISTER								WEEK ENDING *August 26, 19--*
				DEDUCTIONS				
GROSS PAY		FICA TAX	FED. WITH.	UNION DUES	INSURANCE	TOTAL DED.		NET PAY
1	3 8 4 93	3 0 79	4 3 00	1 7 00	4 1 17	1 3 1 96		2 5 2 97	1

Illustration 85C   A pegboard

BUILDING YOUR BUSINESS VOCABULARY

On a sheet of paper, write the headings **Statement Number** and **Words**. Next, choose the words that match the statements. Write each word you choose next to the statement number it matches. Be careful; not all the words listed should be used.

Statements	Words
1. Amounts subtracted from wages	biweekly
2. Gross pay less deductions	deductions
3. Every two weeks	manually
4. Every three months	net pay
5. A deduction a worker may claim for the support of another person	pegboard
	quarterly
6. A form which shows how many withholding allowances a worker claims	gross pay
	W-2 form
7. The Wage and Tax Statement prepared from the employee earnings record at the end of the year	W-4 form
	withholding allowance
	withholding tax
8. By hand	
9. A special writing board which allows you to prepare the payroll check, employee earnings record, and payroll register in one writing	

PROBLEM SOLVING MODEL FOR: *Handling Other Deductions*

STEP 1 ▶ *Record the payroll data in the payroll register.*

STEP 2 ▶ *Foot, verify, and rule the payroll register.*

APPLICATION PROBLEMS

PROBLEM | **85-1** ▶ You are the payroll clerk for Palermo Ceramics, Inc.

Directions

a. Copy this table:

Time Card No.	No. of Allow- ances	Gross Pay		FICA Tax		Federal With. Tax		Union Dues		Health Insurance		Total Deductions		Net Pay	
							Deductions								
1	2	405	89												
2	1	387	80												
3	0	270	00												
4	4	453	78												
5	2	609	00												
	Totals														

CHECKPOINT ✔

85-1 (c)
Total net pay = $1,395.46

b. Complete the payroll. Use a FICA tax rate of 8% and the federal withholding tax table in Job 81 (pages 697–698). Deduct $19.23 for union dues and $48.75 for health insurance from each worker's pay.

c. Check your totals.

PROBLEM | **85-2** ▶ You work as a payroll clerk for Tomahawk Craft Company.

Directions

a. Copy this table:

Time Card No.	No. of Allow- ances	Gross Pay		FICA Tax		Federal With. Tax		Union Dues		Health Insurance		Total Deductions		Net Pay	
							Deductions								
1	0	329	80												
2	1	402	30												
3	3	573	86												
4	2	500	70												
5	4	590	95												
	Totals														

CHECKPOINT ✔

85-2 (c)
Total net pay = $1,612.10

b. Complete the payroll. Use a FICA tax rate of 8% and the federal withholding tax table in Job 81 (pages 697–698). Deduct $27.25 for union dues and $39.89 for health insurance from each worker's pay.

c. Check your totals.

PROBLEM | 85-3 ▶ You are the payroll clerk for Legion Microtechnology Company.

Directions

a. Copy this table:

Time Card No.	No. of Allow-ances	Gross Pay		Deductions						Net Pay	
				FICA Tax	Federal With. Tax	Union Dues	Health Insurance	Total Deductions			
1	4	1085	00								
2	5	1118	90								
3	3	956	78								
4	3	795	60								
5	4	1168	08								
	Totals										

CHECKPOINT ✔

85-3 (c)
Total net pay = $3,643.30

b. Complete the payroll. Use a FICA tax rate of 8% and the federal withholding tax table found in Job 81 (pages 697–698). Deduct $31.50 for union dues from each worker's pay and $52.87 for health insurance from the following workers' pay: 1, 2, and 5. Since 3 and 4 did not join the health insurance plan, do not make any deductions for health insurance from their pay.

c. Check your totals.

Problem 85-4 may be found in the Working Papers.

CHAPTER 16

Reinforcement
Activities

DISCUSSION

The following errors were made in an employee earnings record. Describe one possible problem that could be caused by each error.

1. The social security number was incorrect.
2. The date hired was wrong by one week.
3. The hourly pay rate was wrong by ten cents.

PROFESSIONAL BUSINESS ETHICS

You are a personnel clerk and have discovered that one employee, Aaron Rogers, Employee No. 127, has been receiving $8.61 an hour instead of $6.81 an hour because of an error in his payroll records. The first paycheck with the error was issued on April 1. The last paycheck with the error was issued April 14. Rogers worked 40 hours each of those weeks.

One of your co-workers suggests correcting Aaron Rogers' future paychecks, but saying nothing about the incorrect paychecks. Your co-worker feels that the amount of dollars incorrectly paid is too small to bother with.

Write a memo to your co-worker about your reaction to the suggestion. Use no more than a half sheet of paper for your memo.

APPLIED COMMUNICATIONS

You are a payroll clerk for the Agar Company. The company is growing rapidly. At a payroll department meeting, Ivy Johnson, the department head, announced that she is considering recommending that the payroll operation be computerized to save time and money. After the announcement, the recommendation was heatedly discussed. Some people felt that the computer would eliminate their jobs. Others felt that the computer was needed because of the increase in work that the department was doing.

1. What advantages do you think that the computer might bring to the payroll operation? (List three advantages.)
2. What disadvantages do you think there might be if a computer is used for payroll? (List two disadvantages.)
3. What might you recommend that the company do for its employees to make the changes brought about by the computer as easy to cope with as possible? (List two recommendations.)

Write a memo that summarizes advantages, disadvantages, and recommendations. Use no more than one sheet of paper for your memo.

RECORD KEEPING CAREERS

Many record keepers must continue their education while they are working. This advanced education is often called *adult education*, because it is for adults. It is also called *continuing education*, because it is education that continues after a person's formal education is completed and often while a person is actually working at a job.

There are many reasons why continuing education is important to record keepers. If a company acquires new technology, the workers may need to retrain. If a company adds new products or services, workers may need to retrain. If workers want promotions to more advanced positions, they may need to retrain.

Most communities provide numerous opportunities for continuing education. These may include evening and weekend classes offered by

1. Your high school.
2. A nearby community college.
3. Nearby business colleges.
4. Professional training organizations.

On a sheet of paper:

a. List the names of two organizations in your area that offer adult or continuing education classes for adults.
b. List the names of those classes, offered by the two organizations, that might provide training in record keeping skills or topics.

REVIEWING WHAT YOU HAVE LEARNED

On a sheet of paper, write the headings **Statement Number** and **Words**. Next, choose the words that match the statements. Write each word you choose next to the statement number it completes. Be careful; not all the words listed should be used.

Statements	Words
1. A record in which the total pay, deductions, and net pay for all workers in a business is recorded is called (a, an) _____ .	employee
2. The Wage and Tax Statement is called (a, an) _____ .	employer
3. The amount paid in social security taxes by an employee must be matched by the _____ .	FICA taxes
4. The form an employee uses to tell an employer how many withholding allowances the employee has is called (a, an) _____ .	four
	FWT
	payroll register
	take-home pay
	three
	two
5. A married employee with two dependent children may claim up to _____ withholding allowances.	W-2 form
6. Net pay may also be called _____ .	W-4 form
7. One reason for keeping an employee earnings record for each worker is to tell when that worker has paid the maximum amount of _____ .	withholding allowance
8. Federal income tax deducted from an employee's pay is called _____ .	withholding tax

MASTERY PROBLEM

You are the payroll clerk for Reliable Technology, Inc. The payroll information for the week ending March 3, 19-- is shown below:

Card No.	Name of Employee	No. Allow.	Hours Worked					Pay Per Hour
			M	T	W	TH	F	
1	Lee Chun	1	8	8	8	9	7	$ 9.80
2	Lea Maloney	2	8	10	8	8	8	8.60
3	Yun Sun	0	8	8	8	7	8	8.40
4	Valerie Telos	2	9 1/2	8	8	8 1/2	8 1/2	9.75
5	Regina Vitale	1	8	7 1/4	7 1/4	8 1/2	7 1/4	10.60

Directions

a. Prepare a payroll register with the same column headings as shown in Illustrations 85A and 85B (pages 725–726).
b. Enter the date for the week ending at the top of the payroll register.
c. For each employee, enter the card number, name of the employee, number of allowances, and pay per hour in the correct columns of the payroll register.

CHECKPOINT ✓

(f)
Total net pay = $1,313.20

d. Find the total hours worked for each employee and enter the amount in the Total Hrs. Worked column.

e. Complete the payroll. Use a FICA tax rate of 8% and the federal withholding tax table found in Job 81 (pages 697–698). Deduct $18.00 for union dues and $31.50 for health insurance from each worker's pay.

f. Foot and rule the register. Check the totals by crossfooting.

REVIEWING YOUR BUSINESS VOCABULARY

This activity may be found in the Working Papers.

COMPREHENSIVE PROJECT 6

Comprehensive Project 6 has been designed to reinforce major concepts of this and previous chapters. The Comprehensive Project is found in the Working Papers.

Paying Your Income Taxes

APPLIED MATH PREVIEW

Copy and complete the problem below. Check your work by crossfooting.

1. $24,526.12 - $5,550.00 =	6. $11,589.26	7. $21,308.64
2. $15,107.74 - $6,130.89 =	4,297.19	2,614.58
3. $ 4,078.87 - $3,892.99 =	356.95	641.79
4. $ 2,184.67 - $1,487.22 =	+ 27.83	+ 89.54

BUSINESS TERMS PREVIEW

* Adjusted gross income * Adjustments to gross income *
* Exemptions * Federal income tax * File *
* Form 1099 * Income tax return *
* Internal Revenue Service (IRS) * Itemized deductions *
* Standard deduction * Taxable income *

GOALS

1. To learn how to calculate gross income, adjusted gross income, and taxable income.
2. To learn when to itemize deductions and when to use the standard deduction.
3. To learn how to find federal income taxes from a table.
4. To learn how to use various records to calculate federal income taxes.

The federal government taxes the incomes of U.S. citizens and others each year. The tax paid on income is called the **federal income tax** and is collected by the **Internal Revenue Service**, or IRS. Many states and some cities also tax incomes.

You have learned that a certain amount of federal income taxes are withheld from your paycheck each pay period. This tax is called the federal withholding tax, or FWT. You have also learned that the amount of FWT withheld from your paycheck for the year is reported on a Form W-2. Copies of Form W-2 are sent to you (the employee) and the IRS soon after the year ends.

The federal withholding tax you pay is an estimate of how much you actually owe in federal income taxes. Neither you nor the IRS will know what your real tax for the year is until the year is over. At that time, the IRS requires you to calculate your actual income taxes. You must **file**, or send in a report showing how you calculated the actual taxes owed on your income for last year. This report must be filed no later than April 15 and is called an **income tax return**, or simply a return. You file your return at the nearest office of the Internal Revenue Service.

If the amount of income taxes withheld from your paycheck is larger than the amount of taxes you actually owe, you will get a refund. If the amount withheld is smaller than what you actually owe, you must pay the balance due.

KEY Terms

Federal income tax. Federal government's tax on income.

Internal Revenue Service (IRS). Collects federal income tax.

File. Send in your return to the IRS.

Income tax return. Shows how income taxes were calculated.

SAMPLE PROBLEM

Jill Regan is a single person who works two jobs. She is a full-time accounting clerk at Branston Department Store during the week. On weekends, she is a salesclerk at Collins Jewelry store.

On February 1, Jill receives two Forms W-2 in the mail: one for her full-time job and the other for her weekend job. Jill knows that she does not have to file her federal income tax return until April 15. However, she would like to complete and file her return as soon as possible because she believes that she may get a refund from the government. Jill's Form W-2 from Branston Department Store is shown in Illustration A1. Her form from Collins Jewelry Store is similar.

Like many other people, Jill uses an income tax work sheet to help her gather income tax data and calculate her federal income taxes (see Illustration A2). She uses a pencil to complete the work sheet so that she can make changes and correct errors.

1 Control number	22222	For Official Use Only ▶ OMB No. 1545-0008							

2 Employer's name, address, and ZIP code	6 Statutory employee	Deceased	Pension plan	Legal rep.	942 emp.	Subtotal	Deferred compensation	Void
Branston Department Store 1515 Newhall Road Springfield, IL 62702-1515	☐	☐	☐	☐	☐	☐	☐	☐

	7 Allocated tips	8 Advance EIC payment

	9 Federal income tax withheld 1,508.00	10 Wages, tips, other compensation 14,620.00

3 Employer's identification number 37-6014162W	4 Employer's state I.D. number 37-6014162W	11 Social security tax withheld 906.36	12 Social security wages 14,620.00

5 Employee's social security number 258-18-1972	13 Social security tips	14 Medicare wages and tips 14,620.00

19a Employee's name (first, middle initial, last) Jill R. Regan	15 Medicare tax withheld 212.16	16 Nonqualified plans
	17 See Instrs. for Form W-2	18 Other
7001 Branch Drive Springfield, IL 62703-7001		

19b Employee's address and ZIP code

20	21	22 Dependent care benefits	23 Benefits included in Box 10

24 State income tax 438.60	25 State wages, tips, etc. 14,620.00	26 Name of state ILLINOIS	27 Local income tax	28 Local wages, tips, etc.	29 Name of locality

Copy A For Social Security Administration   Department of the Treasury—Internal Revenue Service

Form **W-2 Wage and Tax Statement**

Illustration A1   Form W-2 for Full-Time Job

Income:			Income Tax from Tax Table		$2,104.00
Salary, Full-time Job		$14,620.00	Federal Income Taxes Withheld:		
Salary, Weekend Job		3,744.00	Full-time Job	$1,508.00	
Commissions, Weekend Job		1,546.27	Weekend Job	+ 104.00	
Savings Account Interest		+ 105.65	Total Income Taxes Withheld		- 1,612.00
Gross Income		$20,015.92	Balance Due		$ 492.00
Adjustments:					
Less: Retirement Deposits		- 438.60			
Adjusted Gross Income		$19,577.32			
Deductions:					
Less: Standard Deduction		- 3,400.00			
		$16,177.32			
Exemptions:					
Less: 1 @ $2,150.00		- 2,150.00			
Taxable Income		$14,027.32			

Illustration A2   Income Tax Work Sheet

Here is how Jill completes the work sheet and finds the amount of her federal income tax:

STEP 1 ▶ *Find gross income.*

Nearly all types of income are taxable by the federal government. For example, income from salaries and wages, tips, bonuses, interest, prize money, rent receipts, and profits from a business are all taxable. On the other hand, gifts, most kinds of money received from inheritance, and most kinds of money received from life and health insurance are not usually taxable.

Jill has kept careful records of the amounts of money she has received and spent during the last year. One record of income is the Form W-2 that she receives from each employer. Another is her check register. Jill deposits all money received in her checking account and writes a brief explanation of each deposit. So, her check register provides a record of all money she receives during the year (see Illustration A3). You can see that recording all money received in your check register will make finding the amount of your income tax a lot easier.

Illustration A3   Part of Jill's Check Register

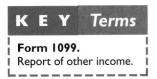

		RECORD ALL CHARGES OR CREDITS THAT AFFECT YOUR ACCOUNT					
NUMBER	DATE	DESCRIPTION OF TRANSACTION	PAYMENT/DEBIT (–)	√ T	FEE (IF ANY) (–)	DEPOSIT/CREDIT (+)	BALANCE $ 246 55
—	19-- 6/3	TO Interest on svgs. acct. FOR	$		$	$ 25 72	+ 25 72
							272 27
542	6/4	TO Red Cross FOR donation	15 00				– 15 00
							257 27

Still another record that Jill uses to find her total income is a **Form 1099**. Jill received a copy of a Form 1099 from her bank (see Illustration A4). The Form 1099 showed the amount of interest that she earned on her savings account for the year. The bank also sent a copy of the Form 1099 to the Internal Revenue Service.

K E Y   Terms

Form 1099.
Report of other income.

9292	☐ VOID	☐ CORRECTED	
PAYER'S name, street address, city, state, and ZIP code	Payer's RTN (optional)	OMB No. 1545-0112	
Market Street Bank 5055 Ballwin Avenue Springfield, IL 62702-5055			**Interest Income**
PAYER'S Federal identification number 37-1978-4455	RECIPIENT'S identification number 258-18-1972	1 Interest income not included in box 3 $ 105.65	**Copy A** For **Internal Revenue Service Center**
RECIPIENT'S name Jill R. Regan		2 Early withdrawal penalty $ 0.00	3 Interest on U.S. Savings Bonds and Treas. obligations $ 0.00
Street address (including apt. no.) 7001 Branch Drive		4 Federal income tax withheld $ 0.00	For Paperwork Reduction Act Notice and instructions for completing this form, **see Instructions for Forms 1099, 1098, 5498, and W-2G.**
City, state, and ZIP code Springfield, IL 62703-7001		5 Foreign tax paid	6 Foreign country or U.S. possession
Account number (optional) 3829783-3	2nd TIN Not. ☐	$ 0.00	

Form **1099-INT**   Department of the Treasury – Internal Revenue Service

Illustration A4   A Form 1099 Showing the Interest Earned

By looking at her check register, Forms W-2, and Forms 1099, Jill finds that her gross income is $20,015.92 (see Illustration A2 on page 736).

Jill records each type of income on her work sheet. She then adds the income amounts and records the total, Gross Income.

Paying Your Income Taxes   737

STEP 2 ▶ *Find adjusted gross income.*

From your gross income, the federal government allows you to subtract certain kinds of expenses. These amounts include losses from a business, payments you make to approved retirement plans, alimony, and penalties for early withdrawal of savings. Amounts that you subtract from gross income are called **adjustments to gross income**.

Jill deposits 3 percent of her full-time salary into an approved individual retirement account at her bank. This amount ($14,620.00 x .03 = $438.60) is an adjustment to her gross income. Jill subtracts the retirement amount from her gross taxable income to find her **adjusted gross income** of $19,577.32 (see Illustration A2 on page 736).

Jill records the retirement deposits under the title *Adjustments* on the work sheet. She subtracts the amount from her gross income.

STEP 3 ▶ *Find taxable income.*

Taxable income is the amount on which you will pay federal income taxes. Taxable income is your adjusted gross income less deductions and exemptions.

Deductions are those expenses that the federal government lets you subtract from your adjusted gross income. What the federal government lets you claim as deductions changes from time to time. Currently, these expenses include interest paid on a home mortgage, property taxes, state and local income taxes, contributions you make to charities, and part of your medical and dental expenses.

To claim the deductions, you must list, or itemize, each deduction on the income tax return. For example, Jill could list the donation that she made to the Red Cross as a deduction (see Illustration A3 on page 737). If you itemize your deductions, you must be careful to keep your canceled checks and receipts so that you can verify these deductions to the IRS, if they ask you to do so.

Jill lists each of her **itemized deductions** by examining her Forms W-2, check register, and the receipts of her expenses she had saved during the year. Her itemized deductions are

Donations	$105.00
State income taxes withheld from full-time job	438.60
State income taxes withheld from part-time job	158.71
Total itemized deductions	$702.31

However, you are alternatively allowed to deduct a fixed amount, called a **standard deduction**, no matter what the dollar amount of your actual deductions is. If the amount of your actual deductions is more than the standard deduction, you can itemize the deductions. If your itemized deductions are less than the standard deduction, you take the standard deduction.

The amounts allowed for the standard deduction and for each exemption are changed often by the federal government. In this text, the amount used for the standard deduction will be $3,400.00 for a single person. Since the standard deduction is more than her itemized deductions, Jill decides to take the standard deduction.

Jill records the standard deduction under the heading *Deductions*. She then subtracts the standard deduction from adjusted gross income.

If Jill had itemized her deductions, she would have listed each one under the heading *Deductions*. She would then have subtracted the total from adjusted gross income.

Exemptions are amounts you may deduct from adjusted gross income based on the number of dependents you list on your form. You may list, or claim, one exemption for yourself, unless another person claims you as an exemption on her or his income tax return. For example, suppose that you are working part-time but are still a dependent of your mother and father. If your parents claim you as an exemption on their income tax return, you may not claim an exemption for yourself on your income tax return.

The amount allowed for an exemption is changed often by the federal government. In this text, the amount used for each exemption will be $2,150.00.

Jill records her exemption under the heading *Exemptions*. She subtracts the amount of the exemption from the amount above it. The result is her taxable income of $14,027.32 (see Illustration A2 on page 736).

K E Y	Terms

Exemptions.
Deductions based on number of dependents claimed.

STEP 4 ▶ *Find the amount of income tax.*

If your taxable income is not over a certain amount, you can use a tax table to figure your income tax. Part of a federal income tax table is shown in Illustration A5.

19-- Tax Table—*Continued*

If Form 1040A, line 22, is—		And you are—			
At least	But less than	Single	Married filing jointly	Married filing separately	Head of a household
			Your tax is—		
14,000					
14,000	14,050	2,104	2,104	2,104	2,104
14,050	14,100	2,111	2,111	2,111	2,111
14,100	14,150	2,119	2,119	2,119	2,119
14,150	14,200	2,126	2,126	2,126	2,126
14,200	14,250	2,134	2,134	2,134	2,134
14,250	14,300	2,141	2,141	2,141	2,141
14,300	14,350	2,149	2,149	2,149	2,149
14,350	14,400	2,156	2,156	2,156	2,156

Illustration A5   Part of a Federal Income Tax Table

To use the table, Jill finds the amount of her taxable income in the table under the headings labeled with the words "At least" and "But less than." Her taxable income is found on the very first line of the table—"At least 14,000", "But less than 14,050." Since Jill is single, she looks across the table to the Single column. The amount there, 2,104 (or $2,104.00), is the federal income tax she owes for the year.

Jill records the taxes owed on the work sheet on a line labeled *Income Tax from Table*.

STEP 5 ▶ *Find the refund or balance due.*

Jill must now find out if the income taxes that were withheld from her wages during the year were less than or more than the amount of tax she actually owes. To do that, she looks at Box 9 of her Forms W-2. When she does, she finds that her total income taxes withheld are $1,612.00 (see Illustration A2 on page 736).

Jill records the withholding amounts for each job under the heading *Federal Income Taxes Withheld* and enters the total withholding amount.

Jill realizes unhappily that the actual amount of taxes owed are more than the estimated amounts withheld from her pay during the year. Jill subtracts the total amount of withholding from the income taxes that she owes. She is going to have to pay the balance due, $492.00 (see Illustration A2 on page 736).

If the income tax amounts withheld from her paychecks had been larger than the amount of taxes she owed, Jill would have received a refund. For example, if the total taxes withheld from Jill's pay had been $2,230.00, Jill would have received a refund of

$2,230.00	Federal income taxes withheld
- 2,104.00	Federal income taxes owed
$ 126.00	Refund

Jill uses the data from the work sheet (and other forms) to complete the federal income tax return form shown in Illustration A6. She mails the return, along with a check for $492.00, to the office of Internal Revenue Service in her area.

𝓑UILDING YOUR BUSINESS VOCABULARY

On a sheet of paper, write the headings **Statement Number** and **Words**. Next, choose the words that match the statement. Write each word you choose next to the statement number it matches. Be careful, not all the words listed will be used.

Form 1040A page 2

Name(s) shown on page 1	Jill R. Regan			Your social security number
				258 18 1972

17 Enter the amount from line 16. **17** 19,577 32

Figure your standard deduction, exemption amount, and taxable income

18a Check if: ☐ You were 65 or older ☐ Blind ☐ Spouse was 65 or older ☐ Blind Enter number of boxes checked ▶ **18a** ☐

b If your parent (or someone else) can claim you as a dependent, check here . . . . ▶ **18b** ☐

c If you are married filing separately and your spouse files Form 1040 and itemizes deductions, see page 35 and check here ▶ **18c** ☐

19 Enter the **standard deduction** shown below for your filing status. **But if you checked any box on line 18a or b**, go to page 35 to find your standard deduction. **If you checked box 18c**, enter -0-.

- Single—$3,400
- Head of household—$5,250
- Married filing jointly or Qualifying widow(er)—$6,000
- Married filing separately—$3,000

19 3,400 00

20 Subtract line 19 from line 17. (If line 19 is more than line 17, enter -0-.) **20** 16,177 32

21 Multiply $2,150 by the total number of exemptions claimed on line 6e. **21** 2,150 00

22 Subtract line 21 from line 20. (If line 21 is more than line 20, enter -0-.) This is your **taxable income**. ▶ **22** 14,027 32

Figure your tax, credits, and payments

If you want the IRS to figure your tax, see the instructions for line 22 on page 36.

23 Find the tax on the amount on line 22. Check if from: ☐ Tax Table (pages 48-53) or ☐ Form 8615 (see page 37). **23** 2,104 00

24a Credit for child and dependent care expenses. Complete and attach Schedule 2. **24a**

b Credit for the elderly or the disabled. Complete and attach Schedule 3. **24b**

c Add lines 24a and 24b. These are your **total credits**. **24c**

25 Subtract line 24c from line 23. (If line 24c is more than line 23, enter -0-.) **25** 2,104 00

26 Advance earned income credit payments from Form W-2. **26**

27 Add lines 25 and 26. This is your **total tax**. ▶ **27** 2,104 00

28a Total Federal income tax withheld. If any tax is from Form(s) 1099, check here . ☐ **28a** 1,612 00

b 19X2 estimated tax payments and amount applied from 19X1 return. **28b**

c **Earned income credit.** Complete and attach Schedule EIC. **28c**

d Add lines 28a, 28b, and 28c. These are your **total payments**. ▶ **28d** 1,612 00

Figure your refund or amount you owe

29 If line 28d is more than line 27, subtract line 27 from line 28d. This is the amount you **overpaid**. **29**

30 Amount of line 29 you want **refunded** to you. **30**

31 Amount of line 29 you want **applied to your 19X3 estimated tax**. **31**

32 If line 27 is more than line 28d, subtract line 28d from line 27. This is the **amount you owe**. Attach check or money order for full amount payable to the "Internal Revenue Service." Write your name, address, social security number, daytime phone number, and "19-- Form 1040A" on it. **32** 492 00

33 Estimated tax penalty (see page 41). **33**

Sign your return

Under penalties of perjury, I declare that I have examined this return and accompanying schedules and statements, and to the best of my knowledge and belief, they are true, correct, and complete. Declaration of preparer (other than the taxpayer) is based on all information of which the preparer has any knowledge.

Your signature ▶ *Jill R. Regan* Date 2/1/-- Your occupation Accounting Clerk

Spouse's signature. If joint return, BOTH must sign. Date Spouse's occupation

Keep a copy of this return for your records.

Paid preparer's use only

Preparer's signature ▶ Date Check if self-employed ☐ Preparer's social security no.

Firm's name (or yours if self-employed) and address E.I. No. ZIP code

Form 1040A page 2

Form 1040A — U.S. Individual Income Tax Return 19--

Department of the Treasury—Internal Revenue Service

IRS Use Only—Do not write or staple in this space.

OMB No. 1545-0085

Label (See page 14.)

Your first name and initial: Jill R. Last name: Regan

If a joint return, spouse's first name and initial Last name

Your social security number: 258 18 1972

Spouse's social security number

Home address (number and street). If you have a P.O. box, see page 15. 7001 Branch Drive Apt. no.

City, town or post office, state, and ZIP code. If you have a foreign address, see page 15. Springfield IL 62703-7001

For Privacy Act and Paperwork Reduction Act Notice, see page 4.

Presidential Election Campaign Fund (See page 15.)

Do you want $1 to go to this fund? ... Yes ☐ No ☒

If a joint return, does your spouse want $1 to go to this fund? ... Yes ☐ No

Note: *Checking "Yes" will not change your tax or reduce your refund.*

Check the box for your filing status
(See page 15.)
Check only one box.

1 ☒ Single
2 ☐ Married filing joint return (even if only one had income).
3 ☐ Married filing separate return. Enter spouse's social security number above and full name here. ▶
4 ☐ Head of household (with qualifying person). (See page 16.) If the qualifying person is a child but not your dependent, enter this child's name here. ▶
5 ☐ Qualifying widow(er) with dependent child (year spouse died ▶ 19___). (See page 17.)

Figure your exemptions
(See page 18.)

If more than seven dependents, see page 21.

6a ☒ **Yourself.** If your parent (or someone else) can claim you as a dependent on his or her tax return, do not check box 6a. But be sure to check the box on line 18b on page 2.

No. of boxes checked on 6a and 6b: 1

b ☐ **Spouse**

c Dependents:

(1) Name (first, initial, and last name)	(2) Check if under age 1	(3) If age 1 or older, dependent's social security number	(4) Dependent's relationship to you	(5) No. of months lived in your home in 19--

No. of your children on 6c who:
- lived with you
- didn't live with you due to divorce or separation (see page 21)

No. of other dependents on 6c

d If your child didn't live with you but is claimed as your dependent under a pre-1985 agreement, check here ▶ ☐

Add numbers entered on lines above: 1

e Total number of exemptions claimed.

Figure your total income

Attach Copy B of your Forms W-2 and 1099-R here.

If you didn't get a W-2, see page 22.

Attach check or money order on top of any Forms W-2 or 1099-R.

7 Wages, salaries, tips, etc. This should be shown in box 10 of your W-2 form(s). Attach Form(s) W-2. **7** 19,910 27

8a Taxable interest income (see page 24). If over $400, also complete and attach Schedule 1, Part I. **8a** 105 65

b Tax-exempt interest. DO NOT include on line 8a. **8b**

9 Dividends. If over $400, also complete and attach Schedule 1, Part II. **9**

10a Total IRA distributions. **10a** **10b** Taxable amount (see page 25). **10b**

11a Total pensions and annuities. **11a** **11b** Taxable amount (see page 25). **11b**

12 Unemployment compensation (see page 29). **12**

13a Social security benefits. **13a** **13b** Taxable amount (see page 29). **13b**

14 Add lines 7 through 13b (far right column). This is your **total income**. ▶ **14** 20,015 92

Figure your adjusted gross income

15a Your IRA deduction from applicable worksheet. **Note:** *Rules for IRAs begin on page 31.* **15a** 438 60

b Spouse's IRA deduction from applicable worksheet. **15b**

c Add lines 15a and 15b. These are your **total adjustments**. **15c** 438 60

16 Subtract line 15c from line 14. **This is your adjusted gross income.** If less than $22,370, see "Earned income credit" on page 39. ▶ **16** 19,577 32

Form 1040A page 1

Statements	Words
1. An alternative fixed amount that you can deduct from your adjusted gross income no matter what the dollar amount of your actual deductions is.	adjusted gross income
	adjustments to gross income
2. The amount left after subtracting adjustments from gross income.	deductions
	exemptions
3. The tax paid on income; it is collected by the Internal Revenue Service.	federal income tax
	file
4. When used in connection with income tax return, it means to send or mail.	Form 1099
	gross income
5. Amounts that the IRS lets you subtract from your gross income.	income tax return
	Internal Revenue Service (IRS)
6. Total income before adjustments, deductions, and exemptions are subtracted.	itemized deductions
	refund
7. The agency of the United States Government that collects income taxes.	standard deduction
	taxable income
8. A list of expenses that you are allowed to deduct on your income tax return.	trial balance
	withholding taxes

9. Amounts deducted from adjusted gross income based on the number of dependents claimed.

10. The result when the amount of income taxes withheld during a year is larger than the amount of income taxes actually owed.

11. A report filed with a government agency that shows how income taxes owed were computed.

12. Adjusted gross income less deductions and exemptions; the amount on which you pay federal income taxes.

13. A report of other income, such as interest and dividends, sent to the taxpayer and IRS by the firm paying income.

PROBLEM SOLVING MODEL FOR: *Completing the Income Tax Work Sheet*

STEP 1 ▶ *Find gross income.*

STEP 2 ▶ *Find adjusted gross income.*

STEP 3 ▶ *Find taxable income.*

STEP 4 ▶ *Find the amount of income tax.*

STEP 5 ▶ *Find the refund or balance due.*

*A*PPLICATION PROBLEMS

PROBLEM | **A-1** ▶ Find the taxable income for each person below by completing the table. The first one is done for you to show you how.

Name	Gross Income	Adjustments to Income	Adjusted Gross Income	Total Deductions	Total Exemptions	Taxable Income
Ex. Brown	17,000.00	2,500.00	14,500.00	3,400.00	2,150.00	8,950.00
(a) Carr	16,500.00	1,500.00		3,400.00	2,150.00	
(b) Durr	21,750.00	425.00		4,145.00	4,300.00	
(c) Eads	23,826.00	975.00		4,683.00	4,300.00	
(d) Finn	20,741.00	0.00		3,400.00	2,150.00	
(e) Gore	22,369.26	387.24		3,400.00	2,150.00	

PROBLEM | **A-2** ▶ Terry Bock uses a tax work sheet to find the federal income tax he owes. Complete a work sheet for Terry by following the steps below. Use Illustration A2 (page 736) as a guide.

a. Find Terry's gross income. Terry's Forms W-2 show that he earned $16,752.00 from a full-time job and $3,245.00 from a part-time job. Terry's Form 1099 shows that he also earned $235.00 in interest on a savings account.

b. Find Terry's adjusted gross income. Terry's check register shows that he deposited $425.00 in an approved individual retirement account at his bank.

c. Find Terry's deductions and exemptions. Terry's check register shows that he can itemize these deductions: donations, $245.00; state income taxes paid on full-time job, $670.08; state income taxes paid on part-time job, $129.80. Instead of itemizing his deductions, Terry could use the standard deduction of $3,400.00. Terry is single and claims one exemption for himself.

d. Find Terry's taxable income.

e. Use the income tax table in Illustration A5 (page 739) to find the federal income taxes owed.

f. Find the refund or balance due. Terry's Form W-2 shows that he had the following amounts withheld from his paychecks last year: federal income taxes withheld from full-time job, $1,820.00; federal income taxes withheld from part-time job, $104.00.

CHECKPOINT
A-2
Tax due = $217.00

APPENDIX

Applied
Math Skills

GOAL

To review the basic math skills needed to solve the problems in the text.

𝒰NDERSTANDING THE WORK

The basic math skills needed to solve the problems in the text are presented on this and the following pages. You may wish to review these skills before you begin the study of record keeping. You may also wish to review these skills as you find the need for them.

MATH SKILL 1 ▶ *Finding the place value of numbers*

Every number contains digits. For example, the number 5433.198 has seven digits in it. Each of these digits has a place value. That is, the value of a digit depends on the position it occupies in a number.

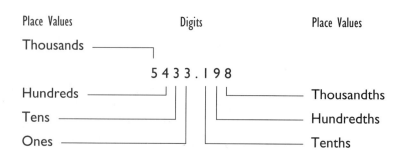

Place Values	Digits	Place Values
Thousands		
	5 4 3 3 . 1 9 8	
Hundreds		Thousandths
Tens		Hundredths
Ones		Tenths

APPLICATION PROBLEMS

Write the place value of each digit underlined below.

1. 194.59<u>7</u>
2. $5<u>8</u>3.12
3. <u>3</u>.419
4. <u>1</u>2.021
5. 0.07<u>8</u>
6. $25.<u>6</u>7

MATH SKILL 2 ▶ *Rounding money amounts*

In business, money amounts are usually rounded to the nearest whole cent, or hundredths of a dollar. Rounding to the nearest cent means that an amount *less* than one-half cent ($0.005) is ignored. An amount of *one-half cent or more* is rounded to a whole penny. For example:

Problem	Explanation
$3.574 is rounded to $3.57	Since the number to the right of the cents position is less than 5, it is ignored.
cents position	
$3.575 is rounded to $3.58	Since the number to the right of the cents position is 5, the value of the cents position is raised from 7 to 8.
cents position	

APPLICATION PROBLEMS

Round these amounts to the nearest cent.

1. $3.685
2. $14.8925
3. $5.093
4. $25.191
5. $4,003.2865
6. $0.049

MATH SKILL 3 ▶ *Adding whole numbers*

When you add, you combine two or more numbers to get one number. The result is called the sum, or total. For example:

```
  1 1  ◄──────── carries
  3,295
+ 4,137
─────────
  7,432  ◄──────── sum or total
```

When the total of a column adds to more than 9, you must carry the tens' digit to the next column to the left. For example, in the problem above, 5 + 7 = 12. The 2 of the 12 is written in the first column. The 10 of the 12 is carried to the next column to the left and added to the 9 and 3 to get 13. Likewise, the 3 of the 13 is written in the second column, and the 10 of the 13 is carried over to the next column to the left and added to the 2 and 1 to get 4.

APPLICATION PROBLEMS

Add these columns.

1.	398	2.	1,058	3.	3,729	4.	10,786	5.	23,498
	+ 167		+ 988		73		308		963
					+ 4,198		2,118		6,071
							+ 63		55
									+ 8,207

MATH SKILL 4 ▶ *Adding decimals*

When adding decimal and money amounts, the important thing to remember is to line up the numbers by the decimal points. Otherwise, the numbers added will not be of the same place value. For example, to add $0.03, $107.35, and $5, write:

$$\begin{array}{r} \$\ \ 0.03 \\ 107.35 \\ +\ \ 5.00 \\ \hline \$112.38 \end{array}$$

Notice that a decimal point and two zeros were added to $5 to make the whole number, 5, line up with the other decimal amounts.

APPLICATION PROBLEMS

Add the numbers below. Line up the numbers by the decimal points first:

1. $68.315 + 54.905 + 4.1 =$
2. $1,089.76 + 0.62 + 42.73 + 732.676 =$
3. $\$31,649.87 + \$31.89 + \$2,018.87 + \$506.73 + \$9.75 + \$0.21 =$
4. $\$201.33 + \$0.45 + \$1,083.95 + \$42,298.51 + \$0.72 =$
5. $\$0.93 + \$659.21 + \$4.51 + \$46,829.31 + \$65.74 =$

MATH SKILL 5 ▶ *Adding numbers with the fractions $^1/_4$, $^1/_2$, and $^3/_4$*

In business, you often have to add numbers that have these fractions: $^1/_4$, $^1/_2$, and $^3/_4$. For example, you may have to add $9 + 7\,^1/_2 + 8\,^1/_4 + 7\,^3/_4$. To do so, it is usually easiest to convert these fractions to decimals first. The decimal equivalents of these fractions are

$$^1/_4 = 0.25 \qquad ^1/_2 = 0.5 \qquad ^3/_4 = 0.75$$

To find the total of $9 + 7\,^1/_2 + 8\,^1/_4 + 7\,^3/_4$, convert the fraction in each number to a decimal and add:

$$\begin{array}{r} 9.00 \\ 7.50 \\ 8.25 \\ 7.75 \\ \hline 32.50 \end{array}$$

Notice that a decimal point and two zeros were added to the 9 to make it line up with the numbers. Notice that a zero was also added to 7.5 to make it line up with the other numbers.

APPLICATION PROBLEMS

Find the total for each problem. Convert any fraction in a number to a decimal first.

1. $7\,^1/_2 + 8\,^1/_2 + 9\,^1/_4 =$
2. $8\,^1/_2 + 7\,^1/_4 + 9\,^1/_2 + 8\,^3/_4 =$
3. $8 + 7\,^1/_2 + 9\,^1/_4 + 8 + 7\,^1/_4 =$
4. $8 + 8 + 7\,^3/_4 + 8\,^3/_4 + 10\,^1/_2 =$

MATH SKILL 6 ▶ *Checking addition*

To check your addition, you should add the numbers again in the opposite direction. For example, suppose that you added 9 + 4 and got 13. To check your work, you would add 4 + 9. Since the answer you got the second time is also 13, you know that you have added correctly.

APPLICATION PROBLEMS

Add to find the totals. Convert any fractions you find to decimals first. Be careful to line up the numbers by the decimal points. Check each problem by adding the numbers in the opposite direction.

1. $40 + 145 + 6 + 1{,}459 =$
2. $40.009 + 6.23 + 0.03 + 780.345 =$
3. $\$17.78 + \$9.87 + \$0.56 + \$301.73 =$
4. $\$1{,}042.08 + \$51.64 + \$0.95 + \$112.23 =$
5. $8\,^1/_2 + 5\,^3/_4 + 7\,^1/_2 + 9\,^1/_4 + 8 =$

MATH SKILL 7 ▶ *Subtracting whole numbers*

Subtraction is the reverse of addition. When you subtract, you find the difference between two amounts. For example:

When the bottom number in one column is too large to subtract from the number above it, you must borrow from the column to the left. For example, in the problem just illustrated, 5 is too large to subtract from 2. So, you borrow 10 from the second column. The 2 then becomes 12 and the 40 in the second column is reduced to 30. Now you can subtract 5 from 12 to get 7. To finish the problem, you subtract the twenty in the second column from the 30 in the same column to get 10.

APPLICATION PROBLEMS

Find the difference in the numbers of each problem by subtracting.

1.	98	2.	139	3.	1,082	4.	3,134	5.	9,215	6.	21,365
	- 14		- 103		- 76		- 1,486		- 4,857		- 19,739

MATH SKILL 8 ▶ *Subtracting decimal numbers*

When you subtract decimal numbers, be careful to line up the numbers by the decimal points first. For example, to subtract $0.03 from $3.50:

$$\begin{array}{r} {\scriptstyle 4\,10} \\ \$3.\cancel{5}\cancel{0} \\ -\ 0.03 \\ \hline \$3.47 \end{array}$$

Notice that since 3 could not be subtracted from 0 in the first column, 10 was borrowed from 50 in the column to the left. Then, 3 was subtracted from 10 to get 7. The 50 in the second column was reduced to 40. Since 0 was subtracted from it, 4 was written in the second column of the answer.

APPLICATION PROBLEMS

Find the difference in the numbers of each problem by subtracting.

1. $4.75	2. $6.32	3. $530.19	4. $3,721.73	5. $32,597.83	6. $42,014.23
-1.43	-3.76	- 209.73	-2,945.86	- 24,638.95	- 39,983.56

MATH SKILL 9 ▶ *Checking subtraction*

To check your answer when subtracting, add the difference to the amount subtracted. The total you get should be the same as the top number. For example:

$3.50 ◀——— top number	$3.47 ◀——— difference
- 0.03 ◀——— amount subtracted	+0.03 ◀——— amount subtracted
$3.47 ◀——— difference	$3.50 ◀——— top number

APPLICATION PROBLEMS

Find the difference in the numbers of each problem. Check your work by adding the difference and the amount subtracted.

1.	458	2.	1,390	3.	12,513	4.	$193.65	5.	$7,414.76	6.	$61,452.31
	- 329		- 887		-9,978		- 73.78		- 3,583.89		- 45,625.53

Multiplying whole numbers

Multiplication is a quick way to add two or more numbers. For example, instead of adding 6 + 6 + 6 + 6, you multiply 6 x 4. The answer is the same for both methods: 24. But, multiplication is much faster.

APPLICATION PROBLEMS

Find the product of the numbers in each problem by multiplying.

1. 8 x 2 =
2. 9 x 6 =
3. 12 x 9 =
4. 23 x 6 =
5. 132 x 14 =
6. 320 x 10 =

MATH SKILL **11** ▶ *Multiplying decimal numbers*

When you multiply decimal numbers, you must place the decimal point in the product correctly. To do that, point off to the left in the product as many decimal places as there are in *both* numbers multiplied. For example, to multiply $23.56 x 1.5:

```
  $ 23.56    Notice that three places were pointed off in the product
  x    1.5   because there are 2 decimal places in one of the numbers
    11780    ($23.56) and 1 decimal place in the other (1.5). However,
     2356    since the last number in the product is less than 5 and
  $35.340    you are working with cents, it should be dropped.
```

APPLICATION PROBLEMS

Find the product by multiplying. Round answers to Problems 3 through 6 to the nearest cent.

1. 132.8 x 7.3 =
2. 39.334 x 5.21 =
3. $12.725 x 6.5 =
4. $9.418 x 5.25 =
5. $235.45 x 52 =
6. $437.89 x 52 =

MATH SKILL **12** ▶ *Multiplying by ¹/₄, ¹/₂, and ³/₄*

In business, you will often have to multiply by the fractions ¹/₄, ¹/₂, and ³/₄. To do this, it is usually easiest to convert the fractions to their decimal equivalents. Then, multiply. If the product is a dollar amount, you may have to round to the nearest cent.

For example, to multiply $24.65 by ¹/₄: first change ¹/₄ to 0.25; then, multiply; finally, round off the product to the nearest whole cent.

```
  $ 24.65
  x   0.25
    12325
     4930
  $6.1625, or $6.16
```

APPLICATION PROBLEMS

Find the product by multiplying. Round answers to the nearest cent, if necessary.

1. $45.80 x $\frac{1}{2}$ =
2. $1,345.23 x $\frac{1}{2}$ =
3. $8.95 x 1 $\frac{1}{2}$ =
4. $12.56 x 2 $\frac{3}{4}$ =
5. $7.54 x 37 $\frac{1}{2}$ =
6. $12.45 x 39 $\frac{3}{4}$ =

MATH SKILL 13 ▶ *Multiplying by a percent*

Many business problems require you to multiply amounts by a percent. Sometimes the percent has a fraction in it. The easiest way to multiply by a percent is to change it to a decimal first. To change a percent to a decimal, move the decimal place in the percent two places to the left and drop the percent sign. For example:

12.5% = 0.12.5 = 0.125   8 $\frac{1}{2}$% = 8.5% = 0.08.5 = 0.085

8% = 0.08.0 = 0.08   7.51% = 0.07.51 = 0.0751

Original Problem	Suggested Problem
1. $458.97 x 8% =	1. $458.97 x 0.08 = $36.7176, or $36.72
2. $500.00 x 8 $\frac{1}{2}$% =	2. $500.00 x 0.085 = $42.50

Notice that in the first problem, the product was rounded to the nearest cent because you are working with an amount of money and the product did not come out to an even cent.

APPLICATION PROBLEMS

Find the product of the numbers in each problem. Change any percents and fractions to decimals before multiplying. Round answers to the nearest cent, if necessary.

1. $567.43 x 8% =
3. $93.89 x 3.5% =
5. $48.76 x 4 $\frac{1}{2}$% =
2. $1,489.64 x 8% =
4. $3,078.76 x 7.5% =
6. $5,918.74 x 7 $\frac{1}{4}$% =

MATH SKILL 14 ▶ *Checking multiplication*

To check your multiplication work, reverse the two numbers you multiplied and multiply again. For example, to check that 5 x 8 = 40, do this: 8 x 5 = 40. Since the product you got when you checked your work was the same as the original product, you know that you have multiplied correctly.

You can also check your multiplication by dividing the product by one of the two numbers. The answer should be the other number. For example, 40 ÷ 8 = 5. Also, 40 ÷ 5 = 8.

APPLICATION PROBLEMS

Find the product of the numbers in each problem. Change any percents and fractions to decimals before multiplying. Check each answer by reversing the numbers and multiplying again. Round answers to the nearest cent, if necessary.

1. $39 \times 7 =$
2. $184 \times 5 =$
3. $\$6.48 \times 1.5 =$
4. $\$14.78 \times 2\,{}^1\!/_2 =$
5. $\$928.78 \times 5\% =$
6. $\$657.42 \times 8\,{}^1\!/_2\% =$

MATH SKILL 15 ▶ *Dividing whole numbers*

Division is the opposite of multiplication. When you divide one number by another, you are finding how many times one number is contained within another. For example, dividing 200 by 50 shows that 50 is contained 4 times within 200. The answer, 4, is called the quotient.

When one number is not divisible by another evenly, there is a remainder. For example, 200 divided by 48 shows that 48 is contained 4 times within 200 with a remainder of 8.

When you are dealing with dollar amounts, you will usually round to the nearest cent. To do that, you must divide until you reach the third place to the right of the decimal place, or the thousandths position. For example, to divide $150.00 by 16:

Solution

```
        9.375
 16)150.000
    144
     6 0
     4 8
     1 20
     1 12
        80
        80
         0
```

Explanation

The quotient shows that 16 is contained within 150, 9.375 times. The quotient, $9.375, should be rounded to the nearest cent, or to **$9.38**.

APPLICATION PROBLEMS

Find the quotient of the numbers in each problem. Round answers to the nearest cent, if necessary.

1. $\$23{,}678.00 \div 12 =$
2. $\$31{,}048.00 \div 12 =$
3. $\$946.00 \div 40 =$
4. $\$45.64 \div 8 =$
5. $\$32{,}750.64 \div 52 =$
6. $\$348.39 \div 6 =$

To check division, you may rework the problem. You may also check division by multiplying the quotient by the number you divided by and then adding the remainder. For example, 200 ÷ 48 = 4, with a remainder of 8. To check this division:

Solution	Explanation
4 x 48 = 192	Multiply the quotient by the number you divided by.
192 + 8 = 200	Add the remainder.

APPLICATION PROBLEMS

Find the quotient of the numbers in each problem. Check your division by reworking each problem.

1. 487.00 ÷ 40 =
2. $26,862.00 ÷ 12 =
3. $27,944.80 ÷ 52 =

4. $18,943.60 ÷ 52 =
5. $758.40 ÷ 40 =
6. $15,499.80 ÷ 12 =

Using
Electronic Spreadsheets

BUSINESS TERMS PREVIEW
• **Cell** • **Software** •

GOALS

1. To learn about computer spreadsheet software.
2. To learn how to create and save spreadsheets.

𝒰NDERSTANDING THE WORK

Spreadsheet **software** is commonly used in business offices. Spreadsheet software lets you prepare tables, such as budgets and payroll registers, easily and quickly.

Spreadsheet software takes the place of a pad of paper and calculator to find the answers to common business problems. For example, spreadsheet software was used by Linda McClain to maintain the list of expenses shown on the computer screen in Illustration C1.

The spreadsheet has both columns and rows. The columns are identified by letter and the rows by number. Data are shown in **cells**, which are where columns and rows meet. For example, the word *Salaries* is found in Cell A5, or where Column A and Row 5 meet. The number 3000.00 is found in B5, or where Column B and Row 5 meet.

To develop the list of expenses, Linda created a spreadsheet that contained
1. A title: Expenses.
2. Column headings: Type and Amount.
3. Row labels: Salaries, Rent, Power, Postage, Telephone, and Other.
4. A formula for adding the expenses and getting the total.
5. The amount for each expense.

Linda entered a formula into Cell B12 and entered the label *Total* into Cell A12. The formula tells the spreadsheet program how to calculate the total of Column B. Formulas will be explained later in this appendix.

Illustration C1   List of expenses on a computer screen

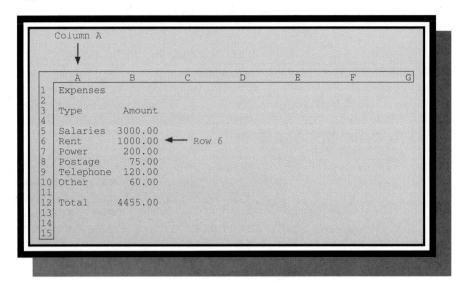

Linda also entered the amounts for each expense in Column B, Rows 5-10. When she did this, the amount in the Total row was calculated automatically by the formula she had entered into Cell B12.

Spreadsheet SKILL 1 ▶ Loading the software into your computer

Each type of computer and each spreadsheet program is somewhat different. Instructions to load spreadsheet programs into your computer will be supplied by your teacher. You should learn how to load your spreadsheet program and quit, or get out of, your spreadsheet program.

Spreadsheet SKILL 2 ▶ Moving the cell pointer

After you load your spreadsheet program, your computer display screen should look similar to Illustration C2.

Illustration C2   The computer screen after loading the spreadsheet

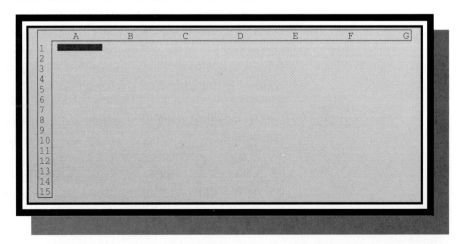

Notice that Cell A1 is highlighted. The highlighted cell is the cell pointer. It tells you where you are in the spreadsheet. The cell pointer tells you that you are at Cell A1, and you may enter data into the cell. To move the cell pointer to other cells in the spreadsheet, use the arrow keys on your keyboard.

APPLICATION PROBLEM

Use the arrow keys on your keyboard to move the cell pointer to the following cells: A10, B10, B2, E5, C15, D20.

Spreadsheet SKILL 3 ▶ *Entering alphabetic data*

You enter alphabetic characters into a cell by
a. Moving the cell pointer to that cell.
b. Keying the characters.
c. Pressing the Enter key.

For example, move the cell pointer to Cell A1. Key the title for the spreadsheet, Expenses. If you make mistakes while entering the characters, use the backspace key to erase the errors. Then, re-enter them correctly. When you are done, press the Enter key. This will insert the characters in Cell A1.

You may spot an error in the cell after pressing the Enter key. If you do, simply key the correct characters over the errors and press the Enter key. The correct characters will be inserted into the cell.

APPLICATION PROBLEM

Practice entering alphabetic characters by entering the column headings and row labels.

Move the cell pointer to Cell A3 using the arrow keys on your keyboard. Key the word *Type* and press the Enter key. Move the cell pointer to Cell B3, key the word *Amount,* and press the Enter key. You have now entered the headings for the two columns.

Move the cell pointer to Column A and enter Salaries in A5, Rent in A6, Power in A7, Postage in A8, Telephone in A9, and Other in A10. When the labels have been entered, enter the word *Total* in Cell A12 and press the Enter key. Do not forget to press the Enter key after each label has been keyed.

Spreadsheet SKILL 4 ▶ *Entering numeric data*

You enter numbers into a cell in the same way as you entered alphabetic characters. You must move the cell pointer to each cell you want, enter a number, and press the Enter key. For example, move the cell pointer to Cell B5. Enter the amount for salaries expense by keying 3000. Then press the Enter key.

Notice that you do not enter commas or dollar signs when entering numeric data. Some spreadsheet programs will show the salaries amount as 3000. Others will show it as 3000.00.

If the amount had been 3120.80, you would have had to enter the numbers 3120, then the decimal point, then 8, and then press the Enter key.

APPLICATION PROBLEM

Practice by entering the rest of the expense amounts. Enter 1000 in B6, 200 in B7, 75 in B8, 120 in B9, and 60 in B10. Press the Enter key after keying each number.

Spreadsheet SKILL 5 ▶ *Entering formulas*

A formula is a set of math steps that are performed by the spreadsheet program. For example, a formula might instruct the spreadsheet program to add the amount in one cell to the amount in another cell and place the answer in a third cell.

Suppose that you had entered $100 in Cell C1 and $50 in Cell C2. You could then move the cell pointer to Cell C3 and key this formula: +C1+C2.

When you press the Enter key, the total of cells C1 and C2, $150, would appear in Cell C3.

You are probably wondering why that first plus sign is needed. Why can't you just enter C1+C2? The answer is that if you keyed C1, the spreadsheet program would think that you were entering alphabetic characters and would not treat C1+C2 as a formula. By entering the + sign first, the program knows that you are entering a formula.

When you enter formulas, you tell spreadsheet programs to add, subtract, multiply, and divide by using these keys on your keyboard:

a. + for addition.   c. * for multiplication.
b. - for subtraction.   d. / for division.

APPLICATION PROBLEM

Practice by entering the formula to find the total of the Amount column in the Expenses spreadsheet. Move the cell pointer to Cell B12, where you want the total to be placed. Then enter the formula by pressing these keys in order: +B5+B6+B7+B8+B9+B10.

After entering the formula, press the Enter key. The total of Column B will appear in Cell B12 as soon as you do.

Using spreadsheet functions in formulas

Many spreadsheet programs let you enter formulas using special math functions such as SUM, COUNT, and AVERAGE. These functions tell the spreadsheet program to perform the function on a range of cells.

For example, to find the sum, or total, of cells B5 through B10, you might enter this formula: @SUM(B5..B10). The formula tells the spreadsheet program to add the amounts found in the range of cells B5 through B10.

Notice the @, or At symbol. Many spreadsheet programs look for the @ symbol to know when to perform a function. If you did not enter @ first, the spreadsheet would treat your formula as alphabetic characters since you would have started with the letters SUM. Notice also that you had to enter two periods between B5 and B10. Many spreadsheet programs use the periods to indicate a range.

APPLICATION PROBLEM

Practice by moving the cell pointer to Cell B12. Enter the formula to find the total of the Amount column: @SUM(B5..B10). Now press the Enter key and the new formula will replace the old one. Notice that the answer, 4455.00, remains the same.

Saving the spreadsheet

You should save it on your data disk so that you can use it again. When you are asked to name the spreadsheet, call it Expenses.

APPLICATION PROBLEM

Practice saving the Expenses spreadsheet several times so that you can do it easily.

Using a Calculator and Computer Keypad

KINDS OF CALCULATORS

Many different models of calculators, both desktop and hand-held, are available. Therefore, it is necessary to refer to the operator's manual for specific instructions and locations of the operating keys for the calculator being used. A typical keyboard of a desktop calculator is shown in Illustration D-1 (see p. 759).

DESKTOP CALCULATOR SETTINGS

Several operating switches on a desktop calculator must be engaged before the calculator will produce the desired results.

The *decimal selector* sets the approximate decimal places necessary for the numbers that will be entered. For example, if the decimal selector is set at 2, both the numbers entered and the answer will have two decimal places. The F setting allows the answer to be unrounded and carried out to the maximum number of decimal places possible.

The *decimal rounding selector* rounds the answers. The down arrow position will drop any digits beyond the last digit desired. The up arrow position will drop any digits beyond the last digit desired and round the last digit up. In the 5/4 position, the calculator rounds the last desired digit up only when the following digit is 5 or greater. If the following digit is less than 5, the last desired digit remains unchanged.

The *GT* or *grand total switch* in the on position accumulates totals.

Illustration D1   Typical desktop calculator keyboard

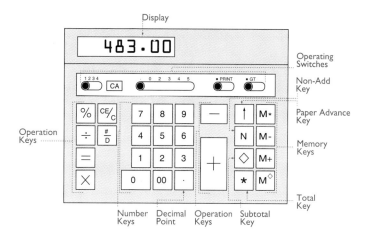

KINDS OF COMPUTER KEYBOARDS

The computer has a keypad on the right side of the keyboard called the *numeric keypad*. Even though several styles of keyboards for the IBM and compatible computers are found, there are two basic layouts for the numeric keypad. The standard layout and enhanced layout are shown in Illustration D-2. On the standard keyboard the directional arrow keys are found on the number keys. To use the numbers, press the key called *Num Lock*. (This key is found above the "7" key.) When the Num Lock is turned on, numbers are entered when the keys on the keypad are pressed. When the Num Lock is off, the arrow, Home, Page Up, Page Down, End, Insert, and Delete keys can be used.

The enhanced keyboards have the arrow keys and the other directional keys mentioned above to the left of the numeric keypad. When using the keypad on an enhanced keyboard, Num Lock can remain on.

The asterisk (*) performs a different function on the computer than the calculator. The asterisk on the calculator is used for the total while the computer uses it for multiplication.

Another difference is the division key. The computer key is the forward slash key (/). The calculator key uses the division key (÷).

Appendix Illustration D2 Standard and enhanced keypads

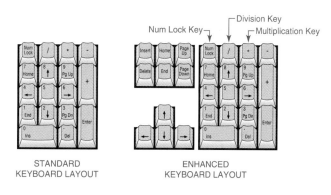

STANDARD
KEYBOARD LAYOUT

ENHANCED
KEYBOARD LAYOUT

TEN-KEY TOUCH SYSTEM

Striking the numbers 0 to 9 on a calculator or numeric keypad without looking at the keyboard is called the *touch system*. Using the touch system develops both speed and accuracy.

The 4, 5, and 6 keys are called the *home row*. If the right hand is used for the keyboard, the index finger is placed on the 4 key, the middle finger on the 5 key, and the ring finger on the 6 key. If the left hand is used, the ring finger is placed on the 4 key, the middle finger on the 5 key, and the index finger on the 6 key.

Place the fingers on the home row keys. Curve the fingers and keep the wrist straight. These keys may feel slightly concaved or the 5 key may have a raised dot. The differences in the home row allow the operator to recognize the home row by touch rather than by sight.

Maintain the position of the fingers on the home row. The finger used to strike the 4 key will also strike the 7 key and the 1 key. Stretch the finger up to reach the 7; then stretch the finger down to reach the 1 key. Visualize the position of these keys.

Again, place the fingers on the home row. Stretch the finger that strikes the 5 key up to reach the 8 key, then down to reach the 2 key. Likewise, stretch the finger that strikes the 6 key up to strike the 9 and down to strike the 3 key. This same finger will stretch down again to hit the decimal point.

If the right hand is used, the thumb will be used to strike the 0 and 00 keys and the little finger to strike the addition key. If the left hand is used, the little finger will be used to strike the 0 and 00 keys and the thumb to strike the addition key.

HAND-HELD CALCULATORS

Hand-held calculators are slightly different from desktop calculators, not only in their size and features but also in their operation. Therefore, the touch system is usually not used on a hand-held calculator. Refer to the operator's manual for specific instructions for the calculator being used.

PERFORMING MATHEMATICAL OPERATIONS

Desktop Calculators   The basic operations of addition, subtraction, multiplication, and division are used frequently on a calculator.

Addition   Each number to be added is called an *addend*. The answer to an addition problem is called the *sum*.

Addition is performed by entering an addend and striking the addition key (+). All numbers are entered on a calculator in the exact order they are given. To enter the number 4,455.65, strike the 4, 4, 5, 5, decimal, 6, and 5 keys in that order, and then strike the addition key. Commas are not entered. Continue in this manner until all addends have been entered. To obtain the sum, strike the total key on the calculator.

Subtraction

The top number or first number of a subtraction problem is called the *minuend*. The number to be subtracted from the minuend is called the *subtrahend*. The answer to a subtraction problem is called the *difference*.

Subtraction is performed by first entering the minuend and striking the addition key (+). The subtrahend is then entered, followed by the minus key (–), followed by the total key.

Multiplication

The number to be multiplied is called the *multiplicand*. The number of times the multiplicand will be multiplied is called the *multiplier*. The answer to a multiplication problem is called the *product*.

Multiplication is performed by entering the multiplicand and striking the multiplication key (x). The multiplier is then entered, followed by the equals key (=). The calculator will automatically multiply and give the product.

Division

The number to be divided is called the *dividend*. The number the dividend will be divided by is called the *divisor*. The answer to a division problem is called the *quotient*.

Division is performed by entering the dividend and striking the division key (÷). The divisor is then entered, followed by the equals key (=). The calculator will automatically divide and give the quotient.

Correcting Errors

If an error is made while using a calculator, several methods of correction may be used. If an incorrect number has been entered and the addition key or equals key has not yet been struck, strike the clear entry (CE) key one time. This key will clear only the last number that was entered. However, if the clear entry key is depressed more than one time, the entire problem will be cleared on some calculators. If an incorrect number has been entered and the addition key has been struck, strike the minus key one time only. This will automatically subtract the last number added, thus removing it from the total.

PERFORMING MATHEMATICAL OPERATIONS

Computers and Hand-Held Calculators

On a computer keypad or a hand-held calculator, addition is performed in much the same way as on a desktop calculator. However, after the + key is depressed, the display usually shows the accumulated total. Therefore, the total key is not found. Some computer programs will not calculate the total until Enter is pressed.

Subtraction is performed differently on many computer keypads and hand-held calculators. The minuend is usually entered, followed by the minus (–) key. Then the subtrahend is entered. Pressing either the + key or the = key will display the difference. Some computer programs will not calculate the difference until Enter is pressed.

Multiplication and division are performed the same way on a computer keypad and hand-held calculator as on a desktop calculator. Keep in mind that computers use the * for multiplication and / for division.

*S*AFETY CONCERNS

Whenever electrical equipment such as a calculator or computer is being operated in a classroom or office, several safety rules apply. These rules protect the operator of the equipment, other persons in the environment, and the equipment itself.

1. Do not unplug equipment by pulling on the electrical cord. Instead, grasp the plug at the outlet and remove it.
2. Do not stretch electrical cords across an aisle where someone might trip over them.
3. Avoid food and beverages near the equipment where a spill might result in an electrical short.
4. Do not attempt to remove the cover of a calculator, computer, or keyboard for any reason while the power is turned on.
5. Do not attempt to repair equipment while it is plugged in.
6. Always turn the power off or unplug equipment when finished using it.

*C*ALCULATION DRILLS

Instructions for desktop calculators: Complete each drill using the touch method. Set the decimal selector at the setting indicated in each drill. Compare the answer on the calculator to the answer in the book. If the two are the same, progress to the next problem. It is not necessary to enter 00 in the cents column if the decimal selector is set at 0-F. However, digits other than zeros in the cents column must be entered preceded by a decimal point.

Instructions for computer keypads: Complete each drill using the touch method. There is no decimal selector on computer keypads. Set the number of decimal places as directed in the instructions for the computer program. In spreadsheets, for example, use the formatting options to set the number of decimal places. When the drill indicates "F" for floating, leave the computer application in its default format. Compare the answer on the computer monitor to the answer in the book. If the two are the same, progress to the next problem. It is not necessary to enter 00 in the cents column. However, digits other than zeros in the cents column must be entered preceded by a decimal point.

D-1 ▶ Performing addition using the home row keys

Decimal Selector—2

4.00	444.00
5.00	555.00
6.00	666.00
5.00	455.00
4.00	466.00
5.00	544.00
6.00	566.00
5.00	655.00
4.00	644.00
5.00	654.00
49.00	5,649.00

DRILL **D-2** ▶ Performing addition using the 0, 1, 4, and 7 keys

Decimal Selector—2

4.00	444.00
7.00	777.00
4.00	111.00
1.00	741.00
4.00	740.00
7.00	101.00
4.00	140.00
1.00	701.00
4.00	700.00
7.00	407.00
43.00	4,862.00

DRILL **D-3** ▶ Performing addition using the 2, 5, and 8 keys

Decimal Selector—2

5.00	588.00
8.00	522.00
5.00	888.00
2.00	222.00
5.00	258.00
8.00	852.00
5.00	225.00
2.00	885.00
5.00	882.00
8.00	228.00
53.00	5,550.00

| DRILL | **D-4** ▶ | Performing addition using the 3, 6, 9, and decimal point keys |

Decimal Selector—2

6.00	666.66
9.00	999.99
6.00	333.33
3.00	666.99
6.36	999.66
3.36	333.66
9.36	696.36
9.63	369.63
6.33	336.69
9.93	963.36
68.97	6,366.33

| DRILL | **D-5** ▶ | Performing subtraction using all number keys |

Decimal Selector—F

456.73	789.01	741.00
- 123.21	- 456.00	- 258.10
333.52	333.01	482.90

| DRILL | **D-6** ▶ | Performing multiplication using all number keys |

Decimal Selector—F

654.05	975.01	487.10
x 12.66	x 27.19	x 30.21
8,280.273	26,510.5219	14,715.291

| DRILL | **D-7** ▶ | Performing division using all number keys |

Decimal Selector—F

900.56	÷	450.28	=	2.
500.25	÷	100.05	=	5.
135.66	÷	6.65	=	20.4
269.155	÷	105.55	=	2.550023685*
985.66	÷	22.66	=	43.49779346*

*Number of decimal places may vary due to machine capacity.

Applied Math Preview Answers

Job 1

1. 215
2. 6,754
3. 230.714
4. $1,204.64
5. $7,591.87

Job 2

1. 338
2. 29.57
3. 2,504.558
4. $63,206.06

Job 3

1. 3,290
2. 43,260
3. 10,000
4. $54
5. $458.90
6. $367
7. $4,800
8. $3.50
9. $0.70
10. $61.70

Job 4

1. 7
2. 124
3. $6.00
4. $4.90
5. $34.00
6. $5.23
7. $12.00
8. $6.05
9. $4.00
10. $165.00

Job 5

1. 0.20
2. 0.25
3. 0.50
4. 0.75

5. 0.29
6. 0.63
7. 0.04
8. 0.12
9. 0.82
10. 0.91
11. 0.70
12. 0.30
13. 0.10
14. 0.52
15. 0.19
16. 0.07
17. 0.03
18. 0.01
19. 0.045
20. 0.0751

Job 6

1. 80%
2. 25%
3. 50%
4. 75%
5. 47%
6. 29%
7. 2%
8. 10%
9. 8%
10. 5%
11. 7%
12. 40%
13. 15%
14. 19%
15. 99%
16. 3%
17. 3.5%
18. 9%
19. 9.5%
20. 7.51%

Job 7

1. $549.20
2. $443.30

3. $384.83
4. $1,214.63
5. $13.80, $111.23, $834.99, $1,631.94, $2,591.96

Job 8

1. $116.65
2. $223.69
3. $1,607.73
4. $929.33
5. $419.54, $517.63, $1,069.33, $870.90, $2,877.40

Job 9

1. $18,593.05
2. $36,171.40
3. $20,510.91
4. $16,865.11
5. $8,957.64, $9,381.79, $73,801.04, $92,140.47

Job 10

1. $478.00
2. $925.18
3. ($309.25)
4. ($387.50)

Job 11

1. $26,000.00
2. $23,400.00
3. $19,500.00
4. $22,289.80
5. $24,500.84
6. $2,000.00
7. $1,313.00
8. $1,545.00
9. $1,877.01
10. $1,188.24

Job 12

1. $0.09
2. $18.00
3. $0.18

4. $4.50
5. $0.09

Job 13

1. $37.89
2. $142.43
3. $364.19
4. $542.76
5. $243.36
6. $687.36
7. $610.31
8. $456.53
9. $269.35

Job 14

1. $450.00
2. $810.00
3. $262.77
4. $150.00
5. $450.00
6. $186.50
7. $851.96
8. $44.39
9. $765.58
10. $1,142.42

Job 15

1. $6,766.20
2a. 47
 b. 170
 c. 214
 d. 248
 e. 236
 f. 216, 158, 182, 332, 915

Job 16

1. $13.61
2. $8.24
3. $11.56
4. $18.31
5. $11.52

Job 17

1. $20.03
2. $14.50
3. $10.01
4. $12.86
5. $177.79
6. $18.16
7. $37.56

Job 18

1. $220.00
2. $160.00
3. $140.00
4. $87.00
5. $29.00
6. $4.25
7. $17.40
8. $8.85
9. $3.46

Job 19

1. $1,663.34
2. $2,127.67
3. $1,254.62
4. $4,811.02
5. $2,315.28

Job 20

1. $8,100.00
2. $1,150.00
3. $50.50
4. $28.50
5. $2,140.00
6. $655.00
7. $32.20
8. $8.12

Job 21

1. $3,750.00
2. $252.40
3. $1.82
4. $336.37
5. $2,359.28

Job 22

1. $9,897.77
2. $3,909.12
 $4,256.04
3. $5,456.10
 $6,170.70
4. $2,593.52
 $3,538.91

Job 23

1. $5,085.29
 $3,506.09
2. $7,190.77
 $3,512.18
3. $1,728.55
 $5,317.30
4. $4,957.26
 $9,402.86

Job 24

1. $813.31
 $702.84
 $607.68
2. $301.72
 $190.54
 $740.54
3. $996.59
 $897.41
 $710.15
4. $2,587.30
 $2,686.05
 $1,738.89

Job 25

1. $1,291.57
2. $869.44

3. $2,026.12
4. $2,705.01

Job 26

1. $535.91
2. $2,407.12
3. $422.62; $372.62
4. $1,518.76; $1,448.76

Job 27

1. $843.03
 $706.86
 $609.68
2. $519.89
 $209.70
 $785.20
3. $210.15
 $966.01
 $584.92

Job 28

1. $3,071.08
 $2,359.81
 $1,952.83
2. $5,012.78
 $3,539.62
 $4,289.62
3. $3,216.78
 $4,172.68
 $3,335.58

Job 29

1. $406.61
 $409.16
 $298.97
 $709.34
2. $614.95
 $790.58
 $786.08
 $577.89
3. $2,893.50
 $2,888.25
 $3,399.35
 $3,413.46

Job 30

1. $96.05
2. $135.08
3. $52.25
4. $41.84
5. $35.03
6. $128.06

Job 31

1. $118.79
2. $80.88
3. $85.24
4. $78.68
5. $57.11
6. $121.21

Job 32
1. $74.35
2. $87.24
3. $52.60
4. $5.82
5. $21.05
6. $121.07

Job 33
1. $118.44
2. $165.43
3. $96.35
4. $84.33

Job 34
1. $14.64
2. $3.18
3. $13.12
4. $5.96
5. $9.45
6. $25.65
7. $8.98
8. $7.38
9. $17.94
10. $26.40
11. $13.50
12. $9.43

Job 35
1. $59.84
2. $9.45
3. $18.36
4. $19.16
5. $20.25
6. $50.75
7. $6.93
8. $24.78

Job 36
1. $4.49
2. $8.16
3. $5.46
4. $10.75
5. $6.33
6. $9.69
7. $8.91
8. $8.97

Job 37
1. $13.87
2. $6.72
3. $16.25
4. $7.81
5. $97.33
6. $7.33
7. $16.90
8. $4.63

Job 38
1. $2.50
2. $45.80
3. $13.99
4. $22.32
5. $8.35
6. $63.19
7. $26.21
8. $2.02

Job 39
1. $1,329.02
2. $1,176.02
3. $5,219.06
4. $3,820.16
5. $2,820.59
6. $16,993.35

Job 40
1. $945.73
2. $733.30
3a. $4,087.02
3b. $3,961.14
4a. $4,187.95
4b. $3,982.25

Job 41
1. 75
2. 65
3. 50
4. 160
5. 180
6. 30
7. 30
8. 44
9. 116
10. 133

Job 42
1. $2,389.00
2. $187.50
3. $915.00
4. $45.00
5. $6,270.00
6. $21,970.00
7. $375.00
8. $905.00
9. $370.00
10. $3,615.00
11. $2,050.00
12. $1,512.00

Job 43
1. $4.34
2. $2.51
3. $5.12
4. $1.54
5. $7.26
6. $22.68
7. $29.20

8. $31.68
9. $35.55
10. $47.12

Job 44
1. March 23
2. July 7
3. February 6
4. May 3
5. December 17
6. September 17
7. February 10
8. November 30
9. October 11
10. June 20

Job 45
1. April 22
2. January 18
3. February 28
4. June 11
5. February 10
6. December 4
7. January 13
8. September 29
9. January 17
10. June 1

Job 46
1.   = $ 75.00
                 =   185.00
                 =   73.00
                 =   106.50
                 =   95.10
   $251.80 + $282.80 = $534.60
2.   = $ 28.00
                 =   64.00
                 =   32.00
                 =   75.00
                 =   226.00
   $594.00 - $169.00 = $425.00

Job 47
1.   = $115.00
                 =   69.00
                 =   73.80
                 =   90.75
                 =   119.75
   $320.80 + $147.50 = $468.30
2.   = $ 35.00
                 =   25.00
                 =   34.30
                 =   59.50
                 =   51.40
   $444.55 - $239.35 = $205.20

Job 48
1. 107
2. 370
3. 1,073
4. 3,297

Job 49

1. 214; 107
2. 1,027; 231
3. 5,610; 1,735
4. 19,551; 2,382

Job 50

1. 79
2. 167
3. 223
4. 729
5. 689
6. 581
7. 978
8. 1,189

Job 51

1. $5,040.75
2. $9,248.25
3. $42,636.50
4. $151,748.00
5. $195,492.15
6. $64,780.80
7. $240,732.10
8. $55,736.80

Job 52

1. $2,794.44
2. $61,848.05
3. $98.10
4. $2,725.95
5. $153,912.54
6. $162,840.00
7. $31,671.00
8. $7,966.28

Job 53

1. $42.10
2. $159.50
3. $687.00
4. $1,359.00
5. $7,240.00
6. $102.00
7. $210.00
8. $328.00
9. $525.00
10. $720.00

Job 54

1. $102,692.10
2. $51,654.57
3. $393.93
4. $1,718.20
5. $6,436.65
6. $276.00
7. $1,037.88
8. $17.08

Job 55

1. 295
2. 691
3. 4,216
4. 2,029

Job 56

1. August 2
2. May 29
3. April 15
4. June 7
5. August 21
6. July 27
7. December 2
8. December 13

Job 57

1. 269
2. 3,815
3. $316.87
4. $0.00

Job 58

1. $2,131.46; $1,086.34; $3,862.52
2. $6,175.96; $6,971.14; $2,799.02
3. $997.05; $284.28; $5,381.16

Job 59

1. $4,682.55; $1,483.50; $3,655.68
2. $552.87; $512.92; $493.09
3. $3,592.17; $3,488.37; $1,911.11

Job 60

1. $4,813.31
2. $9,803.91
3. $21,668.90
4. $17,749.62

Job 61

1. $11,628.81
2. $4,341.37
3. $2,073.39
4. $4,782.49

Job 62

1. Bottom row: $194, $257, $178, $288, $917
   Right column: $215, $173, $161, $173, $195, $917
2. Bottom row: $95.00, $106.29, $57.89, $171.52, $430.70
   Right column: $33.38, $61.93, $88.65, $48.70, $198.04, $430.70

Job 63

1. $16,139.84
2. $22,984.78
3. $17,749.46
4. $19,577.59

Job 64

1. $10,185.70
2. $15,488.47
3. $7,537.70
4. $3,810.98

Job 65

1. Bottom row: 270, 234, 290, 247, 247, 1,041
   Right column: 152, 102, 229, 270, 288, 1,041
2. Bottom row: $118.98, $94.47, $170.59, $246.61, $630.65
   Right column: $115.90, $103.98, $160.34, $146.10, $104.33, $630.65

Job 66

1. $21,965.36
2. $15,914.00
3. $19,743.25
4. $9,078.06

Job 67

1. $13,602.60
2. $12,230.73
3. $845.40
4. $1,144.02
5. $11,273.91
6. $6,516.76

Job 68

1. $5,600.00
2. $4,970.00
3. $1,806.00
4. $5,264.00
5. $6,986.00
6. $7,000.00
7. $4,501.00
8. $2,283.40

Job 69

1. $5,979.98
2. $227,637.99
3. $3,868.26
4. $56,105.78
5. $630.15
6. $26,369.51
7. $52,777.99
8. $28,837.61

Job 70

1. $57,500.00
2. $30,000.00
3. $35,000.00
4. $13,097.25
5. $50,644.30
6. $92,283.06

Job 71

1. $10,294.16
2. $85,126.47

3. $10,078.38
4. $2,096.87
5. $3,985.81
6. $14,417.45

Job 72

1. 28 $\frac{1}{2}$
2. 28
3. 39 $\frac{1}{4}$
4. 61
5. 37 $\frac{1}{2}$

Job 73

1. 36 $\frac{1}{2}$
2. 37 $\frac{1}{4}$
3. 26
4. $326.25
5. $474.30

Job 74

1. 28 $\frac{3}{4}$
2. 42 $\frac{3}{4}$
3. 36 $\frac{1}{2}$
4. $567.00
5. $454.02

Job 75

1. 43 $\frac{1}{4}$
2. 37 $\frac{3}{4}$
3. 40 $\frac{3}{4}$
4. $16.35
5. $12.90
6. $23.025
7. $19.11
8. $17.325
9. $11.775

Job 76

1. 41 $\frac{1}{2}$
2. $13.35
3. $9.60
4. $18.39
5. $19.875
6. $17.175
7. $16.275

Job 77

1. $680.00
2. $705.00
3. $2,283.50
4. $751.56
5. $1,686.48
6. $4,489.56
7. $891.24
8. $2,166.93
9. $1,056.64
10. $791.49

Job 78

1. $80.00
2. $157.50

3. $159.90
4. $100.62
5. $78.48
6. $615.00
7. $987.00
8. $1,919.58
9. $47.00
10. $18.30

Job 79

1. $18.16
2. $27.58
3. $33.16
4. $43.71
5. $24.56
6. $33.99

Job 80

1. $39.17
2. $22.16
3. $38.17
4. $42.26

Job 81

1. $504.73
2. $264.36
3. $64.74
4. $96.60

Job 82

1. 42
2. $8,275.72
3. $2,203.08
4. $15.45
5. $18.24
6. $22.61
7. $35.04
8. $30.31
9. $38.51

Job 83

1. $3,447.92
2.
	= 201
	= 190
	= 120
	= 200
	= 585
397 442 253 204	= 1,296

Job 84

1. $175,946.00
2.
	= 252
	= 224
	= 104
	= 237
	= 554
334 233 469 335	= 1,371

Job 85

1. $127,906.48
2.
	= 227
	= 214
	= 696
	= 2,062
	= 2,273
599 1,726 1,667 1,480	= 5,472

Appendix A

1. $18,976.12
2. $8,976.85
3. $185.88
4. $697.45
5. $363.61
6. $16,271.23
7. $24,654.55

GLOSSARY

◆◆◆

The page number on which the key term first appears is listed following the definition.

A

ABA number A number assigned to banks. 203

account balance Total debits minus total credits. 340

accounting equation Assets equal liabilities plus capital. 610

accounts payable ledger A group of creditor accounts. 483

accounts receivable account A customer account. 340

accounts receivable clerk An employee who keeps records for charge customers. 340

accounts receivable ledger A group of customer accounts. 377

allowance A reduction in price given for damaged merchandise or to correct an overcharge. 406

alphabetically By the alphabet. 26

amount due Principal plus interest owed on the due date of a promissory note. 135

amount financed Installment price less down payment; amount borrowed. 128

amount tendered The amount of cash given to the cashier by the customer. 160

annual Yearly. 107

annual percentage rate The annual finance charge shown as a rate or percentage. 130

assets Things owned with money value. 609

ATM access card A card that allows you to use an ATM to make deposits, withdraw cash, or transfer money (see, also, automated teller machine). 242

audit To verify or check for accuracy and completeness. 599

authorization number Means customer's credit is good. 326

authorize To approve. 111

automated teller machine (ATM) A machine that allows 24-hour banking. 242

B

backordered Out of stock temporarily. 463

badge A special employee card that is read by a badge reader. 635

badge reader A machine that reads employee badges and records the time. 635

balance The amount of stock on hand. 422

balance due When total tax due is greater than estimated tax paid. 599

balance sheet A form that shows that assets equal liabilities plus capital. 610

bank credit cards Credit cards issued by banks. 108

bank deposit Money placed in a bank account. 187

bank reconciliation statement A statement that brings the checkbook and bank statement balances into agreement. 247

bank statement A detailed record from the bank of a checking account. 246

bank statement balance The money remaining in a checking account according to the bank's records. 246

bill A sales slip. 317

billing clerks Employees who spend most of their time preparing customer statements. 358

biweekly Every two weeks. 694

blank endorsement An endorsement consisting of the payee's signature only. 230

budget A plan for receiving and spending money. 59

budget variance report A form that compares budgeted amounts with actual amounts. 92

C

C One hundred. 306

cancelled checks Checks that have been paid by the bank. 232

capital The worth of a business. 603

capital statement A form that shows changes in capital over a period of time. 603

cash box A box in which cash is kept. 150

cash budget A report showing the estimated cash flow of a business. 83

cash count report A form used to find the amount of cash on hand. 175

cash discount Small discount given for early payment. 472

cash flow How money is received and spent over time. 83

cash overage More cash on hand than there should be; when actual currency is more than the balance in the petty cash book. 177

cash payments journal A record of cash payments; a record of expenses paid. 500

cash price The amount an item costs if bought for cash. 126

cash receipts journal A record of all cash received. 392

cash register A machine used to handle money. 157

cash register receipt A written record of transactions printed by a cash register. 157

cash shortage When there is less cash in the register at the end of the day than there should be; when actual currency is less than the balance in the petty cash book. 176

cashier A person who receives and pays out money. 148

cashier's check A check that is guaranteed by the bank. 242

central processing unit The computer system part that processes the data. 26

certificate of deposit A savings account that earns a fixed rate of interest for a fixed period of time. 239

chaining Continuous calculation without clearing. 434

change fund An amount given to a cashier at the beginning of the day for making change. 174

characters A computer word for numbers and letters. 47

charge account A form of credit offered by stores. 107

charge sales Sales made on credit. 322

check A written order by the depositor to his or her bank to pay a company or person. 208

check protector A machine used to write checks. 212

check register A book for recording checks and deposits when stubs are not used. 223

check stub The part of a check that is kept by the depositor. 208

checkbook A book of checks. 207

checkbook balance The money left in a checking account according to the depositor's records. 247

check-cashing privilege card Allows you to cash checks at a store. 166

chronological By date. 117

chronologically By date. 26

classification The name for a group of similar items. 274

classified Grouped together. 68

classify To place in groups. 274

clearinghouse A central place where banks exchange checks. 231

clerk Person who keeps records as a major part of his or her daily work. 480

commission pay A pay plan based on how much an employee sells. 642

commissions A pay plan based on how much is sold. 667

computer printout A document prepared by a computer. 3

computer program Instructions the computer follows to process the data. 26

computer system Input and output devices, and a central porcessing unit. 26

credit When you buy now and pay later; a decrease in a customer account; the column used to record a payment or a return in a customer account. 107

credit application Provides information about your ability to pay your debts. 108

credit card Identifies the person buying on credit. 107

credit card sales slip A sales slip used with bank credit cards. 326

credit card statement A form showing the transactions and balances for a credit card account. 116

credit card verification terminal A device that automatically checks credit cards. 327

credit memo A form that shows that a charge customer has returned merchandise and owes less money; a form used by the seller to show that the balance of an account has been reduced because of a return or an allowance. 348

credit slip A form used to return goods bought with a bank credit card. 330

creditor A source of credit; lender. 107

creditors People or businesses to whom money is owed. 483

crossfooting Adding a row of figures across a business form. 62

currency Bills and coins. 270

cursor A flashing marker on a display screen. 46

customer statement A monthly report listing all transactions in a customer account during the month. 357

cycle billing Billing groups of customers at different times during the month. 358

D

data Information. 7

data base A group of files. 44

data entry clerk A worker who enters data into a computer system. 7

data processing Doing something to data to make it more useful. 18

date of note The day a note is signed. 134

debit The column used to record a charge sale in a customer account. 340

debit cards A card, similar in appearance to a credit card, that automatically deducts funds from the owner's checking account. 164

debit memo A form used by the buyer to notify a creditor of a return or an allowance. 518

debts Another word for liabilities. 609

deductions Amounts subtracted from wages. 684

denomination The value of a coin or bill. 175

deposit slip A form that lists the money deposited in a bank account. 190

detailed audit tape A record of all cash register transactions. 173

discontinued No longer sold by a vendor. 463

division of labor Dividing a job up. 100

documents Letters, bills, and business papers. 34

double-entry system A system in which each transaction has at least one debit and one credit. 537

double ruling A set of lines used to show that the math on a form has been completed. 10

down payment The part of the installment price paid at the time an item is bought. 127

drawee The bank that pays the check. 208

drawer The person who writes the check. 208

drawing Money taken out of the business by the owner. 556

due date The date a note must be paid; the date by which an invoice should be paid. 134

duplicate An exact copy. 150

E

electronic funds transfer The use of a computer to transfer money from one party to another. 242

electronically By computer. 2

embossed Printed in raised characters. 116

employee earnings record A record of an employee's earnings and deductions. 708

endorsement A signature or stamp on the back of a check transferring ownership. 229

enter To record information on a form or into a computer. 2

entry-level jobs Jobs in which first-time workers are placed. 54

estimate A careful guess. 598

estimated tax Estimated amount of income tax and self-employment tax paid to the IRS during the year. 598

estimating Making a careful guess. 59

expenses Costs of operating a business. 556

expiration date The last day on which a credit card can be used. 325

extend an amount To record an amount again in a second column. 62

extended Entered again in a second column. 62

extension Quantity times unit price. 306

F

Federal Insurance Contributions Act (FICA) Law passed by Congress to cover the cost of the social security program. 684

FICA tax Tax collected to pay for social security. 684

field A group of letters and numbers. 44

file A group of records. 44

finance charge The difference between the cash and installment prices of an item. 126

financial statements Summaries of the results of a business. 591

fixed payments Cash payments that are the same from period to period. 83

flextime A plan that allows employees to vary the time they arrive and leave work. 680

foot To add a column and record the total. 9

footing The total of the money column written in small figures. 9

forged signature A name falsely signed by someone else. 202

four-column ledger account A general ledger account with two balance columns. 541

full endorsement An endorsement that names the person to whom a check is transferred. 235

FWT Federal withholding tax. 711

G

general columns Columns in a journal used for many items. 558

general ledger A group of accounts other than customer or creditor accounts. 541

good credit risks People likely to pay their debts. 108

graduated commission When the rate of commission increases as the amount of sales increases. 667

graduated piecework pay A pay plan that increases the amount paid as the number of units of work completed increase. 674

grand total A total of other totals. 151

gross Twelve dozen or 144. 306

gross pay Total wages. 644

guides Used to help find records in a file. 26

H

hourly pay A wage plan that pays workers for each hour they work. 642

I

imprinter A device for recording a credit card sale; a machine that transfers data from a credit card to a sales slip. 116

in rack Where you place your time card when you start work. 632

income Money received from the sale of merchandise or services. 535

income statement A form that shows income, expenses, and net income or net loss. 591

income tax A tax on net income earned. 598

indexing Arranging the parts of a name so that it can be filed. 37

individual checking account A checking account used by only one person. 201

input The first step in the data processing cycle. 19

input device Used to put data into a computer. 25

installment contract A form that describes the time, place, and amounts for an installment purchase. 126

installment plan A form of credit in which you pay for an item in monthly payments. 126

installment price The down payment plus the total of all monthly payments. 128

insufficient funds When there is not enough money in the checking account to pay a check. 216

interest Money paid for the use of money. 133

issue To send out; to give out or ship out. 209

J

joint account An account for two people. 110

joint checking account A checking account used by two or more people. 201

journalize To record in a journal. 387

K

key To enter data using a keyboard. 45

L

leading edge The right side of a check. 232

legible Clear and easy to read. 211

liabilities Amounts owed to creditors. 609

loan clerk A bank clerk who handles bank loans. 141

logging on Identifying yourself as an authorized user of a computer. 425

loose bills and coins Bills and coins that do not fill their wrappers. 189

M

M One thousand. 306

magnetic media Kinds of storage, such as disks, diskettes, and tape. 44

main menu The first menu on a computer. 46

manually By hand. 2

maximum The highest amount of stock. 422

memorandum column A type of column used to help you remember information. 543

menu A list of choices or options on a display screen; a list of computer programs. 46

menu bar A bar on a computer screen that contains the names of other menus. 425

merchandise Goods that a business is selling. 3

merchandising business A business that sells a product. 535

MICR Magnetic Ink Character Recognition. 11

minimum The least amount of stock. 422

money column Column on a form used for recording amounts of money. 9

money market account A savings account that pays higher interest than regular savings and allows withdrawals by check. 239

N

negative cash flow When cash payments are greater than cash receipts. 86

negotiable Transferable to another party. 229

net decrease in capital When withdrawals are greater than net income. 605

net income When income is greater than expenses. 591

net increase in capital When net income is greater than withdrawals. 605

net loss When expenses are greater than income. 591

net pay Gross pay less deductions, or take-home pay. 685

normal balance The side of an account where the balance is usually found. 579

numerically By number. 26

O

OCR Optical Character Recognition. 12

open a file To load a file into computer memory. 44

open order An order not yet received. 441

open order report Lists filled and unfilled purchase requisitions. 440

optical mark recognition Allows pencil marks to be read by special machines. 13

option A choice from a menu. 425

out rack Where you place your time card when you leave work. 632

output The third step in the data processing cycle. 19

output device Used to get data out of a computer. 26

outstanding checks Checks issued by the drawer but not yet paid by the bank. 249

outstanding deposit A deposit not shown on the bank statement. 253

over More than ordered. 463

overcharge A price on the invoice is more than it should be. 406

overcharged When you are charged more than you should be. 118

overtime Time worked beyond 40 hours in a week. 653

overtime rate of pay The rate of pay for any hours beyond 40 hours in a week. 653

P

packing slip A form that describes the contents of a shipment. 462

passwords Secret words that let you use a computer. 425

payee The person or business who receives the check and is paid. 209

payments Amounts spent. 59

payments on account Partial payments of the amount due. 341

payroll register A record of wages earned by a group of workers. 648

pegboard A special writing board that allows you to prepare the payroll check, employee earnings record card, and payroll register in one writing. 726

periodic inventory Actual count of stock on hand. 423

perpetual inventory system Running balance is kept for each item of stock. 423

personal computer A microcomputer. 68

personalized deposit slip A deposit slip on which the depositor's name and address are preprinted. 202

personalized identification number A secret number that allows you to use an automated teller machine. 242

petty Small. 270

petty cash book A form used to record and classify petty cash receipts and payments. 281

petty cash box A storage box for petty cash. 270

petty cash clerk A person who keeps records of petty cash. 270

petty cash fund Currency set aside for making small cash payments. 270

petty cash record Form used to record and classify petty cash payments. 275

petty cash voucher A record of payment from the petty cash fund. 270

piecerate The rate paid for each piece. 673

piecework pay A wage plan that pays workers for each piece of work completed. 642

PIN Personalized identification number used with an ATM. 242

policies Rules or procedures. 166

POS terminal A computer terminal used to record sales. 302

position A job. 2

positive cash flow When cash receipts are greater than cash payments. 86

post To transfer data from one record to another. 385

postdated To record a future date on a document. 211

posting references Abbreviations, such as S1, that show where entries were posted from. 386

prenumbered Numbered in advance. 455

previous balance The balance of an account at the end of the last month. 358

price quotation record A record of vendors, information, and prices relating to one item. 448

principal The amount borrowed on a loan. 134

printer The output device in a computer system. 26

processing The second step in the data processing cycle. 19

promissory note A written promise to pay. 133

prompts Questions or commands on a display screen. 302

proof of cash A form on which you compare how much cash you are supposed to have with what you actually have in the drawer. 176

punching in Having the time you arrive at work printed on your time card. 632

punching out Having the time printed on your time card when you leave work. 632

purchase invoice What the buyer calls the bill from the vendor. 471

purchase on account Buying merchandise on credit. 483

purchase order A form used to order merchandise. 455

purchase order clerk Assists the purchasing agent. 448

purchase requisition Tells the purchasing agent to place an order. 437

purchases journal A record of purchases on account. 491

purchases returns and allowances journal A record of all credit memos received. 519

purchasing agent The buyer for a business. 437

Q

quarter A three-month period; ¹/₄-year or 13 weeks. 82

R

rate of commission The commission percentage. 667

ream About 500 sheets of paper. 306

receipt A form issued for cash received. 149

receipts Amounts of money received. 59

receiving clerk Receives goods and compares with goods ordered. 461

receiving report A form that shows goods ordered and received. 461

reconciled Brought into agreement. 248

record Form on which information is recorded. 2

record clerks Workers trained to store and retrieve data. 34

record keeping jobs Jobs in which workers spend most of their time handling records. 3

refund Money given back to a customer for returned merchandise; when estimated tax paid is greater than total tax due. 165

regular savings account An interest earning account. 239

regular time The first 40 hours worked in a week. 653

regular time rate of pay The rate of pay for the first 40 hours worked in a week. 653

reorder level The point at which stock reaches minimum. 457

replenish the fund Add an amount to the petty cash fund to bring it back to its original balance. 288

restrictive endorsement An endorsement that limits the use of a check. 233

retailers Store owners who sell directly to consumers. 310

retrieve To find a document. 34

revenue Another word for income. 592

running balance The balance found after each entry is made. 340

S

salary A fixed amount of pay. 666

salary plus commission A fixed amount of pay plus the amount of commission. 667

sales invoice A bill; what the vendor calls the bill issued to the buyer. 370

sales journal A record of all charge sales. 384

sales order A form on which a customer's request for merchandise is first recorded. 370

sales returns and allowances journal A journal in which you record credit memos. 406

sales slip A written record of a sale. 115

sales slip register A mechanical device used to record sales. 302

sales tax Percent of selling price collected by retailers for governments. 310

savings account A bank account that earns interest. 238

schedule of accounts payable A list of creditors with the amounts owed to them. 484

schedule of accounts receivable A list of customers who owe money. 380

scrolling Moving up or down on a computer screen. 75

self-employment tax Social security tax for self-employed people. 597

semimonthly Twice a month. 694

service business A business in which a service for a customer is performed. 535

service charge A fee charged for bank services. 239

short Less than ordered. 463

signature card A form used to indicate to the bank which signature to accept on signed checks. 202

slide Entering an amount a column or more off, such as 50 for 5,000. 579

Social Security Act Law that allows qualified persons to receive monthly payments from the federal government. 684

social security number An account number in the social security system. 684

sort To file in some order. 26

source documents Forms from which you get data to enter into the computer. 19

special column A column in a petty cash book for a specific expense; a column in a journal used for only one type of item. 283

special savings account An account with special terms offered only to certain persons. 240

specialization of labor A system in which employees are responsible for a limited range of work. 366

split deposit When part of a check is deposited and part is returned in cash. 234

spreadsheet A computer program that lets you create and enter data into forms. 75

stock Merchandise. 421

stock record A record of each item of stock. 421

stock record clerk A person who keeps track of stock amounts. 422

stop-payment order A form instructing a bank not to pay a check. 242

store To file a document. 34

straight commission Total sales multiplied by the rate of commission. 667

straight piecework pay A pay plan that pays the same amount for each unit of work. 673

stub The part of the receipt or check that stays in the book. 150

subsequent After or following. 128

subtotal A total on which other calculations will be made. 160

surname Last name. 37

T

take-home pay Net pay. 690

tally sheet A checklist of money to be deposited. 189

terms The length of time the customer has to pay a bill, such as 10 days. 371

third-party checks Checks from people other than customers. 166

three-column account An account that has debit, credit, and balance columns. 340

tickler file A chronological file of important dates. 29

time card A record of the hours worked by one employee. 632

time clock A machine that records worker times in and out on time cards. 632

time of note The amount of time for which money is borrowed on a note. 134

trailing edge The left side of a check. 230

transaction Something that happens in a business and that is recorded. 117

transposition error A reversal of digits in a number, such as 45 for 54. 20

traveler's checks A safe form of cash to use when taking a trip. 243

trial balance A form used to prove that debits equal credits in the ledger. 576

triplicate Three copies. 326

U

unauthorized charges Transactions not approved. 118

undercharged When you have been charged less than you should be. 119

unit price The price of each item. 306

universal product code (UPC) A special bar code read by electronic cash registers. 161

UPC See universal product code. 13

update To replace old data with new data. 46

V

variable payments Cash payments that change from period to period. 83

variance A difference. 94

vendor A seller; if the sale is on account, the vendor is also a creditor. 48

verify To check for accuracy. 19

void Unusable. 212

vouch To guarantee that something is correct. 473

voucher The part of the check that shows the purpose of the check and a description of the payment. 219

voucher check A check with a special stub attached. 219

W

W-2 form A statement of a worker's wages, FICA, and withholding taxes prepared once each year by the employer. 716

W-4 form A form that shows how many withholding allowances a worker claims. 695

wage and tax statement W-2 form. 716

wand A scanner that reads bar codes on tags. 302

warning bulletin A list of lost or stolen card numbers. 325

weekly pay A wage plan in which workers are paid for a fixed number of hours per week. 642

wholesaler A business that sells in large quantities to retailers. 370

withdrawal To take money out of an account; cash or other items of value taken for the owner's use. 239

withdrawal slip A bank form used to withdraw money from an account. 241

withholding allowances Deductions claimed for the support of another person. 695

withholding tax An income tax deducted from a worker's wages each payday. 694

work sheet A form used to summarize information for financial statements. 615

INDEX

◆◆

Greek coined money, 421
Incan record keeping ropes, 350
papyrus and record-keeping, 274
scribes, 19

N

Native American heritage, employee, 695
Negative cash flow, *def.* 86
Negotiable, *def.* 229
Net decrease in capital, *def.* 605
Net income, *def.* 591
Net increase in capital, *def.* 605
Net loss, *def.* 591
Net pay, *def.* 683–733, 685
  calculator tip on, 686
  deductions, miscellaneous, 724–729
  employee earnings record, 708–715
  payroll preparation, 702–707
  social security taxes, 683–688
  social security tax table, 689–693
  wage and tax statement, 716–723
  withholding taxes, 694–701
Normal balance, *def.* 579
Numerically, *def.* 26
Numeric data filing, 25–33, *illus.* 27

O

OCR, *def. illus.* 12
Office expense, *def.* 274
Open order, *def.* 441
Open order report, *def.* 440–443
Optical Character Recognition. See OCR
Optical mark recognition, *illus.* 12, *def.* 13
Option, *def.* 425–427
Order, sales, 370, *illus.* 371
Order entry clerk, 2, 54, 336
Order reports, open, 440–443
Output, *def.* 19
Output device, *def.* 26
Out rack, *def.* 632
Outstanding checks, *def.* 249
Outstanding deposit, *def.* 253
Over, *def.* 463
Overcharge, *def.* 406
Overcharged, *def.* 118
Overtime, *def.* 653
  gross pay, 653–659
  payroll register, recording in, 660–665
  on time card, *illus.* 654, 661
Overtime rate of pay, *def.* 653

P

Pacioli, Luca, 536
Packing slip, *def. illus.* 462

Papyrus, record-keeping and, 274
Passwords, *def.* 425–427
Pay
  commission, 642
  gross, 644
  net, 685
  piecework, 642
  take–home, 690
  weekly, 642
Paycheck, *illus.* 230
Payee, *def.* 209
Payment on account, *def.* 341
Payments, *def.* 59
Payroll
  mastery problem, 732–733
Payroll clerk, record keeping of
  gross pay, 631–682
    hourly wages, 642–647
    overtime, 653–665
    payroll register, 648–652, 660–665
    piecework, 673–678
    salaries and commissions, 666–672
    time cards, 631–641
  net pay, 683–733
    deductions, miscellaneous, 724–729
    employee earnings record, 708–715
    payroll preparation, 702–707
    social security taxes, 683–688
    social security tax table, 689–693
    wage and tax statement, 716–723
    withholding taxes, 694–701
Payroll menu, *illus.* 719
Payroll preparation, 702–707
Payroll register, *def.* 648, *illus.* 662, 703, 704, 709, 725–726
  gross pay, 648–652
  overtime, 660–665
  for piecework employees, *illus.* 675
Pegboard, *def.* 726, *illus.* 727
Periodic inventory, *def.* 422
Perpetual inventory system, *def.* 422
Personal budget, 58–67
Personal computer, *def.* 68
Personal Identification Number, *def.* 242
Personalized deposit slip, *def.* 202
Peruvian record-keeping, 119
Petty, *def.* 270
Petty cash book, *def. illus.* 281–287, 282, 289, 291, 293
Petty cash box, *def.* 270
Petty cash clerk, , *def.* 270, 298
Petty cash fund, *def.* 270
  calculator tip for, 293–294
Petty cash receipt, *illus.* 271
Petty cash record, *def.* 275, *illus.* 269–300, 276
  book for, 281–287
  classifying business expenses, 274–280

proving the fund, 272
  replenished overage fund, 292–293
  replenishing and maintaining the fund, 288–296
  replenishing balanced fund, 289–290
  replenishing short fund, 290–291
  writing vouchers, 269–273
Petty cash voucher, *def.* 270, *illus.* 271
Piecerate, *def.* 673
  payroll register for, *illus.* 675
Piecework, gross pay, 673–678
Piecework pay, *def.* 642
PIN. See Personal Identification Number
Policies, *def.* 166
POS display screen, *illus.* 302
Position, *def.* 2
Positive cash flow, *def.* 86
Post, *def.* 385
Postdate, *def.* 211
POS terminal, *def.* 302
  credit slip printed by, *illus.* 349
  sales slip from, *illus.* 324
POS terminals in large store, *illus.* 303
Posting, *illus.* 386, 402
  from purchases journal to creditor account, *illus.* 493
Posting references, *def.* 386
Premium clerk, 54
Prenumbered, *def.* 455
Previous balance, *def.* 358
Price quotation record, *def.* 448, *illus.* 447–454, 449–450
  on computer, *illus.* 451
Principal, *def.* 134
Printer, *def.* 26
Problem-solving skills. See Critical thinking
Processing, *def.* 19
Professional business ethics
  blank endorsement, 265
  check endorsement, 364
  computer anxiety, 53–54
  co-worker's attendance habits, 529
  cultural diversity, 140–141
  employee theft, 444
  incorrect paychecks, 730
  secrecy, 679
Promissory note, *def.* 133, *illus.* 134
Prompts, *def.* 302
Proof of cash, *def.* 176, 180
Proof of cash form, *illus.* 176
  calculator tip for, 177
Proving the petty cash fund, 272
Punching in, *def.* 632
Punching out, *def.* 632
Purchase invoice, *def.* 471–478
  approved, *illus.* 473
  recording, *illus.* 510
  recording,*illus.* 524
  verifying, 474
Purchase on account, *def.* 483

Photo Credits

p. 2, © Phil Jason/Tony Stone Images; p. 8, © Bob Daemmrich; p. 21, © Loren Santow/Tony Stone Images; p. 28, © B. Christensen/Stock, Boston; p. 30, © Jean Francois Causse/Tony Stone Images; p. 46, © Jim Cornfield/Westlight; p. 59, © Mark C. Burnett/Stock, Boston; p. 69, © Barbara Filet/Tony Stone Images; p. 82, © Ken Whitmore/Tony Stone Images; p. 93, © Bob Daemmrich; p. 109, © Mark Richards/Photo Edit; p. 127, © Michael Newman/Photo Edit; p. 134, © Bill Aron/Photo Edit; p. 148, © Mary Kate Denny/Photo Edit; p. 159, © William Warren/Westlight; p. 165, © Bob Daemmrich; p. 181, © Dennis O'Clair/Tony Stone Images; p. 188, © Eric Curry/Westlight; p. 201, © Owen Franken/Stock, Boston; p. 209, System 6 Laminate Desk, KnollOffice, The Knoll Group; p. 217, © Bruce Ayres/Tony Stone Images; p. 224, © Bob Daemmrich/Stock, Boston; p. 230, © Richard Pasley/Stock, Boston; p. 233, © Andrew Sacks/Tony Stone Images; p. 234, © Bob Daemmrich/Stock, Boston; p. 239, © David Young-Wolff/Photo Edit; p. 247, © Victor Watts/Picture Perfect U.S.A.; p. 259, © Jed Share/Westlight; p. 270, © John Neubauer/Photo Edit; p. 275, © Mark Richards/Photo Edit; p. 282, © Walter Urie/Westlight; p. 289, © Jeff Hetler/Stock, Boston; p. 290, © Bob Daemmrich; p. 292, © Craig Aurness/Westlight; p. 304, © Philip Habib/Tony Stone Images; p. 311, © Julie Houck/Stock, Boston; p. 317, © Donovan Reese/Tony Stone Images; p. 318, © Mike McQueen/Tony Stone Images; p. 323, © W. Cody/Westlight; p. 331, © Marc Chamberlain/Tony Stone Images; p. 341, © Bob Daemmrich/Stock, Boston; p. 350, © Andrew Hourmont/Tony Stone Images; p. 358, © Seth Resnick/Stock, Boston; p. 371, © Laurie Rubin/Tony Stone Images; p. 378, © Darrell Wong/Tony Stone Images; p. 387, © H. Richard Johnson/Tony Stone Images; p. 393, © Lawrence Migdale/Stock, Boston; p. 401, © Jim Corwin/Stock, Boston; p. 407, © Aaron Haupt/Stock, Boston; p. 422, © Zefa/Schwertner/The Stock Market; p. 424, © Bob Daemmrich/Stock, Boston; p. 431, © Don Murie/Meyers Photo-Art; p. 438, © Lawrence Migdale/Photo Researchers; p. 440, © Lori Adamski Peek/Tony Stone Images; p. 448, © Ellis Herwig/Stock, Boston; p. 456, © Warren Morgan/Westlight; p. 462, © Mark Richards/Photo Edit; p. 465, © Sepp Seitz/Woodfin Camp; p. 472, © David Madison/Tony Stone Images; p. 485, © Nubar Alexanian/Stock, Boston; p. 494, © Will/Deni McIntyre/Photo Researchers; p. 503, © David Joel/Tony Stone Images; p. 510, © Charles Thatcher/Tony Stone Images; p. 522, © Peter Poulides/Tony Stone Images; p. 535, © Bob Daemmrich/Stock, Boston; p. 542, © Dennis Mac Donald/Photo Edit; p. 549, © Paul Chesley/Tony Stone Images; p. 557, © Lawrence Migdale/Stock, Boston; p. 562, © Bill Ross/Westlight; p. 569, © Christopher Brown/Stock, Boston; p. 577, © Don Murie/Meyers Photo-Art; p. 591, © Cotton Coulson/Woodfin Camp; p. 598, © William Johnson/Stock, Boston; p. 604, © Sue Klemens/Stock, Boston; p. 610, © Dan Bosler/Tony Stone Images; p. 616, © D. Baswick Photographics/Westlight; p. 621, © Grant Taylor/Tony Stone Images; p. 636, © Peter Le Grand/Tony Stone Images; p. 643, © Bruce Ando/Tony Stone Images; p. 648, © Seth Resnick/Stock, Boston; p. 660, © Andy Sacks/Tony Stone Images; p. 668, © Charles Michael Murray/Westlight; p. 674, © Lawrence Migdale/Photo Researchers; p. 685, © Billy E. Barnes/Stock, Boston; p. 690, © Roger Tully/Tony Stone Images; p. 702, © Jeff Persons/Stock, Boston; p. 709, © Arnulf Husmo/Tony Stone Images; p. 717, © D. Mann Ding/Westlight; p. 725, © Ron Watts/Westlight; p. 727, The Reynolds and Reynolds Company